# PEOPLES OF THE
# NEW TESTAMENT
# WORLD

# PEOPLES OF THE NEW TESTAMENT WORLD

## AN ILLUSTRATED GUIDE

WILLIAM A. SIMMONS

**Peoples of the New Testament World: An Illustrated Guide**

ISBN 978-1-56563-877-8

*First Printing—2008*

Design copyright © 2008 Lion Hudson plc/Tim Dowley Associates Ltd

Worldwide co-edition produced by
Lion Hudson plc
Wilkinson House
Jordan Hill Road
Oxford, OX2 8DR, England

Tel: +44 (0) 1865 302750
Fax: +44 (0) 1865 302757
e-mail: coed@lionhudson.com
www.lionhudson.com

*Printed in Singapore*

Library of Congress Cataloging-in-Publication Data
    Simmons, William A., 1954-
        Peoples of the New Testament world : an illustrated guide / William A. Simmons.
            p. cm.
    Includes bibliographical references and indexes.
    ISBN 978-1-56563-877-8 (alk. paper)
    1. Ethnicity in the Bible.  I. Title.
    BS2545.E815S56 2008
225.9'5--dc22
                        2008014875

To

NATHANIEL STEWART SIMMONS

My son and my friend

# Credits

**Photographs**
Jon Arnold: p. 279
British Museum: pp. 22, 23, 236, 307
Tim Dowley Associates: pp. 27, 30, 33, 44, 45,
 46, 47, 50, 55, 67, 68/69, 77, 81, 93, 101,
 135, 139, 140, 151, 158, 162/163, 165, 171,
 175, 177, 179, 183, 187, 188, 190, 193, 199,
 208/209, 210, 211, 212, 214, 217, 219, 225,
 227, 228, 233, 235, 241, 243, 247, 248, 249,
 250, 251, 252, 253, 256, 263, 264, 266, 269,
 277, 279, 283, 284, 286, 296, 299
Israel Government Tourist Office: pp. 59, 83,
 95, 114, 121, 122, 123, 125, 126, 127, 129,
 142, 143, 144, 147, 149, 153, 157, 169, 213,
 215, 281
Zev Radovan: pp. 26, 37, 40, 42, 79, 91, 105,
 145, 191, 292, 295
Jamie Simson: pp. 197, 287

**Illustrations**
Frank Baber: p. 267
Brian Bartles: p. 221
Peter Dennis: p. 78
Jeremy Gower: pp. 21, 136/137
James Macdonald: pp. 99, 319
Alan Parry: pp. 3, 115, 265, 271
Richard Scott: pp. 85, 186
Jean-Jacques Tissot: pp. 61, 71, 103, 109, 110,
 116, 131, 151, 155, 262

**Maps and Charts**
Tim Dowley Associates Ltd

**Cover art**
Young girl offering bunches of grapes. Early
Christian mosaic, 4th CE
Located in the Basilica Patriarcale, Aquileia,
Italy.
Photo Credit: Cameraphoto Arte, Venice / Art
Resource, NY. Used with permission.

# Table of Contents

# Preface

The writers of the New Testament were vitally engaged in communicating their message to their generation. Thus, when speaking of such important groups as the Pharisees, Sadducees, and Zealots, they took much for granted. They assumed that the agendas, ideals, and practices of each group were generally understood by their target audiences. This assumption does carry over to the twenty-first century. Even though the truths of the New Testament are timeless, the language and images employed are deeply rooted in the first-century world. Our present context does not readily afford the tools to fully unpack the riches of their world and vision. Consequently, our ability to make a genuine application of what the first followers of Christ received and passed on is impaired.

Herein lies the central purpose of this work. It seeks to bridge the gap between our world and the world of Jesus and the apostles. Its method will be to delve into the relevant primary documents of the ancient world, dialogue with some of the latest findings of New Testament scholarship, and translate these findings in a way that renders them accessible to serious students of the Bible. The scope of this work encompasses various groups found in the New Testament, whether they are religious, political, or social. Its structure will not follow the pattern usually found in Bible dictionaries or encyclopedias. Instead of simply being placed in alpha-betical or even chronological order, the topics follow a general conceptual framework. After an introductory chapter, which establishes the foundation for the book, the work is roughly divided into two halves. The first half addresses the major Jewish groups of the first century, whereas the second treats the important Greco-Roman groups. John the Baptist and his disciples serve as a link between Judaism and the early church, and the Herodians serve as a transition between the Jewish and Greco-Roman worlds. The presentation on the Greco-Roman world is generally arranged in terms of power, beginning with the Roman imperial rulers and ending with the section on slaves and freedmen and freedwomen.

This arrangement is intended to serve the general purpose of the book. Instead of jumping from topic to topic in an ad hoc manner, it is hoped that, by following up the numerous cross-references, the reader will discern the interconnections that comprise the complex nexus of the world of the New Testament. After a number of these connections have been made, the student should be able to get a feel for the religious, social, and political worlds of the New Testament and how they relate one to another.

Three kinds of bibliography are included in the text, two annotated and one general. The annotated bibliography for the primary documents orients the student to Greek and Latin writers who contribute to the topics at hand. Special attention is given to the Loeb Classical Library collection. To avoid needless repetition, these sources are not included in the annotated bibliographies located at the end of each chapter. These annotated sections do not include every book used in the chapter, nor do they include any journal articles. Rather, they focus on the major monographs and books accessed in the section at hand and usually do not repeat sources described in previous chapters. The general bibliography at the end of the book is comprehensive, including every source relevant to the text, especially all of the journal articles.

Thus this book can be used to supplement general survey courses in the New Testament yet also serve as an orientation for in-depth research. Informed lay persons, pastors, and beginning academics will find this book helpful in leading them to a deeper understanding of God's word.

# Acknowledgments

Interest in writing a book of this kind began during my doctoral studies at the University of St. Andrews. Under the excellent guidance of Professor A. J. M. Wedderburn, I was made keenly aware of the complexities of the world of the New Testament and the diverse social, religious, and political groups that it contained. Continued research only deepened my appreciation for the rich nexus of relationships that we find in the New Testament not only among Jewish groups but among Greco-Roman groups as well.

Understanding the interconnections between these various groups became more and more important to me as I continued my teaching career. The need for a single volume pointing out the elements that defined a particular group, as well as how it compared with and differed from other groups, became apparent.

Dr. Terry L. Cross, dean of the School of Religion at Lee University, opened up opportunity to embark on such a project. He graciously made room in the graduate studies program for a "People Groups of the New Testament World" course. The hard work and interest of the students in the course provided additional insight and affirmation for the present study. Also, the timely comments and calls from my mentor and friend Dr. French L. Arrington helped me see the work through to its completion. Chloe S. Stewart volunteered his time for the first "cold read" of the typescript, and teaching assistant Chris Rouse performed the tedious task of cross-checking the many scriptural references.

Special thanks are due to Dr. Paul Conn, president of Lee University. His commitment to the task of research and its place in higher education is much appreciated.

# Abbreviations

## General

| | |
|---|---|
| B.C.E. | before the Common Era |
| ca. | *circa*, about |
| C.E. | Common Era |
| e.g. | *exempli gratia*, for example |
| i.e. | *id est*, that is |
| KJV | King James Version |
| LXX | Septuagint |
| NIV | New International Version |
| NRSV | New Revised Standard Version |
| NS | new series |
| UBS⁴ | *The Greek New Testament.* United Bible Societies. 4th ed. |

## Primary Sources

### Dead Sea Scrolls

| | |
|---|---|
| CD | Cairo Genizah (copy of *Damascus Document*) |
| 1QH | *Hodayot* or *Thanksgiving Hymns* |
| 1QM | *Milḥamah* or *War Scroll* |
| 1QpHab | *Pesher Habakkuk* |
| 1QS | *Serek Hayaḥad* or *Rule of the Community* |
| 4QMMT | *Miqṣat Maʿaśê ha-Torah* |
| 4QpNah | *Pesher Nahum* |

### Philo

| | |
|---|---|
| Embassy | *On the Embassy to Gaius* |
| Flaccus | *Against Flaccus* |
| Good Person | *That Every Good Person Is Free* |
| Moses | *On the Life of Moses* |
| Spec. Laws | *On the Special Laws* |

### Josephus

| | |
|---|---|
| Ag. Ap. | *Against Apion* |
| Ant. | *Jewish Antiquities* |
| J.W. | *Jewish War* |
| Life | *The Life* |

### Mishnah, Talmud, and Related Literature

| | |
|---|---|
| ʾAbot | *Avot* |
| ʿErub. | *Eruvin* |
| b. | Babylonian Talmud |
| m. | Mishnah |
| Nid. | *Niddah* |
| Šabb. | *Shabbat* |
| Ṭehah. | *Teharot* |
| y. | Jerusalem Talmud |
| Yad. | *Yadayim* |

## Church Fathers

Eusebius

| | |
|---|---|
| Hist. eccl. | *Historia ecclesiastica* (*Ecclesiastical History*) |

Origen
   *Cels.*          *Contra Celsum (Against Celsus)*

## Classical Works

Apuleius
   *Metam.*      *Metamorphoses (The Golden Ass)*
Aristophanes
   *Vesp. Vespae (Wasps)*
Aristotle
   *Eth. nic.*     *Ethica nichomachea (Nichomachean Ethics)*
   *Pol.*        *Politica (Politics)*
Arrian
   *Anab.*      *Anabasis*
Cicero
   *Att.*        *Epistulae ad Atticum (Letters to Atticus)*
   *Fam.*      *Epistulae ad familiares (Letters to His Friends)*
   *Fin.*        *De finibus (On Duties)*
   *Off.*        *De officiis (On Ends)*
   *Prov. cons.*   *De provinciis consularibus (On the Consular Provinces)*
Columella
   *Rust.*      *De re rustica (On Agriculture)*
Demosthenes
   *Timocr.*    *In Timocratem (Against Timocrates)*
Dio Cassius
   *Hist. rom.*   *Historia romana (Roman History)*
Diogenes Laertius
   *Vit. phil.*    *Vitae philosophorum (Lives of Eminent Philosophers)*
Dionysius of Halicarnassus
   *Ant. rom.*     *Antiquitates romanae* (Roman Antiquities)
Herodotus
   *Hist.*       *Historiae (Histories)*
Justinian
   *Dig.*       *Digesta (Digest)*
   *Inst.*       *Institutiones (Institutes)*
Lucretius
   *Rer. nat.*    *De rerum natura (On the Nature of Things)*
Macrobius
   *Sat.*       *Saturnalia*
Menander
   *Epitr.*     *Epitrepontes*
Paulus
   *Sent.*      *Sententiae*
Plato
   *Resp.*     *Respublica (Republic)*
Pliny the Elder
   *Nat.*      *Naturalis historia (Natural History)*
Pliny the Younger
   *Ep.*       *Epistulae (Letters)*
Plutarch (Lives)
   *Alex.*     *Alexander*
   *Caes.*     *Caesar*
   *Crass.*    *Crassus*
   *Galb.*     *Galba*
   *Oth.*      *Otho*
   *Res gest. divi Aug.*  *Res gestae divi Augusti (The Acts of Augustus)*
Seneca
   *Ben.*      *De beneficiis*
   *Ep.*       *Epistulae morales*
   *Ira*       *De ira*
   *Prov.*     *De providentia*

Strabo
  *Geogr.*      *Geographica (Geography)*
Suetonius
  *Vit. Caes.*   *De vita Caesarum (Lives of the Caesars)*
Tacitus
  *Ann.*      *Annales (Annals)*
  *Hist.*      *Historiae (Histories)*
Varro
  *Rust.*      *De re rustica (On Agriculture)*

## Secondary Sources

| | |
|---|---|
| ANRW | *Aufstieg und Niedergang der römischen Welt: Geschichte und Kultur Roms im Spiegel der neueren Forschung.* Edited by H. Temporini and W. Haase. Berlin, New York: de Gruyter, 1972– |
| ATJ | *Ashland Theological Journal* |
| BA | *Biblical Archaeologist* |
| BAR | *Biblical Archaeology Review* |
| BBR | *Bulletin for Biblical Research* |
| Bib | *Biblica* |
| Brev | *Bible Review* |
| BSac | *Bibliotheca Sacra* |
| BTB | *Biblical Theology Bulletin* |
| CBQ | *Catholic Biblical Quarterly* |
| CIRB | *Corpus inscriptionum regni bosporani.* Edited by V. V. Struve. Moscow: Naika, 1965 |
| CRINT | Compendia rerum iudaicarum ad Novum Testamentum |
| EuroJTh | *European Journal of Theology* |
| ExpTim | *Expository Times* |
| GOTR | *Greek Orthodox Theological Review* |
| HTR | *Harvard Theological Review* |
| HUCA | *Hebrew Union College Annual* |
| Int | *Interpretation* |
| JBL | *Journal of Biblical Literature* |
| JETS | *Journal of the Evangelical Theological Society* |
| JJS | *Journal of Jewish Studies* |
| JSNT | *Journal for the Study of the New Testament* |
| JSNTSup | Journal for the Study of the New Testament: Supplement Series |
| JSOTSup | Journal for the Study of the Old Testament: Supplement Series |
| JSPSup | Journal for the Study of the Pseudepigrapha: Supplement Series |
| JTS | *Journal of Theological Studies* |
| NIGTC | New International Greek Testament Commentary |
| NovT | *Novum Testamentum* |
| NTS | New Testament Studies |
| PDM | *Papyri demoticae magicae.* Demotic texts in PGM corpus as collated in H. D. Betz, ed., *The Greek Magical Papyri in Translation, Including the Demotic Spells.* 2d ed. Chicago: University of Chicago Press, 1996– |
| PGM | *Papyri graecae magicae: Die griechische Zauberpapyri.* Edited by K. Preisendanz. 2 vols. Berlin, Leipzig: B. G. Teubner, 1928–1931 |
| PRSt | *Perspectives in Religious Studies* |
| RevExp | *Review and Expositor* |
| RevQ | *Revue de Qumran* |
| SBLDS | Society of Biblical Literature Dissertation Series |
| SBLSP | Society of Biblical Literature Seminar Papers |
| SJLA | Studies in Judaism in Late Antiquity |
| SNTSMS | Society for New Testament Studies Monograph Series |
| SVF | *Stoicorum veterum fragmenta.* H. von Arnim. 4 vols. in 2. New York: Irvington, 1986 |
| TDNT | *Theological Dictionary of the New Testament.* Edited by G. Kittel and G. Friedrich. Translated by G. W. Bromiley. 10 vols. Grand Rapids: Eerdmans, 1964–1976 |
| TNTC | Tyndale New Testament Commentaries |
| TynBul | *Tyndale Bulletin* |
| WBC | Word Biblical Commentary |
| WUNT | Wissenschaftliche Untersuchungen zum Neuen Testament 1974. |

# 1
# Introduction

## THE IMPORTANCE OF THE CONTEXT

Pharisees and Sadducees. Caesars and centurions. Scribes and Samaritans. The names of these groups and others appear throughout the New Testament. Yet what did they really mean in their original contexts? Why did the biblical writers view such labels as useful for conveying the "good news"? If you lived in the first century and you were called a Zealot, what precisely would this have conveyed to those about you? What forces, whether religious, social, or political, could have conspired to bring about such groups? Furthermore, what ideals and beliefs might have led one to identify with a particular group to the exclusion of all others? Finally, how did the existence of these groups relate to the life and ministry of Jesus and the early church?

All of these questions highlight the need to explore the context of the first century in order to advance our understanding of the Scriptures. Such understanding requires knowledge of the historical, religious, and political contexts of the first-century world, or what has been called "the fundamental data of the times."[1] We must seek to own, as much as possible, the values and visions of the ancients so that we may rightly interpret what they thought, felt, said, and did. We must strive to speak their language, all the while realizing that the meanings of words change over time.

1  Cf. Martin Hengel and Roland Deines, "E. P. Sanders' 'Common Judaism,' Jesus, and the Pharisees," *JTS* 46 (1995): 1–70, esp. 2.

When we do so, it becomes clear that some of the most important elements that define the life and times of Jesus came into existence hundreds of years before his birth in Bethlehem. So what might initially appear as historically obscure and arcane eventually comes to be seen as an essential component for understanding the world of the New Testament.

## THE IMPACT OF FOREIGN DOMINATION

If there is any one factor that best explains the complex world in which Jesus and his first followers lived, it is the impact of foreign domination upon the Jews. This factor may be seen as the key element that "strings the beads" so to speak, of the many religious, social, and political realities one encounters in the New Testament. In particular, as Israel repeatedly experienced one national holocaust after another, a singular harsh chord was struck in the minds of many Jews, one that was to resonate to this day. Since they were stripped of the critical factors that define a people, the primal urge to survive was thrust to the fore in the hearts and minds of many Jews in the first century.

Therefore the birth and continuance of the many Jewish groups that one encounters in the New Testament may be viewed as a primary means that Israel employed to secure her existence in the face of brutal oppression.

As will be seen, the crises of conquest and oppression so wracked and fragmented Israel that in the wake of such national trauma, smaller groups of like-minded souls began to coalesce. Though disparate in makeup, agenda, and methods, they all shared a common goal: *the survival of the Jewish people.* Indeed Israel's experiences of exile and oppression birthed a *"mechanism of survival"* that came to characterize her place in the world of the New Testament and beyond.[2]

2  On how the crisis of captivity affected Israel, see Daniel Smith, *The Religion of the Landless: The Social Context of the Babylonian Exile* (Bloomington, Ind.: Meyer-Stone, 1989), esp. 120.

On the other side of the equation, that is, regarding the Greco-Roman world of the first century, the same dynamic is present, if in a different form. The elaborate social and political hierarchy, together with all of the groups composing that hierarchy, may also be viewed through the lens of conquest and domination. From the apex stratum of the Roman imperial rulers to that of the proxies and patrons through whom they ruled, all the way down to the level of slaves and freedmen and freedwomen, the motif of conquest, political and social maneuvering, and the quest for survival informs our understanding of the New Testament.

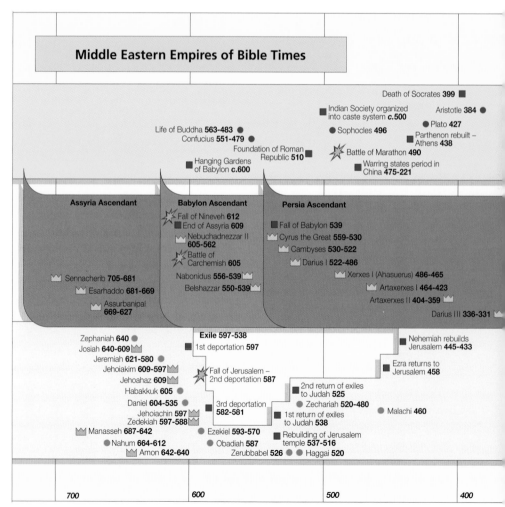

## Middle Eastern Empires of Bible Times

Death of Socrates **399**
Indian Society organized into caste system **c.500**
Aristotle **384**
Life of Buddha **563-483**
Confucius **551-479**
Sophocles **496**
Plato **427**
Parthenon rebuilt – Athens **438**
Foundation of Roman Republic **510**
Battle of Marathon **490**
Hanging Gardens of Babylon **c.600**
Warring states period in China **475-221**

**Assyria Ascendant**

**Babylon Ascendant**

**Persia Ascendant**

Fall of Nineveh **612**
End of Assyria **609**
Nebuchadnezzar II **605-562**
Battle of Carchemish **605**
Fall of Babylon **539**
Cyrus the Great **559-530**
Cambyses **530-522**
Darius I **522-486**
Sennacherib **705-681**
Nabonidus **556-539**
Xerxes I (Ahasuerus) **486-465**
Esarhaddo **681-669**
Belshazzar **550-539**
Artaxerxes I **464-423**
Assurbanipal **669-627**
Artaxerxes II **404-359**
Darius III **336-331**

Zephaniah **640**
Josiah **640-609**
Jeremiah **621-580**
Jehoiakim **609-597**
Jehoahaz **609**
Habakkuk **605**
Daniel **604-535**
Jehoiachin **597**
Zedekiah **597-588**
Manasseh **687-642**
Nahum **664-612**
Amon **642-640**

Exile **597-538**
1st deportation **597**
Fall of Jerusalem – 2nd deportation **587**
3rd deportation **582-581**
Ezekiel **593-570**
Obadiah **587**
Zerubbabel **526**

Nehemiah rebuilds Jerusalem **445-433**
Ezra returns to Jerusalem **458**
2nd return of exiles to Judah **525**
Zechariah **520-480**
Malachi **460**
1st return of exiles to Judah **538**
Rebuilding of Jerusalem temple **537-516**
Haggai **520**

700     600     500     400

Thus, in terms of victors and vanquished, the different Jewish groups under discussion can be understood as renewal movements intended to restore the integrity and continuance of Israel. The complexity and diversity of their approaches for securing Israel's future is astounding. For example, Jeremiah's "build, plant, marry" admonition to the Jews in the exile at first appears to accommodate the ruthless brutality of the Babylonians (Jer 29:4–7). Similarly, the Sadducees at the time of Jesus may well have sought the path of accommodation when confronted by their Roman conquerors. As persons of wealth and influence in Israel, they formed a key nexus for actual-

izing the rule of Rome in the land (Josephus, *Ant.* 13.298). And so the Sadducees were at times pressed into service by the Romans (*Ant.* 18.17), a kind of service that may have called forth the subtleties of diplomacy and compromise with the oppressors of Israel. Such counsel and tactics at first appear to deny Israel's bid for freedom and dignity. But upon closer scrutiny, both Jeremiah and the Sadducees are interested in the same thing: the continuance of the Jewish people in difficult and dangerous times. On the other hand, the Pharisees' approach seems to have accentuated the rituals and traditions that tended to intensify Jewish identity as they saw it (*Ant.* 13.297; Mark 7:1–14; Acts 15:1–5;

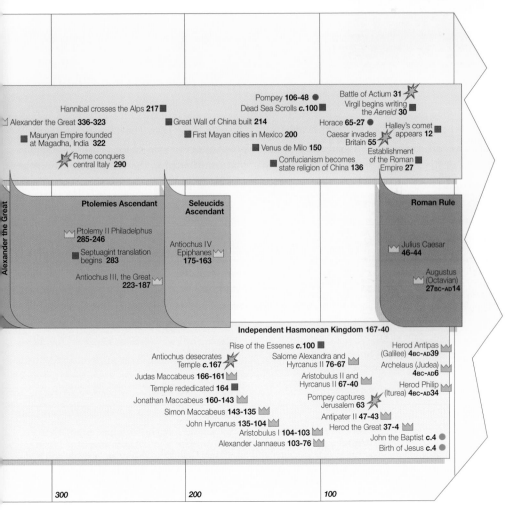

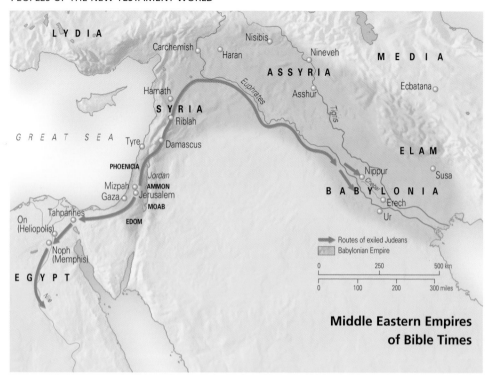

**Middle Eastern Empires
of Bible Times**

*m. Nid.* 1:1–10:8; *m. Zabim* 1:1–5:12), in an effort to stave off Hellenism.[3] Finally, the terror tactics of the Zealots advocated "holy war" to rid Israel of her enemies (*Ant.* 18.9, 23; Mark 15:7; Luke 6:15, 23:18; Acts 1:13).[4] Thus one can see how foreign domination stimulated what might be called a "creativity of survival" on

the part of the Jews. The following section will present an overview of the defining moments that contributed to the rise and development of these groups and others.

## The Babylonian Period

From the very outset, the insightful reader of the New Testament is struck by several facts. The temple built by Solomon no longer exists. In its place is a temple frequently referred to as the second temple or Herod's temple. The geographic and political significance of the twelve tribes of Israel has been obliterated. Jewish worshipers are meeting in "synagogues." Arguably, the ultimate cause of all these factors was the defeat of the Jews by the ancient Babylonians.[5] Indeed the

---

3  The same tendency can be found in the Mishnah (ca. 200 C.E.), in which the early rabbis attribute many sayings to the houses of Hillel and Shammai. These sayings are said to reflect the teachings of the Pharisees prior to 70 C.E. To what extent such sayings in fact reflect the words of Hillel and Shammai cannot be determined. Thus scholars are sharply divided over the legitimacy of applying Mishnaic sayings of the Pharisees to the period prior to the destruction of the temple in 70 C.E. Cf. Jacob Neusner, *The Mishnah: A New Translation* (New Haven: Yale University Press, 1988), xv–xvi, 1077–95, 1108–17.

4  Whether at the time of Jesus the Zealots were in existence as a clearly defined sect is open to debate. That certain Jews, prior to and contemporary with Jesus, were *zealous* for the law and killed those who opposed the sole rule of God cannot be questioned. Cf. Richard A. Horsley and John S. Hanson, *Bandits, Prophets, and Messiahs: Popular Movements at the Time of Jesus* (San Francisco: Harper & Row, 1985), 20.

5  For various views on the significance of the Babylonian captivity for the history of the Jews, see Daniel L. Smith-Christopher, "Reassessing the Historical and Sociological Impact of the Babylonian Exile (597/587–539 B.C.E.)," in *Exile: Old Testament, Jewish, and Christian Conceptions* (ed. James M. Scott; New York: E. J. Brill, 1997), 7–11.

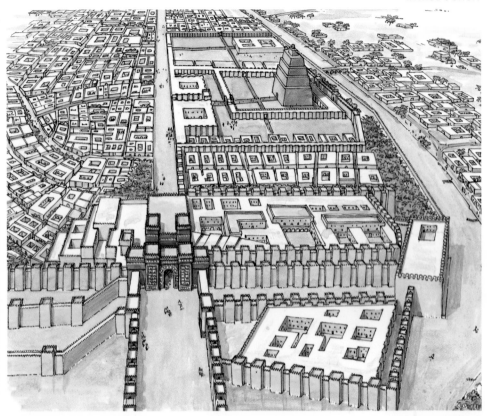

**Artist's impression of Babylon, with the Ishtar Gate in the foreground. The large structure toward the top center is a ziggurat.**

Babylonian captivity seems to have been the most critical event in a long series of events that marked the dramatic demise of Israel and her several rebirths over time. Even the trauma of the Assyrian conquest in 722 B.C.E. failed to establish the formative elements that would determine the future of Israel. The reason is that in some ways the Assyrians were more successful in their conquest of the Jews than were the Babylonians. The former not only destroyed the northern kingdom and deported its people, they also embarked on a campaign to replenish the population from their own stock and the surrounding nations. From this time on, the northern tribes ceased to exist in any definable social or political form and thus did not contribute to the future of Israel in the ways that Judah did. Indeed some scholars hold that the dissolution of the ten northern tribes set the stage for the pivotal role that the Babylonian captivity would play in the lives of the Jews.

In 597 B.C.E. Nebuchadnezzar, king of the Babylonians, overran Judea and captured Jerusalem (Ezek 29:17–18). His goal was to make Israel a subservient vassal of his vast empire. Nebuchadnezzar's initial plan was to undermine the military and political power of the Jews and maintain a virtual slave state in Israel to serve his purposes. He deported the best and the brightest of Israel to Babylon, Daniel and Ezekiel being the most notable (Dan 1:1–6; Ezek 1:1). The precise number of deportees is difficult to determine. One thing is sure: regarding the Babylonian captivity, one should not think in terms of a single mass deportation. On the contrary, the data

21

Panel from the Black Obelisk of Shalmaneser III of Assyria depicting Israelite captives. The kneeling figure is thought to be Jehu, the son of Hanani, king of Israel.

indicate that the Jews experienced at least three deportations while under the yoke of the Babylonians.[6] Second Kings 24:14 indicates that there was an initial deportation of ten thousand captives. Without giving specific figures, 2 Kgs 25:11 contains a succinct if not chilling account of the exile. It simply says that Nebuchadnezzar carried away "the rest" of the people into exile, leaving behind a skeleton crew of the poorest people to farm the land (2 Kgs 24:14). Only the "poorest of the land," "vinedressers," and "plowmen" were left (2 Kgs 25:12; Jer 52:16). Jeremiah 52:28–30 speaks of an incremental removal of captives, totaling forty-six hundred. The difficulty in interpreting these figures is that we do not know whether only the male heads of household are numbered or the figures represent women and children as well. If only the males were recorded, the number of exiles could easily exceed thirty thousand deportees.

Yet the numerical figures do not begin to tell the whole story. As a result of the Babylonian invasion, thousands starved to death while their cities were under siege, and many more were mercilessly slaughtered once the walls of Jerusalem were breached. Additionally, the psychological trauma of the invasion must have been devastating (Lam 2:11–18, 19–21; 5:2–5; 2 Kgs 25:18–27). It has been estimated that the Judah's preinvasion population of about 250,000 had plummeted to a mere 20,000 just before the return of the captives.[7]

Nebuchadnezzar's plan to break the back of the Jews was not limited to carrying off the elite of Israel. He understood that the soul of the Jews lay in her religion and that the tangible symbol of its faith was the temple. In order to subjugate the Jews, he would have to undermine their faith. To that end he robbed the temple of its sacred vessels (Jer 28:1–6). Yet this was only a prelude to more heinous sacrilege.

6 John Bright records mass deportations in the years 597, 587, and 582 B.C.E. (*A History of Israel* [3d ed.; Philadelphia: Westminster, 1981], esp. 345).

7 Ibid., 344.

**Panel from the Black Obelisk of Shalmaneser III depicting Israelites bringing tribute. An inscription on the stele says the Assyrian king received silver, gold, golden tumblers and buckets and tin.**

To keep tabs on the defeated nation and ensure that a steady stream of tribute flowed into Babylon, Nebuchadnezzar appointed Zedekiah as the puppet king of the Jews (2 Kgs 24:17-20). In the power vacuum caused by the exile, Zedekiah saw an opportunity to advance his fortune in the midst of calamity. It appears that he was all too willing to be a vassal of Nebuchadnezzar if it meant he could rule. He paid tribute to Nebuchadnezzar for three years. Yet Zedekiah was not the quisling he appeared to be. In defiance of the counsel of Jeremiah (Jer 27:3-8), Zedekiah made a secret alliance with Egypt in an attempt to cast off the yoke of Babylonian oppression (2 Kgs 24:18-25:7). He was unaware, however, that Nebuchadnezzar was monitoring his every move and had received a report of the Israeli-Egyptian coalition. In response Nebuchadnezzar took drastic action against the Jews, laying siege to the city for eighteen months. He destroyed Jerusalem and pulled down the walls of the holy city (Jer 37:7-10), totally destroying the temple and razing it to the ground. Zedekiah, the last

descendant of David to occupy the throne, was captured. Just before having his eyes gouged out, he was forced to watch the slaughter of his sons. Zedekiah was bound, carried off to Babylon, and died in captivity (2 Kgs 25:7-30).

It is difficult to imagine the trauma inflicted upon the national psyche of the Jews by the Babylonian captivity. The talent drain initiated by Nebuchadnezzar was followed by a merciless attack that severely disrupted the Jews on a number of levels. On a political level, their identity as a nation was shattered. Socially, their leadership structure was deported to Babylon. Religiously, the shining symbol of their devotion to God—the temple—was no more. Jeremiah 50:1-51 echoes the spirit of despair that prevailed among the people.

The terror of total annihilation as a people was burned into the collective memory of Israel. Hanging in the balance was whether Israel would survive the holocaust of captivity. The outcome was by no means certain. The God of Israel had been demeaned in the eyes of the Gentiles. The authenticity of

Israel's faith was on the line (Jer 44:15–19). The anguish of Israel's spirit cries forth from such passages as Lam 1:1–3 and Ps 137:1–6. The prophets speak of the captivity in terms of unimaginable suffering and slavery (Isa 40:2; 41:11–12; Ezek 34:27). The experience serves as a symbol of evil and pain until the end of time (Rev 14:8; 16:9).

For all of these reasons, the people desperately needed some rallying point around which they could rebuild their world. As in times past, the Hebrews turned to their God. Yet this time things were totally different. With the absence of the temple, the priesthood, and the myriad number of sacrifices and rituals, they had lost the most important symbols of their faith. Was there anything left?

The one thing that the ravages of war could not take away from the Jews was their faith in the law of Moses. Indeed, in the wake of the Babylonian captivity, the Torah became the lodestone that drew the Jews together and preserved their identity as a distinct people. Every word, every syllable, indeed every letter of the law, was the breath of the nation, an indispensable lifeline for Jewish ethnicity and faith. Even if the living God seemed to have forsaken them in exile, the Scriptures would sustain them until the time of their deliverance.

It was at this point that much of Israel's fate and practice was determined. With the increased focus on the Torah, critical questions came to the forefront. Precisely what constituted the word of God? How should it be interpreted? What are the implications of Scripture for the daily life of the Jew?

Grave questions mandate sound answers. Yet, as Israel grappled with what it meant to be a true Jew, the answers that evolved varied widely. So, even though the written word did serve as a rallying point for Israel, the nature of the times generated differing schools of interpretation, some so different that they tended to polarize and fragment

the community. In this way the trauma of captivity may have so destabilized the corporate consciousness of the Jews as to instill a disruptive element of decentralization. It is suggested here that it was these polarizing tendencies that ultimately gave rise to the diverse groups within Israel. In time such social and religious factions posed a major challenge to Jesus and his followers (Matt 15:1–6; 2 Cor 3:6).

One of the more positive aspects of the social fragmentation arising from the captivity was the organization of prayer cells for the reading and practice of the Torah. These prayer groups came to be known as "synagogues."[8] In effect the synagogues of the captivity functioned as "alternative sanctuaries," substituting, as far as possible, for the long-lost temple and cult. The distinct role of the synagogue in Jewish worship not only survived the Babylonian captivity but continued throughout the New Testament period.

An overview of the significance of the Babylonian captivity would not be complete without addressing another powerful tool that Israel used to transcend the crisis of the exile. This tool lay not in the organization of the people into various groups or in the ingenious creation of alternate centers of worship such as the synagogues. Rather, the ultimate

---

8   The word "synagogue" appears thirty-four times in the Gospels and twenty-two times throughout the rest of the New Testament. The Greek word is *synagōgē* (συναγωγή), whose verbal form means "to lead together" or "to assemble." It is not certain exactly when the synagogue developed. Roger T. Beckwith believes that this Jewish institution arose as late as the "Great Synagogue" in 152–142 B.C.E. ("The Pre-history and Relationships of the Pharisees, Sadducees, and Essenes: A Tentative Reconstruction," RevQ 11 [1982]: 27). Peter R. Ackroyd does not see conclusive evidence that the synagogue developed during the Babylonian captivity, but he accepts that Ps 137:1–4 and Ezek 8:1; 14:1; 20:1 speak of some kind of religious leadership seeking to establish a venue for worship in the absence of the temple (*Exile and Restoration: A Study of Hebrew Thought of the Sixth Century B.C.* [Philadelphia: Westminster, 1968], 34–35). In any case, to this day the synagogue endures as the premier symbol of Judaism.

**Persian Empire**

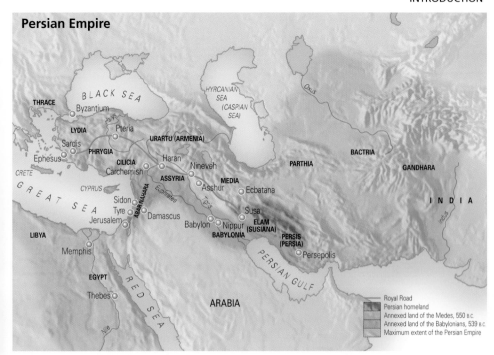

coping mechanism that the Jews employed to overcome their oppression proved to be theological and hermeneutical. They simply, yet seriously, addressed such questions as "Why did this happen?"; "What are the causes of such a national catastrophe for the people of God?"; "Who is to blame for the excruciating pain we are experiencing under the heel of Nebuchadnezzar?"

Israel's own prophets rendered a singular response to all of these haunting queries. They starkly proclaimed that Israel alone was responsible for her undoing (2 Kgs 23:26–27; Jer 1:14–19; 2 Chr 36:13b–17a). For example, Jeremiah makes the shocking proclamation that Nebuchadnezzar is "the servant of the Lord" in punishing Israel for her idolatry (Jer 25:8–12; Ezek 23:1–24). The "Day of the Lord" has visited Israel, and it is not a day of blessing (Jer 13:1–11; 19:1–13). The land will finally enjoy its "Sabbaths" so that it may be restored (2 Chr 36:21–22; Lev 26:34–35). In the meantime, Israel was left to grope after its own restoration in fits and starts. Israel could only hope

and pray for its promised deliverer to reverse its fortunes and grant it a future again.

**The Persian Period**

On October 11, 538 B.C.E., Israel's deliverer did come, but not as she might have expected. Cyrus, king of the Persians, conquered the Babylonians without so much as drawing the sword (Herodotus, *Hist.* 1.188–191). He did so by diverting the waters of the Euphrates River, which coursed under the wall of Babylon and ran straight through the center of the great city. In this way his soldiers were able to walk under the defensive walls and catch the Babylonians off guard as they celebrated a local festival (*Hist.* 1.191–192). The Cyrus Cylinder, unearthed in Babylon in 1879 and presently lodged in the British Museum, states that Cyrus "restored cults and returned exiled peoples to their homes" (lines 30–34).[9] This coincides with

9  For one of the earliest English translations of the Cyrus inscriptions, see Robert William Rogers, *Cuneiform Parallels to the Old Testament* (New York: Eaton & Mains, 1912), 380–84.

25

The Cyrus Cylinder, unearthed in Babylon in 1879, records the fall of Babylon. It declares, "I am Cyrus, king of the world, great king, legitimate king, king of Babylon, king of the four rims of the earth."

Ezra 1:1–6 (cf. also 2 Chr 36:20–21), which indicates that during his very first year in power, Cyrus decreed that the Jews were to be freed and allowed to return to their native land. His decree marked the beginning of the reversal-of-fortune theme found throughout the Scriptures (Jer 51:24; Isa 45:14; Dan 6:24).[10] That is, God would now punish the enemies of Israel that caused the people so much suffering. In an extraordinary use of language, Isaiah calls Cyrus God's shepherd (Isa 44:24–28). For Isaiah, Cyrus is the "Anointed (or 'messiah') of God," an expression previously applied only to David, the king of Israel (45:1). Cyrus's decree is seen as inaugurating a new era for the Jews. From this time on, they shall serve as a "light to the Gentiles" (42:5–9).

Furthermore, Cyrus understood that the return of the Jews to their homeland would be effective only if their temple was restored. And so he ordered that the temple be rebuilt, that all the sacred vessels be returned to the Jews, and that all expenses incurred in rebuilding the temple be drawn from the royal treasury (Ezra 1:2–4; 6:1–5). Zerubbabel was appointed to manage this momentous project (Ezra 3:2, 8; 5:2; Hag 1:1, 14; 2:23), although Sheshbazzar may have played a preliminary role (Ezra 3:10–13, 5:16).

Not everyone was enthusiastic about the Jews' return to the holy land. The regional potentates perceived a shift in the balance of power. Through political intrigue and power brokering, they appealed to Cyrus's successor, Artaxerxes, to halt the restoration efforts of Israel. Yet even Artaxerxes could not permanently frustrate these efforts (Ezra 6:22; 7:12–26), even though he was successful for a season (4:6–24). In the end King Darius swept aside all hindrances to the Jews by adopt-

10  What motivated Cyrus to make such a stunning proclamation is the subject of much debate. Bright speculates that the strategic location of Israel's homeland may have led Cyrus to court the favor of the Jews. Since Palestine could function as a buffer zone between his kingdom and the Egyptians, it would serve his purposes to have grateful subjects relocated in that region. In other words, Cyrus was prompted by geopolitical factors to release the Jews from captivity (*History of Israel*, 362). The degree to which the Jews were "released" is open to debate as well. Nehemiah 9:36–37 speaks of being "slaves in our own land." The Jews were allowed to return to Israel but were under the watchful eye of the Persians.

**The tomb of Cyrus, Pasargadae. Long since empty, it is believed to have contained a golden sarcophagus and table for offerings.**

ing the favorable policies of Cyrus (6:1–12). Darius even discerned the hand of God in the rebuilding of the temple and the refortification of Jerusalem. He calls the God of the Jews "the God of heaven" (6:9) and appeals to the sacrifices and prayers of the Jews to bless his reign and family. Darius summons the cruelest punishment and disaster upon any person or government that attempts to undermine the rebuilding of "this temple of God" (6:7, 11–12). Thus, in spite of the vicissitudes of worldly politics, God's will prevailed in the case of Israel, and this second exodus eventually came to fruition.

In the light of such a gracious offering by Cyrus and the wholehearted support of someone so powerful as Darius, one would have expected that an overwhelming number of Jews would have returned to Israel. This was not the case. Many who had been initially carried away into captivity would have died by now. In addition, many Jews who had been born in Babylon would have been reluctant to leave. The land of the exile was the only home they knew. So, by the spring of 538 B.C.E., it is likely that only a few hundred Jews returned to the land of Israel.[11] Nevertheless, the so-called

---

11   It was this kind of sociopolitical upheaval that contributed significantly to the phenomenon of the diaspora (διασπορά), or the "scattering abroad" of the Jews throughout the world. The great pilgrimages of Jews to Jerusalem (Acts 2:9–11) and the many synagogues throughout the Mediterranean world (Acts 13:14; 14:1; 17:1; 18:4) testify to the Diaspora in New Testament times. On the Jews of the Diaspora, see Shaye J. D. Cohen, *From the Maccabees to the Mishnah* (Philadelphia: Westminster, 1987), 15.

"Golah (exile) lists" of Ezra and Nehemiah speak of several waves of emigrants (Ezra 2:1–70; Neh 7:4–73). Both Ezra and Nehemiah number 42,360 returnees, not including more than 7,000 "menservants and maidservants" (Ezra 2:64–65; Neh 7:66–67). Again, there is some debate as to whether these figures include Jewish women and children or reflect only Jewish male heads of households. If the latter, the number of returnees may have numbered as high as 80,000. Regardless of how we count them, we might have expected a much larger number of Jews to return to their ancestral homeland.

The importance of these initial returnees is not in substance but in symbol. The Jews were being restored again to Israel. Zerubbabel was being empowered to reinstate the cardinal symbol of Judaism in all the earth, that is, the temple. Although the Jews' concern for their own affairs seems to have delayed the completion of the second temple (Hag 1:2–14) and the end product could not compare to the splendor of Solomon's temple (Hag 2:3), the job eventually reached a stage of completion that allowed for the resumption of the cult. It is estimated that the great dedication of the temple and the celebration of the first Passover took place in March 515 B.C.E. (Ezra 6:13–22), setting in motion the presence and program of the second temple. As time and circumstance would have it, this edifice would experience both the sacred and the profane. The pagan Antiochus Epiphanes would later ravish it, and the self-promoting Herod the Great would greatly embellish it. Yet it endured and served as the locus of the Jews' religious expression through the time of Jesus and the early church, only to be destroyed once again by the Romans in 70 C.E. (cf. Dio Cassius, *Hist. rom.* 66.4.1–66.7.2).

For now, the Jews embarked on an exciting new beginning. All that remained was for someone to give a definitive interpretation of the law. Ezra "the scribe" was to fulfill this historic role. He shouldered the burden of reinstating the law in the minds and hearts of not only those who had been carried away into Babylon but also of those who had been left behind.

Perceiving that many of the Jews had intermarried with their pagan neighbors and had corrupted the law as he understood it, Ezra embarked upon a stringent program of ethnic reform based upon the teachings of Torah. Ritual purity, tithing, and Sabbath observance became paramount. Yet at the heart of everything that Ezra said and did was the burning question "Who are the true people of God?"[12]

The societal and religious ramifications of this one question would come to mold the development of Judaism from the time of Ezra until the present. As will be demonstrated, the Pharisees, the Sadducees, and Jesus and his followers all had different answers to this one, paradigm-invoking issue.

It should be kept in mind that racism and an obsession with religious rituals were not the primary motivating factors for Ezra or for those who followed him. On the contrary, for Ezra and for like-minded Jews, an extreme concern for ethnic and religious purity was at the heart of Israel's bid for survival. Desperate times often require desperate measures. The drive to create a future for one's own people can become an all-consuming passion, and this clearly was the case for Ezra and his followers. Yet in setting their course along these lines, members of the newly formed community constructed barriers that excluded some of their own family. In other words, they created communities of outcasts within their own land.

12  Although the answer to this question seems clear enough to Ezra and Nehemiah, Shaye J. D. Cohen argues that historically the identity of the Jews has been more imagined than empirical (*The Beginnings of Jewishness: Boundaries, Varieties, Uncertainties* [Berkeley: University of California Press, 1999], esp. 1–5, 11–12).

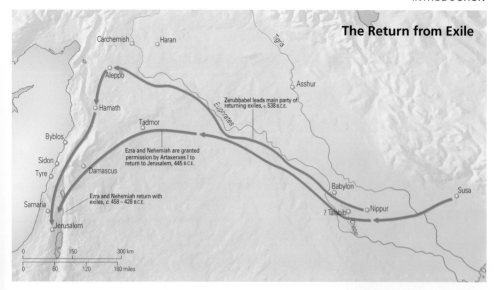

**The Return from Exile**

A particular and long-standing example of this kind of marginalization can be seen in the case of the Samaritans.[13] Because of what the returnees perceived to be racial impurity, the Samaritans were barred from helping rebuild the temple (Ezra 4:1–3). With chilling precision Zerubbabel articulated the official line when he proclaimed, "You have no part with us in building a temple to our God. We alone will build it for the Lord" (Ezra 4:3). This kind of racial factionalism smoldered on for centuries and posed a major task for reconciliation during the ministry of Jesus (John 4:1–19; Luke 10:25–37).

The tendency to ostracize and disenfranchise may not have been confined to those who were of mixed blood. There is some evidence that the returning exiles experienced a degree of culture shock from their own country people upon their initial entry into Israel. Recall that only the poor and unskilled

were left behind in the land and not carried off into captivity. One can only imagine that their poverty and lack of cultural development increased as a result of the social and economic strain brought on by the exile. The 'am ha-'arets, or "people of the land," spoken of in Ezra 4:1–5 may reflect more than a simple ethnic designation for Samaritans. The 'am ha-'arets may be Jews who, from the perspective of Ezra and Nehemiah (cf. Neh 8:1–13:31), had become lax in their understanding and obedience to the law of Moses.

Similarly, the prophet Jeremiah laments, "I thought, 'These are only the poor; they are foolish, for they do not know the way of the Lord, the requirements of their God' " (Jer 5:4). It appears that many of the Jews who had been left behind by Nebuchadnezzar had been reduced to mere subsistence. They had neither the means nor the knowledge to keep all of the commandments of Moses. In other words, the returnees not only rebuffed the mixed-breeds upon their return but may well have been repulsed by the less fortunate of their own kind, that is, the 'am ha-'arets. As we will see, by the time of Jesus, the poor "people of the land" may have constituted a long-standing sector of Jewish society—one

---

13   The Samaritans' version of their origins and development varies considerably from that of the Jews found in the Bible. The latter reports that the Samaritans had embarked on the path of syncretism long before the return of the exiles. The Assyrian conquest, with its deportation of the Jews, and the immigration of Gentiles into the region (cf. 2 Kgs 17:3b–40) created the conditions for ethnic pluralism.

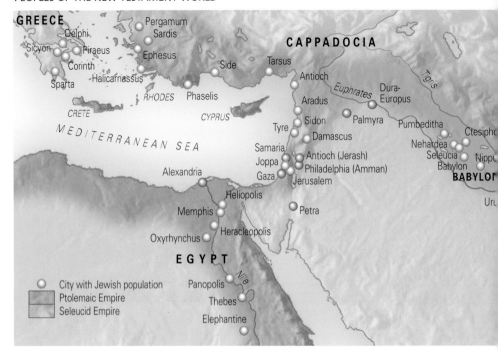

that may have been denigrated by some who viewed themselves as religiously superior. Yet this very group, the *'am ha-'arets*, may have been the most open to the radical new vision of the preacher from Galilee.

In any case, the ethnocentric religious campaign of Ezra and Nehemiah may well have served as the seedbed for the likes of the Pharisees and the more militant Zealots, who emerged much later. Furthermore, as noted, extreme observance of religious guidelines for the purpose of distinguishing oneself from the less observant can easily become an end in itself. That is, the religious life becomes captive to social, political, and ethnic factors and thus ceases to cultivate a more substantial relationship with the living God. From this perspective, well-intended religious practices can degenerate into the most callused casuistry, such as was so painfully seen in some of the Pharisees in Jesus' day (Matt 12:10–14; Luke 11:42–46).

There can be no doubt that the reestablishment of the Jews in their ancestral homeland held forth great promise. In the main, however, such expectations were not realized. Messianic qualities bestowed on Zerubbabel by Haggai would not come to fruition (Hag 2:20–23). Zerubbabel would see the start and finish of the temple's construction, but it would be the "Branch" and not Zerubbabel who would bring the temple to its full significance (Zech 3:8, 6:12). Unfortunately, historical and political circumstances seemed to conspire against the newly planted nation. Still, a struggling, meager existence was in fact an existence, and survival on any terms was viewed as a success.

## The Alexandrian or Greek Period

Even though the life and achievements of Alexander the Great are oft reported, primary sources have not survived. Some of the earliest records are from Plutarch and Arrian, writing in the second century C.E. They in turn depend heavily on two contemporaries of Alexander, Ptolemy and Aristobulus, who wrote their memoirs forty

**The Ptolemaic and Seleucid Empires**

**Alexander the Great (356 B.C.E.– 323 B.C.E.).**

years after Alexander's death. What we can gather is that Alexander was born in 365 B.C.E. to the powerful warrior king Philip of Macedon (Arrian, *Anab.* 1.1.1; Plutarch, *Alex.* 2.1–6; 3.1–5). In less than twenty-five years, the young Alexander would transform his world. He would initiate cultural, political, and philosophical trends that not only molded his world to his own Greek vision but have influenced the course of Western culture to this day.

Philip was very deliberate in the development and training of his young son. He knew that Alexander would inherit his throne and he desired that his son pursue the life of the mind rather than study to make war. Philip sought to make Alexander a wise and powerful statesman, not a warmonger. To this end he employed the great Greek philosopher Aristotle to tutor Alexander. When Alexander was only thirteen years of age, he sat at the feet of the great teacher and learned of Greek literature, art, philosophy, and science (Plutarch, *Alex.* 7.1–5). Alexander came to believe that Greek

culture was the highest model of life that the world had ever known. He also came to believe that he was the supreme exemplar of Greek culture. Alexander was convinced that he was a direct descendant of the superheroes and gods of ancient Greek mythology. He believed that Hercules was the progenitor of his father's side of the family and that his mother descended from the great Achilles (Plutarch, *Alex.* 2.1). He felt that he alone was the embodiment of all the Greek power and spirit of the ages.

In 345 B.C.E., at only twenty years of age, he took over the throne from his father (Arrian, *Anab.* 1.1.1). The teaching of Aristotle had made its mark on the young Alexander. He possessed a burning desire to hellenize (i.e., impose the Greek culture and language on) all the world. Thus he strove to create a "common Greek consciousness" in every corner of the empire. This Zeitgeist, this syncretistic amalgam of Greece and the Orient, was to extend its influence to every facet of life, be it language, political traditions, architecture, the arts, sciences, or philosophy.

31

The method that Alexander chose to actualize his grand vision was not the way of statesmanship and diplomacy, as prescribed by his father. Rather, he chose the path of war. In a meteoric rise to power, spanning a period of only thirteen years, Alexander extended his Greek empire from his homeland in the west to the Tigris and the Euphrates Valley in Persia and continued on eastward to the borders of India (1 Macc 1:1–7; Strabo, *Geogr.* 14.4.27).

His first objective was to sweep the Persians from the map. He did so by defeating Darius in a number of decisive battles, ranging from Troy in the west (334 B.C.E.) to the "Cilician Gates" in the Tarsus Mountains, and by finally bringing the war home to Darius in the very heart of Babylon (Arrian, *Anab.* 7.16.5–18.19.2). Susa, the capital of Babylon, fell in 331 B.C.E. (Josephus, *Ant.* 11.304–305). Alexander's conquest was so complete that Darius had to flee for his life, leaving behind both throne and family.

As was so often the case in the ancient world, Palestine stood in the way of the larger prize, Egypt. Thus, after defeating the Persians, Alexander rolled down the coastal plain, crushing all opposition in his path (*Ant.* 12.1). A seven-month siege ended in the defeat of Tyre, with no serious opposition in the land of the Jews until he came to Gaza. It fell in only two months (*Ant.* 11.325–340). Egypt welcomed Alexander as a "liberator" (1 Macc 10:51–55), paving the way for him to lay the foundation of his model Greek city, Alexandria, in North Africa. Alexandria would prove to be the cultural, intellectual, and mercantile center for the entire southern shore of the Mediterranean. Perhaps more important, Alexandria would serve as the dynamo of Hellenism, infusing the entire region with Greek thought, language, and culture.

This last point brings us to the heart of the issue as far as the Jews are concerned. No other event since the Babylonian captivity threatened Israel's existence more than the legacy of Alexander and his hellenizing campaign. The distinct identity of the Jews was under assault from every quarter. The pressures to assimilate were enormous. The dangers posed by pagan syncretism were on every side.[14] Just as Alexander had planned, the access points for all of these threats to indigenous culture were many and irreversible. For example, Alexander established Greek *poleis*—thoroughly hellenized colonies—throughout the conquered territories, including Israel and Samaria (Josephus, *Ant.* 11.338; *Ag. Ap.* 2.43). The plans for these outposts of Greek culture and language were modeled after the indigenous cities of Greece and included sporting arenas and theaters. The *gymnasium* was installed as a chief means of promoting Greek sports, the arts, and Greek cultural ideals. It was in this setting that appreciation of all things natural, including the exposure of the human body, proved to be so troubling to many Jews throughout the Hellenistic period (*Ant.* 12.241; 15.268–270).

The practical intent of the whole Greek enterprise was to govern and collect revenue from those conquered. Alexander created an elaborate tax-farming system to ensure the flow of cash into his treasuries, amassing an unimaginable surplus of wealth. This kind of tax-farming system was taken up by his successors and applied with egregious effect by the Romans during the time of Jesus (Matt 22:17–21; Mark 12:13–17; Luke 20:20–26). Regarding governance, Israel was viewed as a semiautonomous "temple-state," exempt from tribute on the Sabbath year but otherwise paying taxes to its Gentile masters (*Ant.* 11.338; 13.213). The tenure of the high priest was subject to his Gentile masters, and he was to supervise the collection of

---

14 For the existence of non-Jewish symbols in Judaism and the meaning of their presence among the Jews throughout the ages, see Erwin R. Goodenough, *Jewish Symbols in the Greco-Roman Period* (13 vols.; New York: Pantheon, 1953–1968), 12:132–57.

Acre (Akko), in northern Israel, became a distinctively Hellenistic town following Alexander's visit.

taxes for "the enemy" (*Ant.* 14.143, 190–214). The Jewish aristocracy, represented particularly by the Sadducees, had to continually negotiate and compromise with their civil potentates (*Ant.* 20.248–251; *J.W.* 1.169–170; 2.205). From their perspective, the route of appeasement was judged the best way to secure influence and to retain assets already in hand. Thus the leadership of Israel, as well as that of the temple, became enmeshed in a web of politics and power, a trap from which they would never fully escape (Matt 27:12, 62; Mark 15:1; Luke 23:1–13; John 18:36; 19:6, 15, 21).

Yet by far the most successful and enduring contribution of Alexander's program of Hellenism was the inculcation of the koinē, that is, the "common," Greek language. Koine Greek quickly became the lingua franca of the empire and would remain so through the Roman period. Its infiltration into the Jewish mind and culture is truly astounding. By the third and second centuries B.C.E., the Greek language had spread throughout the land of Israel and its culture. Greek loan words began to work their way into Jewish vocabulary, even finding a home in the Hebrew Scriptures (cf. Dan 3:4). The Jewish historian Josephus wrote all of his major works in Greek. The Jewish aristocracy in Jerusalem began to give Greek names to their children, and it should not be overlooked that Andrew and Philip, two of the twelve apostles, have Greek names.

Certainly the most striking symbol of Hellenism among the Jews was the production of the Septuagint, the Greek translation of the Hebrew Scriptures. This translation became a practical necessity because many Jews of the Diaspora could no longer read the Hebrew text—a testimony to the power of Hellenism. The fact that the translation probably took place during the rule of Ptolemy II (285–247 B.C.E.) reveals how early such a translation was needed. The famous *Letter of Aristeas* (9–51, 121–127, 301–321) tells the tale of how the chief librarian of Alexandria sought the high priest in Jerusalem for help in making the translation (see also Josephus *Ant.* 12.50–57, 86–90, 100).[15] The request was that six bilingual Jewish scholars from each of the twelve tribes undertake the project. These seventy-two scholars (hence the "Septuagint," i.e., "the Seventy," often abbreviated as LXX) were to come to Alexandria and work in complete isolation one from the other. Nevertheless, so the story goes, all finished at precisely the same moment, producing copies that agreed word for word with each other! This apocryphal story was no doubt designed to undermine the natural resistance of some Jews to reading the Hebrew Scriptures in the Greek language. Apocryphal or not, the story worked, for the LXX quickly became the standard Jewish Bible of the Diaspora. It greatly facilitated Gentile interest in Judaism and immeasurably added to the spread of the gospel by the early church, the New Testament writers frequently resorting to the LXX rather than to the Hebrew Masoretic text. Finally, all the New Testament documents are written in Koine Greek.

In summary, Israel was becoming more and more cosmopolitan. This new worldliness not only trafficked in merchandise but also carried on a brisk trade in the world of ideas. Greek thought forms and values were displacing traditional Hebrew ideals at an alarming rate. Key elements of the Hebrew faith were being recast in the garb of pagan Greek philosophers. Perhaps the most notable example is that of Philo of Alexandria, a Jewish scholar and philosopher contemporaneous with Jesus and Paul. Using the allegorical method typical of the Alexandrian school (cf. Philo, *The Posterity of Cain* 1–32), Philo so accommodated Moses and his message to the Greek mind-set that at times he appears more like a Greek philosopher than a Hebrew prophet. For example, in his interpretation of Genesis, Philo is careful to note the distinction between what is perceived by the senses (the physical world) and what is conceived by the mind (the intelligible world) (*On the Creation of the World*[16]). In classic Platonic fashion, he holds that the material world is mutable and subject to change but the intelligible world is immutable. And in the vein of the Stoics, Philo emphasizes that the laws of God are in harmony with the laws of nature and vice versa (*Questions and Answers on Genesis* 4.184; *Questions and Answers on Exodus* 2.19; *On the life of Abraham* 5–6).

The threat posed by Hellenism to Jewish identity and thought continued to increase after the Alexandrian period because the successors of Alexander, the Ptolemies, the Seleucids, and ultimately the Romans, promoted Greek ideals throughout their reigns. For many, the line dividing the Jews from the Gentiles was growing too faint. Thus the critical question for many Jews at this time is captured by Shaye Cohen's question "How far could Judaism go in absorbing foreign ways and ideas before it was untrue to itself and lost its identity?" To the outrage of many Jews, there were some among their own people who cared little for preserving their Jewish identity. Some desired to fully embrace the world of Hellenism, going so far as to mask the sign of circumcision in the gymnasium and at public baths (Josephus, *Ant.* 12.241). Violent conflict was in the making.

### The Syrian Period

Hellenization accelerated during the Syrian period. The oppressive policies of the Ptolemies and the Seleucids increased the pressure on the hapless Israelites. As might be expected, critical aspects of the integrity of Jewish life and culture began to give way under this relentless strain. In an effort to hold on to the law and life, the Jewish people began to divide and subdivide into various factions, each vying for power and security in the midst of a very unstable environment. The Jews were once again at

---

15  For salient portions of the Aristeas text, see Margaret H. Williams, ed., *The Jews among the Greeks and Romans: A Diasporan Sourcebook* (Baltimore: Johns Hopkins University Press, 1998), 120.

16  Cohen, *From the Maccabees to the Mishnah*, 45

the mercy of macropolitics beyond their control. As a nation, there was no option for self-determination. Their bid for survival now operated at a more fundamental level. One powerful family sought ways to depose another powerful family. The disintegration of Alexander's empire clearly hastened this downward spiral toward social anomie.

As often happens, after the untimely death of Alexander in 323 B.C.E. a power struggle ensued among his top military figures (Plutarch, *Alex.* 75.1–77.3; Josephus, *Ant.* 12.1–4). His generals carved up the empire among themselves, but ultimately just two major contenders were left. The Ptolemies had consolidated power in Egypt, and the Seleucids had control in Syria. Once again Israel found itself between the pinchers of two great powers. By 301 B.C.E. the Ptolemies had established their control over Palestine. After a ruthless campaign against Palestine, Ptolemy carried off one hundred thousand Jews to Egypt, forcing thirty thousand into military service as mercenaries (*Ant.* 12.7–8). His easy success over Jerusalem may have been due to the Jewish practice of not taking up arms on the Sabbath, a practice that Agatharchides derides (Josephus, *Ag. Ap.* 1.208; cf. also *Ant.* 12.4). After consolidating power, however, Ptolemy allowed the Jews to live in relative peace, follow their religion, and have a degree of autonomy (*Ant.* 1.9–10).

Yet such peace and stability were short-lived. The balance of power between the Ptolemies and the Seleucids vacillated until the definitive victory of the latter at Panion in 198 B.C.E.[17] Antiochus III (also known as Antiochus the Great) in about 199 B.C.E. aided the Seleucids in their victory over the Ptolemies by initially establishing favor with the Jews (*Ant.* 12.129–133). He then helped rebuild Jerusalem after the conflict with the Ptolemies and exempted the Jews from taxes

for three years. Additionally, he repopulated Jerusalem with those Jews who had been scattered abroad by the ravages of war (*Ant.* 12.139–140, 144). Finally, and perhaps most important, he endorsed the high priesthood of Simon the Just, one of the most admired religious leaders of the time (*Ant.* 12.43).[18]

The benevolence of Antiochus III toward the Jews was for a good reason. As he approached Jerusalem, he was welcomed with open arms, especially by the Jewish leaders who viewed Hellenism as the path to the future (*Ant.* 12.133). Such goodwill toward a conqueror may well reflect the tendency for the religious and political elite of Israel to advance their own fortunes by cooperating with their Hellenistic rulers. The economic and political power of the high priests, the Sadducees, and other wealthy families, such as the Tobiads, would surely increase if the Hellenistic vision of the Seleucids carried the day. For these reasons, they viewed Antiochus III as an opportunity to advance their pro-Hellenic agenda and thus gain the upper hand over Jews who opposed this agenda. Understandably, a seething resentment began to emerge between the Jews who wanted to distance themselves from any pagan influences whatsoever and those who wanted to shed every vestige of Judaism in the interests of economic and political gain. This rift between some wealthy pro-Hellenistic Jews and Jews who viewed themselves as being more zealous for the law and their ancestral customs only increased under Antiochus III's successor.

In 190 B.C.E. the Romans defeated Antiochus III at Magnesia (*Ant.* 12.414). Besides heavy war reparations, his son Antiochus IV was taken as hostage to Rome. During the twelve years he spent there, he gained a healthy respect for imperial power.[19] With the assassination of

---

17  E. P. Sanders, *Judaism: Practice and Belief, 63 B.C.E.–66 C.E.* (Philadelphia: Trinity Press International, 1992), 16.

18  As high priest, Simon the Just worked diligently not only to restore the temple and the city but also to renew the confidence and security of the people. For an impressive eulogy of the beloved Simon, see Sir 50:1–11.

19  Lester L. Grabbe, *Judaism from Cyrus to Hadrian* (London: SCM, 1992), 275.

Antiochus III, the Roman captors of Antiochus IV allowed him to continue the dynasty of the Seleucids in Syria so long as his younger brother took his place as hostage in Rome.

Therefore, in a relatively short period of time, the Jews found themselves under the heel of Ptolemy, Antiochus III, and now his son Antiochus IV. The ego of this last dictator knew no bounds. In a display of gross self-adulation, he dubbed himself Epiphanes, or "Manifest God," a title that irked many Jews beyond measure (*Ant.* 12.234; 1 Macc 1:10). The fact that many Jews referred to him as "Epimanes," or "Moron," is telling. Predictably, the more outrageously Antiochus behaved, the more fractious the infighting became among the Jews. Destabilization breeds discontent.

This degree of acrimony among the Jewish populous under Antiochus IV was a long time coming. As noted, the transition between the Ptolemies and the Seleucids was by no means seamless. Sectors of the Jewish leadership were pro-Ptolemy and others were pro-Seleucid. One faction was committed to Jewish nationalism, as evidenced by a strict observance of the law, whereas another faction desired to cast off the confining bands of Judaism and launch into the heady world of Hellenism. Polarities like these came to determine the relationships between four major Jewish families: the Oniads, the Tobiads, the Simonites, and eventually the Hasmoneans.

The purpose in examining the agendas of these competing clans is not to indulge in the study of arcane ancient feuds. Rather, when viewed collectively, these groups display the kind of political and religious diversity that existed in the society as a whole. Furthermore, these factions reflect themes and tendencies that would persist well into the first century C.E.

The scenario initially unfolds with one high priest, Onias III (of the Oniad family), who served under Antiochus III. Harboring pro-Ptolemaic sentiments, he withheld funds from his Syrian master, squirreling it away in the recesses of the temple treasury (Josephus, *J.W.* 1.31; 7.423). He also seems to have engaged in money laundering with Hyrcanus Tobias (of the Tobiads), who also hated Antiochus III (*Ant.* 12.239; 2 Macc 3:11). Simon (of the Simonites) used this indiscretion to indict Onias III before Antiochus and eventually had himself appointed tax farmer of all of Palestine. He brokered a deal with the Tobiads to sideline the Oniads forever. Yet no sooner had Simon claimed the prize than Antiochus IV came to power and provided new opportunities for intrigue. Jason, the brother of Onias III, reclaimed the high priesthood for the Oniads by offering considerable bribes to Antiochus IV (2 Macc 4:1–10). Jason embraced hellenization with a passion. Second Maccabees 4:9 tells us that his intent was to enroll all Jerusalem as "citizens of Antioch." He reveled in the construction of a gymnasium near the temple precincts and promoted all things Greek. Jason was even able to corrupt the priests who served in the temple. Under his influence, the priests would interrupt their temple duties so that they could watch the athletic competition at the nearby gymnasium (2 Macc 4:10–16). Those who attended the gymnasium "made themselves uncircumcised" (1 Macc 1:15). These words probably refer to a painful surgical procedure employed by some Jews to mask their circumcision.

In the meantime, Menelaus, the brother of Simon, was able to steal the high priesthood back for the Simonites by outbribing Jason. He was able to persuade the wealthy Tobiads to cast their lot against the Oniadthermore, whole. Furthermore, these factions reflect themes and tendencies that would persist well into the first century C.E.

The scenario initially unfolds with one high priest, Onias III (of the Oniad family), who served under Antiochus III. Harboring

Coin of Antiochus IV "Epiphanes," Seleucid king (175–164 B.C.E.). His attempts to hellenize the Jews brought about the Maccabean revolt.

pro-Ptolemaic sentiments, he withheld funds from his Syrian master, squirreling it away in the recesses of the temple treasury (Josephus, *J.W.* 1.31; 7.423). He also seems to have engaged in money laundering with Hyrcanus Tobias (of the Tobiads), who also hated Antiochus III (*Ant.* 12.239; 2 Macc 3:11). Simon (of the Simonites) used this indiscretion to indict Onias III before Antiochus and eventually had himself appointed tax farmer of all of Palestine. He brokered a deal with the Tobiads to sideline the Oniads forever. Yet no sooner had Simon claimed the prize than Antiochus IV came to power and provided new opportunities for intrigue. Jason, the brother of Onias III, reclaimed the high priesthood for the Oniads by offering considerable bribes to Antiochus IV (2 Macc 4:1–10). Jason embraced hellenization with a passion. Second Maccabees 4:9 tells us that his intent was to enroll all Jerusalem as "citizens of Antioch." He reveled in the construction of a gymnasium near the temple precincts and promoted all things Greek. Jason was even able to corrupt the priests who served in the temple. Under his influence, the priests would interrupt their temple duties so that they could watch the athletic competition at the nearby gymnasium (2 Macc 4:10–16). Those who attended the gymnasium "made themselves uncircumcised" (1 Macc 1:15). These words probably refer to a painful surgical procedure employed by some Jews to mask their circumcision.

In the meantime, Menelaus, the brother of Simon, was able to steal the high priesthood back for the Simonites by outbribing Jason. He was able to persuade the wealthy Tobiads to cast their lot against the Oniad clan once again (*Ant.* 12.240; 2 Macc 4:34–35). The hellenizing tendencies of Menelaus sank to new lows. He began selling the golden vessels of the temple on the open market to raise cash (2 Macc 4:23–32). Civil violence erupted in Jerusalem, Jew slaughtering Jew at will. A rumor that Antiochus IV had been killed in an Egyptian campaign only added fuel to the fire. The former Jason of the Oniads now saw a chance to dethrone Menelaus and his Tobiad backers. He launched a military campaign against his own people, killing thousands (2 Macc 5:5–6).

The supposedly dead Antiochus IV, upon hearing of the rebellion in Jerusalem, broke off his attack on Egypt and multiplied the carnage by brutally snuffing out the civil war in the holy city. He then embarked on a "kill or cure" policy with the help of the beleaguered Menelaus. He continued the plundering of the temple, established a citadel for the military occupation of Jerusalem, and began parceling out sections of confiscated land for his Greek mercenaries (*Ant.* 12.243–251; 2 Macc 5:11–16). The disgust of those who opposed Antiochus and his Hellenic program was palpable (1 Macc 1:11–15).

Yet Antiochus continued to accost Jewish sensitivities on a number of levels. Jews were forbidden to observe the law, the temple was defiled and dedicated to Zeus Olympus, and they were coerced to worship Bacchus and perhaps even to venerate Antiochus as a god. They were forbidden to circumcise their children. Those who refused to comply were hideously tortured (*Ant.* 12.250–256; 2 Macc 6:1–7). When an altar was constructed in the temple court and swine offered thereon, the situation reached a flash point for the Jews (1 Macc 1:44–47).

## The Maccabean Period

The Maccabean period occupies a critical place in the life and history of the Jews. Some scholars maintain that this period advanced the development of Judaism more than any other in its history. Factors that eventually led to the formation of such groups as the Pharisees, Sadducees, and Zealots began to coalesce. It was also during this time that elements promising a hope and future for Israel were dashed to the ground. Sadly, the theocratic ideals so prominent at the beginning

of the Maccabean revolt quickly vanished. Within a generation or two, Israel became ensnared in a quagmire of politics and avarice. This time Israel had only itself to blame. The threat to stability and peace did not come from some external Gentile oppressor. Rather, the seeds of Israel's undoing were sown by its own native sons. The consequences of a series of poor choices would seal Israel's fate for millennia—indeed, well into the twentieth century.

The Maccabean period was birthed and sustained through the dramatic, courageous acts of a single Jewish family. The Hasmoneans (thus the designation "Hasmonean period") were a clan of Jews from a priestly line but not at all connected with the high priests of their day. They enjoyed the privileges of the upper class, had roots in Jerusalem, yet maintained a country estate in Modein, twenty miles north of the city (1 Macc 2:1). The leaders of the family—Mattathias, together with his five sons, Judas, Jonathan, Eleazar, Simon, and John (1 Macc 2:2–5; *Ant.* 12.266)—were enraged at the abuses of Antiochus Epiphanes (1 Macc 2:14; *Ant.* 12.267) and harbored nothing but contempt for the quisling high priest, Menelaus. In disgust they left the environs of Jerusalem, hoping to distance themselves from the indignities committed there.

But this was not to be. It appears that in about 168 B.C.E., emissaries of Antiochus came to Modein to enforce the extreme Hellenistic program described above (1 Macc 1:41–50, 2:17–18). They singled out Mattathias as a leader of pious Jews and sought to make a public example of him. In particular, they demanded that he make sacrifice on a pagan altar as a symbol of forsaking his zeal for God and the law. When, upon Mattathias's refusal, a less pious Jew stepped in to offer the sacrifice, Mattathias took the sword, slaughtered the emissaries of Antiochus, and tore down the altar (1 Macc 2:19–25; *Ant.* 12.268–269). Describing the zeal of Mattathias, 1 Macc 2:26–29 relates,

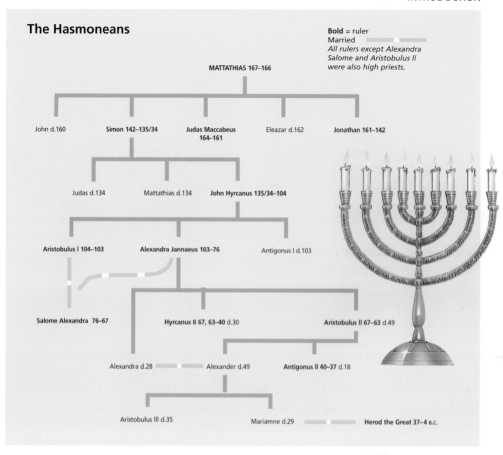

**The Hasmoneans**

Bold = ruler
Married ▨▨▨ ▨▨▨
*All rulers except Alexandra
Salome and Aristobulus II
were also high priests.*

MATTATHIAS 167–166

John d.160 — Simon 142–135/34 — Judas Maccabeus 164–161 — Eleazar d.162 — Jonathan 161–142

Judas d.134 — Mattathias d.134 — John Hyrcanus 135/34–104

Aristobulus I 104–103 — Alexandra Jannaeus 103–76 — Antigonus I d.103

Salome Alexandra 76–67 — Hyrcanus II 67, 63–40 d.30 — Aristobulus II 67–63 d.49

Alexandra d.28 — Alexander d.49 — Antigonus II 40–37 d.18

Aristobulus III d.35 — Mariamne d.29 — Herod the Great 37–4 B.C.

Thus he burned with zeal for the law, just as Phinehas did against Zimri son of Salu. Then Mattathias cried out in the town with a loud voice, saying: "Let every one who is zealous for the law and supports the covenant come out with me!" Then he and his sons fled to the hills and left all that they had in the town. At that time many who were seeking righteousness and justice went down to the wilderness to live there, (NRSV, cf. also *Ant.* 12.271–272).

The mention of "zeal" and "zealous," especially in reference to Phinehas (cf. Num 25:6–8; Ps 106:30), should receive special notice. This same sentiment, the joining of religious zeal with violence, would serve as the paradigm for the entire Maccabean revolt and set the agenda

and methods for many militants to come— for example, Saul of Tarsus (cf. Phil 3:6) and groups such as the Zealots. Mattathias did indeed offer sacrifice, but not in the way that the king's men expected. Inflamed with zeal and acting zealously for the law, Mattathias and his sons, especially Judas, would not hesitate to use lethal force against Gentiles and against all Jews who, in their opinion, lived like Gentiles (1 Macc 3:5–6, 8; *Ant.* 12.278).

These events triggered a popular revolt that would eventually lead to an independent Israel (1 Macc 2:15–30).[20] Leadership for the rebellion quickly passed from Mattathias to his eldest son, Judas Maccabeus, or "the Hammer"

20 Bezalel Bar-Kochva, *Judas Maccabaeus: The Jewish Struggle against the Seleucids* (Cambridge: Cambridge University Press, 1989), 60–62.

**Coins of John Hyrcanus (135–104 B.C.E.), the first Hasmonean to lead an independent Jewish state.**

(*Ant.* 12.279–284). His public defiance was the catalyst that galvanized the pious sentiments of Jews throughout the land. Those who were "zealous for the law" began streaming out of Jerusalem for the purpose of joining the popular revolt that was holed up in the mountains (1 Macc 2:27–30).

Such zeal for the law and religious militancy more than likely established the ideological foundation for the emergence of the Pharisees and the Zealots, who sought to be separate from Gentiles and everything impure by way of a radical piety. First Maccabees 2:42–43 notes that the Hasidim, or "pious ones," participated in the Maccabean revolt. Moreover, the words "but we fight for our lives and our laws" (1 Macc 3:21, NRSV) reveal the close identification between the desire to preserve a distinctive people and the zeal for the law. These two factors fueled the revolt and cast the die for Israel's identity throughout the ages.[21]

21   As Horsley notes, Antiochus Epiphanes planned to crush the uprising quickly, sell off all Jewish survivors into slavery, and confiscate their land for his Gentile mercenaries. "This Seleucid plan shows that what was at stake was not simply the religious freedoms of the Jews, but the very existence of traditional Judean society. The Maccabean revolt was a struggle by the Judean peasantry for their own social-economic survival" (Horsley and Hanson, *Bandits, Prophets, and Messiahs*, 21).

Through a series of brilliant military tactics, Judas accomplished three major objectives. First, by means of guerrilla warfare and terror, he was able to repel the much superior and better-equipped Seleucid army (*Ant.* 12.286). Next, he was able to recapture Jerusalem and rededicate the temple (1 Macc 4.34–59; *Ant.* 12.316–319). Finally, Judas was able to lay the groundwork for a much broader expansion of Maccabean control throughout Judea.

By occupying strategic points around Jerusalem, he cut off the Seleucid garrison stationed there. In December of 165 B.C.E. he and his men were able to retake Jerusalem and celebrate the first Hanukkah, or "dedication," of the temple. Nevertheless, the Seleucid fortress in Jerusalem refused to yield, and the struggle continued throughout the land. Antiochus engaged in negotiations, but it was too late and too little. As Maccabean command passed from Judas to his brother Jonathan and then to Simon, the Seleucid garrison was starved into submission (1 Macc 13:49–52). By 142 B.C.E. the political independence of Israel was secured.

Nearly as soon as the long-cherished victory was won, things began to go terribly wrong. John Hyrcanus (135–104 B.C.E.), the first of the Hasmoneans to lead an independent Jewish state, fell well short of the pious vision of his father, Mattathias. He

# The Hasmonean Kingdom

Tyre

Antiochia

PHOENICIA

Gischala

Seleucia

Ptolemais

Sea of Galilee

Gabara

Hippos

Dium

Sepphoris

Geba

Mount Tabor △

Philoteria

Abila

GALILEE

Gadara

Dora

GILEAD

Strato's Tower

Scythopolis

Pella

SAMARIA

Samaria

Gerasa

Shechem

Apollonia

Mount Gerizim △

Joppa

Arimathea

PEREA

Lydda

Philadelphia

MEDITERRANEAN SEA

Jamnia

JUDEA

Jericho

Emmaus

Samaga

Azotus

Jerusalem

Medeba

Ascalon

PARALIA

Beth-zur

Anthedon

Marisa

Gaza

Hebron

En-gedi

Dead Sea

Orda

Gerar

IDUMEA

MOAB

Raphia

Beersheba

Malatha

NABATEA

Zoar

ninocorura

Jordan

| | Independent Judea after Jonathan's campaigns, 142 B.C. |
| Land conquered by Simon, 142-135 B.C. |
| John Hyrcanus I, 128-104 B.C. |
| Aristobulus I, 104-103 B.C. |
| Alexander Jannaeus, 103-76 B.C. |
| Boundary of Hasmonean kingdom, 76 B.C. |
| ○ Hellenistic city |

0    25    50 km

0    10    20    30 miles

**Coins of Alexander Jannaeus (104–78 B.C.E.), leader of the hellenizing Sadducees.**

unlawfully declared himself high priest (*Ant.* 13.230) and consolidated all religious and political power in his family for nearly one hundred years. Much of his power base lay in foreign mercenaries, the majority of whom were Gentile. He financed these armies with revenue he garnered from conquered territories.[22] According to Josephus, Hyrcanus even robbed King David's tomb of its riches to buy the favor of his enemies (*J.W.* 1.61; cf. also *Ant.* 13.58). Between 135 and 76 B.C.E. the Hasmoneans reclaimed all the Jewish territory held by King David, much of it through the campaigns of the Hasmonean leader Alexander Jannaeus (104–78 B.C.E.), who likewise employed the military might of foreign mercenaries and usurped high-priestly privileges (*Ant.* 13.374–375). Some of the stark differences between the Pharisees and the

Sadducees may have emerged during this period of turmoil (*Ant.* 13.288–298).

One particular incident graphically portrays the sense of betrayal that many Jews felt at the hands of the Hasmoneans. As Alexander attempted to minister at the altar in the temple, the people began pelting him with citrons. Alexander was so enraged that he called forth troops and massacred six thousand of his own people (*Ant.* 13.372–373). Civil war ensued, costing the lives of more than fifty thousand Jews. The situation became so desperate that the opponents of Alexander even called upon their previous oppressors, the Seleucids, for military aid (*Ant.* 13.374–376). Alexander wrangled enough support to repel the Seleucids, this time under the leadership of Demetrius Eucerus. Alexander then had eight hundred of the Jewish resistors crucified (*Ant.* 13.379–383; *J.W.* 1.96–98). The Qumran literature speaks of a "young lion" who executes wrath against those "who seek

22  Martin Goodman, *The Ruling Class of Judaea: The Origins of the Jewish Revolt against Rome,* A.D. *66–70* (Cambridge: Cambridge University Press, 1987), 31.

smooth things" or "those who seek easy interpretations" (4QpNah 1:6–8). This may be a reference to Alexander Jannaeus's battle against the Pharisees who opposed him.

In conclusion, what started as a pious theocratic ideal evolved into political maneuvering and fratricide. Factionalism engendered destabilization, and this created the perfect conditions for a stronger force to intervene. As the Jews struggled to bring their house in order, the Romans came knocking at the door.

## The Roman Period

The Roman period can be described as the "world of the New Testament," for it encompasses the life and times of Jesus Christ as well as the birth and development of the early church. In the main, the Jews once again experienced the lash of an oppressive Gentile regime driven by what Green describes as a "coarse psychological pragmatism."[23] Simply put, if it worked, it was Roman. The Romans did not hesitate to use any means available to enhance their power and wealth. To that end they were great assimilators of the best that Hellenism had to offer in the areas of politics, philosophy, religion, and, especially, military tactics.

This last gift of the Greeks—the advantage of a well-equipped and -trained army—was often the first solution the Romans used to solve problems. Their propensity to strike with a blunt instrument, and to strike hard, would characterize Rome's legacy throughout the ages. Through the use of brute force, coupled with complicated political arrangements, the Romans expanded their power throughout the Mediterranean world for two centuries before the coming of Christ. Their insatiable appetite for more was only whetted by the infighting of the Hasmoneans. The bitter feud between two Hasmonean brothers, Aristobulus II and Hyrcanus II (67–63 B.C.E.) (cf. *Ant.* 20.242–243), provided the context for

23  Peter Green, *Alexander to Actium: The Historical Evolution of the Hellenic Age* (Berkeley: University of California Press, 1990), 661.

direct Roman intervention (*Ant.* 14.77).

This feud over who would be high priest and king represents a much broader struggle (*Ant.* 15.41; *J.W.* 1.153). The Sadducees aligned with Aristobulus whereas the Pharisees and those they represented favored Hyrcanus (*Ant.* 13.405–408). The two factions fought a running battle with each other, once again spilling the blood of fellow Jews to advance their own causes. Aristobulus eventually succeeded in gaining the upper hand (*Ant.* 13.301, 428; 14.1–7), but his office of high priest and the kingdom would soon be torn from his grip by more powerful forces.

A third faction that now entered the fray would play a major role in the life and ministry of Jesus. One Antipater sought to exploit the wounded ego of the deposed Hyrcanus to advance his own political interests (*Ant.* 14.72–77). This Antipater was the father of Herod the Great, who in time would rule with such tyranny at the time of Jesus' birth. Through various alliances with Rome, the Herodian dynasty was to direct the fate of Israel for one hundred and fifty years.

For the most part, the Herodian reign was one of exploitation and oppression of the Jews. Added to all of this misery were the harsh policies of Pontius Pilate, Roman governor of Judea from 26 to 36 C.E. (*Ant.* 18.55–62). He "mixed" the blood of some Galileans with their sacrifices (Luke 13:1), and Barabbas led a Zealot uprising to remove him from power (Mark 15:7). Pilate's cavalier approach to justice, as seen in the mock trial of Jesus, would change the course of history forever (Matt 27:2–27; *Ant.* 18.63–64). Even the callousness of the Roman hierarchy could not stomach Pilate for long. After committing unspeakable atrocities against Samaritan worshipers on Mt. Gerizim, he was recalled to Rome to answer for his crimes (*Ant.* 18.85–89).

In summary, the climate of the Roman period mirrored the repression and brutality of previous regimes. The pious in Israel prayed

Jews pray at Jerusalem's Western Wall. Some of the dressed stones date from Herod's Temple, destroyed by the Romans in 70 C.E.

for the coming of the messiah, and the more militant hatched plots to spread terror among their enemies. Many wrestled with questions of how a Jew should cope with Roman domination. Should one pay taxes to Caesar (Mark 12:14; Luke 20:22; 23:2)? To what extent should a Jew submit to the dictates of an ungodly emperor (Matt 5:39–48; Luke 6:27–36)? It was a time of struggle and turmoil. It was the time of Jesus and the early church.

## INCREASING HELLENIZATION AND THE JEWISH STRUGGLE TO SURVIVE

The centuries of foreign domination and oppression took an enormous toll on the social, the political, and especially the religious life of the Jews. The Assyrian conquest of the ten northern tribes sent a chilling message to the "remnant" in the south. A nation's worst nightmare—its complete dissolution as a people—was not some groundless fear but, rather, a real historic possibility. The foundation stones that defined the identity of Israel as a distinct people were systematically being removed one by one and discarded on the ash heap of history. The geographic and social significance of the tribes was gone. The temple and the cult were no more. Traditional leadership structures were shattered. In this context, the sophisticated and complex elements that form a distinct people were stripped away. All that remained was the primal instinct to survive. For many, the pathway to survival was to intensify any beliefs or practices that stressed Jewishness over against an ever-increasing Gentile encroachment.

In this kind of threatening environment, the impulse to form subgroups of like-minded persons was strong. For those emphasizing separation, any aspect of the law that tended to intensify the identity of the subgroup was raised to the highest importance. In some settings, circumcision, purity regulations, and Sabbath observance took meanings that went beyond their original religious significance. They became means to secure the future of a nation, and in their unrefined form, they

Relief of the Roman triumph that followed the defeat of the Jewish Revolt. The Roman soldiers are bearing a candelabra from Herod's Temple.

**Mosaic from the floor of the third-century synagogue at Tiberias. The figurative design with signs of the zodiac shows the strong Hellenistic influence on the Judaism of the time.**

became extensions of nationalism. Many of these tendencies began to coalesce upon the return of the exiles from the Babylonian captivity. The question "Who is a true Jew?" became the dominant issue for influential postexilic leaders such as Ezra and Nehemiah.[24] Their answer to this question often fell along the lines of ethnicity as interpreted from the law. The more tightly the identity of a particular group is defined, the more exclusive it becomes. As was the case with the Samaritans and the *'am ha-'arets* ("people of the land"), a sense of alienation and disenfranchisement set in among some sectors of Israel.

The thoroughgoing program of Hellenism initiated by Alexander the Great and contin-

ued by his successors accelerated this tendency. Hellenism promoted a creeping erosion of distinctive Jewish culture, thus further blurring the line separating Jew from Gentile. The Hebrew language was being supplanted by Greek. Greek philosophy, education, and fashion were replacing traditional Hebrew elements (*Ant.* 12.241; 2 Macc 4:10–15). In some ways, regarding the official cult in Israel, the marriage of the sacred and the mundane had been consummated. The chief religious figure of the Jews, the high priest, was in many instances a pawn of the oppressors of Israel. The Jewish nobility at times were prone to cooperate with the enemy. Furthermore, the lucrative rewards afforded by the tax-farming system led some Jews to leech their fellow countrymen of the meager resources they possessed (Luke 2:1–5). These tax revenues were increasing the power of

---

24  Today the question "Who is a true Jew?" is as relevant as, and perhaps more problematic than, it was during the time of Ezra and Nehemiah. On the difficulties surrounding Jewish identity in modern times, see Cohen, *Beginnings of Jewishness*, 8–9.

**View of the remains of the settlement at Qumran. The cliffs in the background are honeycombed with caves, in some of which the Dead Sea Scrolls were discovered.**

those who were causing such misery to the Jewish people.

As indicated, the Jewish response to increased Hellenism was varied and often contradictory. The Jewish officials who served as mere functionaries of Gentile empires extended no favor toward religious militants. In general, tax collectors would not have been especially concerned with advancing the fortune of Israel.

On the other hand, there were some whose interpretation of the law and what it requires led them to take a different route. Their passion for Jewish life and land as they saw it was often expressed in terms of rejection and rebellion. In these cases the amalgam of the religious and the militant often came together (*Ant.* 20.186, *J.W.* 2.425; Luke 6:15). The most extreme example of this approach to Hellenism was that of the Zealots, especially

as demonstrated in the fatal rebellion from 66 to 70 C.E. For these Jews, instruments of terror and murder served their purpose of promoting the "sole rule of God." The same agenda was shared by the Hasidim, although they generally followed less militant practices. The Pharisees intensified the requirements of the law in an attempt to stave off the threat of assimilation. They separated themselves from Jews who did not follow their stringent interpretation of Moses and purity. They insulated themselves from all possible sources of defilement by erecting layer upon layer of religious barriers to shut out the profane (*Ant.* 13.297; Matt 9:10–11; Mark 2:16; Luke 5:30). Some, such as the Essenes, including those at Qumran, gave up all hope of attaining holiness while living among common Jews. They abandoned fellowship with their own people to live a monastic life of religious devotion, some

47

even completely withdrawing from society to live in the desert (*Ant.* 18.18–21; 1QS 8:13–16).

As a result of all of these pressures, accumulating over a long period of time, there was an extraordinary degree of diversity within first-century Judaism. Although orbiting about the common core of the law of Moses, differing factions within Judaism took widely varying trajectories. Radical and at times antithetical interpretations of Jewish life and practice inculcated a degree of social polarization and fragmentation within Jewish society. Various sectors of the population became alienated from each other. Jews who welcomed Hellenism were violently rejected by those who did not. Those who pursued ritual purity separated themselves from those who did not. The gist of the matter is that *intercultural* segregation (i.e., between Jews and Gentiles) gradually developed into a type of *intracultural* segregation. Ironically, the intense desire to preserve the integrity of Israel by some religious groups engendered, to some extent, the fragmentation of that identity. Therefore questions such as "Who then can be saved?" (Matt 19:25; Mark 10:26; Luke 13:23, 18:26), "And who is my neighbor?" (Luke 10:29), and "Teacher, which is the greatest commandment in the Law?" (Matt 22:36) were not theological parlor games for many Jews. For them, such issues were at the very heart of Israel's struggle to survive. In the midst of such a troubled and factious world, Jesus came preaching the kingdom of God.

# Annotated Bibliography

Ackroyd, Peter R. *Exile and Restoration: A Study of Hebrew Thought of the Sixth Century B.C.* Philadelphia: Westminster, 1968. This work is a clear historical investigation of how the exile might have informed Hebrew thought in the sixth century. It is exegetically based with numerous references to various positions on the major critical issues.

Bright, John. *A History of Israel.* 3d ed. Philadelphia: Westminster, 1981. This is a standard work on the history of Israel, contained in one volume and accessible to beginning students.

Cohen, Shaye J. D. *The Beginnings of Jewishness: Boundaries, Varieties, Uncertainties.* Berkeley: University of California Press, 1999. This collection of essays addresses the critical question of what precisely constituted a Jew in antiquity and how this identity would have been distinguished from a Gentile. The work has value in presenting the reader with the issues of ethnicity and of an ethnically determined religion in the ancient world.

———. *From the Maccabees to the Mishnah.* Philadelphia: Westminster, 1987. This is a relatively brief yet clearly written work on how national crises and a sense of political and social alienation may have influenced the development of Jewish thought, particularly regarding apocalyptic literature.

Goodenough, Erwin R. *Jewish Symbols in the Greco-Roman Period.* 13 vols. New York: Pantheon, 1953–1968. Encyclopedic in scope and format, this collection of archaeological, textual, and epigraphic material examines the substance and meaning of symbols in Judaism in order to demonstrate that the ever-present diversity found in the Jewish faith defies any attempt to arrive at a single definition of Judaism.

Goodman, Martin. *The Ruling Class of Judaea: The Origins of the Jewish Revolt against Rome, A.D. 66–70.* Cambridge: Cambridge University Press, 1987. This is a good resource for exploring the various causes for the Jewish revolt against Rome in the first century. Goodman's central thesis is that power struggles among the ruling elite in Israel, and particularly the Roman miscue in appointing a ruling elite that had no natural authority over the vast majority of Jews in Israel at the time, led to the revolt. This work grants insight into the Herodian dynasty, especially as set forth by Josephus.

Grabbe, Lester L. *Judaism from Cyrus to Hadrian.* London: SCM, 1992. This clearly structured, one-volume work covers the major events of Judaism during the Second Temple period.

Green, Peter. *Alexander to Actium: The Historical Evolution of the Hellenic Age.* Berkeley: University of California Press, 1990. This thorough, clearly written, but very detailed work on Hellenism and its influence is not intended for the beginner.

Horsley, Richard A., and John S. Hanson. *Bandits, Prophets, and Messiahs: Popular Movements at the Time of Jesus.* San Francisco: Harper & Row, 1985. The authors explore the social and political dynamics of resistance movements in the first century. This is a scholarly work, not for beginners.

Sanders, E. P. *Judaism: Practice and Belief: 63 B.C.E.–66 C.E..* Philadelphia: Trinity Press International, 1992. This excellent work, well researched and argued from the primary sources, is designed for in-depth research.

Smith, Daniel. *The Religion of the Landless: The Social Context of the Babylonian Exile.* Bloomington, Ind.: Meyer-Stone, 1989. Smith provides a good orientation to the holocaust of the Babylonian exile, emphasizing the social factors that shaped Judaism during this period. This fine social and religious study is accessible to the beginning student and gives a good orientation to complex issues.

Williams, Margaret H., ed., *The Jews among the Greeks and Romans: A Diasporan Sourcebook.* Baltimore: Johns Hopkins University Press, 1998. This is a good source for insight into how Jews of the Diaspora sought to maintain their identity among the Greeks and Romans of antiquity. Evidence of syncretism and resistance to assimilation is explored and well presented. The author provides good access to primary sources.

# 2

# The Pharisees—
# Power and Purity

## INTRODUCTION

Perhaps no other religious group played a greater role in the life of Jesus and the early church than the Pharisees. Some form of the word "Pharisee(s)" appears eighty-eight times in the Gospels, eight times in the book of Acts, and once in the Epistles, making a total of ninety-seven occurrences in the New Testament (UBS⁴). As prominent as the

**During prayer Orthodox Jews wear traditional prayer shawls and *tephillim*, small boxes containing verses from Deuteronomy 6, tied to the forehead and hands.**

Pharisees were, it would be a gross simplification, if not a distortion of the truth, to characterize Jesus' ministry as simply "anti-Pharisaic."[1] His vision and agenda cannot be defined as a simple counterpoint to the Pharisees. Furthermore, leading Pharisees of the time, such as Nicodemus and Gamaliel (John 3:1–9; 7:50; 19:39; Acts 5:34–39), did not oppose Jesus, and other Pharisees came to identify with the early Christians (Acts 15:5).

Even so, key aspects of the gospel are set forth in dialogue with the Pharisees. For example, Jesus was frequently in conflict with some Pharisees concerning the proper interpretation of the law of Moses (Matt 15:1–21). Even Jesus' fundamental understanding of God appears radically at odds with that of many Pharisees (Matt 16:6–12; Luke 14:3–35, John 4:1; 11:46–57). Such differences spill over into the birth and development of the early church as well. Acts 15:1–5 indicates that the early church's decision to welcome uncircumcised Gentiles as full members of the community was nearly overturned by some Pharisees. In one way or another, an intense concern with Jewish ethnicity and cultic ritual on the part of some Pharisees plagued the early church throughout the apostolic period (Acts 11:1–3; 15:1–5; Gal. 2:1–15; Phil. 3:2–3).

1   E. P. Sanders, *Paul and Palestinian Judaism: A Comparison of Patterns of Religion* (Philadelphia: Fortress, 1977), 44.

In the end, however, the course of the church was not to be directed along Pharisaic lines (Acts 15:13–29).

The extent to which the Pharisees defined Judaism prior to 70 C.E. is a point of debate among scholars. The very survival of the Pharisees after the destruction of the temple is also open to question, even though the early rabbis claim the Pharisees as their progenitors and purport to preserve their teachings in the Mishnah.[2] Since these teachings survive to this day and form an integral part of modern Judaism, the identity and influence of the Pharisees are a critical issue for both Jewish and Christian scholars. One cannot understand the person and work of Jesus, the story of the early church, and the continued development of Torah Judaism without a thorough knowledge of the Pharisees.

## The Origin of the Pharisees

A critical question that has engaged scholars of Second Temple Judaism and those studying early Christianity concerns the precise identity and origin of the Pharisees. When did this significant group in Judaism arise, and what were the factors that contributed to its emergence? The issue is fraught with problems because of the nature of the sources. Apart from a few allusions in Maccabees and what we are able to sift out of the Qumran literature, the only sources we have concerning the Pharisees are those of Josephus, the writings of the New Testament, and the traditions of the rabbis.[3] Since the presentation of the Pharisees in each of these sources is determined by its literary context, the scholar must proceed with caution.[4] The historical continuity between the sources is not completely demonstrable, and so drawing direct parallels between the sources raises questions.

Perhaps the best way to proceed is along phenomenological lines that seek to identify a common portrait arising out of systemic patterns inherent to the sources. The Maccabees, Josephus, the New Testament, and the early rabbis speak of an identifiable group of Jews who are zealous for the written Torah and the "traditions of the fathers" and at times have considerable influence in the religious and political affairs of the Jews (1 Macc 2:27–30, 42–43; *Ant.* 13.297–298; Mark 7:3–5; *m. 'Abot* 1:1–18).

At points in this long history, covering

2    The order of reception as related by the early rabbis is as follows: God revealed the written *and oral* Torah to Moses. The oral teachings were preserved by the "fathers" and inherited by the Pharisees. After the destruction of the temple in 70 C.E., the traditions were preserved by the early rabbis and finally codified in the Mishnah (ca. 200 C.E.). The Babylonian and Palestinian Talmuds (ca. 400–600 C.E.) are massive commentaries on earlier teachings of the rabbis found in the Mishnah. The self-designated successors of the Pharisees are known as the Tannaim, and their writings are called the Tannaitic literature. For detailed presentations on the order of reception, see Samson H. Levey, "Neusner's *Purities*—Monumental Masterpiece of Mishnaic Learning: An Essay-Review of Jacob Neusner's *A History of the Mishnaic Law of Purities* (22 Volumes)," *Journal of the Academy of Religion* 46 (1978): 338, 342; and Lawrence H. Schiffman, "New Light on the Pharisees: Insights from the Dead Sea Scrolls," *BRev* (1992): 30, 33.

3    Josephus claims to have explored all three major sects in Judaism (the Sadducees, the Pharisees, and the Essenes) and decided to become a Pharisee (*Life* 1.10–12). He mentions the Pharisees twenty times, often in conjunction with the chief priests and always as politically, socially, and religiously influential. On the relationship of the Pharisees to the chief priests, see Urban C. Von Wahlde, "The Relationships between Pharisees and Chief Priests: Some Observations on the Texts in Matthew, John, and Josephus," *NTS* 42 (1996): 506–22.

4    Among scholars who question the accounts of the Pharisees in Josephus, the New Testament, and the rabbinic literature are E. P. Sanders, *Jesus and Judaism* (Philadelphia: Fortress, 1985); and J. Sievers, "Who Were the Pharisees?" in *Hillel and Jesus: Comparative Studies of Two Major Religious Leaders* (ed. James H. Charlesworth and Loren L. Johns; Minneapolis: Fortress, 1997), 135–55. Among those who express more confidence in the reports of Josephus and the rabbis are Jacob Neusner, *From Politics to Piety: The Emergence of Pharisaic Judaism* (Englewood Cliffs, N.J.: Prentice-Hall, 1973); idem, *The Rabbinic Traditions about the Pharisees before 70* (3 vols.; Atlanta: Scholars Press, 1999); and Ellis Rivkin, *A Hidden Revolution: The Pharisees' Search for the Kingdom Within* (Nashville: Abingdon, 1978), esp. 27.

more than three hundred years, these pious are explicitly described as "Pharisees." In other places such persons are called the Hasidim ("pious ones") or the Haberim ("the fellowship"). Scholars are sharply divided over whether all of these groups represent the Pharisees, some stage in the development of the Pharisees, or distinct groups that have no inherent connection to each other.

Despite the various expressions, a general profile seems to emerge that is compatible with what we know of the Pharisees as set forth in the New Testament. It is suggested here that this common portrait of the Pharisees is derived from Judaism's struggle to preserve a single religious heritage in the midst of one national trauma after another. For example, after the destruction of the temple, the rabbinic council at Yavneh (70–125 C.E.) was dedicated to retrieving and consolidating the elements the participants felt best defined their vision of Judaism. In preserving the traditions of the Pharisees as they saw it, the rabbis present a profile that is in many points complementary to what we find in the Gospels and Josephus. "Josephus, the New Testament, and the Tannaitic Literature, though focusing on the Pharisees with different lenses, were looking at the identical object."[5] Whether they were in fact all looking at "the identical object" may be questioned, but there is some consensus among these sources concerning the ideals and praxis of the Pharisees.

It is possible that what may be called proto-Pharisees emerged upon the scene at the beginning of the Hasmonean era, near the end of the Maccabean period. First Maccabees 2:15 indicates that the zeal of Mattathias sparked the popular Jewish revolt against Antiochus Epiphanes in about 168 B.C.E. The agenda and methods of the Maccabean revolt are set forth in 1 Macc 2:24–26 (cf. also 3:1–9). Here we read that these zealous Jews fought for their lives and the law (1 Macc 3:21). Like-minded Hasidim were among those who rallied to the Maccabean cause (1 Macc 2:27–30, 42–43). It is not impossible that these Hasidim were the precursors to the Pharisees. In *Ant.* 13.171 Josephus speaks of the Pharisees in conjunction with Jonathan the Hasmonean (ca. 142 B.C.E.; cf. *Ant.* 13.166, 174). He also talks of the "sect" (Gk. *hairesis*) of the Pharisees and states that they existed by the time of Hyrcanus (135–105 B.C.E.). He records the conflict between the Pharisees and John Hyrcanus wherein Eleazar incited the Pharisees to force Hyrcanus to give up the high priesthood (*Ant.* 13.288–300). In addition, if 4QpNah speaks against the Pharisees from a Sadducean point of view, then this would mean that both groups were well established during the Hasmonean period.[6] These texts show that the Pharisees were in place during the time of the Hasmoneans and possibly as early as the Maccabean revolt.

The emergence of such a major religious party within Israel probably did not occur overnight. Indeed, the religious, political, and social factors that ultimately gave rise to the Pharisees may have already been in place as early as the Babylonian captivity. The threat to Israel and her identity became most acute during this period. It appears that in an effort to counter the religious and cultural syncretism of the time, some Jews embarked on a radical campaign of separation from everything and everyone that did not promote their view of the people of God. The drive to be separate seems to have intensified during the time of Ezra and Nehemiah, about 458 B.C.E. (cf. Ezra 6:1–12; 7:10–28). Their campaign of radical separation may have

---

5  Rivkin, *A Hidden Revolution*, 183. Cf. also Jacob Neusner, *The Idea of Purity in Ancient Judaism: The Haskell Lectures, 1972–1973* (SJLA 1; Leiden: E. J. Brill, 1973), 65.

6  Lawrence H. Schiffman, "Pharisees and Sadducees in *Pesher Nahum*," in Minah le-Nahum (JSOTSup 154; Sheffield, Eng.: Sheffield Academic Press, 1993), 272.

planted the seeds that eventually germinated and grew into the sect of the Pharisees.[7]

## The Babylonian Captivity and the Emergence of the Pharisees

In 597 B.C.E. Nebuchadnezzar, king of the Babylonians, overran Judea and captured Jerusalem. His plan was to reduce Israel to a slave state. To this end he destroyed the temple, confiscating the sacred vessels (Jer 28:1–6), and carried away the most talented Jews to Babylon, including Daniel and Ezekiel. Nebuchadnezzar had no need for the "poorest people of the land," those who "work the vineyards and fields," and so they were left to fend for themselves in the midst of a ravaged nation (2 Kgs 25:12; Jer 52:16). The Jews were devastated politically, socially, and religiously. They needed a rallying point that could hold the people and their faith together.

This quest in response to the holocaust of captivity may well have generated ideals, values, and practices that eventually gave rise to the Pharisees. The crisis of the exile likely forced Israel to adopt strategies for survival that led to the formation of various groups, the Pharisees included. Thus postexilic Israel may have entered into an extraordinary period of "creativity" in ensuring the future of the nation.[8] For Israel, the choices were to adapt or die. The status quo had to be abandoned. Israel would have to embrace radically new ways of seeing itself, its God, and its religion.

One hypothesis that may help to explain the emergence and development of the Pharisees concerns Israel's understanding and practice of the law after the exile.[9] The one thing that the ravages of war could not take from the Jews was their devotion to the law of Moses. In a way that cannot be easily quantified, in the aftermath of the captivity, the law of Moses came to serve for many Jews as the tangible substitute for all that they had lost. To some degree this was the case among the Pharisees.

This intense focus on the law also became the hallmark of Ezra and Nehemiah. For them, strict observance of the law became the definitive sign that distinguished the true Jew from those who had no place in the commonwealth of Israel (Ezra 9:4; Neh 8:3, 18; 9:3). It appears that at this time the proper observance of the Sabbath, circumcision, and purity regulations took on a prominence as never before (Jer 17:19–27; Isa 56:1–8; 58:13–14; Ezek 4:12–15; 22:26). This extraordinary focus on religious code and ritual could have been a seminal factor in the birth and development of the Pharisees.

## EZRA, NEHEMIAH, AND INCIPIENT PHARISAISM

In 538 B.C.E. King Cyrus of the Persians decreed that the Jews were to be allowed to return to their ancestral homeland and to rebuild the temple (Ezra 1:1–6; 6:1–5; 2 Chr 36:20–23; cf. also Herodotus, *Hist.* 1.191–192). The Golah lists of Ezra and Nehemiah grant insight here. "Golah" means "exile" and the "sons of the Golah" refers to the Jews who returned from the Babylonian captivity to resettle in Israel. These lists speak of several waves of emigrants who made the journey, not one mass exodus (Ezra 2:1–70; Neh 7:4–73). The total number of these immigrants is subject to debate. Both Ezra and

---

7    Regarding Ezra and Nehemiah, Lester L. Grabbe states, "The attitudes and perspectives exemplified in the Ezra–Nehemiah reforms, if not the reforms themselves, became an important part of the later religious identity of the Jews" ("Triumph of the Pious or Failure of the Xenophobes? The Ezra-Nehemiah Reforms and Their *Nachgeschichte,*" in *Jewish Local Patriotism and Self-Identification in the Graeco-Roman Period* [ed. Siân Jones and Sarah Pearce; Sheffield, Eng.: Sheffield Academic Press, 1998], 50).

8    Peter R. Ackroyd, *Exile and Restoration: A Study of Hebrew Thought of the Sixth Century B.C.* (Philadelphia: Westminster, 1968), 6.

9    Jacob Neusner, "Exile and Return as the History of Judaism," in James M. Scott, ed., *Exile: Old Testament, Jewish, and Christian Conceptions* (Leiden: E. J. Brill, 1997), 224.

Nehemiah number 42,360 returnees, not including more than 7,000 "menservants and maidservants" (Ezra 2:64–65; Neh 7:66–67).

This incremental return of the Jews from the exile created conditions that could have set the stage for the development of the Pharisees. Some of the earliest returnees of the Golah began to intermarry with the *'am ha-'arets*, or "peoples of the land" (NRSV), the residents of Samaria (Ezra 9:1–5). The latter groups were Jews and half-Jews whom the Babylonians did not think it worthy to carry into exile. The prophet Jeremiah describes the *'am ha-'arets*: "I thought, 'These are only the poor; they are foolish, for they do not know the way of the Lord, the requirements of their God' " (Jer 5:4). Such persons had been without civil or spiritual leadership for over a generation. In the absence of such leadership, the presence of religious and ethnic syncretism is understandable. Some of the earliest returnees from the exile began adopting the syncretistic religious practices of the *'am ha-'arets* and the Samaritans (Exod 34:16; Deut 7:1–4).[10] Fensham speaks of a "double threat" consisting of the disillusion of the racial identity of the Jews as a distinct people and the corruption of cardinal religious principles that defined Judaism at the time.[11] In this context, Ezra and Nehemiah did not view proper ceremonial protocol and the maintenance of ethnic purity as matters of personal choice. Rather, for them, strict observance of the law was the only way that Israel could preserve its identity as a distinct people and thus procure a future.

### Ezra "the Scribe" and the Pharisees

Ezra served as a pivotal figure for reinstating "normative Judaism" among the people once he arrived in Israel in 458 B.C.E. His

role in the history of Israel is succinctly summarized in the words of Ezra 7:10: "For Ezra had devoted himself to the study and observance of the law of the Lord, and to teaching its decrees and laws in Israel." Even Artaxerxes, after recanting his earlier decree (cf. 4:18–22), describes Ezra as "the priest, a teacher of the Law of the God of heaven" (7:12). He officially empowered Ezra to teach "the laws of your God" (7:25) to the people. In this way, the king thoroughly endorsed the exegetical prowess of Ezra.

> This is a copy of the letter King Artaxerxes had given to Ezra the priest and teacher, a man learned in matters concerning the commands and decrees of the Lord for Israel: Artaxerxes, king of kings, To Ezra the priest, a teacher of the Law of the God of heaven: Greetings. (7:11–12)

The intensification of the Torah's importance, as described above, found a ready and willing advocate in Ezra. He enacted reforms that set in motion theological trends that would come to define the Judaism of his day. His reforms, which were affirmed and enforced by Nehemiah, provided fertile ground for the growth of various religious groups, those who were zealous for the law and for the "traditions of the fathers." As noted, it is quite probable that one of these groups was the Pharisees.

Ezra's arrival in the holy land was not a happy one. From his perspective, compromise and apostasy were everywhere. In the midst of religious dereliction and surrounded by Samaritans, *'am ha-'arets*, and the "sons of the Golah" who had joined league with them, Ezra was confronted with the single most vexing question for many Jews even to this day: "Who are the people of God?"

Ezra's answer to this question reveals the true significance of the Golah lists set forth in Ezra 8:1–14. For Ezra, the lists serve as rosters authenticating who are the true "sons of the Exile" and who are not. In particular,

---

10   Hyam Maccoby, "Holiness and Purity: The Holy People in Leviticus and Ezra–Nehemiah," in John F. A. Sawyer, ed., *Reading Leviticus: A Conversation with Mary Douglas* (JSOTSup 227; Sheffield, Eng.: Sheffield Academic Press, 1996), 161.

11   F. Charles Fensham, *The Books of Ezra and Nehemiah* (Grand Rapids: Eerdmans, 1982), 17–18.

An Orthodox Bar Mitzvah at Jerusalem's Western Wall. Note the Torah case and *tephillim*.

those rejected by Ezra and Nehemiah (cf. 10:18–44; Neh 13:23–29) were Jews who "have not kept themselves separate" but have polluted the land by intermarrying with non-Jews (Ezra 9:1–2, 10–12).[12] The priests and Levites were included among this number (9:1; 10:18–44). The horror and dejection of Ezra on this score are set forth in 9:3–15. He tears his garments, pulls out the hair of his head and beard, and falls prostrate before the Lord (9:3–5; cf. also 2 Sam 13:19; Isa 50:6). He cries out that the whole land is "polluted" (Ezra 9:11; cf. also Deut 4:5; Lev 18:25; 20:1–27) and repeatedly speaks about a holy "remnant" (Ezra 9:8, 13, 15).

To correct what he viewed as unfaithfulness to Yahweh, Ezra enacted a program of ethno-religious reformation, made known to the people by way of a scathing sermon delivered in a pouring rain (Ezra 10:10–17). Ezra would require that all who had intermarried with Gentiles take a binding oath before God (10:2–4). As the rain poured down, Ezra arrived at the critical point of his message, saying that those who wanted to be included in the covenant had to "separate" themselves from their wives and children (10:11).[13] Anyone who did not report for the examination of their racial purity would have their homes and possessions confiscated (10:8–9). Furthermore, such persons would be excommunicated from the commonwealth of Israel (10:1–7). Those who were deemed to be racially impure were to be duly noted in print (Ezra 10:18–44).

The theme of separation inherent in Ezra's

message was literally repeated in Nehemiah's reforms as well. It may well be that this theme of religious separation established the paradigm for the emergence of the Pharisees, or "separated ones."

## Nehemiah Continues the Campaign

Nehemiah's abhorrence for racial impurity and neglect of the law was equal to that of Ezra, if not more so (Neh 13:1–3). He records that the law was read aloud from daybreak until noon on the first day, and then "day after day" (8:3, 18; 9:3). Upon hearing the reading of the law, Nehemiah notes that the people were grief-stricken at their failure and neglect of God's word (8:9). The reading of the law leads to a separation from all foreigners and that which is unclean (9:2). A binding oath, strengthened by a curse, is made in order to separate from the heathen and obey the law of God (10:28–30). The separation from all foreigners at the hearing of the law of Moses is stated again in 13:3. In obedience to the law, the feast of booths was renewed (8:13–18), buying and selling on the Sabbath was prohibited, and the observance of the Sabbath's year rest was again required (10:31; 13:15–22). The temple cult, together with the proper protocol for priests and sacrifices, were enforced (10:32–36; 13:10–14). The paying of tithes to the priests and Levites was to be observed (10:37–39). Priestly corruption in the temple was dealt with, and the temple precincts were purified (13:4–9). But the worst abomination, in the view of Nehemiah also, was the marrying of foreign wives, the children of whom could not even speak Hebrew (13:23–24). Nehemiah cursed them, beat them, and pulled out their hair, forcing them to take a binding oath or suffer the wrath of God (13:25–31).

In contrast to those who had succumbed to religious syncretism and racial impurity, the "sons of the Golah" are described as those who have "separated themselves" from for-

---

12 Maccoby notes that the syncretists whom Ezra encountered were a group, larger in number and more powerful than the returning exiles, who threatened the existence of Judaism and monotheistic religion ("Holiness and Purity," 170).

13 The word for "separate" is Heb. badal (בָּדַל), used again in Neh 9:2. The "Sons of the Golah" are described in Ezra 6:21 and 10:16 using Heb. nivdal (נִבְדַּל), a different form of the same word. Hugo Mantel judges these words to be conceptually synonymous with Heb. parash (פָּרַשׁ), "to separate," and Perushim, the "separated ones" or "Pharisees" ("The Dichotomy of Judaism during the Second Temple," HUCA 44/1 [1973]: 55).

eign wives and the abominations that these marriages represent. They had separated themselves "from the unclean practices of their Gentile neighbors" (Ezra 6:21; 10:16). Like those who failed to report for examination of their racial purity, those who did not separate themselves would be cursed, have their property confiscated, and then would be excommunicated from the commonwealth of Israel, with their names noted in print (Ezra 9:1, 10:8). Those who submitted to the reforms and separated themselves "from all foreigners" (lit. "peoples of the land") according to the law were again noted in print (Neh 9:1–2; 10:28). The mixed multitude was to be "excluded" (NIV) or "separated" (NRSV) from the ethnically pure and obedient (Neh 13:3).

### The Theological Platform of Ezra and Nehemiah

Ezra and Nehemiah provided a definitive answer to the question "Who are the people of God?" From their perspective, the issue was resolved by setting forth two stringent criteria: racial purity and the strict observance of the law. Their goal was to preserve the identity of Israel in the aftermath of captivity and to clarify the boundary markers that enhance this identity.[14] Some of the returnees deduced that if the captivity came because of a lack of racial purity and adherence to the law, then security in the land would be granted on the basis of ethnicity and religious purity (Jer 7:7; 30:1–10). Indeed, it was concluded that the former would be a natural result of the latter. Restoration would come through holiness (separation, Deut 14:21) both in one's bloodline and in one's behavior. The primary means for actualizing this kind of separation consisted of the purity regulations set forth

in Lev 11:1–46. In these ways, the Jews could "distinguish" (cf. Lev 11:47) their identity from all others.[15]

### THE THEOLOGY OF "SEPARATION" AND THE EMERGENCE OF THE PHARISEES

The "sons of the Golah" in Ezra and Nehemiah and the Pharisees of a later period understood holiness as separation. For them, the answer to the question "Who is a true Jew?" was drawn from, for example, Lev 20:22–26:

> Keep all my decrees and laws and follow them, so that the land where I am bringing you to live may not vomit you out. 23You must not live according to the customs of the nations I am going to drive out before you. Because they did all these things, I abhorred them. 24But I said to you, "You will possess their land; I will give it to you as an inheritance, a land flowing with milk and honey." I am the Lord your God, who has set you apart from the nations. 25You must therefore make a distinction between clean and unclean animals and between unclean and clean birds. Do not defile yourselves by any animal or bird or anything that moves along the ground—those which I have set apart as unclean for you. 26You are to be holy to me because I, the Lord, am holy, and I have set you apart from the nations to be my own.

As noted, the reforms of Ezra–Nehemiah are concerned with the proper observance of Jewish festivals, tithing, and purity. The same concerns are high on the agenda of the Pharisees (Matt 12:1–5; 23:23; Mark 3:1–6; 7:1–3; Luke 11:42). Ezra and Nehemiah also saw these ritual aspects of the law as binding upon all the people, not just upon the priests while in the temple. The Pharisees may have also understood the Jews as a "kingdom of priests" (Exod 19:6) and may well have believed that

---

14  "The survival of a minority as a group depends on their success in creating a social community with social boundaries" (Daniel Smith, *The Religion of the Landless: The Social Context of the Babylonian Exile* [Bloomington, Ind.: Meyer-Stone, 1989], 64).

15  Here again the Hebrew word *badal* is employed, as it was in Ezra and Nehemiah.

tithing and purity were required of all.[16]

Thus, as in the case of Ezra and Nehemiah, we see in the Pharisees the creation of boundary markers that, from their perspective, clarify the identity of the true people of God. Even though the word "Pharisee" would not be found in the literature for at least another three hundred years, the ideological framework for the sect was already in place soon after the exile. The inauguration of Alexander the Great's campaign of hellenization (323 B.C.E.), together with Antiochus Epiphanes' grotesque interpretation thereof (ca. 190 B.C.E.), could have increased such tendencies toward separation by way of purity.[17] As the Hasmoneans acquired more of the Hellenistic practices they originally sought to destroy, some of these "separatists" fled to the mountains to escape the pollution of Jerusalem.[18] Others, however, chose to live within society, forming "islands of holiness" or, as Schürer regards the Pharisees, an *ecclesiola in ecclesia* (lit. "a little church in the church").[19] They may have been the *Haberim* ("the fellowship"), partaking of the special *haburah*, or "fellowship meal," only with

those who were also in a state of purity.[20] The Haberim may even be the same group as the Pharisees. In summary, the Pharisees represented a religious reformation dedicated to the preservation of the "true Israel" by an intensification of the written Torah and a disciplined practice of the oral Torah. These elements may have been in place many years before the Pharisees arose as a distinct sect in Israel.

## THE PROGRAMMATIC AGENDA OF THE PHARISEES

As was the case with Ezra–Nehemiah, the goal of the Pharisees was to ensure the survival of Israel in the midst of religious compromise and political threat. Their method was through an intensive observance of the Torah and halakhah, that is, "tradition of the elders" (Matt 15:1–3; cf. Gal 1:14). The Pharisees may have viewed these "two Torahs" as of equal authority and binding upon all.[21] This essential link between the Torah and "the traditions" clarifies the broad appeal of the Pharisees. Josephus notes that the Pharisees handed "the teachings" to the people, indicating that the Pharisees believed the traditions of the fathers were applicable to all. Josephus also consistently emphasizes that the sentiments of the people lay with the Pharisees

---

16  Whether the Pharisees required everyone to follow the purity laws prescribed for the priests is a matter of debate. Josephus indicates that they lived somewhat of an ascetic lifestyle and delivered many teachings of the fathers to the people (*Ant.* 13.297; 18.12). Sanders does not believe that purity was a special concern of the Pharisees or that the Pharisees expected all to be in a state of purity. He concedes, however, "that the Pharisees tried to have their views of the law carry the day" (*Jesus and Judaism*, 188; cf. also 182–86).

17  Magen Broshi and Esther Eshel, "The Greek King Is Antiochus IV (4QHistorical Text=4Q248)," *JJS* 48 (1997): 122.

18  Philip Sigal, *From the Origins to the Separation of Christianity* (part 1 of *The Foundations of Judaism from Biblical Origins to the Sixth Century A.D.*; vol. 1 of *The Emergence of Contemporary Judaism*; Pittsburgh: Pickwick, 1980), 327. Cf. also Schiffman, "New Light on the Pharisees," 54.

19  Emil Schürer, *The History of the Jewish People in the Age of Jesus Christ (175 B.C.–A.D. 135)* (rev. and ed. Geza Vermes, Furgus Millar, and Matthew Black; 3 vols. in 4; Edinburgh: T&T Clark, 1973–1987), 2:396.

20  Sanders, *Jesus and Judaism*, 186. But Sanders doubts that the Haberim were identical to the Pharisees (p. 187). For a contrasting view, see Jacob Neusner, *First Century Judaism in Crisis: Yohanan ben Zakkai and the Renaissance of the Torah* (Nashville: Abingdon, 1985), 35.

21  It is this kind of extension of the Torah that was vehemently rejected by the writer of 4QpNah. In this fragment from Qumran, the author berates those who develop *talmud* (תַּלְמוּד), or expanded applications of the Torah. Sanders and Neusner see no evidence that the Pharisees viewed the oral and written Torah as of equal authority. Such a view was held only by later rabbis (cf. E. P. Sanders, *Jewish Law from Jesus to the Mishnah* [London: SCM, 1990], 123; and Neusner, *The Rabbinic Traditions about the Pharisees*, 1:2–3). For contrasting positions, see Rivkin, *A Hidden Revolution*, 184; and Martin Hengel and Roland Deines, "E. P. Sanders' 'Common Judaism,' Jesus, and the Pharisees," *JTS* 46 (1995): 18–19.

**A section from one of the Dead Sea Scrolls discovered at Qumran.**

and not with the Sadducees (*Ant.* 13.297–298, 408–409; 18.15, 17; *J.W.* 2.162).

The extent of Pharisaic influence on first-century Judaism cannot be determined with certainty. If the *dorshe halaqot*, that is, "those who seek smooth things (or 'easy interpretations')," refers to the Pharisees, then the Qumran covenanters felt that the teachings of the Pharisees had been extended to kings, princes, priests, the people, proselytes, cities, and clans (cf. 4QpNah 3–4.7).[22] And if the "the builders of the wall" cited in CD 4:19–20; 8:12–13, 18 also refers to the Pharisees, then their presence and influence extended well back into the second century

B.C.E.[23] According to Josephus, the power of the Pharisees waxed and waned according to whoever was in power at the time. Alexander Jannaeus (104–78 B.C.E.) crucified eight hundred Pharisees who took part in a rebellion, ostensibly because they were representatives of the populace arrayed against him (*Ant.* 13.379–383; *J.W.* 1.96–98). Yet by the time of Alexandra (76–67 B.C.E.), the Pharisees were enjoying an extraordinary resurgence in power. Josephus claims that during her reign the Pharisees were the real power behind the throne, empowered by the queen to follow their practices and the traditions of their fathers and to bind and loose subjects at will (*Ant.* 13.405–410; *J.W.* 1.111) The Gospels also represent the Pharisees as having access to and influence on both Jewish and Roman rulers of the day (Matt 27:62; Mark 12:13; John 7:32, 45; 11:45).

---

22   The Dead Sea Scrolls make a pun by equating the *halakhoth* ("teachings"), perhaps of the of the Pharisees, with *halaqoth* ("lies"). Sanders, however, notes that the Pharisees were a relatively small sect of limited influence and in no way represented common Judaism of the first century (*Jewish Law*, 115). For an opposing view, see Schiffman, "New Light on the Pharisees," 31, 54; and "Pharisees and Sadducees," 281–83.

23   The Tannaitic material of the rabbis (post-200 C.E.) identifies the "builders of the wall" with the Pharisees (cf. *m. 'Abot* 1:1).

The extent of Pharisaic influence, or at least the intent of their influence, may be reflected in the fundamental theological premises of the sect. The Pharisees sought holiness within society as opposed to the reclusive practices of the Qumran community (1QS 8:13–16). The movement seems to have taken the cue for its guiding principle from Exod 19:6: "You will be for me a kingdom of priests and a holy nation. These are the words you are to speak to the Israelites." The words "kingdom," "nation," and "Israelites" may allude to the comprehensive scope of the movement.[24]

In essence, then, the Pharisaic campaign was one of laypersons for laypersons, appealing to the masses to take on the mandate of holiness within society (Lev 11:44–45; 19:2; 20:7). In this regard Josephus refers to the Pharisees as the "people's party," outnumbering all major sects and being the most scrupulous about the traditions (*Ant.* 13.298; 18.15, 17). According to Josephus, the Pharisees represented six thousand heads of households and had the power to oppose kings (*Ant.* 17.41–43).[25] Josephus continues that even when the Sadducees held the upper hand in the temple, the chief priests still followed the dicta of the Pharisees, for they had the favor of the people (*Ant.* 18.17). According to Josephus, even some women of Israel seem to have identified with the Pharisees (*Ant.* 17.41)

It appears that their special understanding of "purity" drove the modus vivendi of the Pharisees. Since the they did not withdraw from society, the purity regulations became immensely important for them. As was the case with Ezra and Nehemiah, purity became the determining factor that distinguished them from the general populace. Therefore cultic regulations, a majority of which are set

forth in Lev 11 and 15, were understood to be applicable to all of life.

But what did "purity" mean for the Pharisees? It had nothing to do with dirt or personal hygiene. Rather, it concerned the proper observance of religious rituals that distinguished the "clean" from the "unclean" (Matt 15:1–20; Mark 7:1–23; Luke 11:37–40).[26] The concept of purity was also defined by the proper observance of the Sabbath as prescribed by the teachings of the fathers (Matt 12:10–14; Mark 3:1–6; Luke 6:7–10; 14:1–6). Meticulous tithing of all things was also part of a Pharisaic regimen (Matt 23:23–27; Luke 11:42). By the time of the codification of the Mishnah, nearly every aspect of life, whether one was picking up a common nail or buying a bushel of wheat, was subject to the rules of purity (*m. 'Erub.* 1:2, 6:2; *m. Šabb.* 1:4–9).[27] Indeed, the two largest portions of the rabbinic traditions about the Pharisees prior to 70 C.E. are entitled *Teharot* ("Purities") and *Qodashim* ("Holy Things").[28]

The "communal order" of the Pharisees was maintained through the sacramental empowering of all of life, and as far as the later rabbinic traditions are concerned, this was particularly the case regarding the eating of food (*m. Ṭehar.* 1:1–3:4; 8:6–9:7; 10:1–8).[29] Since the Gospels express purity concerns in refer-

---

24  Marcus Borg, *Conflict, Holiness, and Politics in the Teachings of Jesus* (New York: Edwin Mellen, 1984), 57.

25  For the influence of the Pharisees among the aristocratic women of Israel, see Tal Ilan, "The Attraction of Aristocratic Women to Pharisaism during the Second Temple Period," *HTR* 88 (1995): 1–33.

26  For an analysis of purity and its varied meanings, see Mary Douglas, *Implicit Meanings: Selected Essays in Anthropology* (2d ed.; New York: Routledge, 1999).

27  The entire sixth division of the Mishnah, entitled "Purities," catalogues the myriad ways one can become impure and how one can attain a state of purity. Cf. Jacob Neusner, *The Mishnah: A New Translation* (New Haven: Yale University Press, 1988), 893–1138.

28  For a list of rabbinic sayings concerning the clean and the unclean, see Jacob Neusner, *The Rabbinic Traditions about the Pharisees*, 3:120–121. Sanders charges that Neusner's view is simply a caricature and not representative of normative Judaism in the first century (*Jewish Law*, 242).

29  Neusner concludes that sixty-seven percent of the later rabbinic traditions about the Pharisees relate wholly or in part to table fellowship (*The Rabbinic Traditions about the Pharisees*, 3:297).

"The Pharisees and Sadducees come to tempt Jesus" by J.-J. Tissot.

ence to common meals and the later rabbis do not refer to any ritual gatherings of the Pharisees about a common table, it appears that the Pharisees ate all of their meals in a state of purity.[30] If so, table fellowship for the Pharisees was not a matter only of nutrition but of spiritual communion. For them, it may well have meant acceptance before God.

30 Sanders rejects the notion that the Pharisees ate all meals in a state of purity. He contends that they only washed their hands with regard to food sacrificed in the temple (*Jewish Law*, 163, 176). For an opposing view, see John C. Poirier, "Why Did the Pharisees Wash Their Hands?" JJS (1996): 217–33.

## JESUS AND THE PHARISEES

In spite of the antipathy between Jesus and the Pharisees so evident in the Gospels, they shared much in common. Indeed, they could be described as theological liberals, for, unlike the Sadducees, who accepted only the Pentateuch as canonical, both Jesus and the Pharisees accepted all of the Hebrew Scriptures, from Genesis to Malachi, as holy writ (Matt 7:12; 11:13; Luke 24:44; John 1:45). Jesus and the Pharisees also endorsed relatively late theological developments, such as belief in the physical resurrection of the dead and in angels and demons (Matt 22:23–33; Luke 20:27; Acts 23:6–10). Finally, and perhaps most important, both Jesus and the Pharisees did not withdraw from society, as was the case with Qumran. They both believed that it was possible to live for God among the people. For all of these reasons, many Pharisees respected Jesus as a fellow teacher, often inviting him to dinner to learn more about his views (Luke 7:37; 11:37; 14:1).

Yet it is precisely in this context—that is, within the context of table fellowship—that the theological agenda of Jesus and that of some of the Pharisees sharply diverged. At table, what affects authentic communion with God became a defining issue between Jesus and some Pharisees of his day. Jesus' deliberate practice of dining with notorious sinners and outcasts was extremely disconcerting to the Pharisees of the Gospels (Matt 9:10–13; Mark 2:15–17; Luke 5:30–39; 7:34; 15:1–2). The fact that he "broke bread" with such pariahs in the name of God and promised them a place in the kingdom was tantamount to blasphemy for these Pharisees. In addition, Jesus' unwashed hands may have meant to them that he took defiled food into his body and thus polluted his whole being (cf. Mark 7:1–23).[31] In place of the carefully crafted understanding of purity held by the Pharisees, Jesus seemed indifferent to the profane and polluting. For him, the law of Moses was an important guide but not a definitive end to what may be known of God. Jesus' clarification of who the Father is transcended the words of Moses (Matt 5:21–22,

27–28, 33–35). If the law was not the final word for Jesus, the "tradition of the elders" was an obstacle to communion with God (Matt 15:2–6; Mark 7:2–13). Thus, for Jesus, the Pharisees were the real polluting leaven that the people had to watch out for (cf. Luke 12:1; Exod 13:6–8). A very harsh indictment appears in Luke 16:15, 18:9–14. Here the Pharisees who oppose Jesus are portrayed as self-justifying, lovers of money who bar others from the kingdom of God while not entering in themselves.

This extraordinary recasting of who God is and what God requires was religiously disruptive on a number of levels, so much so that the Pharisees in league with the chief priests plotted Jesus' destruction (John 7:45–52; 11:47; 18:1–3). Even some of his first followers balked at the radical implications of his theological vision (Acts 11:3; 15:1–2, 6–11; Gal 2:11–15). Yet just as Jesus dismantled the barrier between saint and sinner in Israel, his disciples came to understand that the ancient identifiers of the circumcised and uncircumcised were no longer applicable (Gal 5:6; 6:15; Col 3:11). As Jesus accepted sinners at table, his followers came to believe that God justifies the ungodly and that ethnic and social distinctions are erased in Christ (Rom 4:5; Gal 3:28).

The Pharisees were swept up in the holocaust of 66 C.E. As the Romans demolished Jerusalem and the temple in 70 C.E., the religious and political autonomy of the Pharisees came to an end. Their religious ideals and teachings, however, may not have been extinguished altogether. Their spirit and program may have continued in the life and practices of the proto-rabbis, as attested by the early rabbinic literature and the council at Yavneh. Thus the "separatists" may well have helped in forming the rabbinic tradition, which in time laid the foundation for a significant element of Judaism that survives to this day.[32]

---

31 Poirier asserts that the Pharisees washed their hands before a meal because they did not want to defile their "inward parts," a concern of many Diaspora Jews ("Why Did the Pharisees Wash Their Hands?" 230–32). Indeed, the word "baptized" (ebaptisthē [ἐβαπτίσθη]) in Luke 11:38 may reflect the Pharisaic practice of immersing the entire body in water before a meal (cf. Lev 15:16–17). If Jesus declined to enter the immersion pool as his host had done, the outrage would have been more intense. Cf. also Mason, "Chief Priests, Sadducees, Pharisees, and Sanhedrin," in *The Book of Acts in Its Palestinian Setting* (ed. Richard Bauckham; Grand Rapids: Eerdmans, 1995), 138.

32 For the challenge of defining Judaism and its diverse expressions, see Jacob Neusner, *Judaism: The Evidence of the Mishnah* (Atlanta: Scholars Press, 1988), esp. 1, 22–24.

**SUMMARY**

In many respects, since ages past, the geopolitical landscape had proved inhospitable to the Jews. The threat of extinction was not a remote possibility for them but a real eventuality that lay all too near at hand. Indeed, the northern kingdom had been swallowed up in the shifting sands of time, and who was to say that Judah's hold on existence was more secure?

Under such conditions, the purification and protection of Israel became paramount. Some strategies for survival took the route of separation from all that is "unclean" and combined this with an intensification of signifiers deemed to be authentically Jewish. For example, the reforms of Ezra and Nehemiah understood purity in terms of separation from ethnic uncleanness and ritual defilement. It is possible that the fundamental Pharisaic principle of separation was established at this time. Increased syncretism after the Ezra–Nehemiah revival may have led to a kind of religious expression that eventually evolved into the Pharisees. The birth of the "Great Synagogue" in the second century B.C.E. may be evidence of this kind of religious expression.[33] These Jewish leaders probably were reacting against factors they deemed threatening to faith and practice as they understood it. Their teachings and religious expression may have constituted the germ out of which the Pharisees arose.[34]

33  According to Jewish tradition recorded in the Mishnah, the "Great Synogogue" or "Great Assembly" was made up of those early Jewish rabbis who had received the Torah from the prophets. The first of these rabbis was Simeon the Righteous, who in turn delivered the law of Moses to Antigonos of Sokho (m. 'Abot 1:1–2; see n. 8 above).

34  For a plausible timeline tracing the historical and conceptual development from the time of Ezra–Nehemiah to that of the Pharisees in the first century, see Schiffman, "New Light on the Pharisees," 54. For a list of the names of the rabbis who might have formed the earliest chain of Pharisaic tradition, see Neusner, *The Rabbinic Traditions about the Pharisees*, 1:22.

# Annotated Bibliography

Borg, Marcus. *Conflict, Holiness, and Politics in the Teachings of Jesus*. New York: Edwin Mellen, 1984. This work is a sociopolitical analysis of resistance movements in Second Temple Judaism and how they might relate to the teachings of Jesus. This work is a good source for understanding the various kinds of tensions between the Jews and the Romans of the first century, the conflicts between the various Jewish religious factions of the day, and how Jesus' life and work interacted with these tensions. This informative work may present something of a challenge for beginning students.

Douglas, Mary. *Implicit Meanings: Selected Essays in Anthropology*. 2d ed. New York: Routledge, 1999. This excellent introduction to the concept of purity in religious systems is written from the perspective of a social anthropologist, yet the informed student can readily make applications to biblical studies. The work explores the social-anthropological meanings of purity, food, and table fellowship and the "clean" and the "unclean" in various cross-cultural contexts across the ages.[35]

Neusner, Jacob. *From Politics to Piety: The Emergence of Pharisaic Judaism*. Englewood Cliffs, N.J.: Prentice-Hall, 1973. This was a ground-breaking work on the sociopolitical contexts of emerging Pharisaism and thus serves as a "first read" in this area of research.

———. *The Rabbinic Traditions about the Pharisees before 70*. 3 vols. Atlanta: Scholars Press, 1999. Perhaps the definitive treatment of the rabbinic traditions concerning the Pharisees, this work is very detailed and comprehensive. Though a challenge for beginning scholars, it is so structured that one can glean much information. Volume 3 contains an index covering all three volumes.

Sanders, E. P. *Jesus and Judaism*. Philadelphia: Fortress, 1985. This major work by a very insightful scholar calls into question long-standing premises on the Gospels, the life of Jesus, and Second Temple Judaism. A good orientation to New Testament studies is required in order to make the best use of this valuable work.

———. *Paul and Palestinian Judaism: A Comparison of Patterns of Religion*. Philadelphia: Fortress, 1977. This companion volume to *Jesus and Judaism* seeks to dismantle the long-held belief by some scholars that Judaism is a religion of legalism and works righteousness. In this work Sanders presents and clarifies his important principle of "covenantal nomism."

Schürer, Emil. *The History of the Jewish People in the Age of Jesus Christ (175 B.C.–A.D.. 135)*. Revised and edited by Geza Vermes, Furgus Millar, and Matthew Black. 3 vols. in 4. Vol. 2. Edinburgh: T&T Clark, 1973–1987. This standard reference work provides an encyclopedic look at the historical and religious contexts of the Jews from the Maccabean period until the Bar Kokhba revolt. It is a good starting place for orientation to almost any aspect of Jewish history as it might pertain to the Bible.

Sigal, Philip. *From the Origins to the Separation of Christianity*. Part 1 of *The Foundations of Judaism from Biblical Origins to the Sixth Century A.D..* Vol. 1 of *The Emergence of Contemporary Judaism*. Pittsburgh: Pickwick, 1980. In this solid, comprehensive work on the birth of modern Judaism, Sigal's programmatic style helps coordinate the many facets that gave rise to Judaism. This valuable reference work provides a panoramic view of Israelite history and religion.

Smith, Daniel. *The Religion of the Landless: The Social Context of the Babylonian Exile*. See description at the end of ch. 1.

---

35   For related issues, see John F. A. Sawyer, ed. *Reading Leviticus: A Conversation with Mary Douglas* (JSOTSup 227; Sheffield, Eng.: Sheffield Academic Press, 1996).

# 3
# The Sadducees
# —Priesthood
# and Aristocracy

## INTRODUCTION

Some form of the word "Sadducee" appears fourteen times in the Greek New Testament (UBS[4]).[1] As was the case with the Pharisees, the mere number of references does not reflect the major role that this sect played in the history of Judaism, the life of Jesus, and the experience of the early church. In first-century Judaism, the Sadducees appear to have been the political and religious alternative to the Pharisees. They, too, may be considered a renewal movement whose aim was to cope with the increasing Hellenism and to ensure the survival of their people. The similarity between the Pharisees and the Sadducees ends here, however, for the religious vision and political methods of the Sadducees were of a different nature from those of the Pharisees. As will be discussed below, the Sadducean penchant for accommodating foreign oppressors with the intent of outlasting them was not the path chosen by the Pharisees and in some respects may have proven less successful than the Sadducees' counterparts.

## The Origin of the Sadducees

As with the Pharisees, the primary source material for the Sadducees is limited. The group is explicitly mentioned in Josephus, the New Testament, and the rabbinic literature of the third century C.E. All of these sources assume the existence of the Sadducees as an identifiable group that enjoyed some degree of social and political power during the first century. All of the sources also represent Sadducees as having a following among the general populace.

Josephus lists the Sadducees, along with the Pharisees, Essenes, and the "Fourth Philosophy," as one of the important sects arising at the time of the Maccabeans (*Ant.* 13.171–173).[2] He notes that when the Hasmoneans defeated the forces of Antiochus IV and Jonathan assumed the high priesthood (ca. 161–143 B.C.E.), the

---

[1] The biblical references to the Sadducees are in Matt 3:7; 16:1, 6, 11, 12; 22:23, 34; Mark 12:18; Luke 20:27; Acts 4:1; 5:17; 23:6, 7, 8. The fact that the Pharisees are mentioned much more frequently in the Bible and in Josephus than the Sadducees may mean that the former were deemed more dominant and influential than the latter. Josephus's labeling the Pharisees "the people's party" (*Ant.* 13.298) lends some credence to the Gospels' portrait of these groups.

[2] Josephus's word for "sect" is Gk. *hairesis* (αἵρεσις), from which our contemporary word "heresy" derives. Yet in the first century the word did not refer to cranks, "crackpots," or those who were doctrinally suspect. Rather, "sect" referred to a recognizable group holding particular beliefs that in many points reflected the concerns of the wider society. Luke uses the word to refer to the Pharisees, Sadducees, and early Christians (Acts 5:17; 15:5; 24:5, 14; 26:5; 28:22). On sects of the first century, see Albert Baumgarten, *The Flourishing of Jewish Sects in the Maccabean Era: An Interpretation* (New York: E. J. Brill, 1997), esp. 1, 35, 200; and Anthony J. Saldarini, *Pharisees, Scribes, and Sadducees in Palestinian Society: A Sociological Approach* (Wilmington, Del.: Michael Glazier, 1988), esp. 124.

Sadducees were already in place as one of the major Jewish sects (*Ant.* 13.171–173).[3] Indeed it is likely that the Sadducees came to prominence during this "fog of war," when Jewish sectarianism had reached its zenith.

Pinpointing the origin of the Sadducees with more precision is difficult. The limited number and nature of the sources raise questions. As was the case with the Pharisees, the Sadducees left no independent body of literature, and so we possess no self-testimony of who the Sadducees were and what they believed. We are thus completely dependent upon secondhand accounts of the Sadducees and so are limited by the peculiar visions of these accounts. Josephus, the biblical writers, and the early rabbis all had specialized ways in which they presented the Sadducees. As a Pharisee, Josephus consistently presents them in a negative light (*J.W.* 2.166). By and large, the New Testament views the Sadducees as antagonists of Jesus and his early followers (Matt 16:1–11; Acts 4:1, 5:17). This negative portrait is also carried through to the time of the early rabbis. In their effort to bolster the image of the Pharisees, the rabbis portray the Sadducees as apostates and rubes (*m. 'Erub.* 6:2; *m. Parah* 3:3, 7; *m. Nid.* 4:2). In light of the inherent biases contained in these sources, how can one hope to arrive at an accurate understanding of this ancient Jewish sect?[4]

A possible solution, and the one employed here, is to try to make a distinction between a particular literary bias expressed by a source and a substantial falsification of the data contained in the source. In other words,

even though the sources show signs of flavoring the data to meet their purposes, it is the overall profile of all the sources that merits attention. So even if the combined result of the sources produces a mosaic that lacks clarity, the overall portrait may yet prove recognizable.

On this basis, many theories have been put forward regarding the origin of the Sadducees. For example, it is possible that the emergence of the Sadducees is tied in with the formation of the monastic community at Qumran. Working from the Dead Sea Scrolls manuscript 4QMMT, it has been surmised that Qumran was founded by disaffected Jewish priests not long after the Maccabean revolt. A power struggle may have ensued among the Maccabeans, resulting in the alienation of a number of powerful priests about 168–164 B.C.E. These priests may have become so disgusted with the pro-Pharisaic stance of the Hasmoneans that they withdrew to the desert and preached from a distance, so to speak.[5] If this scenario is correct, then the Qumran community was indeed the birthplace of the Sadducees, and all of the manuscripts produced there were written by their hands. Furthermore, if phrases such as "those who like smooth things" or "the builders of the wall" refer to the Pharisees, then the covenanters at Qumran clearly disliked the Pharisees. Their writings label the Pharisees false teachers whose aim is to dupe the Jewish people from top to bottom, from kings to paupers (cf. 4QpNah 3–4.7). They are the ones who

---

3    The rabbinic material of the second century C.E. echoes Josephus here. The Pharisaic list in *m. 'Abot* 1 indicates that both the Pharisees and the Sadducees came to prominence just after the mid–second century B.C.E.

4    On the challenges facing a historical reconstruction of the Sadducees, see Günter Stemberger, *Jewish Contemporaries of Jesus: Pharisees, Sadducees, Essenes* (trans. Allan W. Mahke; Minneapolis: Fortress, 1995); and Saldarini, *Pharisees, Scribes, and Sadducees*, 299.

5    On this view, see Lawrence H. Schiffman, "The Significance of the Scrolls," BRev 6 (1990): 18–27, esp. 18; and idem, "The New Halakhic Letter (4QMMT) and the Origins of the Dead Sea Sect," BA 53 (1990): 64–73, esp. 69 and 71. For a similar idea, see C. Marvin Pate, *Communities of the Last Days: The Dead Sea Scrolls, the New Testament, and the Story of Israel* (Downers Grove, Ill.: InterVarsity, 2000). He calls the earliest members of Qumran "pro-Zadokites," i.e., early Sadducees (p. 59). For a contrasting opinion, see James C. Vanderkam, "The People of the Dead Sea Scrolls," BRev 7 (1991): 42–47.

**The Shrine of the Book, Jerusalem, where some of the Dead Sea Scrolls are preserved.**

embellish the Torah through the "building of the wall," an expression that no doubt refers to the many additional "traditions of the elders" held by the Pharisees (CD 4:19–20; 8:12–13, 18). Qumran would be defaming the *halakhot* ("teachings") of the Pharisees as so many *halaqot* ("lies").

On the other hand, it could be argued that 4QMMT contains several elements that sound more like the Pharisees than the Sadducees. For example, the author of this ancient document claims the entire Hebrew Scriptures as the canon. It is well known that the Sadducees accepted only the Pentateuch as holy writ (Josephus, *Ant.* 13.297). Also, the writer of 4QMMT is very concerned about purity and emphasizes the need "to separate" (Heb. *parashnu*) from everything and everyone that is unclean. The word "Pharisee" is derived from this Hebrew verb, and it was the Pharisees, not the Sadducees, who were known for their strict observance of purity regulations. It also appears from the Dead Sea Scrolls that the Qumran community believed in the survival of the soul after death and in the future resurrection (1QH III, 19–23; VII, 20), whereas the Sadducees did not (Matt 22:23; Mark 12:18; Luke 20:27; Acts 23:6–8). Finally, those at Qumran adopted an ascetic, monastic lifestyle (1QS VIII, 13–16), but the Sadducees appear to have been drawn from the Jewish aristocracy and to have a penchant for power and wealth (*Ant.* 13.298).

On another score, in light of Josephus's claim that the Jewish sects existed "from the most ancient times" (*Ant.* 18.11), the Sadducees may have roots even more ancient than those of Qumran and the Pharisees.[6] For example, there is evidence that the Sadducees evolved from the ancient priestly line of Zadok, dating back to the time of King David in 1000 B.C.E. (cf. *Ant.* 7.110; 10.152).[7] This

powerful dynasty held the high priesthood until they were deposed in 172 B.C.E. If the Gk. *Saddoukaioi* (Σαδδουκαῖοι) is a translation of the Heb. *tsadhuqim* (i.e., Zadokites), then the connection between the New Testament "Sadducees" and the Old Testament priesthood of Zadok may be on target.

If so, the Sadducees would have drawn from the power and heritage of the Zadokites. The name Zadok appears more than fifty times in the Hebrew Bible, primarily in the books of Samuel, Kings, and Chronicles but also in Ezekiel (cf. 2 Sam 15:24–35; 1 Kgs 1:32–39; 1 Chr 24:3–6; Ezek 43:19). Perhaps the most dramatic deed of Zadok as high priest was to have the Ark of the Covenant brought outside Jerusalem to accompany David. At this time David was fleeing the city in the wake of Absalom's rebellion, and Zadok wanted the symbol of God's power and presence to reside with his king (2 Sam 15:24).

6    Stemberger argues that the Sadducees emerged about seventy-five years prior to the "hellenizing crisis" of 175–152 B.C.E. (*Jewish Contemporaries*, 97). For a similar view, see Roger T. Beckwith, "The Pre-history and Relationships of the Pharisees, Sadducees, and Essenes: A Tentative Reconstruction," RevQ 11 (1982): 9; and Baumgarten, *The Flourishing of Jewish Sects*, 20.

7    Josephus mentions Zadok twenty times in reference to the high priesthood. On the view that the Sadducees sprang from the priesthood of Zadok, see Jacob Neusner, *First Century Judaism in Crisis: Yohanan ben Zakkai and the Renaissance of the Torah* (Nashville: Abingdon, 1985), esp. 36–37. For a contrasting view, see Saldarini, *Pharisees, Scribes, and Sadducees*, 225–26.

Scale model of Herod's Temple, showing the extensive courtyards. There may have been a priestly connection between the Sadducees and the Old Testament priesthood of Zadok that served in Solomon's Temple.

A critical scripture that might connect the Sadducees with Zadok is Ezek 40:46 (cf. also 44:15): "These are the sons of Zadok, who are the only Levites who may draw near to the Lord to minister before him." Whether the Sadducees of the New Testament were direct descendants from Zadok or simply looked to Zadok as a model of dedication is open to debate. What is important here is that Ezekiel's words indicate that Zadok and his descendants were the only Levites suited for the office of high priest. Indeed, most of the biblical references associate Zadok with the high priesthood or with the tribe of Levi serving as priests (2 Chr 31:10; Ezek 48:11; cf. also Sir 51:12). Accordingly, the Sadducees of the New Testament occupy the office of high priest or are in close association with the high priest and his power.

In any case, Zadok and the line of priests that descended from him are presented in the Old Testament as a powerful presence in the religious and political landscape of ancient Israel. This is precisely how Josephus portrays the Sadducees in his writings, and the same holds true for the New Testament. If the Sadducees and the Zadokites are not one and the same group, it appears that they are cut from the same cloth as far as the sources are concerned.

### The Power and Influence of the Sadducees

Josephus claims that the Sadducees numbered less than the Pharisees, yet they constituted the ruling aristocracy in Israel (*Ant.*

18.17).[8] He even mentions one high priest, Ananus, by name, and describes him as a Sadducee (*Ant.* 20.199). Josephus continues to describe the Sadducees in elitist terms, noting that their doctrine was known to "only a few males" (*Ant.* 18.16–17). So it seems that the Sadducees were tied in with the leading families of Israel.[9]

The political ascendancy of the Sadducees over all other Jewish sects may have begun as early as the high priesthood of Jonathan Hyrcanus (152–142 B.C.E.), the younger brother of Judas Maccabee. After taking civil leadership of the Hasmoneans, he initially favored the Pharisees. But when he also sought to take religious leadership of the Jews by assuming the office of high priest, he was opposed by the Pharisees. In particular, one Pharisee by the name of Eleazar publicly challenged the legitimacy of Hyrcanus to assume the high priesthood because his mother was alleged to be a slave (cf. Lev 21:14). Sensing a threat to his power, Hyrcanus switched his allegiance from that of the Pharisees to the party of the Sadducees (*Ant.* 13.288–297). So, at least from the time of Hyrcanus, the Sadducees seem to have had considerable influence on the politics of Israel.

Evidence for the political empowerment of the Sadducees can be seen in the New Testament as well, for Annas and Caiaphas are linked with the party of the Sadducees (*Ant.* 20.198–199; Matt 26:3; Luke 3:2; John 18:13–14; Acts 4:6). As indicated, this association of the high priesthood and the aristocracy of the Sadducees is an important one. Apart from the dominating influence of foreign powers, the high priest, together with the *gerousia*, or "council of elders," served as the governing body for all of Israel (2 Macc 1:10; 4:44; 11:27). It is fairly certain that from the time of Herod the Great until the Jewish revolt against Rome in 64 C.E., the Sadducees controlled the high priesthood and thus wielded great power in Israel. In particular, they were esteemed members of the Sanhedrin, the great high court of the Jews (cf. Acts 4:1–6; 5:17; 23:6–7).

The combined effect of a long, prestigious history and their accumulation of wealth and political influence established the Sadducees as a force to be reckoned with. Imperial Rome, brutal in conquest but politically savvy in governance, understood this from the very beginning of its occupation of Israel. The Romans knew that they needed a go-between in Israel who would cooperate with Caesar yet have influence with the Jews. The power and place that the Sadducees held in Jewish society made them prime candidates to serve as unofficial mediators who appeased the will of Rome yet played an important role for their own people. Thus one could say that, to a large extent, the wealth and influence of the Sadducees determined how they responded to increasing Hellenism. Those who have the most to lose are the most likely to negotiate with threatening powers. Of all of the sects of first-century Judaism, the Sadducees appear to have chosen the route of acceptance and accommodation.

The Romans used two methods to control the high priesthood in Jerusalem. When they managed to rule by proxy through local puppet kings, such as the Herods, they allowed them to appoint and remove the high priests.[10] Thus Herod the Great

---

8    Josephus frequently associates the high priesthood with the household of Boethus, believed to be one of the leading families among the Jews, perhaps dating as far back as the second century B.C.E. (*Ant.* 15.320; 17.78, 339; 19.297; *J.W.* 5.527). For how the house of Boethus may have influenced the doctrine of the Sadducees, see George W. E. Nickelsburg and Michael E. Stone, *Faith and Piety in Early Judaism: Texts and Documents* (Philadelphia: Fortress, 1983), esp. 32.

9    For these reasons, E. P. Sanders concludes, "Not all aristocrats were Sadducees, but it may be that all Sadducees were aristocrats" (*Judaism: Practice and Belief, 63 B.C.E.–66 C.E.* [Philadelphia: Trinity Press International, 1992], 318).

10    For a record of the earliest pact between the Romans, the Jewish leadership, and the high priests, see Josephus, *Ant.* 12.414–419; cf. also 13.259–265. For the Caesars granting authority to the Herods concerning the temple, see *Ant.* 20.222.

The trial of Jesus in the Roman Forum, as envisaged by the French artist J.-J. Tissot. The power of the Sadducees via the high priesthood is reflected in the arrest, trial, and crucifixion of Jesus.

appointed the high priests during his reign, as did all of his successors (*Ant.* 15.11–20; 17.78, 164; 20.15–16; *J.W.* 2.7).[11] In order to consolidate his power, Herod would appoint nonentities to the office of high priest, often selecting foreign candidates from Alexandria or Babylon. He frequently changed the high priests, their tenure lasting no more than five years (*Ant.* 15.41; 17.78, 164). Understandably, many Jews viewed these appointments with contempt.[12] When it became necessary for the Caesar to rule directly to get the job done, Roman officials designated who would be the supreme religious leader of the Jews

(*Ant.* 18.93; 20.6). The Sadducees served as the preferred pool of candidates for these appointments. But since Herod had so diminished worthy candidates, the Romans simply appointed Ananus to the office (*Ant.* 18.26). He and his family would dominate the high priesthood for sixty years.

The combination of Roman civil authority and the role of the high priests empowered the Sadducees in first-century Palestine. Their power via the high priesthood is reflected in the arrest, trial, and crucifixion of Jesus (Luke 19:45–24:53). Moreover, because they were an important component of the Sanhedrin, or Jewish high court, the Sadducees had access to the temple security forces. So, unlike the Pharisees, the Sadducees could immediately enforce their will by way of the temple guard (Acts 4:1).[13]

11   We have an interesting coincidence between Josephus's account and that of the New Testament. He records that King Agrippa appointed Ananus as high priest between the death of Festus and his replacement, Albinus. This is the Ananus who was instrumental in the execution of James, the brother of Jesus (cf. *Ant.* 20.198–202; Acts 12:1–2).

12   For Herod's strategy in appointing high priests, see Martin Goodman, *The Ruling Class of Judaea: The Origins of the Jewish Revolt against Rome, A.D. 66–70* (Cambridge: Cambridge University Press, 1987), esp. 41.

13   For the place and power of the Sadducees in the Sanhedrin, see S. Mason, "Chief Priests, Sadducees, Pharisees, and Sanhedrin in Acts," in *The Book of Acts in Its Palestinian Setting* (ed. Richard Bauckham; Grand Rapids: Eerdmans, 1995), 133–77, esp. 143.

One can imagine that there was a considerable degree of ambivalence among many Jews regarding the high priests of the first century. On the one hand, the high priests were political appointees of their Roman oppressors. On the other hand, the office of high priest was revered for its religious significance. In any case, it is not difficult to see why many pious Jews became disaffected with the temple and the cult at the time of Jesus. One can readily understand why some, such as the Essenes and, to an even greater extent, the community at Qumran, abandoned the official cult altogether and withdrew to the desert and why hoards of disenchanted common folk followed the charismatic figure from Galilee. For many of them, Jesus' cleansing of the temple would have been a powerful symbolic gesture that protested against the compromise and corruption of the temple and its leadership (Matt 21:12–13; Mark 11:15–18; Luke 19:45–47). In light of the general dereliction of a Sadducee-controlled priesthood, Jesus' words about destroying the temple and building a new one must have been received by many as nothing short of the coming of the kingdom of God (John 2:19; Matt 26:61; Mark 14:58).

The delicate position that the Sadducees occupied between their Roman minders and the will of their own people tended, however, toward the maintenance of the status quo. Their tactic for surviving Roman occupation and for (hope against hope) eking out a quasi-kingdom for the Jews was to pursue moderation in all things. The retention of their power and wealth depended upon maintaining a state of equanimity, and their leadership reflected such qualities.

## THE BELIEFS AND PRACTICES OF THE SADDUCEES

Regarding what the Sadducees believed, it could be said that the historical and political circumstances virtually wrote the script for them. After all, Israel had lost its king and its nation status. The Lord seemed distant and detached from the situation on the ground, and their theology reflected this. Josephus portrays the Sadducees as emphasizing the transcendence of God, a God who is disconnected from the affairs of everyday life in Israel. Unlike the Pharisees, they rejected the notion that the providence of God was directing the lives of individuals. Each person has free will and is personally responsible for determining his or her own fate (Ant 13.171–73; J.W. 2.162–165). For the Sadducee, there will be no apocalyptic intervention of God (Ant. 18.16). Nor were they open to fanciful interpretations of Scripture, at least not in the sense of having any binding power upon faith and practice. In a way, one could say that they advocated *sola scriptura*, "scripture alone," and rejected the "traditions of the elders." The teachings of the Pharisees were judged to have a corrupting effect on the understanding of the Scriptures, one that obscured more than enlightened (Ant. 13.297–298).[14] So, for the Sadducees, only what was written down in the law of Moses was thought to be normative for the religious life. Oral tradition did not factor in at all. In a technical sense, the Sadducees could be described as theologically conservative in their assessment of holy writ. The law of Moses, for them, consisted of only the Pentateuch, the first five books of the Bible. Since this section of the Scriptures does not speak of the continued existence of the soul after death or the physical resurrection of the dead, the Sadducees rejected both (Matt 22:23; Mark 12:18; Acts 23:8). Thus Josephus notes that the Sadducees believed "that souls die with the bodies" and that there are no punishments or rewards in Hades (Ant. 18.16; J.W. 2.165).

The New Testament record of the beliefs of the Sadducees affirms what we are able to gather from Josephus. Mark 12:18 states that the Sadducees deny the resurrection of the

---

14   For the different beliefs of the Sadducees and the Pharisees, see Martin Goodman, "A Note on Josephus, the Pharisees, and Ancestral Tradition," *JJS* 50 (1999): 17–20.

dead. In Matt 22:23–33 some Sadducees seek to entrap Jesus on the nature of the physical resurrection by describing the successive deaths of seven brothers who each tried to "raise up children" (NRSV) for the same barren wife (cf. also Luke 20:29–36; Deut 25:5–6).[15]

Their confrontation with Jesus is very plausible. Josephus notes that the Sadducees count it a virtue to dispute with teachers of wisdom (*Ant.* 18.16). Their point is not to obtain an answer to a thorny problem. Rather, they wish to show that Jesus' vision of the kingdom is impossible. If Jesus is wrong about the resurrection, he certainly is wrong about other things as well. In response, Jesus cites Exod 3:6, which states, "I am the God of your father, the God of Abraham, the God of Isaac and the God of Jacob." The present tense contained in the phrase "I am" shows that although the patriarchs were long since dead, nevertheless they enjoy a living relationship with the Father in the present. His words here indicate that the Sadducees were wrong in concluding that physical death ended sentient life. The purpose of this story is to show that the Sadducees who opposed Jesus were not able to capture Jesus with his words in public (Luke 20:39) and so they consorted in private to take him by force (Luke 22:2–5).

The radical difference between the Pharisees and the Sadducees on such issues is presented in Acts as well. In a manner similar to their confrontation with Jesus, the Sadducees confront the early disciples concerning their belief in the resurrection (Acts 4:1–2). Once again, as was the case with Jesus, the issue really has nothing to do with the afterlife. Rather, what these Sadducees are broaching is whether the apostles have a legitimate authority to teach. Paralleling their treatment of Jesus, the Sadducees and the Sanhedrin employ their executive powers to cast the apostles into prison (4:1–7; 5:17–18). The volatile issue of belief in the resurrection of the dead surfaces again in 23:6–9.[16] As Paul stood trial before the Sanhedrin, he realized that it was composed of Sadducees and Pharisees. When he claimed that the cause of his appearance before the court was the question of the resurrection of the dead, a theological free-for-all ensued (23:7–10). The tumult effectively led to a mistrial. The remark by the Pharisees that an angel may have spoken to Paul, or that he might have seen a vision from heaven, rounds out the differences between them and the Sadducees (23:7–9). The Pharisees' belief in the resurrection reflects their belief in life after death. The notion that Paul may have received some kind of divine communication is at odds with the Sadducees' emphasis on the complete transcendence of God and their denial of divine providence.

## THE SADDUCEES AND JESUS—OPPOSITION AND DEMISE

Although the Sadducees and the Pharisees differed with respect to theology and politics, they were joined in their opposition to Jesus and his early followers, according to the Gospels and Acts. For this reason they are often paired together throughout the New Testament (Matt 3:7; 16:1, 6, 11–12). The enmity between the Sadducees and Jesus was not unidirectional. Jesus was very critical of the Sadducees at times (Matt 22:34). John the Baptist was also clearly unimpressed

---

15 The Sadducees might have taken this story from the book of Tobit, which speaks of the deaths of seven husbands in the context of the resurrection (Tob 7:9–18). The Pharisees might have also used this story to support their belief in the resurrection. The Sadducees, however, turned the story on its head, indicating that the belief in the resurrection contradicts Moses' teaching on Levirate marriage (Deut 25:5–6). See Peter G. Bolt, "What Were the Sadducees Reading? An Enquiry into the Literary Background of Mark 12:18–23," *TynBul* 45 (1994): 369–94, esp. 392–93.

16 The rabbis, who claimed to be descendants of the Pharisees, made belief in the resurrection a test of blessedness. Thus *m. Sanhedrin* 10:1 states that "anyone who does not believe in the resurrection of the dead does not have a place in the world to come."

with the sincerity of both groups (Matt 3:7). Similarly, Jesus warned his disciples to be on guard against the corrupt teaching of the Pharisees and the Sadducees (Matt 16:1–12).

After 70 C.E. the Sadducees fade into obscurity. The tightrope they walked between the powers of Rome, on the one hand, and the sacred realm of the temple, on the other, could not withstand the religious and political strain of the times. The equilibrium they sought to maintain was too tenuous to survive the ever-increasing tumult caused by the militants of their day. Unlike the Pharisees, they had no significant following on a popular level, and so their legacy was not carried forward. As indicated, the early rabbis, looking to the Pharisees as their learned and honored predecessors, grant the Sadducees short shrift in their writings. There the hapless Sadducees always come off the losers when pitted against the Pharisees, especially when it comes to purity regulations (cf. *m. Yad.* 4:6–7).

## SUMMARY

Reconstructing the identity and role of the Sadducees in first-century Judaism is difficult because of the nature of the sources. The data are limited and the agenda of each source colors the presentation of the Sadducees. Collation of the various sources, however, paints a portrait that is reflective of much of what we find in the New Testament. From their inception, the Sadducees were associated with power and wealth. They consistently occupied the apex of Jewish aristocracy and religion—the office of the high priest. In some respects, they took a minimalist approach to revelation, accepting only what is explicitly expressed in the Pentateuch. Unlike the Pharisees, they rejected the "traditions of the elders" and did not believe in relatively new theological developments such as belief in the resurrection of the dead or in a myriad number of angels and demons (cf. Acts 23:8).[17] On these points, they were at odds with the theological vision of Jesus and the early church. Their bid for survival in the face of oppression by the Romans was characterized by cooperation. In the wake of the holocaust of 70 C.E., they had no popular following among the Jews, and the Romans had no need of them once Jerusalem and the temple were destroyed. From this point in history, the Sadducees fade into obscurity, their legacy tainted by the early rabbis' endorsement of their erstwhile enemies, the Pharisees.

---

17  Acts 23:8 is the only source indicating that the Sadducees did not believe in angels. But since the Sadducees accepted the Pentateuch, a revelation that speaks of angels, scholars are divided on the meaning of Acts 23. David Daube argues that what the Sadducees rejected was the Pharisaic belief in an intermediate state as an angel or a spirit ("On Acts 23: Sadducees and Angels," *JBL* 109 [1990]: 493). Benedict T. Viviano and Justin Taylor seek a grammatical solution: that the Sadducees rejected the Pharisees' belief that one was resurrected as an angel or as a spirit ("Sadducees, Angels, and Resurrection [Acts 23:8–9]," *JBL* 111 [1992]: 498).

# Annotated Bibliography

Baumgarten, Albert. *The Flourishing of Jewish Sects in the Maccabean Era: An Interpretation*. New York: E. J. Brill, 1997. This excellent work looks to the Maccabean period for the emergence of the major Jewish sects. Extensive use of Josephus and the Qumran literature anchors Baumgarten's heories in primary-source material.

Pate, C. Marvin. *Communities of the Last Days: the Dead Sea Scrolls, the New Testament, and the Story of Israel*. Downers Grove, Ill.: InterVarsity, 2000. Pate provides a good introduction to the Dead Sea Scrolls, particularly regarding how the vision of the desert community might relate to the overall history of Israel and the earliest Christian writings. He uses the general theme of "sin–exile–restoration" to link together Israel's history, the ideals of Qumran, and the message of the Gospels.

Saldarini, Anthony J. Pharisees, *Scribes and Sadducees in Palestinian Society: A Sociological Approach*. Wilmington, Del.: Michael Glazier, 1988. This is a good tool for the study of these sects along the lines of modern social anthropology; this work discusses at length the over reliance on rabbinic literature for the description of these groups and contains a thorough treatment of the scribes' vocation.

Stemberger, Günter. *Jewish Contemporaries of Jesus: Pharisees, Sadducees, Essenes*. Translated by Allan W. Mahke. Minneapolis: Fortress, 1995. Stemberger does not look to social-anthropological theories for an understanding of these ancient Jewish sects but rather seeks to remain within the bounds of the primary documents. Thus he provides a good reservoir of primary materials yet is reticent to put forward theories not explicitly cited in the documents.

# 4
# The Scribes—
# Political Sages

## INTRODUCTION

### The Origin of the Scribes

Unlike the Pharisees and Sadducees, the earliest development of the scribes is not confined to Israel. This is so because the scribes do not simply represent the coalescence of a particular religious or political ideology within Israel. Rather, scribes represent a practical vocation that met the literary and diplomatic needs of ancient civilizations. For example, the presence of scribes in Egypt and Mesopotamia can be traced to as early as the third millennium B.C.E.[1] Similarly, there is evidence for the presence of scribes in Israel long before the Pharisees and Sadducees are spoken of as identifiable groups. Thus the antiquity and universal presence of the scribes expands the sphere of inquiry beyond the scope of any Jewish sect.

When studying the scribes of the ancient world, one is struck by the frequent association of scribes with large urban areas. Perhaps

agrarian societies, where the great majority were illiterate, had no practical need for a scribal class. On the other hand, a centralized nation-state with a well-developed urban center, together with its extensive network of economic and political contexts, would have been in great need of the scribe. In such societies, careful records of treaties had to be drawn up and preserved. Civil law had to be codified, and royal decrees based on the law had to be recorded. So it appears that in antiquity the scribe was an official secretary and archivist whose vocation often required proximity to the ruling elite. Their work, then, drew them into the inner circle of power in the ancient world, and in this way the scribe attained influence that went far beyond that of a copier of manuscripts. Many scribes became royal correspondents and emissaries of the state. As such, they had to be knowledgeable in many areas, such as history, law, diplomacy, philosophy, and religion. In sum, the scribes formed the intellectual elite of the ancient world, reflecting the power and the prestige of the royal court or temple. As cultures evolved to even higher levels of sophistication, the need for specialization also increased. Thus among the scribal class there existed liturgical scribes, fiscal scribes, diplomatic scribes, and so on (2 Chr 24:11; 34:12–13). It is not difficult to understand how a scribal secretary of the king came to function as virtually a secretary of

[1]  The connection between the divine, scribes, and writing is clearly set forth in an ancient Egyptian pictograph of the final judgment. Here a human soul is weighed in a balance while the scribe-god, Thoth, records its fate. Sumerian cuneiform texts show evidence of a scribal class as early as the third millennium B.C.E. On the role of the scribe throughout the ancient world, see Philip R. Davies, *Scribes and Schools: The Canonization of the Hebrew Scriptures* (Louisville: Westminster John Knox, 1998), esp. 24, 20.

**Part of an Egyptian papyrus from 200 B.C.E.**

state. Similarly, one can see how a copier of the Jewish law and the prophets came to function as a religious scholar and teacher in Israel.

### The Scribe in Israel

The fundamental meaning of the Hebrew word for "scribe" connotes "a sent message." This "message" in time became associated with a written message and ultimately with the person who had the skill to write it down. The Greek counterpart to the Hebrew reflects similar ideas designating the persons who specialized in writing and copying important documents.[2] In Israel the scribe was thus a skilled secretary who functioned in various capacities within society, whether as a personal accountant of a wealthy businessman, as the learned attendant in a royal court, or as the recognized expert in the law of God, teaching in the temple and synagogue. This final meaning is the most common in Judaism, generally signifying a "man learned in the Torah" or even a "rabbi." The powerful status of the scribe is displayed in the Aramaic Targumim of the prophets. These translations, dating from at least the first

century C.E. and perhaps earlier, often translated the Hebrew word "prophet" with the Aramaic word for "scribe." The conceptual effect of this substitution is that the scribe is placed on the order of the prophets, interpreting the Torah and speaking forth God's judgment in the present and pronouncing God's will for the future.[3]

All of these functions speak of a highly developed culture, one that needs secretaries and intellects to keep the affairs of state going. This is exactly how Ben Sira, a Jewish sage from the second century B.C.E., portrays the Jewish scribe. He states that the scribe requires freedom from the plough and herd so that he may intently study the law of God, the prophets, and the wisdom literature (Sir 38:24–39:11). Ben Sira adds that the powerful seek the wisdom of the scribes and this insures them a place near the king. Finally, he claims that the scribe shares what he has learned from his own education with those who desire wisdom. The scribe in Israel was, then, highly esteemed, so much so that Enoch, Moses, and Elijah were understood to be great scribes. He was not simply a copyist or secretary. Ben Sira's description parallels what we know of

2    The inherent function of this vocation is contained in the words themselves. The Hebrew word *sopherim*, "the scribes," is derived from *sofer* (סֹפֵר), connoting a sent message. The Gk. *grammateus* (γραμματεύς) is from *gramma* (γράμμα), meaning "something written or drawn."

3    On the role of the scribes in the Targumim, see Robert Hayward, "Some Notes on Scribes and Priests in the Targum of the Prophets," *JJS* 36 (1985): 210–21, esp. 220–21.

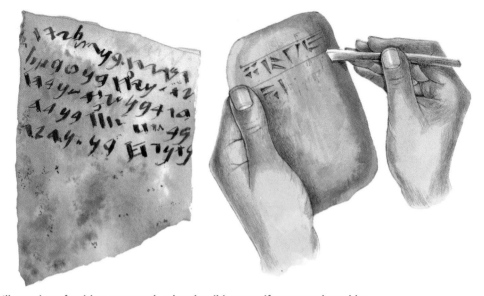

**Illustration of writing on a postherd and scribing cuneiform on a clay tablet.**

the scribes from ancient times. Their social context is primarily urban, not agrarian. The scribes are valued by leaders both civil and religious. And they teach what they have learned to those who earnestly desire wisdom.[4]

There is considerable debate about when this specialized meaning of the word "scribe" came into use in Israel. By way of answer, we know that literacy and scribal activity go hand in hand. Since Israel enjoyed a long literary history, one would expect to find Hebrew scribes from ancient times, and indeed this seems to be the case. Judges 5:14 speaks of a military scribe, and 2 Sam 8:16–17 mentions that David's officials included a "recorder" and a "secretary" (KJV "scribe"; cf. also 2 Sam 20:23–26; 1 Kgs 4:1–6). Also, 1 Chr 18:15–17 contains a list of King David's officials, one of which is explicitly called a scribe. David's uncle, Jonathan, "was a counselor, a man of insight and a scribe" (1 Chr 27:32). The inclusion of this scribe among the high officials in David's court likewise parallels the courtly presence of the scribe found in other ancient cultures.

It has been argued that entire schools of scribes may have existed in Israel even as far back as the reigns of David and Solomon (cf. Josephus, *Ant.* 7.319, 364). This theory rests upon the premise that the Hebrews were a people of the Book; as such, they read the law of God and so needed scribes to copy, interpret, and teach the law. Broken pieces of pottery, or ostraca, have been found at Gezer, Lachish, and Kadesh-barnea. These ancient shards contain sections of the Hebrew alphabet and appear to be the practice pads of pupils studying under scribal masters.[5] Clay bullae—scribal seals used to secure important documents—are being found in increasing number. These seals date at least to the seventh or sixth centuries B.C.E. One of the bullae contains the name of Baruch, the scribe of Jeremiah, and another speaks of Shaphan, mentioned in Jer 36:10, 32.[6] Such evidence is admittedly circumstantial,

4    On the authority of the scribe in the time of Jesus, see Stephen Westerholm, *Jesus and Scribal Authority* (Lund, Swed.: Gleerup, 1978).

5    On the possible existence of scribal schools in ancient Israel, see Davies, *Scribes and Schools*, esp. 78–81.

6    For the significance of the bullae, see J. Andrew Dearman, "My Servants the Scribes: Composition and Context in Jeremiah 36," *JBL* 109 (1990): 403–21. Some of the bullae, found in scriptoria that had been destroyed by fire, dated back to the time of the Babylonian captivity in 587/586 B.C.E. (p. 416).

Relief of Assyrian scribes.

but the ability to read and write appears to have been a vital part of Israel's history from very early on.

It could further be argued that the very process of canonization implies the presence of scribes and, as noted, perhaps even schools of scribes early in Israel's history. Whether there were official scribal schools in Israel dating back as early as the monarchic period cannot be determined for sure. But Josephus says that the law orders that Jewish children be taught to read and write (*Ag. Ap.* 2.204).[7] Thus commitment to literacy was ancient in Israel. All of these points give some indication that scribes were functioning in Israel from a very early date.

As one approaches the period of the prophets, the evidence for scribal activity in Israel increases. Jeremiah 36:10 speaks of a scribe in charge of administrative and fiscal affairs. As noted, the prophet Jeremiah had a personal scribe, Baruch (Jer 36:4, 18, 32).[8] In classic scribal fashion, Baruch not only records the oracles of Jeremiah by way of dictation (36:4) but delivers them to the king (36:14). Isaiah mentions that one of King Hezekiah's highest officials was a scribe named Shebna, charged with managing the treasury (Isa 22:15; 36:3, 22). Second Chronicles 26:11 speaks of a military scribe by the name of Jeiel. Jeremiah 52:25 relates the capture and execution of scribes by Nebuchadnezzar. All of these cases speak of the varied functions of the courtly scribe during the preexilic period. As in other vocations in Jewish culture, the craft appears to have been passed down from father to

son, eventually resulting in whole families of scribes (1 Chr 2:55).[9]

Second Chronicles 34:8 speaks of a scribe named Shaphan, who was under the employ of Josiah; his task was to facilitate the repairs to the temple, particularly regarding the disbursement of funds to the workers (cf. also 2 Chr 34:13). In this respect, Shaphan functioned as a fiscal scribe (cf. 2 Kgs 22:3–5). But Shaphan was clearly more than a fiscal scribe, for he was given a copy of the newly found book of the law (2 Chr 34:14) and commissioned to read it to the king. So, in addition to his close connection with the temple, Shaphan displays another cardinal trait of the Hebrew scribe: he demonstrates expert knowledge of the Torah. Indeed, 2 Chr 34:13 indicates that an entire class of scribes closely associated with the Levites and the temple arose in the later Persian period.

This connection between priestly service in the temple and knowledge of the law is most clearly seen in the book of Ezra. Ezra 7:6 states that Ezra was a scribe (Heb. *sopher*) and priest who was directly descended from the lineage of Aaron. Ezra is described as highly skilled in the law of Moses and an authoritative teacher of the Torah. The fact that Artaxerxes appointed Ezra to lead the Jews back to their homeland (7:6, 10, 14) is an indication of his power and of his proximity to those in power. Thus Ezra more than likely was a powerful official in the employ of the royal court who had been entrusted with the affairs of the Jews while in exile. Ezra was himself empowered to appoint other leaders (7:25–26; chs. 8–10). Again, this description perfectly fits the role of powerful ambassador-scribe that existed in other cultures throughout the ancient world. As priest, leader, and teacher, Ezra is the archetypal scribe (4:8–9).

This portrait of the Jewish scribe continues through the time of the Seleucids and Ptolemies. In about 199 B.C.E. Antiochus III

---

7   Josephus speaks of "sacred scribes" prophesying the birth of Moses (*Ant.* 2.205, 255). Although this statement is no doubt anachronistic, his consistent portrayal of scribes as persons of power and prestige reflects what can be known of the scribes of later ages.

8   Jeremiah used several scribes to disseminate his views and ensure that they were properly interpreted. The employment of a number of courier-scribes parallels what we know of scribal practices from the Lachish ostraca (cf. Dearman, "My Servants the Scribes," 420).

9   For diagrams of scribal family trees, see ibid., 410–11.

**View of the excavated Qumran community settlement, near the Dead Sea.**

wrote to Ptolemy of Egypt about Jewish "temple scribes." He explains to Ptolemy that because of their special position, these scribes of the temple are to be exempt from taxes (Josephus, *Ant.* 12.138–142).

During the Maccabean period, the close connection of the scribes with the law and the priests continued. Judas Maccabeus empowered scribes, some of whom may have been in the service of his army. Such scribes are praised for their piety toward the law and their abhorrence of apostasy and the suppression of Jewish laws by the enemy (1 Macc 5:42; 7:12–13). Second Maccabees 6:18–28 speaks of the scribe and priest Eleazar, who refused to eat swine's flesh from a pagan altar. He sacrificed his own life, accepting a martyr's death rather than be forced to profane the law of God. Here we have the confluence of scribe, priest, purity, and the law, elements present among the scribes at the time of Jesus.

The scribal tradition in Israel continued into the early Roman period, as seen in the Dead Sea Scrolls. In a sense, the Qumran community was a sect of scribal reactionaries that produced and copied more than eight hundred scrolls and fragments of the Bible and other religious literature. This hidden library in the desert addresses the critical role that the scribes played in identifying the Jewish canon. Thus scribal activity in preserving the canon may well have been at work from the time of David right up to the period of Qumran.[10] Josephus confirms the care with which the Jewish scribe copied the Scriptures: "We have given practical proof of our reverence for our own writings. For, although such long ages have now passed, no one has ventured either to add or to remove, or to alter a syllable, and it is also an instinct with every Jew, from the day of his birth to regard them as the decrees of God, to abide by them and if need be to die cheerfully for them" (*Ag. Ap.*, 1.37–43). The very occupation of the scribes as "writing priests" tied in with the process of canonization.

10   On the role of scribes prior to the exile see M. Haran, "Book-Scrolls in Israel in Pre-exilic Times," *JJS* 33 (1982): 161–73; and "More concerning Book-Scrolls in Pre-exilic Times," *JJS* 35 (1984): 84–85.

Thus, long before the Pharisees and Sadducees came together as identifiable religious groups in Israel, the scribes occupied a time-honored place in Jewish society and history as recorders of sacred writ as well as attendants at court.

## THE SCRIBES IN THE NEW TESTAMENT
### Scribes as a Clearly Identifiable Social Group

The New Testament corroborates what we know of the scribes from the Hebrew Scriptures and extra-biblical sources. Some form of the Greek word *grammateus* (NIV, "scribe") appears sixty-six times in the New Testament; most of the occurrences are in the Gospels (sixty-two), the highest concentration in the Gospel of Matthew (twenty-two).[11] That none of these instances contains a detailed explanation of who these scribes were indicates that their identity was taken for granted. By the first century, the scribes were a well-recognized group not only within Israel but also throughout the Mediterranean world. In that they are consistently presented as "*the* scribes" in the Bible (1 Chr 2:55; Jer 8:8; Matt 5:20; Mark 1:22; Luke 5:21; Acts 6:12), they constitute a clearly identifiable social group within Israel.

### The Scribes in the Synoptic Gospels and Acts—Urban Teachers of the Law

In accordance with the predominantly urban role of the ancient scribe, the scribes in the New Testament are frequently located in Jerusalem or are represented as coming from Jerusalem. For example, on more than one occasion, the scribes are described as "those who came down from Jerusalem" en route to Galilee to accuse Jesus (Mark 3:22; cf. Matt 15:1). When not in Jerusalem, the scribes are associated with large cities, such as Capernaum (Mark 2:6, 16; 3:22; 9:14). The

historic connection between the scribes, the temple, and political power in Israel explains their proximity to Jerusalem. "Coming down from Jerusalem" may be understood as code for authoritative representatives of the Sanhedrin, the judicial body that will ultimately secure the death of Jesus.

The Book of Acts contributes to our view of the scribes. Apart from the mention of the Ephesian scribe or "city clerk" in Acts 19:35, all other occurrences of "scribe" in Acts are found in trial scenes (4:5; 6:12; 23:9). Regardless of whether the indicted are Peter and John, Stephen, or Paul, the scribes are in league with the ruling elite of Israel to pass judgment on the Christians. They form part of the Sanhedrin and, as in the Gospels, are linked to the Pharisees and share their belief in the resurrection (23:9).

In accordance with the image of the scribe in the Hebrew Scriptures, the Gospels recognize them as authoritative teachers of the law (Matt 2:4; 23:2–3). Luke's unique nomenclature for the scribes also reflects their authority in the law (Luke 5:17; 7:30; 11:45).[12] This indicates that the authority of the scribes was not derived from a priestly function in the temple or from prophetic inspiration but from their thorough knowledge of the law of Moses.

As experts in the law, the scribes would have naturally taken notice of Jesus' words concerning the law. At times, the Gospels portray some scribes as being genuinely impressed with Jesus' teaching of the law (Mark 12:28–34). On at least one occasion, a scribe expresses an interest in becoming a disciple of Jesus (Matt 8:19). In turn, Jesus affirms scribal teaching when it rightly conveys the meaning of a particular passage (Mark 12:32–33). He even says that the scribes sit in the seat of Moses and function as authoritative teachers of the law (Matt 23:2). In the main, however, the scribes are

---

11   It should be noted that the NIV never uses the word "scribe(s)" in the New Testament, but prefers the phrase "teacher(s) of the law."

12   In these verses Luke describes the scribes as "teachers of the law" (*nomodidaskaloi* [νομοδι-δάσκαλοι]) and "lawyers" (*nomikoi* [νομικοί]).

A scholar carefully unravels one of the Dead Sea Scrolls.

set forth as those who are blind to God's intention in the law and seek to destroy Jesus (Matt 15:1; 26:57; Mark 12:35; 15:1).

## The Relationship of the Scribes to the Chief Priests and Pharisees

The Gospels frequently associate the scribes with the chief priests, especially in the context of opposing Jesus and seeking his death (Matt 16:21; 20:18; 26:3; Mark 8:31; 10:33; 11:18; Luke 9:22; 19:47; 22:2, 66). Indeed, twenty-two verses in the Gospels link the scribes and the chief priests. This close alliance, especially regarding the trial of Jesus (cf. Mark 14:1; 15:1, 31; Matt 26:57; Luke 22:66; 23:10), may indicate that some of the scribes were part of the ruling class of the Sadducees or at least were sympathetic to the cause of the Sadducees.[13]

But the scribes are equally linked with the Pharisees in the Synoptics. The Gospels join the Pharisees with the scribes just about the same number of times as they are joined to the chief priests, a total of twenty-one (Matt 5:20; 12:38; 23:15, 23, 25, 27, 29). This kind of linkage may be traced all the way back to the scribal influence of Ezra and Nehemiah, as mentioned above.[14] In this case the scribes would have been disciples of Ezra and Nehemiah and one and the same as the *sopherim*.[15] It appears, however, that under the pressure of increasing Hellenism, the *sopherim* divided into two factions. One faction may have been more accommodating to Hellenism and survived to New Testament times as the scribes. The other element may have sought to stave off the encroachment of Hellenism by "building a fence" around the law. This group of scribes would have come to be known as the *Hasidim*, the "pious ones," more familiarly recognized as the Pharisees in the Gospels and Acts. If this

---

13   I. Howard Marshall, *The Gospel of Luke: A Commentary on the Greek Text* (NIGTC; Grand Rapids: Eerdmans: 1978), 848–49. Joachim Jeremias considers the scribes one of the three main groups, together with the Sadducees and Pharisees, that composed the Sanhedrin ("γραμματεύς," *TDNT* 1:740–41).

14   Leah Bronner, *Sects and Separatism during the Second Jewish Commonwealth* (New York: Boch, 1967), 38–55.

15   Ellis Rivkin agrees and comments, "A class of *Soferim*, Scribes or exegetes, thus sprang up as a necessary consequence of the canonization of the Pentateuch" (*A Hidden Revolution: The Pharisees' Search for the Kingdom Within* [Nashville: Abingdon, 1978], 185).

scenario is sound, one would expect a close political and ideological association between the scribes and the Pharisees as it appears in the New Testament. For example, Mark 2:16 and Acts 23:9 speak of the "scribes *of the* Pharisees" (NRSV) and may indicate that most of the scribes were Pharisees. Again, in Luke 5:30 we read of "the Pharisees and *their* scribes" (NRSV). So the association of the scribes and the Pharisees in the New Testament is very close. Like the Pharisees, the scribes are teachers of halakhah, the "traditions of the elders," and keepers of the entire Old Testament. It may well be that together with the Pharisees the scribes were instrumental in preserving the religious traditions of the Jews, which in time came to be codified in rabbinic Judaism.[16]

## THE SCRIBES AND JESUS

In the Gospels, the scribes appear as purveyors of conventional Judaism, sharing concerns that were also deemed important by the Pharisees (Mark 9:11; 12:35). For this reason, they are often paired with the Pharisees in opposing Jesus. They question Jesus' authority and challenge him to give a sign that would substantiate his claims (Matt 12:38; cf. also Mark 11:27–28). That they can question authority is a reflection of their own authority, an authority that is not confined to Jerusalem but extends northward into Galilee.[17] Here they castigate

Jesus' disciples for not washing their hands according to the traditions of the elders (Matt 15:1; Mark 7:5). It appears, then, that some of the scribes share the Pharisaic ideal that all Jews must follow the purity regulations as set forth in Levitical law (Mark 7:1–23).

In Mark the scribes are consistently seen as opposing Jesus' teaching authority and that of his disciples. Their challenges and taunts are varied. They question his authority to forgive sins, charging him with blasphemy (Mark 2:6; Matt 9:3; cf. also Luke 5:21).[18] The scribes will use this same charge to secure Jesus' crucifixion.[19] They point out that Jesus' disciples do not have the power to cast out an unclean spirit (Mark 9:14). One scribe apparently tries to entrap Jesus concerning the greatest commandment in the law of Moses. Jesus' response silences not only this critic but all those within earshot (12:28). He then trumps the scribes at their own game by asking a question about how the messiah could be David's son (12:35–37). In 2:16 the scribes and the Pharisees challenge Jesus' practice of eating with tax collectors and sinners (cf. Luke 5:30; 15:2). This incident may likewise address the issue of ritual impurity, but probably much more is at stake here. The tax collectors and sinners were viewed as extortionists, morally profligate, and quislings who served the oppressors of Israel. By enjoying table fellowship with such persons and in the name of God, Jesus was extending divine grace to sinners before repentance. The scribes and the Pharisees share the same religio-political ideals in this regard, viewing Jesus' conduct as betraying the interests of the nation.[20] Indeed, Jesus' final confrontation

16   J. Julius Scott Jr., *Customs and Controversies: The Jewish Backgrounds of the New Testament* (Grand Rapids: Baker, 2000), 168, 173. For the view that the scribes are equal to the Pharisees and that they together constitute the *sopherim*, see Ellis Rivkin, "Scribes, Pharisees, Lawyers, Hypocrites: A Study in Synonymity," *HUCA* 49 (1978): 135, 140–41. Jeremias cautions, however, that on a fundamental level, the scribe reflects a vocation whereas the Pharisees speak to a religious way of life. One did not have to be a Pharisee in order to be a scribe (Matt 23:1–36; Luke 11:39–44) (cf. *TDNT* 1:741). Leaders among the Pharisees may have been scribes, but not every scribe was a Pharisee (John P. Meier, "The Quest for the Historical Pharisee: A Review Essay on Roland Deines, *Die Pharisäer*," *CBQ* 61 [1999]: 716).

17   Christine Schams, *Jewish Scribes in the Second-Temple Period* (JSOTSup 291; Sheffield, Eng.: Sheffield Academic Press, 1998), 150.

18   As guardians of the Torah, the scribes would have felt especially obligated to protect the honor of God. But, for Matthew, to speak evil of Jesus is to speak evil of God. It is the scribe who in the end blasphemes, not Jesus (Donald A. Hagner, *Matthew 1–13* [WBC; Dallas: Word, 1993], 292).

19   Richard J. Dillon, " 'As One Having Authority' (Mark 1:22): The Controversial Distinction of Jesus' Teaching," *CBQ* 57 (1995): 105.

20   Cf. William A. Simmons, *A Theology of Inclusion in Jesus and Paul: The God of Outcasts and Sinners* (Lewiston, N.Y.: Mellen, 1996), 66–87.

in Jerusalem is framed in terms of his conflict with the scribes (Mark 12:35–40).

Jesus' healing on the Sabbath was another point of contention for the scribes as well as the Pharisees (Luke 6:7). In such cases, a scribe would "stand up" to test Jesus because the scribe from Jerusalem viewed himself as the undisputed authority in religion whereas Jesus was simply an untutored charismatic from the hill country of Galilee (Luke 10:25–37).[21] Jesus must provide them with a miraculous sign; otherwise his teaching is contemptible, as they fully believe (Matt 12:38).

Occasionally the Gospels present a scribe in a positive light, as affirming that Jesus has spoken well and said the truth. In turn, Jesus says that this scribe is not far from the kingdom of God (Mark 12:28–34). Yet even this exception furthers Mark's aim to prove that the scribes are utterly clueless about God and God's kingdom.[22] In a summary manner, Luke 11:54 claims that the scribes and Pharisees were waiting to seize upon any saying of Jesus so that they could accuse him.[23]

It seems clear that Jesus did not blindly acknowledge the scribal authority of his day.[24] According to Luke, Jesus deliberately healed on the Sabbath in order to provoke the scribes and Pharisees (Luke 6:7–11). In the Gospels, Jesus mercilessly derides the hypocrisy and mean spirit of the scribes. He portrays them as self-serving, arrogant, and hypocritical (Matt 23:5; Mark 12:40). Jesus charges that they abuse their office by manipulating the law so that

Artist's impression of Jewish High Priest. The Gospels frequently associate the scribes with the chief priests, especially in the context of opposing Jesus and seeking his death.

---

21   Marshall, *Luke*, 442.

22   "One open-minded scribe symbolizes what might have been, but he stands alone" (R. T. France, *The Gospel of Mark: A Commentary on the Greek Text* [NIGTC; Grand Rapids: Eerdmans, 2002], 476).

23   They were "lying in wait for" him, in the sense of a predator waiting for an opportunity to capture its prey (Marshall, *Luke*, 508). Schams notes that in Luke the scribes are never associated with the actual arrest and crucifixion of Jesus. They are, however, very prominent in the trial narrative of Luke (Luke 22:66; 23:1–2, 9–10). For Luke, the real value of the scribe lay in his knowledge and interpretation of the law, not in the execution of the law (*Jewish Scribes*, 168).

24   Westerholm, *Jesus and Scribal Authority*, 128.

they may rob the defenseless. He claims that they are driven by vainglory, covetousness, and power (Mark 12:40; Luke 20:45–47) and accuses them of using subtlety in legal cases to "devour widows' houses." They have the outward appearance of being sincerely religious, but inwardly they harbor corruption and greed (Matt 23:14, 25, 27, 29; Luke 11:44) and fall far short of doing the things that they teach others they ought to do (Luke 11:46). The scribes "will not lift one finger" to help people bear the burden of the law (Luke 11:46), and their pedantic approach to the law undermines any possibility that they will attain the true intent of the law, that is, to demonstrate the love of God toward their fellow human beings. As portrayed in the Gospels, the scribes, together with the Pharisees, in rejecting the words of Jesus and refusing to be baptized by John, have totally missed the will of God (Luke 7:29–30). According to Luke, the crushing irony regarding the scribes is that those who pride themselves in the knowledge of God and his kingdom have in fact locked the door to this knowledge and thrown away the key (Luke 11:52).[25]

In contrast to the flaccid instruction of the scribes, the Gospels characterize Jesus as one who taught with authority (Mark 1:22). This subordination of the scribes to the authoritative teaching of Jesus is important, for it serves as a banner heading descriptive of Jesus' entire public ministry. How Jesus' teaching was perceived as being more authoritative than that of the scribes is not spelled out in detail. No doubt the aspects that ran counter to the halakhic teaching of the scribes are in view here. For example, Jesus' radical teaching on the Sabbath, the clean and the unclean, and the inviolable nature of marriage would have amazed those committed to the status quo. Jesus' teaching is new in contrast to the old teaching of the scribes. Also, his teaching exhibits authority because of his supernatural power to exorcise demons, a power not present among the scribes. In this sense, Jesus demonstrated "authority" (Gk. *exousia* [ἐξουσία]), that is, the entitlement, permission, or even divine commission to act in the freedom of God in order to reclaim the rule of God over creation. The scribes, however, offered only a textbook rendition of the teachings of the fathers (Matt 7:29; Mark 1:22).[26]

Jesus was well aware of the animosity of the scribes and predicted that he would suffer at their hands (Matt 16:21; 20:18; Mark 8:31; Luke 9:22), for they were alarmed at the popularity of Jesus and were afraid of losing their power over the people (Mark 11:18; Luke 19:47–48; 20:19). For these reasons, the scribes conspired with the chief priests on how they might capture Jesus and kill him (Mark 14:1; Luke 22:2). They were successful in their plans and cast their lot with the chief priests in condemning Jesus before Caiaphas and Pilate (Mark 14:43; 15:1; Matt 26:3; 27:41; Luke 22:66; 23:10). According to Mark, the scribes kept up their relentless attack on Jesus to the very end. They even mocked Jesus in his hour of agony on the cross (Mark 15:31).

## SUMMARY

Throughout the ancient world, the scribes are portrayed as the educated elite, associated with large urban centers and often closely joined with the king and his courts. As such, scribes took on a variety of roles, including the administration of finance and the military, as well as those of archivist and copier of important manuscripts. Their most important work was in the roles of ambassadors and counselors to the king. These scribes were very influential in the eyes of the general populace

---

25 "Casuistry in framing laws can well be accomplished by skill in giving the impression of keeping them while avoiding their minute demands. And this reflects lack of love for the people who are forced to bear the yoke while the framers of the law themselves go scot-free" (Marshall, *Luke*, 500; cf. also 299, 507).

26 On how the authority of Jesus differed from that of the scribes, see Dillon, " 'As One Having Authority,' " 92–98; and Hagner, *Matthew 1–13*, 193.

and in forming political policy.

The scribes in Israel demonstrated all these qualities, their power enhanced all the more through their strategic work with the Torah and temple. Like their counterparts in other nations, Jewish scribes held close to large urban areas, especially Jerusalem. Similarly, the scribes in Israel were part of a powerful inner circle of religio-political leaders. As part of the Sanhedrin and as Torah specialists and temple functionaries, their influence spanned the whole gamut of Jewish life in the Second Temple period. Their place in both the sacred and the secular realms meant they had a considerable hand in controlling the popular religious ideology of the people and in influencing their political life.

In the broader scheme of things, it seems likely that the scribes played a strategic role in the Jew's struggle to survive especially after the destruction of the temple in 586 B.C.E. National holocausts such as the Babylonian exile and the subsequent domination by Alexander the Great, followed by the oppression of the Romans, served only to empower the scribes. With the disruption of the temple and cult, the law became the premier unifying factor for the Jews. Those whose occupation was directly tied to the preservation and promotion of the law stood to benefit from this intense preoccupation with the law. So the power and influence of the scribe was in direct proportion to the place that the law held among the people. Although closely associated with the priests and the Pharisees, by the Maccabean period the scribes had gained a position of authority independent of these groups. The scribes became experts on the legal sections of the Hebrew Scriptures and in time produced their own body of *halakhah*, the teaching tradition about the law.[27] Discerners of proverbs and parables, attendants in the courts of potentates, official emissaries to foreign lands—all these roles worked together to develop the literary skills of the scribe and to enhance his public presence (Sir 38:24–39:11).

By the time of Jesus, the vocation of the scribe was well established in Israel. The scribes were viewed as the gatekeepers of the Torah and were in constant conflict with Jesus over its meaning and how it should be applied. Epistemologically, the Gospels leave no doubt concerning who had rightly understood God and God's ways. Jesus' teaching is "from heaven" (Gk. *ex ouranou* [ἐξ οὐρανοῦ]), whereas the teachings of the scribes are "from men" (*ex anthrōpon* [ἐξ ἀνθρώπων]; Mark 11:30–31). The qualitative difference between the teachers and their teachings proved to be irreconcilable. The conflict ultimately resulted in the death of Jesus yet also, in a paradoxical way, aided in the birth of a new spiritual movement, the church.

---

27 Although Westerholm, too, notes the close association of the scribes and the priests, he points out that "by the N.T. period, however, priests, though represented among the sages, do not seem to have played a dominant role, and it is apparent that the authority of the scribes is not dependent on any priestly status" (*Jesus and Scribal Authority*, 28; cf. also 168).

# Annotated Bibliography

Baumgarten, Albert. *The Flourishing of Jewish Sects in the Maccabean Era: An Interpretation.* See description at the end of ch. 3.

Davies, Philip R. *Scribes and Schools: The Canonization of the Hebrew Scriptures.* Louisville: Westminster John Knox, 1998. Davies presents the theory that the Hebrew canon arose from scribal processes that in turn were influenced by the political and social contexts of the day. He clearly presents the case for a scribal class in ancient Israel, but his method presupposes much familiarity with the subject, making it a difficult read for beginners.

Grabbe, Lester L. *An Introduction to First Century Judaism: Jewish Religion and History in the Second Temple Period.* Edinburgh: T & T Clark, 1996. This introduction to first-century Judaism, tracing the critical moments of the Jewish religion and history from after the exile to the beginning of the third century C.E., is accessible to beginners.

Schams, Christine. *Jewish Scribes in the Second-Temple Period.* Journal for the Study of the New Testament: Supplement Series 291; Sheffield, Eng.: Sheffield Academic Press, 1998. This programmatic presentation of the scribe from the Persian period down to the Roman era of the first century describes the evolution of the secretarial scribe of the royal court to the practicing interpreter of the law within Judaism. A scholarly work not intended for beginners, it offers considerable data on the role of scribes in various cultures throughout history.

Scott, J. Julius, Jr. *Customs and Controversies: The Jewish Backgrounds of the New Testament.* Grand Rapids: Baker, 2000. This excellent overview of the intertestamental period focuses on the crises of this era and the Jewish response to them as reflected in their literature. The clear presentation of useful information on the customs, practices, and beliefs of Second Temple Judaism makes this work a good source for beginners.

# 5

# The Zealots—Religious Militancy and the Sole Rule of God

## INTRODUCTION: WORD STUDY AND IDENTIFICATION

The root word for "zealot" literally means "to boil." Our English word "zeal" is derived from the same source.[1] The image of hot, boiling water conveys fervency and passionate commitment, whether to God, a person, or a cause. Although the word can also be used in the negative sense of jealousy and strife (Isa 11:13; Ezek 35:11), more frequently it speaks of the intense love of Yahweh for his people (Exod 20:4–5; 34:12–16; Deut 4:23–24; 5:8–9; 6:14–15; Josh 24:19–20). Indeed, God himself tells Moses that his name is Jealous (Exod 34:14; cf. also 2 Cor 11:2), and Isaiah predicts as well that the promised messiah will be driven by the zeal of the Lord (Isa 9:7).

In time, "zeal" came to be associated with one's complete devotion to Yahweh. For example, Elijah states that he is very "jealous" (Gk. *zēlōn*) for God (1 Kgs 19:10 LXX).[2] One of the earliest examples—perhaps the most important—of this use of "zeal" can

be found in Num 25. In this instance Israel has betrayed its God by cohabiting with the Moabites and embracing idolatrous practices (Num 25:1–2). The wrath of the Lord comes upon the camp, and Moses is instructed to execute every errant male. In full sight of Moses and at the very time the assembly is repenting of their sins, a Jew brazenly takes a Midianite woman into his tent (25:6). Phinehas, the son of a priest, takes hold of a spear and, entering the tent, thrusts both of them through. At that instant the plague is lifted from the children of Israel (25:7–8). The Lord commends and blesses Phinehas because he was zealous for God and displayed the zeal of God in killing those who had sinned. God grants him a covenant of peace and an everlasting priesthood because he has made atonement for the sins of Israel (25:11–13). In this way Phinehas becomes the "archetypal zealot."[3]

From this brief overview it can be seen that the marriage between violence and religious piety in Israel was long-standing. As Israel's struggle to survive intensified, so did the union of militancy and piety. The precise moment, however, when the Zealots emerged as a distinct

---

1   "Zealot" is derived from the Greek word *zēlos* (ζῆλος), which conveys the notion of fervent heat. For a comprehensive treatment of this word, see Martin Hengel, *The Zealots: Investigations into the Jewish Freedom Movement in the Period from Herod I until 70 A.D.* (Edinburgh: T&T Clark, 1989), 59–72.

2   In rendering 1 Kgs 19:10, the LXX translators reflect the importance of religious zeal by retaining the Hebraism *zēlōn ezēlōka*, "zealing I have zealed."

3   Menachim Friedman, "Jewish Zealots: Conservative versus Innovative," in *Jewish Fundamentalism in Comparative Perspective: Religion, Ideology, and the Crisis of Modernity* (ed. Laurence J. Silberstein; New York: New York University Press, 1993), 155.

group in Israel cannot be determined. This is because the Zealots never constituted a highly organized or structured military presence in Israel.[4] It seems that anyone who refused to accept foreign domination and opted for guerrilla warfare as a solution to problems could be classified as a "zealot." But to view such persons as constituting a recognizable religio-political segment of Israel before 66 C.E. may well be premature.[5] On the other hand, there is evidence that several zealot-like groups were already active before the great revolt of 66 C.E. For example, after naming the Pharisees, Sadducees, and the Essenes as the major sects in Israel, Josephus also speaks of the "Fourth Philosophy" (*Ant.* 18.4–25). His characterization of this group and his description of their violent practices can leave little doubt that the "Fourth Philosophy" was composed of zealots of some sort. The fact that Josephus calls these militants a "sect" on the order of the Pharisees and Sadducees indicates that they were identifiable as a group to some degree. Yet his consistent negative portrayal of such persons shows that Josephus did not view zealot ideology and tactics as representative of his people, even though they proved to be very influential (*Ant.* 18.10, 23).[6] Josephus blames these zealots for the downfall of Jerusalem and the holocaust of 70 C.E. (*Ant.* 18.25; *J.W.* 1.10–12; 7.252–274).[7] Thus zealots of some kind are certainly on the scene by the time of Josephus. The militant sentiment that they display, however, may well have been in place much earlier than this period.

## THE ZEAL OF PHINEHAS, THE ZEALOTS, AND THE MACCABEAN REVOLT

Phinehas's example was not lost on subsequent writers in Israel. Psalm 106:28–31 recounts the valor of Phinehas and says that his execution of the Jew and the Midianite "was credited to him as righteousness" (Ps 106:31). Here the justification language of Gen 15:6, originally associated with God's promise to Abraham, is joined with the carnage of Phinehas.[8] Elijah is similarly praised for destroying the prophets of Baal (1 Kgs 18:40; cf. also 1 Macc 2:58 and Sir 48:2). First Maccabees 2:54 commemorates Phinehas's zeal, as do the writings of Ben Sira much later (Sir 45:23–24). Judith 9:4 and *Jubilees* 30:5 praise the zeal of Simeon and Levi for killing the Schechemites who defiled their sister Dinah (Gen 34).

The birth of Zealotism in Israel and the sect of the Pharisees appear to be linked on a number of levels. Their common affirmation of holiness, purity, and zeal for God reflects their kindred spirit. Josephus notes the similarity between the two groups. He records that as resistance movements, both groups expressed extreme veneration for the Law and the Prophets and were willing to lay down their lives in defense of God and God's word. Furthermore, the Zealots and the Pharisees both believed in a blessed afterlife for the faithful, especially those who were martyred in their defense of Yahweh (*Ant.* 18.4, 9, 23).

The historical context of the Maccabean revolt may have given rise to the Zealot movement in Israel in about 168 B.C.E. (1 Macc 2:15–30). It was at this time that Antiochus Epiphanes so radicalized the political and

---

4    For the notion that the Zealots did not exist as an organized party even during Paul's time, see Torrey Seland, "Saul of Tarsus and Early Zealotism: Reading Gal 1:13–14 in Light of Philo's Writings," *Bib* 83 (2002): 449–71.

5    For the view that the militants during the Maccabean revolt, the Hasmonean period, the Jewish uprising in 66 C.E., and the Bar Kokhba revolt in 135 C.E. were all part of the same group that Josephus calls the "Fourth Philosophy," see Mark R. Fairchild, "Paul's Pre-Christian Zealot Associations: A Re-examination of Gal 1:14 and Acts 22:3," *NTS* 45 (1999): 514–32; and S. G. F. Brandon, *Jesus and the Zealots: A Study of the Political Factor in Primitive Christianity* (New York: Charles Scribner's Sons, 1967), esp. 31.

6    On the "zealot syndrome" of such groups, see Friedman, "Jewish Zealots."

7    Brandon, *Jesus and the Zealots*, 34–38.

8    For a complete treatment of the tradition of the zeal of Phinehas from the time of the Maccabees to the period of the rabbinic literature, see Hengel, *The Zealots*, 149–60.

religious context of the Jews that concerted development of zealot sentiment seems plausible. Again, the model of Phinehas is close at hand. The zeal of Mattathias for Yahweh and the law led him to resist the emissaries of Epiphanes and refuse to offer sacrifice on a pagan altar (1 Macc 2:24, 26). Rather than apostatize, Mattathias drew a sword and slew the king's agents. First Maccabees 2:27 records, "Then Mattathias cried out in the town with a loud voice, saying: 'Let every one who is *zealous* for the law and supports the covenant come out with me!' " (NRSV, italics added) With that, he and his sons fled to the mountains, sparking a popular Jewish revolt.

The agenda and methods of the Maccabean revolt are set forth in 1 Macc 2:24–26; 3:5–6, 8. Here we read that these zealous Jews fought for their lives and the law (3:21). By 165 B.C.E. these "freedom fighters" had achieved considerable success. The temple was rededicated to God, and the Jews celebrated their first Hanukkah (4:36–59; 14:9–12, 15). In this way the inauguration of the Hasmonean dynasty had been purchased in blood. There can be little doubt that those who joined Mattathias in *herem*, or "holy war," set the pattern for the eventual emergence of the Zealots as a distinct party in the first century.

Not all the pious took up the sword in their quest for holiness. Many adopted a passive-resistant campaign against incursions into their faith by ever increasing the mandates of the law upon their daily lives. It was this kind of religious resistance that may have eventually evolved into the Pharisees of Jesus' day. Generally, the Pharisees renounced the use of violence in their efforts to spread the kingdom of God. Some did not hesitate, however, to employ violence to further their aims. Some Pharisees "slit the throat" of those who took part in the oppression of their group under Alexander Jannaeus (104–78 B.C.E.) (*Ant.* 13.410). Also, Sadduq the Pharisee joined Judas of Gamala in leading the revolt

In 1968 an ossified foot was discovered in Jerusalem with a spike driven through it. The foot belonged to a crucified man named Yehohanan. This discovery illustrates the nature of crucifixion in New Testament times.

against Rome in 6 C.E. (*J.W.* 2.118; *Ant.* 18.4–9). Indeed, thirty years after the revolt of Judas, Paul the Apostle explicitly identified himself as a Pharisee and spoke of his zealous persecution of the church (Phil 3:5). At his arrest in Jerusalem, Paul is wrongly accused of being a member of the *sikarioi*, zealots who knifed their unsuspecting victims (Acts 21:38; cf. also *J.W.* 2.253–255; *Ant.* 20.186, 210).

## THE SICARII, THE ZEALOTS, AND THE JEWISH REVOLT AGAINST ROME

Infighting within the Hasmoneans' household weakened their hold on power. As was so often the case, the Romans were quick to exploit the situation (*Ant.* 14.29–72; *J.W.* 1.19, 117–159). The imperial war machine, under the direction of Pompey, was able to sweep aside the remnants of the Hasmoneans and capture Jerusalem in 63 B.C.E. Subjugation to a foreign power caused the zealot flame to burn white hot once again.[9]

If at any time zealot sentiment coalesced into an identifiable political-religious party know as the Zealots, it would have been at this time. Discontent among the Jews reached fever

9    On the anti-Roman sentiments of the Zealots, see ibid., 46–50, 59–72.

pitch in the years leading up to 66 C.E., and the power of the Zealots lay in their ability to tap into this discontent. Their touchstone with the masses consisted of two parts: one theological, the other economic. The first issue concerned the sole rule of God over the Jews. At the heart of the Zealot program was the belief in the distinct identity of the Jewish people as defined by their union with Yahweh and revealed in the Torah. So, unlike the Sadducees and, to a lesser extent, the Pharisees, the Zealots did not believe that politics could be defined without including the sovereign rule of God (*Ant.* 18.23). The second issue concerned the exploitation by the rich and powerful and was framed in terms of land valuation and the Roman census.[10] For this cause, the Zealots murdered the principal men of Israel and would suffer indescribable torture before submitting to their enemies (*Ant.* 18.4, 23).

This last description of the Zealots reveals how extreme their members were, especially those who came to be known as the Sicarii. The Sicarii (derived from the Latin *sica*; cf. Justinian, *Inst.* 4.18.5), were so named after the curved knife they kept concealed in the folds of their cloaks (cf. *Ant.* 20.185–186; *J.W.* 7.259–262). Regarding this group Josephus states,

> A new species of banditti was springing up in Jerusalem, the so-called sicarii, who committed murders in broad daylight in the heart of the city. The festivals were their special seasons, when they would mingle with the crowd, carrying short daggers concealed under their clothing, with which they stabbed their enemies. . . . The first to be assassinated by them was Jonathan the high-priest; after his death there were numerous daily murders. (*J.W.* 2.254–256)

As Mattathias had done more than two hundred years earlier, these Zealots were able to consolidate resistance groups and retake Jerusalem from the Romans in about 67 C.E. Josephus uses the word "Zealots" more than fifty times to describe the jumbled amalgam of forces arrayed throughout Judea at this time (*J.W.* 2.651; 4.160–162, 186–400, 503–579). It is difficult to know the number of Jewish combatants who took part in the confused fighting that led to the fall of Jerusalem, but some estimates indicate that as many as ten thousand Zealot fighters and their allies took part in these battles.[11] Once inside the city, Zealot leaders performed deeds that symbolized their intention to make good on their promises to the masses. They burned the government offices that housed tax, census, and loan records. They promised to free all slaves (*J.W.* 2.421–427). They converted the temple into a fortress, holding out against their own people and killing thousands of their countrymen who resisted their cause. Josephus harbors no love for the Zealots, calling them the worst kind of criminals, vile in motive and deed. According to Josephus, no fate, no matter how heinous, could repay the Zealots for the harm they did to their own people (*Ant.* 18.7–10).

Indeed the role that the Zealots were to play in the final days of Jerusalem was both sad and violent. Their Zealot "general," Menachem, son of Judas the Galilean, wrought havoc in Jerusalem by murdering the Jewish elite who collaborated with Rome and by assassinating Ananias the high priest (*J.W.* 2.426, 441–442). When Menachem revealed his aspirations to the throne by entering the temple in royal robes, fellow Zealots turned against him and his. Menachem was killed and his followers escaped to Masada (*J.W.* 2.446–449). Under the direction of their leader, Eleazar,

---

10    On the poor and the Zealots, see Ernst Bammel, "The Poor and the Zealots," in *Jesus and the Politics of His Day* (ed. Ernst Bammel and C. F. D. Moule; Cambridge: Cambridge University Press, 1984), 109–28, esp. 113.

11    For a detailed discussion of the Zealot groups that fought at this time, see Edwin Yamauchi, "Christians and the Jewish Revolts against Rome," *Fides et historia* 23 (1991): 11–30, esp. 14.

This coin dating from the Bar Kokhba revolt features the only known depiction of Herod's Temple. With the fall of Jerusalem in 70 C.E., the Zealots ceased to exist as an organized party. But the spirit of the Zealots surfaced again in the Bar Kokhba revolt of 135 C.E.

66 C.E.[12] To some extent, the issue may be a matter of semantics, for Josephus uses a number of terms—"Fourth Philosophy," "robbers," "Sicarii," "Zealots," and the like—to describe Jewish militants from the time of the Hasmoneans to the fall of Jerusalem in 70 C.E. (cf. *J.W.* 2.254, 425; 4.135–162; *Ant.* 18.9, 23).[13]

In any case, one of Jesus' disciples was called Simon the Canaanite or Simon the Zealot (Matt 10:4; Mark 3:18; Luke 6:15; Acts 1:13).[14] Whether he was a Zealot in the sense of the group that fought the Romans from 66 C.E. onwards cannot be determined. We know that paying taxes to Caesar was a burning issue among the Zealots (*Ant.* 18.3–4; 20.102; *J.W.* 7.253–254; cf. also Luke 2:1–2), as it apparently was at the time of Jesus (Matt 22:15–22; Mark 12:14–17; Luke 20:20–26).[15] Zealot sentiment may also have been present even at the trial and crucifixion of Jesus, for Barabbas was more than likely a zealot revolutionary (Mark 15:6–15; Matt

a descendant of Judas Maccabaeus, this last Zealot band held out until all hope was lost in 73 C.E. (*J.W.* 7.252–253). Josephus describes the last assault by the Romans and Eleazar's last desperate attempt to snatch victory from defeat by ordering all Jewish defenders to commit suicide rather than surrender (*J.W.* 4.399–405; 7.275–400). Such mass suicide is incomprehensible to modern ears. But Eleazar would have known of the thousands of Zealots who had alreadybeen crucified by the Romans (*Ant.* 17.295; *J.W.* 2.75). He probably thought it better to control one's own destiny with a modicum of dignity than to be tortured and crucified in abject humility. Yet even after Masada, the zealot flame was not completely extinguished. It was rekindled during the Bar Kokhba revolt of 132–136 C.E.

## JESUS AND THE ZEALOTS

Although zealot sentiment and actions have a long history among the Jews, the critical question remains as to whether the Zealots existed as a distinguishable group before

12 On whether the Zealots were in place at the time of Jesus, see Richard A. Horsley, "The Death of Jesus," in *Studying the Historical Jesus* (ed. Craig Evans and Bruce Chilton; Leiden: E. J. Brill, 1994), 395–422, cf. esp. 408; and idem, *Jesus and the Spiral of Violence: Popular Jewish Resistance in Roman Palestine* (San Francisco: Harper & Row, 1987), esp. 78–79. Cf. also Morton Smith, "Zealots and Sicarii: Their Origins and Relations," *HTR* 64 (1971): 1–19.

13 For those who take a more synthetic approach, see William Klassen, "Jesus and the Zealot Option," in *The Wisdom of the Cross: Essays in Honor of John Howard Yoder* (ed. Stanley Hauerwas et al.; Grand Rapids: Eerdmans, 1999), 131–49; and Yamauchi, "Christians and the Jewish Revolts against Rome."

14 The phrase *ho Kananaios* (ὁ Καναναῖος) is a transliteration of the Aramaic *qan'ana*, meaning "zealous." Thus Simon the Canaanite is also called Simon the Zealot.

15 The association of the birth of Jesus with the census of 6 C.E. has been a point of contention for New Testament chronology. The word *prōtē* (πρώτη) in Luke 2:2 could mean "before" and thus refer to the beginning of a census completed under Quirinius (I. H. Marshall, *The Gospel of Luke: A Commentary on the Greek Text* [NIGTC; Grand Rapids: Eerdmans, 1978], 98–99). On the birth of Jesus and the census, see J. Vardaman and E. Yamauchi, eds., *Chronos, Kairos, Christos: Nativity and Chronological Studies Presented to Jack Finegan* (Winona Lake, Ind.: Eisenbrauns, 1989).

22:15–22; Luke 20:20–26) together with the two thieves crucified with Jesus (Matt 27:38).

In light of all these factors, the relationship of Jesus to the Zealots, or to Zealot-like groups for that matter, is open to question. His mandate to take up one's cross and follow him seems to reflect the radical vision of the Zealots (Matt 10:38). Similarly, James and John wanted to call down fire on the Samaritans and expressed their willingness to die for the cause (Luke 9:54; Mark 10:38–40). Jesus' cleansing of the temple, with its violent display of turning over tables and driving people out, would have spoken to those of a zealot temperament. The disciples also connected Jesus' actions here with the words in Ps 69:9, "*zeal* for your house consumes me" (italics added; cf. also John 2:17). Jesus' admonitions that he came not to send peace but a sword (Matt 10:34) and that if one did not have a sword, then one should sell one's cloak and buy a weapon (Luke 22:36) would also have been welcomed by the Zealots.[16]

On the other hand, Jesus' words that the kingdom of God suffers violence and the violent take it by force may be a tacit rejection of a religious militancy (Matt 11:12). And unlike the Zealots, his answer to the question of paying taxes to Caesar indicates his belief that the kingdom of God is distinct from the kingdom of this world (Matt 22:21; Mark 12:17; Luke 20:25). His command to love one's enemies would have been antithetical to Zealot doctrine (Matt 5:44; Luke 6:27). Similarly, his counsel to turn the other cheek would have been incomprehensible to a committed Zealot (Matt 5:39). Finally, the Zealots would not have endorsed Jesus' fellowship with tax collectors.

For all of these reasons, it appears that in comparison with the Zealots and groups like them, Jesus and his disciples could be described as apolitical and nonzealot.

## THE ZEALOTS, THE EARLY CHURCH, AND THE APOSTLE PAUL

The early church found itself in a climate of violence and instability. The task of developing a distinct identity, one that would not be labeled subversive to the powers that be, was no small task. The fact that Jesus had preached a kingdom besides the rule of Caesar made matters difficult. That he was crucified as "King of the Jews" under Pontius Pilate made matters more difficult still (Matt 27:37; Mark 15:26; Luke 23:38). Indeed, some of the early Christians were thought to be a Zealot movement bent on the kind of revolt started by the false messiah Theudas (Acts 5:36; *Ant.* 20.97–98). At the time of his arrest in Jerusalem, even Paul was thought to be a Zealot insurrectionist from Egypt (Acts 21:38).

In spite of these challenges and confusion, the early church did not take a Zealot path in its spread of the Gospel. On the contrary, the church was the object of zealot-like persecution by the hands of Saul of Tarsus. In Gal 1:14 and Acts 22:3, Paul uses the Greek word *zēlōtēs* (ζηλωτής) when describing his pre-Christian persecution of the church.[17] Although the word is usually translated as an adjective, "zealous" (KJV, NIV), it is in fact a noun. If taken literally, Paul would be saying that before his conversion to Christ he was an extreme zealot (or Zealot?) for the traditions of his fathers. Here we have almost the same expression used by Josephus to describe a Zealot's devotion to the traditions of the fathers (*Ant.* 12:271). Paul further links this zeal with his intent to destroy the church (Gal 1:13). He even presided over the stoning of Stephen and fully consented to his death (Acts 7:58; 22:20). So, just like Phinehas of old, the pre-Christian Paul may have believed that the killing of apostate Jews and Gentiles credited righteousness to his account. In addition, the close connection between some Pharisees and

---

16 For a sustained argument that Jesus was in fact a Zealot, see S. G. F. Brandon, *Jesus and the Zealots: A Study of the Political Factor in Primitive Christianity* (New York: Charles Scribner's Sons, 1967). For a contrasting view, see Martin Hengel, *Was Jesus a Revolutionist?* (Philadelphia: Fortress, 1971).

17 On Paul's affinity to the Zealots, see James D. G. Dunn, *The Theology of Paul* (Grand Rapids: Eerdmans, 1998), 352–53; and Torrey Seland, "Saul of Tarsus and Early Zealotism: Reading Gal 1:13–14 in Light of Philo's Writings," *Bib* 83 (2002): 449.

**Aerial view of Masada.**

the Zealots lends credence to the notion that Paul may have been a Zealot. Paul makes this connection in Phil 3:5-6, where he claims to have been a Pharisee driven by zeal to persecute the church. Thus the pre-Christian Paul certainly displayed his "zeal" as a good Zealot would, that is, through murderous persecution of the church (Acts 22:4-5).

After his encounter with the risen Lord on the Damascus road, however, Paul relocates the crediting of divine righteousness away from the model of Phinehas back to its more ancient context, that is, the faith of Abraham (Rom 4:3; Gal 3:6). From this time onward, for Paul the kingdom of God is not cast in terms of violence but rather consists of righteousness, peace, and joy in the Holy Spirit (Rom 14:17). Ironically, he spent the rest of his Christian life protecting his churches from the zealous campaign of those he regarded as "Judaizers" (cf. Gal 1:7, 4:17-18, 5:12).[18] Ultimately, Paul suffered at the hands

of Zealot-like Jews who plotted to murder him (Acts 23:12, 21). Their threats led to his transference to Caesarea and then on to Rome, where church tradition indicates that he was executed at the hands of Nero in about 64 C.E.

## SUMMARY

The first believers refused to meld militancy and faith in Christ. They were to submit to civil authorities, support the government with their taxes (Rom 13:1-7), and pray for the Roman imperial rulers (1 Pet 2:13-17). Their commitment to Jesus directed them away from the violence of the Zealots and not toward it. With the fall of Jerusalem in 70 C.E. and that of Masada in 73, the Zealots ceased to exist as an organized party of the first century. But the spirit of the Zealots would surface again in the Bar Kokhba revolt of 135 C.E., a revolt in which the Christians took no part.

---

18  The exact word "Judaizer" does not appear in the Scriptures but rather is derived from the adverb *Ioudaikōs* (Ἰουδαικῶς) found in Gal 2:14. The word speaks of an attempt to force Gentiles to fully convert to Judaism and to follow all Jewish practices. For the various meanings of the phrase "to Judaize" throughout history, see Shaye J. D. Cohen, *The Beginnings of Jewishness: Boundaries, Varieties, Uncertainties* (Berkeley: University of California Press, 1999), 175–197.

# Annotated Bibliography

Bammel, Ernst, and C. F. D. Moule, eds. *Jesus and the Politics of His Day. Cambridge:* Cambridge University Press, 1984. This collection of scholarly essays counters the notion that Jesus and the early Christians were Zealots or sympathetic to their cause. It is a classic study on the dynamics of messianic expectations and politics in the first century C.E.

Brandon, S. G. F. *Jesus and the Zealots: A Study of the Political Factor in Primitive Christianity.* New York: Charles Scribner's Sons, 1967. This thoroughly researched work posits the thesis that Jesus and his first followers were political activists who sympathized with the Zealots.

Hall, John F., and John W. Welch, eds. *Masada and the World of the New Testament.* Provo, Utah: Brigham Young University Studies, 1997. This is a collection of essays on a wide array of subjects concerning Palestinian life in the first century. Among the topics are agriculture, commerce, and religious practices. It is clearly written and well illustrated.

Hengel, Martin. *The Zealots: Investigations into the Jewish Freedom Movements in the Period from Herod I until 70 A.D.* Edinburgh: T&T Clark, 1989. The classic scholarly work on the Zealots, this volume is thoroughly researched and documented and contains an excellent bibliography.

Horsley, Richard A. *Jesus and the Spiral of Violence: Popular Jewish Resistance in Roman Palestine.* San Francisco: Harper & Row, 1987. Horsley emphasizes the effect of Roman oppression and the injustice of the Jewish aristocracy on the common folk of Jesus' day. Jesus is seen to be a political activist who is interested in end-time judgment only in order to affect justice in the here and now. Horsley makes good use of primary documents, especially Josephus, to expose the political and economic oppression of first-century Israel.

Safrai, S. and M. Stern, eds., *The Jewish People in the First Century: Historical Geography, Political History, Social, Cultural, and Religious Life and Institutions.* 2 vols. Compendia rerum iudaicarum ad Novum Testamentum, sec. 1. Philadelphia: Fortress, 1974–1976. This work is a storehouse of data on Jews and their world of the first century. Extremely detailed and plainly written, it is valuable for gleaning data on Jewish life during the early Roman period.

# 6

# The Tax Collectors—
# Pragmatic Opportunists

**INTRODUCTION**

Some form of the word *telōnēs*, "tax collector" appears twenty-one times in the Gospels.[1] The term probably refers to the ancient practice of purchasing a franchise to collect taxes for the state. By opening the enterprise to the private sector, the state would avoid the expense of creating and maintaining the labor force needed to collect taxes. Procedurally, the system worked as follows. The right to collect taxes was offered to the highest bidder, who in turn would guarantee the state's share from his own resources. It was up to the tax collector, then, to meet his quota and also to make a profit on the deal. The tax collector of old was an integral part of a state-run business that in time took on the form of a corporation employing different levels of tax collectors. The person who won the state contract was a chief tax collector who hired out lesser functionaries for the completion of the task. For example, in the New Testament, Zacchaeus was a chief tax collector who supervised regional agents such as Matthew, "the tax collector" (Matt 10:3; Luke 5:27; 19:1–10). In Jesus' day the tax collectors made a living by garnering revenue for the Herods, who in turn paid tribute to Caesar.

The frequent mention of tax collectors in the Synoptics indicates that they formed an identifiable social group in Israel. These tax collectors often appear in contexts that resolve critical issues for the Gospel and early church. In this way, the tax collectors of the Gospels serve as object lessons for a better understanding of the New Testament.

**The Tax Collector in Ancient Society**

The history of the tax collectors' place in society is a long one, and their presence in the Mediterranean world was almost universal. The affairs of state secured their role in every land. Our earliest record of a tax-farming system stems from the ancient Greeks. Demosthenes of Athens (384–322 B.C.E.) mentions tax farmers and the kinds of stress placed upon the state when there was a shortfall in revenue (*Timocr.* 24.96–101). He notes that there were no established standards of accountability for regional tax collectors and that this lack of regulation led to tax fraud and default on tax-farming contracts (*Timocr.* 24.144–146). Xenophon (430–354 B.C.E.) laments the heavy tax burden that wealthy Athenians had to endure and the kinds of economic maneuvering that some citizens employed to avoid taxes (*Oeconomicus* 2.6; 7.10). Aristophanes (450–338 B.C.E.) satirizes the wealthy for feigning poverty so that they might avoid the tax collector (*Ranae* [*Frogs*] 1063–1069). He laments that the

---

1    See Matt 5:46; 9:10-11; 10:3; 11:19; 18:17; 21:31–32; Mark 2:15-16; Luke 3:12; 5:27, 29-30; 7:29, 34; 15:1; 18:10-11, 13; 19:2.

citizens of Athens have to flee their country or be ruined by taxes while the resident aliens have a better life there (*Aves* [*Birds*] 35–37). He lampoons the tax farmer as the bottomless pit of wanton exploitation of the people (*Equites* [*Knights*] 245–249). The Greek system of the *polis*, or "city-state," did nothing to curb the abuses of the tax farmer or the ploys of those who sought to avoid taxation. A decentralized form of government lacked the close supervision needed to stem graft among the tax collectors, and the Greek senate took no measures for accurately determining how much income the state needed for the year. It simply estimated the cost for running the government, published its expectations, and opened the market for bids. Successful bidders and their backers had to first put up half of the expected revenues from their own pockets and sign a contract to pay the rest of the money at the end of the year.[2] To avoid a shortfall and make a hefty profit for their efforts, tax collectors were known to garner all that the market could bear.[3] The absolute monarchs of Egypt effected a closer management of their tax agents. After the money was turned into the national treasury, the pharaoh granted a small percentage of the total proceeds to each tax agent. The rise of the Romans, however, marked the continuance of tax revenue collecting.[4] As was their

Coin of the Roman emperor Augustus. Jewish Palestine circulated its own copper coins, omitting the image of the Roman emperor. But foreign coins, bearing the image of the deified emperor, were also in common circulation.

custom, the Romans patterned their system of tax collection after the Greeks. The senate adopted a laissez-faire approach to taxation by appointing censors to run the tax-farming enterprise in the provinces. The senate also enacted *leges censoriae*, or "tax-farming laws," to manage revenue collection throughout the vast empire. A tax office in Palestine was a long way from Rome, however, and the money collected might pass through several hands before it reached Caesar. Opportunities for corruption and exploitation abounded. For all these reasons, the tax collectors' guild operated under a cloud of suspicion throughout the era, first-century Israel being no exception. Indeed even the great orator Quintilian (ca. 35–95 C.E.) found it a challenge to maintain dignity in speech when force of reason led him to speak ill of tax farmers (*Institutio oratoria* 11.1.86).[5]

Certain individuals and entire families apparently became adept at working the system and gained the confidence of the Roman censors, and for these reasons they were routinely

---

2 The word "tax collector" as it appears in the NIV is a translation of the Gk. *telōnēs* (τελώνης), a compound word derived from *telos* (τέλος, "toll" or "indirect tax") and *ōneomai* (ὠνέομαι, "buy"). In the KJV, τελώνης is nearly always translated "publican," derived from the Latin *publicanus* (cf. Matt 5:46–47; 11:19; 21:31–32; see also Justinian, Dig. 39.4.1). "Chief tax collector" as found in Luke 19:2 is a translation of *architelōnēs* (ἀρχιτελώνης), the arch- root indicating "first" or "principal," as in the sense of rank. For a detailed treatment of tax collectors in the ancient world, see Otto Michel, "τελώνης," *TDNT* 8:88–106.

3 Justinian notes that in the heat of bidding, a tax farmer might pay too much for a franchise. Nevertheless, the agent is held to his bid and must pay it in full, even if from his own resources (*Dig.* 39.4.9).

4 Although Justinian (sixth century C.E.) notes that ancient Roman laws were enacted to curb abuse by tax farmers, they were admittedly "lenient" when compared to similar laws against theft (*Dig.* 39.4.1).

5 "Nobody is unaware of the extent of the audacity and insolence of cliques of tax farmers. This is the reason why the praetor promulgated this edict to control their audacity" (Justinian, *Dig.* 39.4.12).

awarded tax collecting contracts year after year. By the third century B.C.E., a cadre of official tax collectors was well established in Rome. In this way, the tax collectors gradually evolved into an identifiable social group among the people. The nature of their vocation and the corruption associated with it stigmatized the tax collectors. Their experience of marginalization in the wider society, especially within the ethnocentric culture of first-century Israel, further accentuated their identity as a distinct group among the people.

## Tax Collectors in Israel

One of the earliest records of taxation in Israel is found in Josephus' account of the conquest of Antiochus Epiphanes. To reward the Jews for their cooperation, Antiochus lobbied Ptolemy of Egypt on their behalf. He requested that the Jews be relieved of their tax burden for a time so that they might recover from the ravages of war. Those who attended to the temple were to be exempt from all taxes (*Ant.* 12.138–142). In *Ant.* 12.175–185, however, Josephus describes a classic tax-farming system with all of its abuses. Here one Joseph wins the tax-farming contract from Ptolemy through guile and employs savage methods to obtain his due from the peoples of Judea and Samaria. Threats, coercion, and even the mass murder of leading citizens were all part of a day's work for Joseph. Regarding taxes, the Jews would suffer such state-sponsored abuse for much of their existence, especially under the Romans.

Roman taxation of the Jews began with the conquest of Pompey in 63 B.C.E. From this time on, one could argue that Jews experienced a double tax burden.[6] Not only did they pay the Romans their due; they continued to pay tithe,

plus firstfruits, redemption money, and the temple tax (Exod 30:12–16; Matt 17:24–27).[7] Josephus notes that those who "lived as Jews" and followed their "paternal customs" willingly paid an annual tax for the upkeep of the temple (*Ant.* 16.169–170; 18.312–313; *J.W.* 7.218). This tax is not explicitly demanded in the Torah, although the Pharisees appealed to Exod 30:13 as a justification for the tax. There is some evidence that many Jews were reluctant to pay the half-shekel temple tax required of all Jewish males. Furthermore, it is estimated that during the time of Julius Caesar direct taxes on farm produce amounted to 12.5 percent of the total crop. Josephus also speaks of a "house tax" paid in Jerusalem under the Roman governors (*Ant.* 19.299). When one adds to this the custom taxes on goods transported from region to region, the average Jewish farmer could have easily have paid up to 35–40 percent of his annual income in taxes of some kind.[8]

Understandably, the Jews petitioned Archelaus to reduce the tax rate, and after he was removed from power because of his oppressive rule, the Jews made their petition directly to Rome (*J.W.* 2.111; *Ant.* 17.342–344). The tax burden was certainly "onerous" for Judeans, as Tacitus attests (*Ann.* 2.42). On top of all of these established taxes, the *angaria* was another kind of tax that the Jews had to suffer. This tax allowed the Romans to arbitrarily commandeer human and animal labor for public works, with a promise to compensate at a latter date those so taxed. Matthew 5:41; 27:32; Mark 15:21; and Luke 23:26 appear to

---

6    The Jews had to pay land and agricultural taxes, an annual half-shekel poll tax, the temple tax, the tithe income tax (Num 18:21–32), and the "second tithe" every third year (Deut 14:21–29). On the tax burden of Israel during the Roman period, see F. F. Bruce, "Render to Caesar," in *Jesus and the Politics of His Day* (ed. Ernst Bammel and C. F. D. Moule; Cambridge: Cambridge University Press, 1984), 249–63.

7    The total tax burden of Jews in the first century may have equaled 60 drachmas out of a total yearly salary of 210–280 drachmas. For data on the economic context of Israel in the first century, see S. Safrai and M. Stern, eds., *The Jewish People in the First Century: Historical Geography, Political History, Social, Cultural, and Religious Life and Institutions* (2 vols.; CRINT, sec. 1; Philadelphia: Fortress, 1976), esp. 2:698.

8    Just about every imaginable commodity was taxed by the Romans. For a partial list of items subject to tax, see Justinian, *Dig.* 39.4.16.

**Roman milestone from Capernaum. This port was an important location for collecting taxes in the time of Jesus. Matthew lived and had his tax station here.**

tax-farming system of the Romans appears to have ceased by 44 B.C.E.[9] It is clear, however, that Antipater garnered taxes for Cassius in 43 B.C.E. (*J.W.* 1.218–222). Josephus speaks of a "house tax" that was levied upon the Jews (*Ant.* 19.299). During the reign of Archelaus (23 B.C.E.–18 C.E.), Judas the Galilean fomented revolt and demanded that the Jews not pay taxes to Caesar (*J.W.* 2.118). Herod Agrippa II (31–100 C.E.), in an effort to stave off war, chided the Jews for withholding tribute from Rome (*J.W.* 2.286, 403). And at a later period under Domitian (81–96 C.E.), Josephus prided himself in the fact that his lands in Judea had been exempt from taxes (*Life* 1.429). He also notes that the population of Egypt can be deduced from the Roman poll tax levied on that country (*J.W.* 2.385). Luke 2:1 likewise links Roman taxation with a census.[10] All of these factors, together with the burning question of paying taxes to Caesar as set forth in Matt 22:17, Mark 12:14, and Luke 20:22, indicate that some kind of revenue was probably being taken from the Jews at the time of Jesus. Whether they were direct poll taxes required of each person or indirect customs taxes on local commerce cannot be determined with certainty.[11] But the Caesars made sure that a steady stream of cash flowed into Rome from client kings such as

allude to this especially irksome practice. For all of these reasons, those who collected taxes for foreign occupiers were particularly hated.

## Tax Collectors and the Gospels

Josephus states that when Pompey conquered Israel in 63 B.C.E., "he laid the region and Jerusalem under tribute" (*J.W.* 1.154; *Ant.* 14.74). It is difficult to determine the precise program of Roman taxation in Israel, for at times only portions of the country were taxed and at others the main tax base for the Romans was the city of Jerusalem. Some scholars have maintained that, in a technical sense, there were no Roman tax collectors in Israel at the time of Jesus because the classic

9     For those who judge the phrase "tax collectors" to be simply a rhetorical device not referring to a specific social group, see W. O. Walker, "Jesus and the Tax Collector," *JBL* 97 (1978): 221–38; and David Neale, *None but the Sinners: Religious Categories in the Gospel of Luke* (JSNTSup 58; Sheffield, Eng.: JSOT Press, 1991), esp. 115.

10     The Greek word translated census is *apographē* (ἀπογραφή), "a registration." Luke 2:1–5 notes that Joseph and Mary needed to register themselves for the census because Caesar had decreed that the whole world be taxed. The association of the birth of Jesus with the census of 6 C.E. has been a point of contention for New Testament chronology. As mentioned above, the word *prōtē* (πρώτη) in Luke 2:2 could mean "before" and thus refer to the beginning of a census completed under Quirinius. See J. Vardaman and E. Yamauchi, eds., *Chronos, Kairos, Christos: Nativity and Chronological Studies Presented to Jack Finegan* (Winona Lake, Ind.: Eisenbrauns, 1989).

11     Although Justinian's *Digesta* was enacted in 533 C.E., it reflects the principles of Roman law in the first century. The section entitled "Censuses" reveals how meticulous the Romans were in taxing their subjects (*Dig.* 50.15.1–8).

the Herods. The modus operandi was expressed by Aristophanes nearly five hundred years earlier: pay up or be destroyed (*Vesp.* 665–679).

In general, the Romans appointed the wealthiest of the local population to manage the tax-collecting system. If there was a shortfall in taxes collected, the ruling elite were expected to make up the difference from their own pockets. The case would have been no different for Judea. Indeed, the birth of Jesus is tied to the Roman census because an accurate count of the people was a necessary measure to ensure maximum revenue for the state.[12] The fact that taxes on local commerce were being collected by the puppet king Herod Antipas and then ferreted off to Caesar in the form of vassal tribute would have inflamed the zeal of many Jews.

In the Gospels the tax collectors are clearly viewed with disfavor. They are consistently joined with the likes of thieves, robbers, and extortionists (cf. Luke 7:34; 15:1; 18:11, 13; 19:1–7). They love their own kind and care little for others (Matt 5:46). From the perspective of the pious, the tax collectors live like Gentiles (Matt 18:17). Thus, in the view of many, the tax collectors are unrighteous and in need of repentance. This general disdain for the tax collector in the Gospels may be explained on a number of levels.

Politically, the tax collectors may have been judged to be sinners because, by taking taxes from their fellow Jews and passing them on to the Romans, they were indirectly supporting the oppressors of Israel. In effect, they were promoting the demise of the nation.[13] For many in Israel, paying taxes to Caesar

was viewed as an act of treason (Matt 17:24; 22:16–21; Mark 12:17; Luke 20:19–25). In addition, zealous militants, perhaps Zealots themselves, were teaching that Jews who paid taxes to Caesar forfeited their birthright as Jews (*Ant.* 18.9). Such persons would have been viewed as quislings and traitors who betrayed the God of Israel by collaborating with the Romans.

The tax collectors were despised also in terms of religion. As members of a renewal movement struggling to accentuate all things Jewish, many Pharisees would have been doubly offended by the tax collectors. For them, the tax collectors refused to "be separate" from the Roman Gentiles. Such actions may have been seen as a tacit acceptance of paganism and a rejection of the unique identity of the Jewish people.[14] In the view of the Pharisees, the tax collectors would have been in continual contact with "unclean" Gentiles.[15] As part of their occupation, the tax collectors would also have traded in untithed or even Sabbath year produce. In no way, then, did the tax collectors adhere to the literal interpretation of Exod 19:6: "you will be for me a kingdom of priests and a holy nation." From a Pharisaic viewpoint, the tax collectors were classed as "sinners," having no part in the *haburah* ("fellowship meal") or "the fellowship" of the "separatists." The Pharisees would have been particularly incensed at Jesus' acceptance of tax collectors in the name of God.

In the minds of many Jews, however, the real problem with the tax collectors may not have been political or ritual but moral. The message of John the Baptist implies as much. He demands that the tax collectors immediately cease from taking more than what they were

---

12   For a firsthand account on how important the census was to the Caesars, see *Res gestae divi Augusti* (*The Acts of Augustus*) 1.8. In the three censuses that Augustus took during his reign, he numbered four to five million citizens throughout the empire.

13   By deriving their livelihood from the Romans, some pious Jews may have judged the tax collectors as being morally in the same camp as the prostitutes who plied their trade among imperial soldiers. For a possible connection between tax collectors and prostitutes, see J. Gibson, "*Hoi telēnai kai hai pornai* (Tax-Collectors and Prostitutes in First Century Palestine: Matt 21:31)," JTS (1981): 429–33.

14   On the political implications of the tax collectors, see Marcus Borg, *Conflict, Holiness, and Politics in the Teachings of Jesus* (New York: Edwin Mellen, 1984), esp. 86–87, 120–21, 143; and John Riches, *Jesus and the Transformation of Judaism* (London: Darton, Longman & Todd, 1980), 105–6.

15   The later rabbis viewed the tax collectors as "unclean" (cf. m. *Ṭehar.* 7:6).

**"The Calling of Saint Matthew" by J.-J. Tissot.**

required to (Luke 3:12–13).[16] His words seem to indicate that there was a legitimate range of profit for the tax collectors and that they should not abuse their office in this regard.[17] The unscrupulous tax collector could have taken advantage of the fact that the indirect taxes (*portorium*) were the object of much fraud (*Ant.* 17.205; 18.90). The tax rate on many goods

was arbitrarily assigned; often the only standard of regulation was how much the collector thought he could get away with. To make matters worse, the tax collectors' methods were often very intrusive. A person's goods and merchandise could be searched on the spot, with any "undeclared" goods subject to confiscation (Aristophanes, *Vesp.* 655–659); thus tax farmers and toll collectors are represented in the Gospels as those who invent dues for illegal profits. It is for these reasons that their occupation is banned by the Pharisees as immoral. On this score, the tax collectors may have been held in disrepute not only by the Pharisees but by the general population of law-abiding Jews.

16  The word for "appointed" here is Gk. *dia-tetagmenon* (διατεταγμένον), meaning "officially commanded," and may refer to the initial tax quota allotted at the time bids were taken for the right to collect taxes.

17  "Collect . . . nothing more," Gk. *mēden pleon . . . prassete* (μηδὲν πλέον . . . πράσσετε; Luke 3:13). Cf. A. M. Okorie, "The Characterization of the Tax Collectors in the Gospel of Luke," *Currents in Theology and Mission* (1995): 27–32, esp. 28.

## TAX COLLECTORS AND JESUS

Jesus is fully aware of the general disdain for tax collectors. He declares that an obstinate and unrepentant person is to be treated like a tax collector, for the latter is the same as an unbelieving Gentile (Matt 18:17). On the other hand, Jesus' attitude toward tax collectors could not be more unlike that of his contemporaries. Jesus states that the tax collectors who heed him are more righteous than the elders in Israel (Matt 21:31–32; Luke 18:10–13). Therefore, as was the case with John the Baptist (Luke 3:12), Luke specifically notes that the "tax collectors and 'sinners' " were attracted to the words of Jesus and his ministry (Luke 15:1). Jesus even summoned Matthew, or Levi, a tax collector, to be one of his trusted apostles (Matt 9:9; Mark 2:14–15; Luke 5:27–29). His affirmation of Matthew led to further contacts with tax collectors. On one occasion, while Jesus was dining in Matthew's house, a large number of tax collectors were present (Matt 9:10). To the dismay of many, Jesus took the initiative to invite himself to dine with Zacchaeus (Luke 19:1–10). In the minds of many Jews, Zacchaeus, as a "chief tax collector" (v. 2), would have personified everything that was wrong with the profession. On the contrary, Zacchaeus is fair and generous to all, following the law's injunction to make restitution to the ones he has wronged (v. 8).[18] To the astonishment of his detractors, Jesus claims that this chief tax collector is also a child of Abraham. Salvation has come to his house and not to the houses of the leaders of Israel (vv. 9–10).

In the light of these accounts, one can see why Jesus was frequently defamed by the Pharisees as "a friend of tax collectors and 'sinners' " (Matt 9:10–11; Mark 2:15–16; Luke 7:34). Jesus' response is that his mission is not to the well or the righteous but to the sick and to the sinners (Luke 5:31–32). Indeed, the entire fifteenth chapter of Luke may be viewed as a defense against the grumbling of the Pharisees (cf. 15:2). The parable of the Prodigal Son (15:11–32) contrasts Jesus' positive regard for tax collectors with the mean spirit of the Pharisees who challenged him. And the parable of the Pharisee and the Tax Collector in 18:9–14 overturns the conventions of many in Jesus' day.[19] All of these accounts press home the same point. Together with the "sinners," the tax collectors find "sympathetic resonance" with Jesus and his ministry. In the end, it is they, not the religious elite, who find favor with God.[20]

Paradoxically, it is the tax collectors and their business that provide Jesus with one of his greatest object lessons. Some of the Herodians and Pharisees came to Jesus and asked whether it was lawful to pay taxes to Caesar (Matt 22:17–21; Mark 12:14; Luke 20:22–26).[21] The question seeks to entrap Jesus on a number of levels. If Jesus answered "No," then his listeners would understand that Jesus rejected the rule of Rome as the later Zealots did (Josephus, *Ant.* 18.3–4; 20.102; *J.W.* 7.253–254). Zealot-minded Jews believed that the law of Moses granted a divine mandate to resist foreign oppressors.[22]

---

18  Zacchaeus states that he has given half of his income to the poor. The law required that those who made illegal gain were to restore the amount plus one fifth (Lev 6:1–5). Zacchaeus's fourfold restitution reflects his earnestness in this regard. See Thorsten Moritz, "Dinner Talk and Ideology in Luke: The Role of the Sinners," *EuroJTh* 5 (1996): 47–69, esp. 60–62.

19  This parable is found only here in the Gospels and is the only place where the word "justified" appears on the lips of Jesus. Paul and his doctrine of justification by faith may have influenced Luke at this point in his narrative.

20  On the role of tax collectors in Luke, see again Okorie, "The Characterization of the Tax Collectors in the Gospel of Luke," 27–32.

21  The word translated "tribute" is Gk. *kēnsos* (κῆνσος), a loan-word from the Latin *census* (cf. also Matt 22:17). Bruce conjectures that these Herodians and Pharisees must have been pro-Roman, for the Herodians were certainly vassals of Rome ("Render to Caesar," 251, 257).

22  Richard A. Horsley says that this is precisely what Jesus is saying. The "things that are God's" take absolute priority over all, and so Caesar does not have a legitimate claim on anything (*Jesus and the Spiral of Violence: Popular Jewish Resistance in Roman Palestine* [San Francisco: Harper & Row, 1987], 310).

On the other hand, if Jesus answered "Yes," then he would be viewed as one who completely acquiesced in the brutal oppressors of Israel. He also might have labeled himself an idolater in the eyes of some, for Caesar's image was on the coin.[23] Furthermore, to answer "Yes" may have negated his teaching on the in-breaking of the kingdom of God and, in the eyes of some, undermined his authority.

Sensing the issues at stake, Jesus does not answer the question directly. In good rabbinic fashion, he redirects the question toward a deeper meaning. He calls for a coin to be brought forth and asks whose "portrait" (*eikōn* [εἰκών]) and "inscription" (*epigraphē* [ἐπιγραφή]) are on the coin (Matt 22:20). His opponents answer, "Caesar's." It is then that Jesus gives this curious reply: "Give to Caesar what is Caesar's, and to God what is God's" (v. 21). His answer appears to have reconfigured the issues. The question now becomes, "What belongs to God?" It is possible that in this context the mention of the word "image" would have led Jesus' hearers to think of Gen 1:26. If so, Jesus has deftly turned a potentially explosive issue about paying taxes to Caesar into a lesson about committing one's whole self to God. In so doing, the zealot-minded would have heard that taxes have

Coin dating from the time of Pontius Pilate, 30 C.E.

nothing to do with complete devotion to God, and others would have been led to a deeper examination of what it meant to serve the Lord totally. For Jesus, civil authority and "mammon" have their place, but God's place is far and above all these things (Matt 6:24 KJV; cf. Luke 16:9–13).

The meaning of Jesus' acceptance of tax collectors may not, in the end, be primarily political or have anything to do with ritual uncleanness. Rather, this acted parable may be essentially theological in its message. His conduct here may point to the essential character of God and God's gracious offer of redemption to the unworthy. If so, then Jesus would have found a way to transcend the fractious issues of power politics and elevate the thoughts of his listeners to focus on the heart of God.

---

23   Jesus probably asked for a denarius, which bore the image of Tiberius as well as the inscription *TI CAESAR DIVI AVG F AVGUSTUS* ("Tiberius Caesar, Son of the Divine Augustus"). Some Jews viewed paying the tax as tantamount to worshiping Caesar. See further David T. Ball, "What Jesus Really Meant by 'Render unto Caesar,' " *BRev* 19 (2003): 14–17.

# Annotated Bibliography

Borg, Marcus. *Conflict, Holiness, and Politics in the Teachings of Jesus*. See description at the end of ch. 2.

Neale, David. *None but the Sinners: Religious Categories in the Gospel of Luke*. Journal for the Study of the New Testament: Supplement Series 58. Sheffield, Eng.: JSOT Press, 1991. This is a careful analysis of the meaning of "sinners" in Lukan thought and literature.

Riches, John. *Jesus and the Transformation of Judaism*. London: Darton, Longman & Todd, 1980. Riches presents a social and linguistic analysis of how Jesus sought to transform the religious concepts and practices of his day. Jesus rejects all understandings of God that promote militarism, nationalism, and all notions of holiness that stress purity and separation. In place of these, Jesus presents a vision of God that conveys unconditional love and forgiveness for all, regardless of their moral condition or lack of ritual purity.

# 7
# The Sinners— Marginalized and Profligate

## INTRODUCTION: AN ATTEMPT AT IDENTIFICATION

Some form of the word "sinner" appears forty-two times in the New Testament.[1] For the most part, the word functions as a theological description for those considered to be beyond the pale of redemption in Israel and the church (e.g., John 9:16, 24–25, 31; Rom 5:8, 19; Heb 7:26; Jas 4:8; 1 Tim 1:9). It is suggested here that Jesus understood and employed this sense of the word in his public ministry (Luke 6:32–34; 13:2). In the Synoptic Gospels, "sinner" is almost always paired with publicans or tax collectors, as in "tax collectors and 'sinners' " (Matt 9:10; 11:19; Mark 2:15, 16; Luke 5:30; 7:34; 15:1). In these cases one finds the frequent charge of the Pharisees that Jesus was a friend of tax collectors and sinners, a charge that Jesus does not deny (Matt 11:19; Luke 7:34). He shares meals with sinners, and as was the case with the tax collectors, he does so in the name of God (Matt 9:9–13//Mark 2:13–17// Luke 5:27–32). All of these uses indicate that the word "sinners" refers to a distinct social category in the minds of some who lived at the time of Jesus.

The identification of "sinners" in the Gospels entails some of the same problems as that of the 'am ha-'arets, "people of the land."

That is, the meaning of the word depends to some degree on the social and religious contexts in which it is used.[2] Thus, regarding the literary context of the Gospels, the critical question is whether the word "sinners" refers to the Jews who deliberately flout the law of Moses or refers to those who simply "lighten" the Torah for the sake of expediency. The question presents the following possibilities for who the "sinners" are: sinners by way of occupation, Gentiles, nonobservers of the Pharisaic interpretation of the Torah, or Jews who were flagrantly immoral, such as thieves, prostitutes, and murderers.[3]

The first two options appear to be the least likely. The phrase "tax collectors *and* 'sinners' " indicates that the sinners are to be understood as a group distinct from that of tax collectors. Thus those who sin by way of occupation do not seem to be in view here. The notion that "sinners" means "Gentiles" has some support from the New Testament. In a few contexts, the word "sinners" has

---

1 For a detailed discussion of the word "sinner," see K. H. Rengstorf, "ἁμαρτωλός," *TDNT* 1:317–33.

2 For the view that the word "sinners" evidences no semantic consistency in the New Testament and so cannot refer to any distinct social group in Israel, see David A. Neale, *None but the Sinners: Religious Categories in the Gospel of Luke* (JSNTSup 58; Sheffield, Eng.: JSOT Press, 1991), esp. 91–92. For a contrasting view, see Nils Dahl, *Jesus the Christ: The Historical Origins of Christological Doctrine* (Minneapolis: Fortress, 1991), 91.

3 See Marcus Borg, *Conflict, Holiness, and Politics in the Teachings of Jesus* (New York: Edwin Mellen, 1984), esp. 83–84.

become nearly equivalent to "Gentiles." For example, when confronting Peter in Gal 2:15, Paul comments, "We . . . are Jews by birth, and not Gentile sinners." On balance, however, it is doubtful that Jesus was castigated by the Pharisees for having table fellowship with Gentiles. If that were so, statements like those found in Matt 10:5–6 and 15:21–28 would be incomprehensible. Nor would the conflict over the inclusion of Cornelius in the church at Antioch (Acts 10–11) make sense. Likewise, this first great step of the evangelists to take the gospel to the Gentiles as set forth in Acts 11:19–20 would be anticlimactic.

For all of these reasons, the problem of Jesus' association with sinners seems to lie elsewhere. The theory that "sinners" refers to all Israelites who failed to abide by the Pharisaic interpretation of purity is part of a long-standing tradition in Protestant theology. The idea here is that in some way the Pharisees barred the common people from the kingdom of God and that Jesus let them in.

It must be admitted that some Pharisees may well have viewed common folk as beyond redemption. After all, John states that the Pharisees believed the common people were cursed because they did not know the law (John 7:49). Yet in a real sense, the Pharisees could not effectively bar anyone from the kingdom, for the whole purpose of the temple and the myriad number of sacrifices was to take care of sin in the lives of everyday folk.[4]

Yet theological acumen often gives way to the practical ambiguities of life. How the ritually "unclean" would have viewed themselves before God and the Pharisaic program for purity cannot be determined. That is, even though separatists such as the Pharisees and Qumran could not have effectively barred the common folk from the kingdom, many of the economically and spiritually impoverished may have perceived, in the face of this strident piety of the separatists, that something was not right between them and God. If so, then questions such as where one should worship (John 4:20), what would be the signs of the coming messiah (Matt 17:10; 24:1–25:46; Mark 9:11; Luke 21:8–36), what is the greatest commandment (Matt 22:36; Mark 12:28), and how one can be saved (Matt 19:25; Mark 10:17, 26; Luke 10:25; 13:23; 18:18) would have borne down hard on the spiritually perplexed and would have shown a degree of uncertainty among the general populace. In this case, "sinner" in the Gospels would include everyone except the likes of the Pharisees.

To restrict the meaning of "sinners" to non-Pharisees, however. seems to draw the line too finely and cast the net too broadly. The consistent grouping of the sinners with the tax collectors seems to point in another direction. Perhaps, just as the tax collectors were deemed sinners because of graft and extortion, the sinners were also seen as lost because they were genuinely immoral persons.[5] "Sinners" are paired not only with "tax collectors" but also with the likes of prostitutes (Matt 21:31–32). In this sense, the sinners of the Gospels would not be the people of the land or those who were ritually unclean. Rather, they would be moral profligates who had, by their lifestyle, effectively rejected their religious heritage.

## JESUS AND THE SINNERS

The Gospels appear to indicate that Jesus fully accepted the conventional understanding of "sinners," a meaning that was thoroughly moral in nature and not confined to issues of ritual impurity. If this is the case, his offense

---

4    See further Joachim Jeremias, *Jesus' Promise to the Nations* (Naperville, Ill.: Allenson, 1958), esp. 108–13; and Norman H. Young, "Jesus and the Sinners: Some Queries," *JSNT* 24 (1985): 73–75. Cf. also E. P. Sanders, "Jesus and the Sinners," *JSNT* 19 (1983): 5–36; and idem, *Jesus and Judaism* (Philadelphia: Fortress, 1985), 176–211.

5    Sanders may well be correct in asserting that the sinners were the *resha'im*, i.e., the wicked who sinned "willfully and heinously" with no intention of repenting ("Jesus and the Sinners," 8–9).

**"Jesus sat at meat with Matthew" by J.-J. Tissot.**

would not have been that he associated with non-Pharisees or the ritually impure. Rather, the issue regarding sinners would have been that Jesus ate and had fellowship with Jews who were genuinely wicked in the eyes of the general populace.[6] Furthermore, in the name of God, Jesus demonstrated by his deeds that notorious frauds and profligates could experience God's grace even though they had not repented in accordance with the standards of contemporary Judaism.[7] If this is the case, he would have reversed the conventional wisdom

---

6   J. Gibson concludes that tax collectors, sinners, and prostitutes were the portion of Jewish society that was "*de facto* and *de jure*" ostracized from the general populace ("*Hoi telēnai kai hai pornai* [Tax-Collectors and Prostitutes] in First Century Palestine: Matt 21:31," *JTS* 32 [1981]: 429).

7   Sanders is keen to emphasize that the sinners remained unrepentant indefinitely (*Jesus and Judaism*, 25, 45, 206–8, 210, 271; "Jesus and the Sinners," 23–26). But if this were so, then Jesus would not have been taken seriously by the religious leaders or by the masses, for that matter (A. E. Harvey, *Jesus and the Constraints of History: The Bampton Lectures, 1980* [London: Gerald Duckworth, 1982], 50–51). On the dynamic relationship between forgiveness and grace in the ministry of Jesus, see Evelyn R. Thibeaux, " 'Known to Be a Sinner': The Narrative Rhetoric of Luke 7:36–50," *BTB* 23 (1993): 151–60; and James L. Ressequie, "Luke 7:36–50: Making the Familiar Seem Strange," *Int* 46 (1992): 285–90.

**"The Good Shepherd" by J.-J. Tissot.**

would have graphically challenged the premise that separation from sinners constitutes one of the highest virtues. By effectively removing all barriers hindering immediate access to God and his grace, Jesus would have completely undermined the fundamental premise that the only fate awaiting the sinner was the judgment of God. These bold steps would have appeared to defy scriptural injunctions such as Exod 23:7, which says that God will in no way justify the guilty.

In light of these premises, it should be recalled that the immediate context of Jesus' acceptance of sinners was that of sharing a meal with them. Long before first-century Judaism, what one ate and with whom one ate had far-reaching social and religious implications (Dan 1:8–16; 1 Macc 1:62–63; Tob 1:10–12; Jdt 12:1–4, 19). For the pious, meals created and maintained special relationships, clarified the identity of a people, and established boundaries between the things that belong to God and those that are part of this fallen world. This would have been especially true for the Pharisees, who may have insisted on following purity regulations even when not in the temple. This practice may mean that some Pharisees viewed the body as an extension of the temple, and the assembly of the "separated ones" as analogous to the "promised land."[9]

of his day if he declared that the sinners would enter the kingdom of God before "the righteous."[8] Thus the radical vision of God as set forth by Jesus' table fellowship with the morally wicked may have been that if they heeded his message and followed him, they would have a place in the kingdom of God. This would mean that morally wicked persons could receive the grace of God completely independently of the temple and the sacrifices of the priests.

If this view is on target, then Jesus' acceptance of sinners would have been theologically motivated from beginning to end. He

Jesus apparently did not share these views concerning the body and purity and had little regard for the social and religious boundaries of his day. For Jesus, eating together was not an occasion to publicly demonstrate religious separation but an occasion to promote the inclusion of those who had been marginalized. Eating together in the name of God

---

8    For the role that theological reversals play in the ministry of Jesus, especially as recorded by Luke, see Thorsten Moritz, "Dinner Talk and Ideology in Luke: The Role of the Sinners," *EuroJTh* 5 (1996): 47–69.

9    For the social and religious implications of table fellowship, see Mary Douglas, "Deciphering a Meal," in *Implicit Meanings: Selected Essays in Anthropology* (2d ed.; New York: Routledge, 1975), 249, 236–51, 263–69. In Jesus' case, Dunn speaks of his table fellowship with sinners as being of a "quasi-sacred character" (*Jesus' Call to Discipleship* [Cambridge: Cambridge University Press, 1992], 90).

communicated friendship and the opportunity to extend grace to all persons without preconditions, regardless of their moral situation. It meant that God does not desire the death of the wicked but wills to associate with, love, and bestow honor on the ungodly (cf. Luke 15:1–32).[10] In a way that would not become explicitly articulated until years later, that is, in Paul's doctrine that God justifies the ungodly (Rom 4:5), Jesus' table fellowship may have demonstrated this divine willingness to provide whatever was necessary for repentance in the truest sense of the word, that is, a loving response to God's offer of love. And so Jesus' "inspired behavior" may have reflected the righteousness of God in terms that provided the optimal conditions for reconciliation. That is, his conduct not only clarified the true character of God, but also proffered the grace needed to affect authentic reconciliation with God.

## THEOLOGICAL IMPLICATIONS

The sinners in the Gospels, then, may have served as a fulcrum to affect a major paradigm shift in religious ideology, one that was to have momentous consequences for the early church. Through Jesus' relationship with them, holiness as actualized by the Pharisees, and even more radically by

the Qumran community, was cast into question. Jesus' symbol-laden identification with sinners indicated that holiness was not a fragile something that needed to be coddled and protected in a thousand different ways. In one simple, commonplace act—sharing a meal together—Jesus relativized the many purity regulations and clarified holiness as the divine presence that transforms everything coming under its sway. Holiness could now be viewed as "inclusive mercy" and be actualized in ways that ran contrary to the separatist sects of the day. Regarding sinners, in what must have appeared as reckless abandon to some, Jesus' table fellowship completely disregarded traditional categories that distinguished the righteous from the unrighteous, and the repentant from those who showed no conventional signs of repentance. He broke through the categories that separated the clean from the unclean and lifted the dividing wall that distinguished the sinner from the saint. The sinners in the Gospels may well serve as the point where the issue was pressed to its critical conclusions. Through them, Jesus seems to be emphasizing that God does not always have to work within the parameters of Torah and temple. In this way, his theologically laden conduct would have demonstrated Jesus' fundamental understanding of God and would have set in motion principles and practices that would in time birth a new spiritual movement altogether.

---

10   Some view the parables of the lost sheep, lost coin, and lost son of Luke 15 as reflecting the purest form of the gospel: forgiveness without sacrifice or atonement. Yet in all three parables, loss, suffering, and grief are felt by the ones who effect redemption.

# Annotated Bibliography

Douglas, Mary. *Implicit Meanings: Selected Essays in Anthropology.* See description at the end of ch. 2.

Dunn, James D. G. *Jesus' Call to Discipleship.* Cambridge: Cambridge University Press, 1992. Dunn provides a good introduction to the significance of the kingdom in Jesus' preaching and how this significance relates to the call of the contemporary Christian. Jesus is represented as one who breaks boundaries in the interest of including many in the kingdom.

Harvey, A. E. *Jesus and the Constraints of History: The Bampton Lectures, 1980.* London: Gerald Duckworth, 1982. This work is a good orientation to the "quest for the historical Jesus" question and one that takes the Gospel records as historically reliable. In compliance with the "constraints of history," Jesus was called the messiah by his disciples during his earthly ministry, and he accepted this title. Yet as teacher-prophet and miracle worker, Jesus challenged these constraints in order to open up new vistas for the understanding of God and God's kingdom.

Sanders E. P. *Jesus and Judaism.* See description at the end of ch. 2.

# 8

# The "People of the Land"—
# Poverty and Piety

## INTRODUCTION

The impact of events such as the Assyrian and Babylonian captivities sent out tremors that reverberated throughout Israel. Social and political fault lines fractured the people into various groups and subgroups. Certainly, in many cases, the lines of demarcation between some groups were more fluid than static. The group that came to be known as the Samaritans is a case in point. From one perspective, their formation could be viewed as resulting from the intensification of religious norms, particularly by the likes of Ezra and Nehemiah. In this sense, it could be argued that their emergence was not due to any concerted action on their own part. Yet this de facto formation did, indeed, over time result in the birth of a distinct group who eventually became identified as the Samaritans.

A similar social phenomenon holds true for another segment of first-century Judaism, one perhaps more nondescript than that of the Samaritans. In the wake of Nebuchadnezzar's conquest of Jerusalem, not all of Judah was carried away into Babylon. Jews who were not deemed worthy to advance the fortunes of Babylon were left behind. Such persons were marooned, so to speak, long after their Jewish neighbors to the north had undergone a considerable period of amalgamation and syncretism by way of the Assyrians. Leaderless, without temple or cult, these unfortunates

continued on as best they could, eking out an existence somewhere between the plight of the Samaritans and the radical vision of the returnees under the leadership of Ezra and Nehemiah.[1] The group that came to be known as the 'am ha-'arets, the "people of the land," may have emerged from this sector of the Jewish people and their history.[2]

## THE 'AM HA-'ARETS AND THE "LIGHTENING" OF THE TORAH

A precise description of the 'am ha-'arets is not forthcoming. The data at hand will not support a definitive profile of this group. Analyses must therefore fall more in the realm of the descriptive than the empirical. Evidence suggests that many of the 'am ha-'arets, impoverished politically, socially, and especially economically, may have embraced an attitude of practicality regarding the Torah. The rigors of survival on the margins of society may

1    For the sociological consequences of the reforms of Ezra and Nehemiah, see Lester L. Grabbe, "Triumph of the Pious or Failure of the Xenophobes? The Ezra–Nehemiah Reforms and Their *Nachgeschichte*," in *Jewish Local Patriotism and Self-Identification in the Graeco-Roman Period* (ed. Siân Jones and Sarah Pearce; Sheffield, Eng.: Sheffield Academic Press, 1998), esp. 51, 54, 57.

2    The first appearance of the term is in the singular (cf. Jer 1:18; 34:19; 37:2; Ezek 7:27; 22:29; 2 Kgs 23:30). Although the precise nature of this social group remains unclear, the negative connotations that later became associated with the plural form ('am ha-'arets, "peoples of the land") are not present at this early stage.

**Nineteenth-century photograph of Bedouin peasant family in Israel.**

have barred many Jews from endorsing the 'amanah, or "firm agreement," enacted by Ezra and Nehemiah (Neh 9:38; 10:1–29; 13:1–2; Ezra 4:4; 6:19–21; 9:1). Their proximity to the soil may have rendered the finer points of Sabbath observance and ritual purity impractical for many 'am ha-'arets.[3] Peasants who scratched out a living from the soil were continually subject to corpse defilement, were often ritually impure, and often were financially unable to tithe or pay the temple tax. From the viewpoint of the early separatists—those who might be called proto-Pharisees—such Jews

had betrayed the mandates of Yahweh in a time when strict observance of the law was critical for the integrity of the nation. Add to this mix the oppression by foreign powers together with increasing Hellenism, and the notion of keeping every point of the law becomes a luxury enjoyed by a relative few in Israel. Thus economic hardship and a heavy tax burden may have led a good number of Jews to be nonobservant with respect to tithes, the temple tax, and keeping the prohibitions of the Sabbath year.[4] One may also take into account that some Levites were wealthy landowners who served only a few days a year in the temple. Some poorer Jews may have balked

3   For the kinds of struggle that the 'am ha-'arets may have faced, see Aaron Oppenheimer, The 'AM HA-ARETZ: A Study in the Social History of the Jewish People in the Hellenistic-Roman Period (Leiden: E. J. Brill, 1977); and Philip Sigal, From the Origins to the Separation of Christianity (part 1 of The Foundations of Judaism from Biblical Origins to the Sixth Century A.D.; vol. 1 of The Emergence of Contemporary Judaism; Pittsburgh: Pickwick, 1980).

4   On the extraordinary tax burden placed upon the Jews by the Romans at the time of Jesus, see Jacob Neusner, First Century Judaism in Crisis: Yohanan ben Zakkai and the Renaissance of the Torah (Nashville: Abingdon, 1985), 29; and John Riches, Jesus and the Transformation of Judaism (London: Darton, Longman & Todd, 1980), 108.

**Artist's impression of a town street market in New Testament times.**

at paying one-tenth of their income to this religious elite. It is easy to see why some of the *'am ha-'arets* may have been tempted to "lighten" the Torah and ignore the mandates of the "traditions of the elders," and how nonconformist the *'am ha-'arets* would have appeared to groups such as the Pharisees, the Essenes, and those of Qumran, who defined Israel in terms of purity.[5] By the time of Jesus, boundaries distinguishing the religiously observant from those who simply had other priorities would have been even more entrenched.

For example, from the Pharisees' point of view, every Jew who failed to abide by their rigid understanding of purity was categorized as *le-mitsvoth* ("not concerned with ritual purity") and *la-torah* ("ignorant of the law"). From their perspective,

these were "untouchables," "fathers of impurity," whose very clothes were capable of transferring uncleanness. Rabbinic Judaism perpetuated this caricature. Elaborate guidelines on how those in a state of ritual purity could relate to the "people of the land" are set forth in *m. Demai* 2:3, 8, 11. These rituals were deemed necessary for the Haberim, "the fellowship" of the pure. For them, a Pharisaic *haburah* ("fellowship meal") had to be eaten in absolute ritual purity, as set forth in the strictures of Leviticus. For those who partook of such meals, a barrier of holiness had to be erected between the "separated ones" and the *'am ha-'arets*, since the latter conveyed defilement. From the Pharisees' perspective, the *'am ha-'arets* were cut off from the kingdom of God.[6]

---

5    For the basic differences between the Pharisees and the *'am ha-'arets*, see Morton Smith, "The Dead Sea Sect in Relation to Ancient Judaism," *NTS* 7 (1960): 347–60.

6    On this view of first-century Judaism, see Robin Scroggs, "The Earliest Christian Communities as Sectarian Movement," in *Christianity, Judaism, and Other Greco-Roman Cults: Studies for Morton Smith at Sixty* (ed. Jacob Neusner; Leiden: E. J. Brill, 1975), 1–23.

"The Sermon on the Mount" by J.-J. Tissot.

The extent to which the common people would have actually allowed separatist groups to define their relationship to God and temple is open to question.[7] Clearly, the "Sons of Light" at Qumran considered all Jews who were not part of their group to be corrupt and destined for annihilation, especially the priests serving in the temple (cf. 1QM). So, on one level, as a lay movement of reformers, the Pharisees could be regarded as the people's party, enjoying a broad appeal and influence (Josephus, *Ant.* 13.298; 18:15, 17). Conceivably, on at least a symbolic level, the opinion of some powerful Pharisees might have carried considerable weight with the people. If these religious lead-

7   Sanders has consistently set forth a well-thought-out challenge to this portrayal of first-century Judaism. He notes that the Pharisees were relatively few in number, confined to Jerusalem, and not in control of the temple and cult. In any case, he contends that the Pharisees did not represent "normative Judaism" during Jesus' day. See E. P. Sanders, "Jesus and Sinners," *JSNT* 19 (1983): 5–36, esp. 18–20; and idem, *Jesus and Judaism* (London: SCM, 1985), 185–200.

sense of religious superiority, a trait not alien to such groups, then they may have viewed the 'am ha-'arets with a measure of contempt. Also, if the agenda of the Pharisees carried over to the early rabbis of post-70 C.E., as their own literature claims, then the rabbinic view of the 'am ha-'arets is very negative indeed (cf. m. 'Abot 2:5; b. Berakot 47:6; b. Pesaḥim 49b). For the rabbis, the 'am ha-'arets are unclean—even their clothes are unclean—and thus constitute a source of uncleanness (m. Ḥagigah 2:7; m. Ṭehar. 7:2–5; 8:1–2, 5).

The context of the 'am ha-'arets at the time of Jesus was, then, variegated. Persons falling between the cracks that separated the major sects may well have felt some anxiety about their spiritual status before the Lord. Exclusive fellowship meals, complex and rigid classification of the clean and the unclean, extreme separatist groups living in the desert—all of these elements combined may have instilled a religious ambiguity among the 'am ha-'arets and led many in Israel to feel religiously marginalized.[8] The fact that there were two separate routes to the temple—a "high road" for the pure and a "low road" for the 'am ha-'arets—would have

sent a negative message to many worshipers. The social and religious disruption so characteristic of Jesus' day likely led many common Jews to wonder, "Who then can be saved?" (Mark 10:26; Luke 13:23).

## JESUS AND THE 'AM HA-'ARETS

By offering the kingdom to "the poor" (Matt 11:5; Luke 4:18) and the "little ones" (Mark 9:42; Matt 10:42; 18:10, 14), Jesus enacted a religious paradigm that was at odds with some of his contemporaries. His offering of the grace of God apart from the official religious protocol of the temple and packaged quite differently from the Pharisees' viewpoint proved to be very attractive to many common folk, as demonstrated by the tremendous following that Jesus received from the masses (Matt 4:25; Mark 10:1; Luke 5:15). In contrast to the factionalism reflected in some of the major sects of his day, Jesus was communicating that God receives all persons regardless of their state of purity or impurity, their success vis-à-vis the law, or the degree of their moral failure. He thereby may well have set in motion a theological trajectory that in time was destined to travel beyond the religious frontiers of first-century Judaism. Indeed, some of Jesus' earliest followers, such as the Hellenists of Acts 6, may have seized upon this emphasis, creatively interpreting and reapplying it so as to accommodate uncircumcised Gentiles into the people of God.

---

8    Mary Douglas claims that food is a code that communicates social relationships such as rank, inclusion, exclusion, boundaries, and rules to enact transactions that cross boundaries. Those who were excluded from fellowship meals and were made aware of their shortcomings regarding religious heritage would have perceived such boundaries (Mary Douglas, "Deciphering a Meal," in Implicit Meanings: Selected Essays in Anthropology [2d ed.; New York: Routledge, 1999], 249).

# Annotated Bibliography

Neusner, Jacob. *First Century Judaism in Crisis: Yohanan ben Zakkai and the Renaissance of the Torah*. Nashville: Abingdon, 1985. This work by a leading Jewish scholar explores the social and religious dynamics in Israel during the first century, particularly elements that resulted from political and religious oppression. This is a scholarly work that yields insight for the serious student.

Oppenheimer, Aaron. *The 'AM HA-ARETZ: A Study in the Social History of the Jewish People in the Hellenistic-Roman Period*. Leiden: E. J. Brill, 1977. Perhaps the benchmark work on the *'am ha-'arets*, this thoroughly researched study by a leading Jewish scholar requires careful reading.

Schürer, Emil. *The History of the Jewish People in the Age of Jesus Christ (175 B.C.–A.D. 135)*. See description at the end of ch. 2.

Sigal, Philip. *From the Origins to the Separation of Christianity*. See description at the end of ch. 2.

# 9
# The Samaritans—
# Religion and Ethnicity

## INTRODUCTION: THE ASSYRIAN AND BABYLONIAN CAPTIVITIES AND THE EMERGENCE OF THE SAMARITANS

The emergence and identity of the Samaritans is problematic, for ancient texts employ the term "Samaritan" with some degree of ambiguity. Sometimes "Samaritans" refers to residents of a particular geographic region, that is, Samaria. At other times the term refers to a political constituency that opposes the Jewish leadership in Jerusalem. Finally, the term is also used to refer to a distinct ethnoreligious sect that claims that only its version of the Pentateuch is holy writ and that the only legitimate place of worship is on Mt. Gerizim. Compounding the problem is that the Samaritans and the Jews present very different accounts concerning the origin of the Samaritans.[1]

A case can be made from the Hebrew Bible that the emergence of the Samaritans as a distinct people is enmeshed in the geopolitical experience of Israel beginning with the tenth century B.C.E. That is, the origin of the Samaritans may be traced to the division of the northern and southern kingdoms in Israel

shortly after the death of Solomon.[2] In 931 B.C.E. ten of the twelve tribes seceded under King Jeroboam, thus establishing the "divided kingdom"—Israel to the north and Judah to the south (1 Kgs 11:26–12:26). In 883 B.C.E. King Omri of Israel purchased a hill in order to found a new capital city. The name of the hill was Shameron (literally, "a lookout point") (1 Kgs 16:16–22). Some scholars believe that the name Samaria is derived from this word and that the inhabitants of the region came to be known as Samaritans.[3] The kingdom of Israel lasted for over 150 years, and came to an

---

1    One of the earliest accounts of Samaritan origins from a Samaritan point of view dates from the fourteenth century C.E., in the writings of Abu'l Fath, their chronicler. Cf. Abu'l Fath, *Kitab al-Tarikh* (trans. Paul Stenhouse; Sydney, Australia: Mandelbaum Trust, University of Sydney, 1985), esp. 47–48.

2    The Samaritans reject the accounts of their origin as set forth in the Hebrew Bible. Rather, they claim that their roots originate with Joshua's conquest of Canaan, his establishment of governance in Shechem near Mts. Gerizim and Ebal. See the words of the Samaritan chronicler Adler (ca. eighteenth century C.E.) in *Chronicle Adler*, in John Bowman, ed. and trans., *Samaritan Documents Relating to Their History, Religion, and Life* (Pittsburgh: Pickwick, 1977), 89–90. For additional views on how the Samaritans came into existence, see Ingrid Hjelm, *The Samaritans and Early Judaism: A Literary Analysis* (JSOTSup 303; Sheffield, Eng.: Sheffield Academic Press, 2002), 12–75; and Craig A. Evans, "Crisis in the Middle East: Ethnic and Religious Tensions Ran High in Jesus' Day Too," *Christian History* 59 (1998): 20–23.

3    The self-designation of the Samaritans, however, is *Shomrim*, or "keepers" of the Torah (Bowman, *Samaritan Documents*, 93). For a comparison of Jewish and Samaritan versions of Samaritan origins, see Robert T. Anderson and Terry Giles, *The Keepers: An Introduction to the History and Culture of the Samaritans* (Peabody, Mass.: Hendrickson, 2002), 10–19.

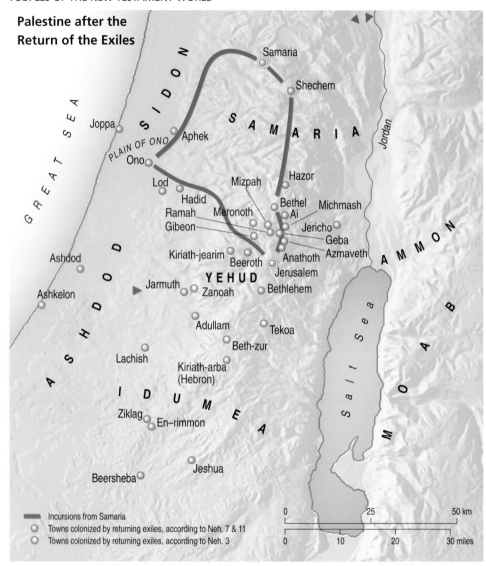

**Palestine after the Return of the Exiles**

GREAT SEA

SIDON

SAMARIA

Samaria

Shechem

Joppa

PLAIN OF ONO

Aphek

Ono

Lod

Hadid

Ramah

Meronoth

Gibeon

Mizpah

Hazor

Bethel

Ai

Michmash

Jericho

Geba

Azmaveth

Kiriath-jearim

Beeroth

Anathoth

YEHUD

Jerusalem

Ashdod

Ashkelon

Jarmuth

Zanoah

Bethlehem

ASHDOD

Adullam

Tekoa

Beth-zur

Lachish

Kiriath-arba
(Hebron)

IDUMEA

Ziklag

En-rimmon

Jeshua

Beersheba

Jordan

AMMON

Salt Sea

MOAB

—— Incursions from Samaria
○ Towns colonized by returning exiles, according to Neh. 7 & 11
○ Towns colonized by returning exiles, according to Neh. 3

0    25    50 km

0   10   20   30 miles

---

end when Shalmaneser, king of Syria, besieged the northern kingdom in 722 B.C.E. (cf. 1 Kgs 11:13, 17; 2 Kgs 18:9).

### THE EFFECT OF THE ASSYRIAN CAPTIVITY ON THE EMERGENCE OF THE SAMARITANS

The Assyrian captivity devastated the national, religious, and cultural identity of the ten northern tribes. The Babylonian captivity of Judah to the south in 587 B.C.E. only compounded the fate of the people who eventually came to be known as the Samaritans. The combined effect of the Assyrian and Babylonian captivities resulted in the partial extinction of a huge segment of the Jewish population in Israel. In time, as will be explained below, with the arrival of colonists, the inhabitants of the land became extremely diverse in their ethnic and religious identities, so much so that Jews returning from the Babylonian exile regarded many as Gentiles (Ezra 4:1–4; Josephus, *Ant.* 11.84–85, 174; cf. also John 4:9; 8:48). Nevertheless, the

**The city of Nablus viewed from the slopes of Mount Gerizim. Since Bible times this area has been associated with the Samaritans.**

Samaritans more than likely are in fact related to the Jews (*Ant.* 11.341; 12.257–264). Whether this relationship is one of ethnicity, religion, or both is open to question. Indeed, the ambiguity inherent in the origin and identity of the Samaritans continues to this day.[4]

A significant distinction between the Assyrian and Babylonian captivities affords some clarity for the admittedly murky origin

of the Samaritans, who are mentioned for the first time in 2 Kgs 17:29. Unlike after the Babylonians' defeat of Judah in the south more than 130 years later, the Assyrians did not simply import the best and the brightest of Israel into their native land. Their strategy was more complex than that of the Babylonians. Sargon, the successor to Shalmaneser, slaughtered tens of thousands of Jews in the northern kingdom and then carried off thousands of Israelites to Assyria (2 Kgs 17:3–6; 18:9; *Ant.* 9.259, 277). Such deportations continued under Esar-haddon and Assurbanipal. After severely depleting the region of Jews, at least five different nationalities were imported into northern Israel.

---

4 For additional debate on the precise origin of the Samaritans, see R. J. Coggins, "Jewish Local Patriotism: The Samaritan Problem," in *Jewish Local Patriotism and Self-Identification in the Graeco-Roman Period* (ed. Siân Jones and Sarah Pearce; Sheffield, Eng.: Sheffield Academic Press, 1998), 66–78; and idem, *Samaritans and Jews: The Origins of Samaritanism Reconsidered* (Atlanta: John Knox, 1975).

Aerial view of Mount Gerizim, which is sacred to the Samaritans. The remains of a temple built by the Samaritans in the time of Nehemiah have been discovered on top of Mount Gerizim.

Second Kings 17:24 lists these as from Babylon, Cuthah, Awa, Hamath, and Sepharvaim (cf. also *Ant.* 9.277–290; 10.184–185; 11.19).[5] The Assyrians thus employed a deliberate strategy to pluralize the Israelite population in the north in order to undermine the cohesion and culture of the Jewish people there.

As a result of all of these disruptions, the peoples of the region of Samaria experienced a considerable degree of destabilization. Religiously, the northern region became a patchwork of different faiths, with a form of Judaism eventually rising to preeminence. Second Kings 17:28–36 explains how veneration of Yahweh became the working paradigm in the midst of such pluralism. As the story goes, harassment by wild beasts led many polytheists to believe that they had offended the God of the Jews. Hence they requested that a Jewish priest establish a worship center at Bethel (2 Kgs 17:28; cf. also *Ant.* 9.288–291). Even though they were polytheists, the biblical record states that the mixed multitude feared Yahweh. In this way a type of Judaism

5    The denigration of the Samaritans by the Jews can be seen in the fact that the Jews called the Samaritans "Cutheans," an appellation the Samaritans despised (cf. *Ant.* 9.290; 11.88, 302). The Samaritans explain the connection with Cuthah by claiming that some of their number fled to Wadi al-Kutha because they were persecuted by the Jews (see the *Chronicle of Abu'l Fath*, in Bowman, *Samaritan Documents*, 123–24). The consistently negative portrayal of the Samaritans in Jewish literature can be seen in Philo, who states that the Samaritans are as "barbarous and uncivilized" as the Germanic tribes (*Embassy* 2.10).

**A Samaritan priest holds aloft the scrolls of the Torah.**

existed in the north, and significant contact with Judah and Jerusalem continued during this time. Second Kings 23:15, 19 reveals that King Josiah of Judah suppressed the "high places" of Samaria (ca. 630 B.C.E.). In addition, 2 Chr 34:9 indicates that revenue was received from "Manasseh and Ephraim" and from the "remnant of Israel" in the north to make repairs to the temple. Finally, Jer 41:5 speaks of persons coming from the north to give offerings in the temple in Jerusalem while it still stood. Thus, even after all the efforts of the Assyrians, it appears that some Jews in the north still maintained a tenuous connection with Jerusalem in Judah.

In summary, the conquest and tactics of the Assyrians clearly exacerbated the tensions that existed between the Jews of Israel and those who resided in Judah. Not only had the two groups been divided by the political breech that resulted from the division of the kingdom in about 931 B.C.E.; now they were further alienated by religious and cultural factors brought on by the Assyrian catastrophe of 722 B.C.E. as well.

## THE EFFECT OF THE BABYLONIAN CAPTIVITY ON THE EMERGENCE OF THE SAMARITANS

The Babylonian captivity weakened further still the feeble connection between the Jews who remained in the north and the Jews in Jerusalem (cf. *Ant.* 10.184). In 597 B.C.E. Nebuchadnezzar, king of the Babylonians, overran the southern kingdom of Judah and captured Jerusalem (2 Kgs 24.10–16; 2 Kgs 25:1–4; *Ant.* 10.131–135; *Ag. Ap.* 1.154). His goal was to make Judah a subservient vassal of his vast empire. As mentioned in an earlier chapter, to this end he robbed the temple of its sacred vessels (Jer 28:1–6) and deported the leading citizens of Israel to Babylon, most notably Daniel and Ezekiel. With the destruction of the temple in Jerusalem, together with the dissolution of the priesthood and the cult, the maintenance of a distinct Jewish identity in the region was nearly impossible. Those who had been compromised racially by the Assyrians, together with those who were not thought worthy to be carried away into Babylon, were cut off from the elements that preserved Jewish blood, faith, and culture.

Paradoxically, this kind of religious and social anomie was increased by the piety of the Jews who had been carried into exile. As noted earlier, to maintain their identity during the captivity, some of the exiles appear to have intensified aspects of the law that they felt defined them as a distinct people. After the exile, Sabbath observance, circumcision, and purity became paramount for many Jews returning from Babylon (Jer 17:19–27; Isa 56:1–8; 58:13–14 f., Ezek 4:12–15, 22:26). In the eyes of the returnees, these elements became the definitive signs of the "true Jew," just as they had been indispensable for the survival of the "sons of the Golah" or the "sons of the Exile" while they were in Babylon (Ezra 6:1–22). Ezra "the scribe" served as the pivotal figure for maintaining "normative Judaism" among the Jews during this period (*Ant.* 11.121–131). His role in Israel is succinctly summarized in Ezra 7:10: "For Ezra had devoted himself to the study and observance of the Law of the LORD, and to teaching its decrees and laws in Israel."

## THE EFFECT OF THE "SONS OF THE EXILE" ON THE EMERGENCE OF THE SAMARITANS

None of this held true, however, for those whose Jewish identities had been ravaged by the Assyrians or for those who were left behind by the Babylonians. They did not have the law or the kind of leadership that Ezra provided for those in exile. The release of Jews from exile in 538 B.C.E. by King Cyrus of Persia (Ezra 1:1–6; 6:1–5; 2 Chr 36:20–21; *Ant.* 11.3–8) did nothing to change this situation. The Golah lists (or "Sons of the Exile") of Ezra and Nehemiah suggest that successive waves of returnees left Babylon for Israel (Ezra 2:1–70; Neh 7:4–73). This incremental return of the Jews created a situation where, before Ezra's arrival, some of the "sons of the Golah" had intermarried with the *'am ha-'arets*, or "peoples of the land," and the residents of Samaria (Ezra 4:1–5; Neh 13:23–24; *Ant.* 11.140). By the time Ezra arrived on the scene, this amalgam of returnees from the exile with the mixed multitude already living in Israel may have been going on for over a generation. From the perspective of Ezra, they were adopting syncretistic religious practices that threatened the purity of Israel's race and religion (Neh 13:1–3; Exod 34:16; Deut 7:1–4).

For all of these reasons, returnees from exile who thought like Ezra rejected those they felt had polluted the race of the Jews and profaned the law. The Golah lists in Ezra 8:1–14 serve this purpose. Any persons who had intermarried with non-Jews, regardless of whether they were priests or Levites, were not included in the Golah lists (cf. Ezra 9:1–2, 10–12; 10:18–44; Neh 13:23–29;

A Samaritan displays part of the 2,000-year-old scroll of the Torah in the synagogue at Nablus.

**Samaritans prepare animal offerings for sacrifice on the altar.**

*Ant.* 11.145–153).[6] Both Ezra and Nehemiah physically acted out their revulsion toward those who had compromised their identity as Jews and even accosted the most grievous offenders (Ezra 9:3–5; Neh 13:25–31; cf. also 2 Sam 13:19). They lamented that as in the days of old, the whole land had been polluted (*Ant.* 11.161–166; Deut 4:5; Lev 18:25–30). In no uncertain terms, they preached that God would bless only the "holy race" (Ezra 9:2, 8–9, 13, 15; 10:10–17; Neh 8:3, 18; 9:3). Those who failed Yahweh in this regard had only one recourse: they had to "separate" from their foreign wives and children and make a binding agreement and covenant to keep all the practices of orthodox Judaism (Ezra 10:2–4, 11; Neh 9:2, 38–10:39; 13:3).[7] Any who refused would have all their possessions seized and be branded as non-Jews having no part in the blessings of the covenant (Ezra 10:1–9; *Ant.* 11.147–148).[8]

6  Those returning exiles who had preceeded Ezra's arrival in the homeland and who themselves had become syncretists, were also excluded from the Golah lists. Thus Maccoby notes that the syncretists whom Ezra encountered were a group larger in number and more powerful than the constituency that sided with Ezra and his reforms. On the role of purity and race in the reforms of Ezra, see Hyam Maccoby, "Holiness and Purity: The Holy People in Leviticus and Ezra–Nehemiah," in *Reading Leviticus: A Conversation with Mary Douglas* (ed. John F. A. Sawyer; JSOTSup 227; Sheffield, Eng.: Sheffield Academic Press, 1996), 153–70.

7  Again Maccoby comments on the critical nature of this decision: "Ezra's decision was at a watershed in the history of Judaism, when the future of monotheism was at stake. It was a matter of deep principle not of ethnic exclusivism, to reject marital links with the 'people of the land' " (ibid., 163). Although Maccoby works hard to extricate Ezra from the charge of "ethnic cleansing," he is concerned about phrases that speak of the corruption of the "holy seed" and the land being "polluted" as a result of the syncretism of the *'am ha-'arets*: "This seems to be the language of adulteration and contamination" (p. 165). Along similar lines, Robert Segal notes that at times in Israel's history, intense nationalism has blurred the distinction between religion and race ("Response to Hyam Maccoby's 'Holiness and Purity,' " in *Reading Leviticus: A Conversation with Mary Douglas* [ed. John F. A. Sawyer; JSOTSup 227; Sheffield, Eng.: Sheffield Academic Press, 1996], 172).

8  The contemporary Samaritan tradition, written a millennium after the events, turns Ezra's record on its head. It was the Jewish exiles who had no Torah, were ignorant of its content, and were corrupted by the deceit of Ezra. See *Chronicle Adler*, in Bowman, *Samaritan Documents*, 102–3. See also Amran Ishak, *The History and Religion of the Samaritans* (Jerusalem: Greek Convent, 1964), esp. 34–35.

**Samaritans read and pray in their synagogue near Nablus, in the West Bank.**

In summary, the reforms of Ezra and Nehemiah were intended to establish a line of demarcation that officially ostracized the mixed multitude who eventually came to be known as the Samaritans. The incident that graphically sets forth this grievous tear in the fabric of Jewish identity occurred when the Samaritans and "the people of the land" tried to help rebuild the temple. Ezra 4:3 records the rejection of this offer:

> But Zerubbabel, Jeshua and the rest of the heads of the families of Israel answered, "You have no part with us in building a temple to our God. We alone will build it for the Lord, the God of Israel, as King Cyrus, the king of Persia, commanded us."

From this point on, those who were rejected sought to frustrate the efforts of the Jews in the rebuilding of the temple and the walls of Jerusalem (Ezra 4:4; *Ant.* 11.19, 173–175).[9] On a political level, they communicated with Xerxes and Artaxerxes in an effort to convince them that the exiles had betrayed their trust and goodwill. They claimed that the Jews were actually seeking to build a kingdom that would eventually threaten Persia (Ezra 4:6–16; *Ant.* 11.19–30). The Samaritans had a degree of success, for Artaxerxes stated that the building of the temple had to be halted (Ezra 4:18–24). Further communication by the Jews, however, led Darius to overturn the command of Artaxerxes, allowing the

---

9    According to Samaritan tradition, the conflict arose over the returnees' failure to recognize that the temple should be built on Mt. Gerizim, not in Jerusalem (see *Chronicle Adler*, in Bowman, *Samaritan Documents*, 89–90; cf. also Ishak, *The History and Religion of the Samaritans*, 30–31). Hence the Jews are labeled "Those Who Went Astray" (see *Chronicle of Abu'l Fath*, in Bowman, *Samaritan Documents*, 123).

building of the temple to be completed (Ezra 6:1–12).

## THE ROLE OF MANASSEH AND THE TEMPLE ON MT. GERIZIM

The conflict concerning the rebuilding of the temple reflects the highly religious nature of the situation. The theme of religious tension is continued throughout the book of Nehemiah, particularly regarding Manasseh, who was married to the daughter of Sanballat, the governor of Samaria.[10] As the son of the high priest in Jerusalem, he would have been next in line to inherit that office. But the notion that a member of a Samaritan family would become high priest was unacceptable to Nehemiah. So, as part of his cleansing of the temple and reinstatement of the temple cult, Nehemiah drove Manasseh from the temple courts (Neh 13:28). Subsequently, in ca. 430 B.C.E., Manasseh fled to Samaria and embarked on the creation of a rival worship cite near Mt. Gerizim (*Ant.* 11.302–310; 12.10; 13.74; John 4:20). Eventually, a hundred years after Manasseh was driven from the temple in Jerusalem, Alexander the Great endorsed the building of a Samaritan temple on Mt. Gerizim in 332 B.C.E. (*Ant.* 11.340–346; 13.74, 256).[11] This temple stood for more than two hundred years, until John Hyrcanus destroyed it in 128 B.C.E. (*Ant.* 13.255–256). It seems that the Samaritans had previously

supported Antiochus Epiphanes in his campaign against Jerusalem (*Ant.* 12.257–58), and Hyrcanus thought it fitting to raze the Samaritans' center of worship when he ousted the Syrians.[12] This event precipitated intense hatred between the Jews and the Samaritans, perhaps more than any other. A cycle of violence ensued that lasted through the first century (*Ant.* 12.156; 20.118–127).

## THE RELIGION OF THE SAMARITANS

Evidence for the common ancestry of the Samaritans and the Jews may also be seen in Samaritan religion. Just as with the Jews, religion plays a critical role in the identity of the Samaritans. Moreover, since Manasseh was of the family of the high priest in Jerusalem, he serves as a link between the beliefs and practices of the Jews at that time and the formation of the Samaritan faith. In particular, since he came from the family of the high priest, his form of Judaism may have contained many Sadducean elements. The fact that many of the priests in Jerusalem "revolted to" Manasseh as he fled to Sanballat in Samaria lends support here (*Ant.* 11.302–312). Indeed, the cardinal tenets of Samaritan faith appear to have much in common with the Sadducees. For example, the Samaritans accepted only the Torah, that is, the five books of Moses, as holy writ.[13] For them, the prophets and wisdom literature were not viewed as of equal authority to the words of Moses. Also, unlike the Pharisees

---

10 Lester L. Grabbe doubts that the conflict between the Samaritans and the Jews could have developed at this early date. He believes that such tension developed during the Seleucid and Hasmonean periods, not at the time of Ezra and Nehemiah ("Triumph of the Pious or Failure of the Xenophobes? The Ezra–Nehemiah Reforms and Their *Nachgeschichte*," in *Jewish Local Patriotism and Self-Identification in the Graeco-Roman Period* [ed. Siân Jones and Sarah Pearce; Sheffield, Eng.: Sheffield Academic Press, 1998], 58, 63). For a contrasting view, see John Macdonald, *The Theology of the Samaritans* (London: SCM, 1964), 24.

11 The literary evidence from this period concerning the Samaritans is meager. See Anderson and Giles, *The Keepers*, 31–331; on the uneven relationship between the Samaritans and Alexander and his successors, see 24–29.

12 The literature from the Maccabean period reflects Jewish animosity toward the Samaritans and their temple. Second Maccabees 6.2 reports that the Samaritan temple was dedicated to "Zeus-the-Friend-of-Strangers."

13 One of the earliest records of Samaritan belief and theology is found in the work of the great Samaritan leader Marqah, dating from the fifth century C.E. The earliest manuscript of Memar Marqah, however, dates from the fourteenth century. Cf. Marqah, Memar Marqah: *The Teaching of the Marqah* (ed. and trans. John MacDonald; 2 vols. in 1; Berlin: Töpelmann, 1963), 1:xx; cf. also Bowman, *Samaritan Documents*, 16; and Anderson and Giles, *The Keepers*, 61, 117.

A Bible scribe in Jaffa copies a Yemenite scroll of the law on parchment using a traditional quill.

but more like the Sadducees, the Samaritans never developed an extensive body of teachings, or *halakhah*. Nothing like the Mishnah, or codification of the "traditions of the elders," exists among the Samaritans.

These are some of the distinctive teachings of the Samaritans:

1. God is one—the absolute unity of God.[14]

2. God created humanity in the image of angels.[15]

3. Moses is the only prophet of God. He received the Torah not on Mt. Sinai (Deut 27:4) but on Mt. Gerizim. The law was given directly to Moses by the hand of an angel. Laying aside a literal interpretation of Deut 34:10, the Samaritans teach that there will never be another prophet like Moses.[16]

4. Mt. Gerizim is the true house of God and contains the twelve stones of Israel

14  Bowman, *Samaritan Documents*, 239. There is some evidence of Islamic syncretism in the Samaritan religion from at least the medieval period onward. Repeated emphasis on radical monism may be due to Moslem influence (cf. Anderson and Giles, *The Keepers*, 116; and MacDonald, *The Theology of the Samaritans*, 38–39).

15  Marqah, *Memar Marqah*, 47.

16  Cf. ibid., 220–21; and *Commentary of Ibrahim ibn Ya'kub*, in Bowman, *Samaritan Documents*, 244–47.

(Deut 27:4). The Samaritans maintain that because of the apostasy of the Jews, the tabernacle was darkened and gradually disappeared. God provided a special cave for the Samaritans so that they could hide the holy vessels and garments. After they were hidden, the cave itself was swallowed up and disappeared. The *Shekinah*, or visible glory of God, will appear in the end time upon Mt. Gerizim and not upon Mt. Zion.

5. The *"Taheb,"* that is, "the one who restores," will appear at the end time (cf. John 4:25). He is mortal and will live for only 110 years. During that time, however, he will destroy all those who have followed the counsel of Ezra, that is, all the Jews who have rejected the Samaritan account of things.[17]

This last tenet once again echoes the conflict between the Jews who returned from the exile and those persons who were not carried away into captivity. Sirach 50:25–26 states, "Two nations my soul detests, and the third is not even a people: Those who live in Seir, and the Philistines, and the foolish people that live in Shechem." For Ben Sira, the "foolish people" was Samaria.

## THE SAMARITANS
## AND THE NEW TESTAMENT

The animosity between the Jews and the Samaritans was well entrenched by the time Jesus began his public ministry. Indeed, to a Jewish mind-set, the harshest slander that Jesus' enemies brought against him was that he was a Samaritan and demon-possessed (John 8:48). At one point in his ministry, Jesus commanded that his disciples not go to the Gentiles or to any

city of the Samaritans (Matt 10:5). This seems to indicate that Jesus viewed the Samaritans racially as somewhere between full-fledged Gentiles and pure-blooded Jews, a view that coincides with the historical and political experiences of the Samaritans as presented in the Hebrew Scriptures. John flatly states that the Jews have no dealings with the Samaritans (John 4:9).

The Samaritans also harbored ill will toward the Jews. As Jesus made his way toward Jerusalem for the last time, he sent some of his disciples into Samaria (Luke 9:51–55). Their goal was that the Samaritans receive them and their master. When the Samaritans heard that Jesus was heading for Jerusalem, however, they refused to provide hospitality for him and his followers. James and John, the "Sons of Thunder" (Mark 3:17), wanted to incinerate the Samaritans by calling down fire from heaven. The allusion to the destruction of the prophets of Baal by Elijah (1 Kgs 18:25–38) or to the fate of Sodom and Gomorrah (Gen 19:24) is revealing. Jesus soundly rejected their request and opted for another route to Jerusalem that bypassed Samaria (Luke 9:55–56).

The fact that the Samaritans rebuffed Jesus when they heard that he was going to Jerusalem is significant. It harks back to the expulsion of Manasseh by Nehemiah and the creation of an alternative shrine on Mt. Gerizim. This controversy over the legitimate place of worship continued to the time of Jesus, as Jesus' dialogue with the Samaritan woman in John 4:19–20 reveals. Here Jesus indicates that the Samaritan religion is obscure and compromised and that God's true plan of salvation has come through the Jews (4:22). Nevertheless, Jesus is not hostile to the Samaritan woman or to her people. His point is simply that the geographic location of any temple, whether it belong to the Samaritans or the Jews, is irrelevant to God. What matters in worship is spirit and truth (4:23–24). His words to her are effectual. Not only is she led to faith; a revival ensues in

---

17  Cf. *Phineas on the Taheb*, in Bowman, *Samaritan Documents*, 263–71. The Samaritan tradition is that Eleazar, the son of Aaron, served God in the tabernacle of Moses and that this tabernacle was brought to Mt. Gerizim (cf. Ishak, *The History and Religion of the Samaritans*, 4–15). For a summary of Samaritan beliefs, see Anderson and Giles, *The Keepers*, 119–125; and MacDonald, *The Theology of the Samaritans*, 359–71.

"The Woman of Samaria at the Well" by the French artist J.-J. Tissot.

Samaria. This positive encounter between Jesus and the Samaritan woman indicates Jesus' position on the Samaritan question. In short, for Jesus, geography, politics, and race are of no consequence to the kingdom of God. This theme of equality and inclusion is carried forth throughout the Gospels, especially regarding the Samaritans. In Luke 10:25–37 a Jewish priest and a Levite fail in their moral duty to help one in distress, but a Samaritan displays the love of God and thus qualifies as the good neighbor. And finally, of the ten men healed of leprosy, only one returned to Jesus in order to give thanks. That grateful one was a Samaritan (Luke 17:11–19).

Jesus' positive regard for Samaritans was epoch-making. In his person and work, ethnic and racial barriers were being transcended in the name of God. Furthermore, Jesus' last commission to evangelize the world explicitly includes Samaria (Acts 1:8). This soon set the paradigm for ministry and evangelism in the early church. Philip, one of "the Seven" in Acts 6, conducted the first transcultural evangelism in Samaria (Acts 8:4–8). The Jewish leadership in Jerusalem endorsed this bold step (Acts 8:14–17). Churches were soon planted in Samaria, and the early Christians had no qualms about traveling through that region (Acts 9:31; 15:3). In Acts 11:19–20 Luke reports that some of "those who had been scattered" (cf. Acts 8:4) as a result of the persecution of Stephen and the Hellenists began to share the gospel with Gentiles. It can be argued, then, that Jesus' contact with Samaritans eventually opened the door to the Gentile mission in the church.[18]

Nevertheless, the geopolitical reality between the Jews and the Samaritans of the time was far different. One of Herod the Great's wives was Malthace, of the Samaritan nation (*Ant.* 17.19–20,

18  For a detailed treatment of how the Hellenists might have served as a historical and theological link between Jesus and Paul, see William A. Simmons, *A Theology of Inclusion in Jesus and Paul* (Lewiston, N.Y.: Mellen, 1996), 88–121.

250; *J.W.* 1.562; 2.39). Through this marriage Herod sought to strengthen political ties with Samaria. To further solidify relations, he conducted extensive building projects throughout Samaria. None of these actions endeared Herod to his Jewish subjects. Furthermore, it appears that the Samaritans supported the brutal campaign of the Roman governor Cumanus (48–52 C.E.) against the Jews (*Ant.* 20.118–122). They and the Herods sided with the Romans in the various conflicts the empire had with the Jews (*J.W.* 1.303; Life 1.269).

Samaria's fate turned for the worse, however, when it was implicated in the Zealot uprising against Rome in 66 C.E. In the confusion of war, the Romans took no time to strain out the Jews from the Samaritans. Vespasian (69–79 C.E.) struck with a blunt instrument, demolishing Samaria and Israel alike (*J.W.* 3.307–315).

Not to be sidelined forever, however, the Samaritans once again aided the Romans in their campaign against the Jews. The Samaritans helped the empire quash the Bar Kokhba rebellion in 135 C.E. As a reward, the Romans helped the Samaritans rebuild their temple, which had been laid waste since the reign of the Hasmoneans, on Mt. Gerizim. As the Roman Empire fragmented, so did relations with the Samaritans. By the end of the fifth century C.E., the Samaritans once again were cast as the enemies of Rome. In 529 C.E. the Romans destroyed the temple on Mt. Gerizim, never to be built again.

## THE SAMARITANS TODAY

At the beginning of the twentieth century, only about 182 Samaritans survived. Today it is estimated that 500 to 1,000 Samaritans live on Mt. Gerizim, near the city of Nablus, and in Holon.[19] This growth is due to the fact that after World War II, the government of Israel classified the Samaritans as Jews. They were included in the "law of return," which allowed Jews of the Diaspora to emigrate to Israel, and in more recent times some Samaritans have married Jewish women who have agreed to live in accordance with Samaritan tradition. Yet many still abide by the older tradition, which allows only Samaritans to marry other Samaritans. The continuance of a distinct population of Samaritans hangs in the balance.

The Samaritans continue to celebrate their ancestral practices. An ornate Torah scroll is the only physical object allowed in their worship services. It is said to be more than three thousand years old, written on the twelfth day after the children of Israel entered into the land of Canaan. The Samaritans still observe Passover and the Feast of Unleavened Bread on Mt. Gerizim.[20] Forms of the Feast of Pentecost, Tabernacles, and Yom Kippur are still observed. All males are circumcised on the eighth day after birth, even if it is the Sabbath. Thus, to this day, core Samaritan beliefs and practices echo many of those practiced in Judaism.

19  The Samaritans have been described as "the smallest religio-ethnical group in existence" (Reinhard Pummer, *The Samaritans* [Leiden: E. J. Brill, 1987], 1). To this day the Samaritans claim to be the true Israelites. They view their meager population as a fulfillment of the prophecy in Deut 28:62, "You who were as numerous as the stars in the sky will be left but few in numbers, because you did not obey the Lord your God" (Ishak, *The History and Religion of the Samaritans*, 4–5).

20  Pictures of the present-day slaughter of the Passover lamb by Samaritans can be found in Pummer, *Samaritans*, plates xxxiv–xxxvii.

# Annotated Bibliography

Anderson, Robert T., and Terry Giles. *The Keepers: An Introduction to the History and Culture of the Samaritans*. Peabody, Mass.: Hendrickson, 2002. This is an excellent introduction to the history and culture of the Samaritans from the Persian period to modern times. It makes good use of primary documents and is clearly written, well organized, and well illustrated, providing a concise yet comprehensive treatment of the Samaritans.

Bowman, John, ed. and trans. *Samaritan Documents Relating to Their History, Religion, and Life*. See description in the Annotated Bibliography of Primary Documents.

Fath, Abu'l. *Kitab al-Tarikh*. See description in the Annotated Bibliography of Primary Documents.

Hjelm, Ingrid. *The Samaritans and Early Judaism: a Literary Analysis.* Journal for the Study of the Old Testament: Supplement Series 303. Sheffield, Eng.: Sheffield Academic Press, 2002. This revisionist work seeks to deconstruct traditional interpretations of Samaritan origins and history. Calling into question the reliability of Samaritan and Jewish Scriptures, it seeks to excise biases in the ancient texts in order to arrive at a more historically reliable record. This works concludes that the Samaritans and the Jews have never formed one nation and that a Jerusalem-based vision of Israel is misleading.

Pummer, Reinhard. *The Samaritans*. Leiden: E. J. Brill, 1987. This general orientation to the history and thought of the Samaritans offers many excellent plates illustrating Samaritan artifacts and contemporary religious practices.

# 10

# John the Baptist and His Disciples—Community and Transition

## INTRODUCTION

When John the Baptist summoned his disciples to come out of the general populace of Israel, he displayed an insider/outsider mentality that was distinctive of many first-century Jewish sects (Josephus, *Ant.* 13.17).[1] Thus by intentionally calling persons to embrace a vision and practice that differed from their fellow Israelites, John and his disciples made up an important group in the New Testament.

According to the Gospels, those who responded to John's call and underwent baptism in water would be incorporated into the true Israel and escape the wrath to come (Matt 3:1–12; Luke 3:1–18). John the Baptist and his disciples viewed themselves as the end-time community of the true Israel. This eschatological community was foundational and preparatory for the Jesus movement, which was soon to follow. The advent of Jesus

and the birth of the church did not, however, end the influence of John and his followers. They continued to be a spiritual presence throughout the apostolic period.

It could therefore be argued that apart from the life and ministry of Jesus, John the Baptist is the most theologically significant figure in the New Testament. For Luke, his birth merits as much attention as that of the messiah (Luke 1:5–80), and Luke is careful to note that John is a blood relative of Jesus (Luke 1:36). In addition, as with the birth of Jesus, supernatural intervention brought about John's entrance into this world. The aged Zacharias and Elizabeth were granted a miracle child whose birth echoed such great figures as Isaac, born to Abraham and Sarah (Gen 15:4–6; 17:19), and Samuel, God's gift to Hanna (1 Sam 1:1–20; Luke 1:5–25, 36, 57–64). Gabriel (Luke 1:11, 19), the angel of the Lord, announced that John's birth marked an extraordinary redemptive moment in God's plan of salvation (Luke 1:16). John would be anointed of the Spirit from his mother's womb and would be a prophetic voice, one on the order of the great prophet Elijah (Luke 1:15, 17). His message would be a "voice of one calling in the desert," and his mission would be to prepare the way for the coming of the messiah (Matt 3:3; Mark 1:3; Luke 3:4; John 1:23). In short, John fulfilled the critical end-time prophecy

---

1    For the significance of an "us"-and-"them" mentality for the development of distinct groups, see Shaye J. D. Cohen, *The Beginnings of Jewishness: Boundaries, Varieties, Uncertainties* (Berkeley: University of California Press, 1999), 5–8. Robert L. Webb defines a "movement" as "a group of people who are unified by a common ideology or programme," and a "sect" as a movement that views itself as distinct from all other people. On these bases, he views John's ministry as creating a sectarian movement (*John the Baptizer and Prophet: A Socio-historical Study* [JSNTSup 62; Sheffield, Eng.: JSOT Press, 1991], esp. 295 n. 85, 353).

A Bedouin shepherd in the Judean wilderness, where John the Baptist exercised his ministry.

of Isa 40:3. Furthermore, in a move that even confounded John, Jesus came to be baptized by him. After he came out of the water, the Father and the Spirit publicly affirmed Jesus as the Son of God (Matt 3:13–17; Mark 1:9–11; Luke 3:21–22). It may well be that John's baptism of Jesus was the first public display of Jesus' total identification with sinners, an identification that eventually would lead to the cross. This awkward moment for John may have been the event that revealed to him that Jesus was the Lamb of God who takes away the sins of the world (John 1:29, 36).[2] In this way, John's baptism marks the beginning of Jesus' public ministry (Luke 3:23).

2    On the theological significance of John's birth, see Lawrence D. Goodall, "None Greater Born of a Woman: The Theological Figure of John the Baptist," *Communio* 24 (fall 1997): 550–62.

Although John testified about Jesus, the latter also testified about John. Jesus proclaimed that among those born of women, John was the greatest prophet of all time (Luke 7:28). Also, John's influence continued after the death and resurrection of the Lord. When the apostles sought to replace Judas, one of the criteria for the candidates was that they had to be a disciple from the time of John's baptism to the ascension of the Jesus (Acts 1:22). Notably, the starting point for qualification was not the beginning of Jesus' public ministry but John's. Furthermore, the great Apollos of Alexandria in North Africa was a disciple of John (Acts 18:24). When Paul ministered in Ephesus on his third missionary journey, he encountered about a dozen disciples who knew only of the baptism of John

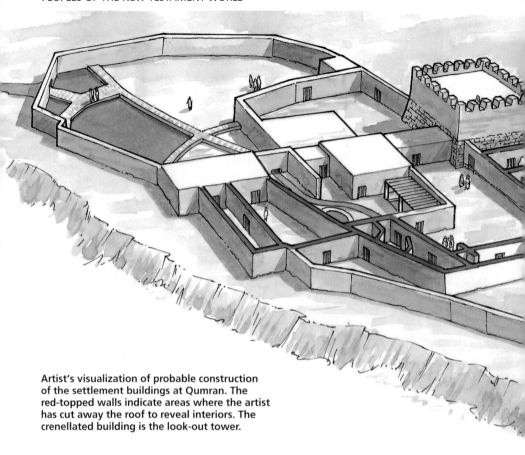

Artist's visualization of probable construction of the settlement buildings at Qumran. The red-topped walls indicate areas where the artist has cut away the roof to reveal interiors. The crenellated building is the look-out tower.

(Acts 19:1–7). So, even by the end of Paul's ministry, the influence of John was still active throughout the Mediterranean world.

Nevertheless, in spite of John's power and prominence, it could also be argued that he is the most enigmatic figure in the New Testament. After presenting a detailed birth narrative, one might expect Luke to give a brief history of the early life of John the Baptist. Nothing of the sort is forthcoming. For example, in Luke 2:41–52 the evangelist presents a cameo of the boy Jesus, now twelve years of age, debating with the teachers of the law in the temple. This short piece on the childhood of Jesus helps bridge the gap of about thirty years between Jesus' birth and his public ministry. Yet no such record is on hand for John. Luke simply says that John

was in the wilderness until the day of his appearing (Luke 3:2). Luke does not explain how John was sustained in the desert or even if John lived with others while there. There are other puzzles to John's life. For example, John was the son of a priest and hence would have been a priest as well (Luke 1:5). Yet he served not one day as a priest in the temple, nor does he give any positive affirmation of the temple and its cult (Matt 3:7; Luke 3:7). John was the greatest of all the prophets but did not perform a single miracle (John 10:41). His appearance and message was so like Elijah's that many believed that he was Elijah reincarnated. Yet John flatly denied that he was Elijah (John 1:21, 25) even though Luke said that he would come in the spirit and power of Elijah (Luke 1:17) and Jesus

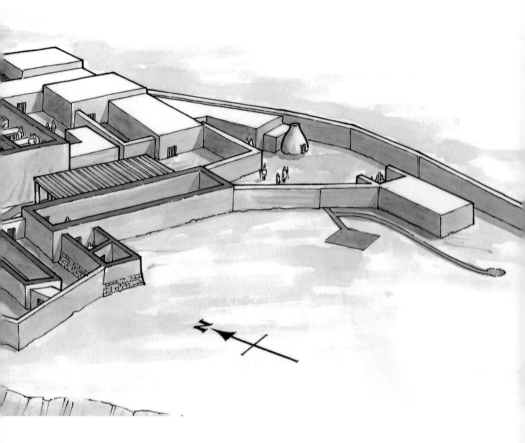

indicated that John had fulfilled the role of Elijah in the end times (Matt 17:10–13; Mark 9:11–13).[3] Although he was immensely popular, John made no claim about himself apart from that of being a witness to the Lamb of God (Mark 1:7–8; Luke 3:16; John 1:6–9, 19–23, 26–27; 3:27–30). Rather, John consistently

deprecated his person and role, emphasizing that one greater than he was coming (Mark 1:7–8; Luke 3:16; John 1:26–27). Compared with Jesus, he was simply a household slave, one not worthy to loosen the straps of his master's sandals (Matt 3:11; Luke 3:16; John 1:27). When his disciples forsook him to follow Jesus, we find not a word of protest on the lips of John (John 1:19–23, 35–39). He was committed to an ascetic lifestyle and lived off the land (Matt 3:8–10; Luke 3:9, 17). Yet the one coming after him, who was greater than he (John 1:30), frequently dined with the rich (Matt 9:10–12; Mark 2:15–17; Luke 5:29–30). John's message was one of apocalyptic judgment whereas Jesus freely offered the kingdom to profligates and sinners (Matt 9:9–17; 11:18–19). John expected the penitent

---

3  Morris M. Fairstein notes that the Mal 5:5 prophecy says Elijah will come before a particular *time* (i.e., the Day of the Lord) but says nothing about Elijah coming before a particular *person* (i.e., the messiah). From this he concludes that at the time of Jesus, the thought that Elijah must come prior to the messiah was not a widespread belief ("Why Do the Scribes Say That Elijah Must come First?" *JBL* 100/1 [1981]: 75–86, esp. 77). On the possible connection between Malachi, Elijah, and John, see Jeffrey A. Trumbower, "The Role of Malachi in the Career of John the Baptist," in *The Gospels and the Scriptures of Israel* (ed. Craig A. Evans and W. Richard Stegner; JSNTSup 104; Sheffield, Eng.: Sheffield Academic Press, 1994), 28–41.

to come to him (Matt 3:5) whereas Jesus went into the towns and cities and sought out those in need of salvation. John's person and word presented a powerful witness to Christ, yet in his darkest hour, he questioned whether Jesus was really the messiah (Matt 11:1–19; Luke 7:18).

In the one person of John, the reader of the New Testament encounters both power and perplexity. In Matthew and Mark, John simply arrives upon the scene without warning, fulfilling his calling as a forerunner to the messiah (Mark 1:1–2; Matt 3:1; cf. Mal 3:1; Isa 40:3).[4] Such is the strange yet salient role that John plays in the New Testament.

## JOSEPHUS AND JOHN THE BAPTIST

The limited number of sources at our disposal renders any study of John and his disciples provisional in nature. Apart from the Gospels and Acts, Josephus is the only first-century source that explicitly mentions John and his followers. His text on John is worth quoting in full:

> Now some of the Jews thought that the destruction of Herod's army came from God, and that very justly, as a punishment of what he did against John, that was called the Baptist, for Herod slew him, who was a good man, and commanded the Jews to exercise virtue, both as to righteousness toward one another, and piety toward God, and so to come to baptism; for that the washing [with water] would be acceptable to him, if they made use of it, not in order to the putting away [or the remission] of some sins [only], but for the purification of the body: supposing still that the soul was thoroughly purified beforehand by

righteousness. Now, when [many] others came in crowds about him, for they were very greatly moved [or pleased] by hearing his words, Herod, who feared lest the great influence John had over the people might put it into his power and inclination to raise a rebellion, (for they seemed ready to do anything he should advise,) thought it best, by putting him to death, to prevent any mischief he might cause, and not bring himself into difficulties, by sparing a man who might make him repent of it when it would be too late. Accordingly he was sent as prisoner, out of Herod's suspicious temper, to Macherus, the citadel I before mentioned, and was there put to death. Now the Jews had an opinion that the destruction of this army was sent as a punishment upon Herod, and a mark of God's displeasure to him. (*Ant.* 18.116–119)

These words are important on a number of levels. The account roughly parallels what is found in the New Testament. Josephus calls John "the Baptist," for he summoned the Jews to submit to water baptism, and this baptism reflected purification of the body and prior cleansing of the soul through righteousness. Josephus also completely affirms the person and ministry of John. John was a "good man," well received by the people, and one who exhorted others to act justly toward one's neighbors and live a devout life toward God. As in the Gospels, Herod Antipas does not fare well when compared with John. Josephus portrays Herod as suspicious of John and fearing his influence over the people. To prevent a popular uprising, Herod makes a preemptive strike against John, having him arrested and ultimately murdering him at one of his desert palaces.

Josephus has embedded his report on John in a section on the political history of Judea,

---

4   "In the Lucan narrative, he [John] appears in the wilderness completely alone—untaught, unmarried, his old father and mother surely dead, without connection to any place, relatives, or sects" (Joan E. Taylor, *The Immerser: John the Baptist within Second Temple Judaism* [Grand Rapids: Eerdmans, 1997], 12).

**Opposite:** Stretch of the Jordan river near one of the traditional sites linked with John's baptisms.

**Steps leading into one of the baptistery cisterns at Qumran.**

Galilee, and surrounding areas, particularly emphasizing the events that led to political turmoil among the Jews. His report comes immediately after his account of Herod's defeat by King Aretas of Syria, to the north (ca. 37 c.e.), and this defeat is directly linked to Herod's treachery against John. Twice Josephus mentions that the Jews believed that Herod had been beaten on the battle-field because he had killed John. According to Josephus, Herod's defeat was a matter of divine vengeance. The fact that Josephus was writing some years after the execution of John speaks of the latter's popularity and staying power in the consciousness of the people.[5]

5    For a discussion on the authenticity of Jose-phus's account of John, see John P. Meier, "John the Baptist in Josephus: Philology and Exegesis," *JBL* 111/2 (1992): 225–37.

## THE GOSPELS, JOHN THE BAPTIST, AND THE DESERT

Luke, at the very close of his birth narrative, states, "And the child grew and became strong in spirit; and he lived in the desert until he appeared publicly to Israel" (Luke 1:80). Nothing more is said to explain who raised John in the desert, nor is there a description of how he was raised there. The Gospel's silence at this critical juncture in the life of John has led to much speculation.

The verb tenses in Luke's account indicate that the growth and spiritual development of John occurred "in the deserts" (Luke 1:80, KJV) until the day he began his public ministry in Israel.[6] The plural "deserts" in Luke may indicate a sojourning in uninhabited places. Generally, Matthew and Mark concur, saying that John was "in the desert" (but note the singular here). John 1:23 implies as much by connecting John the Baptist's ministry with Isa 40:3, which states, "A voice of one calling: 'In the desert prepare the way for the Lord; make straight in the wilderness a highway for our God.' "

The connection between John and Isa 40:3 is important. All three Synoptics point to Isa 40:3 as the foundation for John's calling (Matt 3:3; Mark 1:2–3; Luke 3:4–6). Luke makes the link twice by including an allusion to Isa 40:3 in the hymn of Zacharias (Luke 1:76). Therefore, as far as the biblical record is concerned, the desert setting is indispensable for a proper understanding of John the Baptist.

In identifying what the Gospels meant by "desert," one should not automatically assume that John wandered the barren, scorched sands of the Arabian peninsula.[7] "Desert" in this context may refer not to the barrenness of the Sinai but rather to the basin of the Dead Sea (cf. Josh 15:61; 2 Chr 26:10). Indeed, the Bedouin east of Jerusalem and north of the Dead Sea graze their sheep and goats in this area to this day. Yet it is a harsh and inhospitable environment, amenable only to those who possess special skills that have been passed on from generation to generation. Since Luke indicates that John was raised in this environment from his childhood, who could have taken care of him during this period and passed on these life skills to him?

A tempting inference, not without historical and archaeological support, is that John was raised by the Essenes or some Essene-like community, such as the one at Qumran. John was born in about 4 B.C.E., six months before his cousin, Jesus. When he began his public ministry, he appeared in the northwest region of the Dead Sea—the region where the Qumran community was established. Since the Romans did not destroy Qumran until 68 C.E., John could have spent considerable time with the sect.[8]

The distinction between the community at Qumran and that of the Essenes is of some significance, for, although both groups are similar, they appear not to be identical (cf. Philo, *Good Person* 12.75–87). From what can be gathered from the Dead Sea Scrolls, Qumran was a monastic sect that deliberately isolated itself from external affairs. Josephus, however, who grants more space to his description of the Essenes than to that of the Pharisees and the Sadducees, portrays

---

6    The Greek text has *en tais erēmois* (ἐν ταῖς ἐρήμοις), clearly emphasizing the plural form of "desert."

7    The Hebrew word for "desert" is *midbar* and may refer to arid land that is not suitable for farming yet habitable for humans. The term may thus refer to areas like that of the Qumran community north and west of the Dead Sea.

8    For discussions on whether John was an Essene and whether he was raised at Qumran, see John C. Hutchison, "Was John the Baptist an Essene of Qumran?" *BSac* 159 (2002): 187–200; Hartmut Stegemann, *The Library of Qumran: On the Essenes, Qumran, John the Baptist, and Jesus* (Grand Rapids: Eerdmans, 1998), 224; Otto Betz, "Was John the Baptist an Essene?" *BRev* 6 (1990): 18–25, and William H. Brownlee, "John the Baptist in the New Light of Ancient Scrolls," in *Scrolls and the New Testament* (ed. Krister Stendall and James H. Charlesworth; New York: Crossroad, 1992), 33–53.

The search for fragments in one of the Dead Sea caves above the Qumran settlement.

the Essenes as "dwelling in every city" and having more contact with those outside their group than the other sects he describes (*J.W.* 2.124–126, 132, 567; 3.11; cf. also *Ant.* 13.311; 15.372–379; 17.346; 18.18–22). Moreover, it is now understood that the Essenes were in place fifty years before the founding of Qumran and may have in some way contributed to its establishment.[9] That is, the Essenes may have interpreted Isa 40:3 in terms of their own role in salvation history and so founded Qumran to function like a "publishing house" in the wilderness to "prepare the way for the Lord." Support for this theory can be found in Qumran's *Rule of the Community:*

> And when these have become a community in Israel in compliance with these arrangements they are to be segregated from within the dwelling of the men of sin to walk to the desert in order to open there His path. As it is written: "In the desert, prepare the way of [the Lord], straighten in the steppe a roadway for our God." This is the study of the law which he commanded through the hand of Moses, in order to act in compliance with all that has been revealed from age to age, and according to what the prophets have revealed through his holy spirit. (1QS VIII 12b–16)[10]

Moreover, it is now known that Qumran developed a method for preparing leather manuscripts by using potash from the Dead Sea rather than the organic tannin conventionally employed. This method permitted the community to make many manuscripts

9    Pliny the Elder, *Nat.* 5.15.73, writing in ca. 77 C.E., comments that the Essenes still dwelt on the western shore of the Dead Sea above Engeddi, which, like Jerusalem, was a "heap of ashes" at this time.

10    Quotation taken from Florentino García Martínez and Eibert J. C. Tigchelaar, eds., *The Dead Sea Scrolls Study Edition* (2 vols.; Grand Rapids: Eerdmans, 1997) 1:89–91.

View of the cave where some believe John the Baptist anointed his disciples.

A section from one of the of Dead Sea Scrolls conserved at the Shrine of the Book, Jerusalem.

of the Bible and other literature, many of which have survived to this day as the famous Dead Sea Scrolls, first discovered in 1947. In any case, both groups, the Essenes and Qumran, were located west and north of the Dead Sea and east of the Jordan River, the area where John began his ministry.[11]

In addition to proximity and an extraordinary focus on Isa 40:3, there are other tantalizing parallels between John and the desert communities. In *J.W.* 2.120, Josephus writes of the Essenes, "Marriage they disdain, but they adopt other men's children, while yet pliable and docile, and regard them as their kin and mould them in accordance with their own principles." This description portrays the Essenes as a celibate community willing to take in children to disciple them in accordance with its own religious vision.[12] If John was taken in by the Essenes at a young age, then Luke's "he was in the deserts" statement (Luke 1:80) becomes more comprehensible.[13]

The connection with the Essenes becomes even more appealing when one considers that John the Baptist and the Essenes share points of discipline and lifestyle. In general, both were to some degree reclusive and ascetic (cf. Philo, *Hypothetica* 11.4, 13). Philo notes that some Essenes lived in villages but avoided large cities because of lawlessness and that

11   For the precise location of John's ministry and the problematic meaning of "Bethany beyond the Jordan" (John 1:28), see Markus Öhler, "The Expectation of Elijah and the Presence of the Kingdom of God," *JBL* 118/3 (1999): 461–76; Brownlee, "John the Baptist," 36; and Stegemann, *The Library of Qumran*, 213.

12   But Philo understands that there are no children among the Essenes, natural or otherwise (*Hypothetica* 11.3). It should be noted also that the Qumran community did not adopt children. Cf. Jerome Murphy-O'Connor, "John the Baptist and Jesus: History and Hypotheses," *NTS* 36 (1990): 359–74, esp. 360.

13   1QM 1:3 indicates that the Essenes could have regarded the area around Jerusalem as "wilderness" or "desert."

Aerial view of the settlement site at Qumran, near the Dead Sea, showing the cliffs beyond.

they were all males, were celibate, and owned no personal property, not even clothing (*Good Person* 12.75–87; but cf. *Hypothetica* 11.1, 12–14). He reports that the Essenes did not offer sacrifices in the temple, that they rendered the Scriptures allegorically, intently listening in order of rank, and that they also maintained a constant state of purity (*Good Person* 12.75, 81–83; cf. also 1QS IX, 3–5).They strictly observed the Sabbath, as also noted by Josephus (*J.W.* 2.137–139). Initiates were on strict probation for a year, after which they were permitted to participate in communal immersion. The Essenes, however, did not permit such to partake in communal meals (*Hypothetica* 11.11) until after the second year of probation. Violators of community rule were expelled, which was virtually equivalent to a death sentence for the excommunicants because they often refused to reenter society and would take no food that did not meet the strict purity requirements of the Essenes. Those who blasphemed God and Moses were executed (*J.W.* 2.143–146).[14]

The similarity between John, the Essenes, and Qumran is remarkable. John lived in the desert and followed an ascetic lifestyle. He came "neither eating bread nor drinking wine" (Luke 1:15; 7:33–34; Matt 11:18–19). He ate locusts and wild honey and was clothed in a garment made of camel's hair.[15] For a belt he had a simple strip of leather bound about his waist (Mark 1:6; Matt 3:4). As with the Essenes and Qumran, Isa 40:3 served as the platform for John's calling (cf. 1QS VIII, 13–16). He emphasized that eschatological judgment was coming in fire, as did Qumran and the Essenes (Matt 3:12; Luke 3:11; 1QH XXX, 4–17).

Regarding piety, John practiced water baptism, which in some respects echoes the immersions of the Essenes and Qumran (cf. *J.W.* 2.129, 161). And like the Essenes and Qumran, John did not endorse the temple or the priestly cult in Jerusalem. Finally, the Essenes and the Qumran community espoused messianic and eschatological expectations compatible with the views of John. It appears that the Essenes and Qumran looked for three end-time figures that would usher in the messianic age. First would be a prophetic forerunner (1QS VIII, 3–8), followed by an anointed priest, the "Teacher of Righteousness" (1QpHab I, 13; II, 8; CD I, 11), and then rule by an anointed king (1QS IV, 20–22). As forerunner of the messiah, John testified that Jesus was the anointed end-time priest-king of the Lord (Luke 3:4–5; John 1:31–32).

On the other hand, striking differences do exist between John the Baptist and the Essenes and Qumran.[16] John saw himself as *fulfilling* Isa 40:3. He alone was the voice crying in the wilderness. By way of contrast, the Essenes and Qumran viewed their entire communities as fulfilling this role (1QS VIII, 13–16). John did not totally withdraw from society and form a monastic sect in the desert like the covenanters of Qumran. People responded to his call, but they did not enter into a probationary period of any kind. Sincere repentance evidenced in baptism was enough. In a few respects, however, John led a more austere life than that at Qumran. We read in 1QS VI, 4–6 that the community meal was bread and wine, which John did not eat. Also, the parallels between John and the Essenes on water baptism may be more apparent than real. John baptized others in water on the basis of sins forgiven. His baptism was a once-and-for-all event that prepared the penitent to escape the wrath of God. Members of the Essenes and Qumran repeatedly immersed *themselves* in water so that they might be ritually pure ( 2.129; 4Q414 2 II, 4–7; 4; 4Q512 42–44, 2–6). For them, deliverance from eschatological judgment was based upon membership in the sect, not immersion in water. Furthermore, whereas the covenanters viewed themselves as the exclusive recipients of salvation and the rest of Israel as damned (CD 7:1–13; 4Q491 1–10), John extended salvation to all who repented.

Ultimately, then, regarding the question of John's relationship to the Essenes or to Qumran, the sources are inconclusive. The

---

14 All of these strictures are remarkably similar to those found in the *Rule of the Community* scroll of Qumran (1QS). So, if Qumran was not Essene, it could be described as Essene-like. Yet even here there appears to have been considerable diversity among the Essenes. Josephus notes that some Essenes were celibate whereas others were permitted to marry (*J.W.* 2.160–161). Pliny the Elder states that there are no women among the Essenes and that they renounce all sexual desire. Their recruits come from those who are "tired of life," and so the community has continued for "thousands of ages" (*Nat.* 5.15.73).

15 Philo records that some of the Essenes were skilled at raising honey bees (*Hypothetica* 11.8).

16 Neither the Gospels nor Josephus identify John as an Essene; although Josephus mentions the sect by name and identifies persons who were Essenes, he never connects John with the desert dwellers.

Aerial view of the Jordan meandering toward the Dead Sea.

data point in both directions.[17] It is not impossible that John was a disaffected member of Qumran. That is, in time John may have become disillusioned with the covenanters' extremely restricted vision. No explicit evidence, however, supports this. In the final analysis, it appears that John the Baptist occupied the space between two worlds. He lived and ministered in that nondescript space between the world of common Judaism and the extreme religious piety of the Essenes and those at Qumran. From this perspective, John served as a bridge between the separatist tendencies of radical holiness and the divine initiative to offer grace to the masses.

## JOHN THE BAPTIST
## AS LIVING PARADIGM

John did not witness in word alone, for every aspect of John—location, appearance, and sustenance—"spoke" the message of God. Regarding location, the desert had powerful historical and religious significance for the Jews. It is literally a place apart from the affairs of society and, to that extent, a place to draw near to God. The desert is the place of divine revelation. God appeared to Moses in the desert (Exod 3:1–4). It was in the desert that Israel communed with Yahweh for forty years (Exod 16:35; Num 14:33–34). God spoke to Elijah in the desert and supernaturally provided him with food and drink (1 Kgs 17:1–5). And in a reversal of the exodus, Elijah crossed the Jordan on dry ground so that he might enter the wilderness, and at this point he was translated into heaven (2 Kgs 2:4–11). John is said to have come in the spirit and power of Elijah and to have begun his ministry at the place where Israel crossed the Jordan on dry ground (Josh 3:17; 4:13, 19). Symbolically, those who submitted to John's message and his baptism were on the verge of "crossing over" into a new epoch of God's work in the world.[18]

John's clothing also conveyed an otherworldly message. As mentioned, he wore clothes of camel's hair and a strip of leather about his waist for a belt (Matt 3:4; Mark 1:6). This was different from the white linen robes worn by the Essenes, a point not lost on those who feel that John had no connection with them. His cloak may have been self-made from the camel hair that had been rubbed off on the palm trees at nearby oases. If so, then he may have been continuing the ancient practice of wearing sackcloth made of camel's hair during times of repentance and humility before God (Jonah 3:5–10; Dan 9:3; 1 Kgs 21:27–29; Isa 58:3–5). The Baptist's attire conveyed his message: humble yourselves before God—seek God's face—repent. Finally, the "leather wrap" about his waist may have been an untanned strip of animal hide rather than a refined belt of prepared leather; separation from civil society and its industry is the impression here.[19] His food likewise speaks of a total reliance upon God rather than on the cultivated products of society. He ate what was provided by the land, specifically, locusts and wild honey. Although some have linked the locust with the pods of a tree used for animal fodder (Luke 15:16), more than likely John ate those flying insects considered to be Levitically clean and still eaten by the desert nomads to this day (Lev 11:21–22). All of

---

17   Among those who feel that there is no direct connection between John the Baptist and the Essenes or Qumran, see Taylor, *The Immerser*, 20, 34; Stegemann, *The Library of Qumran*, 222; Hutchison, "Was John the Baptist an Essene?" 192–94. For a contrary position, see Otto Betz, "Was John the Baptist an Essene?" 18, 23; Brownlee, "John the Baptist," 35.

18   On the symbol of the exodus and the ministry of John, see Trumbower, "The Role of Malachi," 30; and Stegemann, *The Library of Qumran*, 58. Stegemann comments, "In a kind of symbolic, prophetic manipulation of signs, John was thereby placing the people of Israel at the transition of the future time of salvation, corresponding to that of the desert generation of Israel that had indeed already been promised salvation, but whose members had to perish before their children could reach the sacred goal" (p. 215).

19   The Greek phrase employed to describe John's belt—*zōnēn dermatinēn* (ζώνην δερματίνην)—may mean simply a strap or strip of raw leather.

of these symbolic references seem to indicate that John wanted to distance himself from the corrupting influence of society while still remaining in contact with it.

A final note on John's diet may yield additional insight. The Synoptics state that John came "neither eating bread nor drinking wine" (Luke 7:33–34; Matt 11:18–19). And the angel Gabriel says to Zechariah in foretelling John's birth, "for he will be great in the sight of the Lord. He is never to take wine or other fermented drink, and he will be filled with the Holy Spirit even from birth" (Luke 1:15). These may simply be general descriptions of his ascetic practice, or they may reflect that John was a Nazarite.[20] Since his miraculous birth parallels the births of Samson and Samuel, both of whom were Nazarites, the notion that John was bound by a Nazarite vow from birth is not without parallel.[21] The Nazarite vow was one of complete consecration to the Lord. Nothing from the grape vine, either vinegar, wine, strong drink, grapes, raisins, or grape seeds, was to be food for a Nazarene. If the vow was for life, the hair was never to be cut. The early rabbis in *m. Nazir* 6:3 instruct that the hair of a Nazarite could be washed, but not combed. If this was the practice during John's day, his hair might have been worn in long dreadlocks, adding to an already striking appearance as one from the wilderness.

---

20 The nature and stipulations of a Nazirite vow are set forth in Num 6:1–21. This vow is described as a special vow of separation to the Lord and can be entered into by both men and women. Those that commit themselves to the vow may not eat or drink anything derived from the grapevine nor cut their hair for the entire period of the vow. They must avoid coming into contact with a dead body (corpse defilement), and if so defiled must start the vow over by completely shaving the head and offering appropriate sacrifices. At the end of the designated period, the Nazarite is to present himself or herself to the priest in the temple, offer sacrifices, completely shave the hair again and burn it on the altar.

21 For some, the Nazirite vow is a lifetime commitment commencing at birth, as it appears to have been for Samuel and Samson (1 Sam 1:11; Judg 13:5–7, 16:17).

## THE MESSAGE AND BAPTISM OF JOHN

Throughout Israel's history, specific Hebrew texts have often incited individuals to take concrete action in the name of Yahweh, like the Pharisees and the Zealots. This may have been the case with John. Some of the most dramatic images and prophecies of the Hebrew Scriptures coalesce in his person and message. The inaugural statement of Luke that "the word of God came to John" echoes the summons of the great prophets of old (Luke 3:2, cf. Gen 15:1; 1 Kgs 17:2; 18:1; Isa 38:4; Jer 1:1–2; Ezek 1:3). Specifically, the word that came to John was the fulfillment of Isa 40:3 and Mal 3:1. These Scriptures serve as the basis for John's calling and also as the content of his message, for he was that voice crying in the wilderness, preparing the way of the Lord (Matt 3:3; Mark 1:3; Luke 3:4; John

**Cross marking a traditional site of John's baptisms in the Jordan.**

1:23). As noted, this epoch-making call was sounded through the voice of Elijah redivivus, so to speak.[22] John fleshed out the end-time role of Elijah in his person, appearance, and message, fulfilling the prophecy of Mal 4:5–6 (cf. also 2 Kgs 1:8). The angel Gabriel affirms this fulfillment to Zechariah, stating that John will come in the spirit and power of Elijah (Luke 1:17). Just as Elijah sought the reformation of Judaism, so, from John's perspective, the goal was nothing less than the spiritual cleansing of Israel, from top to bottom, with no exceptions. Herod, the religious elite, those who tended the temple, the common Jew on the street, and even Roman soldiers were caught up in the message of John. For John, the Pharisees and Sadducees are a swarm of snakes who have, against all odds, received advanced notice that wrath is on the way (Matt 3:7; Luke 3:7).[23] For John, ethnic privilege, even being a natural-born child of Abraham, is of no consequence to God. If God wants children, God can work with rocks instead of patriarchs (Matt 3:9; Luke 3:8).[24] Also, like Elijah, John's message was one of impending apocalyptic judgment. The "Day of the Lord" is at hand, and God's hand wields the fire of judgment (Mal 3:1–3). God's winnowing shovel is already in God's hand; all that remains is to cast the chaff into the fire (Matt 3:12; Luke 3:17; cf. Sir 48:10). The Judge is imminent, and already the ax

has hewn the roots of unproductive trees; they are on the way to the pyre (Matt 3:10; Luke 3:9, 17).[25]

The Baptist also follows the moral mandates found in the end-time prophecy of Mal 3:1–3. Malachi announces that swift justice will be meted out against those who rob workers of their pay, those who oppress widows and orphans, and those who neglect to defend the rights of aliens in the land. Similarly, John calls for the equitable sharing of material goods with those in need. Tax collectors are to resist graft and collect a fair tally from the people. Soldiers are not to abuse their office or resort to extortion for personal gain (Luke 3:10–14).

John's promise of divine retribution against such transgressors would have been very popular for those enduring the injustices of the first century. These injustices included the extraordinary economic burden placed upon the people by heavy taxation from the Romans, combined with the tithes and temple tax expected of good Jews. In addition, the cooperation of the Jewish high priests and the religious elite with their Roman occupiers would have demoralized the general populace of the Jews, who awaited divine deliverance and judgment against those who had wronged them. John promised just this, and the people responded to him en masse, so that at least one political leader feared that John would incite a popular revolt (Matt 14:1–10; Mark 6:16–29; Luke 9:9).

Every surviving source on John connects him and his ministry with water baptism.

22  It appears that at the time of Jesus, the Jews believed that Elijah would be the precursor to the coming of the messiah. See further Morris Fairstein, "Why do the Scribes Say That Elijah Must Come First?" 76; Betz, "Was John the Baptist an Essene?" 25; and Öhler, "The Expectation of Elijah," 461.

23  John's reference to "snakes" may reflect 1QH 2 23.17–18, which speaks of "the hateful creature."

24  John may be making a play on words here in his rejection of the Jewish authorities and the temple priesthood. In Hebrew the word for "children" is banim and the word for "stones" is 'abanim. John may be indicating that the true temple consists of dedicated people, not members of any particular race (Betz, "Was John the Baptist an Essene?" 24).

25  Öhler notes that Malachi is the only Old Testament prophet to compare the judgment of Israel with winnowing out the chaff and burning it in fire ("The Expectation of Elijah," 472). Webb remarks that the Gk. ptuon (πτύον) is actually a winnowing shovel, not a winnowing fork (thrinax [θρινάξ]). His point is that John the Baptist has already separated the wheat from the chaff by his preaching and that all that remains is for Jesus to come in judgment, take his winnowing shovel, and cast the chaff into the fire of judgment (John the Baptizer, 298–99).

**Bedouins winnowing grain.**

All four Gospels, Acts, and Josephus describe John as one who baptized others in the river Jordan. John was so closely linked with what he practiced in ministry that it effectively defined his personal identity. He is repeatedly called "John *the Baptist*" (or "*the Baptizer*," Matt 3:1, emphasis added; cf. 11:11, 12; 14:2; 16:14; 17:13; Mark 6:14, 24, 25; 8:28; Luke 7:20, 28, 33; 9:19; *Ant.* 18.116). In the Fourth Gospel, when the Pharisees ask John to identify himself, his first words are, "I baptize with water" (John 1:26), and later he declares that God commissioned him to perform this very act (John 1:33). There can be little doubt that a primary feature of John's ministry was water baptism.

Nevertheless, scholarship is divided over the meaning and significance of John's baptism. The sacramental use of water has a long history in Judaism. Exodus 30:18–21 describes the ritual ablutions that the priests must undergo in order to serve in the temple. Leviticus sets forth numerous ceremonial washings for the purpose of removing ritual defilement and the corruption associated with leprosy (Lev 15:1–12, 16–24). Often "living water," that is, running or flowing water, is prescribed for the cleansing of the most severe defilements (Lev 14:5–6, 50–52; 15:13; Num 19:20; Deut 21:4). The many *miqvoth*—ceremonial cleansing pools—in and around the temple indicate that the Pharisees practiced ceremonial cleansing before entering the temple. The pious sought to maintain a state of purity by repeated washings (Mark 7:4), which in turn ensured purity at table (Matt 15:2; Mark 7:3). Similarly, the cleansing of impurity by water was a predominant theme in Qumran and among the Essenes. Josephus notes that after predawn prayers and a season of work, community members would clothe themselves in white and immerse themselves in cold water, after which they would be "clean"; the same was done at eventide (*J.W.* 2.128–139). These self-immersions permitted them to eat and pray together. As with the Essenes, the Qumran community practiced repeated ritual washings, maintaining that only their ceremonies were effective for the removal of impurity (4Q512). John's baptism is thus often viewed as a ceremonial cleansing from ritual defilement.

Still, none of the biblical texts related to John's baptism speak of cleansing from ritual impurity. Rather, the emphasis is laid upon repentance and the forgiveness of sins, as Mark 1:4 clearly states: "And so John came, baptizing in the desert region and preaching a baptism of repentance for the forgiveness of sins" (cf. Luke 3:3; Matt 3:1–2). As noted previously, Josephus claims that the washing of the body in John's baptism presupposed the purification of the soul through righteousness (Ant. 18.118). John's baptism, then, was not ceremonial but thoroughly ethical (Luke 3:10–14). John expected a change of conduct, not a change in ritual status. Also, there is no indication that John feared ritual defilement from coming into contact with the common people. This is in stark contrast with the Essenes, who protected themselves from defilement by neophytes of their own sect (J.W. 2.137–140). In addition, the effective agent in John's baptism is not the immersion in water but, rather, the personal confession of sins (Matt 3:6; Mark 1:5). In this respect, John reflected Qumran's insistence that a pure heart must accompany ritual cleansing (1QS III, 1–12). Yet even here there is nothing in Qumran that speaks of "a baptism of repentance for the remission of sins," as we find in John's baptism. There is also no indication that John's baptism was meant to be repeated, as we see in the oft-repeated cleansings of the Old Testament, the Pharisees, and the more extreme Jewish sects. Finally, perhaps the most striking distinction between John's baptism and the

cleansings and immersions as practiced among the Essenes and Qumran is that those who responded to John's call were baptized *by him* (Mark 1:5, 9). This is in stark contrast to the many self-immersions practiced by the Essenes and Qumran.[26]

Perhaps more to the point, John's baptism functioned as a metaphor for the forgiveness of sins that had already occurred as a result of personal contrition before God. In this sense, John's work would have been on the order of the great prophets of old. For example, Isa 1:16–17 states, "wash and make yourselves clean. Take your evil deeds out of my sight! Stop doing wrong, learn to do right! Seek justice, encourage the oppressed. Defend the cause of the fatherless, plead the case of the widow." In a similar vein, Ezekiel preaches, "I will sprinkle clean water on you, and you will be clean; I will cleanse you from all your impurities and from all your idols. I will give you a new heart and put a new spirit in you; I will remove from you your heart of stone and give you a heart of flesh. And I will put my Spirit in you and move you to follow my decrees and be careful to keep my laws" (Ezek 36:25–27). In all these instances, water purification is joined hard with moral transformation.

In addition, John was calling his respondents to come out of the society at large and join in a special renewal movement. His baptism represented an initiation into a select group destined to escape impending judgment. Again, the dire warnings of Mark 3:1–6 and Luke 3:3–14, coupled with the promise of the baptism in the Holy Spirit, lend support here. Just as the ax, winnowing shovel, and fire destroy what is worthless, so the Holy Spirit will yield eschatological judgment, purging away anything that is of no use to the kingdom (cf. 1QS IV, 21). This judgmental yet purgative role of the Spirit is developed further by Luke's

**Opposite: View from inside one of the Dead Sea Scrolls caves at Qumran.**

26  On the distinctions between John's baptism and that of others, see Webb, *John the Baptizer*, 180; and Stegemann, *The Library of Qumran*, 218.

account of John and the early church. In Acts 1:5 Luke links John's words of the coming messianic judgment with the baptism of the Spirit. This could mean that John's ministry of baptism comes to complete fulfillment when the church is baptized in the Spirit at Pentecost. To those who have submitted to the reign of the messiah, the Spirit is a blessing. On the other hand, to those who resist the hand of God in the world, the last days' outpouring of the Spirit is a curse (Isa 32:15–19; 44:3; Ezek 11:19–20; 36:26–27; 37:14; Joel 2:28–29; Zech 12:10).

In sum, what John was doing by baptizing others in the river Jordan was recognizable by his contemporaries but radically different from what they had ever known or experienced. The imagery may have been familiar to many, but in key areas the application was new.

## THE DISCIPLES OF JOHN THE BAPTIST

Our knowledge of the beliefs and practices of John's disciples must be drawn from what we can learn about John. Unlike with the community at Qumran, the sources do not contain any separate literature traceable to the disciples of John. Moreover, there are relatively few places in the New Testament where John's disciples are mentioned (cf. Mark 2:18; 6:29; Matt 11:2; John 1:35–37; 3:25–27; Acts 18:25; 19:1–7).[27] So the beliefs and practices of John's disciples remain sketchy.

This being said, those who followed John must have been highly motivated to hear his message. They had to be willing to forsake home and hearth, at least initially in any case, to go out into the wilderness to John, for he did not come to them. A large part of their motivation was no doubt due to their desire for radical change and justice. Roman oppression, either directly or through a network of client kings, bore down hard on the Jews. Gross insensitivities to the people, such as Pilate's introduction of images into the temple and his skimming of temple

taxes for public works, fueled discontent. Herod Antipas's construction of a city on an ancient Jewish burial ground did not help matters (Josephus, *J.W.* 2.167–77; *Ant.* 18.55–62). Furthermore, John's message for social equity and moral integrity would have been very attractive to many common Jews of the day. His warning that God would soon destroy the wicked and reward the righteous offered hope in the midst of corruption and graft. People were willing to travel to hear John's message, and Matt 3:5 indicates that just about everyone in Judea did just that.

Once they made the journey to him, it would not have taken long for astute hearers to make the connection between their master and Elijah as presented in the oracle of Malachi.[28] If they submitted to baptism, they became part of an eschatological community awaiting the imminent arrival of the kingdom of God. Since John and his disciples moved about the land (John 3:23) and eventually some of his followers made it as far as Ephesus (Acts 19:1–7) and Alexandria in North Africa (Acts 18:24–25), they did not coalesce into a reclusive desert sect as at Qumran. Regarding piety, they were known to fast and were taught special prayers (Mark 2:18; Luke 11:1), just as the covenanters fasted and prayed (cf. 1QS 2:5–15).[29] John's disciples seem to have been more austere in their practices of fasting than that of Jesus and his disciples. Perhaps this was due to the ascetic tendencies of John, tendencies that Jesus did not emulate. At any rate, John's disciples had some concerns about the lack of fasting among Jesus' disciples and made their concerns known to Jesus (Mark 2:18; Luke 5:33). They were dedicated to John both in life and in death (Matt 14:12). Yet it was

---

27 Öhler, "The Expectation of Elijah," 469 n. 31.

28 "We find it almost definite that the followers of John the Baptist believed him to be the eschatological Elijah (Luke 1:17; John 1:21, 25)" (ibid., 473).

29 Betz, "Was John the Baptist an Essene?" 23. There is some speculation that the Lord's Prayer was in fact a prayer that was first taught by John to his disciples.

**"Saint John the Baptist sees Jesus from afar" by J.-J. Tissot.**

this dedication that led them to break away from John and follow after the Lamb of God (John 1:29, 36).

## JESUS AND JOHN THE BAPTIST

Jesus was very different from John in many respects. John was an ascetic in the desert whereas Jesus enjoyed socializing at table in the city (Matt 11:18–19; Luke 7:33–34). John performed no miracle whereas miracles were a major aspect of Jesus' ministry (John 10:41; 2:11). John preached the impending wrath of God whereas Jesus offered mercy and grace to the most profligate of sinners (Matt 21:31). Such differences became so great that in what must have been his darkest hour, John questioned whether Jesus was God's final offer of salvation (Matt 11:2–3; Luke 7:19–20). In spite of all of these differences, there can be no question that Jesus thoroughly endorsed the person and ministry of John, his "relative" (Gk. *syngenis* [συγγενίς]; Luke 1:36). Jesus' implicit affirmation of John can be seen in that, over the protests of John, Jesus insists on being baptized by him (Matt 3:13–17; Mark 1:9–11; Luke 3:21–22).[30] Indeed, Jesus adopts John's baptism for his own ministry, and this in turn sets the pattern for his followers and the church (Rom 6:3; 1 Cor 1:14–16; 6:11; Acts 8:38; 10:48).[31]

Jesus clearly wants the people to understand who John is and how important he is in God's economy. To this end, Jesus asks three

30  Öhler, "The Expectation of Elijah," 473. The inherent tension here is reflected in the apocryphal *Gospel of the Nazarenes*: "Behold, the mother of the Lord and his brethren said to him: John the Baptist baptizes unto the remission of sins, let us go and be baptized by him. But he said to them: Wherein have I sinned that I should go and be baptized by him? Unless what I have said is ignorance (a sin of ignorance)."

31  Stegemann, *The Library of Qumran*, 218.

questions of the crowds in Luke 7:24–26 and Matt 11:7–9. These questions lead the hearers to one conclusion: John is the greatest prophetic voice the world has ever known. John is a burning and shining lamp in a dark world (John 5:30–36). He is the greatest born among women, for he is the last and definitive prophetic word before the inauguration of the kingdom (Matt 11:11–13; Luke 7:28). For Jesus, then, John is the last-days voice of Elijah (Mark 9:9–14). After John, the messianic kingdom is dawning in this present age.[32]

This last point captures the relationship between John and Jesus. John was the living demarcation between the old and the new age. John was a witness to the light, not the light itself (John 1:19–34). He was not the bridegroom but only a friend (John 3:29). He was not the way but only the one who prepared the way (Matt 3:3; Mark 1:3; Luke 3:4; John 1:23). He was not the Christ (John 1:20–23), but in the spirit of Isaiah, he clearly perceived that Jesus was the one who bore the nature of God (Isa 9:6; 42:1–4; 53:1–10). Thus John declares him to be "the Lamb of God, who takes away the sin of the world" (John 1:29, 36). His mission in life was to point to the One who would come after him, the One stronger than he, the One whose sandals he was not worthy to unlatch. John's medium was water, but the Christ would baptize in the Holy Spirit and with fire (Matt 3:11; Mark 1:7; Luke 3:16; John 1:15, 30; 5:33–36).

For all of these reasons, John's relationship to Jesus may be characterized by such words as "transitional," "temporary," and "preparatory."[33] John fully understood the subordinate role he played with respect to Jesus and flatly stated, "He must become greater; I must become less" (John 3:30). Thus John's disciples went on to follow Jesus

as their new master (John 1:35–40).[34] This transference of allegiance is paradigmatic of John's whole person and ministry. His person and word wholly testified to the unique person and work of Jesus the messiah, not only while John was yet living but even after his death as well (John 10:41–42).

## HEROD ANTIPAS AND THE DEATH OF JOHN THE BAPTIST

Like Jesus, John met a violent death at the hands of the political leaders of his day. The Synoptics record that Herod Antipas had John thrown in prison because John railed against his illegal marriage to Herodias, the wife of his half-brother, Philip (Matt 14:1–12; Mark 6:14–29; Luke 6:7–9). In the light of John's use of Malachi and his commitment to ethical living, the Gospels' record is credible. Malachi 2:13–16 is the only place in the Hebrew Scriptures that explicitly speaks against divorce.[35] John may have viewed the words "do not break faith with the wife of your youth" in Mal 2:15 as tailor-made for the sin of Herod. At some point in his career, John publicly condemned Herod and paid the price for it.[36] In time Herodias ensnared her new groom in his own words, and John met a tragic end. Josephus's special interest in John comes to our aid as well, yet from a different viewpoint from the Gospels. As noted above, Josephus has John executed for political reasons rather than for moralizing about the indiscretions of Herod (*Ant.* 18.116–119). Because he feared that the people would do whatever John might bid them to do, Herod arrested John and had him imprisoned in the

---

32  "He was the last, the greatest, the eschatological prophet" (Öhler, "The Expectation of Elijah," 475–76).

33  Webb, *John the Baptizer*, 197.

34  John 3:22–25 indicates that some tension may have existed between the disciples of John and those of Jesus. Issues concerning purity may have arisen between the two groups (cf. esp. John 3:25) (ibid., 75). In the *Pseudo-Clementines*, a third- or fourth-century document, the disciples of John claim that their master was greater than Jesus and that John was the true messiah (Betz, "Was John the Baptist an Essene?" 21).

35  See Trumbower, "The Role of Malachi," 40.

36  Öhler, "The Expectation of Elijah," 472.

Aerial view of Herodion, one of Herod the Great's strongholds, near Bethlehem. Recently a tomb believed to be that of Herod the Great was discovered at this site.

fortress at Machaerus.[37] In light of his recent family history, it seemed the prudent course of action. Zealous youths had torn down the Roman eagle from the temple during his father's reign, and the ensuing riots led his brother to slay three thousand Jews. Judas the Galilean had recently led a popular revolt, and the formation of the Zealot party was well under way. All of this turmoil was linked with religious zeal that echoed the prophet's call for God to destroy the enemies of Israel.[38] The Jewish street was a powder keg that did not afford Herod Antipas the luxury to discriminate between the revivalist and the revolutionary.

37   This fortress was located east of the Dead Sea in Perea, within the jurisdiction of Herod Antipas, the region where John had been baptizing. The fortress, expanded by Herod the Great, contained banquet halls suitable for the feast described in the Synoptics. Cf. also Stegemann, *The Library of Qumran*, 213.

38   "John's preaching a baptism of repentance and forgiveness of sins proved to be lethal. Crowds had gathered around him, and crowds were dangerous" (Ellis Rivkin, "Locating John the Baptizer in Palestinian Judaism: The Political Dimension," in *The Society of Biblical Literature 1983 Seminar Papers* [SBLSP 22; Chico, Calif.: Scholars Press, 1983], 84).

**The Library of Celsus, Ephesus. Paul encountered John's disciples in Ephesus during his third missionary journey.**

The different motives set forth by Josephus have led some scholars to question the Synoptic account.[39] But the two accounts may not be that far off in substance. Jesus leverages the tremendous popularity of John when responding to his opponents, and Josephus states that Herod was a wicked man, so much so that his Roman tenders had to banish him to Lyons in 39 c.e.[40] Also, the ancient Jews did not tend to separate a leader's moral life from the legitimacy of his political rule, as we moderns sometimes are apt to do. John's tirade against Herod would have easily translated into political unrest in his context.[41]

## SUMMARY

Some scholars have lamented that there is a "contemporary forgetfulness of John" in the church today.[42] It is contended that at some level there is a general discomfort with John, with his appearance, message, and manner, and that this has led to a tragic malaise in the church.[43] There can be no question that to slight such a monumental figure as John would be a grave mistake.

This mistake was not made during the life and times of Jesus. John changed the course of Second Temple Judaism. As a "hinge," John functioned as a cardinal (from the Latin *cardo*, "hinge") figure linking the religious economy of Judaism with the radically dynamic spiritual movement founded by Jesus. His most atten-

39   Murphy-O'Connor, "John the Baptist and Jesus," 370–72.

40   Stegemann, *The Library of Qumran*, 213.

41   "The socio-political explanation provided by Josephus and the personal and moral explanation provided by the nt are probably presenting two sides of the complex set of factors which motivated Antipas' arrest of John" (Webb, *John the Baptizer*, 375).

42   Cf. Goodall, "None Greater Born of Woman," 561.

43   "Neglect of John the Baptist is a key symptom of our contemporary malaise; a renewed awareness of his role in the Church is an essential antidote to our ills" (ibid., 550).

tive student and recorder, Luke, notes that the beginning of the Christian age is to be marked not at the start of Jesus' ministry but with John's (Acts 1:22). When Peter encapsulates the life and ministry of Jesus for Cornelius, his starting point is the baptism of John (Acts 10:37b). Luke even joins John's baptism to the seismic shift of the ages, the outpouring of the Holy Spirit at Pentecost (Luke 3:16–17; Acts 1:5). Lest the reader forget, this link between Pentecost and John's baptism is made again in Acts 11:16. In Paul's first recorded sermon, he explicitly cites John as the turning point that led to God's work in Christ (Acts 13:24–25). The magnitude of John's work is demonstrated when Paul encounters John's disciples as far west as Corinth and as late as his third missionary journey (Acts 18:25; 19:1–7). These last accounts indicate that the early church had its hands full in helping far-flung disciples of John make the transition to the Jesus movement.

In the end, the astute reader should be struck with the paradox and pathos of John. He was a confrontational, high-profile prophet whose message claimed him to be nothing more than a voice in the desert and less than a slave compared with what God was doing in Christ. The core message at the start of his ministry was that, in fact, his role in the kingdom of God was ending. Finally, despite the power of God and his tremendous appeal to the people, he died a tragic death. The vindictive plot of an adulteress tapped into the paranoia of Herod Antipas, who had him beheaded at the whim of a dancing girl. John's death represented a defeat in a quantitative, numerical kind of way. Yet the "restoration of all things" (Gk. *apokatastasis pantōn* [ἀποκατάστασις πάντων]), which Jesus implied that John had helped bring about (Matt 17:11–12; cf. also Acts 3:21), cannot be measured quantitatively. John's life and ministry served as a catalyst for the dawn of the new age.[44]

---

44 Thus, when describing the quality of John's work, Goodall states, "Rather, it is ontological. John restored the fullness of Israel in his very self, repristinating the prophetic tradition in all its expectancy and purity" (ibid., 554).

# Annotated Bibliography

Taylor, Joan E. *The Immerser: John the Baptist within Second Temple Judaism*. Grand Rapids: Eerdmans, 1997. This scholarly work seeks to anchor John the Baptist within the milieu of Second Temple Judaism and not within the context of emergent Christianity. John is not an Essene, and his baptism was not to initiate members into a new community but rather to cleanse from ritual impurity, a point that joins John with the Pharisees. This volume is well written and researched, providing valuable access to primary sources, but it is definitely intended for a scholarly audience.

Webb, Robert L. *John the Baptizer and Prophet: A Socio-historical Study*. Journal for the Study of the New Testament: Supplement Series 62. Sheffield, Eng.: JSOT Press, 1991. In this benchmark work on John the Baptist from a sociological perspective, close work with primary sources (especially Josephus and the Dead Sea Scrolls) analyzes the role of ritual immersions in antiquity. John reflects the theme of prophetic judgment and restoration, found in Second Temple Judaism, but is unique in that he intended to initiate a religious sect. This is a highly technical work but rich in its use of primary documents and treatment of contemporary research.

# 11

# The Hebrews— Faith and Dissonance

## INTRODUCTION: WORD STUDY AND IDENTIFICATION

The first instance of the word "Hebrews" (Gk. *Hebraioi*) in the New Testament is found in Acts 6:1. It is here that Luke suddenly inserts the term into his narrative, without any introduction or explanation. The identity of the Hebrews is taken for granted by Luke, and for the most part, modern scholarship follows suit. That is, the lion's share of scholarly comment is directed toward the place of the Hellenists in the early church, with the Hebrews playing supporting roles in the unfolding saga of the newborn faith.[1] For example, it is commonly known that the word *Hebraioi* is found in the LXX (cf. Gen 40:15; 43:32; Exod 1:15), but its meaning is not the same as in Acts 6. The New Testament use of the term does not refer to Jews in general but relates to those who are closely associated with the "Twelve" (cf. Acts 6:2). The *Hebraioi* in Acts are more than likely the Aramaic-speaking portion of the church in Jerusalem together with the apostolic leadership that was originally appointed by Jesus

(Luke 6:13).[2] Apart from these general observations, the major commentaries present no detailed description of the Hebrews in the New Testament.

The Hebrews and the kind of diversity that existed in this group, however, seem to have played a major part in the development of the church's identity. As the Hebrews struggled with what it meant to be Christian while at the same time remaining true to Judaism, the distinct identity of the church began to emerge.[3] In this way the Hebrews may well have been the sector of the first believers that set the ideological and theological parameters for the emerging church.

When one attempts to identify the Hebrews in Acts 6:1, it should be remembered that

---

1    E.g., Hans Conzelmann focuses on the Hellenists to the exclusion of the Hebrews in *Acts of the Apostles* (Philadelphia: Fortress, 1987), 44–45. Ben Witherington does not devote one sentence to identifying the Hebrews but spends ten pages on the Hellenists (*The Acts of the Apostles: A Socio-rhetorical Commentary* [Grand Rapids: Eerdmans, 1998], 240–50).

2    See Joseph Fitzmyer, *The Acts of the Apostles: A New Translation with Introduction and Commentary* (New York: Doubleday, 1998), 345–46. Justo L. González describes the "Hebrews" as the "old guard" in the church ("Reading from My Bicultural Place: Acts 6:1–7," in *Reading from This Place: Social Location and Biblical Interpretation in the United States* [ed. Fernando F. Segovia and Mary Ann Tolbert; Minneapolis: Fortress, 1995], 143). Since the church was newly established, the "old guard" could not have been that old.

3    J. Julius Scott Jr. tags the opening chapters of Acts as reflecting a "self-definition process" and a period of "self-awareness" ("The Church's Progress to the Council of Jerusalem according to the Book of Acts," *BBR* 7 [1997]: 209). James D. G. Dunn also speaks of a "process of redefinition" (*The Acts of the Apostles* [Valley Forge, Pa.: Trinity Press International, 1996], 139).

161

**View of the Old City of Jerusalem from the slopes of the Mount of Olives, showing the Temple Mount area, once the site of Herod's Temple.**

the constituency of the early church was by no means monolithic. Rather, a theological spectrum appears to have been in place from the very beginning.[4] Within this ideological continuum could be found those whose beliefs and practices were barely distinguishable from the Judaism of the day. On the other hand, there were those who espoused a vision that challenged even the theological framework of the young church. The religious and cultural profile of Hebrews in the early church is clarified by examining the place they occupy in this spectrum. It may well be that the Hebrews in

Acts were left of center, so to speak, and had closely bound Christianity to the religion and politics of Israel.[5]

In any case, Acts 6:1 indicates that the Hebrews constituted a recognizable religious group in the early church. This appears to be true for the following reasons. First, Luke clearly contrasts the Hebrews from the Hellenists in a way that indicates that each group has its own identity. Second, when considered closely, the nature of the conflict between the Hebrews and the Hellenists seems to point in this direction: the Hebrews

---

4    "Jewish Christianity is a multifarious phenomenon, in itself a theological spectrum, and in the first century probably consisted of different parties" (Jacob Jervell, *The Unknown Paul: Essays on Luke–Acts and Early Christian History* [Minneapolis: Augsburg, 1984], 29).

5    Jervell gives a serviceable definition of "the Hebrews." He claims that they were "Jewish Christians [who] refuse to separate Christianity from the religious, political, and cultural fate of Israel" and who maintain that "there is but one Israel" (ibid., 33).

and Hellenists are Jews yet differ in ideals and practice. Examination of the text lends support to this understanding of the Hebrews.

In Acts 6, the Hebrews, for whatever reason, find themselves distanced from the Hellenists, so much so that the widows of the latter group are being overlooked by the church's relief program (6:1b).[6] The cause of the neglect could simply have been a breakdown in communication. If the Hellenists were Greek-speaking Jews from the Diaspora, and it appears that they are, then the Hebrews were more than likely Palestinian Jews whose mother tongue was Aramaic. This linguistic diversity could have strained the lines of communication between the two groups. The net result was that the widows of the Hellenists were not receiving their due of support from the church.[7]

This kind of linguistic diversity no doubt caused difficulties for the early church, as it does in any multilingual setting. Luke's solution of the appointment of an entirely new

---

6  F. Scott Spencer thinks that Luke's main point is to reveal the impropriety of the apostles' subordinating the care of widows to the ministry of teaching and prayer. So, for Luke, the way widows are treated serves as a standard of one's character and spiritual growth ("Neglected Widows in Acts 6:1–7," *CBQ* 50 [2001]: 729–30, 732–33).

7  Luke's frequent note that the church was "increasing in number" may explain how the widows of the Hellenists might have fallen between the cracks. It might also explain the increased cultural and ideological diversity in the church. In the end, Ernst Haenchen does not define the Hebrews and Hellenists apart from language (*The Acts of the Apostles: A Commentary* [Philadelphia: Westminster, 1971], 260).

leadership team for the Hellenists, however, does not seem to fit the situation at hand (Acts 6:3–6). Many Jews in Israel and of the Diaspora were bilingual. Designating translators for the Hellenists would have solved a breakdown in communication between the Hebrews and the Hellenists. Thus it may well be that the distinction in language reflects more substantial distinctions between the two groups, differences that fell more along the lines of theological vision and practice than along those of simple linguistic diversity in the church.[8] The harsh experience of Stephen and the seven when compared with that of the Hebrews moves in this direction as well (Acts 6:8–8:4). The fact that the Hebrews initially escaped the severe persecution brought against the Hellenists seems to suggest that more than language was involved in the dispute. That is, the Hebrews may not have shared the ideological and theological distinctions that identified the Hellenists as a target for persecution. Or to emphasize another perspective, at this stage in the development of the early church, the Hebrews may have held and practiced a form of Christianity that did not arouse the ire of some sectors of the Jewish community in Jerusalem.[9] Without trying to tease out the exact nature of the differences between the Hebrews and Hellenists, it may be said that the Hebrews followed the "social-cultural particularism and isolationism" characteristic of some sectors of first-century Judaism whereas the Hellenists

**Opposite: Scale model of Herod's Temple, Jerusalem, looking through the main gates. The area at the bottom is the Court of Women. Beyond that, entered through the Nicanor Gate is the Court of Priests.**

did not.[10] It would not be surprising if such antipathies were present in the early church. After all, factionalism between otherwise like-minded Jews was what sparked the Maccabean revolt and fueled the conflict that led to the destruction of Jerusalem in 70 C.E.

The fact that the geographic locus of the dispute is in Jerusalem and that Luke calls the leadership of the Hebrews "the Twelve" clarifies their identity further still. The Hebrews appear to be composed of the first followers of the historical Jesus in Palestine, including the first apostles, together with all the Aramaic-speaking Jews who had attached themselves to the Jesus movement early on. In short, the Hebrews were the "mother church" that was entrusted with the leadership of the whole church. A major aspect of this leadership would have been the mentoring of the rapidly unfolding development of the new movement. Since at this stage no "belief and practice manual" had been written for the fledgling church, the leaders of the Hebrews would have had to proceed in an ad hoc fashion to some degree. Consequently, when the dispute of Acts 6 arose, authoritative direction comes forth from the Hebrews, not the Hellenists. It is the "Twelve" who call the community of faith to order, set the agenda for the selection of the "deacons," and are in charge of restructuring the leadership of the early church.[11] All of these factors, not the least being their immediate contact with the historical Jesus, may have granted the Hebrews a prestige and authority that would endure throughout the apostolic period and beyond.

---

8    Indeed, even though Dunn labels the two groups "the Greek-speakers" and the "Aramaic-speakers," he sets forth a "second deduction": "Language is a vehicle of culture. And anyone who functions in a single or predominant language is almost certainly a product of the culture which that language embodies" (*Acts*, 81).

9    Gerd Lüdemann summarizes the situation when he identifies the Hebrews of Acts 6 as "Aramaic-speaking Christians who were strict observers of the law [and] fell out with Greek-speaking Christians over the question of the law, and the language barrier added a further element to the dispute" (Early Christianity according to the *Traditions in Acts: A Commentary* [Minneapolis: Fortress, 1989], 78–79).

10   Scott, "The Church's Progress to the Council of Jerusalem," 209.

11   Fitzmyer notes that this is the last time the leadership is called the "Twelve." Henceforth Luke refers to them as the "apostles" (Acts 6:6; 8:1, 14, 18; 9:27; 11:1; 14:4, 14; 15:2, 4, 6, 22, 23; 16:4) (*Acts*, 349).

## THE RELIGIOUS AND SOCIAL CHALLENGE OF THE HEBREWS

The critical issue for the Hebrews appears to have been one that would occupy the early church throughout the first century. In particular, the church in Jerusalem and its leadership wrestled with how the newly founded faith in Jesus related to the Judaism of their day. Jesus' constant appeal to the Hebrew Scriptures, his words about the restoration of Israel, and the promise of the kingdom firmly welded the vision of the new movement to Judaism. At the same time, Jesus' radical vision of the Father, together with its barrier-breaking effects, called into question the religious status quo. The first believers, then, inherited a vision that, though with deep roots in Judaism, contained progressive elements that launched them in new directions. Thus the burning issue for them might have been this challenge: "How and to what extent can we remain true to the ancient faith while at the same time following the lead of the Spirit enjoined by Jesus?" (see Luke 24:48–51; Acts 1:4–9). The conflict between the Hebrews and the Hellenists in Acts 6 appears to fall along these lines.

This kind of dissonance does not appear to have been present during the earliest days of the church. From all accounts, the first believers saw themselves as squarely within the pale of Judaism. For example, the defection of Judas and the plan for his replacement are anchored in the ancient Scriptures of the Jews (Acts 1:15–26). Their reception of the Holy Spirit was understood to be the end-time fulfillment of the ancient prophecy of Joel (Acts 2:1–21). In what can be considered the first Christian sermon, Peter grounds every point in Old Testament imagery (Acts 2:22–39). Everything they experienced and said reinforced the notion that they were simply Judaism on the move. This notion was further strengthened by what the Hebrews practiced religiously, meeting daily for the seasons of prayer in the temple.

The miracle story of Acts 3:1–8 sets forth these aspects of continuity and discontinuity between the Hebrews and first-century Judaism. Here Luke is careful to assert that each day the early believers met in the temple, participating in the prayers, sacrifices, and services (Acts 2:46, 5:42). Adherence to this time-honored Jewish regimen of prayer set the stage for a dramatic healing in the temple, as recorded in Acts 3:1–8. Here the phrases "they went up" and "at the ninth hour" (v. 1, KJV) support the historical accuracy of Luke. The temple was elevated both spatially and conceptually, being "high and lifted up" on a hill but also elevated in the mind of every devout Jew (Isa 6:1; cf. 38:22). The ninth hour of prayer (i.e., 3:00 p.m.) was the time of the evening *Tamid* sacrifice, a continual burnt offering venerated by Jews since the time of Moses (Exod 29:39, 41; Num 28:3–4; Ezek 46:13–15; Dan 9:21; Jdt 9:1; Josephus, *Ant.* 14.65). As Peter and John approach the "temple gate called Beautiful" (v. 2), the charismatic presence of the risen Lord is exercised through his church. A lame beggar is healed and leaps for joy in the temple courts, graphically fulfilling the eschatological imagery of Isaiah that "then will the lame leap like a deer" (Isa 35:6).[12] The major issue here is that as leaders of "the Hebrews," Peter and John actively take part in the Jewish cult, celebrating times of prayer and sacrifice within the temple precincts. The religious implications are that as leaders of the Hebrews, Peter and John still view themselves as adherents to the

---

12  Whether the "Beautiful Gate" is the Nicanor Gate, separating the outer court of the Gentiles from the court of the women, or the Corinthian Gate, of artistically worked bronze, is of no real import for the story (Josephus, *J.W.* 5.201). Witherington sides with the Nicanor Gate, but Bruce admits that we cannot be certain what gate Luke means. In any case, the "Beautiful Gate" signaled a barrier between the court of the Gentiles and the court of the women. An additional barrier separated the latter from the inner court, i.e., the court of Israel, where only male Jewish worshipers were allowed (Witherington, *Acts*, 174; F. F. Bruce, *The Book of Acts* [Grand Rapids: Eerdmans, 1988], 27).

# Ground Plan of Herod's Temple

religion of Israel.

Thus the apostles and their constituency, the Hebrews, clearly understood themselves to be part and parcel with the faith of their birth, and it seemed that their dramatic new life in Jesus the messiah in no way threatened their place in Judaism.[13] At this stage in the church's development, the relationship between the Hebrews and Judaism was seamless, and they were "enjoying the favor of all the people" (Acts 2:42).

Yet the miracle of Acts 3 points in another direction as well. Not all the people rejoiced in the empowerment of Peter and John and in the use of their power. The fact that Peter and John and, soon after, all of the apostles were arrested and imprisoned by the Sanhedrin proves that not all the people favored the church and its preaching that Jesus was the messiah (4:1–22; 5:17–40).

The connection between the first believers and their Jewish contemporaries, then, was certainly not trouble free. In spite of Luke's idyllic scene, there is evidence that some tension had been in place since Pentecost. The fact that the church had to embark upon the liquidation of personal assets to meet the financial and material needs of the community did not bode well (2:44–45; 4:34–35). The economic crisis of the early believers meant that they had to take care of their own widows (6:1–6). This raises the question why they were not able to partake of the common social welfare program administered out of the temple. Could this mean that the first Hebrew believers were being ostracized from the Jewish community at large and had to fend for themselves? Admittedly, such reading between the lines lacks certainty, but by Acts 8 a massive rift between the church and Judaism erupts, and it is not unreasonable to assume that fault lines were in place before this time.

It may have been that, for the Hebrews, the

pressure from without was soon accompanied by tension from within. Their tiff with the Hellenists in Acts 6:1–6 may indicate that the Hebrews sought to steer a middle course between Judaism and the more innovative aspects of the Hellenists. As noted, this middle course may have allowed the Hebrews to escape the first wave of open persecution of the church, as set forth in Acts 8:1–4.

## PETER AND THE CORNELIUS EPISODE

Elements of this possible middle course are still present in Acts 10. A careful study of the Cornelius episode in this chapter shows that even after the scattering of the Hellenists in Acts 8, the religious inertia of the Hebrews was still in place.[14] It appears that the mind-set among some of the Hebrews was that of *Jubilees* 22:16, which states, "Keep yourself separate from the nations, and do not eat with them; and do not imitate their rites, nor associate yourself with them." Ultimately, the encounter between Peter and Cornelius the centurion would change all this.

The prayer life of Peter and Cornelius follows the pattern of devout Jews of the first century, with visions and revelations coming at the sixth and ninth hours. Jewish devotional practice, however, is not the main concern here. Rather, the critical element is that Peter, after all that he had experienced and taught about Christ and the faith, still held on to some ethnocentric, particularizing aspects of Judaism.[15] He still cherished the rites and practices that convey Jewish privi-

---

13  See Dunn, *Acts*, 40; and Scott, "*The Church's Progress to the Council of Jerusalem*," 209.

14  See David S. Dockery, "Acts 6–12: The Christian Mission beyond Jerusalem," *RevExp* 87 (2001): 423–37, esp. 431.

15  The ambivalence toward Jews in Luke–Acts, at times lauding Jews and at others denigrating them, is the subject of much debate. Joseph B. Tyson contends that much of this mixed review of Jews by Luke can be explained if the recipient of his works was a Gentile "Godfearer." He believes that the centurions of Luke 7 and Acts 10 symbolize the mind-set of Theophilus, a Gentile who was both attracted to and repulsed by aspects of Judaism ("Jews and Judaism in Luke–Acts: Reading as a Godfearer," *NTS* 41 [1995]: 19–38, esp. 20–22, 25).

**Aerial view of the Roman amphitheater, Caesarea Maritima. The Jewish historian Josephus left a detailed description of Caesarea.**

lege, separation from Gentiles, and nationalism. For Peter and, as will be seen, for many of the Hebrews, the cardinal principles of Judaism, in particular circumcision and purity regulations (Lev 11; Deut 14), instilled a kind of religious inertia that caused them to lag behind the more progressive elements of the church. The extent of this inertia in the life of Peter can be seen in the extraordinary events required to overcome it. Nothing short of a supernatural vision was needed to get Peter, the apostle to the Hebrews, to move in new directions.

Three times the heavens are opened, revealing a tarp full of clean and unclean animals, the Lord commanding the entranced Peter to kill and eat them (Acts 10:11–16). Peter resists the divine injunction on all occasions, claiming that nothing unclean has ever entered his mouth (10:10–16). Peter judges that the clean animals have been rendered unfit because they have come in contact with the unclean. By extension, he, being a devout Jew (clean), will not become defiled by coming in contact with an uncircumcised Gentile (unclean).[16] These religious traditions were designed to regulate the contact between Jews and Gentiles (cf. 1 Macc 1:62–63), and so the thrice-repeated vision is perfectly employed for the intended affect, that is, to move Peter beyond kosher laws so that he may realize that no person is unclean, even if that person is an uncircumcised Gentile.[17] Through divine revelation, Peter comes to understand that the ethnocentric aspects of first-century Judaism are not to be the pattern for the church. In this way Peter serves as a living paradigm of those Hebrews who were able to break loose from certain ancestral customs that might inhibit the spread of the gospel.

Nevertheless, the impact of Peter's breakthrough is dampened in at least two ways. First, the resistance to full incorporation of the Gentiles is much broader and deeper than that of one person, Peter. Second, as Acts 11 and 15 will show, Peter is no longer the undisputed head of the church in Jerusalem. That honor has now fallen to James, and he proves to be very sensitive to believing Jews who still cherish the law of Moses as the pattern for life and faith.

## THOSE OF THE CIRCUMCISION

Addressing the first issue, Luke subtly reveals that the group that went with Peter to Cornelius's house was not all of the same mind. He mentions that "the circumcised believers" were among the entourage that Peter took along (Acts 10:45). Since all the Jews who went to the house were circumcised, this phrase must represent a specialized subset of the Hebrews.[18] These persons "were astonished" to see that the Gentiles had received the Holy Spirit, their skepticism being overcome only by the manifestation of Spirit-inspired glossolalia (10:46; cf. also 2:4).[19] If "the circumcised believers" are of the same type who came from Judea, stirring up trouble in Antioch, and continued their protest in the church at Jerusalem (cf. 15:1, 8), then their identity becomes clearer. At least some of them are Pharisees who have made some claim upon the newborn faith yet still mandate the "custom taught by Moses" (15:1) for inclusion in the community. For them, Judaism is the primary religious paradigm for salvation regardless of the person and work of Jesus and the universal outpouring of the Spirit. For them, Gentiles must first become Jews, that is, be circumcised and obey the law of Moses, if they hope to be saved.

Even here, however, "the circumcised believers" do not represent a completely homogeneous group. There appears to be a theological spectrum here as well. Some accept the expansion of grace to uncircumcised Gentiles, as set forth in Acts 10. On the other hand, upon his return to Jerusalem, Peter has to vigorously defend his actions

---

16   Mikeal C. Parsons claims that the conjunction "and" (Gk. *kai* [καί]) in the phrase "nothing defiled and unclean" (Acts 10:14) marks a qualitative distinction between "defiled" and "unclean." "Defiled" refers to a Jew who has come in contact with Gentiles, whereas "unclean" refers to the Gentiles themselves, who are unclean by nature (" 'Nothing Defiled AND Unclean': The Conjunction's Function in Acts 10:14," *PRSt* 27 [2001]: 264, 266, 271). Dunn comments that "Peter here is portrayed as through and through loyal to his ancestral traditions" (*Acts*, 137).

17   The present middle form of the word *katalambanomai* (καταλαμβάνομαι) in Acts 10:34 speaks of the gradual illumination of Peter's self-awareness concerning the full inclusion of non-Jews as the people of God. Scott renders this passage, "I am in the process, just now, of coming to realize for myself" (*"The Church's Progress to the Council of Jerusalem,"* 213).

18   The phrase "those of the circumcision" (*hoi ek peritomēs* [οἱ ἐκ περιτομῆς]) appears to be a semitechnical term for Luke, referring to Jews who emphasize the primacy of the law of Moses and circumcision. As will be seen, this same expression will be used to identify Jews who protest the inclusion of uncircumcised Gentiles in the church (Acts 11:2).

19   Luke commonly uses the word *existēmi* (ἐξίστημι) to describe how "amazed" persons were who witnessed the miracles of the early church (Acts 2:7, 12; 3:10; 8:13). The word literally means "to stand out of oneself."

Remains of the Roman port of Caesarea Maritima, where Peter met the centurion Cornelius.

before this group, as seen in 11:1–18. These persons condemn Peter for entering into the house of an unclean Gentile and eating with him (cf. 2 Macc 5:27). Eventually Peter wins over this pocket of resistance by way of his fourfold testimony.[20] Yet it also appears that even then some of those who had been circumcised were so recalcitrant as to disqualify themselves from bearing the name of Christ altogether. These radicals, who traveled from Judea to Antioch (Acts 15:1), evidently claiming to be sent by James (Gal 2:12), indicted the Gentile believers there and intimidated Peter to revert to his separatist ways (Gal 2:12). For these reasons, Paul labels these troublemakers from "the circumcision group" as "false brothers" (Gal 2:4, 12).

## JAMES, THE JERUSALEM COUNCIL OF ACTS 15, AND THE APOSTLE PAUL

Regarding the second issue, the transition of power from Peter to James, Acts 15 comes into play again. Here James comes across as a colorless celebrity, for Luke has made no effort to establish his credentials as head of the church. Yet his authority is unquestioned throughout Luke's narrative, all submitting to his decrees as set forth in Acts 15 and 21.[21] In both instances, James functions as a mediating voice in the church between the circumcision group, who are zealous for the law, and the law-free gospel to the Gentiles being championed by Paul.[22] In response to the extreme demands of the Pharisees present among the

20   Peter recounts his vision, the vision of Cornelius, and the Pentecost-like experience of the Gentiles, posing a final penetrating question to clinch the argument (Acts 11:4–18) (Parsons, " 'Nothing Defiled AND Unclean,' " 267).

21   Jacob Jervell, *Luke and the People of God: A New Look at Luke–Acts* (Minneapolis: Augsburg, 1972), 185–86.

22   For the view that the Jerusalem council was the defining moment for Jewish Christianity, see Jervell, *The Unknown Paul*, 30–33.

171

Hebrews (Acts 15:1) and the rebuttal presented by Paul and Barnabas (15:4, 12), together with the more extended testimony of Peter where he explicitly says that God had cleansed the hearts of the Gentiles by faith (15:7–11), James gives his authoritative judgment (15:19).[23] Even though James decides that the Hebrews should "not make it difficult for the Gentiles," he mandates several restrictions that Gentiles are expected to follow. These restrictions include abstaining from idolatry, sexual immorality, things strangled, and blood.[24] These guidelines were enacted in order to facilitate fellowship between the Hebrews and the Gentiles in the church. Yet it must be noted that nothing is expected of the Hebrews and everything is laid upon the shoulders of the Gentiles. It is they who must grant utmost respect to the sensibilities of their Jewish brethren. And even though the Gentiles were not forced to become proselytes, they must honor "the customs Moses handed down" (Acts 6:14; 21:21; 26:3; 28:17).

James takes a similar law-affirming tack when he seeks to resolve the conflict in Acts 21. At the close of his third missionary journey, Paul travels to Jerusalem to present the Jewish believers with a gift from the Gentile churches, a collection that he has been coordinating for over a year (Rom 15:31). In place of its grateful reception by the church in Jerusalem, James relates some grave concerns harbored by "many thousands" of believing Jews who are "zealous for the law" (Acts 21:20).[25] A rumor has been spread among them that proves to be more grievous than the concerns of Acts 15. It has been said that Paul is prohibiting *Jews* from circumcising their children and is telling them that they should forsake the law of Moses, together with all of its customs (Acts 21:21).

"Zealous for the law" is a loaded phrase and in need of some explication. The joining of zeal for the law and the supposed pollution of the Gentiles in Acts 21 brings to mind the militant "zeal" of Phinehas, who killed a fellow Jew for consorting with a Gentile (Num 25:7–12). Philo noted this kind of politicized zeal: "There are thousands who are zealots for the laws, strictest guardians of the ancestral customs, merciless to those who do anything to subvert them" (*Spec. Laws* 2.253). Such zeal led Paul, before his conversion to Christ, to murder Stephen and to try to destroy the church (Acts 7:58–8:3; 1 Cor 15:9; Gal 1:13, 23). Indeed, at this time, "zeal for the law" in light of Gentile encroachment into Jewish affairs was quite high (cf. Josephus, *Ant.* 20.160–161, 167–170). An uncomfortable silence and a disturbing inactivity characterize the Hebrew Christians when Paul falls into the hands of murderous zealots, as described in Acts 21:30–31.

At any rate, James once again seeks to steer a middle course between the Hebrews who are zealous for the law and Paul's ministry to the Gentiles. His plan is to have Paul take a Nazarite vow together with four other Hebrews and to pay all of the expenses incurred.[26] The

---

23 In effect, James agrees with Peter that the Gentiles should not be required to bare the "yoke" of the law, a burden that he contends no one has borne to divine satisfaction (Acts 15:10).

24 In this instance, James may be reflecting what came to be known in Jewish tradition as the Noahide laws, first explicitly presented in the *Tosefta* of the late second century C.E. The Noahides are considered to be the children of Noah (i.e., Gentiles), and the Noahide laws consist of seven moral mandates that are universally binding upon all humankind. These mandates reject idolatry, sexual immorality, and the consumption of blood. On the origin and content of the Noahide laws, see David Novak, *The Image of the Non-Jew in Judaism: An Historical and Constructive Study of the Noahide Laws* (New York: Edwin Mellen, 1983), esp. 3–35.

25 Dunn thinks that the gift was rejected by the church in Jerusalem because it had been "tainted" by Paul's shameful disrespect for the law of Moses (*Acts*, 284). But Bruce reminds us that Paul was being careful to follow the admonition of the leaders of the church in Jerusalem that he should "remember the poor" (Gal 2:10). Why would James reject something that he had exhorted Paul to do earlier on (*Acts*, 404)?

26 What Paul is being asked to do is no small matter. The stipulations of the vow are set forth in Num 6:1–21. After a period of purification for seven days, the participant was to offer one male lamb, one ewe lamb, and one ram together with accompanying food and drink offerings. The hair was not to be cut for the entire period of the vow, after which it was shorn and presented in the temple as an offering

purpose of this compromise is to prove that Paul is not a hater of the law of Moses and that rumors to this effect are false.

Some scholars doubt that Paul would have agreed to James's request, considering his disdain for certain religious rituals, so clearly expressed in the Epistle to the Galatians. Yet we must not forget how pragmatic and adaptable Paul was willing to become in order to further the gospel. He would often accommodate the concerns of many different groups so that he might present the gospel to them all (1 Cor 9:19–21).

In the end, however, all of the efforts of James and the willingness of Paul come to naught. Some Diaspora Jews, of the politically zealous kind, cry out in the temple that Paul "teaches all men everywhere against our people and our law and this place," and that he has brought Gentiles into the Court of Israel (Acts 21:28–29). Paul is seized upon, beaten, falls into the custody of a Roman centurion, and ceases to be a free man for the rest of the book of Acts (21:31–33). According to Luke, the malice of the Jews who were zealous for the law followed him even while he was in chains. When Paul arrived in Rome as a prisoner, one of his first acts was to call for the leaders of the Jews and to defend himself against the charge that he has profaned Moses and the law (28:17–29).

In summary, just as was the case at the Jerusalem council in Acts 15, James's compromise requires nothing from the Hebrews but everything from Paul and those who promote a law-free mission to the Gentiles.

James sides with Hebrews whose vision is still defined by their interpretation and application of the law of Moses. Even at this relatively late date in the development of the apostolic church, James strives to maintain the Judaic character of the Christian faith.

## SUMMARY

The original apostles, all Jewish, were empowered by a Jewish messiah and were granted the mandate to restore the lost sheep of Israel. These Hebrew believers established their headquarters in Jerusalem, the capital of the Jews, and formed the core of the mother church. The major ideological challenge of the church during this period was how to interpret the radical and dynamic vision of its founder within the framework of historic Judaism. This challenge became even more acute when by 50 C.E. the *Hebraioi* became a numerical minority in the church.[27] Yet they were empowered to establish the thought, practice, and preaching of the early church, and so this thoroughly Jewish core set the agenda for the first generation of Christians. It may well be that James's decisions in Acts 15 and 21, Paul's confrontation with Peter in Gal 2, and the running battle Paul fought against the Judaizers throughout his career all point to the competing ideology of the Hebrews vis-à-vis that of the Hellenists.

---

27   On how quickly the Gentiles became a majority in the church, see Jervell, *The Unknown Paul*, 26–33.

# Annotated Bibliography

Dunn, James D. G. *The Acts of the Apostles*. Valley Forge, Pa.: Trinity Press International, 1996. Containing solid biblical exegesis from a leading British scholar, this work is intended for the English-speaking reader and does not require knowledge of Greek. It includes a thorough introduction, and its lucid style and order communicate to beginners.

Fitzmyer, Joseph. *The Acts of the Apostles: A New Translation with Introduction and Commentary*. New York: Doubleday, 1998. Fitzmyer provides a balanced commentary on the book of Acts with a fresh translation from the original Greek texts. He gives attention to textual variants in the manuscript tradition, and the significance of the Dead Sea Scrolls is brought to bear on this important work. This is the work of an accomplished scholar capable of aiding informed students of the Bible.

Gonzâlez, Justo L. "Reading from My Bicultural Place: Acts 6:1–7." Pages 139–48 in *Reading from This Place: Social Location and Biblical Interpretation in the United States*. Edited by Fernando F. Segovia and Mary Ann Tolbert. Minneapolis: Fortress, 1995. Gonzâlez employs a sociocultural hermeneutic that seeks to move away from a traditional Western European interpretation of the text. It views the Bible as the product of writers who have been molded by their social and historical contexts and posits that no interpretation is complete if it does not permit the cultural voice of the interpreter to come through.

Novak, David. *The Image of the Non-Jew in Judaism: An Historical and Constructive Study of the Noahide Laws*. New York: Edwin Mellen, 1983. The rabbinic reduction of the law to seven moral and religious principles that are universally binding upon all, the so-called Noahide laws, is traced historically from rabbinic times to the present day through meticulous research. The theme of how Jews related to Gentiles throughout history is interwoven throughout the book. Although the reader may experience the feeling of being given too much information on the subject, by the end of the work a general understanding of Jewish philosophy throughout the ages will be obtained.

Witherington, Ben, III. *The Acts of the Apostles: A Socio-rhetorical Commentary*. Grand Rapids: Eerdmans, 1998. This comprehensive treatment of Acts seeks to demonstrate both the historical reliability of Luke and his literary genius. Close work with the original Greek together with detailed documentation from the primary and secondary sources makes this book an excellent reference tool for the serious student of Acts.

# 12

# The Hellenists— Cultures in Transition

## INTRODUCTION: WORD STUDY AND IDENTIFICATION

A critical question of New Testament scholarship is how a thoroughly Jewish messianic movement made the transition to a predominantly Gentile church within a period of only ten years. More precisely, how did a renewal movement that began within first-century Judaism quickly transcend the concerns of Israel and embrace the known world?

In addressing this issue, a primary assertion is that there is a "substantial coherence"

Stone inscription from the balustrade wall around the Temple prohibiting non-Jewish persons from entering the inner courts. It reads: "No foreigner is to enter within the forecourt and the balustrade around the sanctuary. Whoever is caught will have himself to blame for his subsequent death."

between the person and work of Jesus and the first believers of the church.[1] This continuity between founder and followers logically points to a link between the two. The precise nature (historical or ideological?) and mechanism (direct dependence or redacted tradition?) whereby this link was established is, however, open to question. Rephrasing the issue, if the vision of Jesus was confined to "the lost sheep of Israel" (Matt 10:5–6), how did this vision quickly develop into a multilingual, international movement that, within a very short period of time, became predominantly Gentile in its makeup?

The fractious nature of Israel at the time of Jesus may have facilitated such a transition rather than hindered it. The polarization of Jewish society into groups with competing ideologies once again demonstrates that Judaism was anything but monolithic in the first century. Such pluralism may have provided a context for the generative ideals of Jesus to take root and develop in a way that transcended traditional categories in Judaism. It is possible that early Christian Hellenists (NIV, "Grecian Jews"), first mentioned in Acts 6:1, served as a bridge joining the vision of Jesus and that of an expansive church, one that quickly went beyond categories that defined first-century Judaism.

The quest for a link between the historical Jesus and the early church has often been framed in terms of how Jesus may or may not relate to the Apostle Paul.[2] The premise here is that substantial similarities between great religious figures of the same era can hardly be attributed to mere chance and

coincidence.[3] It is at this point that the Hellenists as first encountered in Acts 6 and 7 come into play. Of all the groups on the scene at the dawn of the early church, the Hellenists are likely to have served as the most direct pathway joining the early church with Jesus. Furthermore, the Hellenists may well have been the bridge not only between Jesus and Paul but also to a wider world, one that went beyond the traditional confines of first-century Judaism.[4]

The sudden appearance of two distinct groups in Acts 6:1–6, one called the Hellenists and the other the Hebrews (NIV, "Hebraic Jews"), comes as a shock to the discerning reader.[5] These two groups represent the first rending of the apparently seamless unity of the church as set forth in Acts 1–5.[6] The unity that Luke has consistently portrayed by way of his "with one accord" theme in Acts 1:14; 2:1, 46; 4:24; 5:12 has abruptly come

---

1   E. P. Sanders, *Jesus and Judaism* (Philadelphia: Fortress, 1985), 231. Cf. also Robin Scroggs, "The Earliest Christian Communities as Sectarian Movement," in *Christianity, Judaism and Other Greco-Roman Cults: Studies for Morton Smith at Sixty* (ed. Jacob Neusner; Leiden: E. J. Brill, 1975), 8.

2   See William A. Simmons, *A Theology of Inclusion in Jesus and Paul: The God of Outcasts and Sinners* (Lewiston, N.Y.: Edwin Mellen, 1996).

3   Geza Vermes, *Jesus the Jew: A Historian's Reading of the Gospel* (London: Collins, 1973), 78. "There is, after all, a considerable *a priori* plausibility in the working hypothesis that there was *some* bridge between Jesus and Paul, some group of individuals through whom at least some of the Jesus-tradition was mediated to Paul whether we specify the Hellenists in particular, or include also Peter (Gal 1:18) and other unnamed disciples" (James D. G. Dunn, *Jesus, Paul, and the Law: Studies in Mark and Galatians* [Louisville: John Knox, 1990], 12).

4   For a detailed discussion of the Hellenists and how they may have served as a bridge, see Heikki Räisänen, "The 'Hellenists'—a Bridge between Jesus and Paul?" pages 242–306 in *Torah and Christ: Essays in German and English on the Problem of the Law in Early Christianity* (Helsinki: Finnish Exegetical Society, 1986), esp. 245.

5   "Without warning, 'the whole group . . . of one heart and soul' who pooled their resources to insure that 'there was not a needy person among them' (4:32, 34) becomes two groups—Hebrews and Hellenists—embroiled in conflict arising from the neglect of certain needy persons in the community: Hellenist widows" (F. Scott Spencer, "Neglected Widows in Acts 6:1–7," *CBQ* 50 [2001]: 715).

6   J. Julius Scott Jr., "The Church's Progress to the Council of Jerusalem according to the Book of Acts," *BBR* 7 (1997): 209.

Restored remains of the Hellenistic Jewish synagogue of the Diaspora at Sardis, Asia Minor.

to an end.[7] A more precise inquiry into the nature of this dispute may shed light on the identity of the Hellenists.

There are two main possibilities for the meaning of the Greek word *hellēnistai*, "Hellenists," in Acts 6: it could mean Gentiles, or it could refer to Jews of the Diaspora who spoke Greek rather than Aramaic or Hebrew.[8] If the term refers to Greek-speaking Jews of the Diaspora, is the distinction purely linguistic, or are there cultural, philosophical, and theological differences as well? And if ideological differences are part and parcel with the identity of the Hellenists, did these differences lead to a rift between the

Hellenists and the Hebrews in Acts 6?[9]

In engaging these issues, it is helpful to note that each of "the seven" in Acts 6:5 has a Greek name. This has led some scholars to conclude that Gentiles are meant here. Furthermore, in Acts 11:20 the Hellenists are clearly contrasted with the Hebrews, again leading some to conclude that "Hellenists" in Acts 6 means "Gentiles." Yet if uncircumcised Gentiles were entering the church at this time, much of what follows in Acts would be very difficult to understand. For example, the controversy over circumcision did not arise until the conversion of Cornelius in Acts 10, then reached its peak in Acts 11, and subsequently called forth an entire church council in Acts 15.[10] Also, of "the seven"

7 On the social dynamics of Luke's theology, see Philip F. Esler, *Community and Gospel in Luke–Acts: The Sociological and Political Motivations of Lucan Theology* (SNTSMS 57; Cambridge: Cambridge University Press, 1987), esp. 136–37.

8 For the various meanings of "Hellenists," see H. Windisch, "Ἑλληνιστής," TDNT 2:504–16, esp. 511; C. Craig Hill, *Hellenists and Hebrews: Reappraising Division within the Earliest Church* (Minneapolis: Fortress, 1992), 24; and Francis Watson, *Paul, Judaism, and the Gentiles: A Sociological Approach* (SNTSMS 56; Cambridge: Cambridge University Press, 1986), 27.

9 For a list of scholars who see ideological and theological issues lying behind Acts 6:1–7, see Spencer, "Neglected Widows," 716 n. 3. For feminists' renderings of the passage, see 718 n. 10.

10 For a classic study, see C. F. D. Moule, "Once More, Who Were the Hellenists?" *ExpTim* 70 (1958–1959): 100–102. Cf. also Stephen G. Wilson, *The Gentiles and the Gentile Mission in Luke–Acts* (SNTSMS 23; Cambridge: Cambridge University Press, 1973), 129.

Nicolaus alone is singled out, being described as a "proselyte" from Antioch. This is Luke's way of indicating that Nicolas is different from the rest of the group. He was not a Jew by birth or a resident of Judea. The implication is that the rest of "the seven" were Jews by birth and might have called Judea their home. Finally, if the Hellenists of Acts 6:1 were Gentiles, why did the Hellenists initially preach only to Jews when they were scattered as a result of the persecution of Stephen (Acts 11:19)? Surely they would have felt the freedom to offer the gospel to their own kind.

For these reasons, the Hellenists of Acts 6 do not appear to be Gentiles, but rather are Greek-speaking Jews of the Diaspora who came to settle in Palestine and had been recently converted to Christianity.[11] First-century archaeology and demographics also lend support to this conclusion. Many Jews of the Diaspora returned to Palestine and organized their own synagogues there (Acts 6:9; 9:29).[12] Indeed, one-third of all the inscriptions on ossuaries—boxes containing bones of the deceased—of the Second Temple period are in Greek, with an additional portion written in Greek and Hebrew. This may indicate that as many as ten to fifteen thousand inhabitants of Jerusalem could speak Greek, not counting the hundreds of thousands of Diaspora Jews visiting during the great religious festivals.[13] Since

many dedicated Jews of the Diaspora would immigrate to Israel in their later years with the expectation of being buried in the holy city, taking care of their widows may have put a special strain upon the early church. And if a number of these Hellenistic Jews converted to the faith even as early as Pentecost (Acts 2:41), then the care of Greek-speaking widows may have been a part of the ministry of the church from the very beginning. It is clear that the care of the widows is at the heart of the contention in Acts 6.[14]

The critical issue, however, is whether the distinction between the Hellenists and the Hebrews should be confined to linguistic differences only. In other words, do the Hellenists have a different ideology and/or theology from that of the Hebrews?[15]

The data obtained from the first century are varied and lead in divergent directions. For example, the diversity in ancient Judaism is reflected in substantial differences between various Jewish factions, ranging from the Zealot-like program of the Maccabeans to the Hellenistic syncretism seen among some later Hasmoneans, including the differences between the Pharisees and the Sadducees. Thus the notion that such differences might exist among the Hebrews and Hellenists of Acts 6 is not implausible. Again, some syncretism can be seen in the need for the LXX

---

11   Regarding the number of Jews in the Diaspora in the first century, accurate numbers are not at hand. Philo speaks of not less than a million Jews dwelling in Alexandria and North Africa in the first century (*Flaccus* 43). Josephus speaks of more than eight thousand resident Jews in Rome and four thousand who were expelled under Tiberius (*J.W.* 2.80; *Ant.* 18.83–84; cf. also Tacitus, *Ann.* 2.85). He also notes that three thousand wealthy Jews were slaughtered in Cyrene after the fall of Jerusalem in 70 C.E. (*J.W.* 7.445). Thus the number of Jews living outside Israel in the first century was enormous.

12   Emil Schürer, *The History of the Jewish People in the Age of Jesus Christ (175 B.C.–A.D. 135)* (rev. and ed. Geza Vermes, Furgus Millar, and Matthew Black; 3 vols. in 4; Edinburgh: T&T Clark, 1973–1987), 2:76.

13   Cf. Martin Hengel, *Between Jesus and Paul: Studies in the Earliest History of Christianity* (Philadelphia: Fortress, 1983), 6–7, 55.

14   Spencer argues that the neglect of the widows in Acts 6 is not an isolated "snap shot" but reflective of a larger "widow theme" in Luke. He points to scenes that include Anna (Luke 2:36–38), the widow of Nain (Luke 4:18–21), the persistent widow (Luke 18:1–8), the poor widow (Luke 21:1–4), and the neglected widows (Acts 6:1–6) ("Neglected Widows," 719, 728).

15   On those who claim that the Hellenists are ideologically and theologically different from the Hebrews, see Justo L. González, "Reading from My Bicultural Place: Acts 6:1–7," in *Reading from this Place: Social Location and Biblical Interpretation in the United States* (ed. Fernando F. Segovia and Mary Ann Tolbert; Minneapolis: Fortress, 1995), esp. 142. For a differing view, see Hill, *Hellenists and Hebrews*, 24, 30, 49; Hengel, *Between Jesus and Paul*, 9, 14, 55; and Esler, *Community and Gospel*, 139.

**The Lion Gate, or St. Stephen's Gate, Jerusalem, traditional site of the martyrdom of Stephen.**

and in the incorporation of Greek terms such as *gerousia* ("council of elders") and *archontes* ("rulers") into the synagogue (cf. Philo, *Flaccus* 76). Graffiti from the second and third centuries B.C.E. speak of Jews worshiping at the shrines of Greek and Egyptian gods, and Josephus notes those Jews who promoted the religious oppression of Antiochus IV (*J.W.* 7.50–51).[16] The accommodation of priests in the temple to the Greek gymnasium and the desire to mask the rite of circumcision indicate the influence of Hellenism among the Jews of the Diaspora and among some who resided in Jerusalem (*Ant.* 12:241; 1 Macc 1:15; 2 Macc 4:7–16). That residents of Shechem would appeal to Antiochus to make Zeus the patron god of their city is of interest here as well (*Ant.* 12.257–264). Synagogues within the bounds of Israel and dating to as early as the first century C.E. are adorned with Greco-Roman symbols such as cupids, griffins, eagles, and the sign of the Capricorn.[17] Inscriptions from first-century Jewish synagogues of the Bosporus may also give evidence of religious syncretism in this sector of the Diaspora. One inscription recording the dedication of a slave in the synagogue ends with

16   See Margaret H. Williams, ed., *The Jews among the Greeks and Romans: A Diasporan Sourcebook* (Baltimore: Johns Hopkins University Press, 1998), esp. 116–30.

17   For examples, see Erwin R. Goodenough, *Jewish Symbols in the Graeco-Roman Period* (13 vols.; New York: Pantheon, 1953–1968), 12:42, 132–81.

179

the words "by Zeus, Ge, Helios" (*CIRB* 1123).[18] In addition, Philo adopted the allegorical interpretation of the Alexandrians, rendering much of the Hebrew Scriptures in symbolic terms (*Allegorical Interpretation* 1.1). He emphasizes the spiritual meaning of circumcision (*Spec. Laws* 1.6, 9–10) and argues that Moses' teaching about the Sabbath is reflected in natural law (*Moses* 2.21–22; *On the Cherubim* 87). Indeed, for Philo, the law of Moses is reflected in the law of all other nations (*Moses* 2.25), and Plato is "the sweetest of all writers," who truly understood the nature of wisdom (*Good Person*, 13).[19]

These examples demonstrate a modus vivendi among some Diaspora Jews whereby they accommodated, absorbed, and adopted beliefs and practices of their Gentile neighbors.[20] This may have made some Hellenistic Jews in the church more open to share the gospel with uncircumcised Gentiles than were their Palestinian Hebrew counterparts.

On the other hand, it should not be forgotten that the Jews in Jerusalem who persecuted Stephen were Hellenists (Acts 9:29). The archenemy of the fledgling church was Saul of Tarsus, a Hellenist. And once Saul joined the very people he persecuted, he in turn was persecuted by Hellenistic Jews throughout the Mediterranean world (Acts 13:50; 14:2; 17:5; 18:12; 21:27–32; 2 Cor 11:26). It would be a mistake to think that all Hellenists were extreme syncretists having no special regard for historical Jewish teachings and practices. The great pilgrimages to Jerusalem and the payment of the half-shekel temple tax show the intense fidelity of many Diaspora Jews to Judaism (Josephus, *Ant.* 16:167–168, 172–173). Endorsement of a freewheeling syncretism, then, proves to be incompatible with the very concept of the Diaspora. Faithfulness to their religion is what maintained the distinctive identity of the Jews in their non-Jewish contexts. This was the way generations of Jews had resisted assimilation into Gentile culture, all the while speaking Greek as their first language.

Nonetheless, some Jews of the Diaspora did lighten Torah requirements as a matter of practicality. Perhaps the most famous example is the conversion of King Izates of Adiabene to Judaism. Josephus records that the requirement of circumcision was initially waved for the king in order to make his conversion more amenable, although ultimately the king decided on his own to be circumcised (*Ant.* 20.38–48).[21]

In light of the evidence, it would be wise not to opt for a simple dichotomy between Hellenistic Jews and Palestinian Jews. Such a view does not seem representative of the full range of Jewish expression in the first century. Perhaps the best approach is to look at individual groups within a diverse context and draw inferences from their differences.[22] One inference that presents itself, especially regarding Acts 6, is that diversity within a generally identifiable group such as the Jews can lead to a considerable dissonance among its members. Thus the conflict between *Christian* Hellenists such as Stephen and his

---

18   See also Seth Schwartz, "The Hellenization of Jerusalem and Shechem," in *Jews in a Graeco-Roman World* (ed. Martin Goodman; Oxford: Clarendon, 1998), 37–45.

19   For the Hellenizing tendencies of Philo, see Alan Segal, *Paul the Convert: The Apostolate and the Apostasy of Saul the Pharisee* (New Haven: Yale University Press, 1990), 92; cf. also 85.

20   For the notion that the Noahide laws might evidence how some Diaspora Jews negotiated life among the Gentiles, see David Novak, *The Image of the Non-Jew in Judaism: An Historical and Constructive Study of the Noahide Laws* (New York: Edwin Mellen, 1983), xvii.

21   See N. J. McEleney, "Conversion, Circumcision, and the Law," NTS 20 (1974): 319–41; and John Stambaugh and David Balch, *The Social World of the First Christians* (London: SPCK, 1986), 47–48.

22   Marinus de Jonge claims that the pluralism of first-century Judaism means that we cannot speak of what is typical of Diaspora or Palestinian Judaism. One must concentrate on specific groups and seek to isolate distinct ideas originating with each group (*Christology in Context: The Earliest Christian Response to Jesus* [Philadelphia: Westminster, 1988], 27).

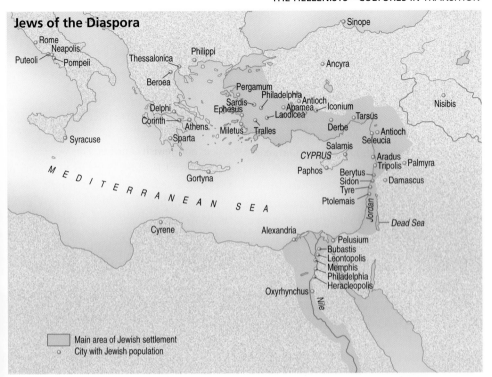

Jews of the Diaspora

- Main area of Jewish settlement
- ○ City with Jewish population

followers and *non-Christian* Hellenists such as Saul is what one might expect in the early church. Furthermore, this kind of tension could be found within a subgroup as well, as might have been the case with the Hellenists and Hebrews of Acts 6. Since the context of the early church was in flux and was characterized by considerable ambiguity and stress, antipathy between the Hellenists and the Hebrews may have arisen and affected the care of the widows in the church.

Even so, the question still remains: what caused the complaint of the Hellenists in Acts 6? Why were separate leadership teams required to solve the problem (Acts 6:3–6)? Why did the Hellenists become the target of severe persecution (8:1–3) whereas, at this stage of the church's development, the Hebrews were left unscathed? Why did some of the Hellenists feel free to evangelize the Gentiles whereas their Hebrew counterparts took this step only after divine intervention (11:19–20; 10:1–11:18)?

In these questions, something more seems to be at hand than a simple language barrier and the occasional spiritualizing tendencies of some Diaspora Jews. That is, the radical steps that Stephen and like-minded Hellenists embarked upon may be traced to the life and ministry of the historical Jesus.[23] Jesus' openness to outsiders, his table fellowship with outcasts and sinners in the name of God, and his affirmation of the marginalized and disenfranchised birthed an extraordinary vision of God that engendered the transcending of barriers based on ethnicity and tradition. It is likely that this theology of inclusion impelled some of the Hellenists in the early church to go beyond the ethnic and religious boundaries that helped define the Judaism of their day. If this was the case, then the Hellenists' field of evangelism in Jerusalem was virtually at their doorstep. The very existence of the court of the Gentiles in the temple indicates

23  David S. Dockery calls Stephen "both paradigm and pioneer" of the new direction of the church ("Acts 6–12: The Christian Mission beyond Jerusalem," *RevExp* 87 [2001]: 425).

that there were many "God-fearing" Gentiles in the city. Yet they were physically separated from full participation in the cult by the *soreg*, or low wall that divided them from the court of the women, which served as another barrier to the court of Israel.[24] Some of the Hellenists in the church may have surmised that if Jesus made no distinction between the righteous and unrighteous in Israel but offered grace to all, the middle wall of partition should be torn down and the Gentiles allowed in (Eph 2:14).[25]

The question of admitting uncircumcised Gentiles into the church may thus lie at the root of the problem in Acts 6. If so, the alienation of the Hellenists from the Hebrews would have been attributable to theological concerns, not simply differences in language and culture. According to Luke's record, the practical effect of this alienation was that the widows of the Hellenists were not obtaining their fair share of financial relief from the church.[26]

The text is unclear on whether the Hebrews' neglect of the widows was inadvertent or deliberate.[27] But the hardship was severe enough to call forth the executive action of the apostles. Their solution for preserving the integrity of the new movement was to grant the Hellenistic faction in the church its own leadership team.

## STEPHEN AND THE SEVEN
### Stephen's Speech and the Theology of the Hellenists

Even though Luke maintains the prestige of the Jerusalem apostles by allowing them to "appoint" (NRSV) Stephen and the seven, it is clear that they do not simply wait on tables as implied in the text (Acts 6:2).[28] On the contrary, Stephen and the seven embark on a Spirit-empowered ministry launching the church in a radical new direction.[29] It is no accident that immediately after the martyrdom of Stephen, another Hellenist, Philip, ministers among the Samaritans. Philip then goes on to bring the Ethiopian eunuch into the fold. This convert may well be the first uncircumcised Gentile accepted into the church (Acts 8:27–39). It is also no accident that Philip is called an "evangelist" by Luke in Acts 21:8.

Thus Acts 6 may well represent a distinct authoritative group in the church that owes its existence to more than the confusion of languages and a laissez-faire attitude toward the law of Moses vis-à-vis the Gentiles. The theology and practice of the Hellenists appear to have differed from their Hebrews counterparts, and this may have been the reason the Hellenists were singled out for persecution. As Acts 8:1 states, all were affected by a severe persecution "except the apostles." Yet a comparison of Acts 9:26, 31 with 11:1–2 indicates that more than just the apostles were present in Jerusalem

---

24  Any Gentiles beyond the *soreg* and any Jews that brought in Gentiles beyond this point were subject to the most severe penalties, even death (Josephus, *Ant.* 15.417).

25  Even if this scenario is sound, it is still difficult to determine just when the question of accepting Gentiles into the church became an issue. Räisänen speculates that if Gentile God-fearers were present on the day of Pentecost (Acts 2:1–13), then the issue may have arisen very early indeed ("*The 'Hellenists,'*" 285).

26  See J. D. G. Dunn, *Unity and Diversity in the New Testament: An Inquiry into the Character of Earliest Christianity* (Philadelphia: Westminster, 1977), 269.

27  To explain the neglect of the widows of the Hellenists, Dockery looks to the rapid growth of the church and the overwork of the Hebrews ("Acts 6–12," 423). Esler believes that the Hebrews had been deliberately mistreating the widows of the Hellenists by misusing their power over the church's finances (*Community and Gospel*, 142). Gerd Theissen asserts that the Hellenists may have contributed more to the fund than the Hebrews and so this grievance would have been particularly hard to take (*The First Followers of Jesus: A Sociological Analysis of the Earliest Christianity* [London: SCM, 1978], 57).

28  As Moule remarks, the function of the seven was not simply "to organize the dole" ("Once More, Who Were the Hellenists?" 100–101).

29  "It was the cultural outlook and theological emphasis of his [Stephen's] group that helped free the Jerusalem Church to leave its isolationism, to move out as witnesses beyond Jerusalem 'to the end of the earth' (cf. Acts 1:8)" (Scott, "The Church's Progress to the Council of Jerusalem," 210).

**Remains of the Hellenistic synagogue of Gamla, northern Israel.**

phrase "except the apostles," then, more than likely refers to the entire Hebrew-speaking church or "the Hebrews" and not just the apostolic leadership.[30] Again, Acts 11:19–24 continues to represent "those who had been scattered" (cf. 8:1) as dispersed throughout the region, yet "the apostles" are unaffected by the persecution and abide freely in Jerusalem. This seems to indicate that the religious ideology and practice of the Hellenists labeled them as targets whereas the Hebrews were still able to be viewed as being within the pale. But predictably, when the Hebrews adopted the same vision and practice as the Hellenists and affirmed uncircumcised Gentiles as full members of the family of God, they too experienced persecution, including death (12:1–2).

What could have been the shape of the Hellenists' theology at this stage? Luke is less than clear here. But a careful study of Stephen's speech in Acts 7:1–53, the longest address in Acts, may reveal the general contours of what the Hellenists believed. Luke may have

connected the speech and the martyrdom of Stephen to the persecution of the Hellenists for this very reason. That is, the speech and the subsequent murder of Stephen speak to the general persecution of the Hellenists, for Stephen is charged with seeking to undermine the law of Moses and promoting the destruction of the temple (6:13–14).[31] Luke clearly states, however, that the charges are false. Accordingly, a close examination of the speech reveals that Stephen does not present a radical critique of the law or the temple.[32] Still, Stephen's words do reject his opponents'

---

30  On the Hebrews escaping the great persecution of Acts 8, see Wilson, *The Gentiles and the Gentile Mission in Luke–Acts*, 142. For an opposing view, see Craig Hill, "Acts 6.1–8.4: Division or Diversity?" in *History, Literature, and Society in the Book of Acts* (ed. Ben Witherington III; Cambridge: Cambridge University Press, 1996), 138.

31  Hengel concludes that these charges explain why the Hellenists are singled out for persecution: "We can conclude from this that the charges against Stephen which Luke mentions in Acts 6:11, 13 f., 'He does not cease to blaspheme against this holy place and the law,' are not Luke's invention but repeat in abbreviated form the accusation of Pharisaic Jews against this Christian minority; they were persecuted because they dared to criticize the temple and Torah, i.e., the two pillars on which Judaism rested" (*Between Jesus and Paul*, 55, 57). Cf. also Seyoon Kim, *The Origin of Paul's Gospel* (Grand Rapids: Eerdmans, 1981), 44.

32  Dockery believes that Stephen intimated that the law of Moses was transitory and that salvation should be offered to uncircumcised Gentiles ("Acts 6–12," 424). For more on the perspective that Stephen rejects both the law and the temple, see Dennis D. Sylva, "The Meaning and Function of Acts 7:46–50," *JBL* 106 (1987): 261–62, 268.

interpretation of the law and roundly criticize their restrictive use of the temple. He emphasizes the transcendence of God and the communion of God with God's people apart from the temple, especially in the wilderness (Acts 7:48; cf. Isa 66:1). God cannot be housed in permanent structures "made by men." For Stephen, such a view of the temple represents a static confining of God's person and work. For him, this view is in stark contrast to the mobile tabernacle of David that followed after the presence of God; it is, rather, a view of the temple that seeks to capture and control the divine presence. For Stephen, to localize the presence of God is tantamount to worshiping a golden calf (Acts 7:40–41).[33] Stephen also appears to make the connection that a misunderstanding and/or misuse of the temple reflect an improper understanding of God. From another perspective, the theological implications of his speech seem to play down the identity markers so descriptive of Judaism as practiced in Jerusalem during the first century.[34]

### The Hellenists and the Gentile Mission

The reference to those who were "scattered" in Acts 8:1 and 11:19 suggests that the same group of Hellenists is being addressed in both places. That is, they are part and parcel with the Stephenite group, and it may be assumed that they share the theology set forth in Stephen's speech. Regarding missionary practice, it appears that some of them took their cue from Philip's evangelization of Samaria and the Ethiopian eunuch. It was this group that took the paradigm-making step of baptizing Gentile Christians, and they were the first to welcome uncircumcised Gentiles as full members of the people of God. Their belief and practice indicate that the Torah and the temple had been made relative to the theology of Jesus, especially as seen in his inclusion of outsiders. Moreover, it is no accident that the arch-persecutor of the Hellenists, Saul, once he converted to the faith, did not go to Jerusalem to become part of the Hebrews. Rather, he joined the Hellenists in Antioch for the very purpose of promoting Gentile missions (19:25–26). Paul's choice may have been determined by his experience on the Damascus road. That is, the Apostle Paul experienced what the outcasts and sinners experienced when they sat at table with Jesus. By extension, he experienced what the Gentiles experienced when they were accepted as full members of the church by the Hellenists. For these reasons, henceforth Paul would teach and preach what the Hellenists had previously embarked upon, if only in an embryonic form. Paul would give his life in service for the very belief and practice that he had formerly persecuted to the death. He would testify to both the Jews and the Gentiles that "God . . . justifies the wicked" (Rom 4:5).

33   On the idea of the temple restricting the presence of God, see John L. Kilgallen, "The Function of Stephen's Speech (Acts 7:2–53)," *Bib* 70 (1989): 177; Sylva, "The Meaning and Function of Acts 7:46–50," 266; and Edvin Larsson, "Temple-Criticism and the Jewish Heritage: Some Reflections on Acts 6–7," *NTS* 39 (1993): 394. For an opposing view, see Hill, "Acts 6.1–8.4: Division or Diversity?" 150.

34   On Stephen's clarification of the law and temple, see Hill, "Acts 6.1–8.4: Division or Diversity?" 147, 151; and Martin Hengel, *Acts and the History of Earliest Christianity* (Philadelphia: Fortress, 1980), 79, 315.

# Annotated Bibliography

Dunn, James D. G. *Jesus, Paul, and the Law: Studies in Mark and Galatians.* Louisville: John Knox, 1990. This work contains upgraded versions of Dunn's previous essays on the subject, tracing the tensions between Judaism and early Christians concerning the law and the historical Jesus. These tensions were expanded by Paul but not created by him. It offers a thorough orientation to how Jesus and Paul relate vis-à-vis the law.

———. *Unity and Diversity in the New Testament: An Inquiry into the Character of Earliest Christianity.* Philadelphia: Westminster, 1977. Dunn points out that early Christianity was not monolithic in its belief and practice, yet emphasizes that diversity fell within the limits of the unifying confession of the church. This is a good introduction to Jewish, Hellenistic, apocalyptic, and early Catholic thought among the first believers.

Esler, Philip F. *Community and Gospel in Luke–Acts: The Sociological and Political Motivations of Lucan Theology.* Society for New Testament Studies Monograph Series 57. Cambridge: Cambridge University Press, 1987. This is a revised dissertation, technical in its presentation but useful for understanding the social stratification in the early church and how this affected communion among the first followers of Jesus. It includes an excellent discussion of the role of table fellowship among the Jews and how the church struggled with bringing Jews and Gentiles together.

Goodenough, Erwin R. *Jewish Symbols in the Greco-Roman Period.* See description at the end of ch. 1.

Hengel, Martin. *Between Jesus and Paul: Studies in the Earliest History of Christianity.* Philadelphia: Fortress, 1983. This is one of the first works of this magnitude completely dedicated to exploring the religious and social contexts of the time between Jesus and Paul. It contains much useful insight into the Hellenists and the hellenizing tendencies of the first believers.

Hill, C. Craig. *Hellenists and Hebrews: Reappraising Division within the Earliest Church.* Minneapolis: Fortress, 1992. Hill counters the notion that there was an ideological rift between the Hebrews and the Hellenists of Acts 6, that the churches of Antioch and Jerusalem were polarized in their belief and practice, and that the Hellenists serve as a bridge between Jesus and Paul.

Räisänen, Heikki. "The 'Hellenists'—a Bridge between Jesus and Paul?" in *Torah and Christ: Essays in German and English on the Problem of the Law in Early Christianity.* Helsinki: Finnish Exegetical Society, 1986. This is an in-depth study of why the Hellenists, not the Hebrews, were the first to accept uncircumcised Gentiles into the church. "Spiritualizing tendencies" of Diaspora Jews and the eschatological urgency of Jesus come into play here. Though not for the beginner, this work reveals much about how Diaspora Judaism related to the early church.

Williams, Margaret H., ed. See description at the end of ch. 1.

# 13
# Charlatans, Exorcists, and Magicians—the Challenge of Syncretism

## INTRODUCTION

### Magic in the Ancient World

The early church was birthed in a world steeped in religious pluralism. Thus, from the time of its inception, the church was confronted with the task of carving out its unique identity in the midst of competing ideologies. As Christianity made inroads throughout the empire, the threat of religious syncretism loomed large before the first believers. The many gods of the Greco-Roman pantheon, as well as the many mystery religions, threatened to inundate the church (Acts 17:15–23;

**Moses and Aaron before Pharaoh. Many of the miracles performed through them were duplicated by the magicians of Egypt.**

1 Cor 8:5). Not only that, but the gospel message was in constant danger of being buried beneath the weight of Greek rhetoric and philosophy (1 Cor 1:12, 17; Col 2:8).

In the midst of all of these worldviews and, in many cases, existing as an essential aspect of them, was the added challenge of magic. From the time of Moses in Exodus to that of the Apostle John on the Isle of Patmos in Revelation, the saints have been hard pressed to differentiate the power of God from magic (Exod 7:11; Josephus, *Ant.* 2.286).[1] For example, many of the miracles performed through Moses and Aaron were duplicated by the magicians of Egypt (*Exod* 7:8–22; *Ant.* 2.284–285).[2] Indeed, after the Israelites left Egypt, Pharaoh was convinced that Moses was a magician (*Ant.* 2.320). Jesus' enemies charged that his supernatural power came from Satan (Matt 12:24; Mark 3:22; Luke 11:15; John 8:48). The first apostles were

---

1   On the extent of magic in the ancient world, see Edwin Yamauchi, "Magic in the Biblical World," *TynBul* 34 (1983): 169–200; and Meir Bar-Ilan, "Witches in the Bible and in the Talmud," in *Approaches to Ancient Judaism: New Series* (ed. Herbert W. Basser and Simcha Fishbane; Atlanta: Scholars Press, 1990–), 5:7–32, esp. 7.

2   For the interrelationship of ancient Judaism and magic, see Jacob Neusner, "Science and Magic, Miracle and Magic in Formative Judaism: The System and the Difference," in *Religion, Science, and Magic: In Concert and in Conflict* (ed. Jacob Neusner, Ernest Frerichs, and Paul Flesher; Oxford: Oxford University Press, 1989), 61–81, esp. 63–66.

similarly maligned (Acts 4:7). Furthermore, the miracle-working power of the Holy Spirit in the church, together with the display of spiritual gifts among its members, could easily have been seen as just another brand of magic in the ancient world. The graft of Simon Magus (Acts 8:9–11), the subterfuge of Elymas the sorcerer (13:8–41), and the antics of the seven sons of Sceva (19:13–16) are proof enough that magicians and their magic were a factor in the early church.

For the people of the first century, the nature of the problem was obvious: if belief in Egyptian magicians and the like is a sin, then why is belief in Moses and Jesus, who perform similar feats, not a sin as well?[3] These issues require a careful examination of the nature and function of magic in the first century.

## The Origin, Definition, and Nature of Magic

Ancient written sources, including the Bible, indicate that magic is a nearly universal phenomenon throughout history.[4] As noted, the Jews encountered magic from earliest times. Saul consulted the witch of Endor (1 Sam 28:7). Second Kings 9:22 ascribes witchcraft to Jezebel, and Ezek 13:17–23 prophesies against witches.[5] Daniel lived among the magicians in Babylon (Dan 1:20; 2:2, 10, 27; 4:7; 5:7, 11, 15; cf. also *Ant.* 10.195–200, 231–240). Josephus notes that Nebuchadnezzar and Belshazzar consulted magicians to interpret dreams and visions (*Ant.* 10.195–200, 231–240). Despite prohibitions in Scripture

(Exod 22:18; Deut 18:10–12; Lev 19:26), some Jews continued to practice magic. The battle against religious syncretism was all too real for the Hebrews, as seen in the occult practices of King Manasseh (2 Kgs 21:2–6). Josephus records that one posing as a magician enticed Drusilla to leave her husband for Felix (*Ant.* 20.142). Elymas (or Bar-Jesus)

**Sculpted figure of the multi-breasted Artemis (Diana) from Ephesus.**

---

3   For the confusion between magic and miracle in the first century, see Susan R. Garrett, "Light on a Dark Subject and Vice Versa: Magic and Magicians in the New Testament," in *Religion, Science, and Magic: In Concert and in Conflict* (ed. Jacob Neusner, Ernest Frerichs, and Paul Flesher; Oxford: Oxford University Press, 1989), 142–65.

4   For an analysis of witchcraft from a social-anthropological point of view, see Jerome H. Neyrey, "Bewitched in Galatia: Paul and Cultural Anthropology," *CBQ* 50 (2001): 72–100, esp. 95.

5   Bar-Ilan, "Witches in the Bible," 9.

**Coin from Ephesus featuring an ancient depiction of the Temple of Artemis, also known as the Artemision, showing the image of Artemis in the center.**

of Acts 13:8 and the charlatan exorcists of Acts 19:14-16 also show that magic was part of the Jewish world of the first century.[6] As the Zealot flame began to wax hot in Israel, Josephus is careful to note that Theudas, the messianic pretender, was a magician (*Ant.* 20.97–99). The practice of magic among some sects of Judaism continued into the rabbinic period and beyond.[7] The *Sepher ha-razim,*

or Book of Mysteries, of the early fourth or late third century C.E. contains many magical formulas.[8] Some scholars argue that the Kabbalah, a Jewish mystical sect, continues the practice of magic to this day.[9]

Magic was also prominent in ancient Greece and Rome. Herodotus traces the origin of magic to the priestly tribe of the *magoi,* one of the six tribes of the Medes and

6  Second Timothy 3:8 identifies the Egyptian magicians who opposed Moses as Jannes and Jambres, names not mentioned in the original report in Exodus. The Qumran materials, however, mention the two magicians (cf. CD 5:17b–19). The continued development of this ancient tradition within Jewish and Christian circles reflects an ongoing concern with magic.

7  For examples of what may be ancient Jewish charms, see Erwin R. Goodenough, *Jewish Symbols in the Greco-Roman Period* (13 vols.; New York: Pantheon, 1953–1968), 2:162–90.

8  These mysteries are said to have been delivered to Noah and claim that the heavens contain seven firmaments ruled by celestial beings waiting to do one's bidding in response to the proper magical spell. See Michael A. Morgan, *Sepher ha-razim: The Book of Mysteries* (Chico, Calif.: Scholars Press, 1983), 17–20.

9  See also Howard Clark Kee, "Magic and Messiah," in *Religion, Science, and Magic: In Concert and in Conflict* (ed. Jacob Neusner, Ernest Frerichs, and Paul Flesher; Oxford: Oxford University Press, 1989), 129.

the Persians (*Hist.* 1.101; cf. also Strabo, *Geogr.* 15.3.1).[10] Although the Persians regarded them as sages and priests (cf. Strabo, *Geogr.* 15.1.68; 3.13–15; Herodotus, *Hist.* 1.132), by the time the *magoi* made their way to Greece in the fifth century B.C.E., they were generally regarded as charlatans and quacks by the intelligentsia. Pliny the Elder concurs, branding the magic of the *magoi* as a detestable art given over to the concoction of poisons and curses (*Nat.* 30.6.16–18; cf. also 28.12.47–49). He notes that the wisest take no stock in the antics of the magicians. The lower classes, however, do not question the magicians' ability to affect the spirit world (*Nat.* 28.3.10–11). Columella concurs and states that enlightened Romans deemed magic a wasteful and superstitious enterprise (Columella, *Rust.* 1.8.6). The *Duodecim tabulae* (*Twelve Tables*) of Roman law, the foundation of Roman jurisprudence, forbade the practice of magic (Pliny the Elder, *Nat.* 28.4.18). Although Tiberius daily consulted an astrologer, he executed any non-Roman magicians in the city and forbade the practice of magic by Roman citizens. Anyone who persisted in the occult was banished from the city (Dio Cassius, *Hist. rom.* 57.15.7–8). Among the Romans, then, a charge of sorcery was a serious offense. Many statesmen and women were indicted on counts of casting spells on the emperor or his officials or simply practicing magical arts of any kind (Tacitus, *Ann.* 2.32; 4.22; 12.22, 59, 65). Indeed, some kind of magical spell seems to have been employed in the assassination of the Roman general Germanicus (Dio Cassius, *Hist. rom.* 57.18.9).

From these examples, however, it can be seen that Roman law did little to curtail the spread of magic throughout the empire. By 150 B.C.E. magic had become thoroughly integrated into the Greco-Roman mystery religions. For example, Apuleius devoted his entire life to magic and extols the feats of powerful magicians. In his *Metamorphoses* (late second century C.E.) he speaks of Lucius, who in an attempt to be transformed into a bird by way of magic is instead changed into an ass. Only after the goddess Isis provides a special garland of roses for him to eat is Lucius changed back into a man again (*Metam.* 137–139, 543–561). Apuleius remarks of a sorceress named Pamphile, "By breathing out certain words and charms over boughs and stones and other frivolous things, [she] can throw all the light of the starry heavens into the bottom of hell, and reduce them again to the old chaos" (*Metam.* 57). Pliny the Elder reveals the pervasive influence of magic among the Romans: "There is no one who is not afraid of becoming the subject of lethal spells" (*Nat.* 28.4.19). Although he is dismissive of magicians and their craft, a careful reading of Pliny shows that he, too, believed in magic to some extent. He notes that all kinds of cures and effects have been procured by magic and that the great mathematician Pythagoras (ca. 582–500 B.C.E.) ascribed powers to certain numbers (*Nat.* 28.6.30–7.46, 18.65–19.69).[11] Even Augustus carried about a sealskin to ward off lightning, and the Roman general Geta resorted to magic to procure water for his men (Suetonius, *Vit. Caes.* 2.90; Dio Cassius, *Hist. rom.* 60.9.4–5). The birth, life, and death of the Caesars were thought to be governed by strange omens and signs (Tacitus, *Hist.* 2.78; Suetonius, *Vit.*

---

10  For the possible connection of the *magoi* with Zoroastrianism, see Howard Clark Kee, *Medicine, Miracle, and Magic in New Testament Times* (SNTSMS 55; Cambridge: Cambridge University Press, 1986), 99. Although the *magoi* are mostly represented as religious figures, they also wielded political power, as evidenced in their overthrow of Cambyses, the son of Cyrus (Herodotus, *Hist.* 3.61–68; Strabo, *Geogr.* 15.3.24).

11  None of Pythagoras's original writings survive, the most complete records stemming from Iamblichus (ca. 300 C.E.) and Diogenes Laertius (mid–third century C.E.). Cf. Iamblichus, *On the Pythagorean Way of Life: Text, Translation, and Notes* (trans. John Dillon and Jackson Hershbell; Atlanta: Scholars Press, 1991); and Diogenes Laertius, *Vit. phil.* 8.1–50.

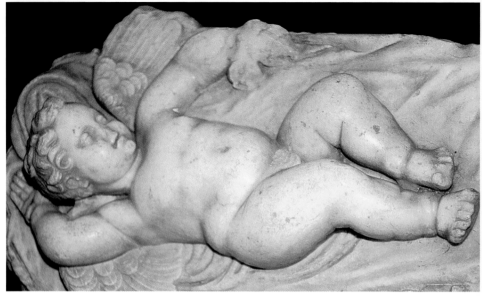

**Sculpture of Eros from Ephesus.**

*Caes.* 2.92–94). In the end, Pliny's remark that the wisest care not a wit for magic is a qualified one, and he concludes that people must decide for themselves if magic is legitimate (*Nat.* 28.5.22–6.30).

Much of what we know of ancient magic comes from a cache of magical scrolls known as the Greek Magical Papyri (*PGM*), including the Egyptian Demotic Magical Papyri (*PDM*).[12] Preserved by the arid climate of Egypt and found at the turn of the twentieth century, these writings contain many incantations, charms, and spells. The earliest spells seem to date to the first century B.C.E., with the most recent and numerous penned in the fourth and fifth centuries C.E.

It is clear from the *PGM* that the effectiveness of incantations and spells depends upon the precise recitation of divine names, such as Isis, Osiris, Zeus, Adonai, Eros, Sabbaoth, and YHWH (*PGM* 1.59; 4.88–93, 1982; 2.115;

3.212; 5.355; 12.90–95; *PDM* 14.585–593, 1110–1129). In addition, the names of spiritual persons and prophets, such as Abraham, Isaac, Jacob, and Jesus, are used in various spells (*PGM* 13.1–343, 815–820; *PDM* 14.225–30, 675–69). Sequences of nonsense letters, and syllables such as "*chi*" and "*abracadabra*," are thought to have special power, especially if said in groups of seven. The apparent notion contained in the magical papyri is that by randomly saying such things, one may eventually hit on the right "password" that will open a portal to the spirit world (*PGM* 2.124–140; 19a.1–15).[13] Once access is obtained, additional charms are brought to bear in an effort to force the spirits to do one's bidding.

Much of the content of the *PGM* is taken up with the immediate concerns of the individual and addresses the full range of human desires. Protection from demons and from mum-

12   This material was first translated into English by K. Preisendanz in *PGM*. For a modern English translation of the *PGM*, including the *PDM*, see Hans Dieter Betz, *The Greek Magical Papyri in Translation, Including the Demotic Spells* (2d ed.; Chicago: University of Chicago Press, 1996–).

13   On the random sequencing of magical formulas, see Clinton E. Arnold, *Ephesians, Power, and Magic: The Concept of Power in Ephesians in the Light of Its Historical Setting* (SNTSMS 63; Cambridge: Cambridge University Press, 1989), 18; and Kee, "Magic and Messiah," 127.

The tone of the *PGM* reveals much about ancient magic. The magician employs spells and fetishes to manipulate and even coerce the gods into granting the desires of the individual. Often the gods and spirits are threatened to grant the requests of the petitioner, and that in a hurry. Many incantations end with the words "Now! Now! Hurry! Hurry!" (*PGM* 4.150, 1593; *PDM* 12.115–119). All means are used to leverage the spirits to do what they are told.[15]

In summary, the data indicate an almost universal belief in the existence of a spirit world among the ancients. This world of gods, demons, and spirits can be made to serve the interests of the individual if one knows secret incantations and practices.[16] So, even though the sources are diverse and span millennia, the central characteristics of magic are fairly consistent. They include:

1. complicated rituals, spells, and recipes;
2. sequential uttering of divine names and nonsense syllables in the hope of hitting on the right "password";
3. an eclectic, syncretistic approach;
4. coercion and manipulation of the deities;
5. requests concerning the immediate desires of the individual.

**Hellenistic faience image from Dor of an Egyptian deity, believed to protect its bearer.**

mies that have come back to life, as well as the destruction of one's enemies, is a common theme (*PGM* 4.86–87, 296–466; 36.161–177; 40.1–18). Frequently an effigy of an enemy would be fashioned, then cursed and broken in the manner of a voodoo doll. Curse formulas were inscribed upon thin sheets of lead, rolled up and nailed to headstones, and placed deep in wells and holes in the ground so that they might be closer to the underworld. Success in business, love, and sporting events is frequently sought (*PGM* 3.275–281; 15.1–21; 35.1–41; *PDM* 14.113–114; 61.1–38).[14]

14  Magical language once used to attract the opposite sex continues to this day. Whenever we call one "charming," "enchanting," or "fascinating" (from the Latin *fascinare*, meaning "to bewitch"), we unwittingly draw upon ancient love charms.

15  For the use of magic for protection and the coercion of the gods and spirits, see Anitra Bingham Kolenkow, "Persons of Power and Their Communities," in *Magic and Divination in the Ancient World* (ed. Leda Ciraolo and Jonathan Seidel; Leiden: E. J. Brill, 2002), 138, 140–43; and Kee, "Magic and Messiah," 127.

16  Arnold encapsulates the major aspects of magic when he states, "The overriding characteristic of the practice of magic throughout the Hellenic world was the cognizance of the spirit world exercising influence over virtually every aspect of life. The goal of the magician was to discern the helpful spirits from the harmful ones and learn the distinct operation and the relative strengths and authority of the spirits. Through this knowledge, means could be constructed (with spoken or written formulas, amulets, etc.) for the manipulation of the spirits in the interest of the individual person" (*Ephesians, Power, and Magic*, 18).

## DIFFERENTIATING MIRACLE
## FROM MAGIC

In spite of the common traits found in ancient magic, its diverse nature defies a single definition. Thus the critical question among concerned scholars is what, if anything, differentiates the magician's art from the sincere devotee of religion.

One school holds that in a technical sense, there is no difference between magic and miracle, between performing extraordinary feats and religion.[17] Absolute definitions are not forthcoming because the determining factor is not the quality of the deed performed (i.e., whether it is of God or the devil) but, rather, the social identity of the one who performs the deed. That is, the sociological principle of "insider" and "outsider" comes into play when we seek a definition of magic. An extraordinary act done by one "in" the group is a "miracle," but such an act done by another that is "outside" the group is "magic." So, the difference between miracle and magic is simply relative to the views of the particular social group that one belongs to. If the group believes a deed is sponsored by God, then it is a miracle. If not, the deed is magic and is inspired by demons.[18] Any group that wants to malign the spiritual credentials of another person or group can simply say that their deeds are magic born of the devil.[19]

On the other hand, some scholars point out that there appears to be qualitative differences between miracle and magic.[20] For example, it is argued that similarity in form does not necessarily mean equality in substance. There are many instances in the Bible that *appear* to be magic. The healing of the woman who touched the hem of Jesus' garment (Matt 9:20–22) and cures effected by Peter's shadow (Acts 5:15) and by handkerchiefs from Paul's body (Acts 19:12) are but a few examples. It is contended, however, that upon closer examination, especially of the context and the flow of the narrative, these biblical miracles have very little in common with the magic of their day. Also, it is maintained that the goals of magic are nearly always bound up with the desires of the individual and not focused upon the welfare of the community. The motives set forth in the *PGM* are painfully egocentric, often seeking erotic love, the vicious destruction of an enemy, or an unfair advantage in sporting events. A single quote from the *PGM* suffices:

> I conjure you all by the god of Abraham, Isaac, and Jacob, that you obey my authority completely, each one of you obeying perfectly, and that you stay beside me and give me favor, influence, victory, and strength, before all, small men and great, as well as gladiators, soldiers, civilians, women, girls, boys, and everybody, Quickly! Quickly! (*PGM* 35.15–20)

Finally, as noted, the tone of the magical spells is totally different from the prayers of those seeking the miraculous intervention of God. The magician threatens, coerces, and even curses the gods if they do not do his or her bidding. On the other hand, regarding miraculous answers to prayer, the supplicant gives priority to the will of God over any individual desires (e.g., Dan 3:12–26; Luke 22:42).[21]

---

17   For a succinct presentation of this position, see Goodenough, *Jewish Symbols in the Greco-Roman Period*, 2:155–61.

18   See Neusner, "Science and Magic, Miracle and Magic," 61–63, 74; John M. Hull, *Hellenistic Magic and the Synoptic Tradition* (London: SCM, 1974); and Morton Smith, *Jesus the Magician* (San Francisco: Harper & Row, 1978).

19   Jesus, the apostles, and John the Baptist are accused of being demon-inspired, and on occasion they cast the charge back into the faces of their enemies (see Matt 11:18//Luke 7:33; Mark 3:23–30; 8:33; Luke 11:24–26; John 6:70; 7:20; 8:48, 52; 10:20). Cf. also Neyrey, "Bewitched in Galatia," 73.

20   See Yamauchi, "Magic in the Biblical World," 123, 175–77; and Kee, "Magic and Messiah," 130–31.

21   "Put simply, in religion one prays to the gods; in magic one commands the gods" (Yamauchi, "Magic in the Biblical World," 175).

View of the stage area from the top tiers of seating of the huge amphitheater at Ephesus, where a riot took place during Paul's visit.

## MAGIC AND THE NEW TESTAMENT

### Jesus the Magician?

As noted, Jesus' enemies sought to marginalize him and his ministry by branding him a sorcerer. They tried to have the people believe that Jesus was a demon-possessed Samaritan who exorcised demons by Beelzebub, the prince of demons (John 8:48; Matt 12:24; Mark 3:22; Luke 11:15). The attempt to link Jesus and his followers with magic continued throughout the apostolic era. The inquisition of Peter and John before the Sanhedrin is a case in point. The words "By what *power*, or in whose *name*, have you done this?" (Acts 4:7, emphasis added) insinuate that Jesus and his disciples are practitioners of the occult. Similarly, Origen's *Contra Celsus* shows us that the program to defame

Jesus and the church was still under way during the period of the early church fathers. In this work, Celsus claimed that according to Roman law, Christianity was an illegal religion. Furthermore, Jesus, the founder of the movement, was libeled as the illegitimate child of a poor Jewish woman and a Roman soldier. Seeking to escape poverty, Jesus went down to Egypt and hired himself out as a common laborer. While there, Jesus learned the magic tricks of the Egyptians and returned to Palestine, arrogantly proclaiming that he was God (*Cels.* 1.29). Through magic Jesus was able to deceive the poor, the ignorant, and the young but was spurned by those of intelligence and social standing (*Cels.* 3.44, 49, 73). The postresurrection appearances of Jesus were

193

the reports of hysterical women, not the sober accounts of credible witnesses (*Cels.* 2.55).[22]

Nevertheless, it appears that at the time of Jesus a social-cultural world was already in place that could differentiate between the occult and the work of God. This is true because, in the end, the historical legacy concerning Jesus and his followers placed them squarely in the camp of the divine and not in that of the devil.[23]

## Magic and the Book of Acts

Luke was aware of what the church faced in its battle against magic. For him, if the power of God in the church could be reduced to mere magic, then the gospel would be viewed as just another form of sorcery. The apostles would then be labeled quacks and shysters with just another "act" to sell. The power of the Holy Spirit would be seen as in league with the spirits of the underworld. The uniquely redemptive presence of the gospel would have been lost amid the spells of sorcerers and the cultic rituals of the mystery religions. In short, for Luke and the first Christian leaders, everything was at stake.

For these reasons, Luke is careful to differentiate the power of the Holy Spirit from that of magic. He does so by establishing a consistent pattern throughout the book of Acts. After he records an extraordinary miracle of the Spirit, it is soon followed by an account of magic. In this way Luke seeks to clarify the work of God in the church from the dark forces present throughout the Mediterranean world. Often his method is to contrast the avaricious and power-hungry motives of the magicians with the altruism of the first believers, who effect healings and deliverance for others through the power of the Spirit. In this way Luke presents every supernatural in-breaking of the kingdom as a benefit to others and as bringing glory to God. It is as if Luke were saying to Theophilus, "You see! The power of the Holy Spirit may look like magic, but it is qualitatively different! And in all cases, God's Spirit is more powerful than anything that the wizards can produce!"

## The Case of Simon Magus

The account of Simon Magus (Acts 8:9–25) occupies a strategic place in the book of Acts and in the history of the early church. Even though Simon is not explicitly called a magician, Luke notes that Simon practiced magic and that for a long time he had astounded the Samaritans by means of his magical deeds (vv. 9, 11). The showmanship so typical of ancient magicians is also attributed to this Simon. Luke says that Simon himself was saying that he was someone great. He successfully convinced the people of this, for they saw him as "the divine power known as the Great Power" (v. 10).[24] Nevertheless,

---

22   For a modern rendition along similar lines, especially regarding the Synoptic tradition as set forth in Mark 7:31–37; 8:22–23, see Smith, *Jesus the Magician*, 84–152. His main thesis is that Jesus was a Jewish goes, i.e., a "trickster" or a "wizard" who used magic to support his claim to be the messiah. Thus Smith judges that the link between Jesus and magic in the Gospels belongs to the earliest stratum of the Synoptic tradition and that it is to be accepted as authentic. According to Smith, Jesus styled his magic after Apollonius of Tyana and cast the Eucharist in terms of the Dionysian cult. For a counter to Smith's arguments, see Kee, *Medicine, Miracle, and Magic*, 112–13, 136–39; and Garrett, "Light on a Dark Subject," 146–48.

23   Garrett claims that this is no accident of history. Jesus and his followers vehemently rejected any connection with magic, and in the end, it was their account that the people believed (ibid., 148). Kee notes, "There is in the gospel narratives no trace of the elaborate multi-named invocations of the gods, the agglomerations of nonsense letters and syllables, the coercive manipulations of the unseen powers which characterize the magical papyri. The aim of the healing is not to force the gods to act, but to share in the fulfillment of God's purpose in the creation and for his people" ("Magic and Messiah," 126).

24   The phrase "The Great Power" is translated from the single Greek word *Megalē* (Μεγάλη) and appears in the text as a proper noun. Luke may be indicating that by means of sorcery Simon was viewed as the Almighty on earth. In the very least, the Samaritans accepted Simon as the authentic channel of divine power and revelation.

Luke's point here is that even Simon had not seen anything like the miracles wrought by the Spirit through Philip (v. 13). He was amazed by the conferral of the Holy Spirit through the laying on of hands by the apostles (v. 17). Simon concluded that the apostles were in the same business as he and that in some way the apostles were able to manipulate the Spirit of God. Thus he offered to buy whatever magical formulas that were necessary to control the Holy Spirit.

Peter's rebuke let Simon (and the reader) know that the magician had it all wrong (vv. 20–23). But instead of repenting and submitting to the Spirit, Simon viewed Peter's words as a classical curse formula and begged him to lift the spell from him (v. 24). From this it appears that Simon's belief (cf. v.13) fell more along the lines of a convinced customer, one who is out to buy one more magical spell, than the faith of a sincere disciple of Christ.[25] In any case, Luke's point is that the power of the Holy Spirit is unidirectional, that is, it flows from the sovereign Lord to his people. The nature of divine power in the church is thus seen to be the exact opposite of magic. So, for Luke, Simon Magus is a magician in the classical sense, and Luke's point in this passage is that he and those like him have no place in the church.[26]

25  On the quality of Simon's belief, see F. F. Bruce, *The Book of Acts* (Grand Rapids: Eerdmans, 1988), 171; and Ben Witherington III, *Acts of the Apostles: A Socio-rhetorical Commentary* (Grand Rapids: Eerdmans: 1998), 288–89.

26  The extrabiblical writings of the early church indicate likewise. Irenaeus (ca. 130–202 C.E.) in *Adversus haereses* (*Against Heresies*) 23.1–5 claims that Simon Magus was the source of all false doctrine, a corrupt mystic priest given to divination and magic. The apocryphal *Acts of Peter* 5:12–6:18; 8:23–29 and the *Pseudo-Clementines* (*Homilies* II 15:1–58; XIII 7:8; *Recognitions* I 12:2) of the second and third centuries C.E. denounce Simon as a wizard, one who is joined to the spirits of the dead. That the legacy of Simon continued for centuries is a testimony to his power and influence in the first-century world. To this day the word "simony" speaks of the unsavory practice of purchasing a religious office.

## Bar-Jesus the Sorcerer

In Acts 13:6–11 Luke records the encounter of Paul and Barnabas with Bar-Jesus. His name literally means "son of Jesus," but since Jesus was a common name in the first century, no relation to the historical Jesus need be assumed. Unlike Simon Magus in 8:9–24, Bar-Jesus is specifically called a magician and a false prophet (vv. 7–8). This last description by Luke may indicate that Bar-Jesus claimed to speak for God. He also appears to have served as one of the attendants in the court of the Roman proconsul Sergius Paulus. Here again Luke is true to the cultural conventions of the time, for such relations were common in the patron-client system of the first century. Moreover, mentioning the name of the proconsul and emphasizing his intelligence serve Luke's purposes. This lets Theophilus know that Paul is well connected with intelligent Roman officials and that such persons are interested in the gospel.

In v. 8 Luke informs us that this magician had a trade name, that is, Elymas, and that this name means "sorcerer."[27] After seeking to bar access to the proconsul and to turn him from the faith, Elymas meets a fate similar to that of Simon Magus. Paul brings to bear the power and authority of the Holy Spirit upon Elymas. Since Paul calls Elymas "a child of the devil," Bar-Jesus is in effect branded "Bar-Satan" and is struck blind for a time (vv. 10–11).

Luke understands that, at least on a superficial level, Paul's words and their consequences resemble the curse formulas of magicians. Therefore he has arranged the flow of the narrative to convey another message. For Luke, the purpose of the story is to show that the gospel is in complete opposition to magic. So, from the opening of the narrative to its close, Paul and Barnabas are associated with the word of God, the Holy Spirit, and faith whereas Bar-Jesus is connected with witchcraft, false prophecy, and

27  It is possible that "Elymas" was derived from the Arabic *alim*, "wise."

Satan. By the time Luke is finished relating the account, the truth of the gospel and the power of the Holy Spirit are set over against false prophecy, Satan, and magic.

## The "Pythoness" of Acts 16

Luke's account in Acts 16:16–40 once again brings up the connection between magic, divination, and profiteering. While in Philippi, the missionary team encounters a "slave girl" (v. 16) whom Luke describes as being possessed by a "Pythian spirit" (Gk. *pneuma pythōna* [πνεῦμα πύθωνα]).[28] It was believed that the god Apollo took the form of a python snake and inspired the prophetesses of Delphi to predict the future. Herodotus makes much of the Pythian priestesses, the definitive counselors of the ancient potentates (*Hist.* 1.13, 19, 47, 54, 65–67).[29] The use of the plural word "owners" in vv. 16b, 19 indicates that this slave girl was jointly owned. Thus her ability to predict the future represented the business concerns of several persons.

Her repeated harangue that Paul and his company are the servants of God pointing the way to salvation at first seems to be on target. If so, then Paul's reaction may be an indication of his short-temperedness (cf. v. 18). The magic jargon of the first century, however, appears to point in another direction. The phrase "Most high God" is frequently found in pagan incantations (*PGM* 2.130–140; 3.570–583). Also, since the Jewish population of Philippi was very low (there was no synagogue there; cf. v. 13) and there would have been few Gentile God-fearers, those who heard her probably would not have equated "Most High God" with the God whom Paul preached but, rather, with the gods mentioned in magical formulas of their day. What's more, as employed in the *PGM* the word "servants"

in v. 17 can also mean "slaves," and "salvation" (NRSV) can refer to healing or extrication from personal problems. It may be, then, that the reason Paul became "so troubled" (cf. v. 18) was that he discerned that the Pythoness was shouting that he and his company were enslaved to spirits just as she was and that they could also serve the personal interests of those in trouble. She billed them as fellow magicians who could tap into the spirit world just as she could. Paul exorcised the spirit "in the name of Jesus Christ," and the missionary team was subsequently brought before the city magistrates for being Jews, disturbing the peace, and teaching customs contrary to Roman practice (vv. 19–21).[30]

With the freeing of the Christian missionaries, Luke has made his point. Once again the superior power of the Spirit is demonstrated vis-à-vis magic. The profit-making potential for the slave girl's masters is gone (v. 19). This will not be the last time in Acts that the power of the Holy Spirit in the gospel destroys the commercial value of magic (cf. 19:19–41).

## Paul's "Extraordinary Miracles" and the Seven Sons of Sceva

Acts 19:11–16 contains two accounts of the supernatural that, upon initial reflection, appear to be unrelated. The first concerns what Luke calls "extraordinary miracles" that God performed through Paul (v. 11). It is the manner in which these miracles take place that makes them extraordinary: items from Paul's clothing seem to effect healing (v. 12). The second account is about the failed attempt of some Jewish exorcists to capitalize on the names of Jesus and Paul (vv. 13–16).

The words "handkerchiefs and aprons" found in v. 12 more than likely refer to leather remnants left over from Paul's tent-making

28  The Greek word for "slave girl" Luke uses here is *paidiskē* (παιδίσκη), which literally means a young female servant.

29  On the oracle of Delphi and Pytho, see J. Keir Howard, "New Testament Exorcism and Its Significance Today," *ExpTim* 96 (1985): 105–9.

30  On the charges brought against Paul and his company, see Craig De Vos, "Finding a Charge That Fits: The Accusation against Paul and Silas at Philippi (Acts 16:19–21)," *JSNT* 74 (1999): 32–84, esp. 54, 58–59.

The Forum, Philippi, Macedonia.

trade.[31] These leather scraps were used as makeshift belts to bind up flowing robes and as sweatbands. In Luke's story, persons who came in contact with these items were healed or delivered of evil spirits.[32]

The efficacy of such items must be evaluated within the religious context of the first believers. The sweatbands may have served as a touchstone for faith, taking on temporary sacramental significance as a point of grace through which God worked his power. Regardless, it must be admitted that in Ephesus, a city steeped in the occult, the miracles effected through Paul's sweatbands appear to be a classic case of magic. Indeed, the "seven sons of Sceva" (v. 14) seem to have taken these "extraordinary miracles" to be just that.

Many in the ancient world believed that the Hebrews had a special connection with the spirit world. It is for this reason that the Greek Magical Papyri contain many corrupted forms of the "ineffable name" of Israel's God (PGM 1.311; 4.1577; 5.102; 7.564; 12.4). Many Jews seem to have taken advantage of this reputation and peddled various kinds of religious cures, especially exorcisms (Josephus, Ant. 8.42–49).[33] The seven sons of the chief priest Sceva appear to fall into this category (v. 13).[34] In any case, in a manner that echoes the procedures of the Greek Magical Papyri,

these religious charlatans attempt to commandeer the power of the name of Jesus and of Paul to influence the spirit world.[35] Once again an attempt to employ the power of the gospel as magic ends in disaster. Instead of coming out of the man, the demon points to the impotence of the exorcists and pommels them bloody (v. 15–16).

For Luke, what at first appears to be Christian magic again turns out to be a very graphic repudiation of sorcery. Luke is careful to state that it was God who performed the healings through Paul and not the scraps of leather (v. 11). No elaborate rituals or spells are found here, nor does Paul seek payment for the healings, which are typical of magicians and their craft. Luke's point is that Christianity cannot be manipulated to serve one's own ends. The following account of the revival in Ephesus supports Luke's point here as well (v. 17–20).

## Magic and Ephesus

The links between magic, the mystery religions, and the local economy in the ancient world are clearly seen in Acts 19:17–41. The conflict between the early Christian missionaries and their opponents in Ephesus teaches much about magic in the first century.

As the third largest city of the empire, Ephesus served as a kind of international center for magic. The world-renowned cult of Artemis (Diana is her Roman name) was located in the heart of the city and was the focus for much of the magical practice and marketing of the region (v. 27). The splendor of the temple of Artemis, considered one of the greatest wonders of the ancient world, was further enhanced through an astronomical quirk of nature: a meteorite that had apparently fallen in the region was under-

---

31  The Greek word translated "tentmaker" in Acts 18:3 is *skēnopoioi* (σκηνοποιοί), a word that literally means "leather workers." Thus Paul and Aquila and Pricilla made leather goods of all kinds, not just tents.

32  These miracles are reminiscent of the healing of the woman who touched the hem of Jesus' garment (Mark 5:27–34) and of those healed when Peter's shadow fell on them (Acts 5:15). Witherington claims that Luke believes in the principle of *mana*, or "sympathetic influence," whereby persons are helped through contact with some item (*Acts*, 577).

33  Luke's Greek word for "exorcists" is *exorkistōn* (ἐξορκιστῶν), found only here in Acts 19:13.

34  Some translations say that Sceva was a high priest. There were, however, no high priests named Sceva before 70 C.E. Their family may have stemmed from a prominent chief priest, or these exorcists may have simply claimed relations with a high priest to bolster their spiritual stature (Witherington, *Acts*, 581).

35  Paris Papyrus 574 says, "I adjure you by Jesus the God of the Hebrews!" We also find "Hail God of Abraham, hail God of Isaac, hail God of Jacob, Jesus Chrestus, Holy Spirit, Son of the Father!" (cf. Witherington, *Acts*, 580 n. 87).

Site of the Temple of Artemis, Ephesus. One column has been reconstructed. The area is now a marsh.

stood to be an image of the goddess Diana, given directly to the Ephesians by the hand of Zeus (v. 35). The connection of the famous *Ephesia grammata* with Artemis complemented her prowess further still. These "Ephesian letters" consisted of small scrolls of magical spells that dated back to the fourth century B.C.E. They were used to ward off demons, ensure success, protect newlyweds, and so on.[36] Although no examples have been found to date, the Greek Magical Papyri speak of the *grammata* as being engraved on images of Artemis/Diana. For all these reasons, many worshiped Artemis as the "queen of the universe," the goddess of the demons of nature and of the dead.

According to Luke, the power of the gospel quickly began to undermine the cultic and commercial interests of those who worshiped Artemis. The debacle of the seven sons of Sceva was the catalyst that started this general dismantling of sorcery in the area (v. 17). Luke says that "many of those who believed now came and openly confessed" their magical practices (v. 18). The word translated "openly confessed" is the Gk. *exomologeō* (ἐξομολογέω) and does not simply mean "repent," although this certainly was the case. Rather, the word means "to confess out loud." Since the mystical power and commercial value of any spell lay in its secrecy, the open confession of the incantations struck a double blow to the magic industry in Ephesus. Once pronounced out loud, the spell lost its potency and hence also lost its commercial value.

36   The *Ephesia grammata* consisted of the following six Greek words: *askion* (ἄσκιον), *kataskion* (κατάσκιον), *lix* (λίξ), *tetrax* (τετράξ), *damnameneus* (δαμναμενεῦς), and *aisia* (ἀίσια) (Arnold, *Ephesians, Power, and Magic*, 15).

Controversy surrounds the phrase "those who believed" in v. 18. The issue here concerns at what point such persons came to faith. The phrase could mean those who had been converted to Christianity for some time and thus had practiced magic for a good while after their conversion. Another possibility is that those who came forward were recently converted and did not yet fully understand the implications of the faith. This was certainly true for some of the believers in Corinth who continued to attend non-Christian worship services after their conversion (1 Cor 10:19–20). On the other hand, Luke may simply be giving another example of how miracle-working power leads to religious revival (cf. Acts 2:4–41; 3:2–4:4). The miracles that had been performed through Paul, together with the reverence and respect that resulted from the overthrow of the exorcists, may have sparked a revival that led to many conversions (vv. 14–17). Ephesians who responded to the call proved the authenticity of their faith by conducting a bonfire of their magical scrolls whereby fifty thousand days' wages went up in smoke (v. 19).

At this point we see most clearly the link between magic, the mystery religions, and merchandising. Again the close connection between the worship of Artemis, magical spells, and the crafting of images of Artemis is in evidence here.

Demetrius, head of the silversmiths' guild, organized a public protest against Paul and his helpers (vv. 23–35). The ensuing riot, however, constituted an illegal assembly as far as Roman law was concerned, and the city clerk was able to regain order and dismiss the mob (vv. 35–41).[37]

37  Ignatius of Antioch's (d. ca. 110 C.E.) comment that once the gospel came to Ephesus, "all magic dissolved" may have been a case of wishful thinking (Ign., *Eph.* 19.3). Clement of Alexandria (ca. 150–215 C.E.), *Protrepticus* (*Exhortation to the Greeks*) 2.1–20, notes that magic was still thriving in Ephesus and the surrounding areas.

## The "Evil Eye" and Drug-Induced Magic

In Gal 3:1, Paul challenges the Galatian believers with the question: "Who has bewitched you." In doing so, he uses a form of the Greek word *baskainō* (βασκαίνω), found only here in the New Testament.[38] The word literally meant "to cast the evil eye" and is generally translated "bewitch."[39] For Paul, the Galatians' defection to the Judaizing heresy is so bizarre that he surmises that they must have fallen prey to the "evil eye." In making this reference, Paul is appealing to the nearly universal belief that a certain look, or a malformed or diseased eye, could cast an evil spell (Pliny the Elder, *Nat.* 28.5.22).[40] Paul's words here may be a roundabout way of referring to his own "thorn in my flesh" (2 Cor 12:7). He may have been suffering from opthalmia, an unpleasant disease common in Galatia. He notes that the Galatians did not shrink back in horror from his "illness" upon first meeting him. On the contrary, Paul says that they would have plucked out their own eyes and given them to Paul if that were possible (Gal 4:15).[41] Also, some of the Judaizers might have referenced Paul's sick eyes in an effort to

38  A form of the word is also found in Deut 28:54 (LXX). Susan Eastman believes that Paul is invoking the Deuteronomic curse of Deut 28:53–57 upon the troublemakers in Galatia ("The Evil Eye and the Curse of the Law: Galatians 3:1 Revisited," *JSNT* 83 [2001]: 69–87, esp. 70).

39  For the varied renderings of the verb here in Gal 3:1, see ibid., 69. The Latin word for "bewitch" is *fascinare*, "to fascinate," which in turn is the transliteration of the Gk. *baskainō* (βασκαίνω) (F. F. Bruce, *The Epistle to the Galatians: A Commentary on the Greek Text* [NIGTC; Grand Rapids: Eerdmans, 1982], 148).

40  Spells protecting one from the "evil eye" may date back to as early as the seventh century B.C.E. The rabbis devised curses to ward off the woe of the "evil eye," and fear of the spell persisted throughout the Middle Ages. Some parts of Italy and Africa still fear the spell-binding power of a malevolent glance. For a history of the "evil eye," see Neyrey, "Bewitched in Galatia," 74 n. 18; and Yamauchi, "Magic in the Biblical World," 187, 190–92.

41  The fact that Paul signed Galatians "with such large letters" (Gal 6:11) may also indicate an eye problem.

discredit him. Paul may be turning the tables on them, saying it is the Judaizers, not he, who have "cast the evil eye" on the Galatians.[42] In Paul's view, such persons merit the twofold anathema expressed in Gal 1:8–9 because they are equivalent to sorcerers, who are satanically inspired. For Paul, the troublemakers in Galatia, like those in 2 Cor 11:3, have appeared as angels of light but have sown seeds of confusion among the Galatian believers. It may be that for Paul, the only antidote for the curse of the evil eye is to once again hold up the cross of Christ before their eyes (Gal 3:1), just as Moses held up the brazen snake in the wilderness to heal those who had been poisoned by serpents (Num 21:9).[43]

In Gal 5:20 Paul lists "witchcraft" (NRSV "sorcery," Gk. *pharmakeia* [φαρμακεία]) as one of the "acts of the sinful nature." Anyone who practices magic will be barred from the kingdom of God (Gal 5:21). This may be another indication that belief in magic and spells was common in Galatia. The word *pharmakeia* originally had the meaning of "drug" or "medicine" but came to take on the idea of "potion" or "elixir." Sorcerers were often employed to mix up poisons to eliminate enemies, espe-

cially of a political kind. In other contexts, the related word *pharmakon* (φάρμακον) described love potions often connected with orgies.[44] John's frequent joining of forms of this word with sexually immoral behavior points in the same direction (Rev 9:21; 18:23; 21:8; 22:15).

## SUMMARY

The early church constantly faced the challenge of syncretism. A significant element of this challenge was the ever-present factor of magic in the first-century world. The writers of the New Testament thus make every effort to differentiate the power of God and the work of the Spirit from that of magic. By and large, the history of the church has followed suit. For example, the *Didache*, an early Christian document that may date back to as early as the first century, explicitly prohibits the practice of magic (*Didache* 2.2). Instead of taking up the coercive and self-seeking methods of the occult, the church's doctrine and practice of prayer consistently reflect reliance upon the divine will, not upon the will of the individual.

---

42   Tom Thatcher, "The Plot of Gal 3:1–18," *JETS* 40 (1997): 401, 410.

43   Eastman, "The Evil Eye and the Curse of the Law," 72.

44   Josephus implies that Cleopatra may have used some kind of spell or potion to entrance Antony with her beauty (*Ant.* 15.93). He also records that Mariamne had a love potion prepared for Herod. Yet her scheme ultimately had the opposite effect, sending Herod into a murderous rage that led to her death (*Ant.* 15.223–229).

# Annotated Bibliography

Arnold, Clinton E. Ephesians, *Power, and Magic: The Concept of Power in Ephesians in the Light of Its Historical Setting*. Society for New Testament Studies Monograph Series 63. Cambridge: Cambridge University Press, 1989. This is a technical, scholarly source on the role of magic in the history and culture of ancient Ephesus that yields insight for serious Bible students.

Betz, H. D. See description in the Annotated Bibliography of Primary Documents.

Ciraolo, Leda, and Jonathan Seidel. *Magic and Divination in the Ancient World*. Leiden: E. J. Brill, 2002. This collection of modern scholarly essays on magic in the ancient world is not for the beginner, but it is a good source for detailed discussion on the place of magic in ancient society.

Kee, Howard Clark. *Medicine, Miracle, and Magic in New Testament Times*. Society for New Testament Studies Monograph Series 55. Cambridge: Cambridge University Press, 1986. This is a good source for gaining insight into how persons of the first century may have differentiated between medicine, miraculous cures, and magical incantations.

*Sepher ha-razim: The Book of the Mysteries.* See description in the Annotated Bibliography of Primary Documents.

Smith, Morton. *Jesus the Magician.* San Francisco: Harper & Row, 1978. This is a modern rendition of Celsus's claim that Jesus was a magician, presented by a leading biblical scholar. Portions of the Synoptic tradition are compared with the words and practices of ancient magicians in an attempt to demonstrate that Jesus was one among many magicians of the ancient world.

# 14
# The Herodians— Politics and Compromise

## INTRODUCTION

The expression "the Herodians" (Gk. *hoi Hērōdianoi*) appears only three times in the New Testament (Mark 3:6; 12:13–17; Matt 22:15–22). The term's association with such powerful figures as Herod the Great and Herod Antipas has led scholars to explore the meaning of this expression in ancient literature for the past two centuries. They generally identify the Herodians in three different ways:[1]

1. a specific sociopolitical group in existence at the time of Jesus;

2. a nondescript association of persons who were generally supportive of the Herods throughout their employ as Roman client kings; or

3. an early Christian term coined to refer to the political leaders who opposed Jesus and were instrumental in bringing about his death.

A study of the phrase in ancient literature indicates that it is most frequently used in reference to the family of Herod and those closely affiliated with it. Indeed, from the time of Origen (ca. 180–250 C.E.), the Herodians have been identified as a Jewish political party that thoroughly supported the Herods, as demonstrated by their willingness to pay tribute to Caesar (Matt 22:15–17).[2] In this sense, the Herodians were a political party that derived its power from Roman imperial rule.[3]

The notion that the term is simply a creation of the early church encounters contrary data. Josephus, *J.W.* 1.319, uses the phrase "the Herodians." He also speaks of a group described as "the ones thinking like Herod" in *Ant.* 14.450. He thus clearly uses the term to designate those who were in some way linked with the Herods. Since the historical contexts of these references are prior to the birth of the church, the phrase "the Herods" would not seem to be an invention of the early church.

---

1 The available sources trace the Herodian family history for a period of almost 220 years (cf. Josephus, *Ant.* 14.8–10; 20.211). As the ruling elite in Israel during this time, the Herods merit a careful study for students of the New Testament. On the important role of the Herods, see K. C. Hanson, "The Herodians and the Mediterranean Kinship, Part 2: Marriage and Divorce," *BTB* 19 (1989): 142–51; idem, "The Herodians and Mediterranean Kinship, Part 3: Economics," *BTB* 20 (1990): 10–21; John P. Meier, "The Historical Jesus and the Historical Herodians," *JBL* 119 (2001): 740–46.

2 On Matthew's portrait of the Herods, see Savas Agourides, "The Birth of Jesus and the Herodian Dynasty: An Understanding of Matthew, Chapter 2," *GOTR* 37 (2001): 135–46.

3 "As for the Herodians, they were not a religious group but a party that promoted the interests of the Herod dynasty and probably hoped for the re-integration of Herod's kingdom under one of his descendants" (F. F. Bruce, "Render to Caesar," in *Jesus and the Politics of His Day* [ed. Ernst Bammel and C. F. D. Moule; Cambridge: Cambridge University Press, 1984], 249–63, esp. 251).

This powerful family influenced the fate of Israel for more than 150 years.[4] The Herodian dynasty orchestrated the demise of John the Baptist, Jesus, and James the brother of John. A thorough study of the Herodians, then, grants much insight into the Gospels and the experience of the early church.

The Herods form a perfect transition from the world of Judaism in the first century to that of the Greco-Roman world of that period. This bridge-building quality of the Herodian family touched the realms of race, religion, and politics. Racially, the Herods arose from Idumean stock (*Ant.* 14.8, 403; *J.W.* 1.123). Thus the Herodian family emerged out of the ill-defined boundary that separated Jacob from Esau, Israel from the Edomites, and the Jews from the Gentiles (cf. Gen 25:30). Religiously, the Herods were, in some sense, proselytes to Judaism and at times sought to strengthen their bond with the Jews through carefully planned marriages to prominent Jewish families (*Ant.* 14.300; 18.109–112). Politically, the Herods curried the favor of the Gentile masters of Israel. They became client kings of Rome who always cast their lot with the emperors and in this way furthered the oppression of the Jewish people. Thus the Herods lived a kind of go-between existence yet were always careful to tie their fate with those in power. In this respect, the Herods were solidly Roman.

## THE HERODIAN DYNASTY

The Herod family tree is very complex and convoluted. This is due to the many politically arranged marriages, many of which were to other members of the Herodian clan. Frequent divorces, polygamous marriages (Herod the Great married ten women), and multiple murders of family members and spouses also add to the confused state of affairs in the Herodian dynasty. For the sake of clarity, the diagram opposite represents the most important members of the Herodians to inform our understanding of the New Testament world.[5]

For the life of Jesus, the field can be narrowed to Herod the Great and Herod Antipas. Herod Agrippa I and Herod Agrippa II factor in the life of the early church, especially in the trials of Paul.

## Antipas (148–? B.C.E.)

Antipas was the progenitor of the Herodian dynasty, but the precise dates of his birth and his death are unknown.[6] He was from among the Edomites, a people descended from Esau and inhabiting the land of Idumea, which lies east of the Jordan River and south of the Dead Sea (*Ant.* 14.8).[7] The Edomites were remote kin to the Jews, yet socially and religiously they were rejected by Israel (Gen 25:30; 32:3; 36:43; Deut 23:7–8; 1 Kgs 11:14; Ps 137:7–9). Historical and political circumstances, however, conspired to draw the Edomites nearer to the fold of Israel. The startling victory of the Maccabeans over the Seleucids birthed the Hasmonean dynasty and reinstated the kingdom of Israel for the first time since the Babylonian captivity. And under John Hyrcanus I (135–104 B.C.E.), the Hasmoneans

---

5 For a comprehensive presentation of all of the endogamous and exogamous marriages of the Herodians, see Peter Richardson, *Herod: King of the Jews and Friend of the Romans* (Minneapolis: Fortress, 1999), 46–51. For the political, religious, and economic factors that determined Herodian kinship relationships, see Hanson, "The Herodians and Mediterranean Kinship, Part 3."

6 Sometimes Antipas is referred to as Antipater I, and his son is referred to as Antipater II. This study will use the terms Antipas and Antipater respectively. For a discussion of the earliest accounts on the origin of the Herods, see Nikos Kokkinos, *The Herodian Dynasty: Origins, Role in Society, and Eclipse* (JSPSup 30; Sheffield, Eng.: Sheffield Academic Press, 1998), esp. 94–108.

4 This time period is reckoned from the ascendancy of Antipas under Alexander Jannaeus (103–76 B.C.E.) to the end of Herod Agrippa II's tenure in 92 C.E.

7 Eusebius questions this account, noting the words of Julius Africanus, who claimed that the family arose from a Philistine slave who served in the temple of Apollo (*Hist. eccl.* 1.6.2).

# Major Figures in the Herodian Family

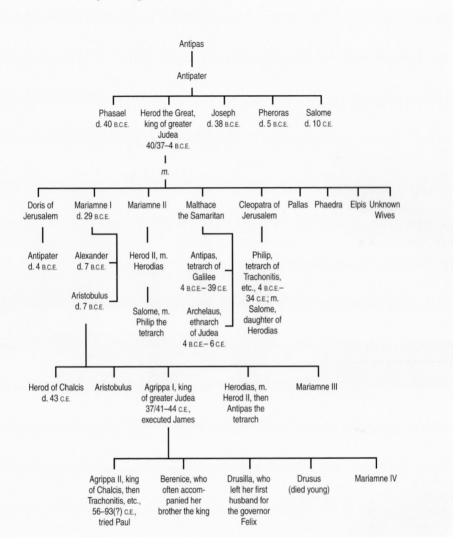

greatly expanded their territory to include the region of Idumea (*Ant.* 14.10–19).

It is at this point that Antipas, the grandfather of Herod the Great and great-grandfather to Herod Antipas, enters into the affairs of the Jews. Josephus claims that Hyrcanus forced the Idumeans to convert to Judaism (*Ant.* 15.254). Thus it is possible that Antipas himself became a proselyte to Judaism at this time. On the other hand, Strabo indicates that the Judaizing of the Idumeans may have been more a matter of cultural assimilation than military conquest. He records that the Nabateans (he makes no distinction between the Idumeans and the Nabateans) often made incursions into Syria, pressing in close to the region of Jericho, before they were finally subdued by the Romans (*Geogr.* 16.4.21). Over time this proximity to Israel may have aided in the assimilation of Jewish practices and beliefs by some Idumeans and eventually come to influence the Herodian family.

205

The reason the nature of Antipas's conversion is an important issue is that the Herods' relationship to Judaism consistently appears more functional and pragmatic than personal or devotional. When power or money were at stake, the Herods did not let their religious convictions stand in the way of advancing their personal fortunes, even at the expense of the Jews whom they ruled. So, if the conduct of the Herods is any measure of their religion, they must have been nominally Jewish, perhaps observing the hallmarks of the religion such as circumcision, Sabbath observance, abstinence from pork, and paying the temple tax.

In any case, the son of John Hyrcanus I, Alexander Jannaeus (103–76 B.C.E.), designated Antipas "general over all Idumea" (*Ant.* 14.10). At this point the bond between the Hasmoneans and the Herods was forged.

## Antipater (100–43 B.C.E.)

The latter period of the Hasmonean dynasty was marked by internal strife and civil war. The Herods were able to capitalize on this instability, gradually aligning themselves with the most powerful factions regardless of whether they were Jewish or Gentile. The real inroads to power were made by Antipater, son of Antipas. In a way that would become the hallmark of the Herodian dynasty, Antipater exploited to his political advantage the infighting of the Jews.

Just before his death in 104 B.C.E., John Hyrcanus I desired his wife to rule, but his son, Aristobulus I, usurped the throne. The deplorable climate of the times can be seen in the fact that Aristobulus I had his mother imprisoned and slowly starved her to death (*Ant.* 13.301–302). Aristobulus I's tenure was short-lived, however. His brother, Alexander Jannaeus (103–76 B.C.E.), was able to wrest control over the people and became high priest and king of Judea (*Ant.* 14.151). The social and political situation worsened. Alexander Jannaeus's oppressive rule, together with his bitter feud with the Pharisees, led to open civil war, resulting in the slaughter of six thousand of his own people in a single day (*Ant.* 13.372–373). After his death, the feuding continued between Alexander Jannaeus's two sons, Aristobulus II and Hyrcanus II. Initially, Aristobulus II gained the upper hand and reached an agreement with Hyrcanus II that if the latter would abandon public life, he could live in dignity as the king's brother (*Ant.* 13.323).

But now Antipater made his bid for power. Antipater, as governor of Idumea, had great power and wealth at his disposal. Sensing instability among the Jews, Antipater cast his lot with Hyrcanus II (*Ant.* 14.8). His plan was to rekindle Hyrcanus II's pretensions to the throne and to convince him to forge an alliance with King Aretas of Nabatea. Together they would lay siege to Jerusalem in order to wrest power from Aristobulus II (*J.W.* 1.126; *Ant.* 14.19).[8]

This regional fracas attracted the attention of the Romans. Antipater was quick to convey his allegiance to the Roman legions even as they marched toward the holy city. The Roman general Pompey employed the efforts of his two legates, Scaurus and Gabinius, to capture Jerusalem in 63 B.C.E. During the campaign, the hapless Aristobulus II took refuge in the temple precincts, and the temple mount was besieged for three months. As the forces loyal to Aristobulus II succumbed to the onslaught of Pompey, the streets of Jerusalem flowed with blood. The priests were cut down at the altar even as they performed their duties. Twelve thousand Jews were mercilessly killed. Pompey and his men defiled the temple by entering into the holy of holies (*J.W.* 1.149–152; *Ant.* 14.66–74). Antipater was party to the entire massacre. When the dust settled, Antipater convinced Pompey that Hyrcanus II would be loyal to Rome, and thus Hyrcanus II was appointed

---

8    D. S. Russell, *The Jews from Alexander to Herod* (Oxford: Oxford University Press, 1967), 76, 84.

Palestine in the Time of Christ

ethnarch and high priest of the Jews (*Ant.* 14.143; *J.W.* 1.194).[9] Gabinius then turned on the Nabateans, the erstwhile allies of Antipater. Ever the pragmatist, Antipater gave provisions to the Romans, all the while encouraging his old ally, King Aretas, to strike a deal with his attackers (*Ant* 14.101–103; *J.W.* 1.178).

Here Antipater revealed the Herodian penchant for playing both sides at once and work-

ing everything to a Herodian advantage. The practical reality was that it was Antipater, not Hyrcanus II, who continued to assist Gabinius, the Roman-appointed governor of Judea, with campaigns in Egypt and with staving off successive attacks from the remnants of Aristobulus II. In this way the Romans came to see that the real help and money lay with Antipater, not with the Hasmonean high priest, Hyrcanus II (*Ant.* 14.98; *J.W.* 1.175–177). In this way the Herodians were carving out a place at Caesar's table, and Antipater looked for opportunities to secure his place in the royal household.

9   "Ethnarch" was the Roman designation for a ruler of a province or a people. Since the term did not entail the same honor and authority as "king," Pompey clearly designated the place and function of Hyrcanus II within the Roman hierarchy.

The opportunity came in 49 B.C.E., when the tensions between Julius Caesar and Pompey exploded into civil war. In typical fashion, Antipater waited until the balance of power tilted in a certain direction, then set his course accordingly. As Caesar triumphed over Pompey, Antipater transferred all of his resources and influence behind the victor (*J.W.* 1.187; *Ant.* 14.127). He was rewarded handsomely by Caesar, who conferred Roman citizenship upon Antipater and graced him with the title *epitropos*, that is, the "trusted administrator or governor" of all Judea (*J.W.* 1.199–200; *Ant.* 14.143).

Caesar realized, however, that he had more than one player on the field in Jerusalem, and he was careful to seek a balance of power among the Jews. To this end, he allowed

Hasmonean influence to continue by permitting Hyrcanus II to stay on as high priest (*J.W.* 1.153). Civil administration, however, was conveyed to Antipater. Caesar, for example, granted huge sums of money to Antipater to rebuild the walls of Jerusalem and strengthen its security forces (*J.W.* 1.201).

Caesar's scheme for power sharing between the Hasmoneans and the Herodians did suc-ceed. In short order many Jews realized that the power of the Hasmoneans was being siphoned off by Antipater, the Idumean, the "half-Jew." To stem the flow and reserve some clout for Hyrcanus II, one Malichus had Antipater poisoned at a banquet in about 43 B.C.E. (*Ant.* 14.281; *J.W.* 1.226).

This treachery proved to be too little and too late. Before his assassination, Antipater

The impressive aqueduct built by Herod the Great to supply drinking water to his port of Caesarea Maritima, named to honor the Roman emperor.

Remains of Herod the Great's winter palace at Tulul El-Alaiq, near Jericho.

had consolidated his control over the Jews by empowering his sons. Phasael was designated governor of Jerusalem, and Herod was appointed ruler over Galilee in 47 B.C.E. (*Ant.* 14.121). The latter proved to be the most adept at staying in the corner of whatever Caesar was in power at the time and at subduing the Jews by way of blessing or curse.

### Herod the Great (73–4 B.C.E.)

Early on, Herod the Great (henceforth called simply "Herod") proved himself the friend of Rome, once again by exploiting the infighting of the Jews. Antigonus, son of Aristobulus II, was the last surviving Hasmonean of the Maccabean kind. That is, Antigonus represented the strain that desired no compromise with Rome or their client kings. He also was the last great hope of the Jews to oust Hyrcanus the high priest and Herod. Antigonus's bid for power succeeded through

an alliance with the Parthians, the archenemies of Rome. Herod and Hyrcanus were driven from Jerusalem; the latter's ears were sheared off so as to disqualify him from ever attaining the high priesthood, and eventually he did not survive the onslaught of Antigonus (*J.W.* 1.271–272; *Ant.* 14.365–369). Herod fled to Rome and used the Parthian-Antigonus alliance to leverage the full support of Octavian and Antony (the two Caesars were reconciled for the moment). Josephus records that in 40 B.C.E., with great fanfare and before the entire Roman senate, the Caesars declared the thirty-three-year-old "Herod the Great" to be "King of the Jews" (*J.W.* 1.281–283, 388; *Ant.* 14.9, 379–389). All that remained was to drive the remnants of the Maccabees out of Jerusalem. Herod the Great was all too eager to lend a hand.

The Roman general Ventidius rolled back the Parthian forces in 39 B.C.E. while Herod strug-

Steps leading to the Temple of Augustus built by Herod the Great in Classical style at Samaria.

gled to retake Judea. With the help of Roman troops, Jerusalem fell after a five-month siege in 37 B.C.E. (*Ant.* 14.394, 421; *J.W.* 1.290; Eusebius, *Hist. eccl.* 1.7.12). King Herod was now empowered by Rome to rule over Judea, Galilee, Perea, and Idumea. To the dismay of the vast majority of the Jews, the Maccabean legacy was over at last. In its place was a totalitarian "half-Jew" who sought to enhance his power by subjugating Israel to Roman rule. Josephus captures the pathos of the Jews when he comments on the fall of the Hasmoneans: "These men lost the government by their dissensions one with another, and it came to Herod, the Son of Antipater, who was of no more than a vulgar family, and of no eminent extraction, but on that was subject to other kings. And this is what history tells us was the end of the Asamonean family" (*Ant* 14.491).

Since Herod was aware that his fortune was tied to the fate of Rome, he gingerly steered a course between the warring factions among the Romans and kept tabs on his enemies among the Jews. At this point in his career, he took every opportunity to aid Marc Antony in the East. He staved off a push by Cleopatra to reinstate Ptolemaic influence in Judea and was ever mindful of Alexandra's (his mother-in-law by way of Mariamne I) attempt to reintroduce Hasmonean presence in the high priesthood. In typical Herodian fashion, when Antony was defeated by Octavian at Actium in 31 B.C.E., Herod switched allegiance to the victor. To demonstrate his commitment to Octavian (soon to be known as Caesar Augustus; cf. Luke 2:1), Herod helped him purge Jerusalem of all Jews hostile to the intent of Rome. Josephus records that Jews of all ages, including women and infants, were slaughtered without mercy, their bodies piled up in heaps (*Ant.* 14.469, 479–480). In this way, Herod the Great, through treachery and

The reconstructed theater at Caesarea Maritima, with columns in the foreground from the Roman harbor built by Herod the Great.

shameless political opportunism, now served as Rome's pawn in Jerusalem.[10] In return, Augustus placed the full might of imperial Rome behind Herod. One can only imagine the ill will that the local Jewish populace had for Herod. He was so hated in Jerusalem that the Romans were forced to keep a permanent garrison there to protect their puppet king.

Herod also exploited the resources of his Jewish subjects to fund his lavish building programs.[11] Since the emperors viewed the building of elaborate palaces as counter to the imperial ethos, Herod needed to be discreet. When he built eight residential palaces, he billed these projects as gifts to the people, not only the Jews but his friends in Rome (*Ant.* 15.363–364). One of his greatest projects was the renovation of the temple (*Ant.* 15.380–387, 391–403; 17.154; *J.W.* 1.401). Work began in 20–19 B.C.E. and continued into the late twenties C.E. (John 2:20), with the entire project completed in 64 C.E.[12] This work brought a tremendous amount of money into Jerusalem and greatly affected its economy. It is estimated that work on the temple employed nearly twenty thousand workers (*Ant* 20.219–221). Herod strengthened defenses throughout the land, building magnificent fortresses at

10  On Herod's complicity with Rome, see John H. Hayes and Sara R. Mandell, *The Jewish People in Classic Antiquity from Alexander to Bar Kochba* (Louisville: Westminster John Knox, 1998), esp. 125; and Stewart Perowne, *The Life and Times of Herod the Great* (Stroud, Glos., Eng.: Sutton, 2003), 64–65.

11  For maps and a chronological list detailing Herod's building projects inside Judea and throughout the Mediterranean world, see Richardson, *Herod*, maps 5 and 6; cf. also pp. 197–202.

12  The extent of Herod's work on the temple can be seen in the fact that the edifice came to be known as "Herod's temple." It was not completed until the time of his great-grandson, King Herod Agrippa II, when Nero was emperor. Herod's renovation of the temple was also part of his plan for defenses, as he rebuilt the fortress of Antonia there (*Ant.* 15.409). Ultimately, these achievements were for naught. In 70 C.E., only six years after its completion, the Romans razed the temple to the ground.

Aerial view of the Roman aqueduct at Caesarea, built by Herod the Great.

Jericho, Herodium, and Machaerus (39–38 B.C.E.), the most famous of which was Masada, near the Dead Sea (*Ant.* 14.296, 369; 16.13; *J.W.* 1.161, 407; 7.285, 303). He erected entire cities and parceled out jobs and land grants to Jews who proved loyal.[13] He built Caesarea Maritima, using the latest technology to construct a lavish harbor there, perhaps the best on the Mediterranean Sea (*Ant.* 15.331–41). Such works were part of Herod's *euergesia*, "good works," meant to impress the emperor.

Herod realized that building projects for the Jews and his patrons in Rome were not enough to solidify his position. He would have to manipulate the religious and political map to his advantage. Herod knew that the death of Hyrcanus put an end to Hasmonean presence in the high priesthood and that this was a sore spot for his Jewish subjects, and so he married the Hasmonean Mariamne I, the grand-daughter of Hyrcanus II (*Ant.* 14.353; 15.23). At the same time, however, he seized the opportunity to control the high priesthood by alternately appointing representatives from different families and abolishing the lifetime tenure of the office (*Ant.* 15.40–41; 17.164, 207). On a political level, he purged the Sanhedrin of the remnants of Hasmonean sentiment and appointed loyal friends to occupy the highest governing body of the Jews.[14]

Herod was ruthless in eliminating opposition both within and without his family. After the defeat of Antony at Actium, Herod feared

13 For a complete catalogue of Herod's building program, see Duane W. Roller, *The Building Program of Herod the Great* (Berkeley: University of California Press, 1998), esp. 94–95. See also Perowne, *The Life and Times of Herod the Great*, 115–28.

14 For a description of the tyranny that Herod held over the Jews, see M. Stern, "The Reign of Herod and the Herodian Dynasty," in *The Jewish People in the First Century: Historical Geography, Political History, Social, Cultural, and Religious Life and Institutions* (ed. S. Safrai and M. Stern; 2 vols.; CRINT, sec. 1; Philadelphia: Fortress, 1974), esp. 1:248, 275.

The unmistakable profile of the slopes of Herodion, the stronghold built by Herod the Great after his flight to Masada in 40 B.C.E.

a Hasmonean resurgence, and so he had the grandfather and the brother of his beloved wife, Mariamne, executed because of their staunch support of the Hasmoneans. When Mariamne chafed at his treachery and did not rejoice at Herod's eventual endorsement by Augustus, Herod began to suspect her of disloyalty. Solome, his sister, fostered these suspicions, and in 29 B.C.E. Herod had the queen executed (J.W. 1.438–443; Ant. 15.222–231). The dissonance created by political expediency and personal grief over the loss of his wife is said to have driven him mad (J.W. 1.444; Ant. 15.240–41). His bloodlust was loosed once again when Herod eventually granted the wish of his mother-in-law, Alexandra, to have her son Aristobulus III installed as high priest. But after witnessing the immense popularity that the seventeen-year-old enjoyed with the Jews and again fearing Hasmonean resurgence, he had Aristobulus drowned as he swam in one of his palace pools (J.W. 1.436; Ant. 20.247–248).

On another occasion, Herod had a golden eagle, the symbol of Roman power, installed over one of the gates in the temple. When Jewish youths tore down this emblem of the empire, Herod rooted out the perpetrators and had them burned alive in public (Ant. 17.149–167). His own children were not spared his wrath born of paranoia. Shortly before his death, he slew three of his sons, Alexander, Aristobulus, and Antipater, born of different mothers, for supposedly plotting to overthrow his throne (Ant. 16.251; 17.187, 349; 18.134; J.W. 1.586). On Herod's murdering ways, Augustus is reported to have said, "I would rather be Herod's pig than his son" (Macrobius, Sat. 2.4.11).[15]

Although recorded only in the Gospel of Matthew, the slaughter of the infants also reflects the dark story of Herod's treachery (cf. Matt 2:1–22). As Matthew has it, near

15  Macrobius (late fourth or early fifth century C.E.?) notes that Augustus's quip was made in response to Herod's slaughtering of the infants in Bethlehem.

Recently discovered tomb, believed to be that of Herod the Great, at Herodion, near Bethlehem.

the end of Herod's life, magi from the east, perhaps motivated by Zoroastrian speculation about a coming king of the Jews, visit his court.[16] To a pathologically insecure Herod, queries about the birth of a Jewish king would have been unwelcome. When he accesses his lieutenants in the Sanhedrin, they counsel that the promised messiah is to be born in Bethlehem (Matt 2:4; Mic 5:2). His plot to employ the magi as spies is not unlike the scheming Herod portrayed by Josephus (Matt 2:12). Realizing that his source for privileged information is lost, he strikes with a blunt instrument, ordering the deaths of all male infants in Bethlehem two years old and under. By casting a wide net, Herod assumes that the promised child will be caught up in

the slaughter (Matt 2:16–18). If the record of Josephus is to be believed, then for Herod, who did not spare his own wife and children, the death of Jewish infants would have been of no concern if it served his interests.

After his death in 4 B.C.E. (cf. *Ant.* 17.150–183, 191), the legacy of Herod the Great was continued through his three sons, Archelaus, Herod Philip, and Herod Antipas.[17] Since Herod had drawn up at least seven wills, at times indicating this son as heir and at times indicating another son, the division of his kingdom was hotly contested.[18]

## Archelaus (23 B.C.E.–18 C.E.)

Herod's first will stated that Herod Antipas was the most worthy son to be king (*Ant.* 17.146). Yet in subsequent codicils, Archelaus

16 Bart D. Ehrman identifies the magi as Assyrian astral scholars (*The New Testament: A Historical Introduction to the Early Christian Writings* [Oxford: Oxford University Press, 2004], 99). See also Richardson, *Herod: King of the Jews*, 296.

17 For an account of Herod's final hours, the great pains that he suffered, and modern diagnoses of the cause of his death, see Nikos Kokkinos, "Herod's Horrid Death," *BAR* 28 (2002): 28–35.

18 Smallwood, *The Jews under Roman Rule*, 104–8.

was designated king, and his two brothers, Herod Antipas and Herod Philip, were to be tetrarchs (*Ant.* 17.188–189). The confusion launched Archelaus and Herod Antipas, together with their respective entourages, on a voyage to Rome in order that they might appeal directly to Augustus Caesar (*Ant.* 17.219–220, 224).[19] Herod Antipas noted that Archelaus had acted as a king without imperial endorsement when he slaughtered many Jews at the Passover festival and that Archelaus also rejoiced at the death of his father, Herod the Great, on the very night that he passed away (*Ant.* 17.230–233). Withholding judgment at that time, Caesar expressed his affirmation for Archelaus and his desire that the wishes of a dying man's will be respected (*Ant.* 17.248). In the end, Augustus struck a mediating position, appointing Archelaus as the ethnarch over Judea, Samaria, and Idumea, the largest and richest territories, whereas Herod Antipas and Herod Philip would be tetrarchs over the remaining areas (*Ant.* 17.318–319). Augustus added one caveat that must have pleased Archelaus. He would become "King of the Jews" if he behaved himself (*Ant.* 17.317). But he did not.

Archelaus, who reigned from 4 B.C.E. to 6 C.E., soon proved to be one of the most treacherous descendants in the Herodian dynasty. His marriage to Glaphyra, once wife to his half-brother Alexander and recently divorced from Juba of Mauretania, in no wise squared with Levirate law or with the Jewish people. In addition, he refused to make amends for the cruelty of his father, Herod the Great. So callous was his response to his people that all of Jerusalem erupted in violence. Archelaus responded by sending his whole army against the Jews, killing three thousand in the temple

alone (*Ant* 17.217–218). The Samaritans fared even worse under his rule and joined with the Jews in making a petition to Caesar to have Archelaus removed from office. In 6 C.E. Archelaus was banished to Vienne in Gaul (*J.W.* 2.111). His territory was then governed directly by Coponius, the Roman procurator, and after him by Pontius Pilate (*Ant* 17.339–44; 18.1–2, 35). Since the Romans still needed a local representative to conduct the census, collect taxes, and serve as a representative in Rome, they chose to work through the high priests and were careful to appoint only those who would serve the purposes of the empire (*Ant.* 18.93; 20.6, 249; *J.W.* 5.114).

The terror of Archelaus is displayed in Matt 2:22–23.[20] Here Joseph is said to be afraid to enter the territory of Archelaus. Instead, warned in a dream, he takes Mary and the child Jesus into Nazareth of Galilee, the domain of Herod Antipas.

## Herod Philip (20 B.C.E.–39 C.E.)

Herod Philip, the son of Herod the Great and Cleopatra of Jerusalem, was raised in Rome, as were his brothers (*Ant.* 17.21; *J.W.* 1.602; *Life* 1.408). Philip proved to be the most peaceable of the family. He did not contest the will of his father as Archelaus and Herod Antipas did, as apparently he was not greedy for more power (*Ant.* 17.219). He ruled from 4 B.C.E. to 34 C.E.; his territory lay east of the Jordan, taking in the northeast portion of Palestine, including the southern part of Lebanon to Damascus. On the west his domain was bordered by the Sea of Galilee and extended south to Decapolis (*Ant.* 17.319; 18.106, 137; *J.W.* 1.668; 3.512). Most of his subjects were Syrian Gentiles, and his area was much hellenized. Yet Josephus records that he went about the region seeking to resolve disputes personally

---

19  While they were away contesting the will, the political situation in Judea rapidly degenerated into open rebellion. Varus, the Roman legate in Syria, however, swept southward and crushed the uprising (Stern, "The Reign of Herod," 280–81).

20  Some scholars have argued that Archelaus is the nobleman who would be made king in the parable of the Talents (Matt 25:14–30; Luke 19:11–27). If so, his harsh treatment of the unworthy stewards could be a symbol of eschatological judgment (ibid., 299).

**View of Herod the Great's north palace, Masada, Israel, from above.**

in an equitable manner (*Ant.* 18.106–108). He did not become embroiled in the kind of political intrigue so characteristic of the Herods. Yet by changing the name of Panias to Caesarea Philippi and having the image of the Caesars struck on the coins of his realm, Herod Philip publicly acknowledged that Rome was in charge. When he died without heirs, Rome ceded his territory to Herod Agrippa I (*Ant.* 18.108, 137; *J.W.* 2.181).

The moderation of Philip may receive some support from the New Testament. Jesus saw the "other side" of the Sea of Galilee as a place of safety, perhaps meaning that he did not view Herod Philip as hostile to him or his followers (Mark 6:46; 7:31; 8:22, 27). Such a setting befits Peter's confession that Jesus was the Christ (Matt 16:13–20; Mark 8:23–30; Luke 9:20). Moreover, Andrew, Peter, and Philip, the disciples of Jesus, came from Bethsaida, in Philip's territory, and it was here that some Greeks contacted the disciple Philip so that they might see Jesus (John 12:20–22). It was also here that after Jesus fed the five thousand, the people sought to make Jesus king by force (John 6:10–15). These incidents seem to reflect a context of stability and a modicum of security compared with the volatility of other areas such as Galilee and Jerusalem.

## Herod Antipas (21 B.C.E.–?)

Herod Antipas, the son of Herod the Great and Malthace the Samaritan, was raised in Rome like his brothers Archelaus and Philip (*Ant.* 17.20; *J.W.* 1.562). Augustus made Herod Antipas tetrarch of Galilee and Perea (Luke 3:1), and he ruled from 4 B.C.E. to 39 C.E. (*Ant.* 17.318; 18.136; *J.W.* 1.668; 2.167). Galilee figured prominently in the ministry of Jesus, and Perea was the venue for the ministry of John the Baptist. Like his forefathers, he sought every opportunity to solidify his standing with Rome, with both Augustus and Tiberius (17–22 C.E.). For example, he built the city of Tiberias

in the emperor's honor (*Ant.* 18.36; *Life* 1.37) and changed the name of the Sea of Galilee to Lake Tiberias to curry the favor of the emperor (*J.W.* 3.57).[21] In this way he became a friend of Tiberius and a member of his inner circle of advisors and allies (*Ant.* 18.36).

It is this Herod who holds such a prominent place in the Gospels—the Herod who had John the Baptist beheaded and conspired with Pilate to have Jesus crucified (Matt 14:3; Mark 6:17; Luke 3:20; John 3:24). Indeed, the first contact between Herod Antipas and John the Baptist was one of conflict. Because John had rebuked Herod for his illegal marriage (Lev 20:21; 18:16) to Herodias, the daughter of his half-brother Aristobulus and the wife of his brother Philip (Matt 14:3 f.; Mark 6:17–18; Luke 3:19; *Ant.* 18.136), Herod Antipas captured John and placed him in prison. Herod Antipas harbored ambivalent feelings about John, for he recognized his piety and was impressed by his preaching. On the other hand, he feared John because of the tremendous influence he had upon the people (Matt 14:5; Mark 6:20).[22] Josephus records that Herod Antipas executed John because he feared that the people would do anything that John might ask them to do (*Ant.* 18.116–119). Josephus does not mention John's rebuke of Herod Antipas but notes that the divorce of his first wife, the daughter of King Aretas of Syria, led to his defeat by Aretas in 36 C.E. (*Ant.* 18.110–112). Josephus reports that "some of the Jews" interpreted this defeat

---

21    The insensitivity of Herod Antipas to the Jews can be seen in the fact that he built the city of Tiberias on an ancient Jewish cemetery. This may be why Jesus not once entered the city (Emil Schürer, *The History of the Jewish People in the Age of Jesus Christ* [175 B.C.–A.D. 135] [rev. and ed. Geza Vermes, Furgus Millar, and Matthew Black; 3 vols. in 4; Edinburgh: T&T Clark, 1973–1987], 2:167). Also, Tiberias was the first city built to be a Greco-Roman *polis* within Israel (Stern, "The Reign of Herod," 286).

22    Harold W. Hoehner notes that Herod Antipas's fear of John was the same as that felt by the chief priests and elders, for they feared to publicly reject John because of the people (Matt 21:26; Mark 11:32; Luke 20:6) (*Herod Antipas; Tetrarch of Galilee* [Grand Rapids: Zondervan, 1980], 163).

The town of Tiberias, built by Herod the Great to honor Mark Antony, viewed from the Sea of Galilee. There is no mention of this important location in the Gospels.

as the judgment of God on Antipas because he had killed the righteous John (*Ant.* 18.116).

The execution of John the Baptist had a profound effect upon Jesus of Nazareth. Initially he withdrew to Herod Philip's territory (Mark 6:30–31) but then moved his ministry back into Galilee (Luke 8:37), which was under the jurisdiction of Herod Antipas. It is as if Jesus took up the apocalyptic ministry of John and brought it back to Herod Antipas's doorstep. Jesus even begins to employ the same eschatological jargon as John in his preaching, calling for repentance, castigating his opponents as a brood of vipers, and warning that the unfruitful will be burned up (Matt 3:2//4:17; 3:7//12:38–39; 3:10//7:19). His preaching is effective, for even Manaen, who was raised with Herod Antipas, and Joanna, the wife of his steward, Chuza, become disciples of Jesus (Acts 13:1; Luke 8:3). The parallel between Jesus and John the Baptist is so close that Herod Antipas wonders if Jesus is not John risen from the dead (Matt 14:1; Mark 6:14–16; Luke 9:7). Some of the Pharisees inform Jesus that Herod Antipas wants him dead, yet Jesus expresses no fear of him. Jesus tells them to report to "that fox" that he, as the Son of God, is directed by the providential hand of the Father (Luke 13:31–33). Just as Herod Antipas had an odd fascination with John, and yet had John killed, he wants to see Jesus as well (Luke 9:9). Just before Herod Antipas hands Jesus over to Pilate, he desires that Jesus do some miracle for him (Luke 23:8).

Pilate was in a position to try Jesus because he had been sent by Rome to rule in Archelaus's stead. Gathering that Jesus was a Galilean, he referred him to Herod Antipas, who was in Jerusalem at the time. Ever careful not to act wrongly regarding Rome, Herod sent him back to Pilate (Luke 23:6–11; *J.W.* 2.169). The upshot of the hearings, according to Luke, was that neither ruler found Jesus guilty of any crime, yet he was sentenced to death anyway (Luke 23:13–25; *Ant.* 18.63–64). Again Luke has Herod Antipas and Pilate congratulating each other for quelling a public uprising (Luke 23:12).

Under Gaius Caligula, the successor to Tiberius, Herod Antipas was retained as tetrarch. The title of "king," however, fell to his nephew Herod Agrippa I. It appears that this

219

nephew's constant accusations against Herod Antipas found a ready ear in Caligula. For example, Herod Agrippa I frequently reported to the emperor that his uncle was growing too close to the Parthians. For this reason, Caligula exiled Herod Antipas to Lugdunum (Lyons) in Gaul in 39 C.E. (*Ant.* 18.252).[23] The precise date of Herod's death is unknown.

## Herod Agrippa I (10? B.C.E.–44 C.E.)

Herod Agrippa I was the son of Aristobulus and Bernice, the brother of Herodias, and the grandson of Herod the Great and Mariamne (*J.W.* 2.178; *Ant.* 18.240, 253; Philo, *Flaccus* 5.25). His life was one of misfortune turned to fortune, time and time again. As a child, he was taken to Rome and schooled in the ways of the empire as the other Herodian offspring had been. As a young man, he soon buried himself in debt and had to flee the city to avoid arrest by his creditors. He became a destitute vagabond who despaired of life until rescued by an old friend, Gaius Caligula (*Ant.* 18.145–150; *J.W.* 2.178–179). Yet an imprudent slip of the tongue, wishing that Tiberius were dead and Gaius were put in his place, landed him in prison (*Ant.* 18.168–169, 185–191). When Gaius became emperor, Herod Agrippa's fortunes turned again for the better, for at that time he was appointed king of the Jews and given the territories of Philip, Lysanius, and Herod Antipas (*Ant.* 18.236–239, 252; *J.W.* 2.183; Philo, *Flaccus* 5.25; Dio Cassius, *Hist. rom.* 59.8.2). Although Gaius was his trusted friend, their bond was greatly tested by Gaius's plan to place a statue of himself in the temple in Jerusalem. Herod Agrippa's diplomatic skill and his love for his people can be seen in his letter to Gaius pleading that no image be brought into sacred precincts of the Jews (Philo, *Embassy* 35.261–42.330; Josephus, *Ant.* 18.256–301).

Four years into Gaius's reign, the senators of Rome conspired to assassinate him (*Ant.* 19.62–114). As he was slain outside the theater, Herod Agrippa bought time in the ensuing chaos to secure his own future. Casting a garment over Gaius's dead body, he announced that Gaius was yet alive and that attendants should go for a physician. Subsequently, while counseling Claudius, the grandnephew of Augustus and nephew of Tiberius, not to yield the government, Agrippa gave a rousing speech to the senate in support of Claudius (*Ant.* 19.236–246). This support of Claudius led to further expansion of his domain. Under Claudius, Herod Agrippa became ruler over all of Palestine, commanding a larger domain than any single Herod before him (*Ant.* 19.274–276, 292, 351; Dio Cassius, *Hist. rom.* 60.8.1–3). Since he was of Hasmonean blood and was more committed to the welfare of the Jews than any of his predecessors, Herod Agrippa was well received by his subjects (*Ant.* 19.328–331). He appointed high priests from the house of Boethus and Ananus (both Sadducees), sought to remain on good terms with the Pharisees, and acknowledged the importance of the Jews in the Diaspora (*Ant.* 19.297–298). For these reasons, Herod Agrippa received high praise in the rabbinic literature (*m. Soṭah* 7:8; *m. Bikkurim* 3:4).

The New Testament presents Herod Agrippa I as an enemy of the church.[24] He had James, the son of Zebedee, executed, and perceiving that "this pleased the Jews," he proceeded to arrest Peter (Acts 12:1–3). When Herod Agrippa learned of the miraculous release of Peter, he suspected complicity and had all the guards executed (Acts 12:19).

Josephus and Luke concur regarding the

---

23  But *J.W.* 2.181–183 says that Herod was banished to Spain. On the misfortune of Herod at the hands of Gaius, see D. Braund, "Four Notes on the Herods," *Classical Quarterly* NS 33/1 (1983): 239–42.

24  "By virtue of his function Agrippa had to handle the Christian problem. Here he appears to have acted with severity, and not in accordance with the Pharisaic school as it found expression in Gamaliel's famous speech in the Sanhedrin" (Stern, "The Reign of Herod," 296). It would be a mistake, however, to characterize the "Pharisaic school" as wholly amenable to Christianity. Gamaliel's star pupil, Saul of Tarsus, was anything but friendly to the first Christians (Acts 7:58–60, 8:1–3; 1 Cor 15:9; Gal 1:13).

**Artist's impression of the harbor and city of Caesarea Maritima, built by Herod the Great. Note the Roman galley entering the harbor, and the probable site of the governor's residence, bottom right.**

sudden death of Herod Agrippa I in 44 C.E. While he was attending a celebration in honor of Claudius in Caesarea and adorned in resplendent attire, the people hailed him as a god. He accepted these accolades, but he suddenly fell ill of an acute stomach ailment and was dead within five days. Both Josephus and Luke suggest his death was divine retribution (*Ant.* 19.343–350; Acts 12.20–23).[25]

### Herod Agrippa II (31–100 C.E.)

The power of Herod Agrippa I raised concerns in Rome, and so his son, Herod Agrippa II, great-great-grandson of Herod the Great, was not awarded the kingdom at his death. Rather,

the realm of Herod Agrippa II increased incrementally. First he was granted by Claudius (ca. 50 C.E.) the kingdom of Chalsis in the far north of Judea, an area corresponding with modern-day Lebanon. Sometime later he was given Philip's tetrarchy (*Ant.* 19.277, 338; 20.15–16). Nero again increased his realm by awarding him Galilee and Perea in 54–55 C.E. (*Ant.* 20.159). In return, Herod Agrippa II changed the name of Caesarea Philippi to Neronias (*Ant.* 20.211).

The power of Herod Agrippa II was enhanced through his sisters. Drusilla married Felix, the Roman freedman who had been made procurator of Judea and was the first before whom Paul stood trial in Caesarea (*Ant.* 20.139, 142–143; Acts 23:23–24:25). Luke is careful to note that Drusilla was "a Jewess" (Acts 24:24) and that Felix was somewhat informed about Christianity by her (Acts 24:22). As Paul spoke to him about righteousness, self-control and

25  Agourides sees this incident as evidence of the pseudomessianic among the Herods. The Jews who called Herod Agrippa I a god were the Herodians who believed him to be the messiah. "The most probable explanation is that people from Tyre and Sidon as well as courtiers of Herod acclaimed his messianic character as a king of godhood"("The Birth of Jesus and the Herodian Dynasty," 139).

221

the final judgment, Felix became fearful and postponed the inquiry until a later date (Acts 24:24–25). Afterwards he sought to extort money from the apostle for the next two years (Acts 24:26). At this point another of Herod Agrippa II's sisters came into play (cf. *Life* 1.343). Bernice became his constant consort, and the liaison between the two was so close that it invited scandal. It was widely believed that Herod Agrippa and Bernice were involved in an incestuous relationship (*Ant.* 20.145). For this reason, he was condemned by both Jews and Christians. The political advantage of Bernice was compounded by the fact that she also became intimate with the emperor Titus. Titus would have married Bernice if not for the anti-Jewish sentiment so entrenched among his subjects (Tacitus, *Ann.* 2.2; Dio Cassius, *Hist. rom.* 66.15.3–5).

After Festus succeeded Felix as procurator, he took up Paul's case. Festus was advised by Bernice and Herod Agrippa II at the trial (Acts 25:13–26:32). In compliance with Paul's appeal to Caesar, Festus sent Paul to Rome.

By 66 C.E. the Jews had had enough of the Romans and their client kings, the Herods. In the revolt that followed, Herod Agrippa II stood solidly behind the Roman army, as had all the Herods before him. He fought side by side with the Roman general Vespasian against the Jews and was wounded in battle (*J.W.* 3.29, 457; 4.14). After the fall of Jerusalem, he and Bernice moved to Rome, where he remained until his death in ca. 100 C.E. His demise marks the end of the Herodian dynasty and its long rule in Judea.

## THE HERODIANS AND THE GOSPELS

In the Gospels the word *Hērōdianoi* always appears in the context of the "conflict sayings" of Jesus, which occur in two contexts:

1. the healing of the man with the withered hand on the Sabbath (Mark 3:1–6);
2. the question of paying taxes to Caesar (Matt 22:15–22; Mark 12:13–17).

In seeking to identify the Herodians as portrayed in the Gospels, it should be noted that in all of these cases, the Herodians are linked with the Pharisees, the Sadducees, and the Sanhedrin (cf. also Luke 23:1–6).[26] The Herodians are persons, then, who are allied with Jesus' opponents—the Pharisees, the Sadducees who were members of the Sanhedrin, and all those in league with Herod Antipas in the condemnation of Jesus.

The association of the Herodians with the Sanhedrin may shed additional light on their identity. After fleeing Herod Antipas's territory for the relative safety of Herod Philip, Jesus warns his disciples to beware of the leaven of the Pharisees and Herod (Mark 8:15).[27] Moreover, Matthew's account of the same incident warns of the leaven of the Pharisees and the Sadducees (Matt 16:6). Since Herod the Great stacked the Sanhedrin with his "friends" and appointed only Sadducees of the family of Boethus as high priests, the link between the Herodians and the Sadducees becomes even stronger (*Ant.* 15.320–322; 17.78, 164–167). The Sadducees in the Sanhedrin and those from the aristocratic household of Boethus may have formed a significant part of the group know as the Herodians.

This is not to say that there is a direct equivalency between the Herodians and the Sadducees. The Greek suffixes -*ianoi* (-ιανοι) or -*einoi*, (-εινοι), much like the Latin equivalent -*iani*, denote members of one's household, or of a governing court, or simply adherents or partisans.[28] Thus the term *Hērōdianoi* in general refers to persons who supported the Herods throughout their long reign; some of them may well have been Boethusian Sadducees of the Sanhedrin.

26  Luke's account concerning tribute to Caesar simply describes those who seek to entrap Jesus as "spies" (Luke 20:20).

27  A textual variant for this verse replaces the word "Herod" with the word "Herodians." For a list of late manuscripts that support this substitution, see UBS[4] 150 n. 15.

28  On the grammatical significance of the Greek and Latin suffixes and the identity of the Herods, see Hoehner, *Herod Antipas*, 332.

The identity of the Herodians and their role in the Gospels may be further clarified within the context of patrons and clients of the first century. Just as the emperor was the patron of the Herods, so the Herods were probably the patrons of the Herodians. This would mean that the Herodians were made up of all persons who believed that their fate and fortunes were bound to the success of the Herodian dynasty. They were prepared to oppose anyone who threatened the well-being of the Herods, whether they were Jews of the Maccabean kind or Jesus the messiah and his followers.

# Annotated Bibliography

Hoehner, Harold W. *Herod Antipas: Tetrarch of Galilee*. Grand Rapids: Zondervan, 1980. This revised dissertation provides valuable information on the political and economic contexts of Herod's day. It discusses in detail how Herod may have related to biblical characters such as Pilate, Archelaus, and John the Baptist and supplies genealogical and chronological tables. Although it is not written for beginners, a careful reading is rewarded.

Kokkinos, Nikos. *The Herodian Dynasty: Origins, Role in Society, and Eclipse*. Journal for the Study of the Pseudepigrapha: Supplement Series 30. Sheffield, Eng.: Sheffield Academic Press, 1998. This revised dissertation thoroughly analyzes the Herodian dynasty, starting with a study of the Idumeans and continuing through to the end of the Herodian line in the second century C.E. It is one of the most comprehensive treatments of the Herodians, including charts, diagrams, and maps that add to one's understanding of their world.

Perowne, Stewart. *The Life and Times of Herod the Great*. Stroud, Glos., Eng.: Sutton, 2003. Extensive knowledge of the archeology and geography of the Middle East has enhanced this study of Herod the Great. This book shows how the entire spectrum of Herod the Great's life, from birth to death, can inform our understanding of the historical Jesus.

Richardson, Peter. Herod: *King of the Jews and Friend of the Romans*. Minneapolis: Fortress, 1999. This balanced work seeks to explain Herod's actions within the sociopolitical climate of the times. Patronage and the role that it played in the building program of Herod are addressed. Archaeological evidence, inscriptions on coins, family trees, and so on, provide a valuable databank for delving into the world of Herod.

Roller, Duane W. *The Building Program of Herod the Great*. Berkeley: University of California Press, 1998. This is a well-presented and well-illustrated work on the vast building program of Herod the Great. Many photos and drawings help the reader appreciate the grandeur of Herod's programs, the revenue it took to complete the projects, and the political capital that Herod gained by contributing to the emperors and patrons of the time.

Schürer, Emil. T*he History of the Jewish People in the Age of Jesus Christ (175 B.C.–A.D. 135)*. See description at the end of ch. 2.

Smallwood, E. Mary. *The Jews under Roman Rule—from Pompey to Diocletian: A Study in Political Relations*. Leiden: E. J. Brill, 1981. This complement to Schürer's work takes the study up to the Jew's relationship to the Romans in the early fourth century C.E. Possible causes of the conflicts between the Jews and the Romans receive special attention, especially the political tensions that led up to the revolt of 66 C.E.

# 15

# The Roman Imperial Rulers— Hierarchy and Empire

## INTRODUCTION

The church was born during the height of the Roman Empire. The first believers preached and worshiped under the rule of Caesar Augustus, and although they were persecuted by Nero and his successors, Christians prospered for the next five hundred years as they negotiated the treacherous landscape of the Roman imperial state. Eventually the Gospel conquered the mighty Roman Empire

**Julius Caesar (49–44 B.C.E.).**

and harnessed its power to shape Western civilization and launch the modern missionary movement. Therefore, in order to gain an understanding of the larger world of the gospel and the church, one must come to understand something about the Roman Empire and its leadership.

The Roman Republic was birthed in 509 B.C.E. and in its ideal was set up to be a representative government. It was composed of a senate drawn from the patricians, or ruling aristocracy, and of the tribunes of the people, representatives who were elected by the common people. In time the senate shared power with two consuls. These two individuals were elected by representative bodies mainly based on wealth and military service.[1] Under this form of republican government, Roman rule greatly expanded through military conquests by such generals as Sulla, Pompey, and Julius Caesar.

The growth of the Republic, however, generated problems that in time became unwieldy. Internal tensions between the senate, ruled by the patricians, and the tribunes of the

---

1    For how the empire was run under the Caesars, see Dio Cassius, *Hist. rom.* 53.12.1–53.16.6. On the basic structure of early Roman government, see Chris Scarre, *Chronicle of Roman Emperors: The Reign by Reign Record of the Rulers of Imperial Rome* (London: Thames & Hudson, 1995), 8. For the duties of Roman civil servants, from the level of consul all the way down to the level of local assessor, see Justinian, *Dig.* 1.10–22.

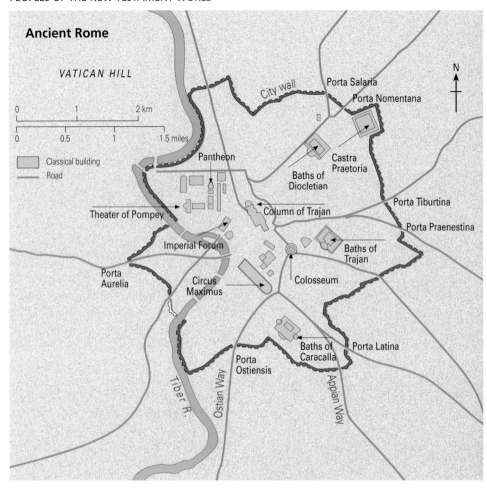

**Ancient Rome**

VATICAN HILL

City wall

Porta Salaria
Porta Nomentana

N

0        1        2 km

0     0.5      1      1.5 miles

Classical building
Road

Pantheon

Castra
Praetoria

Baths of
Diocletian

Theater of Pompey

Column of Trajan

Porta Tiburtina

Porta Praenestina

Imperial Forum

Baths of
Trajan

Porta
Aurelia

Circus
Maximus

Colosseum

Baths of
Caracalla

Porta Latina

Porta
Ostiensis

Tiber R.

Ostian Way

Appian Way

people, representing the interests of the masses, threatened to undo the government altogether. In the midst of this domestic turmoil, certain Roman generals became more powerful on the field of battle.[2] Eventually the Roman senate traded freedom for security and virtually invited the Caesars to take control of the government in the form of a dictatorship (Tacitus, *Ann.* 1.1). Julius Caesar's defeat of Pompey in 48 B.C.E. marked a watershed event in the transference of power from the senate to the emperor (Suetonius, *Vit. Caes.* 1.35.1–2; Plutarch, *Caes.* 51.1–2; Josephus, *Ant.* 19.173). Caesar's famous *Veni, vidi, vici* ("I came, I saw, I conquered") statement announced the end of the Republic (Plutarch, *Caes.* 1.50.2; Suetonius, *Vit. Caes.* 1.37.2). Octavian's victory over Antony in 31 B.C.E. further set the stage for the ascension of the imperial rulers (Suetonius, *Vit. Caes.* 2.17.5; Dio Cassius, *Hist. rom.* 45.6; Josephus, *Ant.* 15.121, 161). For example, as the supreme commander of the empire, Octavian-Augustus had the power to appoint all executive leadership in his domain, from prefects (to govern entire provinces) to procurators (to collect taxes and manage hot spots on a smaller scale).

---

2    In a letter to his favorite slave, Tiro, Cicero reflects the chaos attending the final days leading up to the loss of the Republic to Julius Caesar. He states that he was forced to leave the city and abandon all homes and possessions, fearing all-out civil war was imminent, "when Caesar was seized with a sort of insanity" (*Fam.* 16.12.1–5).

## THE EMPERORS

From the birth of Christ to the end of the apostolic period, there were eleven Roman emperors.[3] Although not all of them are mentioned explicitly in the New Testament, each directly or indirectly played a significant role in the experience of the church.

### Octavian-Augustus (27 B.C.E.–14 C.E.)

On March 15, 44 B.C.E., sixty conspirators joined in the assassination of Julius Caesar as he presided over a meeting of the senate (Suetonius, *Vit. Caes.* 1.79.4–89.1; Josephus, *Ant.* 19.184). This opened the door for Caesar's adoptive son, Octavian, to ascend to the throne. The senate resorted to political maneuverings in an attempt to withhold the consulship from a "mere boy" barely twenty years of age (*Res gest. divi Aug.* 1.1; Dio Cassius, *Hist. rom.* 46.41.4). But Octavian had an army behind him and through force of arms reached his "first settlement" with the senate in 43 B.C.E. (Suetonius, *Vit. Caes.* 2.26.1). Nursing tentative alliances with Antony, Octavian continued to consolidate power until his open breech with and defeat of Antony at Actium in 31 B.C.E. (Dio Cassius, *Hist. rom.* 50.1.1–50.35.6). After returning to Rome, he made a long speech to the senate, feigning democracy and passionately rejecting a *dictatura* ("dictatorship"), but in fact he knew that he was in full control of all aspects of the government (*Res gest. divi Aug.* 1.5; Dio Cassius, *Hist. rom.* 53.3.1–53.10.8). The Republic came to an end (Dio Cassius, *Hist. rom.* 53.17.1) when in 27 B.C.E. Octavian was declared Caesar Augustus, for he was publicly deemed to be more than a mere man (*Res gest. divi* Aug. 5.34; Dio Cassius, *Hist. rom.*

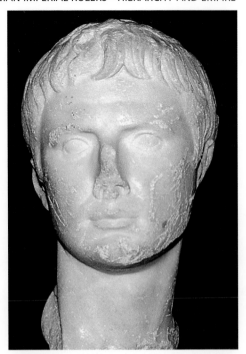

**Octavian-Augustus (27 B.C.E.–14 C.E.)**

53.16.7–8; 53.18.2–3; 53.20.2).[4] As supreme ruler over all the empire, he controlled the senate and the tribunes, was commander in chief of all the military, managed all finances, and appointed all prefects and procurators for the entire empire (Suetonius, *Vit. Caes.* 2.27.1–2.40.5).[5] As *pater patriae,* "father of his country" (*Res gest. divi Aug.* 5.35; Suetonius, *Vit. Caes.* 2.58.2), he levied all taxes and could execute anyone in the empire, from senator to slave. All soldiers swore personal allegiance to him, not to the senate. From the ranks of the most loyal soldiers, Augustus formed the Praetorian Guard, which served as his personal bodyguard, numbering at

3    Augustus (27 B.C.E.–14 C.E.), Tiberius (14–37 C.E.), Caligula (37–41 C.E.), Claudius (41–54 C.E.), Nero (54–68 C.E.), Galba (June 68–January 69 C.E.), Otho (January 15–April 16, 69 C.E.), Vitellius (January 2–December 22, 69 C.E.), Vespasian (69–79 C.E.), Titus (79–81 C.E.), Domitian (81–96 c.e.) (Suetonius, *Vit. Caes.* 6).

4    Caesar was the family name that was carried over from Julius Caesar. The name Augustus is from *augeo,* which can mean "to increase" in dignity or "to wax powerful" (Suetonius, *Vit. Caes.* 2.7.2).

5    Augustus claimed that upon taking office he restored the Republic to the senate and that he was merely "first among equals." Yet in reality, he held absolute power over every person and thing in the empire (cf. *Res gest. divi Aug.* 5.34).

**Tiberius (14–37 C.E.)**

senate, sought to enhance public morality, and encouraged the growth of families by giving tax incentives to have more children, and direct grants to those who already had them (Suetonius, *Vit. Caes.* 2.34).[9] Augustus promoted the growth of families in a long address to equestrians in the Forum, for he feared that childlessness in the leading Roman families had weakened the empire (Dio Cassius, *Hist. rom.* 56.1.2–56.10.3) Through the building of roads and the iron-fisted control of the provinces, his pax romana, "Roman peace," greatly aided the spread of Christianity. His empire-wide census for the purpose of recruiting soldiers and collecting taxes led Joseph and Mary to travel to Bethlehem (Luke 2:1–8) so that they might be registered. It was here that the Savior was born, and this fulfilled the ancient prophecy of Mic 5:2.

After ruling Rome for nearly forty-four years, Augustus passed away at seventy-six years of age in 14 C.E. (cf. *Res gest. divi Aug.* 5.35); his dying words were, "I found Rome of clay; I leave it to you of marble" (Dio Cassius, *Hist. rom.* 56.29.3–5). Augustus was the first and perhaps the greatest of the Caesars, setting a standard of leadership that, unfortunately, was not to be followed by his successors.

least five thousand men.[6] Under his leadership, the Roman Empire reached enormous proportions, annexing Egypt, Achaia, Galatia, and Cyprus between 30 and 22 B.C.E. and finally Judea in 6 C.E. Augustus's only major military setback, and only a temporary one, was the loss of three legions to the Germans under the generalship of Varus (Suetonius, *Vit. Caes.* 3.17.1–2).[7]

Augustus sought to establish justice, setting up in the senate the *clipeus virtutis*, a golden shield inscribed with his virtues (*Res gest. divi Aug.* 5.34).[8] He brought reforms to the

## Tiberius (14–37 C.E.)

According to the Gospels, Jesus' entire adult life and ministry occurred during the reign of Tiberius Caesar. It was under Tiberius that John the Baptist was beheaded, Jesus was crucified, and Saul of Tarsus was converted to the faith. Thus the reign of Tiberius encompasses the seminal events that marked the birth of Christianity.

Tiberius was the adopted stepson of Augustus, and since the latter had no natural-

---

6   For the duties of the prefect or administrative head of the Praetorian Guard, see Justinian, *Dig.* 1.11.1. Cf. also Scarre, *Chronicle of Roman Emperors*, 25.

7   Augustus so mourned the loss of these men that for months he neither shaved nor cut his hair, at times beating his head against a door and shouting, "Quintilius Varus, give me back my legions!" (Suetonius, *Vit. Caes.* 2.23.2).

8   See N. T. Wright, "Paul's Gospel and Caesar's Empire," in *Paul and Politics: Ecclesia, Israel, Imperium, and Interpretation* (ed. Richard A. Horsley; Harrisburg, Pa.: Trinity Press International, 2000), 171.

9   Augustus sought to strengthen marital relationships by enacting laws that favored stable households and made it more difficult to divorce. Cf. John E. Stambaugh, "Social Relationships in the City of the Early Principate: State of the Research," *The Society of Biblical Literature 1980 Seminar Papers* (SBLSP 19; Missoula, Mont.: Scholars Press, 1980), 77.

# Roman Emperors of Bible Times

| YEAR | NAME | NOTES |
|---|---|---|
| 49–44 B.C.E. | Julius Caesar | Died March 14, 44 B.C.E. Murdered by Gaius Cassius and Marcus Brutus. |
| 44–27 B.C.E. | Marc Antony | |
| 27 B.C.E.–14 C.E. | Augustus (Octavianus) | Died August 19, 14 C.E. |
| 14–37 C.E. | Tiberius | Died March 16, 37 C.E. |
| 37–41 C.E. | Gaius Julius Caesar Germanicus (Caligula) | Died January 24, 41 C.E. Widely regarded as insane. Ordered his statue placed in the temple. Murdered by officers of the Praetorian Guard. |
| 41–54 C.E. | Claudius | Murdered by his wife Agrippina so that her natural son (his adopted son) Nero would succeed him. |
| 54–68 C.E. | Nero | Was forced to commit suicide by the Roman Senate. |
| 68–69 C.E. | Galba | Assassinated after seven-month reign. |
| 69 C.E. | Otho | Committed suicide after ruling 90 days. |
| 69 C.E. | Vitellius | Murdered. |
| 69–79 C.E. | Vespasian | |
| August 10, 70 C.E. | | *Destruction of Herod's Temple* |
| 79–81 C.E. | Titus | |
| 81–96 C.E. | Domitian | |

born heirs, Tiberius would become emperor (Suetonius, *Vit. Caes.* 3.15.2; Josephus, *J.W.* 2.168). Augustus was not impressed with his adopted son and was even less enthusiastic about his prospects for leading the empire. Regarding Tiberius he is reported to have said, "Alas for the Roman people, to be ground by jaws that crunch so slowly!" (Suetonius, *Vit. Caes.* 3.21.1–3).[10] His reticence was due to the fact that although Tiberius had proven himself in battle, he showed no talent for public life.[11] He was stiff, arrogant, secretive, and incurably duplicitous in his speech and actions (Dio Cassius, *Hist. rom.* 57.1.1–2.3). Indeed, Tiberius was so inept at social engagement that in 27 C.E. he retired to the island of Capri, never to enter the city of Rome again (Suetonius, *Vit. Caes.* 3.40–44; Dio Cassius, *Hist. rom.* 58.1; Josephus, *Ant.* 18.161–162).[12] The seclusion did not serve Tiberius well; he becoming more reclusive and suspicious as his tenure wore on. From his island enclave, he ordered the killing of thousands whom he thought might be plotting his ruin, tortured slaves to testify against their masters, as well as freemen and citizens, and offered large sums of money to informers (Dio Cassius, *Hist. rom.* 57.19.2;

57.23.1–2; 58.4.8).[13] For example, Sejanus, the power-hungry commander of the Praetorian Guard, was executed together with his son, his daughter, and all of his friends. The trauma of Tiberius's cruelty drove the wife of Sejanus to suicide (Dio Cassius, *Hist. rom.* 58.3.9; 58.11.7; Tacitus, *Ann.* 4.19). Tiberius employed savage means against those whom he feared (Josephus, *Ant.* 18.226), having no respect for life and not even mourning the deaths of his own family members (Suetonius, *Vit. Caes.* 3.52, 60–61, 155; Josephus, *Ant.* 18.181–182; but see Dio Cassius, *Hist. rom.* 57.22.1–3; 58.2.1). At Capri, Tiberius is said to have engaged in all types of sexual deviancy, using his power over life and death to debauch anyone he saw fit (Dio Cassius, *Hist. rom.* 58.22.1–2; Tacitus, *Ann.* 4.19; Suetonius, *Vit. Caes.* 3.62). As John was baptizing in the Jordan River (Luke 3:1) and as Jesus later hung on the cross, an aged Tiberius was living out a profligate life in seclusion (Tacitus, *Ann.* 1.4; 6.51).

As Tiberius approached death at the age of seventy-seven, no one mourned his passing (Josephus, *Ant.* 18.31, 224–225).[14] Indeed, as he hovered between this life and the next, the imperial ring was plucked from his hand to hasten the installation of a new emperor. When he revived for a moment, Macro, the commander of the Praetorian Guard, snuffed out his life to the relief of all those present (Suetonius, *Vit. Caes.* 4.12.1–2; Tacitus, *Ann.* 6.50). The people clamored that his body should be thrown in the river, crying, "Tiberius to the Tiber!" (Suetonius, *Vit. Caes.* 3.75.1).[15]

---

10   When the time came for Augustus to inform the senate concerning his chosen heir, he said, "This I do for reasons of state" (cf. Scarre, *Chronicle of Roman Emperors*, 29).

11   Tiberius's main claim to fame was that through his general Germanicus, he was able to subdue the Germans and thus avenge the loss of the three Roman legions brought about under the leadership of Varus (Suetonius, *Vit. Caes.* 3.20.1). Tacitus, *Ann.* 1.60–61, describes the sad journey of Romans to the site of the massacre six years later. The bones of the legionnaires received a formal burial and the military standards were retrieved (Dio Cassius, *Hist. rom.* 57.18.1; 60.8.7). Augustus deemed it extremely important to retrieve such standards, for the "life" of the legion resided in these emblems (cf. *Res gest. divi Aug.* 5.29). See C. M. Gilliver, *The Roman Art of War* (Stroud, Glos., Eng.: Tempest, 1999), 34.

12   Yet at points Dio Cassius presents Tiberius as very approachable, amenable to the senators, and declining special honors. He claims that Tiberius left for Capri to escape the constant vexation and haughtiness of his mother, Livia (*Hist. rom.* 57.12.5–6).

13   Subsequently Claudius had many of these slave informers and freedmen fed to the lions or returned to their former masters for punishment (Dio Cassius, *Hist. rom.* 60.13.2).

14   Dio Cassius simply states that a public funeral was afforded Tiberius and that Gaius read a eulogy (*Hist. rom.* 58.28.5).

15   The people may here be alluding to the heinous penalty meted out for parricide (the murder of a family member). The murderer was sentenced to be sewn up alive in a leather sack with various animals (a dog, a snake, a cock, and a monkey) and cast into the Tiber River (*Inst.* 4.18.6).

## Gaius Caligula (37–41 C.E.)

The third emperor of Rome (Josephus, *Ant.* 18.33) was born in a military camp and named Gaius Caesar Germanicus. However, since he wore small *caligae*, the hobnailed boots of a legionnaire, the soldiers dubbed him Caligula, "Little Boots" (Tacitus, *Ann.* 1.41; Suetonius, *Vit. Caes.* 4.9). Tragically, this beloved child mascot of the troops would soon grow into a monster. Taking the throne at twenty-five years of age, he became one of the most ruthless emperors of Rome (Dio Cassius, *Hist. rom.* 59.6.1).

His cruelty and megalomania may have their roots in the violence in his own family. The young Caligula was aware that his uncle, Tiberius, had murdered his mother and his two brothers (Tacitus, *Ann.* 6.25).[16] Indeed, Tiberius would have murdered Caligula as well if he had not been dissuaded by Macro, the head of the Praetorian Guard (Philo, *Flaccus* 3.12).[17] Moreover, Tiberius brought Caligula to Capri so that he might engage in all of the sexual depravity so characteristic of the place (Philo, *Flaccus* 3.14, *Embassy* 2.14; Suetonius, *Vit. Caes.* 4.11).

Caligula committed incest with his sisters and often summoned the wives of esteemed senators to his bedchamber; death awaited them and their families if they refused (Suetonius, *Vit. Caes.* 4.25; Dio Cassius, *Hist. rom.* 59.3.3; 59.22.6; 59.26.5). He dressed in outlandish attire, often wearing women's clothing in public (Suetonius, *Vit. Caes.* 4.52). Caligula was an epileptic insomniac who would kill for no good reason (Philo, *Flaccus* 18.182–191). For example, as funds were running low and the beasts of the gladiatorial games needed to be fed, he summoned criminals to stand before him. When asked which ones should be fed to the lions, he quipped, "From bald head to bald head." The line began with one balding victim and ended with another (Suetonius, *Vit. Caes.* 4.27.1–2; Dio Cassius, *Hist. rom.* 59.22.3). Two notebooks entitled "The Sword" and "The Dagger" were found after his death (Suetonius, *Vit. Caes.* 4.49.3; Dio Cassius, *Hist. rom.* 59.26.1). Contained therein were long lists of persons he had earmarked for execution.

Caligula's lust for fantastic gladiatorial games knew no bounds; he would have hundreds of wild beasts slain in a single day and force equestrians to fight and die as gladiators (Dio Cassius, *Hist. rom.* 59.7.1–8; 59.10.1–2). One elaborate prop consisted of an artificial bridge built atop merchant ships, lashed side by side, that spanned the entire Gulf of Naples (Dio Cassius, *Hist. rom.* 59.17.1–11). As he rode at full gallop across the bridge, he called out manically, "Let the games begin!" He adorned his favorite horse, Incitatus, "Flyer," with costly jewels and housed him in a marble room equipped with lavish furnishing. To honor the beast and to show his contempt for the senate, he planned to grant the horse a senatorial post (Dio Cassius, *Hist. rom.* 59.14.7; Suetonius, *Vit. Caes.* 4.55.3).

It has been estimated that such antics squandered more than one hundred million dollars in modern currency, and they quickly depleted the imperial coffers (Dio Cassius, *Hist. rom.* 59.2.4–6). As Tiberius before him, Caligula used overtaxation and extortion to fill the imperial treasury coffers again, convicting and executing the wealthy and then confiscating their estates as penalty (Dio Cassius, *Hist. rom.* 59.10.8; 59.18.1–5; 59.21.1–5). He contrived mock auctions at which wealthy senators were forced to place outrageous bids for a piece of rubbish; this led many to financial ruin and ultimately to suicide (Suetonius, *Vit. Caes.* 4.38.4–4.39).

---

16  Dio Cassius notes that Caligula traversed land and sea to collect with his own hands the bones of his mother and brothers, gave them an honorable burial in Rome, and took vengeance out on all associated with their murders (*Hist. rom.* 59.3.5–7; 59.4.3).

17  Caligula later brought false charges against Macro and forced him to commit suicide (Dio Cassius, *Hist. rom.* 59.10.6)

Luckily, Caligula embarked on few military campaigns, for the ones he did lead were as costly to Rome as to its enemies. On one occasion he drove his legions to the English Channel, and instead of invading the island, he had the soldiers fill their helmets with sea shells, then commanded them to march back to Rome again (Suetonius, *Vit. Caes.* 4.46; Dio Cassius, *Hist. rom.* 59.25.2–5). In 40 C.E. Caligula declared himself divine (Philo, *Embassy*, 12.81), believing himself to be Jupiter, and accepted sacrifices as a god (Dio Cassius, *Hist. rom.* 59.28.8).

He attempted to have his statue erected in the temple in Jerusalem (Philo, *Embassy*, 31.207; 43.346; Tacitus, *Ann.* 12.54). In response, the priests and the scribes incited the people to riot and nearly precipitated all-out war with Rome. The Zealots joined in the fray, since they exploited every opportunity to drive out the Romans (*Ant.* 18.263, 274; *J.W.* 2.192).[18] On the eve of disaster, a petition from Herod Agrippa I persuaded Caligula to reconsider the project. The Syrian legate, Petronius, was contacted, and the statue never reached Jerusalem (Philo, *Embassy* 42.330–337; Josephus, *Ant.* 18.289–301).

In his last days Caligula often talked to statues of the gods and claimed to receive messages from them. In 41 C.E., when he was only twenty-nine, senators and praetorians hatched a conspiracy, and Caligula was assassinated as he left the Palatine Games (Suetonius, *Vit. Caes.* 4.57–59; Josephus, *Ant.* 19.105–161, 185; Dio Cassius, *Hist. rom.* 59.1.1–7). Dio Cassius, concluding his history of Caligula, comments, "Thus Gaius, after doing in three years, nine months, and twenty-eight days all that has been related, learned by actual experience that he was not a god" (*Hist. rom.* 59.30.1).

18  On the "Caligula crisis," see N. H. Taylor, "Palestinian Christianity and the Caligula Crisis, Part 1: Social and Historical Reconstruction," *JSNT* 61 (1996): 101–24, esp. 101, 109–10.

## Claudius (41–54 C.E.)

Claudius ruled during the time of the greatest missionary expansion of the early church and so played a significant role in the experience of the first evangelists. Luke records that he expelled all of the Jews from Rome and that Aquila and Pricilla were caught up in the melee (Acts 18:2).[19] Suetonius explains that the cause of the expulsion was that the Jews were constantly rioting *impulsore Chresto*, "at the instigation of Christ" (*Vit. Caes.* 5.24.14; cf. also Tacitus, *Ann.* 15.44; Acts 24:5).[20] Since the early emperors probably viewed Jews and Christians as members of the same religion (cf. Acts 18:12–16), the name Chresto may well have referred to Christ. Claudius's remarks may indicate, then, that Christianity was making inroads in Rome, Syria, and North Africa as early as 41 C.E. (Acts 8–13). Furthermore, Claudius appointed Felix, one of his freedmen (Tacitus, *Ann.* 12.54), as governor of Judea (Suetonius, *Vit. Caes.* 5.28); Paul would appear for judgment before him (Acts 23:24–24:27). Thus insight into the person and reign of Claudius gives us much information on what the church faced at this time.

After the carnage of Caligula, the senate was reluctant to appoint another Caesar. Nevertheless, it was in the interest of the Praetorian Guard to have an emperor on the throne. Since Augustus was Claudius's great-uncle and Tiberius his uncle, Claudius was in line for the throne (cf. also Josephus,

19  This was not the first time that the Jews were driven from the capital city. Expulsions of the Jews from Rome are recorded as early as 139 B.C.E. The Jews had become so populous and influential in Rome during Tiberius's reign that he, too, had them expelled from the city (Dio Cassius, *Hist. rom.* 57.18.5). Cf. also Gideon Fuks, "Where Have All the Freedmen Gone? On an Anomaly in the Jewish Grave-Inscriptions from Rome," *JJS* 36 (1985): 25–32, esp. 25.

20  For details on the expulsions of the Jews from Rome, see Leonard Victor Rutgers, "Roman Policy toward the Jews: Expulsions from the City of Rome during the First Century C.E.," in *Judaism and Christianity in First-Century Rome* (ed. Karl P. Donfried and Peter Richardson; Grand Rapids: Eerdmans, 1998), 93–116, esp. 105.

*Ant.* 18.165). The generals reckoned that Claudius was a simpleton and so could not do much harm. After all, during the murder of Caligula, Claudius cowered in terror behind curtains and was shocked to be hailed "Caesar" by the killers, whom, for the sake of "justice," he subsequently had executed (Suetonius, *Vit. Caes.* 5.10.1-2; Dio Cassius, *Hist. rom.* 60.1.1-4; 60.2.2). The army had its way, and the senate came under the thumb of another tyrannical Caesar (Josephus, *Ant.* 19.161-165).

Many judged Claudius to be mentally retarded. He stuttered and foamed at the mouth when he spoke, and he had a runny nose (Dio Cassius, *Hist. rom.* 60.2.2). Augustus wrote his mother that Claudius "is wanting and defective in soundness of body and mind" and that he should not appear in public at the games for the sake of possible embarrassment to the family (Suetonius, *Vit. Caes.* 5.4.1-7). Claudius often fell asleep at banquets. When he awoke, he found that his slippers had been placed on his hands by court jesters (*Vit. Caes.* 5.8).

Nevertheless, at the beginning of his rule, he behaved admirably. He reversed many of the injustices committed by Caligula and refused to harm anyone who had abused him during his time as a private citizen. He lived modestly and did not accept bribes from his subjects (Dio Cassius, *Hist. rom.* 60.5.1-60.6.4). Militarily, he successfully directed a campaign against the Britons, traveling to the battlefield in person and subduing many of the regional tribes (Dio Cassius, *Hist. rom.* 60.19.1-60.22.2).

On the other hand, Claudius was gripped by vices that tainted his reign. He was addicted to drink and gambling. He had a bloodlust for gladiatorial games, committing many more persons to death than beasts (Suetonius, *Vit. Caes.* 5.33-34; Dio Cassius, *Hist. rom.* 60.13.1). He was easily induced to panic, especially at the instigation of his

**Claudius (41–54 C.E.)**

freedman Narcissus; this weakness led to many innocent persons losing their lives (Dio Cassius, *Hist. rom.* 60.14.2; 60.29.6).

Claudius's judgments were whimsical and often deadly, fueled by a combination of timidity and suspicion (Tacitus, *Ann.* 11.2; Suetonius, *Vit. Caes.* 5.35-37). For example, he would strip a person of citizenship for not knowing Latin but then grant full Roman citizenship to entire families for no apparent reason (Dio Cassius, *Hist. rom.* 60.17.4-5).[21] He married four times, killing at least one wife for "bigamy." He granted religious freedom to the Jews and exempted them from the draft, yet drove them later from the city (Josephus, *Ant.* 19. 278-291, 299-311; 20.1-14).[22] Claudius enjoyed playing the supreme patron at the games by giving away free tickets to commoners and by awarding the "wooden sword" to worthy contestants

21   For the penalty for Romans who lost their citizenship, see Justinian, *Dig.* 48.22.3.

22   Dio Cassius says that Claudius did not expel the Jews from Rome but forbade them to meet together, as he did all the collegia in the city (*Hist. rom.* 60.6.6).

233

(Suetonius, *Vit. Caes.* 5.22.5).[23] Yet he enjoyed watching the torture of his enemies and once frivolously ordered the death of thirty-five senators (*Vit. Caes.* 5.29.2). He created a sprawling bureaucracy to care for an ever-expanding empire, yet he allowed his freedmen Narcissus and Pallas, whom he appointed chief magistrates, to amass enormous wealth through graft and extortion (Tacitus, *Ann.* 12.53–54; Suetonius, *Vit. Caes.* 5.28).[24] The power of Narcissus and Pallas was beyond that of senators and governors. For example, when Silanus, the governor of Spain, offended Narcissus, the latter invented a dream that "revealed" to Claudius that the governor was plotting to assassinate the emperor. Upon hearing of the dreamt-up "plot," Claudius ordered the execution of Silanus (Dio Cassius, *Hist. rom.* 60.14.4). Planting the same seed of suspicion, Narcissus had Messalina, the wife of Claudius, killed as well (*Hist. rom.* 60.31.5).

Of all of his blunders, however, perhaps the worst was his marriage to his niece, the cunning Agrippina (Tacitus, *Ann.* 12.6–8; Dio Cassius, *Hist. rom.* 60.31.8–60.32.1). More than likely it was she who orchestrated the murder of Claudius by feeding him poisoned mushrooms (Dio Cassius, *Hist. rom.* 60.35.4) and thus paved the way for Nero to come to power (Suetonius, *Vit. Caes.* 5.43–46).[25]

## Nero (54–68 c.e.)

Nero's ascension to the throne was marked by treachery from the beginning. His father, the Roman general Germanicus, was assassinated with the consent of Tiberius (Dio Cassius, *Hist. rom.* 57.18.11). His crime was his

success as a general. In 53 c.e., when he was eleven years of age, his mother Agrippina, the fourth wife of Claudius and sister of Caligula, pressured the emperor to adopt Nero (Tacitus, *Ann.* 12.25–26; Suetonius, *Vit. Caes.* 5.43). Once officially in the family, Agrippina solidified Nero's place among the royals by arranging his marriage to the daughter of Claudius (Tacitus, *Ann.* 12.58).[26] Fearing the emperor would appoint his own son, Britannicus, as heir (Dio Cassius, *Hist. rom.* 60.32.1–2, 5; 34.1), she had Claudius poisoned (Tacitus, *Ann.* 12.67; Suetonius, *Vit. Caes.* 5.43–44). Agrippina relentlessly promoted Nero, all the while pushing Britannicus to the background (Tacitus, *Ann.* 12.68–69). Eventually she drove Nero to eliminate Britannicus in a manner similar to the murder of Claudius (Josephus, *Ant.* 20.150–154). On Britannicus's fourteenth birthday, Nero invited him to a royal banquet. As he fell over dead at "the children's table," Nero explained to the guests that Britannicus had had an epileptic seizure (Dio Cassius, *Hist. rom.* 61.7.4). The concocter of the poison that killed Britannicus was awarded a huge sum of money and a large estate for a job well done (Tacitus, *Ann.* 13.15–17).[27] Thus Nero ascended to the throne, becoming emperor at seventeen years of age (*Ann.* 12.68–69).

Fortunately, Nero had one of the finest tutors of all time, according to Dio Cassius (*Hist. rom.* 61.3.3). Seneca, the Stoic philosopher and onetime senator, was hailed *amicus principis*, "friend of the Emperor."[28] He was also the older brother of Gallio, the Roman proconsul of Achaia who acquitted Paul in Acts 18:12–17 (Tacitus, *Ann.* 15.73;

---

23  The gladiator who received a wooden sword from the emperor was granted freedom.

24  Later, under the reign of Nero, Pallas fell out of favor and was forced to renounce his office (cf. Tacitus, *Ann.* 13.14).

25  Roman law forbade poisonings and parricide (i.e., the murder of family members), and reserved the strictest penalties of the law for such crimes (Justinian, *Dig.* 48.8–9).

26  On the empowering of Nero, see Miriam T. Griffin, *Nero: The End of a Dynasty* (New York: Routledge, 1984), 15.

27  For Roman laws forbidding the concoction of poisons and their use see Justinian, *Dig.* 48.8.3.

28  Ibid., 71. Seneca's full name was Lucius Annaeus Seneca; he lived from 4 b.c.e. to 65 c.e. (Ben Witherington III, *The Acts of the Apostles: A Socio-rhetorical Commentary* [Grand Rapids: Eerdmans, 1998], 551).

Dio Cassius, *Hist. rom.* 61.3.2–3). With effort, Seneca was able to placate Nero's ill temper in the early years of his reign (Tacitus, *Ann.* 13.2). During its first five years, the so-called golden years, Nero sought to restore the reforms of Augustus by denouncing secret trials within the palace and forbidding bribery and extortion (Suetonius, *Vit. Caes.* 6.10.1; Tacitus, *Ann.* 8.4–5).[29]

Nero's rule became more despotic, however, as time wore on, at first in secret and thereafter more openly (Suetonius, *Vit. Caes.* 6.27.1–2). It is said that Nero would slip into the night to murder and plunder (Suetonius, *Vit. Caes.* 6.26.1; Dio Cassius, *Hist. rom.* 61.9.1–4) but by day he took on the manner of *liberalitas* (generosity), *clementia* (mercy), and *comitas* (accessibility).[30] Soon he abandoned all pretense of decency, eventually murdering two of his wives; one of them, Sabina, he kicked to death in the later stages of pregnancy (Suetonius, *Vit. Caes.* 6.35.1–3; Dio Cassius, *Hist. rom.* 62.13.1; 62.28.1–2). Not long after killing Britannicus, he slaughtered his own mother, first attempting to drown her at sea and then dispatching armed assassins to complete the deed (Dio Cassius, *Hist. rom.* 61.13.2–61.14.1). Agrippina, who had worked hard to win him the throne, was thus taken out of the way, for Nero interpreted her political maneuverings as evidence of her own ambitions to rule (Tacitus, *Ann.* 14.8–9). Employing a reign of terror, he forced family members and friends to take their own lives (Josephus, *J.W.* 2.250). On one occasion, he threatened to murder the entire senate (Suetonius, *Vit. Caes.* 6.37.3). He also engaged in all types of sexual distortions, castrating two of his freedmen, Sporos and Doryphorus, to make transsexuals of them.

Nero (54–68 C.E.).

He married them both and publicly led them about as his wives (Suetonius, *Vit. Caes.* 6.28–29; Dio Cassius, *Hist. rom.* 62.28.2–3; 63.13.1–2).

Fiscally, Nero quickly depleted the treasury and resorted to overtaxation and extortion to make up the difference (Dio Cassius, *Hist. rom.* 61.5.5–6). His unbridled avarice led to his most notorious deed. Not long after he voiced that Rome appeared a bit shabby and run down, a fire broke forth in the area of the Circus Maximus on July 19, 64 C.E. The flames raged for nine days, consuming two-thirds of the city (*Hist. rom.* 62.17.1). As the city burned, Nero was witnessed atop a tower, dressed as an actor and playing his beloved lyre. He sang a song dedicated to the sack of Troy (Suetonius, *Vit. Caes.* 6.38; Dio Cassius, *Hist. rom.* 62.18.1), a performance even more distorted than the antics he performed on the stage before a literally captive audience of senators and equestrians (*Hist. rom.* 61.20.1–3). Nero droned on for so long that some senators pretended to faint so that they could be carried away in peace (*Hist. rom.* 63.15.3).

29   On Nero's early years, see William Lane, "Social Perspectives on Roman Christianity during the Formative Years from Nero to Nerva: Romans, Hebrews, 1 Clement," in *Judaism and Christianity in First-Century Rome* (ed. Karl P. Donfried and Peter Richardson; Grand Rapids: Eerdmans, 1998), 196–244, esp. 202.

30   Griffin, *Nero*, 66.

**Coin of Nero (54–68 c.e.).**

Rumor soon spread that Nero had started the fire in order to make room for the construction for his palatial Domus Aurea, "Golden House" (Suetonius, *Vit. Caes.* 6.31). Indeed, Dio Cassius describes how Nero hired arsonists to start fires at different places throughout the city so that no one would know how to contain the blaze (*Hist. rom.* 62.16.1–62.17.3). To assuage the people, he provided disaster relief and built them new homes free of charge. For this purpose, he had to drain funds from all over the empire, worsening the state of revenue. Nevertheless, even as the Apostle Paul neared his execution in the Mamertine prison, Nero's popularity soared among the common people. All that remained was to find a scapegoat for the fire.

Tacitus informs us of Nero's dreadful solution:

Nero substituted as culprits, and punished with the utmost refinements of cruelty, a class of men, loathed for their vices, whom the crowd styled Christians. . . . Vast num-

bers were convicted, not so much on the count of arson as for hatred of the human race. And derision accompanied their end: They were covered with wild beasts' skins and torn to death by dogs; or they were fastened on crosses, and when daylight failed were burned to serve as lamps by night. (*Ann.* 15.44)

Tacitus adds that the *Christiani* were a sect founded by Chrestus, who was justly executed by Pontius Pilate during the reign of Tiberius. Suetonius concurs: "Punishment was inflicted on the Christians, a class of men given to a new and mischievous superstition" (*Vit. Caes.* 6.16.2). Tacitus brands the Christians "a foreign and deadly superstition" (*Ann.* 13.32), and Pliny the Younger speaks of that "wretched cult" (*Ep.* 10.96; cf. also 10.97).[31]

31   Tacitus speaks of Pomponia Graecina, a woman of equestrian rank, who was tried "for alien superstition," probably referring to Christians (*Ann.* 13.32). This trial may have taken place as early as Paul's Epistle to the Romans. If so, then believers would have experienced persecution before Paul's arrival in Rome.

The blood of Christian martyrs was not enough, however, to satiate Nero's wrath. His oppression, heavy taxation, and hatred for the senate led to two assassination attempts in 65 C.E. In the purge that followed, even the great Stoic philosopher Seneca was implicated and forced to commit suicide (Suetonius, *Vit. Caes.* 6.35.5; Dio Cassius, *Hist. rom.* 62.24.1; 62.25.1–3).[32] By 67 C.E. his leadership had deteriorated further still, and this led to the insurrection of Roman generals in Spain and Gaul (Plutarch, *Galb.* 5.2, *Oth.* 20. 2–4; Dio Cassius, *Hist. rom.* 63.23.6). At first Nero expressed no alarm concerning the revolt. He sent a letter to the Senate explaining that he could not come in person because he had a sore throat. Once recovered, he noted, he would continue his musical tour (Dio Cassius, *Hist. rom.* 63.26.2). The severity of the coup became apparent when his trusted advisor and general, Publius Petronius Turpilianus, also joined the revolt (Dio Cassius, *Hist. rom.* 63.27.1). Having lost hope in arms, Nero planned to kill all the senators, burn down the city of Rome, and journey to Alexandria. Once there he would live as a private citizen and follow his musical career (Dio Cassius, *Hist. rom.* 63.27.1). Before he could enact such ill-conceived plans, the Senate declared him an enemy of the state, mobilized the Praetorian Guard against him, and declared Galba the emperor (Dio Cassius, *Hist. rom.* 63.27.2).

Stymied and panicked, Nero failed to respond adequately to these challenges (Suetonius, *Vit. Caes.* 6.42). Appeals to the tribunes, centurions, and even household servants fell on deaf ears. By June of 68 C.E. his imperial power was no more. Fleeing the palace in disguise, he found himself in the storage room of one of his freedmen, Phaon. Snatching up a letter from a servant, he learned that the senate had declared him an enemy of the state (Dio Cassius, *Hist. rom.* 63.27.3; 63.28.1–4). As he prepared to take his own life, his thoughts were still vain and petty, for he cried out, "What an artist the world is losing!"[33] A self-inflicted wound to the throat was ineffectual, and so his private secretary, Epaphroditus, delivered the death stroke for him (Suetonius, *Vit. Caes.* 6.49.2–3; Dio Cassius, *Hist. rom.* 63.29.2).[34]

Nero lived 30 years and 9 months and ruled for 13 years and 8 months (Dio Cassius, *Hist. rom.* 63.29.3; Josephus, *J.W.* 4.491). The empire and its generals waited to see who would take up the reins of power (Josephus, *J.W.* 4.490, 497).

## Galba (68–69 C.E.)

Galba did not stem from the royal family and so his reign marked the end of the Julio-Claudian dynasty, a reign that lasted nearly one hundred years (Suetonius, *Vit. Caes.* 7.2; Dio Cassius, *Hist. rom.* 56.29.1). His initial contact with imperial power was by way of Livia, the wife of Augustus. She favored Galba greatly and bequeathed great sums of money to him, an inheritance that was subsequently revoked by Tiberius (Suetonius, *Vit. Caes.* 7.5).[35] His rise to political power began when Augustus

33 The historians consistently report the pitiful manner in which Nero took his life. After eating some coarse bread and common well water, Nero exclaimed, "So this is my famous cold drink!" He was apparently referring to his habit of drinking water that had been first boiled and then chilled by being plunged into snow (Pliny, *Nat.* 36.40).

34 Epaphroditus went on to become the official secretary of Domitian. Yet as the emperor became more paranoid, he recalled that Epaphroditus had helped Nero commit suicide, and so he condemned Epaphroditus to death (Suetonius, *Vit. Caes.* 8.14.4).

35 As was the case with other emperors, Galba's rise to power was signaled by omens. Dio Cassius records that on the day that Galba assumed the *toga virilis* (a plain white garment worn by male Roman citizens at about 14 to 16 years of age) a lightening bolt struck the capitol, effacing the "C" in "Caesar." The diviners interpreted this to mean that in 100 days (the Roman numeral for "100" being "C") Augustus would attain "to some divine state," that is, die. Even the jealous and suspicious Tiberius intuited that Galba would become emperor (*Hist. rom.* 57.17.2, 63.29.6; Josephus, *Ant.* 18.216). For more on Galba, Otho, Vitellius, and Vespasian see Kenneth Wellesley's *The Year of the Four Emperors* (3d ed.; London: Routledge, 2000).

32 Dio Cassius seems to think that Nero had an influence on Seneca. He claims that Seneca became nearly as debauched and avaricious as Nero, living a double life of hypocrisy (*Hist. rom.* 61.10.1–6; cf. also Tacitus *Ann.* 13.42.6).

appointed him as consul in 33 C.E. He was then made the governor of Upper Germany and subsequently assigned to Africa (Plutarch, *Galb.* 3.3). His last appointment in 61 C.E. was as governor of Hispania Tarraconensis, the largest of the three provinces in Spain, where he ruled for eight years (Suetonius, *Vit. Caes.* 7.6–8). In these posts he earned a reputation for being an effective administrator and a strict disciplinarian.[36]

Galba's decision to revolt in April of 68 was due to a number of factors. Nero's oppression had become increasingly intolerable and on more than one occasion Galba publicly expressed his discontent with the emperor. Fearing Galba's increased power in the west and detecting signs of disloyalty, Nero ordered Galba's assassination. When Galba intercepted the imperial edict mandating his death, his plans to rid the empire of Nero began in earnest. At this time, Otho, the governor of Lusitania in western Spain, cast his lot with Galba by committing his soldiers and fortune to the revolt (Plutarch, *Oth.* 20.2–4). When Galba finally mobilized his forces against Nero, Otho was literally at his side, never failing to express support for Galba on the long march to the Capitol (Plutarch, *Oth.* 20.3). All of this was done in hopes that in time he would be adopted by Galba and ultimately ascend to the throne (Suetonius, *Vit. Caes.* 7.4).[37] Galba received critical aid from another sector of the empire as well. Junius Vindex, proconsul of Gaul, revolted against Nero during Galba's eighth year as governor. Not opting for the throne for himself, Vindex repeatedly urged Galba to join forces

with him, march on Rome and seize power (Suetonius, *Vit. Caes.* 7.92; Plutarch, *Galb.* 4.1–2; Dio Cassius, *Hist. rom.* 63.23.6).[38] Events favorable to Galba were underway in the Capitol as well. Nymphidius Sabinus, the prefect of the Praetorian Guard, persuaded the soldiers to support Galba, promising a large donative (or cash reward) if they forsook Nero in Rome (Plutarch, *Galb.* 2.2).[39]

When Galba publicly announced his intent to overthrow Nero, he refused to take the title of Caesar or Emperor but rather referred to himself as the "General of the Roman Senate and People" (Plutarch, *Galb.* 5.2).[40] Soon after, a terrible miscue by Vindex nearly ended Galba's campaign at the start. Vindex had made a secret pact with Rufus, commander of some of the strongest forces in Germany. The plan was that once Galba was in power, Rufus would govern all of Germany and Vindex would be over Italy. However, before all of their respective troops could be informed of the agreement, the two armies clashed in all out war against each other. Vindex lost 20,000 soldiers in the ill-fated battle and in light of the debacle, took his own life (Plutarch, *Galb.* 6.2–4; Dio Cassius, *Hist. rom.* 63.24.4). Hearing of the disaster, Galba nearly called off his attack, but changed his mind due to the timely report of one Icelus, a freedman recently come from Rome. Icelus

---

36  Galba's punishment of one who had poisoned his ward to prevent him from inheriting his estate serves as a case in point. When Galba ordered that he be crucified, the offender protested that a Roman citizen deserved better. Conceding the point, Galba had the man nailed to a cross that was higher than that of others who had been condemned and painted the cross white (Suetonius, *Vit. Caes.* 7.9).

37  Androgation, the adoption of an adult person, by way of imperial writ was a long standing practice of Roman law (Justinian, *Inst.* 1.11; *Dig.* 1.7.1–2).

38  The decision to vie for the throne was accompanied by good omens such as fully armed but unmanned warships appearing off the coast of Spain, a mule giving birth, and the hair of a young boy turning white as he attended sacrifice with Galba (Dio Cassius, *Hist. rom.* 64.1.3).

39  At one point Sabinus sought to wrest the empire for himself. When the tide began to turn in favor of Galba, however, he was executed by the same praetorians he had initially inspired to revolt (Plutarch, *Galb.* 2.8–9, 13–15).

40  Tacitus notes that Galba became the first to be declared emperor outside the city of Rome (Tacitus, *Hist.* 1.4). Nero mocked Galba's challenge by auctioning off all of Galba's possessions in Spain. Galba countered by selling all of Nero's property within his domain. According to Plutarch, Galba garnered much more from these sales than Nero (*Galb.* 5.4).

informed Galba that the military, the Senate, and the people of Rome had declared him Emperor and that Nero had committed suicide (Plutarch, *Galb.* 7.1). Moreover, Rufus, the victor over Vindex, now threw his full weight behind Galba (Plutarch, *Galb.* 10.3). Galba now had a clear path to power.

Galba's march from Rome to Spain was marked by cruelty and avarice. Upon entering Rome in the fall of 68 C.E., he slaughtered 7,000 unarmed members of the Praetorian Guard (Tacitus, *Hist.* 1.4; Dio Cassius, *Hist. rom.* 64.3.1; Tacitus, *Hist.* 1.20; Plutarch, *Galb.* 15.4). Those of the imperial German guard who survived the initial carnage were reassigned to their native lands without any reward. Galba soon gained a reputation for being stingy at court, mandating that all who had received gifts from Nero must return them to the royal treasury (Suetonius, *Vit. Caes.* 7.12; Dio Cassius, *Hist. rom.* 64.3.4; Plutarch, *Galb.* 16.4). Perhaps worst of all, and no doubt the cause of his eventual downfall, he refused to grant the donative, or special cash reward, for the soldiers who had helped put him in power (Dio Cassius, *Hist. rom.* 64.3.3; Plutarch, *Galb.* 18.2, 23.2). His response to repeated protests in this regard was that he levied his troops; he did not buy them (Suetonius, *Vit. Caes.* 7.16; Tacitus, *Hist.* 1.5).[41]

For all of these reasons, Galba soon became unpopular with both citizen and soldier (Suetonius, *Vit. Caes.* 7.12–13; Tacitus, *Hist.* 1.4). Within two months of his entrance into Rome, disgruntled troops were ready to get rid of him.[42] On January 1, 69 C.E., the army of Upper Germany, totaling seven legions in all, declined to renew its allegiance to Galba (Tacitus, *Hist.* 1.12). Instead they claimed Aulus Vitellius, the governor of Lower Germany, as their leader and emperor (Dio Cassius, *Hist. rom.* 64.4.1).[43] To demonstrate their loyalty to Vitellius, they pulled down statues of Galba, ripped his name from their military standards and replaced it with the name of Vitellius (Plutarch, *Galb.* 22.4, 8). In an attempt to show that he was still in control and not at all alarmed by the defection of the German legions, Galba adopted Piso Frugi Licinianus as his heir and presented him to the praetorian camp as the next emperor (Suetonius, *Vit. Caes.* 7.17; Dio Cassius, *Hist. rom.* 64.5.1).[44]

Otho was crestfallen (Plutarch, *Oth.* 23.3; 24.1). With the adoption of Piso, his hopes of succeeding Galba were dashed. Tacitus sums up the sentiment of Otho by stating, "He was angry toward Galba and jealous of Piso" (*Hist.* 1.21).[45] From that point on he plotted to overthrow the emperor by bribing Galba's personal body guard (the *speculatores*) and ingratiating himself to the entire Praetorian Guard (Tacitus, *Hist.* 1.23).

At this juncture the historians indicate that the signs began to turn against Galba. They note that even as he entered the praetorian camp to announce the adoption of Piso, a frightening thunderstorm unleashed its fury upon the emperor (Plutarch, *Galb.* 23.2). Yet even now, Galba refused to offer gifts of gratitude to the soldiers who had put him in

41   Plutarch notes that the soldiers thought that by making this statement, Galba had established legal precedent for all future emperors. In their minds this meant that they would never again receive special monetary rewards (Plutarch, *Galb.* 18.3–4).

42   For more on Galba's rapid fall from grace see Colin Wells, *The Roman Empire* (2d ed.; Cambridge: Harvard University Press, 1992), 153–56.

43   Galba had personally appointed Vitellius to this post. By surrendering the wealth and luxury of Lower Germany to Vitellius, Galba figured he would not have time or reason to plot treachery.

44   By adopting Piso, Galba claimed that he was following in the footsteps of Augustus, who had adopted Tiberius (Tacitus, *Hist.* 1.15, 18). Plutarch attributes the adoption of Piso to the fact that Galba was still childless at seventy-three years of age and that Piso was a young man and highly favored by the people (*Galb.* 19.1–2).

45   Suetonius notes that Otho was financially motivated to become emperor. Otho had accumulated such crushing debt that the only possible way that he could become solvent was to take the throne by force (*Vit. Caes.* 7.5).

power.[46] On January 15, 69 C.E., Otho judged that the time was right to depose Galba. As he stood at the side of the emperor while he offered sacrifice, Otho heard the ill omen of the diviner. The entrails of the sacrifice revealed that the life of Galba was in imminent danger and that he should exercise extreme caution (Plutarch, *Oth.* 24.2). Visibly shaken by the prophecy, Otho anxiously awaited news from his co-conspirators. He did not have to wait long. A court attendant approached the altar and announced the prearranged password, "Your architects have arrived and are waiting for you" (Plutarch, *Oth.* 24.4; Tacitus, *Hist.* 1.22). Excusing himself from the man that he would soon kill, Otho made a beeline for the praetorian camp (Dio Cassius, *Hist. rom.* 64.5.3; Suetonius, *Vit. Caes.* 7.6). Once there Otho criticized Galba for not following through with the donative, for his severity with which he attacked the German troops upon his entrance into Rome, and for his refusal to accept counsel from those who were wiser than he (Tacitus, *Hist.* 1.37).[47] Since the general soldiery was unarmed while stationed within the city, Otho then ordered that the imperial armory be opened and that each soldier arm himself as best he could (Plutarch, *Oth.* 25.2–3; Suetonius, *Vit. Caes.* 7.14; Tacitus, *Hist.* 1.38).

By this time Galba had gathered that a coup was underway and halted between making good his escape and returning to the palace (Tacitus, *Hist.* 1:32–33). As the general tumult ensued, Galba was caught out in the open while being carried along in his royal litter. A conspirator approached Galba with a bloodied sword claiming to have slain Otho in the melee. This was a ruse intended to get Galba to let down his guard

and come into the open. As Galba gazed upon the feigned assassin he reportedly said, "Who gave you the orders, comrade?" (Suetonius, *Vit. Caes.* 7.19; Tacitus, *Hist.* 1.39; Plutarch, *Galb.* 26.1–2). As the unruly crowds pressed in, Galba tumbled from his litter onto the ground even as praetorian lancers and swordsmen closed in. All of his personal guards fled except one, a centurion by the name of Sempronius Densus. Standing between the fallen emperor and his assailants, Sempronius railed against their treachery before he too was cut to pieces by Otho's forces.[48] At this point Galba is said to have begged for a few days in order to make good on the donative (Tacitus, *Hist.* 1.41). Realizing that his belated plea had been ignored, the aged emperor exposed his neck and commanded, "Strike if it be for the good of Rome!" (Plutarch, *Galb.* 27.1). On January 15 of 69 C.E. Galba was decapitated and his head impaled on a lance and paraded throughout the city (Plutarch, *Galb.* 27.3, *Oth.* 1.2; 3.11–13; Dio Cassius, *Hist. rom.* 64.6.3–5; Suetonius, *Vit. Caes.* 7.19–20; Josephus, *J.W.* 4.494, 546).

Piso, though wounded in the attack, sought refuge in the temple of Vesta. He was soon hunted down, dragged into the open, and slaughtered (Tacitus, *Hist.* 1.41–43).[49] Only four days had elapsed since his adoption by Galba (Plutarch, *Galb.* 24.1; Tacitus, *Hist.* 1.19; Suetonius, *Vit. Caes.* 7.12). Just as with Galba, Piso's head was impaled on a pole and displayed among the standards of the rebel soldiers.[50]

---

46  Tacitus states, "There is no question that their loyalty could have been won by the slightest generosity on the part of this stingy old man" (*Hist.* 1.18).

47  Tacitus has Otho stating, "Galba's house alone is equal to paying the donative which is never given to you, but daily thrown in your teeth" (*Hist.* 1.25). In welcoming the praise of the turncoat praetorians, Tacitus continues that Otho "played in every way the slave to secure the master's place" (*Hist.* 1.31).

48  In tribute to Sempronius, Plutarch states, "No one opposed them or tried to defend the emperor, except one man, and he was the only one, among all the thousands on whom the sun looked down, who was worthy of the Roman empire" (*Galb.* 26.4).

49  Because of his intense jealousy toward Piso, Otho rejoiced more over his death than when he heard that Galba had been slain (Tacitus, *Hist.* 1.44). When shown the severed head of the emperor, Otho reportedly said, "This is nothing, fellow soldiers; show me the head of Piso" (Plutarch, *Oth.* 27.4).

50  Such savagery was indicative of the near total collapse of discipline among the praetorian. The soldiers selected their own prefects and paid bribes to their officers so that they might neglect their duty with impunity (Tacitus, *Hist.* 1.46).

The reign of Galba was short-lived by any account. He lived for 72 years and ruled for no more than nine months from the time he announced his revolt in Spain (Dio Cassius, *Hist. rom.* 64.6.6).[51]

## Otho (January–April 69 C.E.)

Otho's connection to the imperial household came by way of Nero. As a youth Otho became Nero's confidant and friend. He sought to solidify his bond with Nero by joining in the debauchery and antics of the future emperor, even trying to outdo Nero in carousing (Suetonius, *Vit. Caes.* 2.1; 7.2; Plutarch, *Galb.* 19.3–4; Pliny, *Nat.* 13.22). Their friendship dissolved when Otho had an affair with Nero's mistress, Poppaea Sabina (Suetonius, *Vit. Caes.* 7.2). Nero would have executed Otho if not for the protection afforded by Seneca, Nero's tutor (Plutarch, *Galb.* 19.5). Instead, in 59 C.E. Otho was exiled to Lusitania, the westernmost province of Spain, where he served as governor for ten years. He was noted for his balanced and moderate reign and for refusing to exploit the wealth of the province for personal gain (Suetonius, *Vit. Caes.* 7.3; Dio Cassius, *Hist. rom.* 61.11.2).

When Otho took control, the Praetorian Guard smeared their hands and swords in the blood of Galba and Piso to show their loyalty and to receive their cash rewards. The Senate also conferred imperial rights on Otho and hailed him as Caesar, giving him the title of Augustus (Plutarch, *Galb.* 27.5–6; 28.1; *Oth.* 3.1; Tacitus, *Hist.* 1.47; Dio Cassius, *Hist. rom.* 64.6.1).

**Relief of a Roman gladiator.**

Otho's strategy to consolidate his hold on the government was threefold: 1) he indulged the military by granting the long awaited donative and by turning a blind eye to abuses committed by the soldiers against the citizens of Rome; 2) he sought to appease the senators by honoring the Roman constitution and by dismissing any legal claims that had been lodged against them; and 3) he lobbied for the favor of the masses by expressing generosity toward the provinces and by granting citizenship freely (Dio Cassius, *Hist. rom.* 64.8.1–2; Plutarch, *Oth.* 3.2).

Such measures were not altogether successful. The Senate recoiled at his violent seizure of power and always harbored fear of his close relationship with the military (Tacitus, *Hist.* 1.50). They rightly perceived that it was Otho who had taught the Praetorian Guard that one could become Caesar by force of arms (Dio Cassius, *Hist. rom.* 64.9.2). The provinces in turn

---

51   There are some descrepencies concerning the precise length of Galba's reign. Suetonius claims that Galba held power for only seven months (*Vit. Caes.* 7.23). Josephus has seven months and seven days (*J.W.* 4.499). These differences seem to stem from the point of reckoning: nine months from the time of the initial revolt in Spain; seven months from the time that Galba entered the city of Rome. Dio Cassius is aware of the difficulty in determining the actual length of the reigns of Galba, Otho, and Vitellius. He states, "For they did not succeed one another legitimately, but each of them, even while his rival was alive and still ruling, believed himself to be emperor from the moment that he even got a glimpse of the throne" (*Hist. rom.* 66.17.5).

were uneasy about his former relationship with Nero. Their fears were not allayed when Otho adopted Nero's name as part of his imperial title and continued to honor the former dictator in the months to come (Suetonius, *Vit. Caes.* 7.1; Dio Cassius, *Hist. rom.* 64.6.5; Plutarch, *Oth.* 3.1). Otho's inability to stabilize the political arena had an ill effect upon the military as well. The soldiers questioned who really held the most power in the empire.[52]

Otho's tenuous hold on the government quickly began to unravel. The combined forces of Upper and Lower Germany, under the commands of Alienus Caecina and Fabius Valens, respectively, cast their lot with Vitellius (Suetonius, *Vit. Caes.* 7.8; Tacitus, *Hist.* 1.52–53; Josephus, *J.W.* 4.546). Otho initially sought to appease Vitellius by offering to share the throne with him (Dio Cassius, *Hist. rom.* 64.10.1; Tacitus, *Hist.* 1.74–75). When Vitellius flatly rejected the notion of a shared empire, negotiations degenerated into a flurry of threatening letters followed by a declaration of all out war (Plutarch, *Oth.* 4.2–5). Ignoring omens that favored Vitellius, Otho decided, despite being ill prepared for war, that a preemptive strike was his best chance to stay in power (Suetonius, *Vit. Caes.* 7.8–9; Tacitus, *Hist.* 1.90). Although Otho's forces were undisciplined and soft from long seasons of inactivity in Rome, they met with initial success at the first battle of Bedriacum, repelling Caecina at Placentia (Plutarch, *Oth.* 5:4–6; 6.2; Tacitus, *Hist.* 2.11–12, 14; Josephus, *J.W.* 4.547) and then again at Cremona

(Tacitus, *Hist.* 2.21–27).[53] These initial victories, however, ultimately undermined Otho's efforts. His forces let down their guard, became overzealous for battle, and attacked rashly (Tacitus, *Hist.* 2.18). When the legions of Valens, some 40,000 in strength, finally joined forces with Caecina at Cremona, the outcome would be very different (Tacitus, *Hist.* 1.59–60; 2.29–30).

Ignoring his generals' counsel that delaying the attack would be to his advantage, Otho once again opted for a lightning strike against Vitellius at Cremona (Plutarch, *Oth.* 8.4; Tacitus *Hist.* 2.32).[54] His attempt to sabotage Caecina's bridge-building campaign to cross the Po River met with disaster. At what came to be known as the Second Battle of Bedriacum, many of Otho's men were killed, sending panic among his troops (Plutarch, *Oth.* 10.3). As Otho's supply train mixed with the combatants, a false rumor that Vitellius had made a pact with Otho only added to the confusion (Plutarch, *Oth.* 12.1–2; Tacitus, *Hist.* 2.40–41). As the two armies ground against each other, Otho withdrew from Cremona, taking his personal body guard and cavalry back to Rome. This move further demoralized his men at a critical point in the battle (Plutarch, *Oth.* 10.1). Before the day ended, over 40,000 soldiers were slain on both sides, yet Vitellius and his generals had prevailed (Dio Cassius, *Hist. rom.* 64.10.3; Josephus, *J.W.* 4.547). They prepared to make their last push on to Rome to rid the empire of Otho.

Once back in Rome, Otho received the grim news of the defeat. A young soldier fresh from the field announced to Otho that they had been

---

52 The instability of Otho's reign is perhaps best illustrated by the following: While banqueting with eighty senators in the palace, the Praetorian Guard heard a rumor that Otho's life was in danger, suspecting that the spies of Aulus Vitellius were already at work in Rome (Tacitus, *Hist.* 1.80–85). The Praetorian charged the palace with swords drawn, killed Otho's personal guard, and rode directly into the emperor's private banquet hall. Only Otho's impassioned plea for calm prevented the majority of the senators from being slaughtered on the spot (Dio Cassius, *Hist. rom.* 64.9.3; Plutarch, *Oth.* 3.4–8).

53 Plutarch grants a vivid description of this Germanic warrior. He states that Caecina was huge in stature, clothed in animal skins and could only communicate with his Roman overlords in sign language. Yet Caecina was ferocious in battle and the perfect leader to press Vitellius' cause across the Po River (*Oth.* 6.3).

54 Otho's generals, Celsus and Paulinus, argued that the Vitellians were over-extended and that they had no dependable supply lines. They counseled a war of attrition that would eventually drain the enemy of men and material (Tacitus, *Hist.* 2.32, 39).

**The Forum, Rome, administrative center of a mighty empire.**

defeated, that their surviving forces had defected to Vitellius, and that the victors were presently marching toward the city. Otho's guard branded the messenger a liar and a coward and urged Otho to employ his remaining forces in a counterattack. At that point, in order to prove his veracity, the messenger drew his own sword and fell on it, dying at the feet of the emperor (Dio Cassius, *Hist. rom.* 11.2).

The soldier's suicide had a profound and decisive effect upon Otho. Rather than continuing the campaign and needlessly sacrificing the lives of his men, Otho conceded defeat (Dio Cassius, *Hist. rom.* 64.13.1–3; Tacitus, *Hist.* 2.46). He firmly resisted the tear-filled pleas of his soldiers to fight on, explaining that their lives and the welfare of the empire were dearer to him than his own life (Suetonius, *Vit. Caes.* 7.10). Plutarch records Otho as stating, "If I was worthy to be a Roman emperor, I ought to give my life freely for my country" (*Oth.* 25.4).[55] Granting any remaining money he had to his servants, he selected a sharp dagger, placed it beneath his pillow and had a sound night's sleep. In the morning of April 16, 69 C.E., Otho took his own life and so ended his brief and tumultuous reign (Josephus, *J.W.* 4.548). The magnanimity of his death led some of his most loyal soldiers to slay themselves upon his funeral pyre (Suetonius, *Vit. Caes.* 7.12; Tacitus, *Hist.* 2.49). Summing up Otho's life, Dio Cassius records, "Thus after living most disgracefully of all men, he died most nobly; and though he had seized the empire by a most villainous deed, his taking leave of it was most honorable" (64.15.2).[56]

55 Tacitus records similar words of valor. He has Otho saying, "To expose such courageous and brave men as you to further dangers . . . I reckon too great a price for my life" and "Others may hold power longer than I; none shall give it up more bravely" (*Hist.* 2.47).

56 Plutarch adds, "For he lived no more decently than Nero, he died more nobly" (*Oth.* 28.2).

In the end Otho's bid for power lasted only 90 days, and he died before his 37th birthday (Dio Cassius, *Hist. rom.* 64.15.1–2; Suetonius, *Vit. Caes.* 7.11; Plutarch, *Oth.* 27.1–4).

## Vitellius (69 c.e.)

Aulus Vitellius was introduced to the imperial household in an ignoble manner. As a profligate youth, he was raised by Tiberius on the Island of Capri (Dio Cassius, *Hist. rom.* 58.22.1–2; Tacitus, *Ann.* 4.19; Suetonius, *Vit. Caes.* 3.62). Vitellius continued to ingratiate himself to Gaius and Claudius by indulging in shared vices, and he won the favor of Nero by extolling his lyre playing and song (Suetonius, *Vit. Caes.* 7.3–4).[57] For his tireless acclaim of the imperial court, he was awarded the proconsulate of Africa. From there Galba appointed Vitellius governor of Lower Germany, reasoning that he would become so occupied with plundering the riches of Germany that he would have no time for treachery (Suetonius, *Vit. Caes.* 7.7).

The legions of Germany, however, had other plans. Their discontent with Galba led them to claim Vitellius as their emperor and march on Rome. As the brief reigns of Galba and Otho crumbled before him, Vitellius led a hedonistic entourage through Gaul and down the peninsula of Italy, buoyed along by the good omen of an eagle hovering above their standards (Suetonius, *Vit. Caes.* 7.9).[58] Displaying no concern for the tens of thousands who had died in the battle at Bedriacum and not even allowing their corpses to be buried, he arrived in Rome some forty days after the battle. He callously commented that the odor of a dead enemy is sweet but that of a dead citizen is sweeter

(Suetonius, *Vit. Caes.* 7.10; Tacitus, *Hist.* 2.59, 70; Dio Cassius, *Hist. rom.* 65.1.3).

Vitellius entered Rome on April 19, 69 c.e., just three days after the suicide of Otho. In an effort to signal his transition from soldier to statesman, he hurriedly changed out of his general's garb into a senatorial robe (Tacitus, *Hist.* 2.89). Once in the city, the military swore allegiance to Vitellius and the Senate followed suit (Tacitus, *Hist.* 2.56). He refused to accept the titles of Caesar or Augustus, preferring instead the title of Germanicus (Tacitus, *Hist.* 1.62, 2.56; Plutarch, *Galb.* 22.7–8). At his coronation he set the tone of his administration by offering a sacrifice in memory of Nero and by having all listen to renditions of Nero's music (Suetonius, *Vit. Caes.* 7.11).

Vitellius's immediately concerned himself with what to do with the remnants of Otho's army. Those that had survived Bedriacum simply blended in among the legions of Vitellius. Since Otho opted not to continue the fight, his troops were boasting that they had not actually been defeated in battle (Tacitus, *Hist.* 2.66). To prevent these soldiers from regrouping and possibly launching an attack against him, Vitellius redeployed them to distant lands, sending many to Britain, Spain and Dalmatia. In an effort to fortify his position in the city, he elevated his loyal German troops to the Praetorian Guard (Tacitus, *Hist.* 2.66–69, 93–94). His brusque treatment of the defeated as well as his gross insensitivity to the slain would come back to haunt him when Vespasian rose to power.

His tenure as emperor was marked by excessive gluttony, savage revenge against debt collectors, and severe punishment for any diviner that might utter an ill omen against him (Suetonius, *Vit. Caes.* 7.14–15).[59] Dio Cassius states, "The entire period of his reign was nothing but a series of carousals and revels" (*Hist.*

---

57  Tacitus notes that Vitellius willingly accompanied Nero on his singing tours because in his words Vitellius "was the slave and chattel of luxury and gluttony" (*Hist.* 2.71).

58  Some 60,000 men accompanied Vitellius enroute to Rome, not counting the officers, their courtiers and slaves. These victorious hoardes drained the land of its resources and terrorized the citizenry of Rome once they arrived (Tacitus, *Hist.* 2.87–88).

59  Soon after taking power, Vitellius contacted his many creditors and informed them that he had spared their lives in place of his debts (Dio Cassius, *Hist. rom.* 65.5.3).

*rom.* 65.3.1). All soon learned that the only way to power was to plan lavish banquets and orgies in his name, with different cohorts of families hosting breakfast, lunch, or dinner, and then another troupe designated to take care of dessert (Dio Cassius, *Hist. rom.* 65.4.3). The magnitude of his indulgence became so insufferable that one Vibius Crispus, unable to attend a banquet because of illness, quipped, "If I had not fallen ill, I surely should have perished" (Dio Cassius, *Hist. rom.* 65.3.1).

Vitellius knew that he must win as many friends as possible if he were to secure a future as emperor. To that end he squandered large sums of cash on gladiatorial competitions and chariot races in an effort to appease the masses (Tacitus, *Hist.* 2.94–95). He also used his office to extend hastily arranged treaties, grant citizenship to foreigners, reduce taxes where beneficial, and cancel debts to appease potential enemies (Tacitus, *Hist.* 3.55). All of these practices tended to enrage the general soldiery in the field because Vitellius had nothing left to pay the donative. Therefore after eight months of debauchery, corruption and oppression, the disaffected legions were ready for a change (Josephus, *J.W.* 4.592–601).

None of this was lost on Vespasian, one of Vitellius's generals. Vespasian appraised his options by administering to his troops an oath of allegiance to Vitellius. When they remained silent, he knew that the tide had turned against the emperor (Tacitus, *Hist.* 2.74). The first legions to encourage Vespasian to revolt were those stationed along the Danube. Earlier in the year they had been mobilized to fight for Otho, yet when Vitellius prevailed, they were ordered to return to their posts. Vitellius then instilled bad blood among these troops by executing their leading centurions. Consequently, the soldiers viewed Vespasian as a ready means of repaying Vitellius for his cruelty. Tiberius Julius Alexander, prefect of Egypt,

also pledged fealty to Vespasian on July 1 of 69 C.E., the date from which Vespasian reckoned the beginning of his reign (Tacitus, *Hist.* 2.76–77). Two days later, the legions of Judea saluted him as emperor. Mucianus, the governor of Syria, noting that "an army can make an emperor," joined in as well and encouraged Vespasian to seize the throne (Tacitus, *Hist.* 2.76–80; Dio Cassius, *Hist. rom.* 65.8.4; Josephus, *J.W.* 4.32, 605, 621).[60] By mid-July, Herod Agrippa II, the brother of Bernice, had sailed from Rome to join Vespasian in his bid for power (Tacitus, *Hist.* 2.81).

Once Vespasian had placed his son Titus in charge of the campaign against Judea (Tacitus, *Hist.* 2.82), he sent his generals ahead to destroy Vitellius in Rome. In the meantime, Vespasian went to Alexandria to cut off the grain supply in an effort to starve Rome into submission (Suetonius, *Vit. Caes.* 8.5–7; Tacitus, *Hist.* 3.8, 42; Josephus, *J.W.* 4.605). As these momentous events unfolded, good omens signaled that a transference of power was in the making.[61]

Even as the legions began to assert their loyalty to Vespasian, dark omens accompanied Vitellius' reign (Dio Cassius, *Hist. rom.* 65.8.1–2).[62] In desperation, Vitellius sought to hide the magnitude of the desertions to Vespasian by secretly summoning auxiliaries from Germany, Britain

---

60 The armies of Syria had heard that Vitellius was going to grant the choice regions of Syria to the German legions while making the Syrian troops suffer the harsh climate of Germany (Tacitus, *Hist.* 2.80). It was to their advantage to get rid of Vitellius.

61 Tacitus records that a cypress tree fell on his estate only to rise again the next day, growing larger and more luxuriant than ever before. He also speaks of a certain priest of the god of Carmel in Judea, who after examining the entrails of the sacrifice pronounced favor on Vespasian (*Hist.* 2.78; cf. also Dio Cassius, *Hist. rom.* 66.1.2).

62 For example, when Vitellius attempted to bolster his troops to offset the effect of mass defections to Vespasian, a huge flock of birds obscured the sun. Also, as he prepared to meet the forces arrayed against him, a sacrificial bull broke loose from the altar and had to be dispatched unceremoniously (Tacitus, *Hist.* 3.56).

and Spain to fill in the ranks (Tacitus, *Hist.* 2.97). His own Praetorian Guard in Rome had grown soft from overindulgence and a general lack of activity and discipline. They also were ill-affected by the heat of Italy and planned for the upcoming battle in a haphazard and dispirited way. To make matters worse, Caecina, who had fought so valiantly against Otho, was divided in his loyalty, secretly planning to defect to Vespasian at the first opportunity (Tacitus, *Hist.* 2.99–100; 3.2).

On the other side of the equation, the forces of Vespasian were already on the move. Antonius Primus, commander of the forces in Pannonia, embarked on a lightening strike against Vitellius (Dio Cassius, *Hist. rom.* 65.9.3–4), crossing the Alps and seizing Verona even before he could be joined by Mucianus from the east (Tacitus, *Hist.* 3.8; Dio Cassius, *Hist. rom.* 65.9.1–2; 65.18.1; Josephus, *J.W.* 4.632–633). Primus moved on to Bedriacum to meet the forces of Vitellius, who again were entrenched at Cremona (Josephus, *J.W.* 4.635–640). It was here that Caecina sought to surrender and join forces against Vitellius. His German troops would have none of it and so imprisoned their own commander, choosing to fight leaderless against Primus rather than commit treachery (Tacitus, *Hist.* 3.13–15; Dio Cassius, *Hist. rom.* 65.11.1–5; Josephus, *J.W.* 4.635–640).

Vitellius's forces launched a daring night attack against Primus, hoping that the marine assault by General Valens would tip the scales in their favor.[63] The battle raged on until dawn, the combatants often stopping for food and drink and engaging in conversation before fighting on.[64] Thinking that Mucianus had finally arrived and joined the battle against them, those loyal to Vitellius withdrew to the fortified city of Cremona. Holding their shields overhead to repel the missiles of the enemy, Vespasian's men were able to breech the walls of Cremona. Once inside they ravaged the city for four days, after which they burned it to the ground (Tacitus, *Hist.* 3.21–29, 32–34; Dio Cassius, *Hist. rom.* 65.10.2–4; 65.15.1–2; Josephus, *J.W.* 4.642).[65]

The defeat at Cremona sent Vitellius into a panic (Tacitus, *Hist.* 3.54). He withdrew all of his forces to Rome while sending forth conflicting orders; one moment he sent envoys to plead for peace, the next he prepared for a protracted defense of the city (Dio Cassius, *Hist. rom.* 65.16.2–6). His closest aids kept the grim reality from their emperor: the enemy was at the door of the city (Tacitus, *Hist.* 3.56).[66] With defeat inevitable, Vitellius is said to have dressed in mourning as he walked aimlessly throughout the city begging the people to have pity on his wife and family. At one point he offered a dagger to a senator so that he might strike him down. The senator refused and both citizens and soldiers forced Vitellius back to the palace, preparing to make a last stand against Vespasian (Tacitus, *Hist.* 3.68–69, 81–84). In the midst of the chaos, Vespasian's youngest son, Domitian, was spirited away and held in safe keeping until the city was secure (Dio Cassius, *Hist. rom.* 65.17.4; Josephus, *J.W.* 4.649).

Having returned to the palace, Vitellius found it empty. He quickly dressed as a slave and hid in the servants' quarters,

---

63 Vitellius had sent Valens by sea to the shores of Gaul. His mission was to persuade the people to abandon Vespasian and to launch a rear assault on Primus and Mucianus. By the time of his arrival, though, the sentiment of the Gauls was firmly behind Vespasian. Valens was captured at sea and executed, further demoralizing the forces of Vitellius (Tacitus, *Hist.* 3.41–43).

64 Dio Cassius states, "Therefore, not even when night came on, as I stated, would they yield; but, though tired out and for that reason often rested and engaging in conversation together, they nevertheless continued in the struggle" (*Hist. rom.* 65.13.3–5).

65 Vespasian's forces employed the *testudo* or "tortoise" here to good effect. The tactic involved holding the shields overhead and interlocking the edges to create a formidable barrier (Tacitus, *Hist.* 3.29). In a desperate attempt to appease the enemy, the Vitellians fetched Caecina from his bonds, dressed him in noble garments, and forced him to plea for peace. Primus completely ignored his offer and captured the city in late October or early November of 69 C.E. (Tacitus, *Hist.* 3.31).

66 It is estimated that Vespasian's forces entered Rome on about December 20, 69 C.E. Vitellius met his end on that same day (Josephus, *J.W.* 4.645).

stacking furniture against the door in one last attempt to stave off death (Suetonius, *Vit. Caes.* 7.16; Tacitus, *Hist.* 3.85).[67] Once discovered, he begged for his life, claiming that he had information to secure the safety of Vespasian (Suetonius, *Vit. Caes.* 7.17). He was dragged ignominiously from the palace, all the while being mocked and tortured (Josephus, *J.W.* 4.651–652). At one point he is reported to have said, "And yet I was once your emperor" (Dio Cassius, *Hist. rom.* 65.21.2). Enraged, his tormentors slaughtered him and dragged his corpse by a hook, casting the body into the Tiber River (Suetonius, *Vit. Caes.* 7.18). Dio Cassius reckons that the reign of Vitellius lasted ten days short of a year (*Hist. rom.* 65.22.1).

At that point Domitian was brought out of hiding to the cheers of those who favored Vespasian (Tacitus, *Hist.* 3.86). When Mucianus finally arrived in the city, he hoisted Domitian onto a podium and had the boy speak on behalf of his father (Dio Cassius, *Hist. rom.* 65.22.2; Josephus, *J.W.* 4.654). On December 22 of 69 C.E., the Senate went through the motions of conferring all imperial rights and privileges to an emperor who again had taken the throne through force of arms.[68]

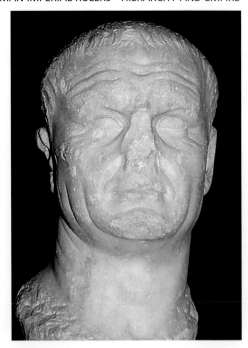

**Vespasian (69–79 C.E.)**

## Vespasian (69–79 C.E.)

After a year of civil war and strife that had seen the rise and fall of three emperors, Vespasian restored peace and civility to the empire (Suetonius, *Vit. Caes.* 8.1).[69] His reign marks the beginning of the Flavian Dynasty, which would continue under his sons Titus and Domitian.

Vespasian was not born to the imperial household but rather was the son of a tax collector, one Sabinus of Asia. He did, however, stem from a long established family and in time was able to ingratiate himself to those who held supreme power. Though reluctant at first to take on the *latus clavus*, that broad stripped toga signaling senatorial aspirations, he quickly rose through the ranks of the Roman hierarchy.[70] Through the powerful

67   Dio Cassius records that Vitellius dressed in shabby clothes and hid in the dog kennel of the palace. When the soldiers discovered him, he was covered in rubbish and blood after being bitten by the hounds in his hiding place (*Hist. rom.* 64.20.2).

68   Wells aptly sums up the situation: "Vespasian had won the throne by force of arms. His troops occupied Rome. Vespasian continued to date his reign from his first acclamation at Alexandria. The Senate by this decree is not conferring power, but legitimizing it. It had done the same for four emperors in a year and a half, and had little *autoritas* of its own left. The Senate, like the city of Rome, was one of the spoils of war" (*The Roman Empire*, 159).

69   Dio Cassius notes that one year and twenty-two days elapsed from the time of Nero's death to the beginning of Vespasian's reign (*Hist. rom.* 66.17.4). Plutarch blames the civil unrest that occurred after the death of Nero not so much on the ambition of those who strove to be emperor but on the greed and lack of restraint of the soldiers. He claims that they killed Nero in order to get the promised reward and then killed Galba because they didn't get it (*Galb.* 1.4; 2.3).

70   Suetonius records that it was only through the chiding of his mother, who claimed that Titus was inferior to his younger brother, that Titus took on the garb of Roman nobility (Suetonius, *Vit. Caes.* 8.2).

**Inscription honoring the emperor Vespasian on the Arch of Titus , Rome.**

freedman, Narcissus, he gained the favor of Claudius and was assigned the legions of Germany. His next command was over the troops in Britain, through whom he subjugated the local tribes and captured the Isle of Wight. Receiving high honors for his service there, he was appointed governor of Africa (Suetonius, *Vit. Caes.* 8.4).[71]

Vespasian, careful to laud Nero's every accomplishment and often holding banquets in his honor (Suetonius, *Vit. Caes.* 8.2), continued to increase in power under Nero. He was honored to accompany Nero on his singing tour of Greece, but when he dozed off during a performance, Nero banished him from the empire. Fearing for his life, Vespasian then went into hiding. However, Vespasian's fortune began to turn for the better with the outbreak of war with Judea in 66 C.E. Nero needed a competent commander to lead the

campaign, and in spite of the insult he had received he appointed Vespasian as general of the armies of the east (Suetonius, *Vit. Caes.* 8.5; Tacitus, *Hist.* 1.10; Dio Cassius, *Hist. rom.* 63.23.1; Josephus, *J.W.* 3.1–4).

In prosecuting the war against the Jews, Vespasian joined forces with his son Titus and also procured the help of Herod Agrippa II (Josephus, *J.W.* 3.29). The combined armies first captured Galilee in the north of Israel (Josephus, *J.W.* 3.110–4.106, 550). They then moved southward, subduing the major towns of Judea in an effort to prepare for the final assault on Jerusalem (Josephus, *J.W.* 3.366–486). At this time Vespasian learned of the suicide of Nero and the rapidly devolving political fates of Galba, Otho and Vitellius (*J.W.* 4.494–495, 502, 588). Leaving the siege of Jerusalem to Titus (Josephus, *J.W.* 4.555, 658), he leveraged the defecting legions of Germany, Syria and Africa to his advantage. Within a year, he would be emperor.

Vespasian remained in Alexandria until Rome was completely secured and all opposi-

---

71  Suetonius notes that Vespasian never lost sight of the practical side of making a living. While in Africa, the future emperor traded in all kinds of livestock and mules and was subsequently called "the Muleteer" by his subjects (Suetonius, *Vit. Caes.* 8.4).

tion was destroyed. He arrived in Rome late in the summer of 70 C.E. (Tacitus, *Hist.* 4.80). His first order of business was to restore the Capitol, which had been all but destroyed by war. To set an example, he immediately commenced clearing away debris with his own hands (Dio Cassius, *Hist. rom.* 66.10.2). Vespasian then made every effort to obtain duplicates of ancient records that had been destroyed in the war, honoring the wills of his fallen enemies and clearing out the backlog of civil suits that had accumulated during the war (Suetonius, *Vit. Caes.* 8.10; Dio Cassius, *Hist. rom.* 66.10.3). In an effort to make the empire solvent, he levied taxes of all kinds, even taxing public urinals (Dio Cassius, *Hist. rom.* 66.14.5).[72]

Vespasian provided free access to senator and citizen alike, posting no guards in the palace, and sought to be evenhanded in his dealings with common folk (Dio Cassius, *Hist. rom.* 66.11.1; Suetonius, *Vit. Caes.* 8.9–10.).[73] He also took steps to foster public education (Dio Cassius, *Hist. rom.* 66.12.1). Seeking to enhance tolerance of public criticism, one of his first official acts was to dismiss the charge of *maiestas*, which had imposed imprisonment or even death upon those who dared to speak against the emperor (Dio Cassius, *Hist. rom.* 66.9.2; Justinian, *Dig.* 48.4.1). He enjoyed a good joke, even at his own expense, and was not easily offended (Suetonius, *Vit. Caes.* 8.15; Dio Cassius, *Hist. rom.* 66.11.2–3).

All in all, Vespasian reigned modestly, being reluctant to accept the title, "Father of his Country" (Suetonius, *Vit. Caes.* 8.12). Dio Cassius notes that Vespasian was neither of noble birth nor rich (*Hist. rom.* 66.10.3), but was a hard worker to the very end. When he

Titus (79–81 C.E.)

became ill of a fever in 79 C.E., he struggled to stand and said, "The emperor ought to die on his feet" (Dio Cassius, *Hist. rom.* 66.17.3). In his final moments, Vespasian reflected upon the Roman practice of deifying their emperors after death. As he breathed his last on June 23, 79 C.E., he quipped, "I am already becoming a god" (Dio Cassius, *Hist. rom.* 66.17.3). He lived to be sixty-nine years of age and reigned nearly ten years. Perhaps the historian Tacitus provides the best epitaph for Vespasian in saying that he was the only emperor who was changed for the better by the office (*Hist.* 1.50).

### Titus (79–81 C.E.)

Because the patronage that Vespasian had received from Claudius was also extended to his sons, Titus was regarded as part of the royal family and received a court education. He studied along side of Britannicus, the son of Claudius, and was present at the time of his poisoning (Dio Cassius, *Hist. rom.* 61.7; Josephus *Ant* 20.153). As a sign of his

---

72  When Titus rebuked his father for taxing even the toilets, Vespasian produced some of the coins gained thereby and quipped, "See, my son, if they have any smell" (Dio Cassius, *Hist. rom.* 66.14.5).

73  Suetonius comments, "Certainly he never took pleasure in the death of anyone, but even wept and sighed over those who suffered merited punishment" (*Vit. Caes.* 8.15).

Arch of Titus, Rome, built to celebrate the emperor's defeat of the Jewish revolt.

true friendship to Britannicus, Titus drank from the same cup that had killed his friend, and was ill for some time thereafter. Never regretting the gesture, Titus had a golden statue of Britannicus erected in the palace and publicly honored him throughout his life (Suetonius, *Vit. Caes.* 8.2). As a member of the imperial court, Titus distinguished himself as an accomplished scholar and artist. He was noted for having an extraordinary memory, being able to perfectly reproduce signatures at a single glance (Suetonius, *Vit. Caes.* 8.3).

Titus's rise to power came by way of his military successes in Germany and Britain, and most notably in Judea (Suetonius, *Vit. Caes.* 8.4). In the spring of 70 C.E. when Vespasian left off the attack of Judea to seize power in Rome, Titus pressed the campaign onward to the capture of Jerusalem (Josephus, *J.W.* 3.8; 4.555, 658; 5.1). He did not lead from afar, but personally engaged in the conflict, repeatedly exposing himself to mortal danger and slaying many of the enemy at close quarters (Josephus, *J.W.* 5.47, 61, 82, 310–311). Since his envoys of peace were ignored by the combatants in Jerusalem, Titus built fortified camps in preparation for

The Amphitheatrum Flavium, Rome, later known as the Colosseum, built by Titus.

a long siege. The Jews fought valiantly against Titus, destroying his siege engines, undermining his ramparts, and making successful forays against the Romans outside the protective walls of Jerusalem (Dio Cassius, *Hist. rom.* 66.4.1–5; Josephus, *J.W.* 5.76–81). Nevertheless, by May of 70 C.E., within a month of commencing the siege, Titus had broken through the outer defensive walls of Jerusalem (Josephus, *J.W.* 5.302).[74] Once his armies were within the perimeter, the Jews once again rejected his offer of clemency (Josephus, *J.W.* 5.114; 6.215).[75] The long and bloody siege dragged on, producing a good number of deserters on both sides of the conflict. The inner defenses, consisting of a second and third defensive wall, proved more formidable than the outer wall, the Jews

74  For a detailed description of the successive walls, towers and battlements protecting Jerusalem, see Josephus, *J.W.* 5.136–176.

75  At times the Jews would feign surrender to get the Romans to let down their guard and draw close to the walls of Jerusalem. Once that was accomplished, they would inflict great damage upon the Romans and mock them for falling into their trap. If it were not for the entreaties of their fellow soldiers, Titus would have executed the soldiers who fell for the ruse (Josephus *J.W.* 5.109–129, 317–329).

The interior of the Colosseum, showing the remains of the tiered seating and the vast vaults beneath the arena.

fighting more ferociously as the Romans drew near the Temple precincts (Dio Cassius, *Hist. rom.* 66.5.3–5; Josephus, *J.W.* 5.89–94, 332–342, 346–347; 6.73). The Jews would not be finally subjugated until August, and victory was only finally secured when the temple was put to the torch (Josephus, *J.W.* 6.165–167, 228, 271).

With the victory of Jerusalem finally in hand, the Romans placed their military standards inside the temple and offered sacrifice there. Heaping words of praise upon Titus, the legions claimed him as their emperor (Josephus, *J.W.* 6.316). Titus raced back to Rome to stem rumors that he was planning to overthrow his father and take control of the empire. Once there, he came before Vespasian unannounced, and while standing alone with open palms said,

"I am here, father; I am here" (Suetonius, *Vit. Caes.* 8.5). Having regained his father's trust, Titus was appointed as prefect of the Praetorian Guard. He used this post to eliminate any opposition to his father and remained a loyal and obedient son in all matters pertaining to the state (Suetonius, *Vit. Caes.* 8.5–6).

Upon Vespasian's death on June 24, 79 C.E., Titus assumed full imperial power. He emulated his father's measured use of executive power, refusing to punish anyone for a charge of maiestas (Dio Cassius, *Hist. rom.* 66.19.1; Suetonius, *Vit. Caes.* 8.9). He lived frugally with regard to his own needs but was known for greatly increasing taxes on some provinces and for accepting bribes (Dio Cassius, *Hist. rom.* 66.19.3). He is said to have appointed corrupt governors as "sponges" so that they could soak up the wealth of their provinces. Once they had become engorged with ill-gotten gain, Titus would then charge them with graft and seize their assets (Suetonius, *Vit. Caes.* 8.16). With such proceeds he built the *Amphitheatrum Flavium*, later to be known as the Colosseum, and sponsored spectacular gladiatorial events there (Dio Cassius, *Hist. rom.* 66.25.1–5). His sexual dalliance with Bernice, the wealthy and powerful sister of Herod Agrippa II, was widely known, and he would have married her if it were not for the protests of his subjects (Dio Cassius, *Hist. rom.* 66.15.4; Tacitus, *Ann.* 2.2). He played the role of chief patron well, considering a day all but lost if he had not used his office for the public good (Suetonius, *Vit. Caes.* 8.8). His response to the two great natural disasters of 79 C.E., the eruption of Mt. Vesuvius and the burning of Rome, was nothing short of magnanimous. He sent cash relief to the victims of the disasters and restored any personal property that was lost. He refused all foreign aid, covering the expense of the relief efforts from funds already on hand (Dio Cassius, *Hist. rom.* 66.22.1–66.24.4).

In 81 C.E. Titus was struck down with a sudden illness. Many interpreted his last words, "I have made but one mistake," to mean that Domitian had finally succeeded in killing the emperor (Dio Cassius, *Hist. rom.* 66.23.3). Even though Titus had earlier discovered Domitian's treachery, he could not bring himself to execute his own brother (Dio Cassius, *Hist. rom.* 66.26.1–3; Suetonius, *Vit. Caes.* 8.9). Titus died at forty-two years of age, after having reigned for twenty-six months.

## Domitian (81–96 C.E.)

In step with Claudius and Nero, Domitian continued to persecute the early church. Eusebius declares that Domitian initiated "the second great persecution against the Christians" (*Hist. eccl.* 3.17). He came to be emperor by default.

**Domitian (81–96 C.E.)**

Since Titus had left no male heirs to succeed him and Domitian was his younger brother, the senate appointed Domitian to the throne (Tacitus, *Hist.* 4.86; *Ann.* 11.11; Josephus, *J.W.* 4.598; *Life* 1.429). He patterned his reign after that of Nero. In his early years, he sought to restore equity to the judicial system, end corruption throughout the provinces, and raise the general level of morality in the empire (Suetonius, *Vit. Caes.* 8.32). Regarding the city officials and provincial governors, Suetonius writes, "At no time were they more honest and just" (*Vit. Caes.* 8.8.2). Domitian strove for fiscal responsibility; he himself regularly declined great sums of money bequeathed to him (*Vit. Caes.* 8.9). He sought to enhance the goodwill of the military by increasing their pay. They in turn fought hard for him, defeating the Germans in several campaigns (*Vit. Caes.* 8.6.2).[76]

76 Domitian's zeal for righteousness was often misguided. In a gross display of feigned piety, he suspected the vestal virgins of violating their vows of chastity and slaughtered them all (Pliny the Younger, *Ep.* 4.11; Suetonius, *Vit. Caes.* 8.8.3–4).

Yet as his tenure increased, Domitian became more lavish, suspicious, and severe (Dio Cassius, *Hist. rom.* 67.1.1). In the construction of his new palace, the Domus Augustana, he had columns of highly polished stone installed so that he could see the reflections of those behind him (Suetonius, *Vit. Caes.* 8.14.4).[77] He employed many secret informers who terrorized the senate with false accusations and mock trials (Tacitus, *Agricola* 41, 45). Domitian increased the gore of gladiatorial combat, initiating night combats that drew dwarfs and women into the bloodbath (Suetonius, *Vit. Caes.* 8.4.1–2; Dio Cassius, *Hist. rom.* 67.8.4). He quickly emptied the imperial treasury for his extensive building programs and patronage (Suetonius, *Vit. Caes.* 8.5). Once again like Nero, the emperor employed extortion and graft to increase revenue to make up for the shortfall (*Vit. Caes.* 8.12.1–2). The Jews became a target of persecution and a convenient source for extracting exorbitant tax revenues (*Vit. Caes.* 8.12.2–3). From 93 C.E. until the end of his reign, Domitian became increasingly paranoid, killing and torturing at will. He murdered and exiled all whom he suspected, regardless of whether they were esteemed members of the senate or members of his own family, often announcing their innocence just before he had them executed (*Vit. Caes.* 8.10–11.3).[78] Claiming to be divine, he demanded that he be worshiped as *Dominus et Deus*, "Emperor and God" (*Vit. Caes.* 8.13.2). Christians and Jews who refused to do so were taxed into penury or executed. No record was kept of those who followed "foreign religions," for in Domitian's eyes they were not worth counting. He had Flavius Clemens, the husband of his niece, killed on the charge that he was an "atheist," an unofficial term for a Christian (Dio Cassius, *Hist. rom.* 67.14.1–3; Suetonius, *Vit. Caes.* 8.15.1).[79] Tradition records that he arrested the Apostle John in Ephesus. Failing to kill John by boiling him in oil, Domitian exiled the apostle to the isle of Patmos, where he worked as a slave until his death (Rev 1:9; Eusebius, *Hist. eccl.* 3.18).

Domitian's demise came in the same way as so many emperors before him. His wife, Domitia, together with his chamberlains and some trusted praetorians, had him assassinated. In a desperate and bloody struggle with his steward Stephanus, Domitian was stabbed to death in 96 C.E. (Suetonius, *Vit. Caes.* 8.17; Dio Cassius, *Hist. rom.* 67.17.1–2).

# PROCONSULS, PREFECTS, PROCURATORS, AND GOVERNORS
## Introduction

When Rome acquired many new territories in the third century B.C.E., it adopted a provincial form of government for them. Originally *provincia* referred to the office that conducted war and was closely associated with Roman generals. In time, however, the annexed territory itself came to be known as the *provincia*, "province." Whenever possible, Rome sought to rule its provinces indirectly through client kings, as Augustus did with the Parthians and the Medes and as was also practiced with the Herods (*Res gest. divi Aug.* 5.33). The Caesars' constant fear was subversion through urban unrest; governance through the local elite

---

77 Since the leading cause of death for an emperor while in office was assassination, such precautions were not unwarranted. Of the twenty-three emperors from Tiberius (14–37 C.E.) to Alexander Severus (222–235 C.E.), it is estimated that seventeen either were assassinated or committed suicide (Barry Baldwin, *The Roman Emperors* [Montreal: Harvest House, 1980], 8).

78 The punishment for high-ranking Roman citizens often was deportation to a remote Mediterranean island (cf. Justinian, *Dig.* 48.22.1–6; 49.4.1). The banishment applied even after death, with the body of the deceased to be buried on the island prison unless specified otherwise by the emperor (*Dig.* 48.24.2).

79 Many Romans regarded the early Christians as atheists because they rejected the gods and goddesses of the Greco-Roman pantheon as well as the many "lords" of the mystery religions (Acts 14:8–19; 17:22–32; 1 Cor 8:4–6). On Domitian's persecution of Jews and Christians, see James C. Walters, "Romans, Jews, and Christians: The Impact of the Romans on Jewish/Christian Relations in First-Century Rome," in *Judaism and Christianity in First-Century Rome* (ed. Karl P. Donfried and Peter Richardson; Grand Rapids: Eerdmans, 1998), 184–85.

was thus the best way to keep the indigenous population under control.[80] The imperial mandate for these *amici*, "friends," of Rome was that they control the indigenous population, collect from them yearly *tributa*, or taxes, and provide quarters for Roman officials and the military. In many cases, however, Rome found it necessary to rule directly through appointed officials. The provincial governors appointed by the Roman senate were called proconsuls and were placed over peaceful areas, as was the case with Sergius Paulus in Crete (Acts 13:7) and Gallio in Achaia (Acts 18:12).[81] The Caesars directly appointed prefects in areas that posed a security risk to the empire. Their primary tasks were to insure military supremacy and execute Roman justice for citizens and allies. If a prefect's portfolio also called for the collection of taxes, he took on the title of "procurator." As such, he supervised the selling of tax-collecting franchises to the *societates publicanorum* ("publicans' guilds").[82] In real terms, the governor had to avoid upsetting local noblemen who could ensure the steady flow of revenue to Rome, nor could he tolerate civil unrest.

The Roman seat of government for Judea was at Caesarea Maritima (Caesarea by the Sea), the great city that Herod built for Caesar. The chief captain Claudius Lysias sent Paul to Caesarea when the proceedings of the Sanhedrin fell through in Acts 23:26. But the Romans also had fortresses in every major city, Jerusalem being

no exception. Since Jerusalem could be especially unruly during the Passover season, Pontius Pilate was stationed at the Fortress Antonia during the trial of Jesus (Josephus, *Ant*. 18.35).

The Caesars were always concerned about provincial governors becoming too powerful, and so they usually limited their tenure to one year. But since the military officers and their troops remained in their assigned area even as the governors were rotated out, it was the Roman generals who posed the real threat to the emperors. Time and again, a general such as Julius Caesar, Mark Antony, or Augustus would amass power on the field and then use it to subjugate the senate back in Rome (*Ant*. 19.243).

Roman rule over Judea was especially troublesome. The Romans' strategy of governing through compliant mediators was frustrated by weak leadership on site and the repeated insurrections of the Jews. For these reasons, the inept leadership of Archelaus motivated Augustus to remove him from office in 6 C.E. From that time until Vespasian destroyed Jerusalem and the temple in 70 C.E., the Jews came under the direct rule of Roman prefects and procurators.[83] During this period there were at least six Roman governors over Judea, the most important of whom were Pontius Pilate, Antonius Felix, and Porcius Festus. Outside Judea, Gallio of Achaia and Sergius Paulus of Cyprus also play significant roles in the New Testament.

## Pontius Pilate (26–36 C.E.)

Pontius Pilate was the procurator under Tiberius, his patron being Sejanus, chief lieutenant to the emperor (Josephus, *Ant*. 18.177).[84] Pilate is most noted for his role

---

80  "It was normal Roman practice in the incorporation of a new province into direct rule to build upon existing institutions, and to depose the existing local leaders from power only when it seemed absolutely necessary" (Martin Goodman, *The Ruling Class of Judaea: The Origins of the Jewish Revolt against Rome, A.D. 66–70* [Cambridge: Cambridge University Press, 1987], 29, cf. also 34).

81  For the duties of proconsuls and governors see Justintian, *Dig*. 1.16.and 1.18.

82  On Roman law and the governance of the provinces, see Adrian Nicholas Sherwin-White, *Roman Society and Roman Law in the New Testament* (Oxford: Clarendon, 1963), 12; and Wolfgang Kunkel, *An Introduction to Roman Legal and Constitutional History* (Oxford: Clarendon, 1973), 40–41.

83  For a graphic description of the siege of Jerusalem and the destruction of the temple by the general Titus, see Dio Cassius, *Hist. rom*. 66.4.1–7.2.

84  Josephus records that Sejanus betrayed the trust of Tiberius and paid the ultimate price for his duplicity (*Ant*. 18.181–185) in 31 C.E., when Tiberius executed Sejanus, many of his associates, and his children; his wife committed suicide (Tacitus, *Ann*. 6.6–9). On Sejanus and Pilate, see Peter Richardson, *Herod: King of the Jews and Friend of the Romans* (Minneapolis: Fortress, 1999), esp. 312.

in the Gospels, conducting the trial of Jesus (Matt 27; Mark 15; Luke 23; John 18:29–19:38; *Ant.* 18.63–64).[85]

No doubt the public outcry over Jesus placed Pilate in a quandary, for he found no civil grounds for Jesus' execution and apparently did not view him as a threat to Roman security (Luke 23:4; John 18:38; 19:4). On the other hand, his standing orders were to maintain peace among the locals. Pilate's referral to Herod Antipas (Luke 23:7–8) might have been a matter of protocol. The Caesars had empowered the Herodian dynasty, and Jesus was under the jurisdiction of Herod Antipas. In any case, Pilate failed in his duty by washing his hands of the incident (Matt 27:24), for he was the supreme Roman commander of the region and responsible for all capital punishments.

Josephus records the gross insensitivity and oppression of Pilate. Pilate sought "to abolish the Jewish laws" by bringing imperial banners into Jerusalem that bore the image of Caesar (Josephus, *Ant.* 18.55–59; *J.W.* 2.169–174). Knowing the sensitivity of the Jews to anything resembling idolatry, especially in the precincts of the temple, Pilate had the ensigns brought in by night. Upon their discovery, the Jews petitioned Pilate to remove the banners, and after a week of protest, Pilate threatened to kill them all. Falling before him and bearing their necks to the sword rather than allow the profanation of Jerusalem, the Jews forced

Inscription from Caesarea naming Pontius Pilate.

Pilate to relent from his folly (*Ant.* 18.55–59; *J.W.* 2.174). On another occasion, Pilate used funds from the temple to build an aqueduct to Jerusalem. When the Jews rioted, Pilate sent his soldiers among them, killing and wounding many (*Ant.* 18.60–62; *J.W.* 9.175–177). Those killed on this occasion may be the ones recorded killed in Luke 13:1. Here Luke states that Pilate slaughtered some Galileans and mixed their blood with that of the sacrifices in the temple.[86] Finally, Pilate's ill treatment of the Samaritans led to his dismissal (*Ant.* 18.85–89). Great numbers of Samaritans had been incited to converge upon Mt. Gerizim to look for vessels that had been buried there by Moses, or so they had been told. Pilate interpreted the amassing of so many zealous Samaritans as a threat to peace. Therefore he sent mounted troops to stop the crowds, slaughtering many Samaritans in the process. After the Samaritans appealed to Vitellius, the

---

85  In *Ant.* 18:63–64, the so-called *Testimonium Flavianum*, Josephus records that Pilate crucified Jesus "the Christ," a doer of miracles, who was subsequently raised from the dead and founded the "sect of the Christians." He continues that these believers "are not extinct at this day." It should be noted that none of the early Church Fathers quote this passage; its first appearance occurred in Eusebius' *Hist. eccl.* 1.11 in the 4th century C.E. The passage also seems to show evidence of interpolations or insertions by an early Christian scribe. For a thorough treatment of the possible authenticity of the text and the history of scholarly debate, see Alice Whealey, *Josephus on Jesus: The Testimonium Flavianum Controversy from Late Antiquity to Modern Times* (Studies in Biblical Literature 36; New York: Lang, 2003).

86  See James M. Dawsey, "Confrontation in the Temple: Luke 19:45–20:47," *PRSt* 11 (1984): 153–165, esp. 161.

**Remains of the *bema* at Corinth.**

Roman prefect of Syria and superior to Pilate, Vitellius ordered him to quit Judea and give an account to Tiberius in Rome. Marcellus was then installed in Pilate's place (*Ant.* 18.89).

## Sergius Paulus (44–47 C.E.)

The Apostle Paul met Sergius Paulus, the proconsul of Cyprus, early in his first missionary journey (Acts 13:4–12). Since Luke only lists his *cognomen* (what he was called by family and friends) and his *nomen gentile* (his family or clan name), omitting his *praenomen* (his first name), it is difficult to determine the identity of this proconsul. We know that the Pauli clan consisted of wealthy landowners of Pisidian Antioch who served the emperors in the first and second centuries C.E. Also, a Latin inscription found in the north of Cyprus and dated to the 40s C.E. speaks of a proconsul by the name of Paulus.[87] This would have been when Paul was on the island, but without further details,

it cannot be determined if this is the proconsul of Acts 13.[88] In any case, Sergius Paulus, ignoring the wiles of Elymas the sorcerer, "believed" and was amazed at the teaching of the Lord (13:12). Whether the proconsul believed unto salvation or was simply convinced that the gospel was more powerful than magic cannot be determined (8:9–24). Yet Luke portrays Paul's first encounter with a Roman proconsul in a positive light. The fact that he and Barnabas traveled immediately to Pisidian Antioch may indicate that Sergius Paulus was so impressed with the Gospel that he referred the missionaries to his family members living in that region. If this is so, then this entire region may have been opened up to the gospel through the influence of Sergius Paulus.

## Gallio (51–53 C.E.)

An inscription at Delphi indicates that Gallio was proconsul of Achaia from 51

---

87 In 1877 an inscription was found in Paphos mentioning Sergius Paulus as proconsul and describing his family's assets in Pisidian Antioch. See F. F. Bruce, *The Book of Acts* (Grand Rapids: Eerdmans, 1988), esp. 248 n. 25, 249.

88 Witherington thinks Paul was preaching to Lucius Sergius Paulus, who served as curator of the Tiber under Claudius three years after his assignment in Cyprus, but we cannot be sure (Witherington, *Acts*, 400; cf. also Bruce, *The Book of Acts*, 248 n. 21).

to 53 C.E.[89] Gallio was the younger brother of Seneca, the esteemed Stoic philosopher and counsel to Nero. Seneca comments that Gallio was wise, amiable, and above flattery (*Naturales quaestiones* 4a, preface 11). Such qualities are in evidence when Gallio examines Paul's case before his judgment seat in Corinth (Acts 18:12–16).[90] The charge brought against Paul by the Jews is that he preaches an illegal religion (18:13). Gallio rejects the accusation and judges that Christianity is a form of Judaism (18:14–15). As such it falls under the category of *religio licita*, "approved religion," a ruling about the Jews that was established by Julius Caesar and upheld by all emperors thereafter.[91] Gallio's decision meant that throughout the empire, Christianity would fall under the same governmental protection as Judaism.

Gallio's fate turned for the worse with the assassination of Nero. His brother Seneca was implicated in the plot to kill the emperor and was forced to commit suicide. As Gallio pleaded for his own life before the senate, he too was framed as a conspirator, and he reportedly committed suicide a year later (Tacitus, *Ann.* 15.63).

## Felix (52–58 C.E.)

Felix's full name was Marcus Antonius Felix, indicating that like his brother Pallas (Josephus, *Ant.* 20.182; *J.W.* 2.247), he was the freedman of Antonia, mother of Claudius Caesar. And just as Claudius made Pallas a high-ranking officer in his administration, Felix was appointed procurator of Judea in 52 C.E. (*Ant.* 20.137; *J.W.* 2.252; *Life* 1.13, 37). He succeeded the hated Ventidius Cumanus, inheriting all of the tumult that Cumanus had engendered under his reign

(*Ant.* 20.103–117). Felix enhanced his power by taking for his third wife Drusilla, the sister of Herod Agrippa I (*Ant.* 20.140–144; cf. Acts 24:24). He became so powerful that he convinced the emperor Claudius to marry his niece Agrippina, who in turn pressured Claudius to adopt her son Nero.

At the end of his third missionary journey, while delivering a large offering to the poor saints in Jerusalem, Paul was accosted by Jews in the temple. Paul then was quickly placed under Roman custody and transported to Caesarea (Acts 21:27–33; 22:23–34).[92] There he was tried by Felix because at this time he was still the Roman procurator of Judea (24:1–27).

Describing the first hearing, Luke notes that Felix "was well acquainted with the Way" (v. 22). His knowledge of Christianity may have come from Drusilla, who sat at Felix's side during Paul's second hearing (v. 24). As Paul joined his defense with the Christian virtues of righteousness, self-control, and judgment, Felix "was afraid," clearly shaken by Paul's words (v. 25). Abruptly ending the proceedings, Felix used Paul's case to curry favor with the Jews. He left Paul in prison for two years, all the while conferring with him so that he might receive a bribe (vv. 26–27).[93]

In light of the constant strife of the Jews during his tenure, Felix's bartering of Paul's fate is understandable, even if not excusable. The dreaded Sicarii murdered and pillaged throughout Judea, and Josephus records that Felix killed them daily (*Ant.* 20.160–68). On the other hand, chafing under the constant admonitions of Jonathan the high priest, Felix bribed some of these assassins to kill

---

89  His active tenure may have been much shorter because of illness (cf. Witherington, *Acts*, 552).

90  Paul's word for the judgment seat of Gallio is *bēma* (βῆμα). He uses the same word in 2 Cor 5:10 when he describes Christians appearing before the judgment seat of Christ.

91  For a detailed discussion of Judaism as *religio licita*, see Witherington, *Acts*, 539–44.

92  The confusion that accompanied Paul's arrest can be seen in the fact that at first he was mistaken for an Egyptian Jew who had led an insurrection against Rome (Acts 21:38). Cf. also *Ant.* 20.167–172; *J.W.* 2.261–263.

93  The sidelining of Paul in prison by Felix may reflect the governor's knowledge of Roman law. Once an appeal has been made, nothing new regarding the case is to occur until proceedings commence again in a higher court (Justinian, *Dig.* 49.7.1).

him (*Ant.* 20.162–164). Crushing a popular uprising of the Jews that was led by a messianic pretender from Egypt, he killed four hundred of the pretender's followers, but Josephus records that the pretender escaped (*Ant.* 20.169–172). Felix's heavy-handed approach to quelling riots between Jews and Syrian Gentiles in Caesarea led to his downfall (*Ant.* 20.173–178, *J.W.* 2.266–70; Tacitus, *Ann.* 12.54). A delegation of Jews appealed to Nero, and Felix was recalled to Rome and replaced by Porcius Festus (*Ant.* 20.182; *J.W.* 2.271). Only the intercession of his powerful and wealthy brother, Pallas, saved his life (*Ant.* 20.182–184). Tacitus commented that Felix "exercised the power of a king with the mind of a slave" (*Hist.* 5.9).

## Porcius Festus (59–62 C.E.)

The civil unrest of the Sicarii continued under Festus (*Ant.* 20.185). He likewise had to send armed forces against a messianic pretender and his followers, killing them all in the process (*Ant.* 20.185–188). His insensitivity to the Jews and their religion became an issue of imperial concern. Herod Agrippa I had built a dining hall that allowed a view of the temple and its proceedings. Offended at his impropriety, the Jews constructed a high wall blocking the view. When this came to the attention of Festus, he gave the order that the wall be torn down. Once again a delegation of Jews traveled to Rome and appealed to Nero. The religious sensitivities of Nero's wife influenced him to side with the Jews, leaving Festus and Herod Agrippa I to live with the consequences (*Ant.* 20.189–195). All in all, Festus did not deal as harshly with the Jews as Felix did (*J.W.* 2.272) and so remained in office until his death, thereafter being replaced by Albinus (*Ant.* 20.197, 200).

In the New Testament, Festus plays a major role as the second procurator to hear Paul's case (Acts 25:1–22). Soon after taking office, he traveled to Jerusalem to establish connections with the Jewish leadership. It was here that he learned of Paul's case, which had been mothballed for two years under Felix's reign (vv. 1–2). Once back in Caesarea, Festus and a contingent from the Sanhedrin heard Paul's defense. Paul quickly sensed that Festus was "at a loss" concerning how to proceed, knew little of Judaism, probably had never heard the name of Jesus, and was exploiting the trial to gain advantage with the Jews (vv. 9, 19–20). Not wanting to be a pawn of provincial politics, Paul invoked his right as a Roman citizen and appealed to Caesar (vv. 11–12).

Paul's use of *provocatio*, the ultimate appeal in the Roman judicial system, effectively ended the jurisdiction of Festus.[94] He knew the penalty for denying an appeal as set forth in the *lex Julia*, which stated,

> Also liable under the *lex Julia* on *vis publica* is anyone who, while holding imperium or office, puts to death or flogs a Roman citizen contrary to his [right of] appeal or orders any of the aforementioned things to be done, or puts [a yoke] on his neck so that he may be tortured. . . . It is provided in the *lex Julia* on *vis publica* that no one is to bind or hinder an accused so as to prevent his attending at Rome within the fixed period. (*Dig.* 48.6.7–8)[95]

Nevertheless, Festus, having found no criminal charges against Paul, did not know what

---

94   The opening sentence of the section entitled "Appeals and Referrals" in Justinian's *Digesta* states, "As everybody knows, the practice of appeals is both frequent and necessary, inasmuch as it corrects the partiality or inexperience of judges" (*Dig.* 49.1.1). Paul's statement "I appeal" constituted the *apud acta*, or oral pronouncement of appeal in the presence of Caesar (*Dig.* 49.1.3).

95   *Provocatio* was an ancient Roman right assuring that citizens could be heard by the people. After the Caesars gained full control, however, the hearings took place before the emperor, not a jury of one's peers. The *provocatio* was not to overturn a verdict already pronounced but rather to obtain a venue for justice over the head, so to speak, of the procurator. "This law, then, protected the citizen both from coercion by a procurator and also from his exercising his right of capital punishment" (Witherington, *Acts*, 724–25).

kind of letter to write to Nero (Acts 25:18, 25), deeming it "unreasonable" (25:27) to send a prisoner without specific charges. He hoped, then, to gain good counsel on this matter from Herod Agrippa II and his sister, Bernice, who were both Jews and thoroughly familiar with Judaism (25:13, 26).

Herod Agrippa II, great-great-grandson of Herod the Great, was at this time king of Chalsis, a territory corresponding to modern Lebanon. He was the confidant of Nero, and his sister Bernice was the consort of Titus (Tacitus, *Ann.* 2.2). Thus Paul's defense, his longest and one that carefully followed the categories of Greek rhetoric, was before royals who had the ear of the emperor.[96] In his address Paul acknowledges that Agrippa is an expert in Judaism (Acts 26:3). Paul even indicates that Agrippa knows something about Jesus, for, unlike the mystery cults, Christianity took place in the public eye (26:26). Once again Paul's preaching proves effective. Festus, moved by Paul's words, interrupts the hearing with the claim that much learning has driven Paul insane (26:24). To fend off Paul's personal address to him, Agrippa asks, "Do you think that in such a short time you can persuade me to be a Christian?" (26:28). With that the hearing ends, and Festus prepares to send Paul to Rome.

---

96 For a careful presentation of the rhetorical devices employed by Paul, see Witherington, *Acts*, 737.

One wonders, however, why Paul would have appealed to Caesar. As a man of letters, he surely was cognizant of the evils of the office. On the other hand, Paul had had good experiences with Roman proconsuls in the past, such as Sergius Paulus and Gallio. Especially since Gallio was the younger brother of Seneca and Nero had ruled so admirably from 54 to 59 C.E., Paul clearly thought that his chances were better in an imperial court. Unfortunately, Nero's state of mind rapidly degenerated in the early 60s C.E. Not only did he make the Christians the scapegoat for the great fire of Rome; subsequent purges drove Seneca to suicide (Tacitus, *Ann.* 15.61–64) and also led to the death of Gallio. According to tradition, Paul fared no better, being executed by Nero in 63–64 C.E.

## SUMMARY

The seeds of liberty sown in the early Roman Republic ultimately led to anarchy. In time the senate traded freedom for security by submitting representative government to the iron-fisted rule of the emperors. Their dictatorial power tended to cruelty and corruption that effectively negated Roman justice, especially when political advantage and money were at stake. The Pax Romana was maintained through the suppression of any and all who even appeared to threaten the status quo, and this included the Christians. For more than three hundred years, until the conversion of Constantine in 312 C.E., the followers of Christ suffered at the hands of the empire.

# Annotated Bibliography

Donfried, Karl P., and Peter Richardson, eds. *Judaism and Christianity in First-Century Rome*. Grand Rapids: Eerdmans, 1998. This collection of eleven scholarly articles focuses on the experience of Jews and Christians living in Rome of the first century. It is not designed for the beginner but contains useful information on the expulsions of the Jews from Rome and how the expulsions may have related to the early Christian communities there.

Goodman, Martin. *The Ruling Class of Judaea: The Origins of the Jewish Revolt against Rome, A.D. 66–70*. See description at the end of ch. 1.

Griffin, Miriam T. *Nero: The End of a Dynasty*. New York: Routledge, 1984. This thoroughly researched work analyzes the climate and factors leading to the empowerment of Nero. Early influences are discussed in order to make sense of his later reign. The negative consequences that eventually brought about his tragic end are investigated.

Richardson, Peter. *Herod: King of the Jews and Friend of the Romans*. See description at the end of ch. 14.

Scarre, Chris. *Chronicle of Roman Emperors: The Reign by Reign Record of the Rulers of Imperial Rome*. London: Thames & Hudson, 1995. Scarre has produced an excellent source book on Roman imperial rulers from the time of Augustus to the abdication of Romulus Augustus in the fifth century C.E. Clearly written and well illustrated, it is a good place to begin an in-depth study of the emperors.

# 16

# The Centurions— the Presence of Roman Military Might

## INTRODUCTION: WORD STUDY AND IDENTIFICATION

Several Greek words meaning "centurion," an important Roman officer, appear a total of twenty times in the New Testament, with the singular possessive appearing only once and the plural three times.[1] The word *hekatontarchos* (ἑκατόνταρχος) literally means "a ruler

over one hundred" (cf. Matt 8:8). Mark consistently uses *kenturiōn* (κεντυρίων), the Greek transliteration of the Latin (cf. Mark 15:39). Once, however, he also uses *spekoulatōr* (σπεκου-λάτωρ), a Greek form of the Latin *speculator*. The *speculator* held the same post as a centurion but was part of a division of the Imperial Guard in Rome. This elite unit was also known as the Praetorian Guard, numbering six thousand. *Speculatores* were often promoted to lead auxiliary armies throughout the provinces,

1    Matt 8:5, 8, 13; 27:54; Mark 15:39, 44, 45; Luke 7:2, 6; 23:47; Acts 10:1, 22; 21:32; 22:25, 26; 23:17, 23; 24:23; 27:1, 6, 11, 31, 43; 28:16.

"John the Baptist and the Pharisees" (Tissot). John was beheaded by a *"speculator."*

**Sculpture of a Roman officer's breastplate.**

especially in trouble spots such as Judea.[2] So, when John the Baptist was beheaded, Herod Antipas dispatched a *speculator* to carry out the task (Mark 6:27). A centurion was a Roman military officer in charge of about one hundred soldiers, with the status of a noncommissioned officer and charged with the responsibilities of a modern army captain.[3]

2    Adrian Nicholas Sherwin-White, *Roman Society and Roman Law in the New Testament* (Oxford: Clarendon, 1963), 124, 155. Members of the Praetorian constituted an elite group among the centurions and were paid twice as much as other centurions (John E. Stambaugh, "Social Relations in the City of the Early Principate: State of Research," in *The Society of Biblical Literature 1980 Seminar Papers* [SBLSP 19; Missoula, Mont.: Scholars Press, 1980], 91).

3    For a detailed description of the various ranks within the Roman army, see Wendy Cotter, "Cornelius, the Roman Army, and Religion," in *Religious Rivalries and the Struggle for Success in Caesarea Maritima* (Waterloo, Ont.: Wilfrid Laurier, 2000), 280–82.

## THE ROMAN CENTURION

The secret of Rome's success was its ability to manage military might to accomplish political goals. Thus the army played a critical role in Rome's overall strategy, and the centurion played a critical role in the army. Though usually not of equestrian rank, centurions were the most important officers in the Roman army. They were the immediate commanders in the field and took the fight to the enemy. There were two kinds: legionnaires and auxiliaries. The legionnaires were recruited from Roman citizens who were born in Rome or Italy, and most often they were appointed by the provincial governor.[4] Auxiliaries were taken from the provinces and could receive citizenship upon completion of service.[5] Unlike officers of higher rank, such as the legates and tribunes, who served for only three or more years, centurions often worked for more than thirty years in the military.[6] Their importance precluded

---

4    David J. Breeze and Brian Dobson, *Roman Officers and Frontiers* (Stuttgart: Franz Steiner, 1993), 156.

5    In 16 B.C.E. Augustus set the terms of service for the legionnaires at sixteen years. Within two decades, enlistment was extended to twenty years (Tacitus, *Ann.* 1.17). The troops under Germanicus revolted against Tiberius in order to have their length of service and pay returned to the standard set by Augustus (Dio Cassius, *Hist. rom.* 57.4.1–4). For the terms of service for centurions, see John Wilkes, *The Roman Army* (Cambridge: Cambridge University Press, 1972), 5.

6    For an ordering of the rank in the Roman military from the level of the Roman governor down to that of the centurion, see William J. Hamblin, "The Roman Army in the First Century," in *Masada and the World of the New Testament* (ed. John F. Hall and John W. Welch; Provo, Utah: Brigham Young University Studies, 1997), 338.

**Replica of a Roman siege engine at Masada, Israel.**

Artist's impression of a Roman centurion and infantryman.

**Replica of a Roman catapult (*ballista*) at Masada, Israel.**

their being selected from young recruits; candidates were usually in their thirties.[7] Thus some centurions were still leading men into battle when they were sixty or seventy years old. These were of the highest rank of centurions, the *pilus prior*, "first javelin/spear," and were invaluable in the *concilia*, or councils of war.[8]

The prime function of the centurion was to convert raw recruits into highly trained fighting men.[9] His command consisted of about eighty to a hundred men, or a "century." Six centurions and their men made up a cohort, and ten cohorts made up a legion.[10] So, all along the chain of command, centurions of various levels were in direct charge of the foot soldiers and cavalrymen. In addition to the training and the leadership on the field of battle, the centurion had to keep track of all military equipment, make timely inspections of troops, post guards, and grant leave. Two military clerks aided the centurion in these tasks.

In addition to these duties, the centurion was to maintain discipline among his soldiers. His splendid ornamented armor and colored sash marked him as a man of authority.[11] He often controlled his men by wielding the symbol of his office, the *vitis*, a twisted vine staff used to beat soldiers who failed in their duty.[12] Punishments ranged from flogging to execution, but most consisted of public humiliation. If a soldier was late for roll call or had a dirty uniform, he was made to stand in the courtyard of the camp for a day, clothed only in civilian dress. Others were given reduced rations, and in more severe cases, an entire century was forced to camp outside the fortress. Since the threat of attack was constant, none of those punished would be able to sleep. Augustus was particularly strict regarding military discipline. He disbanded the entire tenth legion for its insubordination, and if

7  Breeze and Dobson list at least six ways in which a centurion could be recruited from seasoned soldiers with thirteen to twenty years of service (*Roman Officers and Frontiers*, 154–55).

8  Adrian Keith Goldsworthy, *The Roman Army at War: 100 B.C.–A.D. 200* (Oxford: Oxford University Press, 1996), 14–15, 30.

9  For a vivid description of the unmatched discipline and efficiency of the Roman military, see Josephus, *J.W.* 3.70–106.

10  Edward Luttwak, *The Grand Strategy of the Roman Empire: From the First Century A.D. to the Third* (Baltimore: Johns Hopkins University Press, 1979), 13–15.

11  For a detailed description of a centurion's uniform and duties, see Graham Webster, *The Roman Imperial Army of the First and Second Centuries* (Totowa, N.J.: Barnes & Noble, 1985), 130–31; Luttwak, *The Grand Strategy of the Roman Empire*, 130, 153; and Wilkes, *The Roman Army*, 34.

12  The centurion Lucilius was unmerciful in his use of the *vitis*. Upon breaking his staff over the back of a soldier, he commanded, *Cedo alteram!* ("Fetch me another!" [cf. Tacitus, *Ann.* 1.23]). This became his nickname until the entire legion rebelled and lynched him. The soldiers captured all the centurions and meted to each sixty blows with the *vitis*, one for each centurion in the legion (cf. *Ann.* 1.31–32).

a cohort retreated in battle, he "decimated" them by executing every tenth man as chosen by lot (Suetonius, *Vit. Caes.* 2.24.2; Plutarch, *Crass.* 10.2–3).

The rank of centurion was, then, a prestigious position in Roman society. A centurion received better pay and more living expenses in comparison with most Roman soldiers, and a better retirement as well.[13] Augustus boasts that throughout his tenure, he established scores of colonies for his military officers and clients and paid for these lands with his own money (*Res gest. divi Aug.* 3.16; 5.28). Some centurions became quite wealthy, presiding over large households and owning slaves (Matt 8:5–13; cf. Suetonius, *Vit. Caes.* 1.33.1; 1.38.1–2). Thus competition was high for these positions. Some soldiers became centurions by working their way up through the ranks, and the office of centurion became a portal for upward mobility. If a centurion was promoted to the rank of primus pilus ("the first javelin/spear"), an elite group consisting of only about six hundred in the empire, he attained the level of an equestrian.[14] After this promotion, the door was open for becoming a procurator.[15] Needless to say, the goal of every centurion in the empire was to attain the rank of "first spear." Some degree of fairness in promotion was needed to avoid discontent throughout

**Artist's impression of a Roman officer.**

---

13   Centurions joined mutinies against their leaders, however, when they and their men were not paid or were abused or when terms of service were ignored. For examples of how the military was exploited and of the violent reactions that often ensued, see Suetonius, *Vit. Caes.* 3.25.1–2; 4.44.1–2; 4.48.1–2 and Tacitus, *Ann.* 1. 17, 26, 31, 35.

14   The appointment to *primus pilus* was for one year, after which there was a promotion or a reappointment to *primus pilus*. See Breeze and Dobson, *Roman Officers and Frontiers*, 145. Cf. also Cotter, "Cornelius, the Roman Army, and Religion," 281; Stambaugh, "Social Relations in the City," 91.

15   With regard to upward mobility among centurions, see Brian Campbell, *The Roman Army, 31 B.C.–A.D. 337: A Sourcebook* (London: Routledge, 1994), 47–48; Breeze and Dobson, *Roman Officers and Frontiers*, 156.

the ranks. A number of centurions, however, arrived at their positions from the top down. Very wealthy civilians and ex-officials of the empire were often appointed as centurions. The fact that equestrians were attracted to enlist as centurions speaks to the prestige of the office. Some of these centurions entered the office with little or no fighting experience.

It was this kind of patronage that at times led to disasters on the battlefield.[16]

One did not need to be a free-born Roman citizen to become a centurion. Many of these officers were taken from units in outlying provinces, or the auxiliary. Cornelius was of the Cohors Italica (Italian Regiment), which was recruited originally from Italy but with auxiliary units drawn from the provinces (Acts 10:1).[17] In these cases, a letter of recommendation from an influential patron was needed to secure the appointment.[18]

The centurions formed the link between the Roman generals and the foot soldiers. As such they wielded great power, for they could influence entire armies to cast their lot with a particular general and literally make him the next emperor (Suetonius, *Vit. Caes.* 1.58.1–2; Tacitus, *Ann.* 2.76). For example, when the senate refused to grant Augustus his first consulship when he was only twenty years of age, a loyal centurion slapped the hilt of his sword before them all and shouted, "This will make him consul, if you do not!" (Suetonius, *Vit. Caes.* 2.26.1).[19] Not only did the centurions make Caesars; they could unmake them as well, for they were often at the center of plots to assassinate the emperor (Tacitus, *Ann.* 15.50; Dio Cassius, *Hist.* 77.3, Suetonius, *Vit. Caes.* 4.56.1–4.58.3).

In addition to their military prowess, centurions occupied a strategic place in Roman society. They lived and worked at the critical juncture between the imperial might of Rome and the conquered subjects of the provinces. As such they functioned as "soldier ambassadors" mediating the power of Rome in no unclear terms yet were brokers of the peace where possible. A centurion thus had to be able to demonstrate both courage and character in leadership. Polybius notes that the centurion was expected to maintain composure under the pressure of battle and not to act impulsively (*Historiae* [*Histories*] 6.24). At the same time, when the occasion called for it, the centurion could exhibit extraordinary feats of courage, often rallying his beleaguered men to carry the victory against enormous odds (Plutarch, *Caes.* 44). During peacetime, however, he was to wield the threat of force with reserve and good judgment. Nor was the centurion commissioned to take the offensive and seize new ground when the opportunity arose. Rather, his task was to maintain the security of the territory assigned to him. If forced into armed conflict, the centurion was to hold his ground and to die at his post before relinquishing control of the region. His primary mandate was to keep the peace in his designated territory through force of arms. Qualities such as these present the centurion in a positive light in the New Testament.

## THE CENTURION IN THE NEW TESTAMENT

### The Healing of the Centurion's Servant (Matt 8:5–13//Luke 7:1–10)

The first Gentile to whom Jesus ministered was a centurion stationed in Capernaum (Matt. 8:5–13; Luke 7:1–10). According to Luke, this centurion was a God-fearer on the order of Cornelius in Acts 10:1–48. He reverenced the God of the Jews and built a synagogue for them, winning the great favor of the Jewish elders (Luke 7:3–5). His character is reflected in the compassion he had for his ailing servant, his humility before the

---

16  The inherent weakness of patronage in the military can be seen in the debacle of Varus, an equestrian appointed general with little experience, who lost three legions of soldiers to Germanic tribes (Suetonius, *Vit. Caes.* 2.23.2; 3.17.1–2). Tiberius realized that the disaster was due to "rashness and a lack of care" (*Vit. Caes.* 3.13.1).

17  E.g., Josephus notes that the Roman soldiers stationed in Caesarea were mustered from the province of Syria (*Ant.* 19.363; *J.W.* 3.66).

18  Pliny the Younger secured the position of centurion for Metilius Crispus, who had no prior military experience (Pliny, *Ep.* 6.25).

19  A similar force of arms by a centurion was demonstrated when the senate denied Julius Caesar an extension of command. In this instance, a centurion stood before the senate and slapped the hilt of his sword and shouted, "But this will give it!" (Plutarch, *Caes.* 29.5).

**Scale model of the Roman Antonia Fortress, Jerusalem, built to overawe the adjacent Herod's Temple.**

Lord, and the great faith he expressed in the effective authority of Jesus (Matt 8:6, 8–10; Luke 7:2, 6–8). In turn, Jesus commended the faith of this Gentile warrior (Matt 8:10), saying that he had found none in Israel with so great a faith. Although prevented from doing so by the centurion, Jesus was willing to enter into the house of this Gentile (John 18:28; Acts 10:28).[20] In symbol, this centurion serves as a precursor to the reception of the gospel by the Gentiles,[21] and Jesus' openness

to this centurion could have helped some Jewish Christians, such as the Hellenists of Acts 6 and 7, to make the transition to the Gentile mission. In any case, in reference to his encounter with the centurion, Jesus states that Gentiles will partake of the end-time messianic banquet (Matt 8:11–12).

### The Centurion's Confession at the Cross (Mark 15:39//Luke 23:47)

Immediately after the death of Jesus on the cross, the first person to make a confession of faith is a centurion. In Mark 15:39 the centurion confesses, "Surely this man was the Son of God!"[22] Whether the centurion was still thinking of the divinely inspired superheroes

---

20  In the later rabbinic literature, the house of a Gentile is explicitly designated as ritually unclean ('*Ahalot* 18:7).

21  When commenting on Jesus' affirmation of the centurion in Matt 8:11, F. F. Bruce states, "These words now began to find their fulfillment in another centurion" (*The Book of Acts* [Grand Rapids: Eerdmans, 1988], 202). The other centurion Bruce is referencing is Cornelius of Acts 10.

22  Luke records, "Surely this was a righteous man" (Luke 23:47).

269

of the Greco-Roman pantheon or whether he was acknowledging Jesus as the messiah of the Jews is open to question.[23] The past tense verb "was" (Gk. *ēn* [ἦν]) in this verse is of significance here. This may indicate that the soldier was thinking of what Jesus had done in the past, not his present situation on the cross. Instead of affirming the divinity of Jesus, this centurion may simply be acknowledging that Jesus fulfilled his divine commission. Thus the degree to which the centurion believed that Jesus was the supreme sacrifice for the sins of the world cannot be determined. In any case, the centurion clearly desires to honor and affirm Jesus at his death.[24]

## Cornelius the Centurion
### (Acts 10:1-48; 11:1-18; 15:7-11)

Luke is very careful to identify Cornelius as a centurion of the Cohors Italica that was stationed in Caesarea (Acts 10:1). Caesarea was predominantly Gentile in population (Josephus, *J.W.* 3.409), served as the seat of the Roman procurator, and had the largest garrison of Roman troops in Judea. Since there were no legionnaires stationed in Judea at this time, this means that Cornelius was not a Roman by birth but a member of the auxiliary forces drawn from the provinces.[25] His name was probably taken from the Roman general P. Cornelius Sulla, who in 82 B.C.E. freed ten thousand slaves. These freedmen then adopted his gens, or family name, as their own (Dio Cassius, *Hist. rom.* 60.17.7).[26]

Luke describes Cornelius as "God-fearing" (10:2), employing a semitechnical phrase describing Gentiles who worship the God of Israel but are not circumcised (cf. also 13:16, 26, 43; 16:14; 17:4, 17; 18:7).[27] Such persons came to form a vital core of the churches founded by Paul. Cornelius is further described as "devout" because he prayed continually and regularly gave alms to the poor (vv. 2, 22, 35). His good works were received as a "memorial offering before God" (v. 4).[28] For Luke, this may mean that before the arrival of Peter in v. 24, God may have already disregarded the barrier that separated Jews from Gentiles.

These positive acclamations of Cornelius come immediately before the extraordinary vision of Peter as recorded in vv. 9–16. In this vision, in spite of the strictures of Lev 11:1–47, all types of animals that were previously classified as unclean are now declared to be clean. As a result, Peter now comes to understand the message of the vision in vv. 28, 34. Even though it had been previously forbidden for a Jew even to enter the house of a Gentile (vv. 27–29), Peter now states that God is no respecter of persons and that no person is unclean before him.[29] Therefore both

---

23  Shiner claims that the centurion's confession is the definitive unveiling of the "messianic secret." That is, this hardened Roman officer was the first to realize the true identity of Jesus as divine. Cf. Whitney T. Shiner, "The Ambiguous Pronouncement of the Centurion and the Shrouding of Meaning in Mark," *JSNT* 78 (2000): 3–22, esp. 3–4. Concerning the anarthrous noun—Jesus is *a* son of God and not *the* Son of God—see E. C. Colwell, "A Definite Rule for the Use of the Article in the Greek New Testament," *JBL* 52 (1933): 12–21.

24  "In the death of Jesus the centurion sees the sacrifice of a martyr who has perished innocently" (I. Howard Marshall, *The Gospel of Luke: A Commentary on the Greek Text* [Grand Rapids: Eerdmans, 1978], 876).

25  The Cohors Italica was originally established in Italy by Augustus. Once this cohort was moved to Syria, it recruited exclusively from the provinces. See I. Howard Marshall, *The Acts of the Apostles: An Introduction and Commentary* (TNTC; Grand Rapids: Eerdmans, 1980), 183.

26  Bruce, *The Book of Acts*, 201 n. 1.

27  Luke's Greek expression for "God-fearer" is *phoboumenos ton theon* (φοβούμενος τὸν θεόν). For a detailed discussion of "God-fearer," see Ben Witherington III, *The Acts of the Apostles: A Socio-rhetorical Commentary* (Grand Rapids: Eerdmans, 1998), 341–44. Witherington summarizes by stating that "God-fearers" are Gentiles who worship Yahweh and are, to some degree, adherents to Judaism (p. 344).

28  For the thought that such good works took the place of sacrifices in the temple, see Rom 12:1–2; Phil 4:18; Tob 12:12; 1QS 8:1–9.

29  The Greek verb translated "no respecter of persons" is *prosōpolēmptēs* (προσωπολήμπτης), which literally means "accepter of the face" of a person. One's appearance or racial identity is no longer of any consequence for being a member of God's covenant people (cf. Rom 2:11; Eph 6:9; Col 3:25).

Artist's impression of a Roman merchant ship, similar to the vessel in which Paul was carried as a prisoner to Rome.

Jews and Gentiles are fully accepted by God.

Even though Cornelius is clean and acceptable, in Luke's theology he is not saved because salvation comes only through the person and work of Jesus (2:21, 36; 4:12).[30] But during Peter's presentation of the gospel, God preempts his call to repentance by pouring forth the Holy Spirit upon Cornelius and his household. As on the day of Pentecost, these Gentiles speak in glossolalia or "tongues" (cf. 2:2–4). Peter understands this as the authenticating sign that God has fully accepted Cornelius and

his household into the family of God, and so he proceeds to baptize them in water (vv. 44–48). From now on, for Cornelius, the *genius centuriae*, or the spirit that protected his cohort of soldiers, would no longer be some mysterious spirit of the field but the Holy Spirit of God.[31]

Luke's point here is that another Roman centurion has played a critical role in the birth of the church. This long, detailed account in Acts 10 and 11 demonstrates that the gospel is not just for the Jews but for Gentiles as well. Furthermore, the vision of Peter and the reception of Cornelius mean that all of the purity regulations of the Old Testament are

30  "Thus the crucial matter of forgiveness of sins is owed not to that fear of God and performance of justice which makes one acceptable to God, but to faith in Jesus" (John L. Kilgallen, "Clean, Acceptable, Saved: Acts 10," *ExpTim* 109 [1998]: 301). The issue of ritual purity had already been addressed, however, by Jesus in Mark 7:14–19a.

31  For an insightful description of religion within a Roman camp, see Cotter, "Cornelius, the Roman Army, and Religion," 287–97.

of no consequence for those who are in Christ, whether they be Jews or Gentiles. Indeed, the crisis of 15:1–5 was partly resolved by Peter's retelling of the Cornelius story (15:7–11). Cornelius and his kin thus serve as the prototype of the full-fledged mission to the Gentiles that would soon follow.[32] From a sociopolitical perspective, the acceptance of a Gentile centurion into the church contains the same message as the question of paying taxes to Caesar: that the church poses no threat to Rome and one's service to Rome does not bar membership in the church.[33]

## The Apostle Paul and the Centurions (Acts 21:31–40; 22:24–30; 23:10–34)

Beginning with Acts 21:31 and continuing until the end of the book, Luke's account is taken up with Paul's arrest and transport to Rome. As a prisoner of Rome, Paul would be under the direct custody of Roman military officials. The first to be mentioned is the Roman tribune in Jerusalem, Claudius Lysias (23:26). This *chiliarchos*, literally "ruler of a thousand," was a chief centurion charged with leading from six hundred to a thousand Roman soldiers. As keeper of the peace, he clapped Paul in irons and embarked on a confused inquiry, assuming Paul to be an Egyptian zealot who had escaped the justice of Rome (21:37–38). Although initially treating Paul roughly, he saved him from being torn to pieces by the mob in 21:32 and then again in 23:10–11. In the first instance, displaying the clout of his office, he granted Paul's request to speak to the Jews (21:40). The collapse of order this second time convinced Lysias that Paul was the cause of the disruption,

and so he ordered him flogged (22:22–24). A lesser-ranked centurion was to extract a confession from Paul by *quaestionarii*, that is, torturers.[34] Paul was to be flogged with a *mastix* (Gk.), or *flagrum* (Latin), a kind of cat-o'-nine tails made of leather or wire thongs tipped with lead pellets or knucklebones.[35] But just before the first lash fell, Paul informed the centurion of his Roman citizenship, which effectively stopped the inquisition.[36] By immediately informing his commanding officer of Paul's citizenship, the inquisitor and Lysias were both kept from violating Roman law.[37] Since the centurion in command illegally bribed his way to citizenship but Paul is freeborn, he admits his inferior social status to the apostle (23:16). The security of a Roman citizen, one he has illegally put in irons, now rests in the centurion's hands. So, when a lesser centurion escorts Paul's nephew to Lysias with rumors of a plot to assassinate Paul, Lysias takes all the precautions needed to safeguard Paul's life (23:12–22). He commands two centurions to take Paul to Caesarea under cover of darkness. To insure his safety, the centurions are to take a military escort of 470 foot soldiers and cavalry. An official letter to Felix, the prefect of Syria, explains why Paul is being referred to him (23:23–34). After appearing before Felix, spending two years in prison, and then appearing before Festus, Paul appeals to Caesar (24:27; 25:11–12, 21).

As a result of his appeal to Caesar, Paul is handed over to a centurion who is simply called by his *nomen gentile*, Julius (27:1). This

---

32  Luke portrays Peter as authorizing the acceptance of uncircumcised Gentiles into the church. But Stephen, Philip, and other Hellenists may have opened the door to the uncircumcised before the Cornelius event. It is clear that by the end of Acts 10, no Jew will be made unclean through contact with a Gentile. In essence, this is what Paul expresses in Gal 3:28.

33  On the social and political ramifications of Cornelius's conversion, see Cotter, "Cornelius, the Roman Army, and Religion," 283, 301.

34  For the use of centurions in torture, see Suetonius, *Vit. Caes.* 2.27.4. Cf. also Brian Rapske, *The Book of Acts and Paul in Roman Custody* (Grand Rapids: Eerdmans, 1994), 265.

35  The *flagrum* had been known to maim for life or even to kill its victims (Witherington, *Acts*, 677).

36  Paul's claim to citizenship was taken seriously, for to make a false claim could result in death (Suetonius, *Vit. Caes.* 5.25.3).

37  "To bind a Roman citizen is a crime, to flog him an abomination, to slay him almost an act of murder" (Cicero, *Verrine Orations* 1.5.66). It was for this reason that the tribune was afraid once he was informed of Paul's citizenship (*Acts* 22:29).

fact shows that he was a freedman, not in any way indentured to any other person, and that he was a Roman citizen.[38] His name also reveals that one of his ancestors probably gained his freedom and citizenship under the reign of Julius Caesar. Luke also notes that this centurion was of the Imperial Regiment, meaning that the regiment had at one time originated under Augustus, not that it had traveled all the way from Rome. Perhaps Julius was one of the *frumentarii*, official couriers for the emperor who guarded the grain shipments to Rome and were also entrusted with the transport of serious criminals.[39] On the other hand, all the centurion had to do was to present a *diploma publicus*, or official document of requisition (Plutarch, *Galb.* 8.4). He then could have required that all civilian craft and accommodations be at his disposal. The empire would compensate for materials and services at a later date.[40] Paul's Roman citizenship meant that Julius would have regarded Paul as his equal in a civil sense, and no doubt his treatment of Paul with "kindness" reflects this (27:3). Tokens of his care for Paul are seen in that he allowed Paul to seek out fellow believers in Sidon to obtain provisions from them, and to remain above deck (27:3). Initially Julius was more impressed with the ship's owner and navigator than with Paul's prophecies concerning the bad weather, but gradually he began to heed Paul's counsel (27:10-12, 21-28). When some sailors sought to climb into a small dinghy and abandon ship, the centurion apparently obeyed Paul's directives and had it cut away (27:30-32). Paul's exhortation to take some food was also heeded (27:31-38). But most important, when the ship ran aground, the centurion, for the sake of Paul, ignored the usual practice of killing all the prisoners (27:42-43). This was a bold step, for if any of the prisoners had escaped, Julius's life and those of the other soldiers would have been forfeited. After wintering in Malta (28:1-10), the centurion not only allowed Paul to spend a week with Christians in Puteoli but apparently accepted their hospitality as well.[41] Upon arrival in Rome, the centurion would have handed Paul over to the proper authority and his task would have come to an end.

## SUMMARY

The Roman military machine was one of the most oppressive armies the world has ever known. It is somewhat surprising, therefore, that each time a centurion is mentioned in the New Testament, he is presented in a positive light.[42] Centurions serve as examples of sincere faith; they are philanthropists, devout, and protectors of the Apostle Paul. Most important, however, the New Testament represents centurions as leading the way for Gentiles to enter the church.

---

38   Claudius forbade noncitizens from identifying themselves on only a first-name basis. This privilege was offered only to free citizens of Rome (Suetonius, *Vit. Caes.* 5.25.3).

39   William M. Ramsey, *St. Paul the Traveler and the Roman Citizen* (Grand Rapids: Baker, 1966), 315; Bruce, *The Book of Acts*, 477. But Witherington adds that this kind of designation did not come into practice until the second century C.E.; the centurion, on the other hand, might have been commissioned to take Paul to Rome and thus requisitioned a private vessel to that end (*Acts*, 759-60).

40   The compensation for ships and carts would be at the minimum rate. Housing and food were to be supplied for free. The power of requisition was a major source of complaint for Roman subjects (Rapske, *The Book of Acts*, 272-75).

41   The *tabernae*, or roadside inns, were generally poor and increasingly overcrowded as one approached the city of Rome. The offer of free room and board from private homes must have appealed to the centurion.

42   "Other New Testament sources contain references to Roman soldiers, and in particular to Roman centurions, who are depicted stereotypically as disciplined, tough, direct, fair and capable of great heart, and who are also sympathetic to Jesus or early Christian leaders" (Cotter, "Cornelius, the Roman Army, and Religion," 279).

# Annotated Bibliography

Breeze, David J., and Brian Dobson. *Roman Officers and Frontiers*. Stuttgart: Franz Steiner, 1993. This massive work contains research articles that describe in detail the rank, career path, pay, promotions, and so on, of Roman officers, especially those stationed at the northern frontier of the empire in Britain. The reader is given an enormous amount of data on the life and materiel of Roman soldiers in the field.

Campbell, Brian. *The Roman Army, 31B.C.–A.D. 337: A Sourcebook*. London: Routledge, 1994. This is an interesting source in that it is a collection of more than four hundred translated documents from the periods under concern, setting forth the organization, the tactics, and the relationship of the Roman soldiers to the people they conquered. It contains a glossary and an index, which aid the student in accessing this massive collection of primary sources.

Goldsworthy, Adrian Keith. *The Roman Army at War: 100 B.C.–A.D. 200*. Oxford: Oxford University Press, 1996. This revised dissertation seeks to reveal the personal struggles and interactions of combatants, putting a face on the merely historical accounts of battle and focusing on the prime directive of the Roman army, that is, to wage war. It is not for the beginner but is of interest in that it does not describe only weaponry, defenses, and so forth.

Luttwak, Edward. *The Grand Strategy of the Roman Empire: From the First Century A.D. to the Third*. Baltimore: Johns Hopkins University Press, 1979. Luttwak analyzes three basic types of defense strategy employed throughout the various eras of the Roman Empire. Battle tactics for specific campaigns, descriptions of life in the field, fortifications, and so on, are set forth. The technical language is burdensome at points, but the book is well illustrated with many helpful maps and charts.

Webster, Graham. *The Roman Imperial Army of the First and Second Centuries*. Totowa, N.J.: Barnes & Noble, 1985. This classic treatment of the Roman army, encyclopedic in scope, reaches back to the very foundations of the Republic and continues through the height of the empire. Nearly all aspects of the Roman army are addressed, and an index helps the student navigate the prodigious amount of material presented.

# 17

# Patrons, Clients, and Trade Guilds—the Nexus of Politics, Society, and Economics

## INTRODUCTION:
### WORD STUDY AND IDENTIFICATION

The term "patronage," as used in the first century C.E., referred to the nearly universal ordering of social relationships based on the exchange of wealth and influence. This informal system of social stratification had the patron-client relationship at its core. The patron, or *patronus*, possessed a surplus of financial and political capital and thus was in a good position to meet the requests of the one in need, the client. In response to receiving *beneficia*, "favors" or "services," the social expectation of the day required the client to repay the patron in kind if possible, for "only the wise man knows how to return a favor" (Seneca, *Ep.* 81.12). Failing that, the client was to publicly express his or her gratitude to the patron and always seek ways to repay the social debt.[1] The client's obli-

gation to the patron could be relieved through a number of ways. For example, the client might make cash installments, provide various services, lend political support, include the patron in his or her will, or simply sing the praises of the patron at every opportunity.

It becomes clear that the principle of reciprocity lies at the core of the patron-client system. By this kind of exchange of services and influence, mutual interests were served, beginning with the upper echelons of society and continuing on down the chain of relationships to the level of slaves.

## THE SOCIAL DYNAMICS
## OF ROMAN PATRONAGE

The rules governing the patron-client relationship were part and parcel with the social fabric of the day. The patron granted *charites*, "graces," to the client, who in turn was to be "grateful," *eucharistos*, toward the patron. Seneca reports that ideally the patron was to imitate the gods by giving with a pure motive, expecting nothing in return (*Ben.* 4.26.1; 4.28.1). On the other hand, Cicero claims that the expression of gratitude or favor for one's patron was to be the first impulse of a client (*Off.* 1.47–48).[2] This creative tension between altruism and indebtedness was described by Seneca as an unbroken dance of dynamic proportions that can

---

1 For the dynamics of debt and repayment in patronage, see Peter Garnsey and Richard Saller, "Patronal Power Relations," in *Paul and Empire: Religion and Power in Roman Imperial Society* (ed. Richard A. Horsley; Harrisburg, Pa.: Trinity Press International, 1997), 96–103; and Robert R. Kaufman, "The Patron-Client Concept and Macro-politics: Prospects and Problems," *Comparative Studies in Society and History* 16/3 (1974): 284–308. Kaufman notes that there are as many definitions of the patron-client relationship as there are writers on the subject (p. 285 n. 3). "The term 'patronage' refers to a system in which access to goods, positions, or services is enjoyed by means of personal relationships and the exchanging of 'favors' rather than by impersonal and impartial systems of distributions" (David A. DeSilva, "Patronage and Reciprocity: The Context of Grace in the New Testament," *ATJ* [1999]: 32).

2 DeSilva, "Patronage and Reciprocity," 38–39.

be profaned only by the ultimate crime, being *acharistos*, "ungrateful" (*Ben.* 1.3.2–5).[3] For the Roman, to be ungrateful was to be unjust, for the patron deserved praise and thanks. Thus, with respect to ingratitude, Seneca comments, "Homicides, tyrants, traitor there always will be; but worse than all these is the crime of ingratitude" (*Ben.* 1.10.4). A client responding in this way would receive the hatred and scorn of his or her neighbors. If profusely grateful, however, the client would be a good prospect for future benefits from even more powerful patrons. For, in the end, according to Seneca, gratitude is more of a benefit to oneself than to the one who receives the grace. According to him, to have felt gratitude creates an "utterly happy condition of the soul" (*Ep.* 81.19–21). In this way a cycle of relationships was established. Granting a favor enhanced one's power; receiving a favor incurred indebtedness; arriving at some degree of parity was a matter of personal honor. Indeed, this principle of honor and dishonor was deeply ingrained in the Roman psyche. Even among the agrarian classes, giving time and labor to help a neighbor in need was the honorable thing to do. Also, cultivating a reputation along these lines served as a kind of social insurance. If one was generous to others, then they were obligated to help you in times of trouble (*Ben.* 4.18.1).

The practical realization of patronage occurred in the following ways. Wealthy patrons would sponsor public works such as paving roads, building amphitheaters, and the like. These patrons would also pay for public entertainment, usually in the form of athletic competition or gladiatorial combat. At times, the wealthiest of patrons would come to the aid of the people when they suffered from natural disasters such as earth-

quakes or famine. In these ways, the patrons built up their client base, who would inevitably return the favor by supporting them for public office and by erecting monuments and inscriptions in their honor.

To modern ears, the patron-client relationship smacks of blatant favoritism and influence peddling. In a first-century context, however, all transactions that could not be bartered in the common marketplace required a patron. If one required a loan, sought a public office, desired Roman citizenship, sought to purchase property, or simply needed support to pursue the arts, a patron had to be secured. It was simply the way things were done in the world of the New Testament. Indeed, Seneca describes the patron-client relationship as the "practice that constitutes the chief bond of humanity" (*Ben.* 1.4.2). For the Romans, this bond had powerful political overtones. Through the judicious granting of benefits and power to local potentates, the Romans were able to rule the entire known world by proxy. Through the patron-client system, Rome was able to govern vast territories with a minimum amount of administration or official staff.

## THE HIERARCHICAL NATURE OF ROMAN PATRONAGE

The patron-client system was inherently hierarchical, involving parties that were of unequal power and wealth.[4] The bond between patron and client was thus one of

---

3  DeSilva notes that this "creative tension" was rooted in the fact that the duties of the patron and those of the client were expressed separately. The goal of the moralists was that both parties were to act appropriately within their respective spheres so as to maintain the dynamic of reciprocity (ibid., 43, 47).

4  "A patron-client relationship is a particular form of social relationship that involves an exchange of different types of 'goods' based on *a marked inequality of power*" (italics added) (Craig De Vos, "Once a Slave, Always a Slave? Slavery, Manumission, and Relational Patterns in Paul's Letter to Philemon," *JSNT* 82 [2001]: 97). In some cases, however, the parties exchanging benefits would be of equal social standing and were referred to as "friends" rather than clients (Pliny the Younger, *Ep.* 4.22). The rank of *amicus*, "friend," was prestigious enough to encompass patrons of both equal and inferior social status (Stephan Joubert, *Paul as Benefactor: Reciprocity, Strategy, and Theological Reflection in Paul's Collection* [WUNT 124; Tübingen: Mohr Siebeck, 2000], 29).

**This inscription from ancient Corinth reads, "Erastus in return for his aedileship laid [the pavement] at his own expense".**

dependency, with the client depending on the good graces of the patron. The imbalance of power and resources established a pyramid of influence, decreasing in power from apex to base. The emperor was the supreme patron above all other patrons, and the obtaining of *amicitia principum*, friendship with the emperor, was the first step to being appointed a senator (Suetonius, *Vit. Caes.* 8.17.1–19.2; 8.22.1). The senators ranked just below the emperor and served as powerful brokers who arbitrated access to the emperor and all the wealth and power that he represented. Below them were the highest Roman officials appointed by the emperor. They served as prefects, procurators, military officers, and municipal magistrates. They were the *equites*, "knights," of the empire, of equestrian rank. During the time of Augustus, they numbered one thousand in Rome, and every major city had its ruling class. They served as the *curia*, or ruling senate of the city, patterned after the imperial senate in Rome. These subpatrons secured their positions by donating generously to the emperor and to the people. They donated buildings and amphitheaters and

bankrolled gladiatorial games and festivals (Josephus, *Ant.* 15.267–275, 341).[5] The lowest tier of free Roman citizens was the *plebs*, or common folk. These commoners included the small business owners craftspeople who made up the general populace of the empire. Finally, there were the freedmen and freedwomen, who often became clients of their former masters (Justinian, *Dig.* 37.14.1, 5, 9, 16). These persons at times incurred such a debt of gratitude that their quality of life was little better than that of a slave. In any case, they were no longer bound to the lowest stratum of Roman society, that is, the status of the slave class, or *servi*.[6]

This social categorizing of inequality must be viewed contextually. A patron at one level in the hierarchy may be a client to more

5    On subpatrons, see John E. Stambaugh, "Social Relations in the City of the Early Principate: State of Research," in *The Society of Biblical Literature 1980 Seminar Papers* (SBLSP 19; Missoula, Mont.: Scholars Press, 1980), 75–99, esp. 77, 79.

6    The various ranks of Roman society from senator to slave are listed in David W. Gill, "Acts and the Urban Elites," in *The Book of Acts and Its Graeco-Roman Setting* (ed. David W. Gill and Conrad Gempf; Grand Rapids: Eerdmans, 1994), 106–7.

powerful patrons above. For example, Pliny the Younger was a client of the emperor Trajan (111–113 C.E.), yet he served as a powerful patron to clients below him. As such, Pliny would have access to the emperor and would often seek appointments and citizenship for his clients. Pliny thereby played the important role of a broker or mediator in the patron-client system (*Ep.* 6.25).[7]

The entire system was a meritocracy in which not all enjoyed equal benefits. For this reason, one would curry the favor of the most powerful aristocrats. These patrons had the advantage of proximity to the emperor and thus had the greatest chance of extending some benefit to Caesar. It was hoped that there would be a reciprocal blessing from the emperor that would eventually trickle down to the lower clients. And so it went up and down the social ladder of first-century Roman society.

One can see how the system of patronage was highly attractive to those with ambition. Patronage allowed one to enhance one's power through networking. This network of mutually beneficial relationships extended outward from the nuclear family to influential friends, then on to clients, and finally reached the resources of rich patrons. Those who were highly competitive by nature and able to "read between the lines" and do more than what was required stood the chance of acquiring great wealth and power.[8]

### THE EMPEROR AS SUPREME PATRON

As direct beneficiary of the gods, the emperor was considered the patron of all humanity. As such, he was the *euergetēs*, the prime benefactor of the empire and the model for all other patrons in the realm.[9] The examples of imperial beneficence are many, but the die was cast with Julius Caesar. Soon after enunciating his famous "I came, I saw, I conquered" statement, Julius Caesar sought to win the favor of the soldiers and the commoners by bestowing lavish gifts upon all (Plutarch, *Caes.* 1.50.2; Suetonius, *Vit. Caes.* 1.37.2; 1.38.1–2). In this way he set the precedent for venerating the emperor as the patron above all other patrons.[10]

Julius Caesar made the city of Corinth the special object of his patronage. His edict that the ancient city of Corinth be rebuilt earned him special honors there. Indeed, the official designation for Corinth was "the colony of Julius Caesar." Marble busts proclaiming Caesar as patron appeared throughout Corinth, and local coinage was inscribed with words proclaiming the emperor as their patron. The coronation of the emperor, his birthday, the celebration of imperial contests, and the Isthmian Games all exalted Julius Caesar as the supreme patron of Corinth.[11]

Caesar Augustus seems to have continued the patronal tactics of his predecessor, Julius Caesar. The benefits afforded by Augustus to his subjects were security, food, clean water, public housing, and, in some cases, tax rebates. One of the most coveted gifts bestowed by the emperor was Roman citizenship (Suetonius, *Vit. Caes.* 1.42.1; 6.24.2). Full enfranchisement was often granted as a

---

7 "Brokerage—the gift of access to another, often greater patron—was itself a highly valued gift" (DeSilva, "Patronage and Reciprocity," 34).

8 See John K. Chow, *Patronage and Power: A Study of Social Networks in Corinth* (JSNTSup 75; Sheffield, Eng.: Sheffield Academic Press, 1992), 42; and idem, "Patronage in Roman Corinth," in *Paul and Empire: Religion and Power in Roman Imperial Society* (ed. Richard A. Horsley; Harrisburg, Pa.: Trinity Press International, 1997), 125.

9 On the emperor as supreme patron, see Richard Gordon, "The Veil of Power," in *Paul and Empire: Religion and Power in Roman Imperial Society* (ed. Richard A. Horsley; Harrisburg, Pa.: Trinity Press International, 1997), 126–39. Cf. also N. T. Wright, "Paul's Gospel and Caesar's Empire," in *Paul and Politics: Ecclesia, Israel, Imperium, and Interpretation* (ed. Richard A. Horsley; Harrisburg, Pa.: Trinity Press International, 2000), 161.

10 By dedicating the temple to Claudius (41–54 C.E.), the Corinthians demonstrated their continued client relationship with the emperor.

11 Chow, "Patronage in Roman Corinth," 107.

**The remains of the Temple of Apollo, Corinth. Julius Caesar made the city of Corinth a special object of his patronage.**

reward for valiant defense of the empire in battle (Tacitus, *Ann.* 3.40; Josephus *J.W.* 1.194; *Life* 1.423).[12] Augustus also granted honorific titles to those who enhanced his power and wealth, and at times he would award an especially faithful client as head of the Isthmian or Caesarean games. He frequently paid for gladiatorial combats out of his own purse (*Res gest. divi Aug.* 4.22–23). At times he would increase his client base by disbursing a direct cash gift to all male citizens of an entire city (*Res gest. divi Aug.* 3.15, 17; Suetonius, *Vit. Caes.*

2.41.2). It is no wonder that many appeared at the imperial palace with hat in hand, and Augustus was known to make sport on such occasions.[13]

Because he was at the apex of the hierarchical structure, Augustus appointed or approved all officials under him. Regional kings were allowed to rule so far as they submitted to the imperial will and secured a steady flow of tribute money for Rome. Augustus affirmed these royal clients by

---

12  Augustus was reticent, however, to bestow citizenship on persons who were not of Roman blood, for he thought that the granting of citizenship to other nationalities weakened the Roman people (cf. Suetonius, *Vit. Caes.* 2.40.3).

13  Even the rumor that the Augustus had been generous was used to pressure the emperor to give a handout. When Pacuvius Taurus tried this ploy, noting that it was common gossip that Augustus had already given him a large gift, Augustus retorted, "Don't you believe it!" (Macrobius, *Sat.* 2.4.4).

sending contingents of soldiers to serve as their personal bodyguards. Puppet kings such as Herod the Great were careful to cultivate these relationships with the imperial patron (Josephus, *J.W.* 1.400; *Ant.* 15.361). Like other clients of the emperor, Herod expressed his fidelity by forwarding large sums of money to Rome. Anyone who had received direct benefit from the emperor was expected to name him in his or her will (Dio Cassius, *Hist. rom.* 59.15.5–6). Herod followed suit and left a thousand talents of silver to Augustus and half as much to Empress Livia (Josephus, *Ant.* 17.146, 190). In this way the emperors garnered enormous wealth during their lifetimes. Remaining true to the principle of reciprocity, they often returned much of it to the people at their deaths. Throughout his life, Augustus showered cash gifts on citizens, soldiers, and the plebs of Rome (*Res gest. divi Aug.* 3.15, 17). Before his death, Augustus willed the equivalent of more than one and a half billion dollars to the people (cf. *Res gest. divi Aug.* 3.15, 17, and "Summary," 1; Suetonius, *Vit. Caes.* 2.101.1–4).

In a similar fashion, Caligula disbursed millions to the soldiers and the citizens upon his inauguration (Dio Cassius, *Hist. rom.* 59.2.1–3). He cast large sums of money and free tickets to the games from the Julian Basilica for days on end, with many commoners being trampled to death in the ensuing melee (Suetonius, *Vit. Caes.* 4.37.1–3; Dio Cassius, *Hist. rom.* 59.9.6–7; 59.25.5). To celebrate his victory over the Britons, Claudius gave cash to those who were dependent upon public welfare (Dio Cassius, *Hist. rom.* 60.25.7–8). Upon his inauguration, Nero granted about twenty dollars to each male citizen. Suetonius describes the lavish patronage of the emperors; regarding Nero, he states, "Every day all kinds of food, tickets for grain, clothing, gold, silver, precious stones, pearls, paintings, slaves, beasts of burden, even trained wild animals and finally, ships, blocks of houses and farms" were given to faithful clients (*Vit. Caes.* 6.11.2). Nero granted Roman citizenship to his favorite actors, as did Claudius (Suetonius, *Vit. Caes.* 6.12.2; Dio Cassius, *Hist. rom.* 60.7.2). Domitian followed suit by granting cash gifts to all male citizens on three occasions and providing lavish banquets for those of equestrian rank as well as food for commoners (Suetonius, *Vit. Caes.* 8.3.5).[14] The emperor was publicly honored as "the Patron" or "the Benefactor" and worshiped as a god (Tacitus, *Ann.* 4.37–38, 55–56; Suetonius, *Vit. Caes.* 1.76.1–3; 4.60.1; 5.45.1).

Such grand benefaction required an appropriate response. In order to fulfill the "reciprocity ethic," the people were to pledge complete loyalty or faithfulness (Gk. *pistis*) to the emperor. The faithful client must be willing to suffer shame and even death in order to bring honor to his or her patron. Indeed, Seneca exhorts that loyalty is the "holiest good in the human heart" and adds, "Loyalty cries: 'Burn me, slay me, kill me! I shall not betray my trust; and the more urgently torture shall seek to find my secret, the deeper in my heart will I bury it!' " (*Ep.* 88.29).

All this goodwill toward the emperor stems from one unshakable principle. Imperial clients realized that their power and prestige were directly proportional to their access to the emperor. This access was obtained through loyalty and the bestowal of lavish gifts. Therefore clients strove to demonstrate their loyalty to the emperor by extending every benefit and praise that they could manage, constantly competing with one another to gain the favor with those who in turn could benefit them. Augustus was particularly adept at exploiting this state of affairs by pitting one client against another, thus stimulating an ever-increasing flow of benefits to himself (Suetonius, *Vit. Caes.* 2.66.1–2.67.2). Although, according to the strict letter of Roman law, it was illegal to receive bribes and gifts from lesser officials, this was in fact the path to

---

14  Miriam T. Griffin, *Nero: The End of a Dynasty* (New York: Routledge, 1984), 63.

Aerial view of the site of the Roman harbor at Caesarea, built by Herod the Great in honor of the Emperor, the supreme patron.

upward mobility.[15] The patron-client relationship thus lent itself to much graft and corruption. Indeed, there was often a fine line between being a true friend who desires to help another and an exploitive patron seeking to extort favors from a client.[16]

## ROMAN GOVERNORS AND PATRONAGE

The most powerful patrons on a local level were the Roman governors, proconsuls, and client kings. These officials assumed the role of brokers or mediators for the imperial patron. For this reason, the aristocracy indigenous to any particular region viewed the Roman governors as their patrons. They understood that all imperial benefits came by way of the governor, for the latter conveyed the granting of citizenship, confirmation to local offices, the endorsement of building contracts, and the conferral of honorific titles. Consequently, honoring Roman governors as subpatrons of the emperor afforded access to Caesar, enhanced a local aristocracy's prestige in the empire, and garnered real material benefits for them, their families, and the subjects they governed. As client kings, the Herods lavished benefits upon the Caesars. They not only named cities and lakes in honor of the emperor; they even built entire cities for the emperor, complete with temples dedicated to the gods of the Greco-Roman pantheon (*Ant.* 15.331–41, 363–364; 20.211). All of these benefits were simply expressions of the most critical benefits that they could afford: complete loyalty and military support.

### The Trade Guilds:
### *Salutatio, Sportulae, Collegia*

Tacitus notes that the *plebs*, or common people, were, for the most part, excluded from patron-client relationships (*Hist.* 1.4). Since most were very poor, they had no "graces" to extend to

others or any means to repay favors they might receive from a patron. Their poverty, however, provided patrons with an opportunity to display their generosity to the masses. Poor communities would select a patron and pledge to that person their loyalty and political support. The patron in turn would build temples and public improvements at his/her own expense. In return, commoners could render back to the patron the one benefit they did possess—public praise.[17]

This interplay between philanthropy and popular acclaim gave rise to the tradition of the *salutatio*. The *salutatio* entailed the gathering of the *plebs* at the door of the patron at dawn (Suetonius, *Vit. Caes.* 330; Seneca, *Ep.* 47.18). As the patron left his or her estate, the commoners would greet the patron with acclaim. Many would follow the patron about during the day, expressing admiration and granting loud applause for any speeches the patron might make. In return, the patron disbursed food to the *plebs*, and on occasion he granted the *sportulae*. The *sportulae* were often small sums of money to help the common people with daily living expenses and to purchase entrance into theaters, athletic contests, and gladiatorial events. The system was a constant drain upon the wealthy, for, Seneca laments, "A cultivates B and B cultivates C; no one is his own master" (*De brevitate vitae* 2.4). Cicero therefore gives instructions on the proper and improper use of the *sportulae*, commenting that benefits should not be squandered on giving banquets

---

15  Julius Caesar's initial inroads to power were through bribery and corruption (cf. Suetonius, *Vit. Caes.* 1.11.1–1.14.2).

16  On patron, clients, and exploitation, see Alicia Batten, "God in the Letter of James: Patron or Benefactor?" *NTS* 50 (2004): 257–72, esp. 258.

17  Suetonius records a clear description of the reciprocal relationship between the emperor and his clients. Regarding Augustus he records, "With this sum he bought and dedicated in each of the city wards costly statues of the gods, such as Apollo Sandaliarius, Jupiter Tragoedus, and others. To rebuild his house on the Palatine, which had been destroyed by fire, the veterans, the *collegia*, the tribes, and even individuals of other conditions gladly contributed money, each according to his means; but he merely took a little from each pile as a matter of form, not more than a denarius from any of them. On his return from a province they received him not only with prayers and good wishes, but with songs" (*Vit. Caes.* 2.57.1–2.58.2).

and gladiatorial shows but to pay ransom money and help real friends in need (*Off.* 2.52–56). There was also a monthly distribution of *sportulae* from the emperor, usually taking the form of a ration of grain. Since each recipient had to appear in person to collect the monthly dole, the system became very disruptive to the workaday world of the empire. For this reason, Augustus tried to change the allotment to quarterly, but he received such protests from the people that he abandoned the plan (Suetonius, *Vit. Caes.* 2.40.1).

The political implications of the "corn dole" were not lost on those of the first century. Nero was careful to grant each Praetorian Guard a monthly allowance of grain free of charge (*Vit. Caes.* 6.10.2). Dio Cassius notes that even before the conflict between Antony and Octavian-Augustus, the senate had voted not to put the distribution of grain into the hands of one man (*Hist. rom.* 46.39.3). Augustus dispensed cash benefits to every male in the empire, including boys, in order to win the favor of the people. In times of scarcity, he would grant wooden "coupons" that could be redeemed for grain, oil, and other necessities (*Res gest. divi Aug.* 3.18; Suetonius, *Vit. Caes.* 2.41.2). Indeed, Augustus laments that some left off farming altogether because they could eke by on free corn rations. He wanted to abolish the corn dole altogether but feared that it would only be reinstated in the future by some politician seeking popular support (*Vit. Caes.* 2.42.3).[18] The critical importance of the corn dole can be seen in special laws that were enacted to prevent fraud associated with the corn dole and especially to punish those who sought to interrupt the supply of grain to Rome (Justinian, *Dig.* 48.12.1–3).

The truly impoverished *plebs*, or freeborn poor, depended upon the sportulae to have enough grain. So, if the emperor could not supply the need, he was in deep trouble. This is why Vespasian's bid for the throne entailed

**Relief of Mercurius (Hermes), patron deity of trade, merchants, and travelers.**

gaining control of Alexandria so that he could cut off the supply of grain to Rome (Josephus, *J.W.* 2.386; 4.602–607; Dio Cassius, *Hist. rom.* 60.11.1–5). Claudius was publicly cursed and pelted with dry crusts of bread when he could not deliver the accustomed *sportulae* to the people, and under the cover of his guards, he barely escaped the mob (Suetonius, *Vit. Caes.*

---

18  Domitian did abolish the distribution of grain but replaced it with formal dinners provided by wealthy patrons (Suetonius, *Vit. Caes.* 8.7.1).

**View of ancient Ephesus from the theater. The harbor of Bible times extended farther inland than it does today. The silversmiths' guild called a meeting in this theater to protest Paul's disruption of their trade.**

5.18.2; Tacitus, *Ann.* 12.43). When Nero found himself in financial straits, he forbade the giving of lavish public banquets but continued the sportulae (Suetonius, *Vit. Caes.* 6.16.2).

The *plebs* were able to participate in the network of patron-client relations by forming collective associations called *collegia*. The *collegia* were clubs or associations organized around a common cult, interest, or trade and usually numbering forty to three hundred members in urban settings. The societies that gathered members from a single craft functioned like trade guilds. These guilds looked after the needs of their members, helped in funeral arrangements, and promoted the interests of the common craft. Monthly dues were paid to cover burials and also to fund festive dinners to affirm the guilds' members.[19]

As part of the patron-client system, the *collegia* mirrored the hierarchical nature of Roman society. The patron deity occupied the highest level in the society, followed by the patron benefactor, who, more often than not, was a decurion, or city magistrate.[20] Wealthy women of the decurial order also functioned as patrons

19  Garnsey and Saller note that the benefits of a *collegium* included fellowship, business contacts, burial insurance, legal services, and the receiving of city contracts to conduct business ("Patronal Power Relations," 100–101). Cf., on the funerary benefits of the *collegia*, Susan Treggiari, *Roman Freedmen during the Late Republic* (Oxford: Clarendon, 1969), 202–3.

20  For the responsibilities of decurions see Justinian, *Dig.* 50.2.1–2.

of *collegia*, often providing the priests or priestesses for the patron deity.[21] Club leaders came next in status, followed by the common members. The leader of the association was called the *quinquennalis*. He supplied oil to all of the members for bathing before banquets and was eligible for double portions of food. His assistant was eligible for a plate and a half. The *collegia*, in sum, constituted a way for those who held little influence to pool their resources and identities so that they might have more leverage in the wider society.

The collective representation and power of the *collegia* were attractive to Roman patrons. Wealthy patrons would sponsor an entire group, often paying up to fifteen thousand times the monthly dues of the common member for this privilege. In return, the patron would tap into the collective identity of the *collegium*. In addition, the group would have celebratory dinners in honor of the patron and his family. These dinners were conducted in the presence of the patron deity. The guild was obliged to support the patron in all public endeavors. In return, the *collegium* would receive funds and prestige from the patron.

There is some evidence that much of the membership of these *collegia* was composed of freedmen and freedwomen.[22] These were emancipated slaves whose masters had now become their personal patrons. As patrons, these former masters still wielded considerable control over their lives. A sign of their continued authority was that freedmen and freedwomen were forced to take the name of their masters as their own. As clients, freedmen and freedwomen were to express their gratitude by rendering free services to their patrons, never to bring suit against them, and even to grant financial assistance to their former masters in times of crisis.[23] Dionysius of Halicarnassus records that some slaves were freed so that they might return a portion of their *sportulae* to their former masters (*Ant. rom.* 4.24.5). Also, the patron could claim up to half of a client's estate at the time of the latter's death (Dio Cassius, *Hist. rom.* 60.17.7–8). In return for their fidelity, the patron provided legal and financial advice to those that were newly freed. In times of dearth, the patron would provide food and housing to his or her freedmen or freedwomen and seek justice on their behalf when a crime was committed against them.[24]

Even so, the *collegia* gave these newly freed persons collective bargaining power to exercise their will over against more powerful constituencies in society, even against their former masters. Some *collegia* became so powerful that they were able to intimidate political candidates and even corrupt the electoral process. For this reason, the consolidation of the *plebs* into *collegia* raised suspicion in the minds of the emperors (cf. Justinian, *Dig.* 47.22.1–4). They feared that the private meetings of the *collegia* might serve as seedbeds for political unrest. The senate therefore passed legislation banning certain *collegia* that did not have an expressed purpose for the public good.[25] Similarly, Julius Caesar

---

21  Female patrons often sponsored *collegia*. E.g., Eumachia (ca. 213 C.E.) led the fullers' *collegium*. She donated a great meeting hall and supplied a priestess for the cult of Venus. Junia Theodora (43 C.E.) of Corinth is commended for her generosity, and Lydia of Thyatira was the patroness of the church at Philippi (Acts 16:14). Regarding the various gods and goddesses of the *collegia*, the carpenters and woodcutters worshiped Silvanus whereas those in the grain trade honored Ceres and Annona. Minerva was the goddess of handworkers, Vesta of bakers, and Mercurius of businessmen. See Joubert, *Paul as Benefactor*, 33; Stambaugh, "Social Relations in the City," 80–81; Chow, *Patronage and Power*, 66 n. 1; and Gill, "Acts and the Urban Elite," 117.

22  Even slaves were permitted to join a *collegium* with the consent of their masters (Justinian, *Dig.* 47.22.3).

23  Some patrons became so rapacious that laws were enacted to ease the oppression of freedmen and freedwomen (cf. Justinian, *Dig.* 38.2.1–51). Patrons sometimes sought to forcefully restrict the freedom of those they had manumitted (*Dig.* 43.29.1–2). Most of the edicts in the *Digesta* sought to limit the claim that a patron or his descendants had upon the estate of their freedmen and freedwomen (cf. *Dig.* 38.5–15).

24  Chow, "Patronage in Roman Corinth," 120–21.

25  For the power of *collegia* composed of freedmen and freedwomen, see Treggiari, *Roman Freedmen during the Late Republic*, 169–77.

banned the *collegia*, and this ban was reinforced by Augustus and continued under Claudius (Suetonius, *Vit. Caes.* 1.42.3; 2.32.12; Tacitus, *Ann.* 14.17; Dio Cassius, *Hist. rom.* 60.6). In response to Pliny the Younger's request for the formation of a firemen's guild in Nicomedia, the emperor likewise mandated caution. Trajan notes that regardless of how innocently such *collegia* might start, they inevitably led to political action of some kind (*Ep.* 10.33–34).

Luke's record in Acts 19:23–41 proves that such concerns were not misplaced. In this instance, Demetrius, head of the silversmiths' guild, mobilized its members and those from related crafts to riot in protest against Paul and his preaching of the gospel. As chief magistrate of the *collegium*, Demetrius knew that nothing would be done without the blessing of the patron goddess of the guild, Artemis. For this reason, he shrewdly linked Artemis with supposed offenses of Paul and his company (vv. 25–28). Demetrius's intent was to coerce the city magistrates into taking action independent of the provincial government and the Roman proconsul, who heard grievances at regular intervals (vv. 38–41). Since such meetings took place in the amphitheater, he led the rowdy crowd to protest there (v. 29). The "city clerk" realized the danger at hand.[26] As liaison to Rome, his duty was to make sure that all assemblies fell within the bounds of Roman purview. He judged that this gathering was not a "legal assembly" and dismissed the crowd under threat of Roman punishment (vv. 39–41).

As a safeguard against such civil unrest, imperial law forbade *collegia* from meeting more than once a month. Those that met more frequently were subject to punishment. This might explain why the early Christians came under Roman censure. It is possible that the early church was viewed as a *collegium* of slaves and lower-class persons that served another "King."[27] Christianity had not received official status as a *religio licita* (an officially authorized religion). Pliny the Younger informs Trajan that he tortures and executes all members of the "wretched cult" regardless of age or status (*Ep.* 10.96).

## PATRONAGE AND THE ARTS

Wealthy patrons enjoyed surrounding themselves with philosophers, artists, and writers. Such clients added to the prestige of the patron, for they were a reflection of his or her culture and good taste. Moreover, the patron could draw upon the intellectual and artistic capital of such clients. In return, the patrons supported the artists and thinkers so that they could more readily exercise their talents (Suetonius, *Vit. Caes.* 8.18.1). In addition to financial support, artists and philosophers received dinner invitations, clothes, and even parcels of land. The patron would take gifted clients along on trips so that he or she could display their skills abroad. The artistic clients would receive an increased venue for their performances. The grateful client would be ever mindful to compose verses that praised the virtues of a generous patron. More than likely Luke's praise of Theophilus as "most excellent Theophilus" (Gk. *kratiste theophile* [κράτιστε θεόφιλε], Luke 1:3) is the expression of a grateful client toward a wise and generous patron.

## PATRONAGE IN THE NEW TESTAMENT
### Patronage in Corinth

As already explained, the patron-client relationship was part of a social web that interconnected persons of the first century. This appears to have been especially true in Corinth. Since Gallio was the governor of Achaia while Paul was ministering in

---

26  The Greek phrase for "city clerk" is *ho grammateus* (ὁ γραμματεύς). This is the same word used for "scribe" throughout the Scriptures and once again evidences the power and prestige that the scribe occupied across cultures.

27  Slaves were permitted to join *collegia* that were officially recognized by the Roman government. Also, *collegia* associated with recognized religions were permitted. Members of the early church, whether slave or free, may have been viewed as forming an illegal *collegium* (Justinian, *Dig.* 47.22.1–3).

**Ruins of the agora, ancient Corinth. The patron-client system was in effect in Corinth in the New Testament period.**

Corinth, he would have been the supreme Roman patron on the scene and would have been honored as such. Indeed, an inscription in Corinth dating to 52–53 C.E. records the adulation of Anaxilas and Dinippus for the brilliant leadership of Gallio. Another inscription outside the theater speaks of the benevolence of a patron called Erastus, stating, "Erastus laid this pavement at his own expense."[28] This Erastus may be the same person mentioned by Paul in Rom 16:23, where Paul states that Erastus is the Roman *aedilis*, or city director of public works. The patronage of Erastus may have come to the attention of Gallio, who then appointed Erastus *aedilis* of Corinth. Although it cannot be determined, this goodwill between Gallio and Erastus may have led to the favorable

judgment against Paul in Acts 18:12–17.

Clearly the patron-client system was in place in Corinth and may have come to influence the church there. The various factions in the Corinthian church evidenced in the slogans "I am of Paul," "I am of Cephas," "I am of Apollos," and "I am of Christ," may reflect patron-client relationships (1 Cor 1:10–17). These groups within the church may have been claiming different leaders as their patrons to leverage special benefits from them. If this is so, then some of Paul's decisions concerning the church in Corinth become more comprehensible.[29] For example, his refusal to accept financial support from the Corinthians may indicate that Paul would not allow himself to become a client of the Corinthians (1 Cor 9:12). By not entering into a patron-client relationship with the

28  It was the custom to either inscribe the name of, or erect a monument to, any patron who made a large contribution to public works (Dio Cassius, *Hist. rom.* 60.25.3).

29  For how the principle of patronage may relate to Paul and his mission, see Joubert, *Paul as Benefactor*, 23.

Corinthians, he would have maintained his independence from them and perhaps, in his eyes, rendered his ministry more effective.

### Patronage and Paul's Trial before Felix

Paul's trial before the governor Felix in Acts 24:1–27 likewise echoes aspects of the patron-client culture of first-century Rome. Tertullus, the trial lawyer who brought charges against Paul, opens his case with a *captatio benevolentiae*, a recitation of the benefits received from Felix's reign as governor: "When Paul was called in, Tertullus presented his case before Felix: 'We have enjoyed a long period of peace under you, and your foresight has brought about reforms in this nation. Everywhere and in every way, most excellent Felix, we acknowledge this with profound gratitude' " (vv. 2–3).[30] Thus Luke's record reflects the patronal practices of the day. As the client, the lawyer publicly acknowledges the benefits that the governor has done for Israel. The governor is now obliged to return the complement by giving ear to what the lawyer has to say against this troublemaker, the Apostle Paul.

Such collusion between lawyers and governors in the ancient world was common. Powerful lawyers would make public dedications and monuments to governors and pledge to defend the governors against charges of corruption in office. In return, the governors would grant gifts to the lawyers for their loyalty. To modern ears, the mutual exchange of gifts between a judge and a lawyer sounds outrageous. In the culture of patron-client relationships, however, exchanges of gratitude were expected. A lawyer's gifts to a Roman governor demonstrated his support of the regime and thus enhanced his status before the community. The governor's favor for the lawyer demonstrated his sense of justice in doing the appropriate thing.

---

30  Ben Witherington III, *The Acts of the Apostles: A Socio-rhetorical Commentary* (Grand Rapids: Eerdmans, 1998), 705.

Paul did not have access to an expensive trial lawyer, and so he had to defend himself. From the start, Felix would have understood that he would not receive any large cash benefits from Paul. If he were to receive anything, it would have to be extorted under the table. Predictably, v. 26 states that Felix repeatedly sought some money from Paul, often sending for him and talking to him about the matter. Apparently Paul sees this for what it is and declines to enter into this unsavory aspect of the patron-client relationship. Not to be completely denied, Felix then seeks to parlay Paul's predicament into political capital. As Roman patron to the Jews, he leaves Paul in prison as a favor to them. Now the Jews are obligated to affirm his leadership and, by extension, acknowledge the rule of Rome (v. 27).

### Patronage, Jesus, and Pilate

Patron-client relationships explain much about the political interconnections between the governor, Pilate; the client king, Herod Antipas; and the appointed high priest, Caiaphas (Matt 26:57–75; Mark 14:53–72; Luke 22:63–71). Herod Antipas directly owed his position to Caesar Augustus and to his procurator, Pontius Pilate. As the supreme local patron, Pilate had the power to grant special Roman dispensations to Herod. In turn, Caiaphas was indebted to the Roman procurators for his appointment as high priest (Josephus, *Ant.* 18.35, 95). This network of relationships was tailor-made for patronage to hold full sway. Pilate could please his patron, Augustus, by keeping the peace with Herod and the Jews. Regarding Jesus and his trial, it was clear to Pilate that Herod wanted Jesus out of the way. It was equally clear that the unrest of the Jews could be settled by crucifying Jesus (Mark 15:9–20; Luke 23:13–25). So, against his better judgment and in a manner very similar to Felix's treatment of Paul, Pilate endorsed the execution of Jesus. He thereby appeased the Jews and their leadership, fulfilled the imperial commission to keep the peace, and indebted Herod and the Jews to himself. This nexus of mutual benefits makes Luke 23:11–12 more comprehensible: "Then Herod and his soldiers ridiculed and mocked him. Dressing him in an elegant robe, they sent him back to Pilate. That day Herod and Pilate became friends—before this they had been enemies." In the context of patronal relationships, Pilate's decision served the interests of various clients and strengthened his position as well.

## PATRONAGE AND THE EARLY CHURCH

The early church was birthed within the context of patron-client relationships and could in no way escape its influence. Indeed, there is evidence that wealthy patronesses, such as Lydia (Acts 16:14), John Mark's mother (Acts 12:12), and Chloe (1 Cor 1:11), were essential in establishing the early churches. The ideology and jargon of patronal relations helped to form the church's identity and its message. One can readily see how the concepts of "grace" (Gk. *charis*), "graces" (Gk. *charites*), "grateful" (Gk. *eucharistos*), and "faithfulness" or "loyalty" (Gk. *pistis*) were taken over by the first believers and put into the service of the gospel. The Scriptures are replete with references to God the Father as the ultimate patron (Acts 14:7; 17:24–28). For example, God is the source of all benefits (Jas 1:17). God unselfishly graces the just and the unjust and is indebted to no one (Matt 5:45; Luke 6:35; Rom 11:35–36). The Father's matchless gift to all humankind, regardless of race or status, was the gift of his Son, Jesus Christ (John 3:16; Gal 3:28). As mediator, Jesus becomes the broker who grants access to the Father for all who believe in him (John 15:14–16; Rom 5:1–2). He in turn mediates the gift of the Spirit and all of the charismatic gifts that empower the church (Luke 24:49; Acts 1:4–5; Rom 12:3–8; 1 Cor 12:1–31).

The beneficence of the Father and the Son is a reflection of their character and justice

(2 Pet 1:3). As recipients of their grace, believers are to be unwavering in their loyalty to God and unceasing in their praise and thanksgiving (2 Cor 1:11; Heb 12:28; 1 Thess 5:18). The saints must be willing to suffer shame and even die for his name (Acts 14:17; 17:24–28). Indeed, they are to sacrifice their entire beings in gratitude (Rom 12:1–2). The ungrateful can expect to receive the ill consequences due the unfaithful (Heb 6:4–8; Rom 2:4–5).

For the believer, Jesus becomes the model for true giving (Rom 3:22–26; 2 Cor 5:18–21). By helping the poor, the Christian reflects the character of God and thereby receives the honor of an obedient servant (2 Cor 8:1–5; Phil 2:29–30; Rom 12:1–6; Eph 4:7, 11–12).[31] The goal of Christian giving, however, is not to build up one's client base as in the classical patron-client relationships of the first century. Rather, the intent is to be like God in the service of one's neighbor without any thought of being paid back. The community of goods in the first six chapters of Acts reflects this ideal (Acts 2:42–47, 4:32, 34–5:11; 6:1–6), an ideal attempted by the covenanters at Qumran.[32]

In addition to these broad examples of patron-client principles in the Scriptures, there are many practical expressions as well. The benevolent centurions merited divine attention (Luke 7:1–10; Acts 10:1–48). The Gentiles received spiritual riches from the Jews, and so they were obligated to return material blessings (Rom 15:27); Paul therefore orchestrated a massive collection for the poor saints in Jerusalem (Rom 15:26–27; 2 Cor 8–9). In addition, much of the language of Philemon echoes patron-client relationships. Paul reminds Philemon that God used

31  DeSilva, "Patronage and Reciprocity," 52, 67–69.

32  Brian Capper, "Reciprocity and the Ethic of Acts," in *Witness to the Gospel: The Theology of Acts* (ed. I. Howard Marshall and David Peterson; Grand Rapids: Eerdmans, 1998), 506–7, 516.

him to bring salvation to his household. Therefore Philemon should be amenable to Paul's requests for Onesimus and grant "some benefit" to the apostle (Phlm 19–20).

In conclusion, the early church was immersed in a climate of patron-client relationships and reflects the jargon and practices of those relationships. It does not appear, however, that the early believers adopted the patron-client system carte blanche. In many instances, the church appears to have rejected the onerous sense of obligation and the tedious quid pro quo that characterized much of Roman patronage, a trait that ran counter to the love commandment (Jas 2:8–9). Contrary to the conventions of his day, Jesus taught that one should invite the poor to banquets and give to those who are not able to repay (Luke 14:1–24). Luke 7:36–50 represents a revision of patron-client relations within the context of the first century. Jesus, as the supreme benefactor, grants forgiveness, but he does so not as a superior to an inferior, expecting payment in kind. Rather, he counts himself among the poor, and brokers God's grace on their level. The creditor in Luke 7:41–42 forgives both debtors and thus refuses to build up his client base. In these ways, Jesus challenges the entire patron-client system.[33] On the other hand, the profuse expression of gratitude

and love of the one forgiven still makes sense within the world of patrons and clients. Thus Simon the Pharisee can understand what Jesus has done (7:43), yet at the same time he is invited to see things differently.[34]

This critique of patronage carried over into the early church. Paul's counsel to the Ephesian elders that it is more blessed to give than to receive strikes at the core of patron-client relations. James chides his recipients for being overly dependent upon a wealthy patron who was trying to manipulate them as indebted clients (Jas 2:1–13).[35] Paul rebukes Thessalonian believers who might have been loitering about waiting for the *sportulae* of wealthy patrons and refusing to go to work (1 Thess 4:10; 2 Thess 3:6–11).[36] In the end, the Christian gives to others in order to emulate Christ and bring honor and glory to God. In this way, the faith radically reconfigured the dynamics of patronage in the first-century world and undermined the principle of reciprocity, which was so entrenched in the Roman mind. God is the supreme benefactor-friend who gives from the heart out of his innate goodness and care for others. The church is to replicate this benefaction in the world and not uncritically endorse the patronage of its day.

33 On how Jesus called into question critical aspects of the patron-client system, see S. Mason, "Chief Priests, Sadducees, Pharisees, and Sanhedrin in Acts," in *The Book of Acts in Its Palestinian Setting* (ed. Richard Bauckham; Grand Rapids: Eerdmans, 1995), 133–77, esp. 140.

34 On how Jesus tapped into, yet altered, patron-client imagery, see Evelyn R. Thibeaux, " 'Known to Be a Sinner': The Narrative Rhetoric of Luke 7:36–50," *BTB* 23 (1993): 151–60, esp. 155.

35 Alicia Batten, "God in the Letter of James," 257–58, 264–65.

36 On the ill effects of dependence on the corn dole, see R. P. Saller, *Personal Patronage under the Early Empire* (Cambridge: Cambridge University Press, 1982), 12–20.

# Annotated Bibliography

Chow, John K. *Patronage and Power: A Study of Social Networks in Corinth*. Journal for the Study of the New Testament: Supplement Series 75. Sheffield, Eng.: Sheffield Academic Press, 1992. This revised dissertation seeks to explain the many problems of the Corinthian church as arising from social factors, specifically the principle of patronage in the first century. It shows how Paul undermined the oppression of the powerful by emphasizing servanthood and unity. It is technical but accessible to new researchers.

Horsley, Richard A., ed. *Paul and Empire: Religion and Power in Roman Imperial Society*. Harrisburg, Pa.: Trinity Press International, 1997. This is a collection of scholarly articles dealing with social, religious, and political power in the Roman Empire; some are explicitly dedicated to the subject of patronage.

———, ed. *Paul and Politics: Ecclesia, Israel, Imperium, and Interpretation*. Harrisburg, Pa.: Trinity Press International, 2000. This collection of essays addresses how Paul and his theology interface with the many political facets of the church, Israel, the Roman Empire, and contemporary interpretation. Findings are related to contemporary issues such as feminism, colonialism, and hierarchical power structures. The student will have to sift through the offerings to find the articles that address particular research concerns.

Joubert, Stephan. *Paul as Benefactor: Reciprocity, Strategy, and Theological Reflection in Paul's Collection*. Wissenschaftliche Untersuchungen zum Neuen Testament 124. Tübingen: Mohr Siebeck, 2000. This dissertation explores the principle of reciprocity inherent in patronage and relates it to Paul's missionary strategy. It is interesting to see how Paul both adapts and adopts the aspects of patronage found in his world.

Saller, R. P. Personal *Patronage under the Early Empire*. Cambridge: Cambridge University Press, 1982. This is a good source to begin an in-depth study of patronage in the Roman Empire. It is thorough but comprehensible to the serious student.

Treggiari, Susan. *Roman Freedmen during the Late Republic*. Oxford: Clarendon, 1969. Treggiari examines how manumission was brought about in the Roman Republic and the kinds of contributions freedmen made despite the prejudice directed at them by native-born Roman citizens. Treggiari attempts to extricate the values and contributions of Roman freedmen from their consistently negative portrayal in some ancient primary sources. The author includes discussions of manumission, adjustment to a new life of freedom, rights before the law, and life as dictated by custom. This is a good place to explore the personal and social dynamics that freed slaves faced in an ancient elitist society.

# 18

# The Greek Philosophers—
# Faith and Intellect
# in Dialogue

## INTRODUCTION

Just as patron-client relationships determined much of the social world of the first century, so Hellenistic philosophy formed the foundation of the intellectual world during this period. The Hellenistic philosophers were the seminal thinkers who inherited the philosophical tra-

Plato.

ditions of Plato and Aristotle (Cicero, *Fin.* 4.3).[1] The Hellenistic philosophers' contribution to Greco-Roman thought consisted in their creative engagement with these traditions, an engagement that ranged from admiring modification to vehement rejection. Their task was to articulate a reasoned explanation of the cosmos and humankind and to prescribe the kinds of actions best suited for life in this world. Their worldviews not only influenced the life and thought of the early church but have continued to impact ways of seeing and acting to this day.

The New Testament explicitly mentions two schools of Hellenistic philosophy: the Epicureans and the Stoics. Acts 17:18 states,

> A group of Epicurean and Stoic philosophers began to dispute with him. Some of them asked, "What is this babbler trying to say?" Others remarked, "He seems to be advocating foreign gods." They said this because Paul was preaching the good news about Jesus and the resurrection.

1    Plato established his philosophical school, the Academy, in Athens in 369 B.C.E. and died in 347. Aristotle, the tutor of Alexander the Great, studied at the Academy from 367 to 347 B.C.E. and developed his own philosophical system; he died in 322. Within the first decade of the fourth century B.C.E., both Epicureanism and Stoicism had been established in Athens as well. Thus, roughly within one generation, the two great founding fathers of Greek philosophy and two of the most prominent of the Hellenistic philosophies had made their mark on the intellectual world.

In this instance, Paul had the opportunity to debate the merits of the gospel with these two important schools while he was in Athens. Although this is the only recorded encounter between an apostle and Hellenistic philosophers, it is likely that the beliefs and practices of such groups form the background of much of what we find in the New Testament. It will be seen that categories of philosophical thought are especially relevant in interpreting the epistles of Paul.

## THE EPICUREANS

### Introduction

Epicurus was born on the island of Samos in 341 B.C.E. and established a society of like-minded friends in Athens in about 307 B.C.E. He and members of his school resided at a secluded villa on the outskirts of the city that came to be known as the "Garden" (Diogenes Laertius, *Vit. phil.* 10.10–11).[2] The setting reflected a fundamental premise of Epicurus: that the path to truth entailed withdrawing from the multitudes and seeking the contemplative life (*Vit. phil.* 10.143; Lucretius, *Rer. nat.* 2.1–20). It was here, the Garden, that Epicurus remained for the entirety of his life, steadily cultivating a philosophical movement that came to affect the whole Greco-Roman world. Indeed, his most devoted disciples commonly referred to him as the "savior," for they felt that Epicurus had unlocked the secrets of existence. All of his works, including the thirty-seven scrolls entitled On Nature, were composed at this intellectual retreat.

### Central Beliefs

Epicurus rejected the Platonic and Aristotelian models of philosophy that had come to dominate his world. He judged their cerebral abstractions and enshrining of the "gods" with providential control over life as major causes of human misery (*Vit. phil.* 10.77; *Rer. nat.* 1.62, 80).[3] Epicurus exhorts, "Bear this well in mind, and you will immediately perceive that nature is free and uncontrolled by proud masters and runs the universe by herself without the aid of gods" (*Rer. nat.* 2.1090). Rather than resort to the internal motions of the mind and the cogitations of experts in the fields of science, medicine, and theology, Epicurus advocated a practical, commonsense reading of the world (*Vit. phil.* 10.31–32).[4] For him, it was the individual, regardless of one's station in life, who served as the locus for truth. This truth was not mediated from within but from without (*Rer. nat.* 6.921). Truth came to the individual from his or her environment by way of the five senses: sight, sound, taste, smell, and touch.

Epicurus believed that the physical senses, rather than pure logic, serve as accurate guides to truth (*Rer. nat.* 4.469–484; Cicero, *Fin.* 1.63).[5] Epicurus was a thoroughgoing materialist (*Vit. phil.* 10.67). All of reality was composed of two elements: atoms and void (*Rer. nat.* 1.329, 430–435; *Vit. phil.* 10.39–40). In a manner that sounds surprisingly modern, Epicurus claimed that all entities were made of tiny, innumerable particles that were indestructible.[6] These "atoms" were always in motion, falling through the

2  None of Epicurus's writings have survived, and thus we depend upon later writers to relate his beliefs. The major witnesses are Lucretius (95–55 B.C.E.), *De rerum natura* (*On the Nature of Things*); the works of Cicero (106–43 B.C.E.); and Diogenes Laertius (ca. 200 C.E.), *Vitae philosophorum* (*Lives of Eminent Philosophers*).

3  "Nothing disquieted Epicurus more profoundly than the notion that supernatural beings control phenomena or that they can affect human affairs" (A. A. Long, *Hellenistic Philosophy: Stoics, Epicureans, Skeptics* [New York: Charles Scribner's Sons, 1974], 41).

4  On the pragmatism of Epicurus, see Julia E. Annas, *Hellenistic Philosophy of Mind* (Berkeley: University of California Press, 1992), esp. 123.

5  For Cicero, the senses can discern only the quality of a thing and make no firm judgment regarding morals; this is left to reason (*Fin.* 2.36–37).

6  Cicero takes exception to Epicurus here, claiming that his knowledge is "second hand," being totally dependent upon Democritus, and that where it varies from the latter, it comes into error (*Fin.* 1.17–18).

void at a constant rate, and as a result of tiny "swerves," they collide together to form all entities that exist (*Vit. phil.* 10.40–43, 61–62; *Rer. nat.* 2.62–65; Cicero, *Fin.* 1.19). Therefore anything that was real was corporeal; that is, it had a body of some sort. Consequently, the human senses are able to detect stimuli from these bodies and interpret their meaning for life (*Vit. phil.* 10.31–32). In the end, however, everything will run its course and dissolve into ruin (*Rer. nat.* 5.91–95).

For these reasons, Epicurus rejected the classical Greek pantheon. Yet he was not an atheist in the strictest sense of the word, for he states, "For verily there are gods, and the knowledge of them is manifest; but they are not such as the multitude believe, seeing that men do not steadfastly maintain the notions they form respecting them" (*Vit. phil.* 10.123; *Rer. nat.* 5.146–165). His point was that the popular understanding of the gods was bound by myth, for it failed to understand that the deities were formed of the finest atomic particles and they had no concern for the affairs of humans.

Presupposing the eternity of matter, Epicurus claimed that nothing can come forth from nothing (*Rer. nat.* 1.156, 265; *Vit. phil.* 10.41). The worlds were formed by the collisions of innumerable atoms. These compounds of accident ensure the existence of other worlds just like our own (*Rer. nat.* 2.1075–1076; 5.416–431; *Vit. phil.* 10.45, 89). The gods were formed in a similar fashion. They were created by the convergence of the very finest atoms and occupy the interstices between the worlds. Since the universe is unbounded, their number is unlimited (*Rer. nat.* 5). Similar to Aristotle's "Unmoved Mover," the gods are totally indifferent to what occurs on earth.[7] This sublime detachment is what preserves their eternal happiness (*Vit. phil.* 10.76, 81; *Rer. nat.* 3.20–24). Thus, for Epicurus,

everything is determined by the fateful creation of compounds, but there is no teleology. That is, creation is not moving toward some predetermined end willed by the gods.

The soul and the mind are able to affect the movements of objects, that is, to move the limbs, eyes, tongue, and so on. And injury to any part of the body affects the soul and the mind. According to Epicurus, these phenomena attest to the essential corporeality of the mind and the soul. He surmised that both the soul and the mind are composed of very fine atoms that are dispersed throughout the physical body by way of heated breath. In a letter to Herodotus, Epicurus explains, "Soul is a body, the parts of which are fine, distributed throughout the whole aggregate. It resembles most closely breath mixed with heat" (*Vit. phil.* 10.63; *Rer. nat.* 3.161–180, 231). The soul and the mind make up a single physical compound, yet the mind has preeminent authority over the soul (*Rer. nat.* 3.136–140, 396). They cannot exist apart from the body. When the body dies, the mind and the soul dissolve into their respective atomic parts and therefore cease to exist (*Rer. nat.* 3). Thus there is no life after death. For Epicurus, death has no meaning for the enlightened person (*Vit. phil.* 10.81–82; *Rer. nat.* 3.830, 925–930): "Death is nothing to us; for the body, when it has been resolved into its elements, has no feeling, and that which has no feeling is nothing to us" (*Vit. phil.* 10.124; cf. also Cicero, *Fin.* 2.100). The fear of death is just another ancient myth that torments the ignorant: "It is nothing, then, either to the living or to the dead, for with the living it is not and the dead exist no longer" (*Vit. phil.* 10.139; cf. also 125, 133). The dissolution of the soul at death means that there is neither final judgment nor punishment for ill deeds done in this life. "Hell" describes the life of those who dread a judgment and fear a punishment that will never come.[8]

---

7    "Similar" here does not mean "the same." For Aristotle, the Unmoved Mover was the ultimate cause of all events in the universe. For Epicurus, all events are caused by the random collision of atoms, and the gods have nothing to do with either this process or its outcome.

8    See N. Clayton Croy, "Hellenistic Philosophies and the Preaching of the Resurrection (ACTS 17:18, 32)," *NovT* 39 (1997): 21–39.

Thoughts are merely ultrafine particles that penetrate through to the mind from the environment (*Vit. phil.* 10.48–50). The life of the mind would be a product of pure chance if it were not for two factors. The first is that at birth we are endowed with "seeds" that move us in particular directions. The second is the phenomenon of "atomic swerve." As atoms fall through the void and penetrate to the mind, they collide and deviate from the path traveled (*Rer. nat.* 2.216, 240–250). This deviation enables the mind to influence which seeds come to fruition, and this in turn directs our conduct and the choices we make. So, even though Epicurus's universe is determined by atomic combinations, the atomic swerve provides for free will and moral development. The slight deviation in the path of atoms breaks the "lock-step" pattern of cause and effect that leads to fatalism (*Vit. phil.* 10.133–134). In some way, the "seeds" of the body, the atoms of the mind, and the atoms that come to it from without combine in such a way as to provide for free choice and moral accountability.[9]

Regarding what should guide individual moral choice Epicurus once again looks to nature. Since all creatures choose pleasure and avoid pain, he concludes that the pursuit of pleasure is the highest good (*Vit. phil.* 10.118, 126, 139; Cicero, *Fin.* 1.22).[10] According to Diogenes Laertius, he stated, "We say that pleasure is the starting-point and the end of living blissfully. For we recognize pleasure as a good which is primary and innate. We begin every act of choice and avoidance from pleasure that we return using our experience of pleasure as the criterion of every good thing" (*Vit.*

Aristotle.

*phil.* 10.128–129; cf. also Cicero, *Fin.* 1.29, 42).[11] Epicurus also taught that pleasure is to be found both in rest and in motion (*Vit. phil.* 10.136).

The pursuit of pleasure is not, however, the life of the debauched, characterized by unbridled wantonness and gluttony (*Vit. phil.* 10.131–132). The profligate lifestyle does not remove the fear of death, the myth of the gods, and the dread of final judgment (*Vit. phil.* 10.142; *Rer. nat.* 5.1194–2000).[12] Rather, what Epicurus meant by pleasure was "freedom from pain in the body and from disturbance

9    Annas concludes that in the end Epicurus is not a "reductivist"—that is, he does not view humans as merely the outworking of chemical formulas (*Hellenistic Philosophy of Mind*, 127). "Epicurus clearly has great reliance on our commonsense view of ourselves as free, developing agents" (p. 130).

10    Cicero, however, claims that the first instinct of animals is not the pursuit of pleasure but self-preservation, which is entirely different from what Epicurus envisions (*Fin.* 2.33).

11    Cicero, however, concluded that the pursuit of pleasure as the highest good was the fatal flaw of Epicureanism. Such a philosophy was beneath the dignity of man, for nature had endowed humans for higher ends than mere pleasure (*Fin.* 1.23; 2.111).

12    Cicero argues that Epicurus cannot extricate all hedonistic elements from his understanding of pleasure (*Fin.* 2.12–14, 20–21, 23, 30, 117). Indeed, Epicureanism soon became identified with the excesses of some of his students and degenerated into hedonism. For this reason, it lost most of its appeal in the decades following the death of Epicurus (Croy, "Hellenistic Philosophies and the Preaching of the Resurrection," 31).

**The Stoa, Athens, from which the "Stoics" derived their name.**

in the mind" (*Vit. phil.* 10.131–132). So, if a particular pleasure will ultimately lead to pain, it must not be chosen. On the other hand, if an experience of pain will lead to pleasure, it is to be selected (*Vit. phil.* 10.129–130; Cicero, *Fin.* 1.36–37). What ultimately matters is the removal of disquietude in the mind and of pain in the body. Thus, in the end, virtues are not to be chosen because they are morally upright in themselves. They are to be chosen insofar as they lead to personal pleasure (Cicero, *Fin.* 1.42–54). Epicurus taught, "For the virtues are naturally linked with living pleasurably, and living pleasurably is inseparable from them" (*Vit. phil.* 10.132). In the end, the ethics of Epicurus are dictated by the pleasure of the individual. As Torquatus exclaimed when defending Epicurus against the attacks of Cicero: "Here indeed is the royal road to happiness—open, simple, and direct! For clearly man can have no greater good than complete freedom from pain and sorrow coupled with the enjoyment of the highest bodily and mental pleasures" (Cicero, *Fin.* 1.57).

The radical individualism of Epicurean ethics feeds into Epicurus's notions of justice and injustice. Technically, he did not develop

a communal ethic at all. The rights of others are recognized so far as they are advantages to the self. On the other hand, justice amounts to a kind of pact between friends not to harm or be harmed (*Vit. phil.* 10.139).[13] This justice is contextualized and defined by what a particular people might deem advantageous at the time (*Vit. phil.* 10.149–153). Justice is further defined as the degree to which an action grants personal peace of mind (*Vit. phil.* 10.144). As Diogenes Laertius states, "In order to obtain security from other men any means whatsoever of procuring this was a natural good" (*Vit. phil.* 10.141). On the other hand, he deems the acquisition of friends to be the surest path to happiness (*Vit. phil.* 10.148).[14]

13   Or as Long and Sedley explain, "Natural justice is a symbol or expression of expediency, to prevent one man from harming or being harmed by another" (A. A. Long and D. N. Sedley, *Translations of the Principle Sources with Philosophical Commentary* [vol. 1 of *The Hellenistic Philosophers*; Cambridge: Cambridge University Press, 1987], 134–35.)

14   Torquatus sets forth the critical bond between friendship and pleasure when he states, "All that has been said about the essential connexion of the virtues with pleasure must be repeated about friendship" (Cicero, *Fin.* 1.68). But Cicero questions the substance of any friendship that seeks the benefit of the self (*Fin.* 2.82–85).

## The Epicureans and Christianity

The relationship of Epicureanism and the Christianity of the first century is one of contrasts. The points of contradiction are too many to list here. Even a cursory understanding of the faith reveals the great ideological rift between the two. The belief that God is eternal and did in fact create all other entities, both material and immaterial, out of nothing strikes at the very foundation of Epicureanism (Gen 1–2). Also, the belief that God is sovereign over creation and is directing the entire cosmos and the destinies of all individuals toward his will would be rejected by Epicurus (Rom 8:18–32). The principle that personal ethics are determined by the character of the transcendent God and not by what might be deemed advantageous to the individual turns Epicurean ethics on its head. The Christian doctrine of life after death and the belief of a final judgment entailing reward for the righteous and punishment for the wicked would have been very disturbing to Epicurus. For all these reasons, much of what Paul said at the Areopagus in Athens would have fallen on deaf ears.[15] Again, the Epicureans would have rejected words about the eternal Creator God who will resurrect the dead and render judgment on the last day (Acts 17:24–26, 30–31). It is likely that a lion's share of the mocking of Paul and his message on that day came from the Epicureans. On the other hand, Paul's message would have been much more amenable to the Stoics who were present to hear him speak at the Areopagus.

## THE STOICS

### Introduction

Zeno, the founder of Stoicism, was born in the city of Citium on the island of Cyprus in 334 B.C.E. and died in Athens, his adopted home, in 262 B.C.E. As in the case of Epicurus, his contemporary, Zeno moved to Athens in 300 B.C.E.

and began conducting lectures there. A cadre of disciples quickly gathered about his person and teachings, and early on they came to be known as "the Zenonians." In time, however, since Zeno preferred teaching among the painted colonnade in central Athens, known in Greek as the *stoa poikilē*, his adherents came to be known as the "Stoics" (Diogenes Laertius, *Vit. phil.* 7.5). Zeno's deliberate choice of an open space for his lectures in the center of a cosmopolitan area reflects a major aspect of his philosophy. Unlike the esoteric, contemplative theories of Plato and Aristotle and the reclusive hermitage of Epicurus, Zeno meant his thoughts to enter the public domain and become the practical guide for living in a complex world. He was successful to this end in that Stoicism became the dominant Hellenistic philosophy in the Greco-Roman world until the end of the empire and beyond. By the first century C.E., Stoicism had attained institutional status, being thoroughly integrated into Greco-Roman thought, culture, and politics. The popularity and success of Seneca (4 B.C.E.–65 C.E.), the Stoic senator who tutored Nero, reflect the power and public acclaim of Stoicism during this period.[16] The early church was enveloped in a world of thought characterized, in broad strokes, by the founding principles of Plato and Aristotle yet further refined by the Stoics. It will be seen that critical issues in Stoicism paralleled and at times converged with Christian thought from the time of Paul through the time of the church fathers.[17]

### Central Beliefs

As was the case with Epicurus, almost none of Zeno's original writings remain. What may be

---

15  The word "Areopagus" literally means "the hill of Ares" and referred not only to a promontory near the Acropolis in Athens but also to the municipal council that met there.

16  The horrid abuses of Nero's later reign can in no way be attributed to Seneca. If anything, Nero's most successful period, 54–62 C.E., owes much to the moderating influence of Stoicism as mediated by Seneca. Cf. Christopher Gill, "The School in the Roman Period," in *The Cambridge Guide to the Stoics* (ed. Brad Inwood; Cambridge: Cambridge University Press, 2003), 34–35.

17  For a thorough parallel between Paul and the Stoics, see Troels Engberg-Pedersen, *Paul and the Stoics* (Edinburgh: T&T Clark, 2000).

known of his teachings comes from secondary sources, some of which were written many years after his death.[18] In general, Zeno posited that philosophy consisted of three parts: the physical, the ethical, and the logical (*Vit. phil.* 7.39; cf. also Seneca, *Ep.* 89.9).[19] In his basic teachings, Zeno was eclectic, affirming the aspects of Plato, Aristotle, and the Cynics that served his purposes and rejecting ideas that did not fit his scheme of things. For example, Zeno accepted Plato's theory of a "divine craftsman" and that God was the "soul of the world" directing all things toward a determined end (*Vit. phil.* 7.70). Yet he rejected Plato's notion of an "ideal world" and claimed that human senses guided by reason are capable of attaining truth (*Vit. phil.* 7.42, 46, 52–54; Cicero, *Fin.* 3.17–18).[20] From Aristotle, and on this point agreeing with Epicurus, Zeno accepted a physicalist view of the universe. Thinking it impossible that a non-physical object could affect or move a physical object, Zeno concluded that everything is made of material parts, including the soul. Yet again, Zeno rendered a thoroughgoing critique of Platonic and Aristotelian metaphysics, anchoring his philosophy more in human rationalism than in theories about the transcendent.

In sum, then, Zeno conceived of the cosmos as a single entity, unified in all of its parts, governed by "divine reason" or the *logos* (*Vit. phil.* 7.134). The divine logos, or reason, permeates all of the cosmos and is inherent in human beings as well (*Vit. phil.* 7.139). In effect, the cosmos is a living being animated by the "world soul," or *pneuma*, which is the "creative fire" that gives life to everything (cf. *Vit. phil.* 7.142–143). The active principle of the *pneuma*, then, is what gives life and sensibility to humans as well. This essential continuity between the living cosmos and human beings is what makes the rational analysis of existence possible. Living in harmony with the *logos/pneuma* vis-à-vis the mind and the body is the bedrock of Zeno's ethic (Cicero, *Fin.* 3.20–23; 4.14–15). The unifying quality of the *logos* not only infuses the entire cosmos but is also reflected in each part that makes up the universe.

## Stoic Theology

Unlike Epicurus, Zeno believed that the gods were responsible for the creation and disposition of all things. Zeno, however, "demythologized" the Greek pantheon, subsuming all gods into one divine *logos*. Diogenes Laertius encapsulates Stoic thought here by stating, "God, Mind, Fate, Zeus are all one, and he is called by many other names" (*Vit. phil.* 7.135, 147). God created the four elements (fire, water, air, and earth) and continually orders all things, and this is "Fate" (*Vit. phil.* 7.136–137, 149). Nature is a firelike artistic spirit that holds the world together, gives it beauty and form, and creates and causes all things to move and grow (*Vit. phil.* 7.148–149, 158). This reflects the world soul and its teleological effect espoused by Plato in *Leges* (*Laws*) 10. Yet the inherent pantheism of the Stoics rejected the transcendence of Aristotle's Unmoved Mover, which affects the world through the heavenly bodies and the stars (Aristotle, *Physica* [*Physics*] ii). For Aristotle, God is above the cosmos; for the Stoics, God is the cosmos.

For the Stoics, anything that exists must be able to act or be acted upon, and this requires a body. Since God certainly exists, God must have a body as well. In fact, God/Nature is the "active principle" composed of

---

18   The three major sources are Cicero, *De finibus* (*On Ends*), Diogenes Laertius, *Vitae philosophorum* (*Lives of Eminent Philosophers*), and *SVF*. Cicero's work contains the Stoic ethics of Chrysippus (232–206 B.C.E.), the careful compiler of Zeno's work and considered to be the greatest of his students. Diogenes Laertius (280–207 B.C.E.) provides a careful synopsis of Stoic teachings. *SVF* presents a collection of Stoic teachings from various sources throughout the ages.

19   For some points of continuity between Epicureanism and the Stoics, see Cicero, *Fin.* 1.62.

20   Although Cicero praises the philosophical structure of Stoicism, thus counting it more difficult to refute than Epicureanism (*Fin.* 3.2, 74–75), he devotes the fourth book of his *De finibus* to a refutation of the Stoics.

The Areopagus, or "Mars Hill," Athens, lies at the foot of the Acropolis.

fire and air. All else is passive matter made up of earth and water. It is the admixture of the divine *pneuma*, or the heated breath of the *logos*, with matter that gives the world form and coherence (Diogenes Laertius, *SVF* 2.299–300). Augustine comments, "For the Stoics thought that fire, i.e., one of the four material elements of which this visible world is composed, was both animate and intelligent, the maker of the world and of all things contained in it, that it was in fact God" (*SVF* 2.423). Yet the good Stoic is a worshiper of God, following all of the sacrifices, prayers, and rites that they judge should be afforded to the divine (*Vit. phil.* 7.119, 124).

## Stoic Anthropology

The human, as part of the ordered universe, is corporeal, yet it is energized by the fiery *pneuma* of the *logos*. Unlike the Epicureans, some Stoics believed that the souls of the wise would survive death for a time, then would be dissolved in the general conflagration that would consume the world (*Vit. phil.* 7.157).

At birth the soul is a blank slate. In time, however, through the five senses of the body, the soul receives impressions from the environment like the marks left on a tablet of wax (*Vit. phil.* 7.156–158). As Diogenes Laertius explains, "Impression leads the way; then thought, which is able to speak, expresses in discourse what it experiences as a result of the impression" (*Vit. phil.* 7.49). The highest part of the soul, the *hēgemonikon*, is the governing principle of reason that permits articulate expression of the sense perceptions that are taken in from without (*Vit. phil.* 7.88; Lucretius, *Rer. nat.* 4.722–730). This governing principle of the mind is located in the heart, as previously posited by Aristotle (*Vit. phil.* 7.159). Unlike the animals, the *hēgemonikon* enables the rational soul to see connections and articulate how these connections relate to one another. As the controlling principle of the mind, the *hēgemonikon* coordinates all the other faculties of the body.[21] In this way,

---

21  For a critique of the Stoics' inordinate emphasis of mind over body, see Cicero, *Fin.* 4.25–32.

the ordered universe governed by the laws of cause and effect are made known to the wise man (*Vit. phil.* 7.88). Zeno labeled as "knowledge" sense perceptions that could not be "destroyed by reason." Perceptions that could be dislodged by right thinking he called "ignorance" (Cicero, *SVF* 1.60). Thus, in a manner that would have been amenable to Epicurus, Zeno's epistemology is empirical in nature.

The central role of logic (or the science of right thinking), as expressed through rhetoric (the science of right speaking), cannot be underestimated in Stoicism. Logic opened the path to truth. Dialectic, or the practice of posing the right questions that lead to the right answers, was the method of Stoicism (*Vit. phil.* 7.41–82). So, for the Stoic, the truly wise man is a master dialectician (*Vit. phil.* 7.83). If the Stoic affirms the logic inherent in Nature and rightly articulates this knowledge in proper rhetoric, he cannot err.

## Stoic Ethics

Stoic ethics arise out of Stoicism's epistemology. Like Socrates, Zeno affirmed that knowledge and goodness go hand in hand and that the person who really knows as he or she ought will live the good life.[22] Virtues are an end in themselves and seek no reward apart from the pleasure of living rightly in accordance with Nature (Cicero, *Fin.* 2.45). This premise presupposes a modicum of free will on the part of the individual. Indeed, the Stoics proffered that the good life is possible because, once again, the *hēgemonikon* constitutes an "internal cause" that is able to engage and ethically process all "external causes" coming in from the environment. In a discriminating manner, the *hēgemonikon* is able to select the good out of the causal nexus of the universe and thereby alter the lockstep cause-and-effect pattern of Nature (*Vit. phil.* 7.86).

All of this means that the Stoic seeks to lead

a life "in agreement with Nature" as far as its good intents are concerned (*Vit. phil.* 7.89). For Nature is active as a good agent in the plant and animal world as well as in humans. In this way Nature seeks to bring about its benevolent will in a providential manner (*Vit. phil.* 7.85–89). Nature instructs us to reject what is harmful and affirm what is good. For this reason, Chrysippus makes a proper understanding of theology prerequisite to the development of sound moral conduct.[23] Or as Cicero would have it, the Stoic seeks a life lived "from the recommendation of Nature" (*SVF* 1.181). This is the life of virtue, for "virtue is the state of mind which tends to make the whole of life harmonious" (*Vit. phil.* 7.89). For the Stoic, Nature teaches four primary virtues that lead to personal happiness: practical wisdom, self-restraint, justice, and courage (*Vit. phil.* 7.89; Seneca, *Ep.* 88.29; Cicero, *Ep.* 2.46–47). Indeed, it was Nature that endowed us with the ability to rationally choose the virtuous life (Seneca, *SVF* 3.219). Seneca aptly summarizes the dependence of virtue on reason: "It is reason alone that is unchangeable, that holds fast to its decisions. For reason is not a slave to the senses, but a ruler over them. Reason is equal to reason, as one straight line to another; therefore virtue also is equal to virtue. Virtue is nothing else than right reason. All virtues are reasons. Reasons are reasons, if they are right reasons" (*Ep.* 66.32).

This is why, of the three kinds of life, that is, the contemplative, the practical, and the rational, the last should be sought above all others (*Vit. phil.* 7.130). So, for the Stoic, reason and providence come together in harmony and open the way to ethical development (*Vit. phil.* 7.88–89; Cicero, *Fin.* 3.24). This is the primary goal of life (Cicero, *Fin.* 3.26, 31). Moreover, such an ethical life is something that the Stoic wants to do, not something he or she has to do

---

22  "The human good is understanding the world correctly, in theory and in practice" (Engberg-Pedersen, *Paul and the Stoics*, 66).

23  See J. Louis Martyn, "De-apocalypticizing Paul: An Essay Focused on *Paul and the Stoics* by Troels Engberg-Pedersen," *JSNT* 86 (2002): 61–102, esp. 74–75.

**Cicero delivers an oration in the Roman senate.**

(*Vit. phil.* 7.89). Moral development has nothing to do with wealth, social standing, or political power. Human well-being consists of physical and mental discipline and living within one's means as dictated by Nature. Simplicity and self-sufficiency are the hallmarks of the virtuous man or woman.

The Stoic's concept of justice and injustice flows out of this thoroughgoing ethical rationalism. To live in harmony with Nature is to forsake a thoroughly egocentric life and continually make choices for the good on the basis of reason as mediated through Nature (*Vit. phil.* 7.99; Cicero, *Fin.* 3.63; but see also 3.16–17). The perfectly wise person, then, is not simply to be guided by pleasure or self-preservation. Rather, he or she is to always choose appropriate acts that lead to justice (*Vit. phil.* 7.108). Thus the Stoic ethic takes on a corporate dimension, because the good Stoic always does his or her civic duty and seeks the advantage of all (Cicero, *Fin.* 3.64). A central tenet here is that one should treat friends as one would wish to be treated (*Vit. phil.* 7.124; Cicero, *Fin.* 3.70). Also, to put an end to jealously and render adultery meaningless, there should be a community of wives in which all are free to choose their own partners (*Vit. phil.* 7.131).

For the Stoic, all virtues are interconnected. To possess one mandates the possession of all (*Vit. phil.* 7.125–128). This also means, however, that the slightest imperfection in one area leads

to the failure of the entire ethical system. Thus, for the virtuous Stoic, there are no degrees of success here. Either one is completely virtuous or one is unjust. Diogenes Laertius expresses the austerity of Stoic ethics: "Nor again, are there degrees of justice and injustice, and the same rule applies to the other virtues" (*Vit. phil.* 7.127; but see Cicero, *Fin.* 4.66). Only by extreme effort and education could one hope to approximate the life of a Stoic sage. In the end, if one foresees that personal circumstances render the ethical life impossible, then the good Stoic is to emulate Socrates and "quit life" in a reasonable manner (*Vit. phil.* 7.130; Seneca, *Prov.* 6.4–9).[24] For this reason, Dio Cassius reports that conditions had become so intolerable during the reign of Claudius "that excellence no longer meant anything else than dying nobly" (*Hist. rom.* 60.16.7). In this case, Nature summons to suicide in the way that Seneca was summoned in the light of Nero's atrocities (Cicero, *Fin.* 3.60; Suetonius, *Vit. Caes.* 6.35.5; Dio Cassius, *Hist. rom.* 62.25.1).[25] As Seneca counseled regarding death,

---

24   The extent to which suicide was viewed as a virtue is reflected in Tacitus: "Caninius Rebilus, who in juristic knowledge and extent of fortune ranked with the greatest, escaped the tortures of age and sickness by letting the blood from his arteries; though, from the unmasculine vices for which he was infamous, he had been thought incapable of the firmness of committing suicide" (*Ann.* 13. 30).

25   Tacitus explains that Nero had prepared a poison for Seneca, but because of a simple diet of fruit gathered from the fields, he escaped the deadly elixir (*Ann.* 15.45).

"There is no difference whether death comes to us, or whether we go to death (*Ep.* 69.6, cf. also 70.7–9; 77.7–9). This cold, dispassionate quality of Stoic ethics is by design. Since the *logos* in the individual is "connate," or integral to the *logos* of the universe, then, after doing the best one can, the good Stoic accepts all outcomes of Nature without care or grief. If one is convinced that Fate has had its way, then emotions have no place in the nexus of cause and effect. "Passion, or emotion, is defined by Zeno as an irrational and unnatural movement in the soul, or again as impulse in excess. . . . And grief or pain they hold to be an irrational mental contraction" (Diogenes Laertius, *Vit. phil.* 7.110, 111). Strong emotions such as fear, depression, and irrational elation are thus evidence of an imbalance between the soul and Nature and so should be avoided (*Vit. phil.* 7.112–115). Such passions are not to be controlled; rather, they are to be eradicated (*Vit. phil.* 7.117–118). If not rooted out, strong passions will lead to madness and self-destruction (*Vit. phil.* 7.124; cf. also Seneca, *Ep.* 74.34).[26]

## Stoic Historiography

For the Stoic, God, unlike everything else in the universe, is ungenerated, indestructible, and the Creator of all. At times God absorbs all of reality into himself by fire and then re-creates a new cosmos by the same means (*Vit. phil.* 7.134, 136). In this way the activity of the *logos*, Nature, God, *pneuma*, or Fate is eternally coming about through an endless series of world cycles that begin and end with pure fire. Therefore, even though the Stoic is teleological in outlook, believing that everything is working out the will of Nature, the understanding of time and history, in the end, is cyclical (*Vit. phil.* 7.141).

Regarding the present, everything can be explained by the interrelationship between cause and effect. Thus, for the Stoic, nothing happens completely by accident because everything can be attributed to previous causes. To this extent, every event is determined by Fate. Thus Seneca queries, "What, then, is the part of a good man? To offer himself to Fate" (*Prov.* 5.8). Ultimately, what is to come is a cosmic conflagration where the souls of the sages may endure for a while and otherwise everything is destroyed (*Vit. phil.* 7.157).[27]

## The Stoics and Christianity

Just as the points of contrast between Epicureanism and Christianity were too numerous to mention, the points of comparison between Stoicism and Christianity cannot be listed here. Clearly, many aspects of Stoicism are represented in the thought and practice of the early church. The Logos as eternal Creator of all things is presented in John's prologue (John 1:1–14). Also, the conceptual structure of Paul's theology reflects Stoic philosophy. For example, the idea that the qualities of the invisible God are evident in nature is espoused by Paul in Rom 1:18–25. Furthermore, Rom 2:14–15 sets forth the belief in some kind of "common grace," mediated in nature and in human nature, that endows every individual with the ability to discern what is appropriate and what is not. Paul's use of the Greek phrase *logikēn latreian* (λογικὴν λατρείαν) in Rom 12:1–2 points to the necessity of correct reason to discern what is right and wrong.[28] The idea of personal moral development is also inherent in the faith (2 Pet 1:5–7). These are but a few examples from among many that parallel Stoic

---

26 The connection between emotions and disease should not be surprising, for, as Seneca taught, the soul is a body and emotions are "bodily things" that contort the physical body and can become "diseases of the spirit" (*Ep.* 106.5–6).

27 Since some Stoics believed that the souls of good men survived for a time after death, perhaps Paul's words about the afterlife in Acts 17:32 would have been amenable to some of the Stoics present on that occasion.

28 Engberg-Pedersen argues that the "deep structure" common to the Stoics and Paul basically entails moving away from the self toward God in order to become part of a new community (*Paul and the Stoics*, 13, 34–60). For a contrasting view, see Philip F. Esler, "Paul and Stoicism: Romans 12 as a Test Case," *NTS* 50 (2004): 106–24.

belief and Christian faith.

The critical question here, however, concerns the precise nature of the church's dependence on Stoicism. It has been argued that each of the parallels above can be found in the Hebrew Scriptures as well. Also at issue is this question: even if the first believers did employ Stoic categories, to what extent did they endorse Stoic theology and epistemology? Although the Stoics and John both speak of the *logos*, John's conception is essentially different from the impersonal, pantheistic Nature of the Stoics. Also, the cardinal doctrines that became so instrumental in the formation of Christianity—sin, atonement, the incarnation, the final judgment by the living God—find no place in the school of the Stoics. A similar contrast can be found regarding personal ethics. Virtue, for the Stoic, is the happy product of human rationalism. The good Stoic makes progress morally by continual practice. For Paul, virtue is a fruit of the Spirit that results not from practice but from spiritual conversion and the unmerited grace of God (Gal 5:22–23; 6:15; 2 Cor 5:17). Stoic teaching on how one should relate to others is generally presented on a theoretical level and does not grapple with the practical issues of living in community as found in Rom 14:1–15:4. Truly empathizing with the pain of others (cf. Rom 12:15) was deemed weak and unworthy of a true Stoic, perhaps even a sign of mental illness (cf. *Vit. phil.* 7:110–115; Cicero, *Fin.* 3:35). For the Stoic, there is also no continuance of personal identity after the grave, and there is absolutely no belief in the resurrection of the physical body. The last point explains the impasse that Paul experienced with the Stoics at the Areopagus in Athens. All went well when he preached in generalities about a wise and benevolent God who provides for us in nature (Acts 17:24–29). But as soon as he spoke of a personal judgment by Jesus Christ and the resurrection of the dead, everything

fell apart (Acts 17:30–33). In Acts 17:18 the Stoics and the Epicureans judge Paul to be a self-interested amateur, a "seed-picker" (NIV "babbler," Gk. *spermologos* [σπερμολόγος]), going about the Mediterranean world gathering up this bit of knowledge and then a bit of that. For the Areopagites, Paul is driven by a pursuit of money, not truth.[29]

Paul's session with the philosophers in Athens may be the key to understanding the early church's relationship to Stoicism. That is, the relationship may well be more one of form than of substance. Regarding form, there can be no question that Paul employs aspects of Stoic rhetoric in his epistles. Paul's use of diatribe, or the practice of arguing with an imaginary opponent, is almost a given in New Testament studies.[30] For, just as Socrates used the pedagogical diatribe to point out the errors of his pupils so that he might lead them to truth, so does Paul. Time after time in Romans, Paul raises false premises or conclusions, only to follow with "May it not be!" (Gk. *mē genoito* [μὴ γένοιτο]).[31] As a good Stoic teacher, Paul confronts his imaginary interlocutor, whether Jew or Gentile,

---

29   Being accepted as a noted philosopher was one of the fastest ways to accumulate wealth in the ancient world. Seneca is said to have garnered great wealth as a philosopher and rhetorician (Tacitus, *Ann.* 13.42.6). "One particularly upwardly mobile group was composed of rhetoricians and sophists, who made enough money from their students to become important members of the moneyed class in the larger cities of both east and west" (John E. Stambaugh, "Social Relations in the City of the Early Principate: State of Research," in *The Society of Biblical Literature 1980 Seminar Papers* [SBLSP 19; Missoula, Mont.: Scholars Press, 1980], 80; cf. also Croy, "Hellenistic Philosophies and the Preaching of the Resurrection," 23).

30   Rudolf Bultmann was one of the first to point out Paul's dependence on Stoic diatribe. See Stanley K. Stowers, *The Diatribe and Paul's Letter to the Romans* (SBLDS 57; Chico, Calif.: Scholars Press, 1981), esp. 176; and idem, *A Critical Reassessment of Paul and the Diatribe: The Dialogical Element in Paul's Letter to the Romans* (New Haven: Yale University Press, 1979).

31   Paul employs this stylistic device no less than ten times in Romans (cf. Rom 3:4, 6, 31; 6:2, 15; 7:7, 13; 9:14; 11:1, 11).

saved or unsaved, for the purpose of pointing out his or her arrogance and pretense. The goal is that they may make progress in their moral development (Phil 1:6, 9–11, 25). Harmful passions are to be denied through crucifying the flesh (Rom 6:12; Gal 5:24; Titus 2:12; 3:3).[32] Paul thus offers a higher way of living that is very similar to the practice of the Stoics.

Paul, however, does not view the Christian as reaching up to attain righteousness as the Stoics exhorted. Rather, it is God who has reached down to us and granted to us the righteousness of his Son as a free gift (Rom 3:24–26). The harsh inflexibility of Stoic perfectionism is not to be found in Paul. It is the Spirit that perfects, it is the righteousness of Christ that justifies, and it is the atonement of Christ that covers the moral shortcomings of the converted (Rom 4:24–25; 5:1–2; 8:1–4). Also for Paul, the gospel is not a pattern for living as derived from Nature. Rather, it is an apocalyptic invasion of the kingdom of God that mandates obedience in the light of impending judgment. The leading of the Spirit and the resultant evidence of the fruit of the Spirit (Gal 5:18–23) are categorical imperatives for the believer, not options.[33] Finally, the Stoics presented something that was reasonable, whereas Paul glories in the foolishness of the cross. The message of the cross is not at all agreeable to the Greek philosophers of Paul's day (1 Cor 1:18–21).

---

32   Again Engberg-Pedersen stresses Paul's integral dependence on the Stoics here (cf. *Paul and the Stoics*, 38, 105, 119, 154, 227).

33   Thus Martyn's general critique of Engberg-Pedersen is that he divorces Paul's theology and cosmology from his ethics. In short, Engberg-Pedersen has "de-apocalyticized" Paul and made him into a modern Stoic. See Martyn, "De-apocalypticizing Paul," esp. 69–72, 86, 88, 91. Cf. Engberg-Pedersen, *Paul and the Stoics*, 17, 304.

## SUMMARY

Hellenistic philosophy offered powerful paradigms for interpreting the world and for prescribing how one should live in it. It is clear that the early Christians found Stoicism more amenable to the faith than the precepts of Epicurus. Yet even here the Christians appear to have simply adopted Stoic rhetorical styles and adapted Stoic concepts to serve the gospel. When the Stoic vision intersected with Christian faith or values, it seems that the apostles were careful to fill the Stoic form with Christian content. In any case, Hellenistic philosophy was such a part of the first-century world that, for good or for ill, the Christians could not afford to ignore it. For example, Tertullian noted that Zeno taught that God and matter were of two different essences and that the Logos or Reason created the universe and instilled order in it (SVF 1.155, 160; cf. also Seneca, *Prov.* 1.2–4). On the other hand, Origen attacked the empiricism of Zeno, and Justin Martyr focused his polemic on the Stoic's notion of Fate. Justin felt that the inherent determinism in Stoicism undermined the Christian doctrine of individual moral accountability (SVF 2.108, 926).

On balance, the verdict of history is that the Hellenistic philosophers were too earthbound to address the more complex issues of the human soul. This general lack of transcendence gave no answer to the human longing for personal immortality. The Hellenistic philosophers prescribed an austere moral regimen yet afforded no power for the attainment of their goals or solace for those who, for whatever reasons, did not meet the success demanded by the system. So, even though the early Christians adopted and then adapted certain aspects of Hellenistic philosophy, it was they who eventually dominated the ideology and practice of the Roman world.

# Annotated Bibliography

Annas, Julia E. *Hellenistic Philosophy of Mind.* Berkeley: University of California Press, 1992. This is an analysis of the major teachings of the Epicureans and Stoics as it relates to their philosophy of the mind, claiming that the mind is a physical component of the body. It offers a good introduction to some of the central doctrines of the Epicureans and Stoics, but it is not intended for the beginner.

Engberg-Pedersen, Troels. *Paul and the Stoics.* Edinburgh: T&T Clark, 2000. This complex and thorough work evaluates the continuity and contribution of Paul's thought through the matrix of Stoic ethics. Paul is placed more squarely in the Greco-Roman thought world than in the world of Judaism. It entertains a good dialogue with contemporary Pauline scholars but is not designed for beginners.

Long, A. A. *Hellenistic Philosophy: Stoics, Epicureans, Skeptics.* New York: Charles Scribner's Sons, 1974. Long offers a programmatic presentation of the major aspects of the Stoics, Epicureans, and, to a lesser extent, the Skeptics. It is a good source for understanding the basic ideas of these philosophies.

Long, A. A., and D. N. Sedley. *Translations of the Principle Sources with Philosophical Commentary.* Vol. 1 of *The Hellenistic Philosophers.* Cambridge: Cambridge University Press, 1987. This is a thorough presentation of the major Hellenistic philosophical schools from the time of Alexander the Great to the end of the Roman Republic. The Epicureans and Stoics receive special attention, and this volume does not assume a thoroughgoing knowledge of the ancient world. It is an excellent source for a beginning researcher, since it offers a detailed analysis of the great schools of Greek thought in a readable format.

# 19
# Slaves and Freed Persons—Church and Culture in Tension

## INTRODUCTION: THE NATURE OF THE SOURCES

Primary sources on the origin and nature of slavery in the ancient world are limited for a number of reasons.[1] The historians of ancient Greece and Rome were attracted to the lives of the Caesars, great senators, and persons of equestrian rank.[2] It was thought that recording the plight of slaves was beneath the calling of a historian, and so such persons fell into the category of "subhistory."[3]

Nevertheless, perhaps one of the most interesting windows on slavery in the ancient world is found in Seneca, *Ep.* 47, which parodies the boorishness of Roman masters toward the quiet dignity and character of their slaves.[4] He exhorts masters to treat slaves well because they are humans, unpretentious friends, and fellow members of a common household who should be judged on the basis of their character and not on the basis of their station in life (*Ep.* 47.1, 10, 14–16). Seneca laments that slaves are made to stand in silence and watch as their masters gorge themselves throughout the night. He rebukes debauched Romans who force their slaves to play the part of male prostitutes and who severely beat their faithful servants for the slightest infraction (*Ep.* 47.2, 5, 8). Seneca counsels that slaves should be led to serve out of love and not out of fear, and he warns that Fate could change a senator into a slave overnight (*Ep.* 47.11–12, 18–19).[5]

Nevertheless, Seneca's point in this epistle is to set forth the Stoic ideal of how slavery ought to be carried on; he is not arguing that slavery is morally wrong or that it should

---

1 The secondary literature, however, on the subject of slavery is immense. Entire monographs are required for bibliographies on the subject. Cf. Joseph C. Miller, *Slavery and Slaving in World History: A Bibliography, 1900–1991* (Milford, N.Y.: Kraus International, 1993).

2 The senators numbered about six hundred and wore special togas with a wide stripe as well as special shoes to distinguish them from all other classes. The second highest rank was the knights, or equestrian order. Of the equestrians, there were more than a thousand in Rome at the time of Augustus, and each city had its wealthy equestrians who ran the municipal government (John E. Stambaugh, "Social Relations in the City of the Early Principate: State of Research," in *The Society of Biblical Literature 1980 Seminar Papers* [SBLSP 19; Missoula, Mont.: Scholars Press, 1980], 76–77, 84).

3 The voice of slaves was therefore by and large silenced in ancient historiography. See J. Albert Harrill, *The Manumission of Slaves in Early Christianity* (Tübingen: J. C. B. Mohr, 1995), esp. 25.

4 "I do not wish to involve my self in too large a question, and to discuss the treatment of slaves, towards whom we Romans are excessively haughty, cruel, and insulting" (Seneca, *Ep.* 47.12).

5 In a patronizing manner, Seneca urges patience toward prisoners of war who may have been accomplished citizens in their native lands one day, only to find themselves field hands or manual laborers the next. He advises that such newly made slaves deserve some time to adjust to their unbidden station in life (*Ira* 3.29.1–2).

**Assyrian relief depicting prisoners who would be employed as slaves by their captors.**

be abolished altogether. Also, at no point in his tirade against the abuse of slaves does he allow them to speak for themselves. Similarly personal letters addressed to slave owners—for instance, some letters from Cicero and the Apostle Paul's letter to Philemon—give us only half of the dialogue and contain nothing of the views of the slaves themselves. So, in order to gain insight into slavery of the first century, the researcher must settle for anecdotal comments from antiquity and for whatever can be gleaned from Greco-Roman law and the socioeconomic analysis of slave cultures of the time.[6]

## THE ORIGIN AND NUMBER OF SLAVES IN ANTIQUITY

Highly stratified, authoritarian cultures that were steeped in patronage lent themselves to the bane of slavery.[7] Indeed, Justinian's *Institutiones* (*Institutes*) (that is, the Roman summary of justice first published in 533 C.E.) repeatedly emphasizes that "slavery is an institution of the law of all peoples" (*Inst.* 1.3.2; 1.5). So, for the Romans, slavery was integral to the social structure of antiquity. This held true for the Jews as well. Even though the Hebrews were prohibited from making slaves of their

6    E.g., Pliny the Younger explains that his slave quarters, though shabby in comparison with the rest of his estate, can be made to house guests, if required (*Ep.* 2.17).

7    On the nearly ubiquitous presence of slavery in the ancient world, see Craig S. De Vos, "Once a Slave, Always a Slave?" Slavery, Manumission, and Relational Patterns in Paul's Letter to Philemon," *JSNT* 82 (2001): 89–105.

own people (Exod 25:39–46), they did enslave those they had conquered (Exod 12:43–44; Lev 22:11; 25:44–46). Also, any Jew who could not repay debts was subject to indentured slavery (Lev 25:39–43; Josephus, *Ant.* 16.1–4).[8] From ancient times, then, the institution of slavery was well entrenched in both the Jewish and the Gentile world.

The sources of slaves in the ancient world were many. They included piracy, infant exposure, prisoners of war, and, in some cases, the breeding of slaves (Justinian, *Dig.* 1.5.5; *Inst.* 1.3.4; 1 Tim 1:10; Dionysius of Halicarnassus, *Ant. rom.* 4.24.1–2; Suetonius, *Vit. Caes.* 3.9.1–2; cf. also *Barnabas* 19:5).[9] In the last instance, the offspring of these slaves were classed as "chattel slaves" (cf. Columella, *Rust.* 1.8.19; Varro, *Rust.* 1.17.5–6).[10] Abandonment was a particularly grievous means of obtaining slaves.[11] Unwanted children would be left in an area known for this purpose, to be taken in by slave traders (cf. Pliny the Younger, *Ep.* 10.65–66). For example, in Menander's *Epitrepontes*, the abandonment of a baby in the forest is taken for granted. In this satirical play, the real issue at stake concerns who owns the jewels or trinkets that were left with the infant when it was abandoned (*Epitr.* 240–355). Tertullian (ca. 180 C.E.) berates the Roman aristocracy for killing infants and the elderly by exposure (*Apologeticus* [*Apology*] 6–8). More often than not, these so-called *alumni* would be raised as prostitutes (Columella, *Rust.* 1.8.1).[12] Even a strange form of tax evasion served as a source of slaves. A noncitizen might sell himself or herself as a slave to a benevolent Roman citizen in the hopes of future manumission (Justinian, *Dig.* 1.5.21). In this case, the freedman/-woman would then be exempt from the heavy Roman taxes levied against noncitizens. Early Christians were able to turn the bane of slavery into a kind of ministry. First Clement 55:2 explains that some Christians even sold themselves into slavery and used the price of their own lives to help the poor.

Yet by far the most productive source of slaves was warfare, in accordance with Aristotle's dictum that the "things" conquered in war belong to the conquerors (*Pol.* 1.12.16). For him, the equitable acquisition of slaves is like warfare or hunting (*Pol.* 1.2.23). Indeed, the *Institutiones* of Justinian maintains that the word *servus* (Latin for "slave") is from the verb servare, "to save." The point here is that Roman military commanders should "save" some captives for the slave trade rather than kill them on the spot. Commercially, of such slaves it was said that they were captured by force of arms (*ab hostibus manu capiantur*) (Justinian, *Dig.* 1.5.4; *Inst.* 1.3.3). These unfortunates were also deemed to be chattel slaves, that is, persons to be sold as property and treated as such. As in the purchase of livestock, they were disrobed, their teeth were examined, and they were prodded to see if they were fit for labor (Seneca, *Ep.*

---

8    On slavery among the Hebrews, see Paul V. M. Flesher, *Oxen, Women, or Citizens? Slaves in the System of the Mishnah* (Atlanta: Scholars Press, 1988), 17, 16–25; and Benjamin G. Wright III, "'*Ebd*/*doulos*: Terms and Social Status in the Meeting of Hebrew Biblical and Hellenistic Roman Culture," in "Slavery in Text and Interpretation" (ed. Allen Dwight Callahan, Richard A. Horsley, and Abraham Smith), *Semeia* 83–84 (1998): 83–112.

9    In noting the vicissitudes of Fate regarding slavery, Seneca recalls that for a time the noble Plato and Diogenes were sold into slavery after being kidnapped by pirates or shanghaied while making a journey abroad (*Ep.* 47.12).

10    For insight on the procuring of children for the purpose of slavery, see Everett Ferguson, *Backgrounds of Early Christianity* (2d ed.; Grand Rapids: Eerdmans, 1993), 58. Some children were sold into slavery because their parents were no longer able to care for them (Jo-Ann Shelton, *As the Romans Did: A Sourcebook in Roman Social History* [2d ed.; New York: Oxford University Press, 1998], 163).

11    On the interrelationship of child abandonment and slavery, see W. V. Harris, "Child-Exposure in the Roman Empire," *JHS* 84 (1994): 1–22.

12    For the abuse of female slaves in antiquity, see Sarah B. Pomeroy, *Goddesses, Whores, Wives, and Slaves: Women in Classical Antiquity* (New York: Schocken, 1975), esp. 191–93; and Jennifer A. Glancy, "Obstacles to Slave Participation in the Corinthian Church," *JBL* 117 (1998): 481–501.

80.9). Female captives faced a particularly grim future. Since the majority of women in ancient Rome had few marketable skills and little formal education, their prospects as future slaves were daunting. The Jews were not exempt from being victims of such atrocities. The population of Jewish slaves in Rome greatly increased after the defeat of Israel by Vespasian and Titus in 70 C.E.[13] The Roman conquests of Israel from 63 B.C.E. to 135 C.E. resulted in a huge cache of Jewish slaves, the majority of whom were sent to Rome and sold at retail. The enslavement of Jews has a history that reaches much further back than the birth of Rome, as the stories of Joseph, Moses, and the exodus graphically portray (Gen 37:28; Exod 1:8–14).

This system of the capturing and selling of persons composed a significant part of the Roman economy of the first century. *Canabae*, private profiteers, would follow the Roman legions into battle and await the wholesale auction of humans that was sure to follow. These poor wretches would then be transported to retail markets for personal gain.[14] As in a well-oiled machine, one part served to advance the next. In this way, the expansion of the Roman Empire brought in a steady flow of slaves from Egypt, Asia, and Greece who, in turn, supplied the labor to keep the empire running.

Because of the fragmentary nature of the sources, no accurate count of the number of slaves in the first century is obtainable. One is forced to extrapolate from the data available and then settle for informed estimates. When all things are considered, it appears that the number of enslaved persons in the empire was staggering. Those captured and enslaved by the imperial armies numbered in the hundreds of thousands, if not in the millions. For example, when recording the Roman defeat of the Helvetians, Tacitus simply says, "Many thousands were massacred, many thousands sold into slavery" (*Hist.* 1.68). Seneca records that a proposal to make slaves wear distinctive dress was defeated on the grounds that it would inform the slaves of how numerous they were and how few the senators were (*De clementia* 1.24.1). Pliny the Elder records that in 8 B.C.E. Gaius Caecilius Isidorus, a freedman of Gaius Caecilius, freed 4,116 of his own slaves when he died. Pliny goes on to speak of "legions of slaves" dwelling under one roof, so to speak—so many slaves that an attendant had to be hired to memorize their faces and names (*Nat.* 33.6.26). All senators and equestrians maintained a retinue of slaves, who were considered to be part of an aristocrat's *familia*. For example, the city prefect of Rome, Pedanius Secundus (61 C.E.), owned four hundred household slaves. After he was murdered by one of them, the senate counseled to execute all of his household slaves in accordance with Roman practice (Tacitus, *Ann.* 14.42–44).[15] This was done so that the senators "might live solitary amid their numbers, secure amid their anxieties" (*Ann.* 14.44). Even the enlightened Seneca, who railed against the mistreatment of slaves, brought along a "cart load" of slaves when venturing into the field to study and write (*Ep.* 87.2). The Roman orator and lawyer Crassus (91 B.C.E.) was deemed to be the second wealthiest citizen of his time (Pliny the Elder, *Nat.* 33.47.135). Among the many

---

13   For the wholesale enslavement of Jews after the fall of Jerusalem in 70 C.E., see E. Mary Smallwood, *The Jews under Roman Rule—from Pompey to Diocletian: A Study in Political Relations* (Leiden: E. J. Brill, 1981), esp. 131; and Gideon Fuks, "Where Have All the Freedmen Gone? On an Anomaly in the Jewish Grave-Inscriptions from Rome," *JJS* 36 (1985): 25–32, esp. 28.

14   On the *canabae* and the prisoners of war who were made slaves, see Richard A. Horsley, "The Slave Systems of Classical Antiquity and Their Reluctant Recognition by Modern Scholars," in "Slavery in Text and Interpretation" (ed. Allen Dwight Callahan, Richard A. Horsley, and Abraham Smith), *Semeia* 83–84 (1998): 19–66, esp. 39; and Harrill, *Manumission of Slaves*, 32–34.

15   Tacitus notes that the measure to execute all the slaves of the household where the murder occurred was passed during the reign of Nero (*Ann.* 13.32).

slaves whom he owned, five hundred were specialists skilled in architecture (Plutarch, *Crass.* 1.4).[16] Plutarch describes the immensity of his wealth:

> And though he owned numberless silver mines, and highly valuable tracts of land with the laborers upon them, nevertheless one might regard all this as nothing compared with the value of his slaves; so many and so capable were the slaves he possessed,—readers, amanuenses, silversmiths, stewards, table-servants; and he himself directed their education, and took part in it himself as a teacher, and, in a word, he thought that the chief duty of the master was to care for his slaves as the living implements of household management. (*Crass.* 1.5–6)

The wealthiest slave owner was the Caesar himself, employing tens of thousands of slaves in public works and agriculture. For example, Augustus purchased twenty thousand slaves and put them to work as oarsmen to help in his campaign against Pompey (Suetonius, *Vit. Caes.* 2.16.1). This was a dangerous practice, however, for, in times of instability, slaves would band together and revolt against their captors (Tacitus, *Ann.* 2.39; Columella, *Rust.* 1.8.18). The most famous of these revolts, led by Spartacus from 73 to 71 B.C.E., may have involved as many as fifty thousand escaped slaves (Plutarch, *Crass.* 8.5–6). Augustus therefore kept his slave army separate from the regular legions and did not arm them to the same extent as his other soldiers (Suetonius, *Vit. Caes.* 2.25.2). About a third of Pompey's army was composed of escaped slaves. After Augustus defeated Pompey, he returned thirty thousand of these slaves to their masters for punishment, considering this to be one of his "benefits" to the people (*Res gest. divi Aug.* 4.25). In times of dearth, when the general populace tended to be

unruly, Augustus would banish the slaves from the precincts of Rome in order to make his task of governing more manageable (Suetonius, *Vit. Caes.* 2.42.3). Such precautions betray the latent fear that the ruling class harbored regarding slaves. Such fears were not unfounded. Despite Augustus's stratagems to mitigate the power of freedmen soldiers, these mutinied soon after his death and rallied entire legions to their cause (Tacitus, *Ann.* 1.31). Tiberius, too, was challenged by slave revolts within Italy, and the general populace was growing increasingly fearful of the great number of slaves at large (Tacitus, *Ann.* 4.27). Also, slaves were eager to indict their rich masters and plunder their wealth in times of political unrest. This was especially true during the civil war occasioned by the brief reigns of Galba, Otho, and Vitellius (68–69 C.E.) (Tacitus, *Hist.* 4.1; *Ann.* 3.36).

On a different front, powerful imperial slaves could prove useful to the emperor in undermining the ambitions of senators and generals. At times the emperor would appoint one of his manumitted slaves to be a governor over an entire region. In this way the consolidated power of an ambitious citizen would be undercut in a single stroke (Suetonius, *Vit. Caes.* 5.24.1–2). For example, Felix, the Roman procurator over Syria and Judea, mentioned in Acts 24:22–27, was the freedman of Claudius (Tacitus, *Hist.* 5.9).

Piecing together accounts such as these, disparate as they are, provides some basis for estimating the number of slaves in the first century.[17] For example, it is estimated that as much as one-third of the population of large cities, such as Rome and Athens, was enslaved. In Italy at the time of Augustus, two to three million persons may have been enslaved out of a total population of seven

---

16   For more on highly skilled slaves and remuneration for their services, see Justinian, *Dig.* 1.7.6.

17   E.g., Varro gives estimates on the number of slaves needed to work a farm, depending upon the size of the estate (*Rust.* 1.18.1–8). Putting together such data yields informed estimates.

million. Empire-wide, perhaps as many as one in six persons were enslaved.[18]

## HISTORICAL OVERVIEW
### Slavery in the Old Testament

The Bible states that slavery has existed from the dawn of civilization. The Scriptures, however, nowhere contain an unqualified endorsement of slavery. Although it was tolerated among God's people, slavery is always portrayed in tragic terms, whether this tragedy is on a personal or a national level. For example, the earliest form of the Hebrew word for "slave" ('ebedh [עֶבֶד]), is found in Gen 9:25: "Cursed be Canaan! The lowest of slaves will he be to his brothers." Here the Lord pronounces judgment upon Canaan for his personal moral failure, and this judgment is expressed in terms of slavery. On a national level, the prophets continually point to Israel's rebellion against Yahweh as the cause of its captivity in Babylon (Isa 1:2–31; Ezra 5:12). In other cases, such as that of Joseph and of all the Jews enslaved in Egypt, enslavement resulted from the sin and oppression of others (Gen 37:28; Exod 1:8–14). In all events, deliverance from bondage is the work of the Lord, symbolizing his will to save from all that oppresses his people (Judg 6:12; Acts 7:10). Slavery in the Scriptures, then, is presented as punishment for moral failure on a personal or on a national level or as the consequence of oppressive indebtedness (Josephus, Ant. 3.282).

The inherent evil of slavery can be seen in the fact that the Jews were prohibited from enslaving fellow Jews. As previously noted, Lev 25:44–46 speaks of Jews taking slaves from the nations but not obtaining slaves from among their Jewish brethren:

> Your male and female slaves are to come from the nations around you; from them you may buy slaves. You may also buy some of the temporary residents living among you and members of their clans born in your country, and they will become your property. You can will them to your children as inherited property and can make them slaves for life, but you must not rule over your fellow Israelites ruthlessly.

Nevertheless, it must be admitted that a limited prohibition of slavery is a far cry from manumission. Even the wisdom of Solomon could not end the bane of slavery in Israel, for he took slaves from the Canaanites and the Babylonians (Isa 14:2; 1 Kgs 9:32).

### Slavery among the Ancient Greeks and Romans

Unlike the qualified but consistently negative appraisal of slavery in the Old Testament, Plato (427–327 B.C.E.) thoroughly rationalized, and to that extent sought to legitimize, slavery. Although chafing at the enslavement of fellow Greeks, Plato took the enslavement of foreigners as a given, an inherent aspect of the ordering of men (cf. Plato, Resp. 5). Aristotle (384–322 B.C.E.) adjusted Plato's view at a strategic point. In broad strokes, he affirmed Plato's rule of intelligence over the irrational and maintained that this is simply a given in society. Yet Aristotle maintained that slavery was "contrary to nature" and in that sense was unjust (Pol. 1.2.3, 8; cf. also Justinian Inst. 1.3.2). With respect to the civil or social order of humankind, however, Aristotle conceded that slavery was simply a factor of power and authority. This hierarchy begins with the fundamental unit of society—the individual household, which is perfectly suited for the employ of slaves (Pol. 1.2.1). Aristotle argued that a household needs tools to have its work done; some tools are lifeless tools, and others are "living tools," that is, slaves (Pol. 1.2.4). So, for Aristotle, the slave is a living tool and thus constitutes

---

18   On the number of slaves in the empire, see Ferguson, *Backgrounds of Early Christianity*, 44–46; and Stambaugh, "Social Relations in the City," 84.

an article of property that belongs to his or her master (*Pol.* 1.2.5–6; 1.3.1). Aristotle also concluded that certain ethnic groups were biologically predisposed to become slaves, and he spoke of "natural slaves," consisting of persons of the least virtue and lacking in skills (*Pol.* 1.1.4.2–3). Possessing reason in a limited degree, slaves differ little from animals, for they cannot know true happiness or follow a purposeful life (*Eth. nic.* 10.6.8). Nature has framed the body of slaves for work and in this way dictates that slavery is both expedient and just (*Pol.* 1.2.15).

With this last point Aristotle has interjected an element of race into his understanding of slavery. As he explains, "Authority and subordination are conditions not only inevitable but also expedient; in some cases things are marked out from the moment of birth to rule or to be ruled" (*Pol.* 1.2.8). Following suit, Cicero, the great Roman orator of the first century, claimed that Jews and Syrians were particularly suited for enslavement (*Prov. cons.* 5.10).

In the end, the abstract philosophizing of Plato and Aristotle endorsed slavery as a necessary contradiction in a less than perfect world and at points interjected the element of race.

### Slaves and Slavery in the First Century

Slavery in the first century world was not monolithic. The Greeks and the Romans differed in their understanding of what it meant to be a slave, the classification of slaves, and the rules for governing them. Instead of clear-cut division between free citizens and a kind of slave caste, there was a continuum between the state of complete freedom and that of total slavery. "Dependent labor" took many forms, from the state of those who could not repay debts to the state of those who functioned as the clients of the rich and powerful. Some slaves were entrusted with great power and were able, even in a slave state, to garner social prestige and

wealth. For example, Pallas, the freedman of Claudius, was counted as one of the wealthiest men in the entire empire (Pliny the Elder, *Nat.* 33.47.135). To some degree, all peasants and surfs were slaves, since they did not own the soil they worked and they forfeited the lion's share of their labor to the landed gentry. The lot of a truly destitute freeborn plebeian was often worse than that of a slave. Such a person was not able to compete with the slaves for manual labor, nor was he or she able to procure skilled jobs that usually went to foreign workers. For all these reasons, it is difficult to arrive at a single definition for slavery in the ancient world.[19]

This ambiguity may be traced back to Aristotle, who often appears contradictory in his discourses on slavery and expresses a considerable degree of dissonance in this regard. For example, he realizes that his "slaves by nature" principle does not square with his premise that prisoners of war are, in effect, slaves of the victors. The inherent contradiction lay in the fact that freeborn Greeks could be taken captive but, according to Aristotle, are not slaves by nature (*Pol.* 1.2.18). Aristotle also realizes that the freeperson and the slave are both essentially human. Political and social factors have made one a slave and the other a free person (*Pol.* 1.2.3). For Aristotle, a slave is a human being, yet in an offense to that humanity, the slave is classed as property that belongs to another. Furthermore, as a human, the slave must possess a modicum of reason and thereby be capable of virtue to some degree. But these qualities do not carry the day for Aristotle, for he maintains that the slave does not possess the deliberative part of the soul (*Pol.* 1.5.3). Still, he cannot deny that the master and the

19   For the various forms of slavery in the Roman Empire, see Allen Dwight Callahan, Richard A. Horsley, and Abraham Smith, "Introduction: The Slavery of New Testament Studies," in "Slavery in Text and Interpretation" (ed. Allen Dwight Callahan, Richard A. Horsley, and Abraham Smith), *Semeia* 83–84 (1998): 1–3; and Horsley, "The Slave Systems of Classical Antiquity," 19–20.

slave are essentially bound by mutual interests and should seek the benefit and enlightenment of each other (*Pol.* 1.2.20). Thinking in another direction, Aristotle claims that the slave is simply part of the master's body and so the relationship between the master and the slave must be tyrannical because the master's interests are always of prime concern (*Eth. nic.* 8.10.4–5). In the end, despite this back-and-forth reasoning about slaves and their nature, Aristotle concludes that there can be no true friendship between master and slave: "Master and slave have nothing in common: a slave is a living tool, just as a tool is an inanimate slave" (*Eth. nic.* 8.11.6).

This dictum, however, was not always followed in the Greco-Roman world. Cicero developed a close bond with his slave-amanuensis, Tiro, and constantly expressed anxiety over Tiro's declining health (Cicero, *Fam.* 16.1–22; Cf. also *Att.* 1.12.4).[20] When Cicero finally freed Tiro, his brother, Quintus Cicero, wrote that "I jumped for joy" upon hearing of Tiro's emancipation (*Fam.* 16.16). Pliny the Younger records that enormous gifts were willed to some slaves out of true love for them and their service (*Ep.* 6.3). For these reasons, some slaves were loyal to their masters, refusing to betray them even when tortured (Tacitus, *Hist.* 1.3). Some took their own lives on the occasion of their master's death, leaping upon the funeral pyre in an expression of unending fidelity (Tacitus, *Ann.* 14.9).

It appears, then, that Aristotle's position that slavery was "contrary to nature" yet a "necessary contradiction in society" vexed the

Romans in their attempt to define and regulate slavery. His statement that "the slave is a living tool and a tool is a lifeless slave" encapsulates the critical issue at stake. For the Romans, the troubling question regarding slavery was whether a slave was a "thing" or a "person."

This intellectual and moral dissonance is reflected in Justinian's *Digesta*, a sixth-century C.E. summary of Roman law.[21] Here a slave is classified as a "thing" (*res*), and thus a slave is an object to be bought and sold (*mancipium*) (*Dig.* 21.1.23). Yet the Digest also defines a slave as a "bodily object" (*res corporales*) (*Dig.* 1.8.1).[22] And Justinian's *Institutiones* (533 C.E.) echoes Aristotle in claiming that slavery is "contrary to the law of nature" and states, "By the law of nature all men were initially born free" (*Inst.* 1.3.2; 1.5; cf. also *Dig.* 1.5.3–4).[23] In light of these ambiguities, the critical question for some Romans was whether a mortal (i.e., a person) who is able to talk intelligibly (i.e. able to reason) can really be just a tool (in other words, a "thing").

For these reasons, the absolute *dominium*, or complete subjugation, of one person's life and will to another was awkward for some Romans, at least on an intellectual level (cf. *Inst.* 1.5.1). In the end, however, sheer pragmatism won out over moral ambiguity in the Roman mind.

---

20   On the value of Tiro to Cicero, the latter writes, "Your services to me are past all reckoning—at home, in the forum, in the City, in my province, in private as in public affairs, in my literary pursuits and performances" (*Fam.* 16.4.3). Cicero also considered Tiro a fellow teacher of his students (*Fam.* 16.10.2). In the interest of Tiro's health, Cicero exhorts, "Put everything else aside; be the slave of your body" (*Fam.* 16.4.4). In another letter, however, he vents his ire toward one of his freedmen, Hilarus, who seems to be exploiting Cicero's name to commit fraud (*Att.* 1.12.2–3).

21   The Byzantine emperor Justinian I (482–565 C.E.) compiled the statutes of Roman law from the time of Augustus to his own day. This work came to be known as the *Digesta Justiniani* (*Digest of Justinian*) (533 C.E.), and together three other legal works, the *Codex constitutionum* (*Code*) (530 C.E.), the *Institutiones* (*Institutes*) (533 C.E.), and the *Novellae constitutiones* (*Novels*), it subsequently came to be known as the *Corpus juris civilis* (*Body of Civil Law*). The most important portion of this collection is the *Digesta*. The *Digesta* is considered by many to be the most important single legal document in Western civilization.

22   On Roman law and slavery, see S. Scott Bartchy, *First Century Slavery and 1 Corinthians 7:21*, 29 (Atlanta: Scholars Press, 1973), 39.

23   These conflicting elements of "mortal object" and "born free" were previously reflected in Varro (116–27 B.C.E.) who asserted that there are three kinds of tools: inarticulate tools (oxen), mute tools (carts), and articulate tools (slaves) (*Rust.* 1.17.1–2).

Regarding all of humanity, the *Institutiones* flatly states, "The main classification in the law of persons is this: all men are either free or slaves" (*Inst.* 1.3). Thus, on a practical level, the Romans endorsed Aristotle's defining the slave as a "living tool." Also, they came to interpret the word *dominium* to mean the full legal power of the master over the slave: "Owners hold the power of life and death over slaves, and owners get whatever slaves acquire" (*Inst.* 1.8).[24] This entails ownership, use of another person for personal profit, and the master's complete discretion in selling the slave, even though the Romans again maintained that this arrangement was "contrary to the law of nature" (*Inst.* 1.3.2). Therefore the Romans' legal provisions allowed for the renting of slaves, the ownership of slaves by several persons, and the compensation of the original owner if a slave was damaged while working for another (cf. Acts 16:16–19).[25]

Regarding a slave as a "thing" is particularly evident in the area of human sexual relationships. Under Roman law, the paring of male and female slaves does not constitute *matrimonium* (marriage) but *contubernium* (the mating of concubines). The children of such arrangements, the so-called *nati* or *facti*, belonged to the slave owner, not to the slave parents (*Inst.* 1.3.4).[26] Columella remarks that an especially prolific slave woman would be rewarded by being exempted from work or even emancipated (*Rust.* 1.8.19).

On the other hand, despite this "living tool" rhetoric, Roman law clearly regarded slaves as human beings. According to the law, the slave occupies the same legal status as a freeborn child. In a Roman home, the freedom of a son and that of a slave are determined by the will of the father. Neither the slave nor the son could own anything without the special dispensation of the father/master (cf. Gal 4:1). The slave is to be cared for in the same manner as a son is cared for, and the deliberate killing of either is deemed to be murder. For example, when Claudius heard that sick and exhausted slaves were abandoned on an island to die, he decreed that all such slaves were free and, if they recovered, were not to be returned to their masters (*Dig.* 40.8.2; Suetonius, *Vit. Caes.* 5.25.1–2; Dio Cassius, *Hist. rom.* 60.29.7a).

The essential humanity of the slave can be seen in the Roman laws governing emancipation. If a slave was freed, he or she could become a Roman citizen. On the other hand, if a Roman citizen committed certain crimes, he or she could be punished by being made a slave (*Inst.* 4.18.2). At times these laws created the awkward situation where some slaves had Roman citizens as parents. That is, the children of a slave would be slaves, but the parent might go on to be freed and attain citizenship. The parent's freedom did not alter the slave status of the children. They remained slaves.

In conclusion, slavery was part and parcel with the Greco-Roman world. Both the Greeks and the Romans suffered considerable philosophical tension over the question of whether a slave was a thing or a person. Yet such dissonance did nothing to affect the practical reality of slavery in society and culture. Slavery was a powerful given that colored all of mortal life and, in the thinking of some, even the afterlife. Epigraphs from ancient

---

24  The consistency of Roman law can be seen in the fact that masters are liable for the crimes that their slaves might commit against others. The master must pay for the damages the slave has incurred, or if the damages exceed the value of the slave, the slave is to be forfeited into the hands of the offended (*Inst.* 4.8.1–3).

25  Cf. Shelton, *As the Romans Did*, 166, for the precise wording of a rental contract from Oxyrhynchus, dating from ca. 186 C.E.

26  If the mother was free, then the children were born free even if the father of the children was a slave. The rationale was that the child should not be held liable for the calamity of the mother (*Inst.* 1.4). Also, if a woman was free at the time of conception but had become a slave by the time of birth, the child was understood to be freeborn (*Dig.* 1.5.5).

tombstones indicate that some believed that the master/slave relationship survived the grave. One such inscription reads, "To you even now under the earth, yes master, I remain as faithful as before."[27]

Regardless of the great range of experiences found among slaves of the first century, the life of a slave under Roman law was, in the main, grim. Often slaves were trained as gladiators to die in the arena (Tacitus, *Ann.* 3.43; Dio Cassius, *Hist. rom.* 60.30.2). The accidental breaking of a crystal cup could lead to the cruelest death (Suetonius, *Vit. Caes.* 2.68.2).[28] Slight infractions could result in a slave being kept in irons in a strong house between his or her work details (Columella, *Rust.* 1.8.18). Even though Seneca lamented the inordinate punishment of slaves, he advocated beating those who had failed the will of their masters (*Ira* 3.32.1–3). A slave had no freedom of movement or of independent residence. He or she was subject to seizure by anyone at anytime. Legal rights were not attached to the slave per se, but to how the Roman master treated the slave before the law. Only the master of the slave or an appointee of the master could represent the concerns of a slave in court (*Dig.* 49.1.15, 18). Personal representation was out of the question. If slaves were required to give testimony in court, they were tortured first to rid them of lies that they would surely tell under oath (Tacitus, *Ann.* 1.23; 3.14). Needless to say, the scales of justice rarely tipped in favor of an aggrieved slave.

## FREEDMEN AND FREEDWOMEN

Despite the many instances of genuine concern for the welfare of slaves and the examples of their loyalty to their masters, the slave of the first century, by and large, lived to be free.[29] Fortunately, the manumission of slaves was common among the Romans, especially in the first century. The manumission of slaves reflected the Greco-Roman virtue of *liberalitas*, "liberality," and thus the freeing of slaves was viewed favorably by many (Dionysius of Halicarnassus, *Ant. rom.* 4.24.6). Although the number is contested, it has been estimated that perhaps up to 90 percent of those who lived in Rome were descendants of slaves.[30]

Although some slave owners released their slaves out of the goodness of their hearts and others granted freedom based upon the personal merits and talents of the slave, many slave owners were motivated to manumit for increased profits (Dionysius of Halicarnassus, *Ant. rom.* 4.24.4–5).[31] The maintenance of slaves was expensive, their labor being more costly than the tools they used (Columella, *Rust.* 1.8.9). So, in many cases, it was financially advantageous to free slaves rather than keep them on as forced labor. During the reign of Augustus, economic hard times led to the manumission of many slaves. Augustus even limited the number of slaves who could be freed, for the state was obligated to supply food

---

27 On epigraphic evidence reflecting slavery in the first century, see Harrill, *Manumission of Slaves*, 22.

28 Seneca records that Vedius Pollio ordered a slave boy thrown into his pond of giant lampreys for breaking a crystal cup in the presence of Caesar Augustus. In response, Augustus ordered that all the crystal cups be broken before Vedius, the pond be filled in, and the boy released unharmed (*Ira* 3.40.1–4).

29 "The goal of any slave's life was manumission, a kind of ultimate participation in social mobility" (Stambaugh, "Social Relations in the City," 86).

30 Philo informs us that many of these captives were Jews. Josephus records that eight thousand Jews in Rome petitioned Augustus so that they might follow their religious customs (*J.W.* 2.80; *Ant.* 17.300). More than five hundred Jewish grave inscriptions found in the catacombs of Rome evidence the high Jewish population of the capital city. On the presence of Jewish freedmen and freedwomen in ancient Rome, see Margaret H. Williams, "The Structure of the Jewish Community in Rome," in *Jews in a Graeco-Roman World* (ed. Martin Goodman; Oxford: Clarendon, 1998), 215–28.

31 The motives for freeing slaves were many and often self-serving. Masters who had broken the law would often free slaves who would otherwise bring incriminating evidence against them (Dionysius of Halicarnassus, *Ant. rom.* 4.24.5). Cf. also Susan Treggiari, *Roman Freedmen during the Late Republic* (Oxford: Clarendon, 1969), 18.

for freedmen and freedwomen (Suetonius, *Vit. Caes.* 2.42.2–3). Even the promise of freedom, however, was leveraged to increase productivity for the master. The slave's possible emancipation in the future was conditioned upon complete obedience and superior productivity in the present. Rarely would a slave be released scot-free, but slave owners would often become the patrons of their freed slaves. The *praenomen* and *nomen gentilicum* of the former owner would be transferred to the freedmen and freedwomen. In this way, the relationship of the freedmen and freedwomen to their former owners was preserved.[32] These new patrons could then attach all kinds of conditions on their newly freed slaves, conditions that kept benefits flowing into their pockets. For example, if the freedman (or freedwoman) died without having children of his own, his entire estate would automatically revert back to his former owner. Even if he did have offspring, the former owner could garner up to one half of all the freedman's possessions and even designate that the wealth be given to one of the patron's own family members (*Inst.* 3.7.1–3; 3.8). Some "patrons" even garnered the meager corn dole from their freedmen and freedwomen (Dionysius of Halicarnassus, *Ant. rom.* 4.24.5). One of the more onerous conditions of manumission was that the offspring of freedmen and freedwomen—that is, those who were born to parents while they were still in the bonds of slavery—still belonged to the masters (*Inst.* 1.4). So, in many cases, freedom for slaves meant more money and benefits for their former masters.

The freeing of slaves in the Roman Empire could be accomplished through various means (*Inst.* 1.5.1–2). Formally, the slave owner could take the initiative and contact a local magistrate for a legal contract. This formal arrangement was required for Roman citizenship. On the other hand, a slave owner could simply write a letter, witnessed by another family member or close friend, declaring the freedom of a slave (*Dig.* 40.2.7, 16–25). This kind of arrangement engendered a quasi-free state in which the former master still exercised much control over the freedman/-woman. Some slaves were able to purchase their own freedom in the following way. Very skilled slaves were a much-sought-after "commodity." Such persons were awarded benefits (the *peculium*) in the form of money or property to secure their services, and in time, often by denying food to themselves, were able to purchase their freedom (Seneca, *Ep.* 80.4–5; cf. also Suetonius, *Vit. Caes.* 8.16.3; *Dig.* 37.15.3; 40.1.4).[33] Another means of freedom was "sacral manumission." The famous oracle of Delphi clearly evidences this practice. Since the slave could not enter into legally binding contracts, the god Apollo served as the legal representative effecting a contract of freedom on behalf of the slave. Proceeds from the sale of the slave would be dedicated to the temple, and the transaction would be duly noted in the public records.[34]

Officially, there were two kinds of freed slaves: those with full enfranchisement and those with what was known as Junian Latin manumission (*Inst.* 1.5.3). The latter case attached caveats that greatly restricted freedom. For example, such freedmen and freedwomen were allowed to enter into commercial contracts but could not marry a Roman citizen or obtain an official Roman will upon his or her death. And if they behaved themselves in an unruly manner, especially with regard to their former masters, their freedom could be

32 Stambaugh, "Social Relations in the City," 86–87. The manumission of Hebrew slaves among the Hebrews did not follow this practice. All relationship between the Hebrew master and slave was dissolved at the point of manumission (Flesher, *Oxen, Women, or Citizens?* 140).

33 Roman law was very detailed in defining the *peculium* and how it was to be regulated. The entirety of book 15 of the *Digest* is devoted to the *peculium*.

34 Ferguson, *Backgrounds of Early Christianity*, 202.

revoked (Tacitus, *Ann.* 13.26–27).[35]

Such addenda almost render the status of freedman and freedwoman into a subcategory of slavery. Freedom was often "purchased" by making legally binding oaths that forced the freedman/-woman to render services to the patron and his or her family.[36] In these cases, freedmen and freedwomen became clients of their former masters, and their fate depended upon the benevolence of their patrons. For example, the freedman/-woman might have to pay a percentage of income to the former owner or pledge to take care of the master in old age (a kind of social-security plan).[37] By way of a *paramonē* contract, all of these conditions would be legally binding, often making the freed slave's life little different from the days of enslavement. For these reasons, there are documented cases of freedmen and freedwomen being financially worse off than when they were slaves. And finally, if the freed person showed ingratitude to his or her former master, the former slave could be punished by Roman law (*Dig.* 37.15.3–4, 9).

Still, the rights of freedmen and freedwomen far exceeded those of slaves. Most important, freed slaves could serve as their own legal representatives before the law. They were also not subject to arbitrary seizure as "property" and could not be made slaves again without due process of law. That is, they would have to commit a crime worthy of slavery to receive that penalty, but this applied to citizens as well (*Inst.* 1.12.1). Freedom of movement and residence was also granted, which meant that they could follow their own vocations in life. Some freedmen and freedwomen became enormously wealthy (Pliny the Elder, *Nat.* 33.47.135). Their path to upward mobility may have been helped by the popularity of celibacy among the Romans and their tendency to have low birth rates.[38] Others were highly educated, especially those from Greece who had been made captives of war. As freed people these slave-scholars played a major role in spreading the Greek culture and arts throughout Rome. Some of these freedmen went on to become powerful Roman statesmen and took their place among the ruling elite. For example, Epictetus (55–135 C.E.), the philosopher-slave, was a member of the imperial household, or *familia Caesaris*, and was certainly more powerful and enjoyed a higher status than most Roman citizens. Pliny the Elder enumerates a list of freedmen who became scientists, grammarians, and statesmen. He laments that their power and wealth exceeded those of many freeborn Romans (*Nat.* 35.58).[39]

Some freedmen and freedwomen became so wealthy as to become the social superiors of senators and equestrians.[40] For example, to the vexation of Agrippina, Nero took in Acte, a freedwoman, as his mistress, and Vespasian all but married the freedwoman Caenis (Tacitus, *Ann.* 13.12–13; Suetonius,

35    On the rights of patrons over their freedmen and freedwomen, see *Dig.* 37.14.1–28. By the time of the *Institutiones*, a third type of manumission, that of "capitulated aliens," had been abolished, for it proved too severe even for the Romans (*Inst.* 1.5.3). The stipulations of the Junian Latin manumissions were done away with as well by this time. All freedmen and freedwomen were awarded full Roman citizenship by the time of the *Institutiones* in 533 C.E.

36    See "The Services of Freedmen" (*Dig.* 38.1.1–51). Here all kinds of benefits continued to flow to the patron from former slaves, such as the promise to give thousands of hours of free labor, or to forward a percentage of the freed slave's total income, or even to leave part of one's estate to one's former master and his or her offspring.

37    For this reason, some freedmen sought to pass themselves off as freeborn. The wealthy freedman Cerylus changed his name to Laches to hide his former identity as a slave and was chided by Vespasian in verse for his ruse (Suetonius, *Vit. Caes.* 8.23.1).

38    Augustus tried to reverse this tendency by penalizing the unmarried and those who opted not to have children (Tacitus, *Ann.* 3.25).

39    Callahan, Horsley, and Smith, however, categorically deny any possibility for slaves to advance socially: "Between the two classes of the Empire, the wealthy *honestiores* and the impoverished *humiliores* lay not a ladder but a chasm" ("Introduction," 5).

40    "A freedman could gain great wealth and imitate the prerogatives of the upper ranks. A slave in the imperial household might enjoy considerable administrative responsibility and hence political power" (Stambaugh, "Social Relations in the City," 75).

*Vit. Caes.* 8.3; Dio Cassius, *Hist. rom.* 61.7.1–3). Augustus held many of his freedmen in high honor, confiding with them concerning matters of state (Suetonius, *Vit. Caes.* 2.67.1). The emperor Claudius appointed three freedmen, Narcissus, Pallas and Callistus, to the top posts of his administration. Through bribes and the selling of offices and citizenship, these freedmen became three of the most powerful and richest men in antiquity (Dio Cassius, *Hist. rom.* 60.17.8). Dio Cassius estimates that Pallas was worth more than four hundred million sesterces in common currency and held great power over kings and cities (*Hist. rom.* 62.14.2–3).[41] Pallas was also the brother of the freedman Antonius Felix who was appointed procurator over Judea and before whom Paul was tried in Acts 24:24–25. Felix garnered additional power by marrying the daughter of Herod Agrippa I. Seneca notes the ironic reversal of Callistus, once he was freed and powerful, turning away his former master from his door, refusing to grant him the morning *sportulae* due a common plebeian (*Ep.* 47).

In many ways, however, manumission did little to alter cultural biases against slaves. Freedmen and freedwomen often were held in contempt by free Romans as crude, ill-mannered, and gaudy.[42] Furthermore, class prejudice was a given for those who never had a chance at freedom. Tacitus lamented that Roman children were being raised by slaves and not by their natural mothers. He saw this as a threat to Roman society (*Dialogus de oratoribus* 28–29). Menander stereotyped slaves as lazy, cowardly, and prone to crime (*Epitr.* 202–211).

Such prejudice was not confined, however, to free Roman citizens. Much class diversity existed even among the slave population, for not all slaves viewed their fellow slaves as equals. Slaves who worked in the mines or built roads were scorned by what might be called white-collar slaves, those who worked as business managers, scribes, educators, and physicians (Columella, *Rust.* 1.8.15).

These last points bring up the interrelationship between race and manumission. Despite Cicero's claim that Jews and Syrians were "born to be slaves" (*Prov. cons.* 5:10), there is some evidence that the Jews could prove troublesome as slaves. Their concerns about ritual purity and strict observance of the Sabbath may have tended to get in the way of many slave tasks. For these reasons, it appears that Jews were frequently freed in Roman antiquity, perhaps more than any other single group. For example, Philo notes that even during the time of Augustus, a large Jewish settlement of freedmen and freedwomen existed in trans-Tiberian Rome (*Embassy*, 155). Acts 6:9 speaks of the "synagogue of the Libertines" in Jerusalem. The Greek word rendered "Libertines" is *Libertinoi* (Λιβερτῖνοι), which is a direct transliteration of the Latin *libertini*, pointing to freed slaves who came out of a Roman context.[43] John Chrysostom lends support here and claims that the attendants of this synagogue were in fact freedmen and freedwomen from Rome (*Homiliae in Acta apostolorum* 15 on Acts 6:9).

Still, these Jewish freedmen and freedwomen did not escape racial prejudice and persecution. For example, Tiberius expelled four thousand Jews of the libertinum genus (i.e., freedmen and freedwomen) from Rome and forced them to battle brigands on the isle of Sardinia. Tacitus notes that if these

---

41 It appears that Pallas had long forgotten his humble beginnings, for he originated a motion, one that was forwarded to the senate by Claudius, that stated that any Roman citizen who married a slave without the owner's knowledge should lose his or her citizenship and be regarded as a slave (Tacitus, *Ann.* 12.53).

42 For continued prejudice against freedmen, see De Vos, "Once a Slave, Always a Slave?" 95. Cf. also Stambaugh, "Social Relations in the City," 84–85.

43 Suetonius instructs that in a technical sense "libertine" does not refer to a freedman or freedwoman per se but to the offspring of those who had been freed, a point of which the emperor Claudius was not cognizant (*Vit. Caes.* 5.24.1–2).

Jewish freedmen perished, it would be a "cheap loss" because the Jews were viewed as superstitious and practitioners of strange rites (*Ann.* 2.85). Because of such atrocities, many Jewish freed slaves sought to hide their previous lives by adopting purely Roman names. Of the hundreds of inscriptions in Jewish catacombs in Rome, not one makes an explicit reference to the deceased as a freedman/-woman.

## SLAVERY IN THE NEW TESTAMENT

At the time of Jesus' birth, the practice of slavery permeated every corner of the Roman Empire. Indeed, the church emerged in a world steeped in the bane of slavery. Furthermore, at no point does the New Testament present a thoroughgoing attack on the institution of slavery. For example, Jesus frequently speaks of slaves and masters without passing any judgment on this social arrangement (Matt 6:24; 18:27–35; 24:45–51; Mark 12:1–11; Luke 7:1–10; 12:42–47; 14:21). One of his most poignant injunctions is that no servant can serve two masters (Luke 16:13).

The Epistles continue in like manner. The sheer number of slaves in the first century guaranteed that many slaves were incorporated into the church. This point is particularly applicable to the church in Corinth. The city appears to have functioned as a clearinghouse for slaves, for a large market near the temple of Apollo served as a place for the buying and selling of slaves. Paul's explicit counsel to slaves in 1 Cor 7:20–24 shows that slaves composed a significant portion of the church in Corinth (cf. also 1 Cor 1:20, 26). It is equally clear from these passages that conversion did not automatically entail manumission from slavery. In the first-century church, becoming a Christian delivered one from the bondage of sin but not from socially endorsed enslavement to other persons.

The influx of slaves into the church undoubtedly created all kinds of tensions for the fledgling movement. Some of these new

Roman slave badge. The Latin inscription is translated: "Seize me if I should try to escape and send me back to my master."

converts may have been sexual concubines, and their newly found faith did not alter the expectations of their masters. Paul's injunctions concerning sexual morality in 1 Cor 5–7 would have brought such tensions into bold relief. So, even though the moral landscape was changing for the church, the curse of slavery was still in place. As a distinctively Christian ethic struggled to emerge from the fog of first-century pluralism, Christian slaves were told to be obedient to their masters, even to those who were difficult to serve (Eph 6:6; Col 3:22; 1 Pet 2:18). Some Christians even owned slaves, as the Epistle to Philemon demonstrates.

All of this sounds alarming to modern ears. We would prefer an unqualified rejection of slavery by Jesus and his first followers. For whatever reasons, such is not forthcoming in the New Testament. Perhaps the fact that the gospel was first and foremost a spiritual revolution and not a social/economic revolution supplies some solace here. The seismic shock of an empire-wide slave revolt in the name of Christ not only would have led to wholesale slaughter at the hands of Roman legionnaires (as every slave revolt had ended) but may have impeded the simple gospel message that each person must be born again.[44] Furthermore, slave resistance to the cruelty of their masters was well known and widespread. It ranged from cold-blooded murder, to feigning illness to avoid work, to constantly pilfering and sabotaging the enterprises of those who oppressed them. While this was understandable in the light of the oppression that slaves suffered, the early church would not have been well served by being associated with this kind of resistance. Peter exhorts Christian slaves to submit to their masters, even if it means suffering unjustly. He argues that such was the experience of Christ, who should serve as every believer's example, whether slave or freedman or freedwoman. Yet Peter contends that there is hope. There will be an eschatological judgment at which God will punish all oppressors (1 Pet 2:18–25).[45]

Nevertheless, it would be a mistake to believe that Jesus and the early church simply endorsed the status quo regarding slavery. The exhortations to obedience and hard work may in fact have had freedom in view. Often high productivity was the surest and quickest way to obtain one's freedom. Also, the New Testament never represents enslavement to another human as being good. Continuing the metaphor of the Old Testament, it represents slavery as something evil. Specifically, the metaphor of slavery represents bondage to sin, death, and the flesh (Rom 8:15, 21; Gal 2:4; 4:3; Heb 2:15; 2 Pet 2:19). The slavery practiced by Babylon is typified as the arch sin in Rev 18:4. The only positive image of slavery found

in the New Testament portrays believers as bound to the Lord or enslaved to one another in Christian service (Luke 4:8; 16:13; Mark 9:35). Moreover, it could be argued that the Christian message transformed the essential nature of the slave/master relationship.[46] The slave is to obey and work as unto God and not as unto men (Eph 6:6–8). In this way, all labor becomes a form of ministry. The gospel makes all human relationships relative to God. The believing slave becomes the Lord's freedman/-woman, and the believing master becomes the Lord's slave (Eph 6:10). Although not an unmitigated emancipation proclamation, 1 Cor 7:21 urges Christian slaves to obtain their freedom if they are able. Similarly, Paul exhorts Philemon that Onesimus will now return "no longer as a slave, but better than a slave, as a dear brother" (Phlm 16).[47] And in Phlm 21 Paul says, "Confident of your obedience, I write to you, knowing that you will *do even more* than I ask" (emphasis added). Even if Paul is not seeking a legally binding manumission of Onesimus, he is certainly seeking a qualitative change in relationship between Philemon and Onesimus. In accordance with the rules of hospitality, Philemon is to receive Onesimus as he would receive the Apostle Paul, that is, as an equal.[48]

---

44   The slave revolt led by Spartacus (73–71 B.C.E.) resulted in the deaths of tens of thousands of escaped slaves. Of those who survived the battle, six thousand were crucified; their flaming crosses lined the Appian Way, leading into the city of Rome (Plutarch, *Crass.* 11.7–8).

45   On the lot of slaves in the early church, see Edgar Krentz, "Order in the 'House' of God: The Haustafel in 1 Peter 2:11–3:12," *Common Life in the Early Church: Essays Honoring Graydon F. Snyder* (ed. Julian V. Hills; Harrisburg, Pa.: Trinity Press International, 1998), 279–86, esp. 282–83.

46   For a brief summary of how Christian apologists used the Scriptures to fight slavery, see Horsley, "The Slave Systems of Classical Antiquity," 23.

47   Under Roman law, those who harbored runaway slaves were subject to severe penalties. Such penalties were waived if the fugitive was returned to his/her owner within twenty days (Justinian, *Dig.* 7.1). For more on Roman law and fugitive slaves see Ernst Levy, *Pauli Sententiae: a Palingenesia of the Opening Titles as a Specimen of Research in West Roman Vulgar Law* (New York: Augustus M. Kelley Publishers, 1969), 110–19.

48   The full intent of Paul's words concerning the possible emancipation of slaves in the church is, however, open to interpretation. For contrasting views, see Harrill, *Manumission of Slaves*, 68; Allen Dwight Callahan, " 'Brother Saul': An Ambivalent Witness to Freedom," in "Slavery in Text and Interpretation" (ed. Allen Dwight Callahan, Richard A. Horsley, and Abraham Smith), *Semeia* 83–84 (1998): 235; De Vos, "Once a Slave, Always a Slave ?" 102–3.

Perhaps the most intriguing passage in the New Testament regarding slavery is found in Gal 3:28. Here Paul proclaims, "There is neither Jew nor Greek, slave nor free, male nor female, for you are all one in Christ Jesus." Some contend that Paul's words are only of soteriological significance and do not address social elements at all.[49] Yet the requirements of the law were the same for the Jew and the Greek as well as for males and females. Since what God requires is the same for all people regardless of race or gender, might not Paul be here speaking to the socially imposed distinctions that are of no consequence to God (Acts 10:34; Rom 2:11)? If such distinctions are of no matter to God, what significance, if any, should they have for the people of God?

Although the precise meaning of Paul's words concerning slavery is open to debate, the liberating message of the gospel appears to have been extremely attractive to slaves of the first century. To be adopted into one family—one that shares the common hope of eternal inheritance—must have been a welcome message to the disenfranchised. To have equal access to God, to partake of the gifts of the Spirit, to be equally indwelt and empowered by the divine regardless of one's social status in the world would have been appealing to the slave community (Rom 5:1–2; 1 Cor 6:19–20; 12:1–28; Heb 4:13).[50]

It thus appears that, to some degree, the seeds of emancipation were sown by the gospel of the first century. Some Christian documents indicate that these seeds may have taken root very early in the experience of the church. For example, Clement and Hermas indicate that some believers sold themselves into slavery to purchase the freedom of others (*1 Clement* 55.2; Shepherd of Hermas, *Similitude* 1:8).[51] And it may be no accident of history that the church is the first legitimate context mentioned by the Institutiones for the emancipation of slaves (*Inst.* 1.5). This section of the *Institutiones* also includes a revision of previous Roman law, a revision that awarded unqualified, full, Roman citizenship to all freedmen and freedwomen regardless of their past or the disposition of their former masters (*Inst.* 1.7; 3.7.4).

---

49 The inherent egalitarian theme of Gal 3:28 was not lost on African American activists (cf. Callahan, " 'Brother Saul,' " 236–39). Ben Witherington III notes that regarding Gal 3:28, meaning is truly in the eye of the beholder. For an overview of the varied interpretations of this passage, see his *Women in the Earliest Churches* (SNTSMS 59; Cambridge: Cambridge University Press, 1988), 77.

50 H. D. Betz, "Spirit, Freedom, and Law: Paul's Message to the Galatian Churches," *Svensk exegetisk årsbok* 39 (1974): 151–52. At the same time, it must not be assumed that the church was devoid of aristocrats. Paul was friends with the "Asiarchs" (Acts 19:31), Publius on Malta (27:7–8), and Dionysius of Athens (17:34). Erastus was the Roman *aedilis*, or magistrate, in Corinth (Rom 16:23). As such he would have been the supervisor of public works and all activities associated with the market place. Cf. David W. Gill, "Acts and the Urban Elites," in *The Book of Acts and Its Graeco-Roman Setting* (ed. David W. Gill and Conrad Gempf; Grand Rapids: Eerdmans, 1994), 106–7. Yet M. Barth comments that salvation is also a "social act" that creates solidarity between those who were once estranged ("The Kerygma of Galatians," *Int* 21 [1967]: 138, 141–42).

51 It also appears that some churches raised money to buy the freedom of slaves who had converted to Christ (cf. Callahan, Horsley, and Smith, *Slavery in Text and Interpretation*, 100–101; and idem, "Introduction," 7).

# Annotated Bibliography

Callahan, Allen Dwight, Richard A. Horsley, and Abraham Smith, eds. "Slavery in Text and Interpretation." *Semeia* 83–84 (1998). This excellent collection of scholarly articles addressing slavery in the New Testament period makes available to the determined student a large amount of information.

Ferguson, Everett. *Backgrounds of Early Christianity*. 2d ed. Grand Rapids: Eerdmans, 1993. This is a good reference work for beginning students who are seeking information on the political, social, and religious backgrounds of the New Testament. It contains good documentation and includes primary sources for further research.

Harrill, J. Albert. *The Manumission of Slaves in Early Christianity*. Tübingen: J. C. B. Mohr, 1995. This revised doctoral thesis addresses slavery in the ancient world from a New Testament perspective, especially within the context of 1 Cor 7. It is valuable for insight into how the early church grappled with the presence of slaves within its midst and into the problem of slavery in general.

Miller, Joseph C. *Slavery and Slaving in World History: A Bibliography, 1900–1991*. Milford, N.Y.: Kraus International, 1993. This comprehensive, multidisciplinary listing of works dedicated to the study of slavery covers nearly the entirety of the twentieth century. More than ten thousand entries are geographically arranged by nation.

Pomeroy, Sarah B. *Goddesses, Whores, Wives, and Slaves: Women in Classical Antiquity*. New York: Schocken, 1975. This early feminist work on the role of women in antiquity traces their role in society through the Hellenistic period and into the early Roman period. Attention is given to the oppression and misrepresentation of women, especially those not of equestrian class, throughout these ages and to the possible causes for the systemic inequality in ancient societies.

Shelton, Jo-Ann. *As the Romans Did: A Sourcebook in Roman Social History*. 2d ed. New York: Oxford University Press, 1998. This is a good source on life in general in the Roman Empire. It is very eclectic in its topics, which include, for example, patron client relationships, Roman domestic life, occupations, slaves, and freed persons. Not presuming an extensive knowledge of Roman history, the book contains many discussions helpful to the beginner. A good subject index and cross-referencing help the reader make connections between the many and varied topics.

Treggiari, Susan. *Roman Freedmen during the Late Republic*. See description at the end of ch. 17.

Witherington, Ben, III. *Women in the Earliest Churches*. Society for New Testament Studies Monograph Series 59. Cambridge: Cambridge University Press, 1988. This balanced, well-researched work provides a good introduction to women in the Greco-Roman Empire, their portrayal, their role in the New Testament, and how women functioned in the church through the third century C.E. It is a handy source for the pursuit of feminist studies and for understanding how this field relates to an understanding of the New Testament.

# 20
# Conclusion

Galatians 4:4-states, "But when the time had fully come, God sent his Son, born of a woman, born under law, to redeem those under law, that we might receive the full rights of sons." The word for "time" in this verse (Gk. *chronos* [χρόνος]), does not refer to a specific time, as in the sense of an hour or a particular day. Rather, Paul is addressing the entire context into which Christ was born. This context was extremely pluralistic regarding nearly every element that defines a culture. For the Jews, the political climate reflected centuries of conflict with the superpowers of the world. The ravages of war had not only altered their geopolitical place in the world but also bore down hard on their national psyche. Indeed, the constant threat of virtual extinction ever loomed large before the Jews, driving them in a multitude of directions that proved to be both constructive and destructive. In the midst of such pressures, the Jews were in no way unified in their bid to preserve their identity. Factions such as the Herodians and the tax collectors sought to capitalize upon the consequences of conquest. Others such as the Sadducees attempted a compromise with Israel's oppressors, hoping to eke out a future, no matter how tenuous that prospect might appear. The Pharisees trusted in a religious program designed to insulate them from the pollution of the Gentiles that threatened to inundate both them and their people.

The Zealots followed the path of unmitigated violence against the Romans and against any Jew who failed to share their radical ideals. And always, lurking somewhere between the prospects of national life and death, was the pernicious encroachment of Hellenization, which incrementally ground away at the foundations of Judaism.

So, all in all, it should be noted that the "time" that Paul spoke of was an extremely fractious one that engendered social, political, and religious anomie. It was a climate that radicalized visions and the methods employed to bring them to pass. It was a world that bred all kinds of dissonance that too frequently degenerated into religious bigotry, racial prejudice, and perhaps, worst of all, the horrid fratricide that accompanies such extreme times. During this "time" the Samaritans grappled to secure their identity somewhere along the ill-defined boundary that separated the Jews from the Gentiles. The *'am ha-'arets*, or "people of the land," gave top priority to securing their daily bread. Many of the poor left the fastidious observance of the Torah to those who had the time and inclination to pursue such matters.

Above it all reigned the civil potentates who carefully groomed their clients. The culture of patronage favored their place in society, and they had been schooled from birth to take full advantage of the system.

Below them, all of the imperial magistrates and military officers competed to negotiate the myriad routes to upward mobility. At the lowest tier were the slaves, whose lives and destinies were at the disposal of their masters. In the interstices between all of these groups dwelt the lawless and the insurgents, the sinners and the profligate, the magicians and the shysters.

In the midst of this "time" God sent his Son, Jesus. He came not as one who was disconnected from the diverse elements that composed his world. Rather, his life and ministry engaged the entire nexus of his day, from the Caesars to the slaves. In this way he served as the lodestone that drew together all of the disparate parts of the first-century world. The Roman authorities, the Jewish religious elite, the common people, societal misfits—in short, all the players on the stage—followed a script that was, in a specialized context, determined by him.

Like a divine spotlight, Jesus accentuated the faint and strained interconnections of the different factions of the time and cast them in bold relief. In so doing, he at once became the victim and the victor of all of the competing sectors and thereby launched a spiritual awakening that birthed the church of the first century. These first believers did not opt to become religious recluses but sought to actualize the "great commission" (Matt 28:18–20; Acts 1:8) by entering the web of relationships that made up the "time" that Paul spoke of in Gal 4:4.

For all of these reasons, every serious student of the word will make every effort to reenter the world of the New Testament. He or she will thereby come to understand the intricate connections of the varied groups that made up that "time" and so be better able to convey that ancient vision to their present generation.

# Annotated Bibliography
## of Primary Documents

*The Ante-Nicene Fathers*. Edited by Alexander Roberts and James Donaldson. 10 vols. Peabody, Mass.: Hendrickson, 1994. This standard presentation of the early church fathers contains an adequate introduction and little commentary.

Arnim, H. von. *Stoicorum veterum fragmenta*. 4 vols. in 2. New York: Irvington, 1986. This is an English translation of von Arnim's four-volume collection (1903–1924) of Stoic teachings by ancient philosophers and early Christian apologists. Although it is helpful for grasping the range of Stoic expression throughout the ages, a lack of organizational structure makes it difficult to extract specific information from this work.

Betz, H. D. *The Greek Magical Papyri in Translation, Including the Demotic Spells*. 2d ed. Chicago: University of Chicago Press, 1996–. Betz provides a modern translation of this important cache of papyri containing magical spells and incantations employed during the Second Temple period. A good introduction orients the beginner to the material, and a thorough topical index helps one navigate through the hundreds of magical formulas presented.

Bowman, John, ed. and trans. *Samaritan Documents Relating to Their History, Religion, and Life*. Pittsburgh: Pickwick, 1977. This is one of the few sources to collate the primary documents of the Samaritans. The Samaritan version of the Bible, their chroniclers, and Samaritan commentaries on sacred Scripture are included as well as explanatory notes by the editor that help contextualize the materials.

Chrysostom, John. *The Homilies on the Acts of the Apostles*. 2 vols. Oxford: John Henry Parker, 1851. This simple, straightforward presentation of Chrysostom's commentary on the Book of Acts grants insight into the ecclesiastical and doctrinal concerns of the fourth-century church.

*1–2 Clement*. In vol. 1 of *The Apostolic Fathers*. Edited by T. E. Page et al. Translated by Kirsopp Lake. 2 vols. Loeb Classical Library. Cambridge: Harvard University Press, 1912–1913. Repr., 1976–1985. This is a clear translation of Clement's epistles from the original Greek with brief explanatory notes and references to the Bible.

Eusebius. *Ecclesiastical History*. Edited by G. P. Goold. Translated by Kirsopp Lake and J. E. L. Oulton. 2 vols. Loeb Classical Library. Cambridge: Harvard University Press, 1994. Written by Eusebius, the leading historian and theologian of the fourth century, the *Ecclesiastical History* is the first great history of the church and is essential reading for gaining insight into the belief and practice of the apostolic and early postapostolic church

and the role that the early church councils played in the formation of doctrine. The great persecutions against the church are also a focus of Eusebius's work.

Fath, Abu'l. *Kitab al-Tarikh*. Translated by Paul Stenhouse. Sydney, Australia: Mandelbaum Trust, University of Sydney, 1985. A large portion of this work by one of the major chroniclers of Samaritan history is a polemic against Jewish versions of Samaritan origins and belief, granting the reader good insight into a Samaritan perspective on important issues related to the people and their history.

García Martínez, Florentino, and Eibert J. C. Tigchelaar, eds. *The Dead Sea Scrolls Study Edition*. Grand Rapids: Eerdmans, 1998. In this very handy and clearly presented presentation of the literature of Qumran, the structured organization and index help the reader find texts of interest amidst the hundreds of fragments contained in the work.

Iamblichus. *On the Pythagorean Way of Life: Text, Translation, and Notes*. Translated by John Dillon and Jackson Hershbell. Atlanta: Scholars Press, 1991. Iamblichus is one of the few sources from antiquity reflecting something of the life and beliefs of Pythagoras. This third-century work is not a biography of Pythagoras but a reflection on the influence of the philosopher-magician in producing a good life compatible with the cosmos and the gods.

Ignatius. *Epistle to the Ephesians*. In vol. 1 of *The Apostolic Fathers*. Edited by T. E. Page et al. Translated by Kirsopp Lake. 2 vols. Loeb Classical Library. Cambridge: Harvard University Press, 1912–1913. Repr., 1976–1985.

Irenaeus. *Against the Heresies*. Translated by Dominic J. Unger. New York: Paulist, 1992–. This is a clear, straightforward translation of an important work by this mid-second-century saint, who provides information on the church's battle with syncretism.

Justinian. *The Digest*. Translated and edited by Alan Watson. 2 vols. Philadelphia: University of Pennsylvania Press, 1985. This is a translation from the Latin *Digesta Justiniani*, a voluminous work containing the primary Roman legal statutes dating from the time of Augustus until the time of Justinian in the sixth century C.E. A glossary helps to explain many of the Latin legal terms found in the work. The *Digest* is an indispensable tool for understanding the civil law of the Roman Empire.

———. *Institutes*. Translated by Peter Birks and Grant McLeod. Ithaca, N.Y.: Cornell University Press, 1987. This is a translation of and introduction to Emperor Justinian's summation of Roman law (533 C.E.). Some scholars consider this condensed work, originally intended as a brief manual for students of the sixth century C.E., one of the most influential documents for the development of the Western system of jurisprudence. Explanatory notes and an index help the student take advantage of this important work.

Josephus, Flavius. *The Works*. Translated by William Whiston. Grand Rapids: Baker, 1974. This is a standard translation of this important first-century work by a leading Jewish leader of the time. A thorough outline, an index, and consistent enumeration of paragraphs make this work a good resource for gaining insight into the history and thought of the Jewish people as these unfolded down to the first century C.E.

Macrobius. *The Saturnalia*. Translated and edited by Percival Vaughn Davies. New York: Columbia University Press, 1969. This late-fourth-or early-fifth-century C.E. work presents a dialogue between the greats of the past (Augustus, Cicero, etc.) on a collage of topics ranging from philosophy to power politics in imperial Rome. The material is presented anecdotally but contains a great number of historical references, some to personages of the Bible, in an interesting and often amusing format.

Marqah. *Memar Marqah: The Teaching of Marqah*. Edited and translated by John MacDonald. 2 vols. in 1. Berlin: Töpelmann, 1963. MacDonald provides one of the few English translations of the great Samaritan chronicler Marqah (fifth century C.E.), recording the main points of Samaritan history and belief.

Neusner, Jacob. *The Mishnah: A New Translation*. New Haven: Yale University Press, 1988. This is a very helpful collection and translation of these early rabbinic writings by an eminent Jewish scholar. The six divisions of the Mishnah and their subcategories, followed by an explanatory introduction and a topical index at the end of the book, aid the student in navigating the often bewildering array of religious teachings found in the Mishnah.

Origen. *Contra Celsum*. Translated by Henry Chadwick. Cambridge: Cambridge University Press, 1953. Origen in this work conducts a sustained attack on Celsus, who lampooned the person and life of Jesus by portraying him as a magician, trained in Egypt, who duped his people after he returned to Israel.

Philo. *The Works: Complete and Unabridged*. Translated by C. D. Yonge. Peabody, Mass.: Hendrickson, 2004. This is a very handy one-volume presentation of Philo's works. The complete outline, the numbering of chapters and lines, and the index at the end help the student find his or her way in this important Jewish work of the first century.

Schneemelcher, Wilhelm, ed. *New Testament Apocrypha*. Translated by R. McL. Wilson. 2 vols. Louisville: John Knox, 1991–1992. This is a modern translation of the pseudepigrapha, which reflect the creativity of the early Christian centuries and display the challenges the church faced from Gnosticism and the formulation of the church's cardinal doctrines.

*Sepher ha-razim: The Book of the Mysteries*. Translated by Michael A. Morgan. Chico, Calif.: Scholars Press, 1983. Jewish magical formulas, sectarian in nature and dating from the early fourth or late third centuries C.E., show the syncretism and diverse expression found in the rabbinic period.

Skehan, Patrick W., trans. and ed., and Alexander A. Di Lella, ed. *The Wisdom of Ben Sira: A New Translation with Notes*. New York: Doubleday, 1987. This is a clear presentation of the second-century B.C.E. Jewish work, also known as Ben Sira, Sirach, or simply Ecclesiasticus, a collection of ethical teachings arranged in the manner of proverbs and intended to direct one in living wisely regarding oneself, God, and neighbor. It grants insight into the religious mind-set of pious Jews just before the Maccabean period.

## Loeb Classical Library Works

The Loeb Classical Library is a monumental collection of English translations of the major Greek and Latin works spanning fourteen hundred years. It comprises nearly a century of scholarly work, presently consists of more than 250 volumes, and is still a work in progress, with new translations in the offing. The original Greek or Latin text appears on the left page, and the English rendering is on the right. Explanatory notes are few, but occasional cross-references help tie in other relevant portions of the corpus. The works are usually divided into books, chapters, and lines, yet this system is not uniformly followed throughout the entire collection. Brief introductions and glossaries in some volumes help bring the first-time reader up to speed, but limited indexes require that the student read widely to glean pertinent information. Yet the Loeb Classical Library is an indispensable reservoir of primary documents for the serious researcher of the Greek and Latin masters.

*The Apostolic Fathers*. Edited by T. E. Page et al. Translated by Kirsopp Lake. 2 vols. Loeb Classical Library. Cambridge: Harvard University Press, 1912–1913. Repr., 1976–1985.

Apuleius. *Metamorphoses (The Golden Ass)*. Edited by T. E. Page. Translated by W. Adlington. 2 vols. Loeb Classical Library. Cambridge: Harvard University Press, 1965.

Aristophanes. *Acharnians; Knights*. Translated and edited by Jeffery Henderson. Loeb Classical Library. Cambridge: Harvard University Press, 1998.

———. *Clouds; Wasps; Peace*. Edited and translated by Jeffery Henderson. Loeb Classical Library. Cambridge: Harvard University Press, 1998.

———. *The Peace; The Birds; The Frogs*. Edited by G. P. Goold. Translated by B. B. Rogers. Loeb Classical Library. Cambridge: Harvard University Press, 1996.

Aristotle. *Nicomachean Ethics*. Edited by G . P. Goold. Translated by H. Rackham. Loeb Classical Library. Cambridge: Harvard University Press, 1994.

———. *The Physics*. Translated by P. H. Wicksteed and F. M. Cornford. 2 vols. Loeb Classical Library. Cambridge: Harvard University Press, 1993–1995.

———. *Politics*. Edited by G. P. Goold. Translated by H. Rackham. Loeb Classical Library. Cambridge: Harvard University Press, 1998.

Arrian. *Anabasis of Alexander*. Translated by P. A. Brunt. 2 vols. Loeb Classical Library. Cambridge: Harvard University Press, 1976–1983.

Augustus. *Res gestae*. Edited by G. P. Goold. Translated by F. W. Shipley. Loeb Classical Library. Cambridge: Harvard University Press, 1998.

Cato. *On Agriculture*. Varro. *On Agriculture*. Edited by G. P. Goold. Translated by W. D. Hooper and H. B. Ash.

Loeb Classical Library. Cambridge: Harvard University Press, 1999.

Cicero. *Letters to Atticus*. Translated and edited by D. R. Shackleton Bailey. 3 vols. Loeb Classical Library. Cambridge: Harvard University Press, 1999.

———. *The Letters to His Friends (Epistolae ad familiares)*. Translated by W. Glynn Williams. 3 vols. Loeb Classical Library. Cambridge: Harvard University Press, 1965.

———. *On Duties (De officiis)*. Edited by G. P. Goold. Translated by Walter Miller. Loeb Classical Library. Cambridge: Harvard University Press, 1997.

———. *On Ends (De finibus)*. Edited by G. P. Goold. Translated by H. Rackham. Loeb Classical Library. Cambridge: Harvard University Press, 1999.

———. *Orations: In Catilinam I-IV, Pro Murena, Pro Sulla, Pro Flacco*. Edited by G. P. Goold. Translated by C. MacDonald. Loeb Classical Library. Cambridge: Harvard University Press, 1996.

———. *Orations: Pro Caelio, De provinciis consularibus, Pro Balbo*. Edited by G. P. Goold. Translated by R. Gardner. Loeb Classical Library. Cambridge: Harvard University Press, 1999.

Clement of Alexandria. *The Exhortation to the Greeks, The Rich Man's Salvation, To the Newly Baptized (Fragment)*. Edited by G. P. Goold. Translated by G. W. Butterworth. Loeb Classical Library. Cambridge: Harvard University Press, 1979.

Columella. *On Agriculture*. Edited by G. P. Goold. Edited and translated by Harrison Boyd Ash. 3 vols. Loeb Classical Library. Cambridge: Harvard University Press, 1993.

*Demosthenes*. 7 vols. Vols. 4–6. Edited by G. P. Goold. Translated by A. T. Murray. Loeb Classical Library. Cambridge: Harvard University Press, 1998.

*Didache*. In vol. 1 of *The Apostolic Fathers*. Edited by T. E. Page et al. Translated by Kirsopp Lake. 2 vols. Loeb Classical Library. Cambridge: Harvard University Press, 1912–1913. Repr., 1976–1985.

Dio Cassius. *Roman History*. Edited by Jeffrey Henderson. Translated by Earnest Cary. 9 vols. Loeb Classical Library. Cambridge: Harvard University Press, 2000. (Volume 7 is printed as if it began with book 61, but it in fact begins with 60.29.1. So the book and chapter headings of vol. 7 are incorrect until p. 82 of the text.)

Diogenes Laertius. *Lives of Eminent Philosophers*. Edited by T. E. Page. Translated by R. D. Hicks. 2 vols. Loeb Classical Library. Cambridge: Harvard University Press, 1965.

Dionysius of Halicarnassus. *Roman Antiquities*. Edited by G. P. Goold. Translated by Earnest Cary. 7 vols. Loeb Classical Library. Cambridge: Harvard University Press, 1993.

Eusebius. *Ecclesiastical History*. Edited by G. P. Goold. Translated by Kirsopp Lake and J. E. L. Oulton. 2 vols. Loeb Classical Library. Cambridge: Harvard University Press, 1994.

Herodotus. *Histories*. Translated by A. D. Godley. 4 vols. Loeb Classical Library. Cambridge: Harvard University Press, 1961–1966.

———. *The Persian Wars*. Edited by T. E. Page. Translated by A. D. Godley. 4 vols. Loeb Classical Library. Cambridge: Harvard University Press, 1961–1966.

Ignatius. *Epistle to the Ephesians*. In vol. 1 of *The Apostolic Fathers*. Edited by T. E. Page et al. Translated

by Kirsopp Lake. 2 vols. Loeb Classical Library. Cambridge: Harvard University Press, 1912–1913. Repr., 1976–1985.

Lucretius. *De rerum natura*. Edited by T. E. Page. Translated by W. H. D. Rouse. Loeb Classical Library. Cambridge: Harvard University Press, 1966.

Macrobius. *The Saturnalia*. Translated and edited by Percival Vaughn Davies. New York: Columbia University Press, 1969.

Menander. *Aspis, Georgos, Dis Exapaton, Dyskolos, Encheiridion, Eptrepontes*. Edited and translated by W. G. Arnott. Loeb Classical Library. Cambridge: Harvard University Press, 1997.

Plato. *The Republic*. Edited by G. P. Goold. Translated by Paul Shorey. 2 vols. Loeb Classical Library. Cambridge: Harvard University Press, 1994.

Pliny the Elder. *Natural History*. Edited by G. P. Goold. Translated by H. Rackham. 10 vols. Loeb Classical Library. Cambridge: Harvard University Press, 2000.

Pliny the Younger. *The Letters*. Edited by E. H. Warmington. Translated by Betty Radice. 2 vols. Loeb Classical Library. Cambridge: Harvard University Press, 1969.

Plutarch. *Lives*. Edited by G. P. Goold. Translated by Bernadotte Perrin. 11 vols. Loeb Classical Library. Cambridge: Harvard University Press, 1999.

Polybius. *The Histories*. Edited by G. P. Goold. Translated by W. R. Paton. 6 vols. Loeb Classical Library. Cambridge: Harvard University Press, 1995.

Quintilian. *Institutio oratoria*. Edited by G. P. Goold. Translated by H. E. Butler. 5 vols. Loeb Classical Library. Cambridge: Harvard University Press, 1995.

Seneca. *Ad Lucillum epistulae morales*. Edited by G. P. Goold. Translated by Richard M. Gummere. 3 vols. Loeb Classical Library. Cambridge: Harvard University Press, 1989.

———. *Epistles*. Edited by G. P. Goold. Translated by Richard M. Gummere. 3 vols. Loeb Classical Library. Cambridge: Harvard University Press, 1996.

———. *Moral Essays*. Edited by G. P. Goold. Translated by John W. Basore. 3 vols. Loeb Classical Library. Cambridge: Harvard University Press, 1996.

———. *Naturales quaestiones*. Edited by E. H. Warmington. Translated by Thomas H. Corcoran. Loeb Classical Library. Cambridge: Harvard University Press, 1972.

Strabo. *The Geography*. Edited by T. E. Page. Translated by Horace Leonard Jones. 8 vols. Loeb Classical Library. Cambridge: Harvard University Press, 1966.

Suetonius. *The Lives of the Caesars*. Edited by E. H. Warmington. Translated by J. C. Rolfe. 2 vols. Loeb Classical Library. Cambridge: Harvard University Press, 1970.

Tacitus. *Agricola*. Translated by M. Hutton. Revised by R. M. Ogilvie. *Germania*. Translated by M. Hutton. Revised by E. H. Warmington. *Dialogus*. Translated by W. Peterson. Revised by M. Winterbottom. Rev. ed. Loeb Classical Library. Cambridge: Harvard University Press, 1970.

———. *Histories*. Translated by Clifford H. Moore. *Annals*. Translated by John Jackson. 3 vols. Loeb Classical Library. Cambridge: Harvard University Press, 1969.

Xenophon. *Memorabilia and Oeconomicus; Symposium and Apologia*. Translated by E. C. Marchant and O. J. Todd. Loeb Classical Library. Cambridge: Harvard University Press, 1965.

# General Bibliography

Abraham, Israel. *Studies in Pharisaism and the Gospels.* New York: KTAV, 1967.

Ackroyd, Peter R. *Exile and Restoration: A Study of Hebrew Thought of the Sixth Century B.C.* Philadelphia: Westminster, 1968.

———. *Israel under Babylon and Persia.* Oxford: Oxford University Press, 1970.

Agourides, Savas. "The Birth of Jesus and the Herodian Dynasty: An Understanding of Matthew, Chapter 2." *Greek Orthodox Theological Review* 37 (2001): 135–46.

Aland, Barbara, et al. *The Greek New Testament.* 4th ed. Stuttgart: Deutsche Bibelgesellschaft, 2001.

Anderson, Robert T., and Terry Giles, *The Keepers: An Introduction to the History and Culture of the Samaritans.* Peabody, Mass.: Hendrickson, 2002.

Annas, Julia E. *Hellenistic Philosophy of Mind.* Berkeley: University of California Press, 1992.

*The Ante-Nicene Fathers.* Edited by Alexander Roberts and James Donaldson. 10 vols. Grand Rapids: Eerdmans, 1969–1973.

*The Apostolic Fathers.* Edited by T. E. Page et al. Translated by Kirsopp Lake. 2 vols. Loeb Classical Library. Cambridge: Harvard University Press, 1912–1913. Repr., 1976–1985.

Applebaum, S. "Economic Life in Palestine." Pages 631–700 in vol. 2 of *The Jewish People in the First Century: Historical Geography, Political History, Social, Cultural, and Religious Life and Institutions.* Edited by S. Safrai and M. Stern. 2 vols. Compendia rerum iudaicarum ad Novum Testamentum, sec. 1. Philadelphia: Fortress, 1974–1976.

Apuleius. *Metamorphoses (The Golden Ass).* Edited by T. E. Page. Translated by W. Adlington. 2 vols. Loeb Classical Library. Cambridge: Harvard University Press, 1965.

Aristophanes. *Acharnians; Knights.* Translated and edited by Jeffery Henderson. Loeb Classical Library. Cambridge: Harvard University Press, 1998.

———. *Clouds; Wasps; Peace.* Edited and translated by Jeffery Henderson. Loeb Classical Library. Cambridge: Harvard University Press, 1998.

———. *The Peace; The Birds; The Frogs.* Edited by G. P. Goold. Translated by B. B. Rogers. Loeb Classical Library. Cambridge: Harvard University Press, 1996.

Aristotle. *Nicomachean Ethics.* Edited by G . P. Goold. Translated by H. Rackham. Loeb Classical Library. Cambridge: Harvard University Press, 1994.

———. *The Physics.* Translated by P. H. Wicksteed and F. M. Cornford. 2 vols. Loeb Classical Library. Cambridge: Harvard University Press, 1993–1995.

———. *Politics.* Edited by G. P. Goold. Translated by H. Rackham. Loeb Classical Library. Cambridge: Harvard University Press, 1998.

Arnim, J. von. *Stoicorum veterum fragmenta.* 4 vols. in 2. New York: Irvington, 1986.

Arnold, Clinton E. *Ephesians, Power, and Magic: The Concept of Power in Ephesians in the Light of Its Historical Setting.* Society for New Testament Studies Monograph Series 63. Cambridge: Cambridge University Press, 1989.

Arrian. *Anabasis of Alexander.* Translated by P. A. Brunt. 2 vols. Loeb Classical Library. Cambridge: Harvard University Press, 1976–1983.

Augustus. *Res gestae.* Edited by G. P. Goold. Translated by F. W. Shipley. Loeb Classical Library. Cambridge: Harvard University Press, 1998.

Aune, David E. "Magic in Early Christianity." *Aufstieg und Niedergang der römischen Welt: Geschichte und Kultur Roms im Spiegel der neueren Forschung.* 23.2:1507–57. Part 2, Principat 23.2. Edited by H. Temporini and W. Haase. New York: de Gruyter, 1980.

Baldwin, Barry. *The Roman Emperors.* Montreal: Harvest House, 1980.

Ball, David T. "What Jesus Really Meant by 'Render unto Caesar.' " *Bible Review* 19 (2003): 14–17.

Bammel, Ernst. "The Poor and the Zealots." Pages 109–28 in *Jesus and the Politics of His Day.* Edited by Ernst Bammel and C. F. D. Moule. Cambridge: Cambridge University Press, 1984.

Bammel, Ernst, and C. F. D. Moule, eds. *Jesus and the Politics of His Day.* Cambridge: Cambridge University Press, 1984.

Bar-Ilan, Meir. "Witches in the Bible and in the Talmud." Pages 7–32 in vol. 5 of *Approaches to Ancient Judaism: New Series.* Edited by Herbert W. Basser and Simcha Fishbane. Atlanta: Scholars Press, 1990–.

Bar-Kochva, Bezalel. *Judas Maccabaeus: The Jewish Struggle against the Seleucids.* Cambridge: Cambridge University Press, 1989.

Bartchy, S. Scott. *First Century Slavery and 1 Corinthians 7:21, 29.* Atlanta: Scholars Press, 1973.

Barth, M. "The Kerygma of Galatians." *Interpretation* 21 (1967): 131–46.

Batten, Alicia. "God in the Letter of James: Patron or Benefactor?" *New Testament Studies* 50 (2004): 257–72.

Baumgarten, Albert. *The Flourishing of Jewish Sects in the Maccabean Era: An Interpretation.* New York: E. J. Brill, 1997.

———. "The Pharisaic-Sadducean Controversies about Purity and the Qumran Tests." *Journal of Jewish Studies* 31 (1980): 157–70.

Beckwith, Roger T. "The Pre-history and Relationships of the Pharisees, Sadducees, and Essenes: A Tentative Reconstruction." *Revue de Qumran* 11 (1982): 3–46.

Bennett, W. J., Jr. "The Herodians of Mark's Gospel." *Novum Testamentum* 17 (1975): 9–14.

Betz, H. D. *The Greek Magical Papyri in Translation, Including the Demotic Spells.* 2d ed. Chicago: University of Chicago Press, 1996–.

———. "Spirit, Freedom, and Law: Paul's Message to the Galatian Churches." *Svensk exegetisk årsbok* 39 (1974): 145–60.

Betz, Otto. "Was John the Baptist an Essene?" *Bible Review* 6 (1990): 18–25.

Bolt, Peter G. "What Were the Sadducees Reading? An Enquiry into the Literary Background of Mark 12:18–23." *Tyndale Bulletin* 45 (1994): 369–94.

Borg, Marcus. *Conflict, Holiness, and Politics in the Teachings of Jesus.* New York: Edwin Mellen, 1984.

Bowman, John, ed. and trans. *Samaritan Documents Relating to Their History, Religion, and Life.* Pittsburgh: Pickwick, 1977.

Brandon, S. G. F. *Jesus and the Zealots: A Study of the Political Factor in Primitive Christianity.* New York: Charles Scribner's Sons, 1967.

Braund, D. "Four Notes on the Herods." *Classical Quarterly* NS 33/1 (1983): 239–42.

Breeze, David J., and Brian Dobson. *Roman Officers and Frontiers.* Stuttgart: Franz Steiner, 1993.

Bright, John. *A History of Israel.* 3d ed. Philadelphia: Westminster, 1981.

Bronner, Leah. *Sects and Separatism during the Second Jewish Commonwealth.* New York: Boch, 1967.

Broshi, Magen, and Esther Eshel. "The Greek King Is Antiochus IV (4QHistorical Text=4Q248)." *Journal of Jewish Studies* 48 (1997): 120–29.

Brownlee, William H. "John the Baptist in the New Light of Ancient Scrolls." Pages 33–53 in *Scrolls and the New Testament.* Edited by Krister Stendall and James H. Charlesworth. New York: Crossroad, 1992.

Bruce, F. F. *The Book of Acts.* Grand Rapids: Eerdmans, 1988.

———. *The Epistle to the Galatians: A Commentary on the Greek Text.* New International Greek Testament Commentary. Grand Rapids: Eerdmans, 1982.

———. *New Testament History.* Garden City, N.Y.: Doubleday, 1971.

———. *Paul and Jesus.* Grand Rapids: Baker, 1974.

———. "Render to Caesar." Pages 249–63 in *Jesus and the Politics of His Day.* Edited by Ernst Bammel and C. F. D. Moule. Cambridge: Cambridge University Press, 1984.

Callahan, Allen Dwight. " 'Brother Saul': An Ambivalent Witness to Freedom." In *"Slavery in Text and Interpretation."* Edited by Allen Dwight Callahan, Richard A. Horsley, and Abraham Smith. *Semeia* 83–84 (1998): 235–50.

Callahan, Allen Dwight, Richard A. Horsley, and Abraham Smith. "Introduction: The Slavery of New Testament Studies." In *"Slavery in Text and Interpretation."*

Edited by Allen Dwight Callahan, Richard A. Horsley, and Abraham Smith. *Semeia* 83–84 (1998): 1–15.

Campbell, Brian. *The Roman Army, 31 BC–AD 337: A Sourcebook.* London: Routledge, 1994.

Capper, Brian. "Reciprocity and the Ethic of Acts." Pages 499–518 in *Witness to the Gospel: The Theology of Acts.* Edited by I. Howard Marshall and David Peterson. Grand Rapids: Eerdmans, 1998.

Cato. *On Agriculture.* Varro. *On Agriculture.* Edited by G. P. Goold. Translated by W. D. Hooper and H. B. Ash. Loeb Classical Library. Cambridge: Harvard University Press, 1999.

Chilton, B. D. *Judaic Approaches to the Gospels.* Atlanta: Scholars Press, 1994.

Chrysostom, John. *The Homilies on the Acts of the Apostles.* 2 vols. Oxford: John Henry Parker, 1851.

Chow, John K. *Patronage and Power: A Study of Social Networks in Corinth.* Journal for the Study of the New Testament: Supplement Series 75. Sheffield, Eng.: Sheffield Academic Press, 1992.

———. "Patronage in Roman Corinth." Pages 104–125 in *Paul and Empire: Religion and Power in Roman Imperial Society.* Edited by Richard A. Horsley. Harrisburg, Pa.: Trinity Press International, 1997.

Cicero. *Letters to Atticus.* Translated and edited by D. R. Shackleton Bailey. 3 vols. Loeb Classical Library. Cambridge: Harvard University Press, 1999.

———. *The Letters to His Friends (Epistolae ad familiares).* Translated by W. Glynn Williams. 3 vols. Loeb Classical Library. Cambridge: Harvard University Press, 1965.

———. *On Duties (De officiis).* Edited by G. P. Goold. Translated by Walter Miller. Loeb Classical Library. Cambridge: Harvard University Press, 1997.

———. *On Ends (De finibus).* Edited by G. P. Goold. Translated by H. Rackham. Loeb Classical Library. Cambridge: Harvard University Press, 1999.

———. *Orations: In Catilinam I–IV, Pro Murena, Pro Sulla, Pro Flacco.* Edited by G. P. Goold. Translated by C. MacDonald. Loeb Classical Library. Cambridge: Harvard University Press, 1996.

———. *Orations: Pro Caelio, De provinciis consularibus, Pro Balbo.* Edited by G. P. Goold. Translated by R. Gardner. Loeb Classical Library. Cambridge: Harvard University Press, 1999.

Ciraolo, Leda, and Jonathan Seidel. *Magic and Divination in the Ancient World.* Leiden: E. J. Brill, 2002.

Clark, Gordon H. *Selections from Hellenistic Philosophy.* New York: F. S. Crofts, 1940.

*1–2 Clement.* In vol. 1 of *The Apostolic Fathers.* Edited by T. E. Page et al. Translated by Kirsopp Lake. 2 vols. Loeb Classical Library. Cambridge: Harvard University Press, 1912–1913. Repr., 1976–1985.

Clement of Alexandria. *The Exhortation to the Greeks, The Rich Man's Salvation, To the Newly Baptized (Fragment).* Edited by G. P. Goold. Translated by G. W. Butterworth. Loeb Classical Library. Cambridge: Harvard University Press, 1979.

Coggins, R. J. "Jewish Local Patriotism: The Samaritan Problem." Pages 66–78 in *Jewish Local Patriotism and Self-Identification in the Graeco-Roman Period.* Edited by Siân Jones and Sarah Pearce. Sheffield, Eng.: Sheffield Academic Press, 1998.

———. *Samaritans and Jews: The Origins of Samaritanism Reconsidered*. Atlanta: John Knox, 1975.

Cohen, Shaye J. D. *The Beginnings of Jewishness: Boundaries, Varieties, Uncertainties*. Berkeley: University of California Press, 1999.

———. *From the Maccabees to the Mishnah*. Philadelphia: Westminster, 1987.

Cohn-Sherbok, D. M. "Jesus' Defense of the Resurrection of the Dead." *Journal for the Study of the New Testament* 11 (1981): 64–73.

Colwell, E. C. "A Definite Rule for the Use of the Article in the Greek New Testament." *Journal of Biblical Literature* 52 (1933): 12–21.

Columella. *On Agriculture*. Edited by G. P. Goold. Edited and translated by Harrison Boyd Ash. 3 vols. Loeb Classical Library. Cambridge: Harvard University Press, 1993.

Conzelmann, Hans. *Acts of the Apostles*. Philadelphia: Fortress, 1987.

Cotter, Wendy. "Cornelius, the Roman Army, and Religion." Pages 279–301 in *Religious Rivalries and the Struggle for Success in Caesarea Maritima*. Waterloo, Ont.: Wilfrid Laurier, 2000.

Crawford, Robert G. "A Parable of the Atonement (Luke 15)." *Evangelical Quarterly* 50 (1978): 2–7.

Croy, N. Clayton. "Hellenistic Philosophies and the Preaching of the Resurrection (ACTS 17:18, 32)." *Novum Testamentum* 39 (1997): 21–39.

Dahl, Nils. *Jesus the Christ: The Historical Origins of Christological Doctrine*. Minneapolis: Fortress, 1991.

Daube, David. "On Acts 23: Sadducees and Angels." *Journal of Biblical Literature* 109 (1990): 493–97.

Davies, Philip R. *Scribes and Schools: The Canonization of the Hebrew Scriptures*. Louisville: Westminster John Knox, 1998.

Davis, David B. *The Problem of Slavery in Western Culture*. Ithaca, N.Y.: Cornell University Press, 1966.

Dawsey, James M. "Confrontation in the Temple: Luke 19:45–20:47." *Perspectives in Religious Studies* 11 (1984): 153–65.

Dearman, J. Andrew. "My Servants the Scribes: Composition and Context in Jeremiah 36." *Journal of Biblical Literature* 109 (1990): 403–21.

Demosthenes. *Against Timocrates*. In vol. 3 of *Demosthenes*. Edited by G. P. Goold. Translated by J. H. Vince. 7 vols. Loeb Classical Library. Cambridge: Harvard University Press, 1998.

DeSilva, David A. "Patronage and Reciprocity: The Context of Grace in the New Testament." *Ashland Theological Journal* 31 (1999): 32–84.

De Vos, Craig S. "Finding a Charge That Fits: The Accusation against Paul and Silas at Philippi (Acts 16:19–21)." *Journal for the Study of the New Testament* 74 (1999): 32–84.

———. "Once a Slave, Always a Slave? Slavery, Manumission, and Relational Patterns in Paul's Letter to Philemon." *Journal for the Study of the New Testament* 82 (2001): 89–105.

*Didache*. In vol. 1 of *The Apostolic Fathers*. Edited by T. E. Page et al. Translated by Kirsopp Lake. 2 vols. Loeb Classical Library. Cambridge: Harvard University Press, 1912–1913. Repr., 1976–1985.

Dietzfelbinger, Christian. *Die Berufung des Paulus als Ursprung seiner Theologie*. Wissenschaftliche Monographien zum Alten und Neuen Testament 58. Neukirchen-Vluyn: Neukirchener Verlag, 1985.

Dio Cassius. *Roman History*. Edited by Jeffrey Henderson. Translated by Earnest Cary. 9 vols. Loeb Classical Library. Cambridge: Harvard University Press, 2000.

Diogenes Laertius. *Lives of Eminent Philosophers*. Edited by T. E. Page. Translated by R. D. Hicks. 2 vols. Loeb Classical Library. Cambridge: Harvard University Press, 1965.

Dionysius of Halicarnassus. *Roman Antiquities*. Edited by G. P. Goold. Translated by Earnest Cary. 7 vols. Loeb Classical Library. Cambridge: Harvard University Press, 1993.

Dillon, Richard J. " 'As One Having Authority' (Mark 1:22): The Controversial Distinction of Jesus' Teaching." *Catholic Biblical Quarterly* 57 (1995): 92–113.

Dockery, David S. "Acts 6–12: The Christian Mission beyond Jerusalem." *Review and Expositor* 87 (2001): 423–37.

Donahue, John R. "Tax Collectors and Sinners: An Attempt at Identification." *Catholic Biblical Quarterly* 33 (1971): 39–61.

Donfried, Karl P., and Peter Richardson, eds. *Judaism and Christianity in First-Century Rome*. Grand Rapids: Eerdmans, 1998.

Douglas, Mary. "Deciphering a Meal." Pages 231–51 in *Implicit Meanings: Selected Essays in Anthropology*. 2d ed. New York: Routledge, 1999.

Douglas, Mary. *Implicit Meanings: Selected Essays in Anthropology*. 2d ed. New York: Routledge, 1999.

Dunn, James D. G. *The Acts of the Apostles*. Valley Forge, Pa.: Trinity Press International, 1996.

———. *Jesus' Call to Discipleship*. Cambridge: Cambridge University Press, 1992.

———. *Jesus, Paul, and the Law: Studies in Mark and Galatians*. Louisville: John Knox, 1990.

———. "The Justice of God." *Journal of Theological Studies* 43 (1992): 1–22.

———. *The Theology of Paul*. Grand Rapids: Eerdmans, 1998.

———. *Unity and Diversity in the New Testament: An Inquiry into the Character of Earliest Christianity*. Philadelphia: Westminster, 1977.

Eastman, Susan. "The Evil Eye and the Curse of the Law: Galatians 3:1 Revisited." *Journal for the Study of the New Testament* 83 (2001): 69–87.

Ehrman, Bart D. *The New Testament: A Historical Introduction to the Early Christian Writings*. Oxford: Oxford University Press, 2004.

Engberg-Pedersen, Troels. *Paul and the Stoics*. Edinburgh: T&T Clark, 2000.

Epictetus. *Discourses (Dissertationes)*. Translated by W. A. Oldfather. 3 vols. Loeb Classical Library. Cambridge: Harvard University Press, 1996.

Esler, Philip F. *Community and Gospel in Luke–Acts: The Sociological and Political Motivations of Lucan Theology*. Society for New Testament Studies Monograph Series 57. Cambridge: Cambridge University Press, 1987.

———. "Paul and Stoicism: Romans 12 as a Test Case." *New Testament Studies* 50 (2004): 106–24.

Eusebius. *Ecclesiastical History*. Edited by G. P. Goold. Translated by Kirsopp Lake and J. E. L. Oulton. 2 vols. Loeb Classical Library. Cambridge: Harvard University Press, 1994.

Evans, Craig A. "Crisis in the Middle East: Ethnic and Religious Tensions Ran High in Jesus' Day Too." *Christian History* 59 (1998): 20–23.

Fairchild, Mark R. "Paul's Pre-Christian Zealot Associations: A Re-examination of Gal 1:14 and Acts 22:3." *New Testament Studies* 45 (1999): 514–32.

Fairstein, Morris M. "Why Do the Scribes Say That Elijah Must Come First?" *Journal of Biblical Literature* 100/1 (1981): 75–86.

Farrar, F. W. *The Herods*. New York: E. R. Herrick, 1900.

Fath, Abu'l. *Kitab al-Tarikh*. Translated by Paul Stenhouse. Sydney, Australia: Mandelbaum Trust, University of Sydney, 1985.

Feldman, Steven, and Nancy E. Roth. "The Short List: The New Testament Figures Known to History." *Biblical Archaeology Review* 28 (2002): 34–37.

Fensham, F. Charles. *The Books of Ezra and Nehemiah*. Grand Rapids: Eerdmans, 1982.

Ferguson, Everett. *Backgrounds of Early Christianity*. 2d ed. Grand Rapids: Eerdmans, 1993.

Fiedler, Peter. *Jesus und die Sünde*. Beiträge zur biblischen Exegese und Theologie 3. Frankfurt: Peter Lang, 1976.

Fine, Steven. "A Note on Ossuary Burial and the Resurrection of the Dead in First-Century Jerusalem." *Journal of Jewish Studies* 51 (2000): 69–76.

Fitzmyer, Joseph. *The Acts of the Apostles: A New Translation with Introduction and Commentary*. New York: Doubleday, 1998.

———. *Studies in the Dead Sea Scrolls and Christian Origins*. Grand Rapids: Eerdmans, 2000.

Flesher, Paul V. M. *Oxen, Women, or Citizens? Slaves in the System of the Mishnah*. Atlanta: Scholars Press, 1988.

France, R. T. *The Gospel of Mark: A Commentary on the Greek Text*. The New International Greek Commentary. Grand Rapids: Eerdmans, 2002.

Freyne, Sean. *The World of the New Testament*. Wilmington, Del.: Michael Glazier, 1980.

Friedman, Menachim. "Jewish Zealots: Conservative versus Innovative." Pages 148–63 in *Jewish Fundamentalism in Comparative Perspective: Religion, Ideology, and the Crisis of Modernity*. Edited by Laurence J. Silberstein. New York: New York University Press, 1993.

Fuks, Gideon. "Where Have all the Freedmen Gone? On an Anomaly in the Jewish Grave-Inscriptions from Rome." *Journal of Jewish Studies* 36 (1985): 25–32.

García Martínez, Florentino. *The Dead Sea Scrolls Translated: The Qumran Texts in English*. 2d ed. Grand Rapids: Eerdmans, 1996

García Martínez, Florentino, and Eibert J. C. Tigchelaar, eds. *The Dead Sea Scrolls Study Edition*. Grand Rapids: Eerdmans, 1998.

Garnsey, Peter, and Richard Saller. "Patronal Power Relations." Pages 96–103 in *Paul and Empire: Religion and Power in Roman Imperial Society*. Edited by Richard A. Horsley. Harrisburg, Pa.: Trinity Press International, 1997.

Garrett, Susan R. "Light on a Dark Subject and Vice Versa: Magic and Magicians in the New Testament." Pages 142–65 in *Religion, Science, and Magic: In Concert and in Conflict*. Edited by Jacob Neusner, Ernest Frerichs, and Paul Flesher. Oxford: Oxford University Press, 1989.

Gibson, J. "*Hoi telōnai kai hai pornai* (Tax-Collectors and Prostitutes in First Century Palestine: Matt 21:31)." *Journal of Theological Studies* 32 (1981): 429–33.

Gill, Christopher. "The School in the Roman Period." Pages 33–58 in *The Cambridge Guide to the Stoics*. Edited by Brad Inwood. Cambridge: Cambridge University Press, 2003.

Gill, David W. "Acts and the Urban Elites." Pages 105–18 in *The Book of Acts and Its Graeco-Roman Setting*. Edited by David W. Gill and Conrad Gempf. Grand Rapids: Eerdmans, 1994.

Gilliver, C. M. *The Roman Art of War*. Stroud, Glos., Eng.: Tempest, 1999.

Glancy, Jennifer A. "Obstacles to Slave Participation in the Corinthian Church." *Journal of Biblical Literature* 117 (1998): 481–501.

Goldsworthy, Adrian Keith. *The Roman Army at War: 100 B.C.–A.D. 200*. Oxford: Oxford University Press, 1996.

González, Justo L. "Reading from My Bicultural Place: Acts 6:1–7." Pages 139–48 in *Reading from This Place: Social Location and Biblical Interpretation in the United States*. Edited by Fernando F. Segovia and Mary Ann Tolbert. Minneapolis: Fortress, 1995.

Goodall, Lawrence D. "None Greater Born of a Woman: The Theological Figure of John the Baptist." *Communio* 24 (fall 1997): 550–62.

Goodenough, Erwin R. *Jewish Symbols in the Greco-Roman Period*. 13 vols. New York: Pantheon, 1953–1968.

Goodman, Martin. "A Note on Josephus, the Pharisees, and Ancestral Tradition." *Journal of Jewish Studies* 50 (1999): 17–20.

———. *The Ruling Class of Judaea: The Origins of the Jewish Revolt against Rome, A.D. 66–70*. Cambridge: Cambridge University Press, 1987.

Gordon, Richard. "The Veil of Power." Pages 126–39 in *Paul and Empire: Religion and Power in Roman Imperial Society*. Edited by Richard A. Horsley. Harrisburg, Pa.: Trinity Press International, 1997.

Grabbe, Lester L. *An Introduction to First Century Judaism: Jewish Religion and History in the Second Temple Period*. Edinburgh: T&T Clark, 1996.

———. *Judaism from Cyrus to Hadrian*. London: SCM, 1992.

———. "Triumph of the Pious or Failure of the Xenophobes? The Ezra–Nehemiah Reforms and Their *Nachgeschichte*." Pages 50–65 in *Jewish Local Patriotism and Self-Identification in the Graeco-Roman Period*. Edited by Siân Jones and Sarah Pearce; Sheffield, Eng.: Sheffield Academic Press, 1998.

Green, Peter. *Alexander to Actium: The Historical Evolution of the Hellenic Age*. Berkeley: University of California Press, 1990.

Griffin, Miriam T. *Nero: The End of a Dynasty*. New York: Routledge, 1984.

331

Gundry, Robert H. *A Survey of the New Testament*. 4th ed. Grand Rapids: Zondervan, 2003.

Haenchen, Ernst. *The Act of the Apostles: A Commentary*. Philadelphia: Westminster, 1971.

Hagner, Donald A. *Matthew 1–13*. Word Biblical Commentary. Dallas: Word, 1993.

Hall, John F., and John W. Welch, eds. *Masada and the World of the New Testament*. Provo, Utah: Brigham Young University Studies, 1997.

Hamblin, William J. "The Roman Army in the First Century." Pages 337–49 in *Masada and the World of the New Testament*. Edited by John F. Hall and John W. Welch. Provo, Utah: Brigham Young University Studies, 1997.

Hanson, K. C. "The Herodians and Mediterranean Kinship, Part 3: Economics," *Biblical Theology Bulletin* 20 (1990): 10–21.

———. "The Herodians and the Mediterranean Kinship, Part 2: Marriage and Divorce." *Biblical Theology Bulletin* 19 (1989): 142–51.

Haran, M. "Book-Scrolls in Israel in Pre-exilic Times." *Journal of Jewish Studies* 33 (1982): 161–73.

———. "More concerning Book-Scrolls in Pre-exilic Times." *Journal of Jewish Studies* 35 (1984): 84–85.

Harrill, J. Albert. *The Manumission of Slaves in Early Christianity*. Tübingen: J. C. B. Mohr, 1995.

Harris, Stephen L. *The New Testament: A Student's Introduction*. Mountain View, Calif.: Mayfield, 1988.

Harris, W. V. "Child-Exposure in the Roman Empire," *Journal of Hellenic Studies* 84 (1994): 1–22.

Harvey, A. E. *Jesus and the Constraints of History:* The Bampton Lectures, 1980. London: Gerald Duckworth, 1982.

Hayes, John H., and Sara R. Mandell. *The Jewish People in Classic Antiquity from Alexander to Bar Kochba*. Louisville: Westminster John Knox, 1998.

Hayward, Robert. "Some Notes on Scribes and Priests in the Targum of the Prophets." *Journal of Jewish Studies* 36 (1985): 210–21.

Hendriksen, William. *Exposition of the Gospel according to Mark*. Grand Rapids: Baker, 1975.

Hengel, Martin. *Acts and the History of Earliest Christianity*. Philadelphia: Fortress, 1980.

———. *Between Jesus and Paul: Studies in the Earliest History of Christianity*. Philadelphia: Fortress, 1983.

———. *Judaism and Hellenism: Studies in Their Encounter in Palestine during the Early Hellenistic Period*. Minneapolis: Fortress, 1974.

———. *The Pre-Christian Paul*. Philadelphia: Trinity Press International, 1991.

———. *Was Jesus a Revolutionist?* Philadelphia: Fortress, 1971.

———. *The Zealots: Investigations into the Jewish Freedom Movements in the Period from Herod I until 70 A.D.* Edinburgh: T&T Clark, 1989.

Hengel, Martin, and Roland Deines. "E. P. Sanders' 'Common Judaism,' Jesus, and the Pharisees." *Journal of Theological Studies* 46 (1995): 1–70.

Herodotus. *Histories*. Translated by A. D. Godley. 4 vols. Loeb Classical Library. Cambridge: Harvard University Press, 1961–1966.

———. *The Persian Wars*. Edited by T. E. Page. Translated by A. D. Godley. 4 vols. Loeb Classical Library. Cambridge: Harvard University Press, 1961–1966.

Hicks, R. D. *Stoic and Epicurean*. New York: Charles Scribner's Sons, 1910.

Hill, C. Craig. "Acts 6.1–8.4: Division or Diversity?" Pages 129–53 in *History, Literature, and Society in the Book of Acts*. Edited by Ben Witherington III. Cambridge: Cambridge University Press, 1996.

———. *Hellenists and Hebrews: Reappraising Division within the Earliest Church*. Minneapolis: Fortress, 1992.

Hills, Julian V., ed. *Common Life in the Early Church: Essays Honoring Graydon F. Snyder*. Harrisburg, Pa.: Trinity Press International, 1998.

Hjelm, Ingrid. *The Samaritans and Early Judaism: A Literary Analysis*. Journal for the Study of the Old Testament: Supplement Series 303. Sheffield, Eng.: Sheffield Academic Press, 2002.

Hoehner, Harold W. *Herod Antipas: Tetrarch of Galilee*. Grand Rapids: Zondervan, 1980.

Hofius, Otto. *Jesu Tischgemeinschaft mit den Sünder*. Stuttgart: Calver, 1967.

Horsley, Richard A. "The Death of Jesus." Pages 395–422 in *Studying the Historical Jesus*. Edited by Craig Evans and Bruce Chilton. Leiden: E. J. Brill, 1994.

———. *Jesus and the Spiral of Violence: Popular Jewish Resistance in Roman Palestine*. San Francisco: Harper & Row, 1987.

———. "The Slave Systems of Classical Antiquity and Their Reluctant Recognition by Modern Scholars." In "Slavery in Text and Interpretation." Edited by Allen Dwight Callahan, Richard A. Horsley, and Abraham Smith. *Semeia* 83–84 (1998): 19–66.

Horsley, Richard A., ed. *Paul and Empire: Religion and Power in Roman Imperial Society*. Harrisburg, Pa.: Trinity Press International, 1997.

Horsley, Richard A., ed. *Paul and Politics: Ecclesia, Israel, Imperium, and Interpretation: Essays in Honor of Krister Stendahl*. Harrisburg, Pa: Trinity Press International, 2000.

Horsley, Richard A., and John S. Hanson. *Bandits, Prophets, and Messiahs: Popular Movements at the Time of Jesus*. San Francisco: Harper & Row, 1985.

Howard, J. Keir. "New Testament Exorcism and Its Significance Today." *Expository Times* 96 (1985): 105–9.

Hull, John M. *Hellenistic Magic and the Synoptic Tradition*. London: SCM, 1974.

Hutchison, John C. "Was John the Baptist an Essene of Qumran?" *Bibliotheca sacra* 159 (2002): 187–200.

Iamblichus. *On the Pythagorean Way of Life: Text, Translation, and Notes*. Translated by John Dillon and Jackson Hershbell. Atlanta: Scholars Press, 1991.

Ilan, Tal. "The Attraction of Aristocratic Women to Pharisaism during the Second Temple Period." *Harvard Theological Review* 88 (1995): 1–33.

Ignatius. *Epistle to the Ephesians*. In vol. 1 of *The Apostolic Fathers*. Edited by T. E. Page et al. Translated by Kirsopp Lake. 2 vols. Loeb Classical Library. Cambridge: Harvard University Press, 1912–1913. Repr., 1976–1985.

Irenaeus. *Against the Heresies*. Translated by Dominic J. Unger. New York: Paulist, 1992–.

Ishak, Amran. *The History and Religion of the Samaritans*. Jerusalem: Greek Convent, 1964.

Jackson, Kent P. "Revolutionaries in the First Century." Pages 129–40 in *Masada and the World of the New Testament*. Edited by John F. Hall and John W. Welch. Provo, Utah: Brigham Young University Studies, 1997.

Jaffee, Martin S. *Early Judaism*. Upper Saddle River, N.J.: Prentice-Hall, 1997.

Japhet, Sara. *1 and 2 Chronicles: A Commentary*. Louisville: John Knox, 1993.

Jeremias, Joachim. "γραμματεύς." Pages 740–41 in vol. 1 of *Theological Dictionary of the New Testament*. Edited by G. Kittel and G. Friedrich. Translated by G. W. Bromiley. 10 vols. Grand Rapids: Eerdmans, 1964–1976.

———. *Jesus' Promise to the Nations*. Naperville, Ill.: Allenson, 1958.

Jervell, Jacob. *Luke and the People of God: A New Look at Luke–Acts*. Minneapolis: Augsburg, 1972.

———. *The Unknown Paul: Essays on Luke–Acts and Early Christian History*. Minneapolis: Augsburg, 1984.

Jonge, Marinus de. *Christology in Context: The Earliest Christian Response to Jesus*. Philadelphia: Westminster, 1988.

Josephus, Flavius. *The Works*. Translated by William Whiston. Grand Rapids: Baker, 1974.

Joubert, Stephan. *Paul as Benefactor: Reciprocity, Strategy, and Theological Reflection in Paul's Collection*. Wissenschaftliche Untersuchungen zum Neuen Testament 124. Tübingen: Mohr Siebeck, 2000.

Judd, Daniel K. "Suicide at Masada and in the World of the New Testament." Pages 378–91 in *Masada and the World of the New Testament*. Edited by John F. Hall and John W. Welch. Provo, Utah: Brigham Young University Studies, 1997.

Justinian. *The Digest*. Translated and edited by Alan Watson. 2 vols. Philadelphia: University of Pennsylvania Press, 1985.

———. *Institutes*. Translated by Peter Birks and Grant McLeod. Ithaca, N.Y.: Cornell University Press, 1987.

Kaufman, Robert R. "The Patron-Client Concept and Macro-politics: Prospects and Problems." *Comparative Studies in Society and History* 16 (1974): 284–308.

Kee, Howard Clark. "Magic and Messiah." Pages 121–41 in *Religion, Science, and Magic: In Concert and in Conflict*. Edited by Jacob Neusner, Ernest Frerichs, and Paul Flesher. Oxford: Oxford University Press, 1989.

———. *Medicine, Miracle, and Magic in New Testament Times*. Society for New Testament Studies Monograph Series 55. Cambridge: Cambridge University Press, 1986.

Keown, Gerald L., Pamela J. Scalise, and Thomas G. Smothers, eds. *Jeremiah 23–52*. Waco, Tex.: Word, 1995.

Kilgallen, John L. "Clean, Acceptable, Saved: Acts 10." *Expository Times* 109 (1998): 301–2.

———. "The Function of Stephen's Speech (Acts 7:2–53)," *Biblica* 70 (1989): 173–93.

Kim, Seyoon. *The Origin of Paul's Gospel*. Grand Rapids: Eerdmans, 1981.

Klassen William. "Jesus and the Zealot Option." Pages 131–49 in *The Wisdom of the Cross: Essays in Honor of John Howard Yoder*. Edited by Stanley Hauerwas et al. Grand Rapids: Eerdmans, 1999.

Klausner, Joseph. *From Jesus to Paul*. London: Allen & Unwin, 1944.

Kokkinos, Nikos. *The Herodian Dynasty: Origins, Role in Society, and Eclipse*. Journal for the Study of the Pseudepigrapha: Supplement Series 30. Sheffield, Eng.: Sheffield Academic Press, 1998.

———. "Herod's Horrid Death." *Biblical Archaeology Review* 28 (2002): 28–35.

Kolenkow, Anitra Bingham. "Persons of Power and Their Communities." Pages 133–44 in *Magic and Divination in the Ancient World*. Edited by Leda Ciraolo and Jonathan Seidel. Leiden: E. J. Brill, 2002.

Kraft, Heinrich. *Die Entstehung des Christentums*. Darmstadt: Wissenschaftliche Buchgesellschaft, 1981.

Krentz, Edgar. "Order in the 'House' of God: The Haustafel in 1 Peter 2:11–3:12." Pages 279–86 in *Common Life in the Early Church: Essays Honoring Graydon F. Snyder*. Edited by Julian V. Hills. Harrisburg, Pa.: Trinity Press International, 1998.

Kraft, Robert A., and George W. E. Nickelsburg. *Early Judaism and Its Modern Interpreters*. Philadelphia: Fortress, 1986.

Kunkel, Wolfgang. *An Introduction to Roman Legal and Constitutional History*. Oxford: Clarendon, 1973.

Kuhrt, Amélie. "The Cyrus Cylinder and Achawmenid Imperial Policy." *Journal for the Study of the Old Testament* 25 (1983): 83–97.

Lacey, D. R. de. "In Search of a Pharisee." *Tyndale Bulletin* 43 (1992): 353–72.

Lane, William. "Social Perspectives on Roman Christianity during the Formative Years from Nero to Nerva: Romans, Hebrews, 1 Clement." Pages 196–244 in *Judaism and Christianity in First-Century Rome*. Edited by Karl P. Donfried and Peter Richardson. Grand Rapid: Eerdmans, 1998.

Larsson, Edvin. "Temple-Criticism and the Jewish Heritage: Some Reflections on Acts 6–7." *New Testament Studies* 39 (1993): 379–95.

Levy, Ernst. *Pauli Sententiae: a Palingenesia of the Opening Titles as a Specimen of Research in West Roman Vulgar Law*. New York: Augustus M. Kelley Publishers, 1969.

Levey, Samson H. "Neusner's *Purities*—Monumental Masterpiece of Mishnaic Learning: An Essay-Review of Jacob Neusner's *A History of the Mishnaic Law of Purities* (22 Volumes)." *Journal of the Academy of Religion* 46 (1978): 337–59.

Long, A. A. *Hellenistic Philosophy: Stoics, Epicureans, Skeptics*. New York: Charles Scribner's Sons, 1974.

Long, A. A., and D. N. Sedley. *Translations of the Principle Sources with Philosophical Commentary*. Vol. 1 of *The Hellenistic Philosophers*. Cambridge: Cambridge University Press, 1987.

Lucretius. *De rerum natura*. Edited by T. E. Page. Translated by W. H. D. Rouse. Loeb Classical Library. Cambridge: Harvard University Press, 1966.

Lüdemann, Gerd. *Early Christianity according to the Traditions in Acts: A Commentary*. Minneapolis: Fortress, 1989.

Ludwig, Charles. *Ludwig's Handbook of New Testament Rulers and Cities.* Denver, Col.: Accent, 1983.

Luttwak, Edward. *The Grand Strategy of the Roman Empire: From the First Century A.D. to the Third.* Baltimore: Johns Hopkins University Press, 1979.

Maccoby, Hyam. "Holiness and Purity: The Holy People in Leviticus and Ezra–Nehemiah." Pages 153–70 in *Reading Leviticus: A Conversation with Mary Douglas.* Edited by John F. A. Sawyer. Journal for the Study of the Old Testament: Supplement Series 227. Sheffield, Eng.: Sheffield Academic Press, 1996.

MacDonald, John. *The Theology of the Samaritans.* London: SCM, 1964.

Macrobius. *The Saturnalia.* Translated and edited by Percival Vaughn Davies. New York: Columbia University Press, 1969.

Mandell, Sara. "Who Paid the Temple Tax When the Jews Were under Roman Rule?" *Harvard Theological Review* 77 (1984): 223–32.

Mann, Jacob. "Rabbinic Studies in the Synoptic Gospels." *Hebrew Union College Annual* 1 (1924): 323–55.

Mantel, Hugo. "The Dichotomy of Judaism during the Second Temple." *Hebrew Union College Annual* 44/1 (1973): 55–87.

Marqah. *Memar Marqah: The Teaching of Marqah.* Edited and translated by John MacDonald. 2 vols. in 1. Berlin: Töpelmann, 1963.

Marshall, I. Howard. *The Acts of the Apostles: An Introduction and Commentary.* Tyndale New Testament Commentaries. Grand Rapids: Eerdmans, 1980.

———. *The Gospel of Luke: A Commentary on the Greek Text.* New International Greek Testament Commentary. Grand Rapids: Eerdmans: 1978.

Martyn, J. Louis. "De-apocalypticizing Paul: An Essay Focused on Paul and the Stoics by Troels Engberg-Pedersen." *Journal for the Study of the New Testament* 86 (2002): 61–102.

Mason, S. "Chief Priests, Sadducees, Pharisees, and Sanhedrin in Acts." Pages 133–77 in *The Book of Acts in Its Palestinian Setting.* Edited by Richard Bauckham. Grand Rapids: Eerdmans, 1995.

McEleney, N. J. "Conversion, Circumcision, and the Law." *New Testament Studies* 20 (1974): 319–41.

Meier, John P. "The Historical Jesus and the Historical Herodians," *Journal of Biblical Literature* 119 (2001): 740–46.

———. "John the Baptist in Josephus: Philology and Exegesis." *Journal of Biblical Literature* 111/2 (1992): 225–37.

———. "The Quest for the Historical Pharisee: A Review Essay on Roland Deines, *Die Pharisäer.*" *Catholic Biblical Quarterly* 61 (1999): 713–22.

Menander. *Aspis, Georgos, Dis Exapaton, Dyskolos, Encheiridion, Eptrepontes.* Edited by G. P. Goold and W. G. Arnott. Translated by W. G. Arnott. Loeb Classical Library. Cambridge: Harvard University Press, 1997.

Meyer, Ben F. *The Aims of Jesus.* London: SCM, 1979.

Meyer, F. B. *John the Baptist.* London: Marshall, Morgan & Scott, 1954.

Michel, Otto. "τελώνης." Pages 88–106 in vol. 8 of *Theological Dictionary of the New Testament.* Edited by G. Kittel and G. Friedrich. Translated by G. W. Bromiley. 10 vols. Grand Rapids: Eerdmans, 1964–1976.

Miller, Joseph C. *Slavery and Slaving in World History: A Bibliography, 1900–1991.* Milford, N.Y.: Kraus International, 1993.

Morris, Leon. *The Gospel according to Matthew.* Grand Rapids: Eerdmans, 1992.

Morgan, Michael A. *Sepher ha-razim: The Book of Mysteries.* Chico, Calif.: Scholars Press, 1983.

Moule, C. F. D. "Once More, Who Were the Hellenists?" *Expository Times* 70 (1958–1959): 100–102.

Moritz, Thorsten. "Dinner Talk and Ideology in Luke: The Role of the Sinners." *European Journal of Theology* 5 (1996): 47–69.

Mulder, Martin Jan, ed., *Mikra: Text, Translation, Reading, and Interpretation of the Hebrew Bible in Ancient Judaism and Early Christianity.* Philadelphia: Fortress, 1988.

Murphy-O'Connor, Jerome. "John the Baptist and Jesus: History and Hypotheses." *New Testament Studies* 36 (1990): 359–74.

Neale, David. *None but the Sinners: Religious Categories in the Gospel of Luke.* Journal for the Study of the New Testament: Supplement Series 58. Sheffield, Eng.: JSOT Press, 1991.

Neusner, Jacob. "Exile and Return as the History of Judaism." Pages 221–237 in *Exile: Old Testament, Jewish, and Christian Conceptions.* Edited by James M. Scott. New York: E. J. Brill, 1997.

———. "The Fellowship (*haberim*) in the Second Jewish Commonwealth." *Harvard Theological Review* 53 (1960): 125–42.

———. *First Century Judaism in Crisis: Yohanan ben Zakkai and the Renaissance of the Torah.* Nashville: Abingdon, 1985.

———. *From Politics to Piety: The Emergence of Pharisaic Judaism.* Englewood Cliffs, N.J.: Prentice-Hall, 1973.

———. *The Idea of Purity in Ancient Judaism: The Haskell Lectures, 1972–1973.* Leiden: E. J. Brill, 1973.

———. *Judaism: The Evidence of the Mishnah.* Atlanta: Scholars Press, 1988.

———. *The Mishnah: A New Translation.* New Haven: Yale University Press, 1988.

———. *Purity in Rabbinic Judaism—a Systematic Account: The Sources, Media, Effects, and Removal of Uncleanness.* Atlanta: Scholars Press, 1994.

———. *The Rabbinic Traditions about the Pharisees before 70.* 3 vols. Atlanta: Scholars Press, 1999.

———. "Science and Magic, Miracle and Magic in Formative Judaism: The System and the Difference." Pages 61–81 in *Religion, Science, and Magic: In Concert and in Conflict.* Edited by Jacob Neusner, Ernest Frerichs, and Paul Flesher. Oxford: Oxford University Press, 1989.

Newman, Robert C. "Breadmaking with Jesus." *Journal of the Evangelical Society* 40 (1997): 1–13.

Newsome, James D. *By the Waters of Babylon: An Introduction to the History and Theology of the Exile.* Atlanta: John Knox, 1979.

———. *Greeks, Romans, Jews: Currents of Culture and Belief in the New World.* Philadelphia: Trinity Press International, 1992.

Neyrey, Jerome H. "Bewitched in Galatia: Paul and Cultural Anthropology." *Catholic Biblical Quarterly* 50 (2001): 72–100.

Nickelsburg, George W. E., and Michael E. Stone. *Faith and Piety in Early Judaism: Texts and Documents.* Philadelphia: Fortress, 1983.

Novak, David. *The Image of the Non-Jew in Judaism: An Historical and Constructive Study of the Noahide Laws.* New York: Edwin Mellen, 1983.

Öhler, Markus. "The Expectation of Elijah and the Presence of the Kingdom of God." *Journal of Biblical Literature* 118/3 (1999): 461–76.

Okorie, A. M. "The Characterization of the Tax Collectors in the Gospel of Luke." *Currents in Theology and Mission* (1995): 27–32.

Oppenheimer, Aaron. *The 'AM HA-ARETZ: A Study in the Social History of the Jewish People in the Hellenistic-Roman Period.* Leiden: E. J. Brill, 1977.

Origen. *Contra Celsum.* Translated by Henry Chadwick. Cambridge: Cambridge University Press, 1953.

Parker, Pierson. "Jesus, John the Baptist, and the Herods." *Perspectives in Religious Studies* 8 (1981): 4–11.

Parsons, Mikeal C. " 'Nothing Defiled AND Unclean': The Conjunction's Function in Acts 10:14." *Perspectives in Religious Studies* 27 (2001): 263–74.

Pate, C. Marvin. *Communities of the Last Days: The Dead Sea Scrolls, the New Testament, and the Story of Israel.* Downers Grove, Ill.: InterVarsity, 2000.

Perowne, Stewart. *The Life and Times of Herod the Great.* Stroud, Glos., Eng.: Sutton, 2003.

Pfeiffer, Charles. *Old Testament History.* Grand Rapids: Baker, 1973.

Philo. Translated by F. H. Colson, G. H. Whitaker, and Ralph Marcus. 12 vols. Loeb Classical Library. Cambridge: Harvard University Press, 1971.

Philo. *The Works: Complete and Unabridged.* Translated by C. D. Yonge. Peabody, Mass.: Hendrickson, 2004.

Plato. *The Republic.* Edited by G. P. Goold. Translated by Paul Shorey. 2 vols. Loeb Classical Library. Cambridge: Harvard University Press, 1994.

Pliny the Elder. *Natural History.* Edited by G. P. Goold. Translated by H. Rackham. 10 vols. Loeb Classical Library. Cambridge: Harvard University Press, 2000.

Pliny the Younger. *The Letters.* Edited by E. H. Warmington. Translated by Betty Radice. 2 vols. Loeb Classical Library. Cambridge: Harvard University Press, 1969.

Plutarch. *Lives.* Translated by Bernadotte Perrin. 11 vols. Loeb Classical Library. Cambridge: Harvard University Press, 1914–1997.

Poirier, John C. "Why Did the Pharisees Wash Their Hands?" *Journal of Jewish Studies* 47 (1996): 217–33.

Polybius. *The Histories.* Edited by G. P. Goold. Translated by W. R. Paton. 6 vols. Loeb Classical Library. Cambridge: Harvard University Press, 1995.

Pomeroy, Sarah B. *Goddesses, Whores, Wives, and Slaves: Women in Classical Antiquity.* New York: Schocken, 1975.

Price, James L. *The New Testament: Its History and Theology.* New York: Macmillan, 1987.

Pummer, Reinhard. *The Samaritans.* Leiden: E. J. Brill, 1987.

Quintilian. *Institutio oratoria.* Edited by G. P. Goold. Translated by H. E. Butler. 5 vols. Loeb Classical Library. Cambridge: Harvard University Press, 1995.

Räisänen, Heikki. "The 'Hellenists'—a Bridge between Jesus and Paul?" Pages 242–306 in *Torah and Christ: Essays in German and English on the Problem of the Law in Early Christianity.* Helsinki: Finnish Exegetical Society, 1986.

Ramsey, William M. *St. Paul the Traveler and the Roman Citizen.* Grand Rapids: Baker, 1966.

Rapske, Brian. *The Book of Acts and Paul in Roman Custody.* Grand Rapids: Eerdmans, 1994.

Rengstorf, K. H. "ἁμαρτωλός." Pages 317–33 in vol. 1 of *Theological Dictionary of the New Testament.* Edited by G. Kittel and G. Friedrich. Translated by G. W. Bromiley. 10 vols. Grand Rapids: Eerdmans, 1964–1976.

Ressequie, James L. "Luke 7:36–50: Making the Familiar Seem Strange." *Interpretation* 46 (1992): 285–90.

Richardson, Peter. *Herod: King of the Jews and Friend of the Romans.* Minneapolis: Fortress, 1999.

Riches, John. *Jesus and the Transformation of Judaism.* London: Darton, Longman & Todd, 1980.

———. *The World of Jesus: First Century Judaism in Crisis.* Cambridge: Cambridge University Press, 1990.

Rivkin, Ellis. *A Hidden Revolution: The Pharisees' Search for the Kingdom Within.* Nashville: Abingdon, 1978.

———. "Locating John the Baptizer in Palestinian Judaism: The Political Dimension." Pages 79–86 in *SBL Seminar Papers, 1983.* Society of Biblical Literature Seminar Papers 22. Chico, Calif.: Scholars Press, 1983.

———. "Scribes, Pharisees, Lawyers, Hypocrites: A Study in Synonymity." *Hebrew Union College Annual* 49 (1978): 135–42.

Rogers, Robert William. *Cuneiform Parallels to the Old Testament.* New York: Eaton & Mains, 1912.

Roller, Duane W. *The Building Program of Herod the Great.* Berkeley: University of California Press, 1998.

Romm, James. *Herodotus.* New Haven: Yale University Press, 1998.

Russell, D. S. *Between the Testaments.* Philadelphia: Fortress, 1960.

———. *The Jews from Alexander to Herod.* Oxford: Oxford University Press, 1967.

Rutgers, Leonard Victor. "Roman Policy toward the Jews: Expulsions from the City of Rome during the First Century C.E." Pages 93–116 in *Judaism and Christianity in First-Century Rome.* Edited by Karl P. Donfried and Peter Richardson. Grand Rapids: Eerdmans, 1998.

Safrai, S., and M. Stern, eds. *The Jewish People in the First Century: Historical Geography, Political History, Social, Cultural, and Religious Life and Institutions.* 2 vols. Philadelphia: Fortress, 1976.

Saldarini, Anthony J. *Pharisees, Scribes, and Sadducees in Palestinian Society: A Sociological Approach.* Wilmington, Del.: Michael Glazier, 1988.

Saller, R. P. *Personal Patronage under the Early Empire.* Cambridge: Cambridge University Press, 1982.

Sanders, E. P. *Jesus and Judaism.* Philadelphia: Fortress, 1985.

———. "Jesus and the Sinners." *Journal for the Study of the New Testament* 19 (1983): 5–36.

———. *Jewish Law from Jesus to the Mishnah*. London: SCM, 1990.

———. *Judaism: Practice and Belief, 63 B.C.E.–66 C.E.*. Philadelphia: Trinity Press International, 1992.

———. *Paul and Palestinian Judaism: A Comparison of Patterns of Religion*. Philadelphia: Fortress, 1977.

Sandmel, Samuel. *Herod: Profile of a Tyrant*. Philadelphia: Lippincott, 1967.

———. *Philo of Alexandria: An Introduction*. Oxford: Oxford University Press, 1979.

Saunders, Jason L. *Greek and Roman Philosophy after Aristotle*. New York: Free Press, 1966.

Scarre, Chris. *Chronicle of Roman Emperors: The Reign by Reign Record of the Rulers of Imperial Rome*. London: Thames & Hudson, 1995.

Schams, Christine. *Jewish Scribes in the Second-Temple Period*. Journal for the Study of the New Testament: Supplement Series 291. Sheffield, Eng.: Sheffield Academic Press, 1998.

Schiffman, Lawrence H. "The New Halakhic Letter (4QMMT) and the Origins of the Dead Sea Sect." *Biblical Archaeologist* 53 (1990): 64–73.

———. "New Light on the Pharisees: Insights from the Dead Sea Scrolls." *Bible Review* 8 (1992): 30–33, 54.

———. "Pharisees and Sadducees in *Pesher Nahum*." Pages 272–90 in Minah le-Nahum. Journal for the Study of the Old Testament: Supplement Series 154. Sheffield, Eng.: Sheffield Academic Press, 1993.

———. "The Significance of the Scrolls." *Bible Review* 6 (1990): 18–27.

———. *Text and Traditions: A Source Reader for the Study of Second Temple and Rabbinic Judaism*. Hoboken, N.J.: KTAV, 1998.

Schillebeeckx, Edward. *Christ: The Experience of Jesus as Lord*. New York: Seabury, 1980.

Schneemelcher, Wilhelm, ed. *New Testament Apocrypha*. Translated by R. McL. Wilson. 2 vols. Louisville: John Knox, 1991–1992.

Schürer, Emil. *The History of the Jewish People in the Age of Jesus Christ (175 B.C.–A.D. 135)*. Revised and edited by Geza Vermes, Furgus Millar, and Matthew Black. 3 vols. in 4. Vol. 2. Edinburgh: T&T Clark, 1973–1987.

Schwartz, Seth, "The Hellenization of Jerusalem and Shechem." Pages 37–45 in *Jews in a Graeco-Roman World*. Edited by Martin Goodman. Oxford: Clarendon, 1998.

Scott, J. Julius, Jr. "The Church's Progress to the Council of Jerusalem according to the Book of Acts." *Bulletin for Biblical Research* 7 (1997): 205–24.

———. *Customs and Controversies: The Jewish Backgrounds of the New Testament*. Grand Rapids: Baker, 2000.

Scroggs, Robin. "The Earliest Christian Communities as Sectarian Movement." Pages 1–23 in *Christianity, Judaism, and Other Greco-Roman Cults: Studies for Morton Smith at Sixty*. Edited by Jacob Neusner. Leiden: E. J. Brill, 1975.

Seland, Torrey. "Saul of Tarsus and Early Zealotism: Reading Gal 1:13–14 in Light of Philo's Writings." *Biblica* 83 (2002): 449–71.

*Seneca*. Translated by John W. Basore. Loeb Classical Library. Cambridge: Harvard University Press, 1989.

Sedley, David. "The School from Zeno to Arius Didymus." Pages 7–32 in *The Cambridge Companion to the Stoics*. Edited by Brad Inwood. Cambridge: Cambridge University Press, 2003.

*Sepher ha-razim: The Book of the Mysteries*. Translated by Michael A. Morgan. Chico, Calif.: Scholars Press, 1983.

Segal, Alan. *Paul the Convert: The Apostolate and the Apostasy of Saul the Pharisee*. New Haven: Yale University Press, 1990.

Segal, Robert. "Response to Hyam Maccoby's 'Holiness and Purity.' " Pages 171–73 in *Reading Leviticus: A Conversation with Mary Douglas*. Edited by John F. A. Sawyer. Journal for the Study of the Old Testament: Supplement Series 227. Sheffield, Eng.: Sheffield Academic Press, 1996.

Shelton, Jo-Ann. *As the Romans Did: A Sourcebook in Roman Social History*. 2d ed. New York: Oxford University Press, 1998.

Sherwin-White, Adrian Nicholas. *Roman Society and Roman Law in the New Testament*. Oxford: Clarendon, 1963.

Shiner, Whitney T. "The Ambiguous Pronouncement of the Centurion and the Shrouding of Meaning in Mark." *Journal for the Study of the New Testament* 78 (2000): 3–22.

Sievers, Joseph. "Who Were the Pharisees?" Pages 135–55 in *Hillel and Jesus: Comparative Studies of Two Major Religious Leaders*. Edited by James H. Charlesworth and Loren L. Johns. Minneapolis: Fortress, 1997.

Sigal, Phillip. *From the Origins to the Separation of Christianity*. Part 1 of *The Foundations of Judaism from Biblical Origins to the Sixth Century A.D.* Vol. 1 of *The Emergence of Contemporary Judaism*. Pittsburgh: Pickwick, 1980.

Simmons, William A. *A Theology of Inclusion in Jesus and Paul: The God of Outcasts and Sinners*. Lewiston, N.Y.: Edwin Mellen, 1996.

Simon, Marcel. *Jewish Sects at the Time of Jesus*. Translated by James H. Farley. Philadelphia: Fortress, 1967.

Skehan, Patrick W., trans. and ed., and Alexander A. Di Lella, ed. *The Wisdom of Ben Sira: A New Translation with Notes*. New York: Doubleday, 1987.

Smallwood, E. Mary. *The Jews under Roman Rule—from Pompey to Diocletian: A Study in Political Relations*. Leiden: E. J. Brill, 1981.

Smith, Daniel. *The Religion of the Landless: The Social Context of the Babylonian Exile*. Bloomington, Ind.: Meyer-Stone, 1989.

Smith, Morton. "The Dead Sea Sect in Relation to Ancient Judaism." *New Testament Studies* 7 (1960): 347–60.

———. *Jesus the Magician*. San Francisco: Harper & Row, 1978.

———. "Zealots and Sicarii: Their Origins and Relations." *Harvard Theological Review* 64 (1971): 1–19.

Smith-Christopher, Daniel L. "Reassessing the Historical and Sociological Impact of the Babylonian Exile

(597/587–539 B.C.E.)." Pages 7–35 in *Exile: Old Testament, Jewish, and Christian Conceptions*. Edited by James M. Scott. New York: E. J. Brill, 1997.

Spencer, F. Scott. "Neglected Widows in Acts 6:1–7." *Catholic Biblical Quarterly* 50 (2001): 715–35.

Stambaugh, John, and David Balch. *The Social World of the First Christians*. London: SPCK, 1986.

Stambaugh, John E. "Social Relations in the City of the Early Principate: State of Research." Pages 75–99 in *SBL Seminar Papers*, 1980. Society of Biblical Literature Seminar Papers 19. Missoula, Mont.: Scholars Press, 1980.

Stegemann, Hartmut. *The Library of Qumran: On the Essenes, Qumran, John the Baptist, and Jesus*. Grand Rapids: Eerdmans, 1998.

Stemberger, Günter. *Jewish Contemporaries of Jesus: Pharisees, Sadducees, Essenes*. Translated by Allan W. Mahke. Minneapolis: Fortress, 1995.

Stern, M. "The Reign of Herod and the Herodian Dynasty." Pages 216–307 in vol. 1 of *The Jewish People in the First Century: Historical Geography, Political History, Social, Cultural, and Religious Life and Institutions*. Edited by S. Safrai and M. Stern. 2 vols. Compendia rerum iudaicarum ad Novum Testamentum, sec. 1. Philadelphia: Fortress, 1974–1976.

Stone, Michael E., ed. *Jewish Writings of the Second Temple Period: Apocrypha, Pseudepigrapha, Qumran Sectarian Writings, Philo, Josephus*. Compendia rerum iudaicarum ad Novum Testamentum, sec. 2. Philadelphia: Fortress, 1984.

Stowers, Stanley K. *A Critical Reassessment of Paul and the Diatribe: The Dialogical Element in Paul's Letter to the Romans*. New Haven: Yale University Press, 1979.

———. *The Diatribe and Paul's Letter to the Romans*. Society of Biblical Literature Dissertation Series 57. Chico, Calif.: Scholars Press, 1981.

Strabo. *The Geography*. Edited by T. E. Page. Translated by Horace Leonard Jones. 8 vols. Loeb Classical Library. Cambridge: Harvard University Press, 1966.

Strack, Hermann L. and Paul Billerbeck. *Das Evangelium nach Markus, Lukas, und Johannes und die Apostelgeschichte*. Vol. 2 of *Kommentar zum Neuen Testament aus Talmud und Midrash*. Munich: C. H. Beck, 1924.

Stumpff, Albrecht. "ζῆλος, ζηλόω, κτλ." Pages 877–88 in vol. 2 of *Theological Dictionary of the New Testament*. Edited by G. Kittel and G. Friedrich. Translated by G. W. Bromiley. 10 vols. Grand Rapids: Eerdmans, 1964–1976.

Suetonius. *Lives of the Caesars*. Edited by E. H. Warmington. Translated by J. C. Rolfe. 2 vols. Loeb Classical Library. Cambridge: Harvard University Press, 1970.

Sweet, J. P. M. "The Zealots and Jesus." Pages 1–9 in *Jesus and the Politics of His Day*. Edited by Ernst Bammel and C. F. D. Moule. Cambridge: Cambridge University Press, 1984.

Sylva, Dennis D. "The Meaning and Function of Acts 7:46–50." *Journal of Biblical Literature* 106 (1987): 261–75.

Tacitus. *Agricola*. Translated by M. Hutton. Revised by R. M. Ogilvie. *Germania*. Translated by M. Hutton. Revised by E. H. Warmington. *Dialogus*. Translated by W. Peterson. Revised by M. Winterbottom. Rev. ed. Loeb Classical Library. Cambridge: Harvard University Press, 1970.

———. *Histories*. Translated by Clifford H. Moore. *Annals*. Translated by John Jackson. 3 vols. Loeb Classical Library. Cambridge: Harvard University Press, 1969.

Tannehill, Robert C. "The Gospel of Mark as Narrative Christology." *Semeia* 16 (1979): 57–95.

Taylor, Joan E. *The Immerser: John the Baptist within Second Temple Judaism*. Grand Rapids: Eerdmans, 1997.

Taylor, N. H. "Palestinian Christianity and the Caligula Crisis, Part 1: Social and Historical Reconstruction." *Journal for the Study of the New Testament* 61 (1996): 101–24.

Teasdale, Andrew. "Herod the Great's Building Program." Pages 85–98 in *Masada and the World of the New Testament*. Edited by John F. Hall and John W. Welch. Provo, Utah: Brigham Young University Studies, 1997.

Tenney, Merrill C. *New Testament Survey*. Revised by Walter M. Dunnett. Grand Rapids: Eerdmans, 1985.

Tertullian. *The Prescriptions against the Heretics*. Translated and edited by S. L. Greenslade. Philadelphia: Westminster, 1956.

Thatcher, Tom. "The Plot of Gal 3:1–18." *Journal of the Evangelical Theological Society* 40 (1997): 401–10.

Theissen, Gerd. *The First Followers of Jesus: A Sociological Analysis of the Earliest Christianity*. London: SCM, 1978.

———. *The Shadow of the Galilean: The Quest of the Historical Jesus in Narrative Form*. Philadelphia: Fortress, 1986.

———. *Sociology of Early Palestinian Christianity*. Philadelphia: Fortress, 1978.

Thibeaux, Evelyn R. " 'Known to Be a Sinner': The Narrative Rhetoric of Luke 7:36–50." *Biblical Theology Bulletin* 23 (1993): 151–60.

Trautmann, Maria. *Zeichenhafte Handlungen Jesu: Ein Beitrag zur Frage nach dem geschichtlichen Jesu*. Forschung zur Bibel 37. Würzburg: Echter, 1980.

Treggiari, Susan. *Roman Freedmen during the Late Republic*. Oxford: Clarendon, 1969.

Trumbower, Jeffrey A. "The Role of Malachi in the Career of John the Baptist." Pages 28–41 in *The Gospels and the Scriptures of Israel*. Edited by Craig A. Evans and W. Richard Stegner. Journal for the Study of the New Testament: Supplement Series 104. Sheffield, Eng.: Sheffield Academic Press, 1994.

Tyson, Joseph B. "Jews and Judaism in Luke–Acts: Reading as a Godfearer." *New Testament Studies* 41 (1995): 19–38.

Vanderkam, James C. "The People of the Dead Sea Scrolls." *Bible Review* 7 (1991): 42–47.

Vardaman, J., and E. Yamauchi, eds. *Chronos, Kairos, Christos: Nativity and Chronological Studies Presented to Jack Finegan*. Winona Lake, Ind.: Eisenbrauns, 1989.

Vermes, Geza. *The Dead Sea Scrolls in English*. 3d ed. Sheffield, Eng.: JSOT Press, 1987.

————. *Jesus the Jew: A Historian's Reading of the Gospel*. London: Collins, 1973.

Viviano, Benedict T., and Justin Taylor. "Sadducees, Angels, and Resurrection (Acts 23:8–9)." *Journal of Biblical Literature* 111 (1992): 496–98.

Von Wahlde, Urban C. "The Relationships between Pharisees and Chief Priests: Some Observations on the Texts in Matthew, John, and Josephus." *New Testament Studies* 42 (1996): 506–22.

Walker, W. O. "Jesus and the Tax Collector." *Journal of Biblical Literature* 97 (1978): 221–38.

Walters, James C. "Romans, Jews, and Christians: The Impact of the Romans on Jewish/Christian Relations in First-Century Rome." Pages 175–95 in *Judaism and Christianity in First-Century Rome*. Edited by Karl P. Donfried and Peter Richardson. Grand Rapids: Eerdmans, 1998.

Watson, Francis. *Paul, Judaism, and the Gentiles: A Sociological Approach*. Society for New Testament Studies Monograph Series 56. Cambridge: Cambridge University Press, 1986.

Webb, Robert L. *John the Baptizer and Prophet: A Socio-historical Study*. Journal for the Study of the New Testament: Supplement Series 62. Sheffield, Eng.: JSOT Press, 1991.

Webster, Graham. *The Roman Imperial Army of the First and Second Centuries*. Totowa, N.J.: Barnes & Noble, 1985.

Wedderburn, A. J. M. "Paul and Jesus: Similarity and Continuity." *New Testament Studies* 34 (1988): 189–203.

Wellesley, Kenneth. *The Year of the Four Emperors*. 3d ed. London: Routledge, 2000.

Wells, Colin. *The Roman Empire*. 2d ed. Cambridge: Harvard University Press, 1992.

Westerholm, Stephen. *Jesus and Scribal Authority*. Lund, Swed.: Gleerup, 1978.

Whealey, Alice. *Josephus on Jesus: The Testimonium Flavianum Controversy from Late Antiquity to Modern Times*. Studies in Biblical Literature 36. New York: Peter Lang, 2003).

Wilkes, John. *The Roman Army*. Cambridge: Cambridge University Press, 1972.

Williams, Margaret H. "The Structure of the Jewish Community in Rome." Pages 215–28 in *Jews in a Graeco-Roman World*. Edited by Martin Goodman. Oxford: Clarendon, 1998.

————, ed., *The Jews among the Greeks and Romans: A Diasporan Sourcebook*. Baltimore: Johns Hopkins University Press, 1998.

Williamson, Ronald. *Jews in the Hellenistic World: Philo*. Cambridge: Cambridge University Press, 1989.

Wilson, Stephen G. *The Gentiles and the Gentile Mission in Luke–Acts*. Society for New Testament Studies Monograph Series 23. Cambridge: Cambridge University Press, 1973.

Windisch, H. "Ἑλληνιστής." Pages 504–16 in vol. 2 of *Theological Dictionary of the New Testament*. Edited by G. Kittel and G. Friedrich. Translated by G. W. Bromiley. 10 vols. Grand Rapids: Eerdmans, 1964–1976.

Witherington, Ben, III. *The Acts of the Apostles: A Socio-rhetorical Commentary*. Grand Rapids: Eerdmans, 1998.

————. *Women in the Earliest Churches*. Society for New Testament Studies Monograph Series 59. Cambridge: Cambridge University Press, 1988.

Wright, Benjamin G., III. "'*Ebd/doulos*: Terms and Social Status in the Meeting of Hebrew Biblical and Hellenistic Roman Culture." In "Slavery in Text and Interpretation." Edited by Allen Dwight Callahan, Richard A. Horsley, and Abraham Smith. *Semeia* 83–84 (1998): 83–112.

Wright, N. T. "Paul's Gospel and Caesar's Empire." Pages 160–83 in *Paul and Politics: Ecclesia, Israel, Imperium, and Interpretation*. Edited by Richard A. Horsley. Harrisburg, Pa.: Trinity Press International, 2000.

Young, Norman H. "Jesus and the Sinners: Some Queries." *Journal for the Study of the New Testament* 24 (1985): 73–75.

Xenophon. *Memorabilia and Oeconomicus; Symposium and Apologia*. Translated by E. C. Marchant and O. J. Todd. Loeb Classical Library. Cambridge: Harvard University Press, 1965.

Yamauchi, Edwin. "Christians and the Jewish Revolts against Rome." *Fides et historia* 23 (1991): 11–30.

————. "Magic in the Biblical World." *Tyndale Bulletin* 34 (1983): 169–200.

# Illustrations

# Subjects Index

# Important Persons Index